THE GERMANIC LANGUAGES

Routledge Language Family Descriptions

In this series:

Also available in paperback:

THE
GERMANIC
LANGUAGES

EDITED BY
Ekkehard König
and
Johan van der Auwera

LONDON AND NEW YORK

First published in 1994
by Routledge
11 New Fetter Lane, London EC4P 4EE

Simultaneously published in the USA and Canada
by Routledge
29 West 35th Street, New York, NY 10001

First published in paperback 2002

Routledge is an imprint of the Taylor & Francis Group

Selection and editorial matter © 1994 Ekkehard König and Johan van der Auwera

Typeset in 10/12 Times by Solidus (Bristol) Limited
Printed in Great Britain by T J International Ltd, Padstow, Cornwall

Index compiled by Indexing Specialists, Hove, East Sussex, BN3 2DJ, UK.

British Library Cataloguing in Publication Data
A catalogue record for this book is available from the British Library

Library of Congress Cataloging-in-Publication Data
The Germanic Languages / edited by Ekkehard König and Johan van der Auwera
    p.   cm. — (Routledge language family desciptions)
    Includes bibliographical references and index.
    1. Germanic languages. I. König, Ekkehard II. van der Auwera,
    Johan III. Series
    PD73.G38   1994   92-37152
    430—dc20   CIP

ISBN 0-415-05768-X (Hbk)
ISBN 0-415-28079-6 (Pbk)

Contents

List of Contributors

Erik Andersson, Department of Swedish, Åbo Akademi, Åbo, Finland.

John Ole Askedal, Department of Germanic Studies, University of Oslo, Oslo, Norway.

Michael P. Barnes, Department of Scandinavian Studies, University College London, London, UK.

Georges De Schutter, Linguistics (GER), University of Antwerp, Antwerp, Belgium.

Bruce Donaldson, Department of Germanic Studies and Russian, University of Melbourne, Melbourne, Victoria, Australia.

Peter Eisenberg, Department of German, University of Potsdam, Potsdam, FRG.

Jan Terje Faarlund, Department of Scandinavian Studies, University of Trondheim, Dragvoll, Norway.

Hartmut Haberland, Department of Languages and Culture, Roskilde University, Roskilde, Denmark.

Carol Henriksen, Department of Languages and Culture, Roskilde University, Roskilde, Denmark.

Jarich Hoekstra, Frisian Academy, Leeuwarden, The Netherlands.

Neil G. Jacobs, Department of Judaic and Near Eastern Languages and Literatures, Ohio State University, Columbus, Ohio, USA.

Ans van Kemenade, Department of English, Free University of Amsterdam, Amsterdam, The Netherlands.

Ekkehard König, Institute of English Philology, Free University of Berlin, Berlin, FRG.

Winfred P. Lehmann, Linguistics Research Center, University of Texas at Austin, Austin, Texas, USA.

Silke Van Ness, Department of Germanic Languages and Literatures, State University of New York at Albany, New York, USA.

Ellen F. Prince, Department of Linguistics, University of Pennsylvania, Philadelphia, Pennsylvania, USA.

Aad Quak, Department of Old Germanic Philology, University of Amsterdam, Amsterdam, The Netherlands.

Suzanne Romaine, Merton College, University of Oxford, Oxford, UK.

Höskuldur Thráinsson, Department of Linguistics, Harvard University, Cambridge, Massachusetts, USA; University of Iceland, Reykjavik, Iceland.

Peter M. Tiersma, Loyola Law School, University of California, Los Angeles, USA.

Johan van der Auwera, Belgian National Science Fund, Linguistics (GER), University of Antwerp, Antwerp, Belgium.

Marijke J. van der Wal, Department of Dutch Language and Literature, Leyden University, Leyden, The Netherlands.

Eivind Weyhe, Fróðskaparsetur Føroya, Tórshavn, Faroe Islands.

Preface

In its basic structure and organization, this work follows the model of B. Comrie (ed.) *The World's Major Languages* (London: Routledge, 1987) and, more specifically, that of M. Harris and N. Vincent (eds) *The Romance Languages* (London: Routledge, 1988). As in the book on Romance languages, the goal is to present a comprehensive but compact overview of the structure of all members of a language family in a discursive style of narrative and within a framework that stresses common ground and convergent features in traditional and current linguistic theorizing rather than controversies and mutually incompatible views. The book includes four chapters on earlier stages of Germanic languages: a chapter on Gothic, our major source of information for the reconstruction of Proto-Germanic, a chapter on Old Norse, the source of all Scandinavian languages and a chapter on Old and Middle English, as well as a chapter on the early stages of Continental West Germanic, i.e. the historical source of German, Dutch, Frisian, Yiddish and Afrikaans.

The modern Germanic languages as they are spoken today are treated in twelve different chapters. The distinctions and differentiations underlying these twelve chapters are, of course, to a certain extent arbitrary and controversial. There are, after all, no purely linguistic criteria for deciding in a given case whether we should speak of two varieties of a single language or of two different languages. There is a separate chapter on Pennsylvania German, but not on Swiss German. Faroese and Frisian are treated as separate Germanic languages, but Neo-Norwegian and Dano-Norwegian are regarded as two varieties of one language. In all of these twelve chapters some attention is given to diachronic developments, but since there are four separate historical chapters dealing with the earlier stages of Germanic languages, the main focus is on the synchrony.

Finally, there is a chapter on Germanic creoles and both the term 'Germanic creoles', which is not an established one, and the inclusion of that chapter require some justification. This chapter mainly treats English-based creoles, but it also includes some discussion of German- and Dutch-based creoles. Although not Germanic languages in their grammatical structure, such pidgins and creoles derive a major part of their vocabulary from Germanic. Moreover, it has been suggested, though not generally accepted, that Middle English is a creole, since extensive borrowing from French and Latin could be regarded as undermining its historical continuity and identity as a Germanic language. A further reason for including this chapter is the fact that pidgins and creoles provide interesting insights into the nature of linguistic change in general.

Each chapter is written by one or several experts on the language in question and in many cases these experts are also native speakers of the relevant language. As in the two other books mentioned above, there are no footnotes, few or no references and there is only a very limited bibliography, a select list of essential reference works and further reading, comprising maximally 15 to 20 items. Hence authors have not been able to refer properly to the sources they have used and to indicate precisely which of the ideas presented are their own and which were borrowed from others. We hope that such information will be obvious to the specialist and that it will be of no interest to the general reader. The inclusion of a fair portrayal of previous and ongoing scholarship would have easily doubled the size of the book.

Each chapter is tightly structured on the basis of a common scheme. There is thus a certain uniformity not only in the major sections for each chapter (introduction, phonology, morphology, syntax, lexis), but also in the range of topics covered in each section. On the other hand, the authors were given sufficient leeway to discuss the core topics, as well as all the other topics they wanted to include, in as much detail as they considered appropriate. This means that the individual chapters differ in the amount of attention given to certain core and non-core topics, depending on the expertise of the author in a certain domain, on the amount of information available for a specific language and on the assessment of the importance of a topic made by the author. Such divergence is natural and even useful, given the fact that our knowledge about the languages covered in this book varies enormously from case to case. English and German are among the best described languages of the world, whereas many essentially descriptive problems have yet to be solved for Faroese or Neo-Norwegian. It is also for this reason that some, but not all, authors were able to go beyond a mere descriptive sketch and to give a general typological characterization of 'their' language on the basis of a constant comparison with the other languages covered in this book.

What are the possible uses of this book? First of all, it will provide a comprehensive and compact source of information for all Germanic languages. There are, of course, many excellent grammars available for English, German or Dutch, but such grammars as exist for Faroese, Norwegian or Swedish are either fairly old, limited in their scope or not easily accessible to those who do not speak a Scandinavian language.

Second, the book can be used as a basis for all kinds of comparative work within the Germanic family, for typological and contrastive work as well as work on language contact. In contrast to the situation in Romance linguistics, there are hardly any works which give a comprehensive overview of all Germanic languages and provide the basis for any kind of comparative insight. Those interested in pursuing a specific phenomenon across the various chapters will find information (a) on features that are typical of Germanic languages; (b) on parameters of variation and major differences between members of this family; and (c) on pervasive tendencies of phonological, morphological and syntactic change.

The distinction between weak and strong verbs, the phonological opposition between related tense and lax vowels, the use of word order to distinguish interrogative sentences from declarative ones, the verb-second phenomenon and the inflectional contrast between only two tenses are typically Germanic features. Not all Germanic languages exhibit these features anymore and in that sense Icelandic, Swedish and Dutch are typical representatives of this family, whereas English and Afrikaans are not.

Major differences between the Germanic languages can be found *inter alia* in the inflectional morphology, in the coding of grammatical relations, in the form and use of reflexive markers and in the conditions for passivization. While Icelandic and to a lesser extent German have preserved many of the inflectional categories of Proto-Germanic, English and Afrikaans have lost most of these distinctions and have moved away from the inflectional type to the isolating morphological type. As far as the identification of grammatical relations (subject, object) is concerned, an interesting contrast can be found within the Germanic family. In German the only relevant factor is case: the subject is the constituent coded in the nominative case regardless of its position. In English, and interestingly enough also in Icelandic, that is in a language preserving the traditional Germanic case system, it is the position before the finite verb (in unmarked declarative sentences) that identifies subjects. In order words, Icelandic has a wide variety of dative, accusative and even genitive subjects, so that case marking is to a certain extent ornamental.

The form of reflexive markers and the constraints on the use of these expressions also differ widely across Germanic languages. Some languages (Old English, Frisian, Old Dutch, Afrikaans) have no reflexive markers at all. The Scandinavian languages have verbal affixes in addition to pronouns, whereas German and Yiddish only have reflexive pronouns. In contrast to all of these languages, English employs complex expressions (pronoun + *self*) to indicate co-reference between two noun phrases in the same clause. Moreover, the Germanic languages differ widely as regards the differentiations made within the system of reflexive markers and the domain in which the markers are used.

Another fascinating area for further comparative work is the system of voice. In German, for example, both intransitive and transitive verbs may passivize, but in the latter case a morphological condition is relevant: only accusative objects of a corresponding active sentence may show up as

subjects of a passive counterpart with *werden*. Dative objects may correspond
to subjects in a passive sentence with the auxiliary *bekommen*. In English the
relevant conditions for passivization are configurational ones: there must be
a noun phrase following, but not necessarily adjacent to, the verb in the
corresponding active sentence that can be selected as subject of the passive
sentence.

It goes without saying that the Germanic languages also provide a valuable
field for the study of all kinds of diachronic processes: the development of
reflexive markers, the development of tense systems and the attrition of
inflectional systems are particularly interesting areas for such historical
investigations. Again an example will illustrate the type of information
available to those who pursue certain phenomena across the various chapters.
In addition to the two-term contrast between the past and the non-past tense,
which was their original endowment, all Germanic languages have developed
a perfect from underlying resultative constructions. In some Germanic
languages this new category has undergone or is undergoing a further
development into a narrative tense. In German this development is still under
way. In Afrikaans and Yiddish the perfect has completely replaced and thus
ousted the past tense. In English and in nearly all Scandinavian languages
there is still a clear semantic opposition between the perfect and the past
tense.

As regards the intended level of readership, we have tried to ensure that the
book is both sufficiently clear and expository for it to be used for general
reference or as a text book for undergraduate or graduate courses in linguistics
or any of the relevant philologies. On the other hand, we also hope that it will
offer information and occasional insights to scholars in linguistics and allied
disciplines.

All abbreviations used in this book more than once are given in the list
following this preface. An asterisk in front of a construction indicates that the
construction is ungrammatical. In the diachronic chapters, however, the
asterisk is used to indicate that the relevant form of a word is reconstructed
rather than actually attested, and to avoid confusion with this latter usage a
double asterisk is used for ungrammatical forms in the section on Yiddish
phonology. Occasionally, an asterisk will also be found following a construction or symbol, but such usage will be explained in the text. In the chapters
with several authors the division of labor was the following: 'The Germanic
languages': North and East Germanic (Carol Henriksen), Introduction, West
Germanic (Johan van der Auwera); 'Old and Middle Continental West
Germanic': Introduction, Old and Middle Dutch (Marijke van der Wal), Old
and Middle High German, Old Saxon and Middle Low German (Aad Quak);
'Yiddish': Phonology (Neil Jacobs), Syntax (Ellen Prince), Introduction,
Morphology, Lexis (Johan van der Auwera).

In conclusion, we would like to acknowledge the cooperation of the
individual contributors in preparing the final versions of their chapters (more

or less) on time and for respecting guidelines and deadlines. For comments on earlier versions of the relevant chapters, we are grateful to Ernst Ebbinghaus (Gothic), Jan Ragnar Hagland and Trygve Skomedal (Old and Middle Scandinavian), Andrew R. W. Baxter (Old and Middle English), Kjartan G. Ottósson (Icelandic), Svein Lie, Oddrun Grønvik and Rolf Theil Endresen (Norwegian), Kirsten Gregerson (Danish), Lars Heltoft (Danish), John Hawkins and Edgar Schneider (English). Finally, we would like to thank our editor, Jonathan Price, for his enthusiasm and patience, and our copy editor, Marguerite Nesling, for her expertise.

Ekkehard König
Free University of Berlin

Johan van der Auwera
Belgian National Science Fund and
University of Antwerp

List of Abbreviations

A	answer	Gmc	Germanic
abl.	ablative	Go.	Gothic
acc.	accusative	HA	Hebrew/Aramaic
adj.	adjective	imp.	imperative
adv.	adverb	ind.	indicative
AdvP.	adverb phrase	indef.	indefinite
Afr.	Afrikaans	indir.	indirect
aux.	auxiliary	inf.	infinitive
BM	*Bokmål* Norwegian	instr.	instrumental
Br.	British	intr.	intransitive
C	consonant	IPA	International Phonetic
com.	common		Association
CYid.	Central Yiddish	Ir.	Irish
Dan.	Danish	Lat.	Latin
dat.	dative	lit.	literally
def.	definite	Lith.	Lithuanian
det.	determiner	m.	masculine
dim.	diminutive	MEng. etc.	Middle English etc.
dir.	direct	MHG	Middle High German
Du.	Dutch	MLG	Middle Low German
EN	East Norwegian	n.	neuter
Eng.	English	N	noun
exc.	exclusive	NEYid.	Northeastern Yiddish
EYid.	Eastern Yiddish	NN	New Norwegian
f.	feminine	nom.	nominative
fam.	familiar	non-imp.	non-imperative
fin.	finite	NP	noun phrase
Fris.	Frisian	O/obj.	object
gen.	genitive	obl.	oblique
Ger.	German	OEng. etc	Old English etc.
Gk	Greek	OHG	Old High German

ON	Old Norse	Sem.	Semitic
part.	participle	SEN	Southeast Norwegian
PG	Pennsylvania German	SEYid.	Southeastern Yiddish
PGmc	Proto-Germanic	sg.	singular
PIE	Proto-Indo-European	Slav.	Slavic
pl.	plural	SPE	*The Sound Pattern of*
pol.	polite		*English* (N. Chomsky
Pol.	Polish		and M. Halle, 1968,
poss.	possessive		New York: Harper &
PP	prepositional phrase		Row)
pp.	past participle	StGer. etc	Standard German etc.
pr.	primary (object)	su.	subject
pres.	present	subj.	subjunctive
pret.	preterite	sup.	supine
PYid.	Proto-Yiddish	SVO etc	subject – verb – object
Q	question		etc.
refl.	reflexive	tr.	transitive
RM	*Riksmål* Norwegian	V	vowel or verb
RP	Received	VLat.	Vulgar Latin
	Pronunciation	voc.	vocative
S	sentence/clause or	VP	verb phrase
	subject	V2	verb-second
SAdv.	sentence adverb	WFris.	West Frisian
Sax.	Saxon	WYid.	Western Yiddish
sec.	secondary (object)	Yid.	Yiddish

1 The Germanic Languages

Carol Henriksen and Johan van der Auwera

Of the 4,000 to 6,000 languages presently spoken in the world, the Germanic languages form a very small subset. For the purposes of this book, there are only twelve modern Germanic languages, and even with the inclusion of varieties like Luxembourgish and Swiss German, and perhaps some 40 to 50 creoles, the membership remains modest. In terms of numbers of speakers, the Germanic group scores much better, for there are at least 450 million native speakers, which is approximately one twelfth of the world's population. Still, even within Indo-European, the Romance languages with an estimated 580 million native speakers rank higher. What the Germanic languages are unrivalled in, however, is their geographical distribution. While originally these languages were confined to a small part of Europe, colonizers and immigrants successfully implanted them, particularly English, in the Americas, Africa (e.g. South Africa), Asia (e.g. India), as well as in the Pacific (e.g. Australia). Moreover, English has become the world's most important international language, serving commerce, culture, diplomacy, and science, including linguistics.

The modest beginnings of this evolution seem to be found in the southern Baltic region (northern Germany, the Danish Isles, southern Scandinavia), which according to accepted opinion had been settled by speakers of Indo-European around 1000 BC. They encountered speakers of non-Indo-European origin, gradually changed their Proto-Indo-European into Proto-Germanic, and dispersed beyond the original homeland to occupy the region from the North Sea stretching to the River Vistula in Poland by 500 BC. The language spoken during this period is attested only indirectly, in the foreign words, usually proper names, used by Greek and Latin authors, and in early loans in neighbouring and co-territorial languages, especially Finno-Ugric and Baltic. The earliest direct records are Scandinavian runic inscriptions from the beginning of the third century AD.

It is customary to divide Germanic into East Germanic, with Gothic as its prominent member, North Germanic, with Icelandic, Faroese, Norwegian, Danish and Swedish, and West Germanic (sometimes 'South Germanic'), with German, Yiddish, Pennsylvania German, Dutch, Afrikaans, Frisian and

1

English. If we relate this variety to the one Common Germanic language of two thousand years ago, we face the question of how we got from the one parent language to the three branches and to the dozen or so descendant languages.

One factor to bear in mind is that every language is inherently variable. A language only exists through speakers that speak an idiolect, and typically share a dialect – and sociolect – with the people with whom they communicate most often or want to be associated. Thus some degree of dialectal variation must have prevailed in Common Germanic too, an assumption plausible also on purely linguistic grounds. Standard methods of linguistic reconstruction sometimes lead to two reconstructed forms rather than only one, suggesting that Common Germanic allowed both. Thus the inherent linguistic variation within Common Germanic itself may safely be taken as a partial explanation of later diffusion, in particular, of the distinction between North and West Germanic.

A second factor responsible for the variety in Germanic is migration. When speakers move away from their homeland and cut or strongly diminish communication with those who stay behind, the inherent tendency for dialect variation increases. The migrants, moreover, may come into contact with speakers of another language, which may alienate either language, in varying degrees, from the language of the previous generations. It may also lead to the disappearance of one or even both of the languages. A distinction may be made in terms of the language variety with which the migrants left. Did they leave with Common Germanic, with a branch of Germanic like relatively undifferentiated North Germanic, or with a fully differentiated separate Germanic language like English? Germanic illustrates each of these types and scenarios.

Towards the end of the pre-Christian era, Germanic tribes, including the Vandals, Burgundians and Goths, left the Common Germanic homeland. The Goths, the only ones that left any significant linguistic records, moved to the Baltic shores east of the Oder, some of them moving on to the Balkans around AD 200, and from there westward to Italy, France and Spain. Because of the initially eastern orientation of the migration, the language of the Goths is called 'East Germanic', and because it is generally taken to have separated from Common Germanic, it is considered a branch, on the same level as West and North Germanic.

Migrations that lead to increased linguistic diversity took place with respect to both North Germanic and West Germanic. During the Viking Age (c.800–c.1050) speakers of North Germanic settled in Iceland, Greenland, the Faroes, the Shetlands, the Hebrides and the Orkney Islands, parts of Ireland, Scotland, England, the Isle of Man and Normandy, along the shores of Finland and Estonia, and even in Novgorod, Kiev and Constantinople. Only in the case of Iceland and the Faroes did these migrations eventually lead to separate modern languages. In Finland, North Germanic was to be retained as a variant of Swedish, and in all other areas North Germanic was gradually given up. As for West Germanic, tribal groups of Angles, Saxons and Jutes invaded England during the fifth and sixth centuries, and the Langobard(ic) (Lombard) tribe moved into Italy. Whereas the southward expansion proved unsuccessful (by the end of the first millenium Langobardic was basically extinct), the westward expansion led to modern English.

The third type of migration resulted primarily from the exploration and colonization of the world by Europeans from the fifteenth century onwards. Its strongest effect was to spread English around the globe. In terms of the fragmentation of Germanic, it led to the creation of colonial variants of Dutch, German and English, and to several creoles, especially of English. A special case is the development of Yiddish. The main form, Eastern Yiddish, is the result of the eastward migration of German-speaking Jews to Slavic territories from the twelfth to the sixteenth century, and from there back to the west (Europe, Palestine-Israel, and the general migration poles of the Americas, South Africa and Australia) in the nineteenth and twentieth centuries.

A third factor needed to explain how one ancestral language relates to a dozen descendant languages is standardization. Without this concept one would still not know why Swedish, Danish and Norwegian are considered different languages, even though mutual intelligibility is very high, whereas some northern and southern dialects of German, which are hardly mutually intelligible, are not considered separate languages. Standardization is the process whereby a community, typically a literate one, imposes a uniformity on its language in response to a growing desire of political, religious or cultural authorities for improved communication across dialects. The standard which then emerges is typically based on dialects that are (a) spoken in the economically and culturally strongest region; (b) deemed 'authentic' in a way that satisfies a sense of national identity in search of a national language; and/ or (c) more highly cross-dialectally intelligible than others. Early catalysts were the printing press; the attention for the native vernacular as opposed to Latin during the Renaissance, giving rise to the first grammars, dictionaries and academies; the Bible translations of the Reformation; and the appearance of strong centralized governments. One or more of these factors were at work in the making of standard Danish, Swedish, German, Dutch and English, and to a small extent Icelandic. The nationalism of the nineteenth and early twentieth centuries was the major impulse for the development of Afrikaans, Faroese, Norwegian, and again Icelandic. Norwegian even has two standards, one based on the Danish-influenced language spoken by the élite, and the other reconstructed from conservative, 'pure' dialects. In the case of the languages without a nation state – Pennsylvania German, Yiddish and Frisian – standardization is a part of language promotion and maintenance efforts, initiated primarily by small numbers of nineteenth- and twentieth-century literary figures, journalists and linguists.

East Germanic

The first of the Germanic tribes to migrate from the Danish Isles and southern Sweden were the Goths, who presumably departed from the Common Germanic area around 100 BC. After crossing the Baltic they were joined by the Rugians, the Vandals and the Burgundians. Together these tribes constitute the eastern branch of Germanic known to us primarily from biblical translations from around AD 350. These translations, the majority of which have been attributed to Wulfila, the Bishop of the Western Goths, were undertaken after the Goths had settled on the Black Sea and become Christians.

The manuscript fragments which have come down to us containing a translation of the Bible into Gothic are not contemporary with Wulfila but were transcribed in Italy around AD 500. The most important are the *Codex Argenteus* in the University Library in Uppsala (330 leaves, of which 187 are still preserved, of the four Gospels), the *Codex Carolinus* in the library in Wolfenbüttel (four leaves containing about 42 verses from the Epistle to the Romans), the *Codices Ambrosiani*, 5 fragments in the Ambrosian Library in Milan (185 leaves containing portions of Epistles, a small fragment of a Gothic Calendar, St Matthew, Nehemiah and a commentary on St John), the *Codex Turinensis* in Turin (4 damaged leaves containing fragments of Epistles), and the *Codex Gissensis*, discovered in Egypt near the ancient town of Antinoë (a double sheet of parchment containing fragments from St Luke in Latin and Gothic).

Due to the early migration of the Gothic tribes, the language of the Goths developed differently from that of the West and North Germanic peoples, and as a consequence of subsequent migration into Italy, France and Spain, the Goths gradually became absorbed by other tribes and nations, thus leaving us with little more than Wulfila's Bible translation as evidence of an East Germanic variety of the Germanic languages.

North Germanic

'Common Scandinavian' is a term often used for the Germanic language spoken in Scandinavia in the period after the 'Great Migrations' in which the organization of power was still local and tribal (*c*.550–*c*.1050). According to the historians Jordanes (*c*.550) and Procopius (*c*.554), there were many small tribal kings in the area which is now Scandinavia, all rivalling to extend their domain at the expense of the others. Of these, the dynasties of the Skjoldungs in Denmark and the Ynglings in Sweden and Norway were the most prominent. Like Common Germanic, Common Scandinavian is attested in runic inscriptions.

The language of the Viking Age (800–1050) was still relatively uniform, referred to as *dǫnsk tunga* 'Danish tongue' well into the Middle Ages. Since there are no native manuscripts from this period, our knowledge of the language derives from foreign texts, loanwords in other languages, place-names datable to this period, runic inscriptions, and later manuscripts, which either go back to an earlier oral tradition or are copies of earlier documents now lost.

Regarding the runic inscriptions, it is interesting to note that there are no or very few Danish inscriptions from around 600 to 800 and only a few, though very important ones, from Norway and Sweden. Around 800 we encounter a revival of runic writing in Denmark, but now in a new alphabet, the younger *futhark*. During this period there are 412 Danish inscriptions, 240 of them on stones erected by wealthy families to commemorate their dead. The younger *futhark* reached Norway around 800, but only a few inscriptions are preserved from this area. Runic writing is also found in the British Isles, Greenland and the Faroes, but in Iceland it is surprisingly sparse and late. Sweden became the great home of runic epigraphy in the younger *futhark* with more than 2,500 preserved inscriptions, testifying to the wealth and power of the leading families and at the same time providing valuable information concerning the fates of those who fell abroad on Viking expeditions. The fragments of poetry found in the runic inscriptions belong to the rich poetic tradition represented in the later Old Icelandic manuscripts.

Since the peoples of the north were linked together primarily by sea routes, it is easy to see how three separate centres of power began to emerge, a southern one (Denmark), a Baltic one (Sweden) and an Atlantic one (Norway). The Danish kings controlled the approaches to the Baltic, the Swedes occupied the region around Lake Mälar, and the Norwegians controlled the fjords, primarily those on the west coast where navigation was best and access to foreign wealth close at hand. The establishment of a Danish archbishopric of the Roman Catholic Church in Lund in 1104, a Norwegian archbishopric in Trondheim (Nidaros) in 1152, and a corresponding Swedish archbishopric in Uppsala in 1164 reflects this political division of Scandinavia into Danish, Norwegian and Swedish kingdoms.

Towards the end of the Viking Age we find a gradual splitting up of Common Scandinavian, initially into two branches: East Scandinavian, comprising the kingdom of Denmark and the southern two-thirds of Sweden and adjacent parts of Norway; and West Scandinavian, comprising most of Norway and the Norwegian settlements in the North Atlantic, in particular Iceland.

East Scandinavian

The East Scandinavian branch is not so much a distinct language as the sum of the innovations that encompassed Denmark, most of Sweden, and adjacent parts of Norway at the end of the Viking Age, splitting during the Middle Ages (1050–1340) into Old Danish, Old Swedish and Old Gutnish, the written language of the island of Gotland. Of these, only Danish and Swedish survived the later processes of political centralization and linguistic standardization.

Danish

Danish (*dansk*) is the official language of the kingdom of Denmark (comprising Denmark, the Faroe Islands and Greenland), where it is native to the majority of a population of over 5 million. Danish is also the first language or 'cultural language' of some 50,000 inhabitants in German Schleswig-Holstein, south of the Danish border.

Modern Standard Danish developed on the basis of the written language of the Reformation, further influenced during the seventeenth and eighteenth centuries by the spoken language of the influential citizens of Copenhagen, the economic and cultural centre of the emerging nation state.

The history of the Danish language falls into three major periods: Old Danish (*c*.800–*c*.1100), corresponding roughly to the Viking Age; Middle Danish (*c*.1100–*c*.1525), corresponding to the Middle Ages; and Modern Danish (after *c*.1525), the period after the Reformation and up to modern times.

Danish is the Scandinavian language that has moved farthest away from its Common Scandinavian roots, primarily due to Denmark's geographic location, which forms a bridge between the Nordic countries and the European mainland.

Swedish

Swedish (*svenska*) is spoken as the official language of Sweden by a population of some 8.5 million inhabitants. It is also the first language of some 300,000 speakers in Finland (on the semi-independent Åland Islands and on the west and south coast) and the second language of various linguistic minorities, altogether up to a million, mostly recent immigrants but also indigenous Finns and Saamis (Lapps).

Prior to the Viking Age it is difficult to distinguish Swedish from Danish, but after *c*.800 the East Scandinavian languages begin to separate, with a major cleavage taking place after extensive Danish innovations around 1300.

Modern Standard Swedish developed in the Mälar-Uppland region, the location of the chief centres of government and learning since the Middle Ages (Stockholm and Uppsala), but the standard language was also influenced by the dialect of the Götaland region immediately to the south. While the cultivated pronunciation of Stockholm enjoys considerable prestige, there are also strongly resistant regional norms, particularly those of southern Sweden (*skånska*) and Finland (*finlandssvenska*).

The history of the Swedish language falls into two major periods: an Old Swedish period covering the Viking Age and the Middle Ages, further subdivided into the runic period (*c*.800–*c*.1225), the classical period (*c*.1225–*c*.1375) and the younger period (*c*.1375–*c*.1526); and a Modern Swedish period with Older Modern Swedish from *c*.1526 to *c*.1732 and Younger Modern Swedish from *c*.1732 to the present.

West Scandinavian

We can assume that there was regional variation even in the Common Scandinavian period, but by the Viking Age a split is observable between the more conservative west facing the Atlantic and the more innovative east that looked to the Baltic. The West Scandinavian branch of Common Scandinavian consists of Old Norwegian and Old Icelandic, the latter deriving from a form of West Norwegian brought across the ocean and developed in relative isolation after the period of settlement (870–930). Otherwise West Scandinavian covered what is present-day Norway, the provinces of Jämtland, Herjedalen, and Bohuslän, now belonging to Sweden, the western isles of Shetland, the Faroes, the Orkneys, the Hebrides, the Isle of Man, coastal areas of Scotland and Ireland, and Greenland.

Icelandic

Icelandic (*íslenska*) is the West Scandinavian language that has been spoken on Iceland ever since the country was settled over a thousand years ago. Today Modern Icelandic is spoken by a population of close to 260,000.

Since the Icelandic settlers came from different localities along the extensive coastal stretch from northern Norway all the way down to the south, as well as from the British Isles, it is hardly possible that the early language was free of variation. In spite of this, Icelandic has never shown any real tendency to split into dialects. Today regional variation in pronunciation and vocabulary is so insignificant that it would be misleading to speak of Icelandic dialects.

The modern standard is a direct continuation of the language of the original settlers, most strongly influenced by the language of southwestern Norway. During the first 200 years there was no marked difference between Norwegian and Icelandic. Cultural ties between the two countries were strong, even into the fourteenth century. However, in the wake of the Kalmar Union, the political union of Denmark, Norway and Sweden between 1397 and 1523, Icelandic and Norwegian went their separate ways. While Danish became the official language of the State and Church in Norway, the Icelanders translated the Bible and other religious literature into their own native Icelandic.

Icelandic is the most conservative of the Scandinavian languages and represents a unique case of linguistic continuity in that it has retained its original inflectional system and core vocabulary relatively unaltered up to this very day. Various developments in pronunciation make it possible, however, to speak of Old Icelandic (up to *c.*1550) and Modern Icelandic periods (from *c.*1550), less clearly also of Middle Icelandic (*c.*1350–*c.*1550).

Norwegian

Norwegian (*norsk*) in two varieties, Neo-Norwegian (*nynorsk*) and Dano-Norwegian (*bokmål*), is the language of over 4 million inhabitants of Norway, including somewhat more than 20,000 Saamis (most of them bilingual). Both

Neo-Norwegian and Dano-Norwegian are official languages in Norway. Both are used by national and local officials, and citizens writing to a public institution have the right to receive an answer in the language of their own letter. School districts choose one of the official languages as the language of instruction and teach the parallel language in separate classes.

During the period in which Danish was the written language of Norway (1380–1814), most Norwegians spoke their local dialects and pronounced Danish using their own Norwegian sounds. The lack of a strong native norm explains in part why the Norwegian dialects were able to thrive on a much larger scale than in Denmark or Sweden. They are still very much alive and socially acceptable even outside the geographic area in which they are spoken.

Since for historical reasons there was no standard Norwegian alternative, such a standard had to be created, either on the basis of the popular dialects or through gradual changes in the Danish norm in the direction of the spoken Norwegian of the urban educated classes. As a result two modern standards developed. The written standard of Neo-Norwegian was established on the basis of the local dialects by the linguist and poet Ivar Aasen in the middle of the nineteenth century. It was officially recognized in 1885 and spread rapidly through the western and midland regions, being taught today as a first language to somewhat less than one fifth of the Norwegian schoolchildren and as a second language to the rest. Dano-Norwegian, or 'book language', is the first language of the majority of the population. Linguistically it is the result of the gradual Norwegianization of the Danish standard which was inherited from the period prior to Norway's independence.

Although it was originally hoped that the two standards could be amalgamated into one 'United Norwegian' (*samnorsk*), this seems farther away today than some years ago, the current solution being peaceful co-existence. The presence and daily use of two standard languages and numerous local dialects does not seriously affect communication in Norway, a country which is exemplary today when it comes to the question of linguistic tolerance.

Faroese

Faroese (*føroyskt*) is the first language of the approximately 47,000 inhabitants of a small group of islands in the North Atlantic, midway between Scotland and Iceland (18 in all, of which one is uninhabited), and along with Danish it is one of the official languages of the Faroe Islands. The Faroes, previously under the Norwegian crown, officially became of part of Denmark in 1816, receiving semi-independent political status in 1948. Unlike Denmark proper, for example, they have not chosen membership in the European Community.

As a West Scandinavian language, Faroese is related to Icelandic and several of the West Norwegian dialects. It has developed into its present form from the language spoken by the Norwegians who colonized the islands in the early 800s. Although there is significant variation in pronunciation from island to island, there are no true dialects.

In contrast to Icelandic, the Faroese written tradition is recent and sparse. Aside from a few Faroese characteristics in some of the Old Norwegian texts from the Middle Ages, the earliest texts in Faroese are three ballads recorded around 1773 by J. C. Svabo, the first to record Faroese folk ballads and to collect material for a Faroese dictionary. In 1846 a literary orthography was devised by V. U. Hammershaimb, based on the Icelandic tradition, and in the 1870s a group of Faroese students in Copenhagen began writing creatively in the language. From these beginnings, Faroese was transformed in the course of a century from a mere spoken language into a language used in schools, newspapers, churches, radio and public administration.

The development of a native literary tradition has been slow, but today there exists a sizeable body of Faroese poetry, fiction, educational material and journalism.

West Germanic

Whereas the origin of the modern North Germanic languages can be traced back to one relatively homogeneous North Germanic parent language, the case for a similar parentage of the West Germanic languages is less clear. It has been suggested instead that ancient West Germanic only existed as a conglomerate of three dialect groups, sometimes referred to after Tacitus as 'Ingwaeonic', 'Istwaeonic' and 'Herminonic' or, in modern terms, 'North Sea Germanic', 'Rhine-Weser Germanic, and 'Elbe Germanic'. This tripartite division bears no direct relation to the division of the modern descendant languages, however. Thus standard (High) German is related to two of these hypothetical dialect groups, namely Istwaeonic and Herminonic. English, Frisian, and to a lesser extent Low German and Dutch, can arguably all be traced back to Ingwaeonic, but because of the geographical discontinuity and because of the Viking and Norman French invasions in the ninth to eleventh centuries and resulting language interference, English developed in an idiosyncratic way such that modern English is strongly estranged from both its Anglo-Saxon ancestor and its modern continental Ingwaeonic counterparts. Interestingly, in the case of English insularity lacked the conservative effect it had for North Germanic, Romance (cf. Sardinian as the most conservative Romance language), Celtic (cf. the fact that Celtic, once spoken over vast areas of continental Europe, now only survives on islands – Britain, Ireland – and a peninsula – Brittany) and, within Germanic, for the conservative insular variety of North Frisian.

German

German (*Deutsch*) is spoken as an official language of the Federal Republic of Germany, as of 1990 united with the former German Democratic Republic (close to 80 million native speakers), Austria (7.5 million), Liechtenstein (15,000), the larger part of Switzerland (4.2 million out of a total of 6.4 million), South Tyrol and a few isolated villages further south in Italy (270,000), the part of Belgium along the border with Germany (65,000), and Luxembourg, which recognizes both the non-indigenous Standard German and the native *Lëtzebuergesch* (360,000), traditionally a Central Franconian dialect. The Swiss, Tyrolean, Belgian and Luxembourg speakers are all in varying degrees diglossic in the local variety and Standard German, as well as bilingual in a Romance language. German is also spoken by autochthonous minorities in Belgium, primarily on the southern side of its border with Luxembourg (estimates vary between 1,000 and 30,000), the French Lorraine (some 300,000) and Alsace (perhaps 1 million), the Danish southern Jutland (20,000), ancient immigrant groups in Eastern Europe, especially the former Soviet Union (1.2 million), Romania (400,000) and Hungary (250,000), in former German colonies (Namibia, Togo, Cameroon), and by a millionfold of relatively recent immigrants especially to the Americas and Australia, most of these again both diglossic and bilingual. German furthermore functions as the second language for the indigenous minorities, Frisian (12,000), Danish (up to 50,000) and Sorbian (anywhere between 20,000 and 100,000) in Germany; Slovene (17,000), Croatian (18,000) and Hungarian (4,000) in Austria; some of the French, Italian, and Romantsch-speaking Swiss (more than a million, 600,000, and 40,000, respectively), and for several millions of foreign nationals residing within the German speech area.

The German dialects go back to the dialects of the West Germanic tribes, Franks, Saxons, Hermunduri (Thuringians), Alemanni, Suebi (Swabians) and Bavarians, who settled in the area roughly corresponding to Germany west of the Elbe and Saale, present-day Austria and German-speaking Switzerland. From the time of Charlemagne up to the eighteenth century, a colonizing and merchandizing movement took these dialects eastward, primarily into Bohemia, Slovakia, Upper Saxony, Silesia, Mecklenburg, Brandenburg, Pomerania, Lithuania, Latvia and Estonia, and even created linguistic enclaves as far east as the Volga or southeast as the Romanian Banat. With the resettlements in the aftermath of the Second World War, some of the eastward expansion was undone, so that except for some isolated speakers and enclaves and some border regions, the German/Slavic–Hungarian border has joined the modern state borders of Germany and Austria.

The dialects of German subdivide into Low German (*Niederdeutsch*, *Plattdeutsch*) and High German (*Hochdeutsch*). The former are spoken in the north of Germany, the latter in the centre and the south. In linguistic terms, the criterion is the degree to which the dialects have been affected by the so-called 'High German Consonant Shift': Low German has not been affected by it, 'Central' German partially, and Southern or 'Upper' German (almost) completely. Modern Standard German developed primarily on the basis of the late medieval chancery language of the court of Saxony and the East Central dialect area around Dresden. In the course of the sixteenth and seventeenth centuries this written language gained gradual acceptance throughout the entire German-speaking area, in part because of the economic power of Saxony and the position of the dialect, intermediate between Low and Upper German and thus more widely comprehensible than either, and in part because Luther made it the language of the Reformation. In this process of geographical expansion, the emerging Modern German standard ousted – but was also influenced by – competing regional standards, the Low German standard of the Hanseatic League in the north, and the Upper German 'Common German' (*gemeines Deutsch*) in the south. The spoken standard spread much later and is based on the North German pronunciation of the written standard, bearing witness to the fact that by the end of the eighteenth century Saxony had lost political power and cultural prestige to Prussia. The expansion of the spoken standard was never completed, however: both in Switzerland and in Luxembourg the local dialects, when spoken, have the social prestige normally associated with a standard language.

High German is documented first in runic inscriptions and glosses, and later in clerical texts, a phase called Old High German (until *c*.1100), followed by Middle High German (until 1400 or 1500), the period of courtly and epic poetry, then Early New High German (until *c*.1650), which laid the foundations of the modern New High German (from *c*.1650). For Low German, one distinguishes between Old Low German or Old Saxon (until *c*.1100), Middle Low German (until 1400 or 1500), contemporaneous with the heyday of the Hanseatic League, and thereafter New Low German.

Yiddish

Yiddish (ייִדיש *yidish* 'Jewish') is one of many Jewish languages and in quantitative terms it used to be the most important one. The origin of Yiddish is traced back to medieval Germany, where Jewish settlers adopted the local German as well as adapted it, mixing it partly with elements of Hebrew and Aramaic, which were kept for religious purposes. These Jews are called 'Ashkenazic', after the Hebrew word *Ashkenaz*, roughly meaning 'Germany', different from 'Sephardic', the other large European group, named after *Sepharad* 'Spain'. From the twelfth to the sixteenth century Ashkenazic groups spread towards Slavic territories (especially present-day Poland, the Ukraine, Byelorussia and Russia, but also Lithuania), and their language absorbed elements from Slavic. From the seventeenth century onwards, their language differed sufficiently from that of the Jews that had stayed in German-speaking areas to justify the modern terms 'Eastern Yiddish' and 'Western Yiddish'. The latter variant began to decline towards the end of the eighteenth century and disappeared nearly completely during the nineteenth century. In the east, however, the nineteenth century saw the language strengthened: instead of, or in addition to, using Hebrew, German or a Slavic language, artists, religious propagandists, socialists, and Zionists turned to the language actually spoken by the Jewish masses, which was Yiddish. In 1908, at a Conference for the Yiddish Language in Czernowitz (today in the Ukraine), Yiddish was accepted as 'a national language of the Jewish people'. Yiddish continued to flourish in literature, the theatre and the press, and it became a language of education, especially in interwar Poland, with Vilnius (now in Lithuania) and Warsaw as its intellectual centres, and a standard language developing on the basis of both Lithuanian and Polish Yiddish dialects. Westward migrations, which started as early as the second half of the seventeenth century and gathered momentum from the end of the nineteenth century, had also taken the language overseas, primarily to North America. On the verge of the Second World War, North America probably had at least three million speakers of Yiddish, while more than seven million had stayed in Eastern Europe, another million being spread over western Europe, Palestine, Central and South America, Africa, Asia and Australia. This meant that more than half of the total Jewish population of the world spoke Yiddish. But then came the Holocaust of six million Jews, subsequent dispersion of the survivors over both the typical immigration countries and western Europe, and linguistic assimilation, partially forced but largely spontaneous, especially to Russian in the former Soviet Union, to English in North America, and to Hebrew in the state of Israel, which was founded in 1948 with Hebrew as its official language. Today Yiddish is estimated to have between one and three million speakers, half of them in the United States, but in every country that has a Jewish population, Yiddish speakers form a minority, usually secular and not passing on the language to the following generation. It is chiefly in orthodox communities that Yiddish is maintained, but then primarily as a spoken in-group language, with Hebrew for religion and the local co-territorial language for contact with outsiders.

Throughout its entire history, speakers of Yiddish have attained high levels of bilingualism. Yiddish has always used a version of the Aramaic alphabet, employing its own orthographical rules. The periodization of Yiddish distinguishes between Early Yiddish (up to *c*.1250), evidenced by glosses only; Old Yiddish (*c*.1250 to *c*.1500); Middle Yiddish (*c*.1500 to *c*.1700), the period when the centre of gravity moved east; and New or Modern Yiddish (from *c*.1700). Sometimes Middle Yiddish is not distinguished and the period of Old Yiddish extended.

Pennsylvania German

Pennsylvania German (*Pensilfaanish, Deitsch*), also popularly known as 'Pennsylvania Dutch' or just 'Dutch', has an estimated 300,000 native speakers chiefly in the United States of America. These speakers descend from German colonists who hailed from all regions of German-speaking Europe, but primarily from the Palatinate (the *Pfalz*), and settled mostly in the eastern part of Pennsylvania during the seventeenth and eighteenth centuries. The first groups consisted primarily of religious sects, but later waves were increasingly comprised of economic migrants. From their primary settlements in Pennsylvania, sectarian groups moved to Maryland, West Virginia, Virginia and North Carolina, but also to the Midwest, Canada and even Central and South America. These groups have kept the language up to the present day.

On the continuum between dialect and language Pennsylvania German gravitates more towards the dialect pole than any other Germanic 'language' treated in this book. The reason for not just calling it a dialect is that it underwent both spontaneous uniformization (dialect levelling) and some standardization efforts, and that it marginally also functions for written communication. All speakers are bilingual in English, and earlier generations diglossic in High German, which was – and still is – used for liturgy. Among secular speakers, the language is in a state of attrition, but in some Old Order Amish and Mennonite communities, for which language is synonymous with religion and which have a high birth-rate, there is no immediate threat to continuity.

Dutch

Dutch (*Nederlands* 'Netherlandic', earlier *Dietsch* or *Duytsch* '(language) of the people' – as distinguished from Latin – and *Nederduytsch* 'low Dutch' – as distinguished from German) is the official language of the Netherlands, where it is native to the majority of a population of some fourteen million, with the exception of two or three hundred thousand Frisians and diverse ethnic minorities of seven hundred thousand. It is also an official language of Belgium, where it is the native language in the Flemish community counting up to six million native speakers, thus forming the majority of the population, also comprising *c.*3.7 million French-speaking Belgians, 900,000 foreign nationals, and up to 90,000 German-speaking Belgians. Dutch is a school language for many Dutch and Belgians that do not have Dutch as their native language, but the level of competence in Dutch differs enormously, with native Frisians reaching the highest levels of bilingualism. The Brussels conurbation is north of the French–Dutch language border and was thus originally Dutch-speaking, but it is now officially bilingual and the dominant language of its inhabitants has become French. This is one language change among others in the vicinity of the language border which together with a general revival of Dutch plagued twentieth-century Belgium with ethnic and political conflict. A Dutch dialect is still spoken by a dwindling minority in the northwestern corner of France (French Flanders) and it is the language of administration and education in the Dutch Antilles and in Surinam (formerly Dutch Guyana). Afrikaans is sometimes considered to be a creole of Dutch (see p. 15) and *Negerhollands* is the name of a virtually extinct Dutch creole on the Virgin Islands.

Dutch derives from Old (West) Low Franconian (*c*.400 to *c*.1100), the language associated with the tribal settlements from the fourth to the ninth century in what is now The Netherlands and Dutch-speaking Belgium, except for Frisian and Saxon settlements in the north and east of the Netherlands respectively. In view of its later development Old Low Franconian is also called 'Old Dutch'. There are few direct records of this language. Its Middle Dutch successor (*c*.1100 to *c*.1500) is well documented from the end of the twelfth century, especially in the western (Flemish) and centre (Brabantic) dialects of the economically more prosperous southern area, now Belgium. Standard Dutch is the variety of Modern Dutch (from *c*.1600 onwards, after the sixteenth century as a transition period with Middle Dutch) based primarily on the dialect of the Amsterdam region after it had become the capital of an independent nation. After the separation of the north, the south saw its upper layers of society and their transactions in the field of culture, education, administration and religion become increasingly romanized, a process which started in the Middle Ages, and when Belgium acquired its independence in 1830 it only had French as a national language. When Dutch slowly reassumed its social prestige and came to be used again for more forms of communication during the late nineteenth and twentieth centuries, the northern standard was accepted.

Afrikaans
Afrikaans is one of the two official languages of the Republic of South Africa, where it has some 5 million native speakers, i.e. 14 per cent of the total population of 36.5 million, including the inhabitants of the homelands. A little less than half of them are whites, called *Afrikaners*, formerly *Boers* 'farmers', while the other half are Cape Coloureds (*Kaapse kleurlingen*), who are descended from the original Dutch settlers, indigenous Hottentots, and Indian, Malay and Black slaves. Some further tens of thousands of native speakers live in Namibia, the former German colony of South West Africa, under the control of South Africa from 1914 to 1990, also consisting of both whites and people of mixed race. In both South Africa and Namibia, especially in the rural areas, Afrikaans further serves as a lingua franca for hundreds of thousands of people of all races. As an official language, Afrikaans is in competition with English, the mother tongue of a little less than 3 million, mostly white but some Coloureds and many of the 1 million Indians living in the country. Afrikaans is also the second language of the majority of Afrikaners and Coloureds and many Blacks. Afrikaans and English coexist with several indigenous languages, especially Sotho (9 million), Zulu (7 million) and Xhosa (7 million), all of them Bantu.

South Africa is the result of Dutch and British expansion into the interior of southern Africa from Cape Town, founded in 1652 by the Dutch East India Company. Cape Town is now the legislative capital of the republic as well as of the Cape Province, the largest of the country's four provinces. As Dutch settlement proceeded along the southern coast in an easterly direction throughout the eighteenth century, so their language spread across southern Africa. In 1806 the British took over the Cape – after an earlier brief occupation from 1795–1803 – and started to encourage British emigration to the territory. As a result the Cape Province became bilingual, though Afrikaans remained dominant in the rural areas, mainly because it had become the mother tongue of the Cape Coloured.

The provinces of the Orange Free State, Transvaal and Natal are the result of the *Great Trek*, which took place in the latter half of the 1830s. The *Trek* was the attempt of the Boers to find farmland beyond the reach of the British authority and the English language. Natal was annexed by the British as early as 1843, but the Orange Free State and Transvaal enjoyed the status of independent republics until their defeat by the British in the Boer War of 1899–1901. When founded in the middle of the century, their white population was overwhelmingly Afrikaans-speaking, although the discovery of diamonds and gold in the 1870s and 1880s in these areas attracted many non-Afrikaans-speaking immigrants. These historical events explain why the white population of Natal is predominantly English-speaking, whereas that of Transvaal and the Orange Free State speaks predominantly Afrikaans, especially in the rural areas but also in some cities, as Boers later became city dwellers. In the administrative capital of Pretoria the dominant language is also Afrikaans, since the government and its bureaucracy has been manned chiefly by Afrikaners since the victory of the National Party in the election of 1948. The language of commerce, however, is English.

It is now generally agreed that the Dutch spoken at the Cape had become a separate idiom by the early nineteenth century ('Cape Dutch'), but the first written records did not appear until half a century later and only in 1925 did the parliament officially adopt Afrikaans as the country's other official language. There is still some disagreement as to whether Afrikaans is an essentially spontaneous development of seventeenth-century Dutch dialects, influenced by neighbouring and co-territorial indigenous and colonial languages, or more of a creole developed by the non-Dutch inhabitants of the Cape. Independently of whether Afrikaans is to be regarded as a creole of Dutch or not, however, certain sectors of the non-white population speak a variety of Afrikaans called *Oorlams*, dialects which betray a greater number of creole features than standard Afrikaans. Because most native speakers of Afrikaans are bilingual in English and because the two languages are not geographically separated, the latter is in the process of exerting a tremendous influence on the former.

Frisian

Modern Frisian exists as three mutually unintelligible varieties: (a) West Frisian (*Frysk*), spoken in the northern Dutch province of *Fryslân* (*Friesland*) by four hundred thousand people, half of whom have it as their mother tongue; (b) East Frisian or Saterlandic (*Friisk*), spoken in the three villages of Saterland, an islet in a moorland area between Bremen and the Dutch border, probably only by a thousand speakers; and (c) North Frisian (*Friisk, Frasch, Fresk*), spoken on the islands and the northwestern coast of Schleswig-Holstein by up to ten thousand people. Most of the speakers of Frisian are bilingual in Dutch (West Frisian), Low and High German (East and North Frisian), and even in the Jutish dialect of Danish (northern North Frisian). Each of the varieties is in decline, East Frisian more than North Frisian and both more than West Frisian. Especially during the last two decades, language-preservation attempts have been undertaken, which have resulted in little more than a dictionary and an occasional publication for East Frisian; a regular publication scheme and tuition for North Frisian; and, for West Frisian, regular publications, access to the media of radio and television, mandatory tuition and local governments' assessments of Frisian as an asset.

The present geographical location is essentially the result of the gradual reduction of a Frisian territory once stretching continuously along the North Sea coast from North Holland to the Weser and discontinuously extending into the North Frisian area. The oldest direct records are from the late thirteenth century in the variant now called 'Old Frisian'. For post-1550 records one uses the term 'Modern (New) Frisian' or 'Middle Frisian', and in the latter case 'Modern Frisian' takes over from 1800 onwards.

English

From the middle of the fifth century, Germanic federates of Jutes, Angles and Saxons left the Danish and German North Sea coast and settled in England, the Angles in the north and the Saxons in the south, except for Kent, which was seized by the Jutes. The native Celts retained control of most of Cornwall, Wales, Scotland and Ireland, but in England they gradually assimilated to the newcomers. The West Germanic dialects spoken then are now referred to collectively as Anglo-Saxon or Old English (up to *c*.1150), first documented in runic inscriptions, with literary, documentary and religious texts from the eighth century onwards, mostly from the southern, so-called 'West Saxon' area. From the end of the eighth century until the beginning of the eleventh century, the Anglo-Saxon population was itself the victim of an invasion, namely by Vikings, who established themselves in the east of England in the area called the 'Danelaw', merged with the earlier inhabitants and influenced the language, especially the lexicon. A third invasion which shaped the English language, again primarily its lexicon but also the orthography, started in 1066 when the Norman French duke, William the Conqueror, forcefully seized the throne of England and started to colonize the land and introduce a French-speaking administration, nobility and clergy. French was to remain the prestige language until the fourteenth century. The lexical and ortho-graphical changes together with a levelling of the Anglo-Saxon inflectional system characterize the 'Middle English' period, conventionally taken to extend from *c*.1150 to *c*.1500, the beginning of 'Modern English'. The latter is the period of the enormous geographical dispersion. In nearby Cornwall, Wales, Scotland and Ireland, English nearly ousted Celtic, and on the Shetlands and Orkneys English replaced the descendant of Old Norwegian called *Norn*. With Britannia's and later the United States' rule of the waves, English was exported around the globe, with the creation of numerous English-based creoles as a side-effect. Today more than 300 million people have English as their native language, and a similar number may have it as a daily second language, and many more as the lingua franca for science, international trade and politics.

The most important predominantly English-speaking areas are the United States (240 million), the United Kingdom (56 million), Canada (24 million), Australia (17 million), Ireland (3.5 million) and New Zealand (3.2 million), though none of them is linguistically homogeneous. Furthermore, English is an official language in a number of countries that lie, or used to lie, in the British colonial or United States' spheres of influence, where it either has substantial numbers of native speakers (e.g. South Africa with nearly 3 million) but more often of second-language speakers (e.g. the Philippines with 11 million), and where it is co-territorial with indigenous languages, other western languages (e.g. Cameroon with French, and South Africa with Afrikaans) or with creoles (e.g. Jamaica).

There are many national variants of English, differing primarily in pronunciation and less so in grammar and spelling. British English has a standard that originated in the London dialect area, but has now become a sociolect, associated with the educated upper classes and often heard on radio and television.

Into the Twenty-first Century

Most of the Germanic languages are not 'endangered species'. On the contrary, most of them lead the protected life of a national language of one or more states. English will most likely increase its role as an international language, and within Europe the liberalization in Eastern Europe will probably revitalize German as a lingua franca. The three Germanic languages that are not associated with a modern state will have a harder time surviving through the next century, however. The fate of Pennsylvania German and Yiddish probably depends on whether or not the sectarian lifestyle of Amish, Mennonite and Jewish communities will continue to attract followers. Most threatened perhaps is Frisian, since it has neither a state nor a religion to support it.

A Note on the Numbers

Estimating the numbers of first- and second-language speakers is very difficult. Our numbers are estimates based on the sources listed in the references or on the expert opinions of some of the contributors to this volume.

References and Further Reading *Nothing on English*

Barbour, S. and Stevenson, P. (1990) *Variation in German*, Cambridge: Cambridge University Press.

Born, J. and Dickgießer, S. (1989) *Deutschsprachige Minderheiten. Ein Überblick über den Stand der Forschung für 27 Länder*, Mannheim: Institut für deutsche Sprache.

Braunmüller, K. (1991) *Die skandinavischen Sprachen im Überblick*, Tübingen: Francke.

Comrie, B. (ed.) (1987) *The World's Major Languages*, London: Routledge.

Harris, M. and Vincent N. (eds) (1988) *The Romance Languages*, London: Routledge.

Haugen, E. (1976) *The Scandinavian Languages. An Introduction to Their History*, London: Faber and Faber.

—— (1982) *Scandinavian Language Structures. A Comparative Historical Survey*, Tübingen: Niemeyer.

Hutterer, C. J. (1975) *Die germanischen Sprachen. Ihre Geschichte in Grundzügen*, Budapest: Akadémiai Kiadó.

Kern, R. (ed.) (1990) *Deutsch als Umgangs – und Muttersprache in der Europäischen Gemeinschaft*, Brussels: Europäisches Büro für Sprachminderheiten – Belgisches Komitee.

Kloss, H. (1978) *Die Entwicklung neuer germanischer Kultursprachen seit 1800*, Sprache der Gegenwart 37, Düsseldorf: Pädagogischer Verlag Schwann.

Molde, B. and Karker, A. (eds) (1983) *Språkene i Norden. Språken i Norden. Sprogene i Norden*, Copenhagen: Gyldendal.

Russ, C. V. J. (ed.) (1990) *The Dialects of Modern German*, London: Routledge.

Stephens, M. (1976) *Linguistic Minorities in Western Europe*, Llandysul: Gomer Press.

Vikør, L. (1993) *The Nordic Languages: Their Status and Interrelations*, Oslo: Novus.

2 Gothic and the Reconstruction of Proto-Germanic

Winfred P. Lehmann

2.1 Introduction

Gothic is the language of two Germanic peoples, the Visigoths and the Ostrogoths, known from the early centuries of our era. Except for a few runic inscriptions, Gothic provides us with our earliest Germanic texts. The texts are chiefly translations of the New Testament and fragments of the Old Testament, ascribed to Wulfila (*c*. 300–82/3), and a few other materials from the sixth century. Because it precedes other extensive Germanic texts by three or four centuries, by even more those in North Germanic, Gothic is important for reconstruction of Proto-Germanic as well as for the information it gives us on its society and their language.

Like all early texts, those in Gothic present many problems. These have given rise to an enormous bibliography that has by no means provided solutions. Our information on Wulfila is slight. The origin of the Gothic alphabet is undocumented and spelling conventions are disputed. The text of the Greek Bible used for the translation is unknown. Only parts of the translation have come down to us, so that the stock of words and forms is not great. And the manuscripts that have preserved the translation were written in northern Italy, the Balkans or southern France, apparently in the early sixth century, possibly even by Ostrogothic scribes in contrast with the Visigoth Wulfila who produced the translation in the fourth century.

Moreover, the early history of the Goths is obscure. As a result, their relationships to the other Germanic peoples is unclear. Traditionally, as reported to us by a sixth-century historian, Procopius, they moved from Götland in eastern Sweden to the coastal area near the mouth of the Vistula in the first century before our era; Tacitus in the *Germania* of AD 98 reports Gotones in this area at his time (chapter 44). Around AD 200 they migrated to southern Russia, some going on to the Black Sea, in the region around the Sea of Azov. There two distinct groups can be recognized, the Visi ('good') and

19

the Ostrogoths ('Eastern Goths'). Subsequently the designation Visigoths was introduced and came to be interpreted as 'Western Goths', as indeed they were geographically in the Eastern Empire and later in their location in Spain from the fifth century. With other Germanic groups, whose languages we know only from names – the Burgundians, the Vandals, the Rugians – the Goths and their language are referred to as East Germanic, in contrast with the North Germanic peoples and languages of Scandinavia, and the West Germanic of central Europe. But differences in time of the texts brought about by shifts and realignments of the identifiable Germanic groups leave this classification open to many questions.

In the fourth century the Goths were in close touch with the Eastern Empire. Captives in battle were Christianized, and the new religion was introduced in other ways as well. Wulfila's grandparents were taken captive in a raid on the Cappadocian village, Sadagolthina, in AD 264. Brought up in the faith, Wulfila came with a delegation to the imperial court c. AD 336/7; there he was influenced by Bishop Eusebius to embrace the Homoean doctrine, a view of the relation of Christ to God the Father similar to that of Arianism. Probably in part because of his missionary efforts, the Goths as a group were Arians; as the Visigoths settled in the west towards the end of the fourth century, and the Ostrogoths a century later, they were at odds with the dominant Athanasian doctrines of the western Church. The doctrinal differences led to conflict. The Goths were destroyed as important political groups, the Ostrogoths by an army of the Eastern Empire under Belisarius in 555, the Visigoths by the Moslems in AD 711.

The Language in Relation to Proto-Germanic and the Other Germanic Dialects

According to tradition the Goths maintained an aristocratic culture that reflected many characteristics of Indo-European society. They supported poets who preserved accounts of their valiant men, such as the king, Ermaneric, who came to be central figures in the medieval literature of the West and North Germanic peoples. The poets created a major role for Attila, ruler of the Huns, glorified as Etzel in the High German *Nibelungenlied*, and for Theodoric, the founder of the Ostrogothic empire in northern Italy, celebrated as Dietrich von Bern. The language maintains many military, legal and political terms, such as *draúhti*- 'army' in derivatives, **maþl* 'assembly', and the possibility of creating poetic terms known in other Indo-European literary traditions, as in the compound *mana-sēþs* 'world' < 'seed of men'. Such retentions of the earlier culture as well as archaic characteristics in the language support the view that Gothic can be taken as the chief source for reconstructing Proto-Germanic.

The other Germanic languages have undergone phonological and morphological changes not found in Gothic. The voiced sibilant /z/ has become a resonant, as in Old High German *mēro*, Old Icelandic *meiri*, as opposed to

Gothic *maiza* 'more'. Long /ē/ has been lowered, as in Old Icelandic *mækir*, Old English *mǣce* as opposed to Gothic *mēki* 'short sword'. The West Germanic languages have been especially innovative, as in lengthening consonants before resonants, e.g. Old English *settan*, Old High German *setzen* as opposed to Gothic *-satjan* and Old Icelandic *setja* 'set'. And as in this example, Gothic does not exhibit umlaut. Morphologically it maintains reduplication in many verbs and, like North Germanic, the reflex of the Indo-European second-person singular perfect form, as in *namt* 'thou didst take' as opposed to Old English *nōme*, Old High German *nāmi*. The Indo-European middle-passive is still preserved. Unfortunately for the determining of syntactic patterns, the Bible translation is very literal, so that it provides little information on syntax.

As might be expected, Gothic of the fourth to sixth century has also undergone changes from Proto-Germanic of the period before our era. Among innovations, Proto-Germanic /i, u/ have been lowered before /r/ and /h/, where the lowered vowels are written ‹aí, aú›. Moreover, strong verbs exhibit no variation between voiceless and voiced fricatives, as in *slaha, slōh, slōhun,* **slahans* 'strike'. Some specialists attribute the lack of contrast to absence of application of Verner's law in Gothic, by which voiceless fricatives became voiced if the Indo-European accent did not precede them, as in Old High German *slahan, sluoh, sluogum, gislagan*. But regularization is more likely, in view of the contrast in common words that are likely to maintain irregularities, like *áih* vs *áigun* 'have', or in derivatives, such as **frawardjan* 'destroy' versus *waírþan* 'become'.

2.2 Phonology

The Gothic alphabet, like the Greek and other early alphabets, also served to indicate numerals. There was no symbol for zero, and accordingly 27 symbols were adequate, those representing 1–9, 10–90, 100–900. In early Greek systems, each of these had a phonetic value. When there was no sound in Gothic corresponding to that in Greek, the symbol was none the less maintained for its use as numeral; for example, the symbol for koppa, representing 90, was kept even though Gothic had no back velar voiceless stop.

Wulfila or other designers of the Gothic alphabet made ingenious use of some superfluous symbols. For the [kʷ] sound they used the symbol representing 6, which in Greek stood for [w] or [v]; in our texts it is transliterated as ‹q›. For [hʷ] they used the symbol representing 700, which is transliterated as the ligature ‹ƕ›. On the other hand, the symbol representing 5 was selected for long Gothic [eː], leaving no likely symbol for the short [e], for which the ‹ai› digraph was selected. Since short [e], [o] were represented by ‹ai, au› the symbols ‹e, o› represent long vowels /eː, oː/. Because these vowels are always long, some handbooks do not indicate the length with a macron. The digraph ‹ei› is used to represent long /iː/.

The readings of ‹ai› and ‹au› are disputed. From borrowed names we know that they represented [ɛ] and [ɔ], the pronunciation of the digraphs in Greek of the time, e.g. *Aíleisabaíþ* Gk *Elisábet*, *apaústaúlus* Gk *apóstolos*. But many words with [ay, aw] diphthongs in the other Germanic dialects are also written with the digraphs, e.g. *áins*, Ger. *eins* 'one', *áugō*, Ger. *Auge* 'eye'. Still others have different cognate elements, e.g. *saian*, Ger. *säen* 'sow', *sauil*, Ger. *Sonne* 'sun'. The digraphs then may have had three different pronunciations: [ɛ, ay, ɛː, ɔ, aw, ɔː]. Yet specialists who insist on one pronunciation argue that framers of an alphabet would be unlikely to use symbols with more than one value. A solution is likely only if we discover new inscriptions or manuscripts. As here, specialists may use acute accent marks to distinguish the readings.

While the order of the alphabetic symbols and their values correspond to those in Greek, the shapes have several origins. Those for ‹h› and ‹r› were based on Latin. The alphabet then, like other elements of Gothic society, reflects the combination of influences of the Greeks and the Latins on Germanic culture that led to the Gothic culture we know.

The Consonant System

We assume nineteen consonantal phonemes for Gothic, four of which are differently interpreted by some specialists (Table 2.1). The series /b, d, g/ has stop articulation initially, finally and when doubled, fricative articulation between vowels. The other consonants have one principal allophone, except for /n/, which has a velar variant before velars.

The status of /j/ and /w/ is disputed, some interpreters taking them as variants of /i, u/. In most contexts they stand in complementary distribution, for example, only [w] before vowels, only [u] under accent between consonants. Direct contrasts for /i/ vs /j/ are found with proper names, e.g. *Maria* vs *kunja* 'kin'; for /u/ vs /w/ the contrasts are clear, as in *gáidw* 'lack', *faíhu* 'property'. Yet the positions in which contrasts are found are so limited that we may assume single phonemes for the resonants in Proto-Germanic.

The status of ‹q› /kʷ/ and ‹ƕ› /hʷ/ is also disputed, some taking them as clusters of two phonemes. Clusters of consonant plus *w* occur only with

Table 2.1   The consonant system

p	t		k	k^w ‹q›
b	d	z	g	
f	þ	s	h	h^w ‹ƕ›
m	n			
l	r	*j*	w	

Note: The four italicized phonemes are those which are differently interpreted by some specialists. ‹ƕ› is the Gothic letter which represents the complex consonant [hw].

dentals, as in *twái* 'two'; the unique form *bidagwa* 'beggar' is taken as an error. Moreover, they pattern with single consonants, as in the past tense *sagq* [saŋkʷ] 'sank', where interpretation as a cluster would require a three-consonant sequence. Similarly, in the initial cluster of *qrammiþa* 'dampness', which would be unique if taken as /kwr/, though the cluster may be an error for /kr-/. We assume the same consonant system for late Proto-Germanic, except that /i, u/ included the consonantal variants [y, w], Gothic *j* and *w*. Moreover, before the fixing of the accent, [z] was a variant of /s/.

The Vowel System

The vowel system of sixth century Gothic consisted of five short and five long vowels: /i, e, a, o, u, iː, eː, aː, oː, uː/, plus at least one diphthong /iw/ and probably /ay, aw/ as well. But there are problems.

As noted above, [i, e] [o, u] were virtually in complementary distribution, the open counterparts standing before /h, hʷ, r/, the close elsewhere, e.g. with PGmc /e/ *qiman*, cf. OHG *queman* 'come' but with PGmc /i/ in *gataíhun*, cf. OHG *zigun* 'showed'. An early form of Gothic may have had a short vowel system consisting of three members: /a/, plus /i, u/ with allophonic variants. But the variants came to stand before other consonants as well, as did [e] in *aíþþau* 'or' < *eh-þ-*, and [i] before *r, h* as in *hiri* 'here', *nih* 'and not'. Accordingly, by the time our manuscripts were written, the language included five short vowels. Borrowings reflect this system, as in *aípiskaúpus*, Gk *epískopos* 'bishop', with /e/ and /o/ before /p/.

Proto-Germanic on the other hand had a vowel system consisting of four short and four long vowels; the two low back vowels had fallen together. The system is generally represented with short /a/ and long /oː/ as a result of the later introduction of short /o/ and long /aː/. After the Proto-Germanic period, short /o/ resulted from lowering of some /u/; long /aː/ arose from compensatory lengthening upon loss of nasal before voiceless fricatives, as in *þāho* 'clay', OHG *dāhā*, cf. Lith. *tánkus* 'thick'.

A new long close /eː/ arose in Proto-Germanic through compensatory lengthening, upon loss of nasal as in *mēs*, OHG *mias* 'table' < VLat. *mēsa*, Lat. *mensa*, and of laryngeal as in *fēra*, OHG *fiara* 'side' < PIE (*s*)*peHyr-*. Proto-Germanic /ē/ was then lowered, generally written /æ/, so that the language had a long vowel system of six members. The two long *e* vowels fell together in Gothic; Old English *lætan* 'let' corresponds to Gothic *-lētan*, while Old English *mēse* reflects the close long /ē/, often called *ē²*, as in Gothic *mēsa* 'table', yielding the system of five long vowels indicated above.

Early Gothic had the diphthongs /ay, aw, ey/, as in *áins* 'one', cf. OLat. *oinos*, *áukan* 'increase', cf. Lat. *augere*, and *kiusa* 'test', cf. Gk *geúomai* 'taste'.

Accentuation and Syllable Weight

Unfortunately we have no means for determining the intonational pattern of sentences. We can however determine the accentuation of individual words. Since voiceless fricatives are manifested even in forms that have voiced fricatives in the other Germanic dialects, we conclude that Gothic had fixed accent on stem syllables, usually initial, as in: *wisan, was, wēsum* 'be' in contrast with Old English *wesan, wæs, wǣron*. The variation between singular and plural of the past is maintained to this day in *was, were*.

Other evidence supports the assumption of initial accent on words. The particle *anda* 'along' has maintained its second vowel in nouns, which had principal stress on the first syllable, but has lost it in verbs, which have principal stress on the stem; the difference is indicated in 1 Timothy 6:12 **andhaíháist þamma gōdin andaháita** 'you have confessed the good confession'. Similarly, because of the initial strong stress on nouns, vowels were lost or weakened in final syllables, as in the accusative singular *haúrn* 'horn' in contrast with *horna* of the Gallehus runic inscription dated about AD 325.

Moreover, enclitics, especially the connective particle *u(h)* 'and' can be placed between prefixes and verb stems, as in *at-uh-gaf* 'and he gave to', suggesting that those prefixes carried a secondary stress. On the basis of this evidence we assume three degrees of stress: strong, mid, and weak.

Syllables are light if they contain only a long vowel, or a short vowel, also when ending in a consonant; otherwise they are heavy. Heavy syllables were followed in Proto-Germanic by a vowel + consonant variant of resonants. The effect is attested in *-ja*-stems of nouns and verbs, as illustrated in Table 2.3.

2.3 Morphology

Phonological Variation in Morphological Sets

Gothic, like Proto-Germanic, makes heavy use of the vocalic variation inherited from Proto-Indo-European that is known as ablaut. The varying vowels are the result of sound changes. In treatment of ablaut they are referred to as grades, with *e*-grade as basic (often called 'normal'), plus the variants: *o*-grade, lengthened grade, and zero grade. Ablaut is especially prominent in strong verbs, as in: *waírþan, warþ, waúrþun, waúrþans* 'become'. A paradigm has been constructed with four principal parts. Classes I–V have *e*-grade in the present and the infinitive, *o*-grade (PGmc, Go. *a*) in the past singular indicative, and zero grade in the past plural and subjunctive as well as the past participle. Classes IV and V have lengthened grade in the third principal part. Classes VI and VII observe different patterns.

While verbs of the first five classes have one basic pattern, they are classified into five groups in accordance with the structure of their stem (Table 2.2). Such alternation is also found in derivation, as in **(fra)wardjan* 'destroy', which illustrates Indo-European use of the *o*-grade in deriving

Table 2.2 The basic pattern of strong verbs classes I–V

		Present	Past singular	Past plural	Past participle
Proto-Indo-European		e	o	Ø	Ø
Proto-Germanic		e	a	Ø	Ø
Gothic	I	ei	ái	i	i
	II	iu	áu	u	u
	III	i/aí+l/m/n/r	a+	u/aú+	u/aú+
	IV	i/aíR	aR	ēR	u/aúR
	V	iC	aC	ēC	iC

Note: R = resonants, C = all other consonants.

causatives and factitives. Reflexes of ablaut variation in endings are also maintained, as in the nominative *brōþar* as opposed to the genitive *brōþrs* 'brother'. Although such patterns of vowel variation are attested in some derived verbs, in nouns and endings, derivational morphology relies more heavily on affixation than on ablaut in both Proto-Germanic and Gothic.

Morphological Classes
Like the other Indo-European languages, Gothic distinguishes nominals and verbals inflectionally as opposed to uninflected words. The nominals in turn may be subclassified into nouns, pronouns and adjectives, which include some forms of numerals. Nouns, adjectives and non-personal pronouns are inflected for gender, number and case. There are three genders: masculine, feminine, neuter. There are three numbers: singular, plural and dual, though the dual is preserved only in the personal pronouns, and in first- and second-person verbs of active voice. There are five cases: nominative, accusative, genitive, dative, and vocative, which has the same form as the nominative or accusative. Scholars who assume a Proto-Indo-European based on Indo-Iranian and Greek posit further cases for Proto-Germanic, of which only residues remain in Gothic; the residues may be derived from derivational as well as from inflectional forms.

The Nominal Group
Proto-Indo-European distinguished athematic nouns (nouns made up of a base without a suffix before inflectional endings) and thematic nouns (nouns with base followed by *e/o* and inflectional endings). In Germanic the thematic nouns have become more prominent; consonant stems like *hatis* 'hate' have become thematic. The *-n-* stems have, however, maintained their prominence; a second adjective inflection has been built on them.

Nouns have six major classes of inflection, plus two subgroups of the *a*-stems. The *n*-stems have also developed separate inflections for *-ōn* and *-īn*

Table 2.3   The principal noun classes

	PGmc *stem*	a	*a-stems* ja	-ja	ō	i	u	n	consonant
Base		dag	har	haírd	gib	gast	sunu	gum	baúrg
Singular									
Nom.	az	dags	harjis	haírdeis	giba	gasts	sunus	guma	baúrgs
Acc.	an	dag	hari	haírdi	giba	gast	sunu	guman	baúrg
Gen.	e/as	dagis	harjis	haírdeis	gibōs	gastis	sunaus	gumins	baúrgs
Dat.	ái	daga	harja	haírdja	gibai	gasta	sunau	gumin	baúrg
Voc.	e	–	–	haírdi	–		sunu		
Plural									
Nom.	ōzez	dagōs	harjōs	haírdjōs	gibōs	gastei	sunjus	gumans	baúrgs
Acc.	anz	dagans	harjans	haírdjans	gibōs	gastins	sununs	gumans	baúrgs
Gen.	ō/ēn	dagē	harjē	haírdjē	gibō	gastē	suniwē	gumanē	baúrgē
Dat.	amaz	dagam	harjam	haírdjam	gibōm	gastim	sunum	gumam	baúrgim

subgroups; these and other details must be left to the handbooks. In Germanic grammars the classes are designated, as in Table 2.3, with labels representing their Proto-Germanic stem vowels or consonants. The Proto-Germanic endings are listed in the first column. The *a*-stems are masculine and neuter. The neuter nominative singular has the ending of the accusative; the nominative plural has an *-a* ending. The *ō*-stems are feminine. The other classes may have any one of the genders. A full set of forms is given for each declension.

Pronouns

Like the other Indo-European languages, Gothic has various sets of pronouns. The personal pronouns are derived from comparable forms in Proto-Indo-European, though some have been enlarged with suffixes, such as the accusative singular *-k < -ge*. For example, the accusative *mik* 'me' corresponds to Greek (*e*)*mé* + *-ge*, with loss of final *-e*. Like the pronouns in the parent language, they maintain the shift in stem between nominative and oblique cases. Many of the forms have been analogically modified; *unsis* is found beside the accusative/dative *uns* (see Table 2.4).

Possessive adjectives are based on the genitive stems, e.g. *meins*, *þeins*, *unsar*, *izwar*; they are inflected like strong adjectives.

An anaphoric pronoun for the third person is based on a root *i* (possibly merged with *e*); it is inflected for case, number and gender, though not all forms are attested (Table 2.5). The interrogative pronoun, found only in the singular, is based on Proto-Indo-European *kʷo-*. In contrast with the other Germanic dialects, a distinct feminine has been developed (Table 2.6).

The neuter also includes a form *hʷē*, which is interpreted as an instrumental, as in *hʷē wasjaíþ* 'with what you clothe yourself'. A comparable form

Table 2.4   The personal pronouns

	I	we	we two	thou	you	you two	self
Nom.	ik	weis	wit	þu	jus		
Acc.	mik	uns	ugkis	þik	izwis	igkis	sik
Gen.	meina	unsara		þeina	izwara	igkara	seina
Dat.	mis	uns	ugkis	þis	izwis	igkis	sis

Table 2.5   The anaphoric pronoun 'he, she, it'

| | *Singular* | | | *Plural* | | |
	m.	f.	n.	m.	f.	n.
Nom.	is	si	ita	eis		ija
Acc.	ina	ija	ita	ins	ijōs	
Gen.	is	izōs	is	izē	izō	
Dat.	imma	izái	imma	im	im	im

Table 2.6   The interrogative pronoun

	m.	f.	n.
Nom.	hʷas	hʷō	hʷa
Acc.	hʷana	hʷō	hʷa
Gen.	hʷis		hʷis
Dat.	hʷamma	hʷizái	hʷamma

is found in the neuter demonstrative, but, apart from compounds, only in the phrase *ni þē haldis* 'by no means' (< 'not rather than that'). It is a residual comparative construction of the OV pattern, paralleled in *neo dana halt* of the Old High German *Hildebrandslied*, both giving testimony to the early verb-final structure of Proto-Germanic.

The usual relative pronoun is made with -*ei* suffixed to the simple demonstrative, i.e. *saei, sōei, þatei*. The suffix may also be added to other pronouns, as in *ikei* 'I, who', and *ei* may be used alone as a clause connective meaning 'that, so that'. The creation of this relative pronoun in contrast with the adaptation of the interrogative in English and of the demonstrative in German provides evidence that postposed relative clauses were developed only in the individual Germanic dialects rather than inherited from Proto-Indo-European or Proto-Germanic.

Table 2.7   The two adjective declensions in the masculine

	Strong Singular	Plural	Weak Singular	Plural
Nom.	blinds	blind**ái**	blinda	blindans
Acc.	blind**ana**	blindans	blindan	blindans
Gen.	*blindis	*blind**áizē**	blindins	*blindanē
Dat.	blind**amma**	blindáim	blindin	*blindam

Adjectives
Like the other Germanic languages, Gothic has two adjective inflections. One is based on the inflection of the noun, with possible *ja*-stems, *i*-stems and *u*-stems, though *o/ā*-stems are most prominent. This inflection is labelled strong. It includes some endings that are taken over from pronouns.

The other inflection is a Germanic innovation based on the inflection of *n*-stems. It indicates definiteness. Its meaning developed from the function of *n*-stems in some Indo-European languages to indicate specific individuals; such forms could then become personal names, e.g., Gk *Plátōn* 'Plato' (< 'the broad-shouldered individual'). Germanic shares the development of a definite adjective inflection with Slavic and Baltic, though in those branches the affixed element is a demonstrative. When definite articles were introduced into Germanic, possibly by influence from Latin which in turn had been influenced by Greek, and this earlier by Egyptian, weak (definite declension) endings accompanied the definite article; in time the adjective endings lost their distinctiveness. When maintained, as in Modern Standard German, the weak endings are reduced to *-e* and *-en*. To illustrate the two declensions, the masculine forms for each are given in Table 2.7.

Comparison is made with the suffixes *-iz-* and *-ōz-*, as in *managizō* 'more' and *garaíhtōza* 'juster', and in the superlative with *-ist-* and *-ōst-*, as in *managistans* 'most' and *armōstái* 'poorest'. Since comparatives refer to specific individuals, the comparative is inflected in the weak declension; the superlative is inflected either weak or strong.

Determiners
Gothic had no articles. The Greek article is represented in some contexts by the simple demonstrative; in such passages the translator apparently intended to express emphasis. The early runic inscriptions also contain no article; accordingly we assume that there was none in Proto-Germanic.

Demonstratives
The simple demonstrative is formed with reflexes of Proto-Indo-European **so, sā, tad*. Similar paradigms are found in the other Germanic dialects;

Table 2.8 The demonstrative pronoun

| | *Singular* | | | *Plural* | | |
	m.	f.	n.	m.	f.	n.
Nom.	sa	sō	þata	þái	þōs	þō
Acc.	þana	þō	þata	þans	þōs	þō
Gen.	þis	þizōs	þis	þizē	þizō	þizē
Dat.	þamma	þizái	þamma	þáim	þáim	þáim

accordingly we can assume the forms also for Proto-Germanic (Table 2.8).

An extended form of the demonstrative is made with the affix -(*u*)*h* 'and, then', i.e., *sah, sōh, þatuh*. The affix is assumed to be a cognate of Latin -*que* 'and'. This demonstrative is occasionally used as a relative pronoun.

Quantifiers
Quantifiers are treated in Gothic grammar as indefinites; for example, *sums, suma, sum* 'someone' is inflected like a strong, rather than a weak, adjective. Its negative is represented by phrases consisting of *ni* 'not' and *áins*, 'one, $h^w as$ 'who', or *manna* 'man' followed by the enclitic particle *hun* 'any', e.g. *ni* . . . *áinshun, áinōhun, áinhun* 'no one'; they are treated as pronouns, though *áinshun* is also accompanied by nouns in the genitive. Two items represent 'each': $h^w azuh$, $h^w ōh$, $h^w ah$ and less commonly $h^w arjizuh$, which is made up of $h^w arjis$ 'who' and -*uh*.

Numerals
Cardinal numerals have the bases found in other Indo-European languages, e.g., *áins, twái, *þreis, fidwōr, fimf, saíhs, sibun, ahtau, niun, taíhun*. The first three are inflected in all genders and cases, though as illustrated with '3' not all forms are attested.

The numerals for 11 and 12 are made as in Lithuanian with a suffix meaning 'additional' based on Proto-Indo-European *leyk^w*- 'leave over': **áinlif, twalif*; the other teen numerals attested have the additive pattern of VO languages, *fidwortaíhun* '14', **fimftaíhun* '15'.

The numerals from 20–60 are made with simple cardinals plus **tigjus* '-ty', e.g. *twaím tigum* '(with) twenty'; those from 70–100 with -*tēhund*, e.g. *sibuntēhund* '70', *taíhuntēhund* '100'. The hundreds are made with cardinals plus the neuter plural *hunda*, e.g. *fimf hunda* '500'.

The ordinals are based on the cardinals, except for *fruma* 'first' and *anþar* 'second', e.g. *þridja* 'third', *saíhsta* 'sixth'.

The Verb

Gothic verbs are inflected for three persons, for three numbers – with the dual only in first and second persons, for present and preterite tenses; for indicative, subjunctive and imperative moods; and for active and passive voice, though passive forms are found only in the present tense. The subjunctive is based on the Indo-European optative; some handbooks maintain the designation, though to indicate parallelism with other Germanic dialects the term 'subjunctive' is generally used. Passives are also made with forms of *wisan* and *waírþan* plus the preterite participle.

Aspectual Expression

While Gothic has a tense system, derivational patterns, such as the *-nan* verbs, also indicate manner of action (*Aktionsart*). Yet expression of such verbal meaning is one of the most debated features of the language, as is treatment of aspectual expression in linguistic handbooks.

Some linguists use the term 'aspect' generally, while others insist on restricting it to languages like Russian, in which parallel forms are found for the so-called perfective and imperfective aspects. It is useful to distinguish between aspect with such a meaning and *Aktionsart* 'manner of action', which is expressed through means such as derivation. Those who make the distinction posit only *Aktionsart* for Gothic.

Strong and Weak Verbs

Gothic verbs fall into two groups: those called strong indicate tense through internal marking based on ablaut; those called weak are largely derived and indicate tense through a *d*-affix. The strong verbs consist of seven classes, for which we here use Roman numerals; the weak verbs consist of four, for which we use Arabic numerals. This twofold distinction sets Germanic off from other Indo-European languages; Latin, for example, has four conjugations, the third of which includes verbs such as those making up the strong group in Germanic. The two other western groups, Greek and Celtic, have even less distinct classes.

The Strong Verbs

The strong verbs consist of two sets as determined by their ablaut patterning. Of the seven Germanic classes, the first five are parallel in their ablaut patterning, as illustrated in Table 2.2; the forms have adapted the ablaut vowels *e* vs *o*, and zero, though the fourth and fifth classes employ lengthened grade in the preterite forms other than the singular indicative.

The two remaining classes are difficult to analyse; their pattern may have been determined by laryngeal bases. By such an analysis the normal grade was applied in the past, while the present and the past participle have zero grade, e.g. Proto-Germanic *a* vs *ō* vs *ō* vs *a* of class VI, and *ay* vs *ēy* vs *ēy* vs *ay* among others of class VII, e.g., *swaran, swōr* 'swear', *háitan, haíháit* 'be named'. This hypothesis is difficult to verify because few verbs in the two classes have bases that are similarly modified in other Indo-European languages. Verbs of class VII show reduplication in the past tense. Its presence has been taken by some as persistence of the widespread pattern in Indo-Iranian and Greek. It may also be the result of internal spread, for parallel verbs in the other Germanic dialects provide only a few forms that have been interpreted as reflexes of reduplicated forms. For the most part the other dialects form the stem vowel in the past tense of class VII verbs with reflexes of Proto-Germanic $\bar{e}^2$.

The Weak Verbs

Gothic has four classes of weak verbs, distinguished by their suffixes: class 1 *i/j*; class 2 *ō*; class 3 *ái*; class 4 *na/ō*. The last two may also be characterized semantically; class 3 verbs are stative; class 4 verbs are inchoative or medio-passive. Class 1 verbs result from various sources, notably causatives or factitives, e.g. *lagjan* 'lay', and denominatives based on nouns or adjectives, e.g. *háiljan* 'heal'. Class 2 verbs are also chiefly denominatives.

The Verbal Paradigm

Many forms of the class IV strong verb *niman* 'take' are attested; it is therefore useful for illustrating the paradigm (Table 2.9). The active voice has two tenses and three moods, but only present forms are found for the passive.

The forms of weak verbs are comparable, though the affix must be taken into consideration. And in the first class the second- and third-person singular and the second plural must be noted for variation of the resonant marking the root. The present singular forms are given in Table 2.10.

The forms of the weak past are characteristic only in the singular indicative. For *lagjan* the first and third singular are *lagida*, the second singular *lagidēs*.

Table 2.9 The verbal paradigm as illustrated by the class IV strong verb *niman*

	Active Present			Past		Passive Present	
	Indicative	Subjunctive	Imperative	Indicative	Subjunctive	Indicative	Subjunctive
1 Singular	nima	nimáu		nam	*nēmjáu	nimada	nimáidau
2	nimis	*nimáis	nim	namt	nēmeis	nimaza	nimáizau
3	nimiþ	nimái	nimadau	nam	nēmi	nimada	nimáidau
1 Dual	nimōs	*nimáiwa		nēmu			
2	nimats	*nimáits	*nimats	*nēmuts			
1 Plural	nimam	*nimáima	*nimam	nēmum	*nēmeima	nimanda	nimáindau
2	nimiþ	nimáiþ	nimiþ	nēmuþ	*nēmeiþ		
3	nimand	nimáina		nēmun	nēmeina		

Table 2.10   The present singular of weak verbs

	Class 1			Class 2	Class 3	Class 4
1 sg.	lagja	stōja	sōkja	salbō	haba	fullna
2 sg.	lagjis	stōjis	sōkeis	salbōs	habáis	fullnis
3 sg.	lagjiþ	stōjiþ	sōkeiþ	salbōþ	habáiþ	fullniþ

There are three non-finite forms, the infinitive, e.g. *niman*, the present participle, *nimands*, the past participle, **numans*. The present participle is inflected like a weak adjective, though the feminine ends in *-ei*, e.g. *nimandei*.

Preterite-presents
The Germanic languages have a small group of verbs that are inflected as past-tense forms but have present meaning. They arose when in the shift from an Indo-European aspect system to the Germanic tense system the lexical meaning rather than the aspectual meaning underwent change. For example, *wáit* 'I know' is based on the perfect (preterite) form of the Proto-Indo-European root **weyd-* 'see'; the aspectual meaning 'I have completed seeing' was not shifted to the preterite meaning 'I have seen' but rather to 'I know' – for, one who has seen knows. Among other members of the group are *kann* 'I know, I can' from 'I have recognized', *ōg* 'I fear' from 'I have suffered in spirit'.

Somewhat similarly, the verb forms *wiljau*, *wileis*, *wili* 'want' are historically optative, but are used as indicatives.

The present-tense forms of the verb *be* are made from the Proto-Indo-European root **ʔes-* 'be', e.g. *im* 'I am', *is* 'thou art', *ist* 'is'. The infinitive and past tense are made from the root Proto-Indo-European **wes-* 'exist', e.g. *was, wast, was,* inf. *wisan,* pres. part. *wisands.*

Uninflected Words
There are four classes of uninflected words: adverbs, prepositions, conjunctions and interjections. Among these the class of adverbs has the most members, some of which are noted here.

Adverbs derived from adjectives are made with the suffix *-ō* that is a reflex of Proto-Indo-European *-ōd*, and identified by some scholars as an ablative, e.g. *galeikō* 'similarly'; as a more likely explanation it is a form from which the ablative in some nouns arose, notably in Sanskrit and Latin. The suffix *-ba* is used to derive adverbs of manner from adjectives, e.g. *ubilaba* 'evilly'. Adverbs of place form a set of related items using several suffixes, e.g. *inn* 'into', *inna* 'within', *innaþrō* 'from within', *hʷaþ* 'where to', *hʷaþrō* 'from where'.

Prepositions are found that govern any of the oblique cases, or also several cases, such as *ana* 'on, at' governing the dative and the accusative, *in* governing all three cases, with the meaning 'because of' when followed by the genitive. They are also used as prefixes in compounding, e.g. *faura-gaggja* 'steward' < 'one going ahead'. When such prefixes are found with verbs, a particle may be placed between the two segments, e.g. *us-nu-gibiþ* 'now give (out)'. The position of the separating particle indicates that such verbal compounds are not fixed yet. This conclusion is supported by the position of the accent in such compounds in Modern German, where the prefix has been weakened in verbs, e.g. *erlauben* 'permit', but not in nouns, e.g. *Urlaub* 'furlough'.

Many conjunctions are in use to indicate the relationships between clauses. They do not govern modal forms, which in Gothic have the function of expressing modality rather than subordination.

Simple conjunction is indicated by *jah* 'and, also', *uh* 'and', and *nih* 'and not'. Disjunction is expressed by *þau(h)* and *aíþþau* < **aif-þau*, cf. Eng. *if*, 'or', as well as by the correlatives *andizuh ... aíþþau* 'either ... or'. Adversative relationship is expressed by *iþ, þan, aþþan, akei* 'but' and *ak* 'but, on the contrary'.

For indicating conditional relationships *jabái* 'if' and *nibá(i)* 'if not' are used, and for indicating concessive relations, *þaúhjabái* 'even if', *swēþaúh* 'to be sure'.

To indicate purpose, many conjunctions in *-ei* are found, including *ei, þatei, þēei, þei* 'that', *swaei* and *swaswē* 'so that'. The conjunction *swē* is used for comparison with the meaning 'as' and temporally 'as, when'. Other temporal conjunctions are *þan, þandē* 'whenever, as long as', *biþē, miþþanei* 'while', *sunsei (suns-ei)* 'as soon as', *untē* 'until'.

Causal relationship is expressed by *allis, áuk, untē, raíhtis* 'for, because'; result by *eiþan, nu, nuh, nunu, þanuh, þannu, þaruh* 'therefore, accordingly'.

This large array of conjunctions, most newly created for these uses in Gothic or Proto-Germanic, provides further evidence that means for expressing clausal interrelationships in Proto-Germanic had to be created, as we have noted with relative markers. When the basic order of sentences shifted from the Proto-Indo-European Object–Verb (OV) to Verb–Object (VO) in Proto-Germanic and its dialects, subordinate clauses came to be postposed; markers were then essential to indicate their relationship with the principal clause. The need was even greater because clausal interrelationships were not expressed through verbal forms, for example, subjunctives in contrast with indicatives.

Only a few interjections are included in the texts: *o* 'oh', *sai* 'behold', *wai* 'alas', as well as the three forms modified for number, *hiri, hirjats, hirjiþ* 'come here'.

2.4   Syntax

The many syntactic studies have been chiefly concerned with determining the function of morphological elements and categories, such as the uses of the various case forms, especially where they differ from the Greek. The space allotted does not permit summaries of the results; on the whole the functions of grammatical classes and categories in Gothic are in accordance with those of the other Indo-European languages, and equivalent to those in the other Germanic languages.

Because of the literal translation, the word order of our texts is for the most part that of the Greek original. Citing the order of sentence constituents or the structure of nominal and verbal groups merely provides a description of these structures in Biblical Greek. Only deviations from the Greek can be used to determine the native order, especially when they accord with the patterning of other early Germanic texts, such as the runic inscriptions. We therefore examine such deviations to determine the native syntax, also for its information on the syntax of Proto-Germanic.

These deviations indicate that Gothic retained many patterns of Object–Verb (OV) syntax. In OV languages, e.g. Japanese, Turkish, governing elements occupy the same position with regard to the element governed as does the principal governing element, the verb. Accordingly adpositions follow nouns as postpositions, rather than precede them as prepositions. And in the comparison of inequality construction, the adjective follows the standard rather than precedes it, as in English. Because they are equivalent to objects, complements (object clauses), and also adverbial clauses, precede the principal clause. Moreover, nominal modifiers, such as relative clauses, genitives and adjectives, precede nouns. Residues of OV patterns in a VO language inform us of the previous structure of the language.

OV Order in Government Constructions

While the order of most clauses maintains that of Greek, in positive sentences with predicate adjectives the auxiliary follows the adjective, as in *siuks ist* 'is sick' (John 11:3). Since many predicate adjective constructions correspond to intransitive verbs in Greek, we may assume that the Gothic pattern is native. The order of such sentences is that of verb-final languages.

Comparative constructions support the assumption of earlier OV order, e.g., *managáim sparwam batizans sijuþ jus* (lit.) 'than many sparrows better are you' = 'you are better than many sparrows' (Matthew 10:31). Here the Greek does not have a comparative, but rather a verb: *pollôn strouthíōn diaphérete humeîs* 'of (from) many sparrows differ you'. While the Gothic pattern differs from the Greek, examples like this illustrate the difficulty of determining the native order. The preposed standard in the comparative construction is indeed as in OV syntax; but the noun phrase also precedes the verb in Greek and may have provided the pattern for the Gothic order. Other comparatives with standards in the dative, such as *máiza imma* 'more than he' (Matthew 11:11) also have the order of the Greek.

OV Order in Participal Constructions

Attempts have been made to determine the native syntactic pattern through analysis of texts other than the Bible translation. But these, except for the Commentary on the Gospel of John, are short; the Commentary also is conceded to be heavily influenced by Greek, whether or not it is a translation. Yet it includes much subordination through the use of participial constructions, as in *jah þa leikinōn us wambái munans gabaúrþ in tweifl gadráus* (lit.) 'and the corporeal from womb thinking birth into doubt fell' = 'because he thought of the corporeal birth from the womb, he doubted'. Such use of participial clauses preposed to the principal verb is characteristic of OV languages. This frequent pattern in the Commentary then provides further support for assumption of OV as the native word order. We must conclude, however, on the basis of the numerous conjunctions in the biblical texts and other constructions discussed below that the language had been shifting from OV to VO patterning.

The Infinitive as Verbal Noun

A construction that has attracted considerable attention is the use of the infinitive to translate passive infinitives of Greek, as in *háit nu witan þamma hláiwa* 'command now guarding [(to) guard] for that tomb' for Greek *kéleuson oûn asphalisthênai tòn táphon* 'command that the tomb be guarded'. Such use of infinitives as object, and also as subject, indicates that the so-called infinitive actually was a verbal noun; this analysis is supported by its origin in an accusative suffix, Proto-Germanic *-onom*. The present participle used as noun maintains similar evidence, for, when nominal, it is used with the genitive, as in *þans fijands galgins Xristaus* 'those hating of the cross of Christ' in contrast with its use of *fijands* when adjectival with a following dative. Such verbal noun constructions are characteristic of OV structure.

Negation and Interrogation

Negation is marked by the particle *ni* or the suffixed form *nih*. These typically stand before the verb.

Interrogation is marked by the enclitic *-u* generally placed on verbs, as in *wileiz-u* 'do you wish' (Luke 6:54). In negative sentences, however, it may be enclitic to *ni*, as in *ni-u gamēliþ ist*? 'Is it not written?' (Mark 11:17). This marker assumes a positive reply. The markers for a negative reply are *ja-u* and *ibái*, as in *ibái mag blinds blindana tiuhan* 'can a blind person lead a blind person?' The position of the particles is often that of the Greek. Yet the placing of interrogative *-u* after verbs may be taken as a residue of OV order; such verbal modifiers are postposed to the verb in OV languages.

Subordination

Subordination is indicated by conjunctions that do not govern the modal form of the verb, as noted above. Accordingly the construction of complex sentences is still highly paratactic as in OV languages.

Relative constructions, as we have indicated, are typically introduced by pronouns or particles suffixed by -*ei*. These often reproduce parallel relatives in Greek. The marker may however be used by itself, as in *from þamma daga ei háusidēdum* 'from the day that we heard it' (Colossians 1:9). It then functions as if indicating the focus of the sentence. This force is found when it is used with *ik* and *þu*, as in *þu h*ʷ*as is þuei stōjis* 'thou who art – thou-who judgest > who are you that you judge?'

Relative constructions then have something of the pattern found in Hittite, Vedic Sanskrit, early Greek and early Latin, where the relativizer is essentially a focusing particle. In Hittite and Latin the particle is based on PIE k^w-, in Sanskrit and Greek on *yo*-. The focusing particle was placed in the clause that complemented the principal clause, as in the examples here, and eventually developed as the relative pronoun. The differing relative markers in the Germanic dialects, e.g. Ger. *der*, *die*, *das*, Eng. *who*, *which*, *that*, indicate that Proto-Germanic had no single marker, and that each of its dialects developed its own.

Passivization

Greek passive constructions may be translated with the Gothic medio-passive in the present, with forms of -*nan* verbs, and with periphrastic constructions made with the preterite participle and forms of *wisan* and *waírþan*. The periphrastic forms still maintain some of their literal value, and accordingly are not actually elements of the verbal system. The perfect passive is translated with forms of *wisan* 'be' in most occurrences; the aorist on the other hand was more commonly translated with *waírþan* 'become'. Presumably the difference in selection was made because *wisan* like the perfect indicates a state rather than a process. Development of such periphrastic forms gives further indication that the language was moving to VO patterning.

2.5   Lexis

In spite of its limited corpus, Gothic maintains words that are not attested in the other Germanic dialects, e.g. *amsas* 'shoulders', *aljis** 'other', *háihs** 'one-eyed', *miliþ* 'honey', and also the word for 'ruler' borrowed from Celtic *reiks*. Gaps in attestation, as of *mōþar 'mother', for which *aiþei* is used, may be a result of our small corpus. The word *atta* is used for 'father'; its cognate *fadar* is attested only once.

The vocabulary includes terms that were borrowed into Proto-Germanic from Celtic, some of which belong in the military sphere, e.g. *brunjō* 'breastplate', *eisarn** 'iron', *kēlikn* 'tower'; others have to do with legal and social arrangements, e.g. *áiþs** 'oath', *ambahts* 'servant', *arbi* 'inheritance', *dulgs** 'debtor', *freis* 'free'. (Placement of * after a word indicates that the form, usually the base of a noun or verb, is not attested, but that another form of that word is attested, such as the dative plural, so that the base form can be provided with reasonable assurance.) These suggest that the Germanic peoples were in contact with Celts in the period before our era, and were culturally influenced by them.

Words borrowed into Proto-Germanic from Latin reflect trading, presumably in the centuries surrounding the beginning of our era: *akeit** 'vinegar', *asilus** 'ass', *assarjus** '(name of a) coin', *áurkeis** 'a pot', *katils** 'kettle', *káupōn* 'trade'. Latin words were also taken from the general vocabulary, such as *káisar** 'emperor'.

Subsequently Gothic borrowed many ecclesiastical terms. Some of these are found in two forms, the first, for example, *diabulus* 'devil' assumed to be borrowed before the time of Wulfila, who presumably used the form *diabaúlus*. Among such terms borrowed from Greek are: *aggilus* 'angel', *aíkklēsjō* 'congregation', *paska* 'Easter'. Yet the *-us* ending indicates the influence of Latin, from which terms were introduced by early missionaries. The basic vocabulary, however, remains Germanic.

Further Reading

Bennett, W. H. (1960) *The Gothic Commentary on the Gospel of John (Skeireins aiwaggeljons þairh iohannen*, a decipherment, edition, and translation), New York: Modern Language Association.

Braune, W. and Ebbinghaus, E. A. (1981) *Gotische Grammatik*, 19th edn (with Readings and Glossary), Tübingen: Niemeyer.

Lehmann, W. P. (1986) *A Gothic Etymological Dictionary* (based on Sigmund Feist, *Vergleichendes Wörterbuch der Gotischen Sprache*, 3rd edn, with a bibliography prepared under the direction of H.-J. J. Hewitt), Leyden: Brill.

Scardigli, P. (1973) *Die Goten: Sprache und Kultur*, trans. B. Vollmann, Munich: Beck.

Streitberg, W. (1920) *Gotisches Elementarbuch*, 5th and 6th edns, Heidelberg: Winter.

—— (ed.) (1919–28) *Die Gotische Bibel*, 2 vols, I. *Der Gotische Text*, II. *Gotisch-Griechisch-Deutsches Wörterbuch*, Heidelberg: Winter.

Tollenaere, F. de and Jones, R. L. (1976) *Word-indices and Word-lists to the Gothic Bible and Minor Fragments*, Leyden: Brill.

3 Old and Middle Scandinavian

Jan Terje Faarlund

3.1 Introduction

The Scandinavian languages are the North Germanic languages spoken in Scandinavia. Sometimes, and especially in the Scandinavian countries, the term 'Scandinavian' is used in a narrow sense to refer to the mutually comprehensible dialects and standard languages of Denmark, Norway and Sweden (including parts of Finland). The term 'Nordic' is then used in a wider sense to include Icelandic and Faroese. In this chapter 'Scandinavian' will be used in the wide sense.

The first detectable dialect split between East and West Scandinavian is due to sound changes that may have taken place by the seventh century. The common Scandinavian language of the period prior to that is called Ancient Scandinavian. The East Scandinavian dialects were spoken in Denmark and Sweden. West Scandinavian included the dialects spoken in Norway and in the Norse settlements in the West (Iceland, the Faroe Islands, the Shetland and Orkney Islands, the Isle of Man, parts of Scotland, and Greenland). The present-day descendants of West Scandinavian are Icelandic, Faroese and Norwegian. Of these, Norwegian has changed most radically, partly under the influence from neighbouring Swedish and Danish, but mainly as part of a common mainland Scandinavian linguistic development.

We can distinguish three periods in the history of Scandinavian: Ancient Scandinavian, until the seventh century, with no known or significant dialect differences; Old Scandinavian, seventh to fifteenth century, with two main dialect areas, West Scandinavian (Old Icelandic and Old Norwegian) and East Scandinavian (Old Danish and Old Swedish); and the modern Scandinavian languages, from the fifteenth century to the present. Old West Scandinavian is commonly referred to as 'Old Norse'.

Old Norse is by far the best attested variety of Old Scandinavian. 'Classical' Old Norse is the language found in the Icelandic sagas from the twelfth and thirteenth centuries. There is also a standardized spelling adopted for Old Icelandic, used in edited texts from the classical period. This chapter will be structured primarily as a synchronic description of classical Old Norse: where relevant, I will make diachronic digressions in either direction,

38

and where there are significant East Scandinavian deviations, those will be dealt with.

Quite frequently, the term 'Middle' Norwegian etc. is used of the last couple of centuries before the Reformation (mid-sixteenth century). This is a chronological term rather than a linguistic one. Linguistically, it was in many ways a period of transition, and it is impossible to define a sufficiently uniform 'middle' stage of Scandinavian. It was a period where many of the changes that led to the modern system took place, but at different times in the different areas of Scandinavia. The changes that took place usually started in Danish, followed by Swedish and East Norwegian, then West Norwegian, and finally Icelandic, which is the most conservative of the Scandinavian languages.

The Scandinavian languages and dialects of today differ mainly in terms of how far they have moved away from Old Scandinavian in various parts of the system. Therefore it is not possible to state the dates where a given change took place. For example, monophthongization of /ai/ to /eː/ had taken place in Jutland by the year 1000, while the diphthong still exists in many Norwegian dialects. Similarly, there are still dialects in mainland Scandinavia that have a separate dative case or number agreement in verbs, although such features started to disappear from the written languages towards the end of the 'middle' period and are now absent from all the standard languages of mainland Scandinavia.

3.2 Phonology

Orthography

Old Scandinavian is recorded in two different scripts, the runic script (the *Futhark*) and the Roman alphabet, which came into use with the introduction of Christianity shortly after the turn of the millennium. With certain additions the latter was made quite suitable as a means of representing the sounds and phonemes of Old Norse. The ‹þ› and later the ‹ð› for the voiced counterpart were borrowed from Old English. The ‹y› for the front, high labial vowel was also borrowed from Anglo-Saxon. Digraphs were used to represent the

Table 3.1   Vowel phonemes of Old Norse

	i	í	y	ý	u	ú	e	é	ø	œ	o	ó	æ	a	á	ǫ
High	+	+	+	+	+	+	−	−	−	−	−	−	−	−	−	−
Low	−	−	−	−	−	−	−	−	−	−	−	−	+	+	+	+
Back	−	−	−	−	+	+	−	−	−	−	+	+	−	+	+	+
Labial	−	−	+	+	+	+	−	−	+	+	+	+	−	−	−	+
Long	−	+	−	+	−	+	−	+	−	+	−	+	+	−	+	−

rich vowel system of Old Scandinavian. In addition various diacritics were occasionally adopted both for vowel quality and quantity. In the standardized spelling used in edited texts and adopted here, the acute accent ′ is used to denote long vowels. The letters used and their phonetic value can be seen from Tables 3.1 and 3.3.

Vowels

Old Norse Vowel System

The vowel phonemes of Old Norse can be represented as in Table 3.1, where the vowels are given in the standard orthography. The main redundancy in the system is that non-low back vowels are always labial. There are seven pairs distinguished by length only. Early in the period the short /æ/ merged with /e/. The long variant of /ǫ/ merged with /á/ early in the thirteenth century, and is represented by that letter in most of the classical texts. In a later development, in Norwegian and Swedish, the labial /á/ also tended to become higher, and thus it would come closer to /ó/. This vowel would in turn move up and threaten to merge with /ú/, which then would move forward and become a high central vowel.

The /i/ and the /u/ can also occur in a non-syllabic position and function as semivowels, /j/ and /w/ (the latter written ⟨v⟩). In Ancient Scandinavian, /j/ was lost word initially, ár 'year' (< *jara), and /w/ was lost in front of stressed labial vowels, ulfr 'wolf' (< *wulfaz).

This vowel system has evolved from the Ancient Scandinavian system through the process of umlaut. Ancient Scandinavian had the five canonical vowels /i, u, e, o, a/, which could be long or short. In stressed syllables preceding unstressed syllables with the vowel /i/ (syllabic or semivowel) the back vowels would have a fronted allophone: /u/ > [y], /o/ > [ø], /a/ > [æ], /au/ > [ey]. Similarly, an /u/ in a following syllable would cause labialization, particularly /a/ > [ɒ], but occasionally also /i/ > [y] and /e/ > [ø] caused by a following semivowel. There was also an a-umlaut, which was a lowering of high vowels preceding an unstressed /a/. During the period from c. AD 500 to 700, called the 'syncopation period', Scandinavian underwent some important phonological changes, such as the loss of vowels in unstressed syllables. This loss led to the phonologization of certain allophonic variants. For example, the plural of land was phonologically *landu, pronounced with a labialized ('rounded') root vowel, *[lɒndu]. When the final vowel was lost, the labialized root vowel became the mark of the plural for this class of nouns, and the [ɒ] became a phoneme, written ⟨ǫ⟩.

In general, there are more umlaut effects in the West than in the East. In the eastern dialects of East Scandinavian there is no a-umlaut, and only a few traces of u-umlaut. The i-umlaut, however, seems to have extended throughout Scandinavia. All of these umlaut rules were productive at a period prior to that covered by our written records; therefore it is not possible to describe the rules accurately. The *i*-umlaut has great consequences for the inflectional morphology of the Scandinavian languages, and is the basis of important morphophonemic alterations, which will be treated in the section on morphology (pp. 45–53). It was – at least during a certain period – sensitive to syllable structure, therefore it did not apply in words with a short root syllable where the /i/ was lost: *staðr* 'place' (< *staðiz*). The *a*-umlaut has mainly affected the lexicon, and plays a less important role in the grammar of the languages.

One umlaut rule is still a synchronic rule of Old Norse, however, namely the so-called younger *u*-umlaut, which changes /a/ to /ǫ/ in front of an unstressed /u/ in an inflectional ending, as in *dǫgum*, the dative plural of *dagr* 'day'. This rule is most consistently applied in Icelandic and in western Norwegian, less so in eastern Norwegian, and in East Scandinavian only in specific environments, such as across a nasal consonant.

Breaking is another effect of unstressed vowels on stressed root vowels. *A*-breaking would change a short /e/ in a root syllable to /ia/ under the influence of a following /a/, as in *hjarta* 'heart'. *U*-breaking is the *u*-umlauted variant of this, caused by an original /u/ in the following syllable: *jǫrð* 'earth' (< *erþu*). By this process, initial /j/ was reintroduced into the language, after the loss of word-initial /j/ in Ancient Scandinavian.

Diphthongs

There are three diphthongs in Old Norse: /æi/, /ǫu/, /æy/. The first one has developed from Ancient Scandinavian /ai/ through a raising of the first element under the influence from the second (some kind of *i*-umlaut): /ǫu/ comes from /au/ through labialization of the first element under influence from the /u/ (some kind of *u*-umlaut); /æy/ is the *i*-umlaut of /au/. /æ/ in /æy/ was furthermore labialized, and the diphthong developed into /øy/. In East Scandinavian the diphthongs were monophthongized early on: /ai/ > /æi/ > /eː/, /au/ > /ǫu/ > /øː/, /ey/ > /øy/ > /øː/. The trend started in Jutland and spread gradually east through Denmark and then north through southern and central Sweden and to parts of eastern Norway. By 1100 the diphthongs were monophthongized in all of Denmark and most of Sweden.

Vowels in Unstressed Syllables

The inventory of vowels in unstressed syllables is much smaller than that in stressed syllables. Instead of the sixteen phonemes of Table 3.1, there is only a contrast of three vowel phonemes in Old Norse, see Table 3.2. There is no length opposition, /a/ is distinguished from the other two by the feature [+ low]. The relevant feature is [± low] rather than [± high], which is shown by the fact that in many manuscripts, especially early Icelandic ones, the unstressed vowels are spelt ‹e› and ‹o› instead of ‹i› and ‹u›. /u/ is distinguished from the other two by the feature [+ labial]. This is shown by the fact that an unstressed /a/ becomes /u/ under *u*-umlaut, as in *kǫlluðu*

Table 3.2   Vowels in unstressed syllables

	i	u	a
Low	–	–	+
Labial	–	+	–

'called (3 pl.)', from *kalla* + *ðu*. (If the distinctive feature were [± back], there would be nothing for the *u*-umlaut to change.)

In Old Swedish and in eastern and northwestern dialects of Old Norwegian the use of -*i*/-*u* vs. -*e*/-*o* in unstressed syllables is determined by a principle of vowel harmony. Root syllables with a [+ high] vowel are followed by *i* and *u* in an unstressed syllable, as in *flutti* 'moved' and *bitu* 'bit (3 pl.)'; and root syllables with a [–high, –low] vowel are followed by *e* and *o*: *dœmde* 'judged, sentenced' and *tóko* 'took (3 pl.)'. (After low root vowels the picture is less consistent.)

Consonants
The consonant phonemes of Old Norse are represented as in Table 3.3, where the consonants are given in the standard orthography. The non-strident non-sonorants form three groups of three consonants each: the labials, the velars, and the dentals [–labial, –velar]. Each of these has a voiceless stop (/p, t, k/), a voiced stop (/b, d, g/), and a fricative (/f, þ, h/). In the labials and dentals the feature [± continuant] takes precedence over [± voice]; there is a voice opposition in the stops, and no voice opposition in the fricatives. That means that [f] and [v], and [θ] and [ð] are in complementary distribution. The voiceless fricatives are used word initially, and the voiced ones word medially and finally. The letter ⟨f⟩ is used for both the voiced and the voiceless variant, as in *fara* [fara] 'go' and *hafa* [hava] 'have', whereas there are separate letters for the two dental allophones, as in *þaðan* 'thence'. In the velar series [+ voice] takes precedence over [± continuant]; there is a continuant opposition

Table 3.3   Consonant phonemes of Old Norse

	p	b	f	t	d	þ	k	g	h	s	m	n	r	l
Sonorant	–	–	–	–	–	–	–	–	–	–	+	+	+	+
Continuant	–	–	+	–	–	+	–	0	+	+	–	–	+	+
Velar	–	–	–	–	–	–	+	+	+	–	–	–	–	–
Labial	+	+	+	–	–	–	–	–	–	–	+	–	–	–
Strident	–	–	–	–	–	–	–	–	–	+	–	–	+	–
Voiced	–	+	0	–	+	0	–	+	–	–	+	+	+	+

between the two voiceless consonants, /k/ and /h/, while the voiced /g/ may be a stop or a fricative depending on the environment.

By the Old Scandinavian period, the /h/ had been lost in all positions except word initially. Thus an /h/ which was the result of final devoicing of a fricative /g/ would also be lost: *mag > *mah > má 'may, can'. In Norwegian and East Scandinavian the /h/ was lost everywhere except word initially before vowels and semivowels. This created a difference between Old Icelandic and Old Norwegian, as in hlutr 'part', hringr 'ring', hníga 'sink', etc. vs lutr, ringr, níga, etc.

A nasal preceding a final stop (which was devoiced) was generally assimilated to that stop in the West, but not in the East. Thus the past tense of binda 'bind' was bant (< band through final devoicing) in the East, but batt in the West.

A synchronic rule of Old Scandinavian is the assimilation of /r/ to a preceding /s/, /n/, or /l/. This takes place whenever a suffix starting with /r/ is added to a stem which ends in one of those consonants. In the case of /l/ and /n/ the rule does not apply after short stressed vowels: cf. stóll (< stól+r) 'table', ketill (< ketil+r) 'kettle', vs telr 'tells'. In most cases /nn/ changes to /ð/ before /r/, as in maðr (< mann+r) 'man'.

In Danish post-vocalic voiceless stops began to be voiced in the twelfth century, and later the voiced stops would develop into fricatives. Together with the vowel reduction mentioned above, this would lead to the character-istic Danish development: mata > made > maðe 'feed'. (The present-day orthography represents the middle stage.)

Towards the end of the thirteenth century certain consonant clusters began to be unacceptable, in particular final clusters ending in /r/. Since the /r/ in most cases was an inflectional ending, it was not easily dropped. Instead, an epenthetic vowel was inserted, bœndr > bœnder 'farmers'. The vowel would often be written ‹æ›. In western Norwegian and Icelandic an ‹u› was used.

Prosody

Stress
There is a distinction between stressed and unstressed syllables in Old Scandinavian. As we have already seen, the two kinds of syllables have a different inventory of distinctive vowel qualities. The stress is normally on the root syllable of a word; in most cases that is the first syllable. In compound words, the first element (or sometimes the second) has the primary stress, while the other element has a secondary stress. Certain prefixes may also have primary stress, in which case the root has secondary stress.

Quantity
Syllable quantity plays no significant part in the synchronic phonology of Old Scandinavian, but it did play a certain role in the derivational morphology of

Ancient Scandinavian (see below, pp. 48 and 51), and it has far-reaching consequences for the subsequent development of the sound systems of the Scandinavian dialects. As we have seen, vowels may be short or long, and consonants may occur in clusters or be geminated. In stressed syllables, a short or a long vowel may be followed by none, one, or two (or more) consonants. Stressed syllables may thus be short, long, or 'overlong'.

In eastern Norwegian and western Swedish bisyllabic words have undergone certain phonological processes that are sensitive to the quantity of the root syllable, often referred to as *vowel balance*. On the one hand these processes have created new morphological patterns and distinctions in those dialects, and on the other hand they have set them off from the other Old Scandinavian dialects.

One such process is *vowel reduction*, which in these dialects affects only words with a long root syllable. After a long stressed syllable an unstressed vowel is reduced, while it is maintained after a short syllable. In eastern Norwegian this has led to the so-called 'cleft infinitive', with the ending *-a* after originally short root syllables (*vera* 'be') and *-e* after long root syllables (*kaste* 'throw'). In some of the Norwegian dialects the reduced vowel was completely dropped. In some words with a short root syllable the root vowel assimilated to the final vowel: *gatu > gutu* 'road'. The basis for these processes is the fact that a final syllable following a short root syllable receives some of the word stress, and is therefore better preserved. In some dialects such words probably had a 'balanced' stress.

In the further development of Scandinavian an important restructuring of the syllable structures took place. In West Scandinavian and Swedish an interdependency between stress and quantity arose; a stressed syllable had to be long. This means that the short stressed syllables were lengthened, either through lengthening of the vowel or through gemination of the consonant, depending on the actual consonants involved, and on the dialect. This change can be described as follows: The syllable boundary shifted towards the left, so that the last one of post-vocalic consonants can no longer count as part of the preceding syllable, and a long syllable is defined as a bi-moraic syllable. Thus a word like *fé* 'cattle' has still two morae, but now it counts as a long syllable and can still constitute a stressed syllable. /hol/ 'hole' is reanalysed as /ho-l/ and becomes mono-moraic, therefore it changes into /hoːl/ or /holl/, and /koma/ 'come' might become /koːma/ or /komma/. At the same time overlong syllables were also abolished, mostly through shortening of the vowel: *nátt > natt* 'night'.

In Danish a different development took place; short vowels in stressed, open syllables were lengthened, /fara/ > /faːre/ 'go, travel'. This did away with one type of short stressed syllables. On the other hand, all geminate consonants were shortened, *þakk > tak* 'thanks', which gave rise to a new type of short stressed syllables in monosyllabic words. In monosyllabic words with a short vowel plus a short consonant, the vowel would either remain short or be lengthened, as in /skip/ > /skiːb/ 'ship'.

Tone

In most Norwegian and Swedish dialects there is today a distinction of two word tones in words of more than one syllable. These tones have never been recorded in writing, therefore we have only indirect evidence of their origin. The tonal difference was originally a difference between the pitch contour of monosyllabic and bisyllabic words. The two tones are therefore called 'single' (') and 'double' (") tone, respectively. In the modern languages there are also bisyllabic words with the single tone. These are mainly of three origins: they are loan words; they are monosyllabic roots with the definite article attached to them, /'baːde/ (*bad* + *et*) 'the bath'; or they are words that have become bisyllabic through the insertion of an epenthetic vowel, /'biter/ (< *bítr*) 'bites (pres.)'. Words which were also bisyllabic in early Old Scandinavian have the double tone: /"bade/ 'bathe (inf.)', /"biter/ (< *bítar*) 'bites, bits (m. pl.)'. These facts indicate that the tonal distinction must have arisen before the definite article changed from being a clitic to becoming a suffix, and before the epenthetic vowel was introduced in final consonant clusters ending in an *r*, which means no later than early thirteenth century.

3.3   Morphology

Historically, most nouns and verbs consist of three elements: the root (or a derived stem), a stem suffix and an inflectional ending. The concatenation of the root and the stem suffix is not a productive process in Old Scandinavian; in the verbs it reflects older (mostly Common Germanic) derivational processes. For many classes of words the stem suffix is not even directly discernible on Old Scandinavian; it may have disappeared through phonological development, or it may have merged with the root or the inflectional ending, and hence it plays a role only in determining the inflectional class of the word. In some cases a stem suffix may have left its traces in the form of an umlauted root vowel.

In some of the inflectional categories there are minor differences in the actual forms in the various dialects of Old Scandinavian. The examples and patterns given in this section are from Old Norse. For a complete survey of eastern Scandinavian deviations, the reader is referred to standard historical grammars of those languages.

The Nominal Group

Nouns

Old Scandinavian nouns are divided into stem classes depending on the original Proto-Germanic stem suffix. One possibility was for the stem suffix to end in one of the vowels *a, ō, i, u*. These nouns form the strong declensions. Then the stem suffix might have ended in an *n* preceded by *a, ō, i*. Those are the weak declensions. In addition there are a few nouns that have stems

Table 3.4   Development of masculine *a*-stem nouns

	Singular		Plural	
Nom.	*armaz	> armr	*armōr	> armar
Acc.	*arma	> arm	*armanz	> arma
Gen.	*armas	> arms	*armō	> arma
Dat.	*armē	> armi	*armumz	> ǫrmum

Note: The Ancient Scandinavian forms of this particular noun are reconstructed.

ending in *nd* or *r*, as well as roots without stem endings.

There are three genders in Old Scandinavian. The gender of the noun partly depends on its stem class: *a*-stems are masculine or neuter, *ō*-stems are feminine, *i*-stems are masculine or feminine, *u*-stems are masculine (originally also neuter and feminine). The gender of *n*-stems depends on the preceding vowel as in the vowel stems. *nd*-stems are masculine, and *r*-stems and athematic stems are masculine or feminine.

Nouns have two numbers – the original dual having been replaced by the plural – and four cases: nominative, accusative, dative and genitive. The two categories, number and case, are expressed syncretically by one inflectional ending. There are thus at most eight different endings for a given noun. In the plural the ending *a* is generalized in the genitive and *um* in the dative for all classes. The forms of the noun *armr* 'arm' as derived from Ancient Scandinavian are shown in Table 3.4. The stem vowel is *a*, and the noun is masculine. The Ancient Scandinavian forms of this particular noun are reconstructed, but most of the forms are attested with other nouns of the same stem class. As can be seen, the stem vowel *a* had merged with the inflectional ending in some of the forms as early as Ancient Scandinavian. The major changes from Ancient Scandinavian to Old Scandinavian are the loss of an unstressed short vowel except when followed by a double consonant; the shortening of long unstressed vowels; and the change /z/ > /r/. In the dative plural there is *u*-umlaut (see section 3.2). Neuter nouns have no ending in the nominative/accusative. In the plural the stem vowel appeared as *u* in Ancient Scandinavian, which caused *u*-umlaut of an /a/ in the root, and was then lost: *land* 'land', plural *lǫnd*.

The *ō*-stems are all feminine. In Ancient Scandinavian the stem vowel appears as *u* in the nominative singular, which would cause *u*-umlaut of an *a* in the root. There is no ending in the nominative singular; the genitive singular ends in *ar*, and the dative singular in *u* or Ø. In the plural, these nouns have the same ending for the nominative and the accusative.

Masculine *i*-stems have basically the same original inflectional endings as the *a*-stems, the main difference being that whenever the stem vowel is visible, it shows up as *i*. The stem vowel causes *i*-umlaut where possible in

Table 3.5   Declension of masculine *an*-stem

	Singular	Plural
Nom.	granni	grannar
Acc.	granna	granna
Gen.	granna	granna
Dat.	granna	grǫnnum

most nouns with a long root syllable: *gestr* 'guest', pl. *gestir*. Some nouns have a genitive in *ar*: *staðar* 'place's' (no umlaut in a short syllable). Feminine *i*-stems always have the genitive in *ar*.

During and before the transition from Ancient Scandinavian to Old Scandinavian there was a fluctuation between *ō*-stems and feminine *i*-stems. On the one hand, the *ō*-stem pattern without the *r* in the nominative and with the same ending for nominative and accusative in the plural was considered a feminine pattern. On the other hand, several original *ō*-stems adopted the plural ending *ir*, while the feminine *i*-stems developed a specifically feminine declension type. This development continues into modern Norwegian and is still going on, since the plural ending *er* (< *ir*) is being generalized to all feminine nouns, while *ar* is being generalized to all masculines. In the modern dialects, then, the stem vowel, which is now to be analysed as part of the plural ending, is determined by the gender of the noun, while originally the gender of a noun was determined by its stem class.

The *u*-stems make up a minor class in Old Scandinavian, and they are all masculines. The stem vowel shows up only in the accusative plural, but has left its trace in the form of *u*-umlaut in other forms. The genitive singular has the ending *ar* and has no *u*-umlaut. The nominative singular ends in *ir* and the dative singular in *i*, both with *i*-umlaut.

In the *n*-stems the *n* of the stem suffix has disappeared in most Old Scandinavian forms. In the singular, those nouns end in a vowel, and all the oblique cases have the same form. In the plural the nominative is based on the strong declensions, and the dative has the ending *um*. The forms of the masculine *an*-stem noun *granni* 'neighbour' are shown in Table 3.5.

Feminine *ōn*-stems have the ending *a* in the nominative singular (*saga* 'story'), and *u* for the other singular forms (*sǫgu*). Nominative and accusative plural are identical in the feminine gender (*sǫgur*). In the genitive plural the stem consonant *n* shows up (*sagna*). Neuter *an*-stems have the ending *a* throughout the singular (*auga* 'eye'), and *u* in the nominative/accusative plural (*augu*). *in*-stems end in *i* in all cases in the singular (*gleði* 'happiness, joy'), and probably also in the plural except the dative, where there would be an *um*-ending. Most of these nouns are abstracts, however, derived (diachronically) from adjectives (*glað* + *in*), and are therefore rarely used in the plural.

Table 3.6   Personal pronouns proper

	Singular			Dual		Plural	
Nom.	ek	þú		vit	it	vér	ér
Acc.	mik	þik	sik	okkr	ykkr	oss	yðr
Gen.	mín	þín	sín	okkar	ykkar	vár	yðar
Dat.	mér	þér	sér	okkr	ykkr	oss	yðr

Some nouns have originally an *ij* or a *w* preceding the stem suffix *a(n)* or *ō(n)*. In these nouns, any stem vowel that can undergo umlaut does so, also in those forms where the *ij* or *w* is lost. There is therefore no morphophonemic change of stem vowel in these nouns. Thus an original *a* has become *ǫ* in words with *w* (*sǫngr* < **sangwaz* 'song'), and *e* in words with *ij* (*stef* < **stafija* 'refrain' 'verse'). In words with a short root syllable, *ij* was reduced to the semivowel *j*. In these words, the semivowels appear in Old Norse only when they are followed by a vowel with different feature values. Thus *j* appears only in front of *a* and *u* (*stef*, gen. pl. *stefja*, dat. pl. *stefjum*). And *w* appears only in front of *a* and *i* (*sǫngr*, dat. sg. *sǫngvi*, nom. pl. *sǫngvar*). After a long root syllable the semivowel *j* was lost and only *i* remained. This in turn was deleted before another vowel, but was maintained before a consonant and word finally. Thus the neuter *a*-stem *kvæði* 'poem' keeps the *i* in all forms except in the genitive and dative plural, where it is followed by *a* and *u*, respectively.

Pronouns

The set of personal pronouns in Old Scandinavian is made up of three separate morphological systems. First, there is the system of personal pronouns proper, where there is a distinction of three numbers (the dual still exists in this system) and four cases, but no gender distinction (Table 3.6). These are the pronouns used for the first and second person, and for the third-person reflexive. As in other Indo-European languages, there is a high degree of suppletion. The reflexive forms (*sik* etc.) are used also for the dual and the plural. Since pronouns are often unstressed, especially when postposed to the verb, various clitic forms appear. Thus in poetry, the first-person singular may appear simply as a suffix *-k* on the verb. (The cliticization of the reflexive pronoun is treated in the section on verbal morphology.)

In some dialects, especially in western Norway, the nominative of the first and second persons dual and plural following a finite verb were reanalysed, whereby the verbal ending was analysed as an initial consonant of the pronoun: *hafið ér* > *hafi þér* 'have you', similarly *hǫfum vér* > *hǫfu mér* 'have we'. Subsequently, this was restored as *hafið þér*, and the new pronoun form was used also in other positions: *þér hafið*. The first-person plurals in *m* still

Table 3.7   Third-person pronouns

	Masculine	Feminine
Nom.	hann	hon
Acc.	hann	hana
Gen.	hans	hennar
Dat.	honum	henni

Table 3.8   Distal demonstratives

| | *Singular* | | | *Plural* | | |
	m.	f.	n.	m.	f.	n.
Nom.	sá	sú	þat	þeir	þær	þau
Acc.	þann	þá	þat	þá	þær	þau
Gen.	þess	þeirrar	þess	þeirra	þeirra	þeirra
Dat.	þeim	þeirra	því	þeim	þeim	þeim

exist in some varieties of Norwegian, and second-person plurals in *þ* or *d* (< *þ*) are general in modern Icelandic and Norwegian. In Old Swedish, the verbal ending for the second-person plural was *in*, which led to the form *ni* for the second-person plural by a similar reanalysis.

Second, there is the system of third-person personal pronouns, with gender distinctions, developed from a common Germanic demonstrative root with the prefix *h-* (Table 3.7). In Scandinavian, this system is used only in the singular, and only for the masculine and the feminine genders. The genitives function as possessive pronouns and adjectives. Third, demonstrative pronouns are used to fill in the gaps: third-person singular neuter and third-person plural all genders.

The demonstratives consist of a distal and a proximal series. The distal series is made up of two stems, *sa*, which is used only for the nominative singular of the masculine and the feminine, and *þa* (Table 3.8). As mentioned above, the neuter and the plural forms are used also to fill in the personal-pronoun system.

The proximal demonstratives were originally formed on the basis of the distal system above with the a suffix *-si* or *-a*, or both, as in the Ancient Scandinavian accusative singular masculine *þansi*. This system is not consistently attested anywhere at any time, and very early the root and the suffix began to merge into a new root with highly irregular declensions. Thus the forms of this demonstrative vary greatly historically and geographically.

Old Scandinavian has a complicated system of interrogative and quantifying pronouns. The most important ones can be divided into three groups on a morphological and semantic basis: the ones formed on the basis of *hver* are either interrogatives ('what, who, which') or universal quantifiers ('each, every'). When a selection is made from a pair, the root *hvár* is used. The existential quantifier is *nokkorr* 'some, any', which is often written as *nǫkkur* (< *nekkvarr* < **ne wait hwarjaz* 'I do not know who' (cf. Lat. *nescio quis*)). The negative quantifier is *engi* 'none' (< *né einn-gi* 'not one at-all'). In addition, *sumr* 'some' and *einn* 'some, one' have adjectival declensions.

The Adjectival Declensions

Originally, adjectives were inflected as nouns, but already in Proto-Germanic some pronominal forms were adopted, which gave rise to the adjectival declension, which therefore is a mixture of a nominal and a pronominal declension. The specifically pronominal forms are the following:

	Singular			Plural		
	m.	f.	n.	m.	f.	n.
Nom.			t	ir		
Acc.	(a)n	a	t			
Gen.		rar		ra	ra	ra
Dat.	um	ri	u			

The other forms are nominal *a*-stems in the masculine and neuter, and nominal *ō*-stems in the feminine. This declension is used when the adjective is a predicate or when it is a modifier in an indefinite noun phrase. This is also called the 'strong declension'. With definite noun phrases, the 'weak declension' is used. This corresponds to the nominal *an*-stems in the masculine and neuter singular, and to the *ōn*-stems in the feminine singular; in the plural for all genders it has *um* in the dative and *u* in all the other cases. With the comparative of adjectives and present participles the feminine singular and the plural of all genders are inflected as nominal *in*-stems.

The adjectival declension is also used for the definite article and for the possessives. The origin of the definite article in Scandinavian is the demonstrative *hin*, originally 'that one over there' or 'the other'. Since this particular root ends in *n*, the assimilations of *r* to *n* apply (see section 3.2): sg. nom. m. *hinn*, dat. f. *hinni*. The *n* of the root assimilates to the neuter ending *t*, whereupon *tt* is shortened (probably due to unstressed position): *hit*.

The definite article has a form without an initial *h* which is cliticized to the noun. This results in a definite form of the noun consisting of a nominal root + nominal case ending + *in* + adjectival case ending, as in *hest-s-in-s* 'the horse's'. In the cliticization process the *i* of the article is lost if the noun ends in an unstressed vowel (*saga-n* 'the story') or in the plural *r* (*sǫgur-nar* 'the stories'). In the dative plural *-um-inum* is generally shortened to *unum* (*hestunum*).

For first- and second-person possessors there are possessives based on the genitive form of the personal pronouns: *hestr okkarr* 'the horse (nom.) belonging to the two of us'. For third-person possessors the genitives of the third-person pronouns or demonstratives are used without further inflection: *hestr hans* 'his horse' and *hestar þeirra* 'their horses'.

Comparison

There are two regular systems of comparison in Old Scandinavian. Most adjectives add *-ar* for the comparative and *-ast* for the superlative: *ríkr–ríkari–ríkastr* 'powerful'. This is the productive system; but there is a smaller group of adjectives that take *-r* and *-st* with *i*-umlaut (caused by a lost *i* preceding the ending): *langr–lengri–lengstr* 'long'.

The Verbal Group

As in other Germanic languages, there is a distinction between weak and strong verbs. The weak verbs originally consisted of a root plus a stem suffix, and the past tense is expressed by adding a dental suffix to the stem suffix. The strong verbs have no stem suffix, and the past tense is expressed through *ablaut* alternations in the root. The tense system has only one opposition: past vs non-past (present).

Stem Classes

In Proto-Germanic there were three stem suffixes that formed the basis of weak verb stems: $\bar{o}$, *ija* and $\bar{e}$. In the non-past forms the inflectional ending was added to these stems. In the past tense, the suffix *d* was added before the inflectional ending. This *-d* had various allophonic values depending on the stem class and the environment. The suffix *-ō* was shortened and changed to *a*, and the dental suffix was a fricative: **kall-ō-d-ō > kallaða* 'called (1 sg.)'. The *a* of the *ija*-stems disappeared, and after short root syllables also the *i*. The *j* remains in front of *a* or *u*, otherwise it was lost too, as in all past-tense forms, **wal-i-d-ō > valda* 'chose'. In non-past forms the semivowel caused *i*-umlaut, as in the infinitive *velja*, but also where the *j* was lost, as in the present tense *velr*. After long root syllables *ij* was maintained and caused umlaut throughout, but was subsequently lost: **dōm-ij-d-ō > dœmda* 'judged'. The $\bar{e}$-stems developed the same way as the long *ija*-stems, except that there is no umlaut, **wak-ē-d-ō > vakta* 'was awake'.

The strong verbs form their past tense by means of vowel ablaut. In each ablaut series there is one root vowel for the non-past, and maximally three root vowels (or diphthongs) for the past: one for the indicative singular, one for the indicative plural and the subjunctive, and one for the participle. In some series the latter two have the same root vowel. Regular strong verbs are conjugated according to one of the six series shown in Table 3.9.

In West Scandinavian, the *jú* of class II appears as *jó* in front of dental consonants (*skjóta* 'shoot'); and the root vowel of the past participle of most verbs of classes II and III underwent *a*-umlaut and became *o* (*kropinn*). In

Table 3.9 Ablaut series in strong verbs

	Non-past	Past ind. sg.	ind. pl.	part.	Sample verb
Class I	*ei > í	*oi > ei	i	i	bíta 'bite'
Class II	*eu > jú	*ou > au	u	u	krjúpa 'creep'
Class III	e	*o > a	u	u	bresta 'break'
Class IV	e	*o > a	*ē > á	u	nema 'take'
Class V	e	*o > a	*ē > á	e	gefa 'give'
Class VI	*o > a	ó	ó	*o > a	fara 'go'

class III there are different root vowels in the non-past stem: *i* before a nasal (*vinna* 'win'); some verbs have a *w*-suffix and *u*-umlaut (*slyngva* 'sling'), and some have breaking (*bjarga* 'save').

In addition to these regular classes there are reduplicating and preterite-present conjugations, and some other irregular verbs, such as *vera* 'be'.

Inflectional Categories
The non-past stem is followed by an inflectional ending indicating first of all whether the verb is in a finite or a non-finite form. The inflectional endings of finite forms indicate mood, number and person. There are three moods: indicative, subjunctive and imperative; and there are two numbers and three persons. The plural form of the verb is used also with dual subjects. The vowel of the stem suffix is always deleted in front of an inflectional ending that begins with a vowel.

The infinitive is formed by adding *a* (< *an*) to the stem: *far+a > fara* 'go', *dœmi+a > dœma* 'judge'. If the root ends in *á*, no infinitive ending is added: *fá* 'get, receive'. The present participle is formed by adding *and* to the stem: *farandi, dœmandi*.

The present indicative has the endings shown in Table 3.10. The *-r* of the singular is originally *-iz*, where the *i* has caused *i*-umlaut in the root in West Scandinavian. By analogy, the umlauted root vowel is used also in the first person. In Old Swedish the first-person singular also has the same ending as the second- and third-person singular, and the second-person plural ends in *-in*.

Table 3.10 The present indicative

1 sg.	Ø	kalla	vel	dœmi	vaki	fer
2 sg.	-r	kallar	velr	dœmir	vakir	ferr
3 sg.	-r	kallar	velr	dœmir	vakir	ferr
1 pl.	-um	kǫllum	veljum	dœmum	vǫkum	fǫrum
2 pl.	-ið	kallið	velið	dœmið	vakið	farið
3 pl.	-a	kalla	velja	dœma	vaka	fara

The present subjunctive has the ending *a* for the first-person singular. The other forms are characterized by an *i* (< *$\bar{e}$*) which does not cause umlaut: 1 sg. *-a*, 2 sg. *-ir*, 3 sg. *-i*; 1 pl. *-im*, 2 pl. *-ið*, 3 pl. *-i*. The imperative exists only in the non-past, and has a separate form only for the second-person singular, which is the stem of the verb (only the root in the *ija*-class). For the other forms, the imperative forms are the same as the indicative.

In the past tense, as we have seen, the singular indicative of strong verbs has a separate stem. This stem receives no ending for the first and third persons, and *-t* for the second person: 1 sg. *gaf*, 2 sg. *gaft*, 3 sg. *gaf* 'gave'. For the indicative of weak verbs and for the subjunctive of all verbs, the singular endings are the same as in the present subjunctive: *-a*, *-ir*, *-i*: *valda*, *valdir*, *valdi* 'chose (sg. ind.)'. Although the subjunctive endings are the same in the present and the past, they have a different historical origin: in the past tense it is derived from *i*, which therefore has caused umlaut (except in the *ō*-stems): *velda*, *veldir*, *veldi* and *gæfa*, *gæfir*, *gæfi* 'gave (sg. subj.)'. In the plural, for all verbs, the indicative is characterized by the vowel *u*, and the subjunctive by *i*: *gáfum*, *gáfuð*, *gáfum* and *gæfim*, *gæfið*, *gæfi* 'gave'. The past participle of weak verbs has the dental suffix, and that of strong verbs has the suffix *-in*, to which the adjectival declensional ending is added: *valdr*, *gefinn*.

A couple of modal verbs have a past infinitive in *u*, which is used after matrix verbs in a past tense, cf. *Hann kvezk fara vilja* 'He says he wants to go' with the matrix verb *kvezk* and the infinitive *vilja* 'want' in the present, and *Hann kvazk fara vildu* 'He said he wanted to go'. (For the forms *kvezk* and *kvazk*, see below.)

Reflexive Forms

The verb acquired a reflexive or medial form through the cliticization of the reflexive personal pronoun: *kalla sik* > *kallask* 'call oneself, be called'. In the first-person singular the ending *-umk* was used (< *$\bar{o}$* + *mik*, where the *ō* did not change to *a* because of the following *m*). Otherwise the ending *-sk* was generalized to all other persons and cases very early on (see section 3.4). Eventually it also replaced the first-person singular ending. In the cliticization process a final *r* of the verbal ending is lost: *kallar sik* > *kallask*; a final *ð* becomes *t*, and the combination *tsk* is usually spelt ‹zk›: *kallið+sk* > *kallizk*. Eventually *sk* was replaced by *st*, and finally reduced to *s* in East Norwegian and East Scandinavian. The reflexive forms also underwent a semantic change, and acquired more and more of a passive-like meaning, until they today are used as regular passive forms.

3.4   Syntax

The Nominal Group

The Structure of the Noun Phrase
The head of the noun phrase is a noun: *þau hin stóru skip, er áðr hǫfðu siglt*
(lit.) 'those the big ships, that earlier had sailed'. The head noun may, however
be deleted under recoverability; thus the example just given is followed by a
sentence with the noun phrase *hit fyrra* 'the former'. In other cases an
adjective is the head without any noun being understood or deleted: *snústu frá
illu ok ger gott* 'Turn away from evil and do good'.

Old Scandinavian generally has a rather free word order. This is true also
at the phrasal level. It is therefore impossible to state absolute rules about the
order of the elements of a noun phrase. Certain general principles do apply,
however, and certain strong tendencies can be observed. The non-cliticized
definite article usually precedes an adjective, and the clitic article can only be
attached at the end of common nouns. In general, the noun and the adjective
can only be separated by a definite article (the only exception to this is
discussed below). It is therefore convenient to treat the head noun together
with any modifying adjectives and definite articles as one unit. For reasons of
convenience I will refer to this unit as the 'nucleus'. Other parts of the noun
phrase are determiners, quantifiers and postnominal modifiers, that is
prepositional phrases, clauses and any other extraposed material. The relative
order of nuclei, determiners and quantifiers is variable, depending on scope
and complexity.

Within the nucleus, the adjective may precede or follow the noun: *eldar
stórir* (lit.) 'fires great', *mikinn her* 'big army'. The unmarked order in definite
noun phrases is for adjectives to precede appellatives and to follow proper
names. Adjectives have a special definite form (the 'weak' form, cf. section
3.3), which has to be used in definite noun phrases. In addition, definiteness
is expressed by means of one, both or neither of the definite articles. If the
order is noun–adjective, only one article can occur between them. The
following structures of definite noun–adjective nuclei can then be found ('+'
means cliticization): N ADJ: *Ólafr digri* 'stout Olaf'; N+DET ADJ: *hafit
mikla* 'the big ocean'; N DET ADJ: *Vínland hit góða* 'Good Vinland'; ADJ
N: *(sá) mildi konungr* '(that) gentle king'; DET ADJ N: *hinn digri maðr* 'the
stout man'; ADJ N+DET: *digri maðrinn*; DET ADJ N+DET: *hinn hvíti
bjǫrninn* 'the white bear'.

Determiners are demonstratives and possessives. The determiner may
precede or follow the nucleus: *sá hinn helgi maðr* (lit.) 'that the holy man',
mínir góðu vinir 'my good friends', *maðr þessi* (lit.) 'man this', *móðir mín*
(lit.) 'mother mine', *þræll konungs* (lit.) 'slave king's'. There is usually at
most one determiner in a noun phrase, but a genitive phrase may co-occur
with a demonstrative: *þessi orð hans* (lit.) 'these words his'. If the noun phrase

contains a restrictive relative clause, a determiner is obligatory, either preceding the nucleus, *einn sá maðr, er þar var* 'one of the men who were there' (lit. 'one that man who there was'), or immediately preceding the relative clause, *ǫllum hǫfðingjum þeim er váru í ríki hans* (lit.) 'all chiefs those who were in his kingdom'.

Quantifiers may also precede or follow the nucleus: *sumir bœndr* 'some farmers', *tólf ina spǫkustu menn* (lit.) 'twelve the wisest men', *berserki sína tolf* 'his twelve berserks' (lit. 'berserks his twelve'), *þau fylki ǫll* 'all those counties' (lit. 'those counties all'). The word *einn*, which eventually developed into the indefinite article, behaves syntactically and semantically as a quantifier: *son einn* 'a/one son'.

Certain category types always follow the nucleus, determiners and quantifiers. Those are adnominal prepositional phrases, *vitrastr maðr í Svíaveldi* 'wisest man in Sweden', relative clauses, *sá hinn mæti gimsteinn er þú ferr með* 'that costly jewel which you carry'. Other elements may also occupy the final position in a noun phrase, such as conjoined adjectives: *húskytja nǫkkur lítil og auð* 'some small and empty hovel' (lit. 'hovel some small and empty'). A peculiar feature of Old Scandinavian is the possibility of extraposing the second conjunct of a conjoined phrase. When this is done to adjectival phrases, the second conjunct is extraposed to the end of the noun phrase: *einn lítill sveinn ok fátœkr* 'a small and poor boy' (lit. 'a small boy and poor').

Two nouns or noun phrases may combine into an appositive construction, where one specifies or modifies the other. A common type of apposition is the combination of a proper name and a title or the name of a function, as in *Ólafr konungr* 'King Olaf'. The rule is that the name precedes the title in such cases. Other types of appositions are combinations of pronouns with nouns, as in *þeir brœðr* 'the brothers (together)' (lit. 'they brothers'). This construction may also be used with a noun in the singular, or with a name, as in *þeir Ólafr* (lit.) 'they Olaf', which means 'Olaf and his men'. Nominal subordinate sentences introduced by *at* are often appositive to a demonstrative pronoun: *ræð ek þat, at vér vindim segl várt* (lit.) 'suggest I that, that we hoist sail ours'. The case and position of this pronoun serves to indicate the grammatical role of the clause.

Noun phrases may be discontinuous in Old Scandinavian. Those elements that may occur as postnominal modifiers (see above) may also be moved further to the right, so that other material separates them from the rest of the noun phrase, as for example a relative clause: *Fjǫlnar var sá nefndr er son var Yngvifreys* 'the one who was the son of Yngvifrey was called Fjolnar' (lit. 'Fjolnar was that (one) called who son was Yngvifrey's'). Note incidentally that this relative clause also contains a discontinuous noun phrase, since the genitive *Yngvifreys* is separated from *son*. The second conjunct may be moved out of its noun phrase: *Þórir fór eptir um daginn ok hans lið út til skipa sinna* 'Thori and his people went out to his ships the next day' (lit. 'Thori went after in the day and his people out to ships his').

Noun phrases may also be divided in other ways, for example between the noun and the adjective: *góðan eigum vér konung* 'we have a good king' (lit. 'good have we king'); between the determiner and the noun: *þeirrar skaltu konu biðja* 'you shall ask for that woman' (lit. 'that shall-you woman ask'); or between the quantifier and the noun: *færi sé englar sendir í heim* 'fewer angels be sent to Earth' (lit. 'fewer be angels sent in earth'). In such cases the quantifier is in the normal, unmarked position of the noun phrase, whereas the noun occupies a position further to the right. This is seen most clearly in quantified questions, such as *hversu margar vildir þú kýr eiga?* 'how many heads of cattle would you like to have?' (lit. 'how many would you cattle own?') where the noun phrase (*hversu margar kýr*) contains a question word. It is the quantifier, *margar*, which stays with the question word, *hversu*, in the front position, whereas the noun, *kýr*, occupies what would be a normal object position in a sentence where the object is not questioned.

Zero Anaphora

Old Scandinavian allows empty argument positions when the content of the argument is unspecified. Thus weather verbs are used without subjects, as well as other verbs when they express natural processes: *gerði myrkt* 'it got dark' (lit. 'made dark'). Also other verbs may be used without a subject: *ekki sá skipit fyrir laufinu* 'did not see the ship (acc.) for foliage'. This sentence can only be interpreted as 'one did not see the ship', and not as 'he did not see the ship'. This is because Old Scandinavian is not a true 'pro-drop' language. On the other hand, it does not have an expletive element to fill empty subject positions.

Argument phrases can also be omitted when they are clearly recoverable from the context, as in *þú munt eigi segja hersǫgu, nema sǫnn sé* 'you shall not tell news from the war unless (it) be true', or when they have no reference, as in *hér hefr upp sǫgu Heiðreks konungs* 'here starts King Heidrek's saga' (lit. 'here lifts up saga (acc.) Heidrek's king's'). In Modern Scandinavian, on the other hand, the subject is obligatory in tensed sentences except under certain syntactically specifiable conditions.

Deletion of a noun phrase in the second conjunct is permitted regardless of case and grammatical role of the identical noun phrases. Thus not only subjects are deleted under identity with subjects, as in Modern Scandinavian, but an accusative object in the second conjunct may be deleted under identity with a preceding accusative object: *síðan fluttu þeir líkit upp með ánni ok grófu þar niðr* 'afterwards they moved the corpse up along the river and buried (it) there'; an accusative object may also be deleted under identity with a preceding dative: *Einarr Þambarskelfir fór með líki Magnúss konungs ok flutti til Niðaróss* 'Einar Þambarskelfi transported King Magnus's body (dat.) and moved (it) to Nidaros'.

Reflexives

The reflexive pronoun has the same forms for all numbers and genders, but three cases are distinguished (there is no nominative form). As a general rule, the reflexive is controlled by a nominative subject: *hann nefndi sik Ólaf* 'he called himself Olaf'. In infinitival clauses the reflexive is governed by the matrix subject: *Þórr hugði at verja sik* 'Thor meant to defend himself'. Also in finite clauses a reflexive pronoun may be governed by the subject of a higher sentence: *Sigmundr biðr þá, at þeir mundu hjálpa sér* 'Sigmund asks them, that they shall help himself'.

The reflexive possessive is used mainly with a nominative subject as its antecedent: *var hann kallaðr Ólafr eptir fǫðurfǫður sínum* 'he was called Olaf after his (paternal) grandfather'. This reflexive may also be governed by other noun phrases, as in *Ólafr konungr þakkaði henni vel orð sín* 'King Olaf thanked her very much for her words', where *sín* has as its antecedent the immediately preceding dative phrase *henni*. The reflexive may even occur in a nominative phrase, with a non-nominative phrase as its antecedent, as in *þykkir honum eigi sín fǫr góð* 'his voyage does not seem good to him' (lit. 'seems him (dat.) not his (refl.) voyage (nom.) good'), where the antecedent of *sín* is the dative *honum*. In the modern languages these latter two uses of the reflexive would be ungrammatical.

Instead of the reflexive pronoun, it is more common with certain verbs to use the reflexive form: *hann lagðisk í rekkju* 'he went to bed' (lit. 'he laid-himself in bed'), *Kálfr klæddisk skjótt* (lit.) 'Kalf dressed-himself quickly'. This form has no case distinction; hence it can be used not only with verbs that take an accusative object, as above, but also with verbs that take a dative, *sumir kómusk á ǫnnur skip* 'some made it onto other ships' (*koma* + dative = 'bring'). The same suffix is also used for the second person: *sakask eigi þú* 'don't injure yourself', and eventually also for the first person (instead of the older *mk*): *ek skal giptask bónda einum* 'I shall marry a farmer'.

The Verbal Group

There is no absolute way of defining auxiliaries as a morphosyntactic category in Old Scandinavian. The most obvious auxiliaries are those verbs that are used with a past participle of the main verb to form grammatical categories. *hafa* 'have' is used with the neuter form of the past participle to form the perfect: *vér hǫfum fengit mikinn skaða* 'we have suffered a great injury'. But the participle may also agree with the object: *mik hefir Helgi hingat sendan* (lit.) 'me has Helgi hither sent (m. acc.)'. *vera* 'be' (past tense *var*) is used with the past participle of some intransitive verbs to form the perfect: *nú er hér kominn Egill* 'now Egil has come here' (lit. 'now is hither come (m. nom.) Egil (nom.)'). The subject may also be omitted with such participles: *gengit var á þingit* 'they/one went to the assembly' (lit. 'gone was to the assembly'). This can be analysed either as an impersonal passive or as a subjectless sentence in the perfect tense. Other intransitive verbs are also used with *vera* without a subject: *lesit er á bókum* (lit.) 'read is in books'. Here only a passive interpretation is possible, since this verb does not take *vera* as an auxiliary in the perfect. The regular passive of transitive verbs is formed with either *vera* as in the former examples, or with its inchoative counterpart *verða* 'become' (past tense *varð*): *senn váru hafrar heim um reknir* 'soon the rams were driven home' (lit. 'soon were rams home (particle) driven'), *af því varð bœn hans heyrð* 'therefore his prayer was heard' (lit. 'of that became prayer his heard').

The auxiliary *munu* combines with the infinitive of the main verb to form the future: *þú munt vera konungr yfir Noregi at eilífu* 'you shall be king of Norway for ever'. Other verbs also mainly combine with a bare infinitive, and may justifiably be classed as modal auxiliaries, such as *kunna* 'can, be able to', *mega* 'be able to', *þora* 'dare', *skulu* 'shall'.

Grammatical Relations

Case Assignment

The major means for marking grammatical relations in Old Scandinavian is by means of morphological case marking. All four cases are used for noun-phrase arguments of verbs. In *hon skyldi bera ǫl víkingum* 'she was to bring beer to (the) vikings', the nominative (*hon*), the accusative (*ǫl*), and the dative (*víkingum*) are represented as governed by the same verb *bera* 'bring, carry'. As will be demonstrated below, there is little evidence that Old Scandinavian has a separate VP node to the exclusion of the subject. All argument phrases seem to be governed by the verb directly, and thereby to be represented at the same level of structure. The change from such a flat structure into a hierarchical NP–VP structure constitutes a major syntactic change in Scandinavian.

The argument phrase and its governor do not need to be adjacent. In *hǫgg þú af tvær alnar hverju stórtré* 'cut two ells off each large tree' (lit. 'cut you (nom.) off two ells (acc.) each big-tree (dat.)') there are two governors, the verb *hǫggva* and the preposition *af*. The verb is specified for nominative and accusative, and the preposition for dative.

It is not implausible to assume that the case systems we know from some Indo-European languages have as their origin a system where each case morpheme (perhaps originally a postposition) corresponds to a particular semantic role. In Old Scandinavian enough remains of such a 'pristine' semantically based case system for there to be a high degree of correlation between morphological case and semantic role. Thus, the dative is regularly used for such roles as instrumental: *þeim reið Goðgestr konungr* 'King Godgest rode (on) it'; recipient: *hon skyldi bera ǫl víkingum* 'she was to bring beer to (the) vikings', *Ólafr konungr þakkaði henni* 'King Olaf thanked her'; and ablative: *þeir fletta hann klæðum* 'they stripped him of his clothes (dat.)'. The accusative generally expresses the theme role: *nú tekr hann hestinn* 'now he takes the horse', *Þorbjǫrn átti fé lítit* 'Thorbjorn had little money'. Some verbs take a genitive phrase. They are verbs with very many different types of meaning, yet most of them imply a partitive reading of the argument. But since Old Scandinavian has already moved away from a pristine case system, 'partitive' has to be understood in a very wide sense. Besides the genuine partitive meaning which is found in expressions like 'all of us', and 'the king's head', it is extended to denote partial objects, as in 'provide some goods', 'try out (the effects of) a method', and by further extension to denote totally unaffected objects, in the sense that the referent of the noun phrase is unaware of its role, as with verbs like 'desire', 'look for', 'wait for', 'miss', 'avenge', 'mention', etc. Note that the use of the genitive case is specified in the lexical entry for the verb, and thus does not depend on the role of the argument in each specific instance. A few examples of the use of genitive objects with verbs may include: *hann var ekki skáld ok hann hafði þeirrar listar eigi fengit* 'he was no bard, and he had not received any such skills (gen.)', *heraðsmenn leituðu hennar* 'men from her district looked for her (gen.)'. Thus, with some exceptions, the accusative, dative and genitive cases correspond fairly well to specific semantic roles.

The nominative is of course primarily the case of the agent role, as shown by most of the preceding example sentences. However, the nominative may also correspond to any other semantic role, as in *Þorbjǫrn átti fé lítit* 'Thorbjorn had little money', and of course in common sentence types like *Ólafr var snimma gǫrviligr maðr* 'Olaf was early an accomplished man'. What these and other uses of the nominative case have in common, however, is that the nominative expresses whatever semantic role is highest on a role hierarchy with at least the following steps: agent > recipient > theme. When there is an agent, it of course is the first role. In the sentence above with the verb *eiga* (past tense *átti*) 'possess, own', the owner is recipient, and the object owned is theme. There is thus a certain redundancy in the lexicon of languages like Old Scandinavian. Not only are the semantic roles to some extent predictable from the meaning of the verb, but the cases with which the verb combines are largely predictable from the roles.

Occasionally the nominative phrase may be absent, *bítr vel á um daginn* '(the fish) bites well during the daytime'. Such sentences have verbs that normally would take an agent, but in these cases the agent is not expressed (see the section on zero anaphora, p. 56). But then there are even verbs that hardly ever combine with a nominative noun phrase: *mun þik kala* 'you will be cold' (lit. 'shall you (acc.) freeze'); *minnir mik hinnar konunnar* 'I remember that woman' (lit. 'reminds me (acc.) that woman (gen.)'). Here an understood agent is less easily inferred; therefore some other noun phrase would be the highest role on the hierarchy and thereby be in the nominative. The generalization about the nominative as the case of the highest role can be salvaged if it is possible to imagine some understood agent also in these latter examples, and perhaps that is how our ancestors saw the world. In any case *minna* can be glossed as 'remind' rather than 'remember'. A stative verb like *sofa* 'sleep', on the other hand, always has a nominative associated with the theme role; with this verb the theme is the first role since one does not conceive of an outside force being the agent of sleep.

When the predicate of an independent sentence is an adjective, a copula verb is required. The phrase referring to the entity that has the property denoted by the adjective may be said to have the theme role. No adjective combines with the accusative, and it seems that with adjectives the nominative has the same function that the accusative does with verbs: it expresses the theme role. Furthermore, some adjectives combine with other roles and cases as well. Adjectives expressing emotional states often combine with a dative phrase and a role expressing the source of the emotion, that is instrument. This role then is expressed by the dative: *Guðrún varð fegin kvámu hans* 'Gudrun was happy about his arrival (dat.)'. Some adjectives also combine with a genitive with a partitive meaning, corresponding to what we find with some verbs: *er Haraldr konungr varð þessa tíðenda víss* 'when King Harald was informed about this news (gen.)'.

Most varieties of modern Scandinavian have lost the original Scandinavian case system, and the standard languages of mainland Scandinavia all have the same reduced case system that we find in English (cf. chapters 8, 9, 10). There are, however, some dialects in the central regions of Norway, and parts of western Sweden, that have retained a separate dative case. I will refer to these dialects as Central Scandinavian. In these dialects three cases – nominative, accusative, and dative – are distinguished. The nominative is used for the subject; the accusative is used for the direct object of most verbs and some prepositions; the dative is used for the indirect object, the direct object of some verbs, and with some prepositions and adjectives.

The nominative stands out from the other cases in this system, too: it is the only case form that is tied to a specific structural position. This is clearly different from association with the first role, as in Old Scandinavian. In Modern Norwegian, all tensed clauses (except imperative sentences) have a subject, that is, a nominative phrase. If an agent is not expressed, for example, the sentence still ends up having a nominative phrase. All of the nominative-less sentences discussed above therefore have modern equivalents with nominative subjects: *ekki sá skipit fyrir laufinu* > *skipet kunne ikkje sjåast* 'the ship could not be seen'; *bítr vel á um daginn* > *det bit godt om dagen* 'the fish bites well in the daytime' (lit. 'it bites well in the day'); *mun þik kala* > *du vil frysa* 'you (nom.) will be cold'.

Also in Central Scandinavian, the genitive case is generally lost. The genitive governed by verbs, adjectives and prepositions has been replaced by the accusative, which means that the distinction between partitive and non-partitive theme arguments is lost. There has been a considerable redistribution of the functions of the dative and the accusative. In general, the accusative has encroached upon the area of the dative as a direct object. For example, the instrument role is now expressed by the accusative rather than by the dative.

Generally speaking, the dative case is used for the recipient and the ablative, and the accusative for the theme. However, the dative is used for the instrument role when it is the argument of prepositions or adjectives. *Ho var redd bikkjen* 'she was afraid of the dog (dat.)'.

One main difference between Old Norse and Central Scandinavian is that in the latter, subjects of passive sentences are always in the nominative, even those which correspond to datives in active sentences: *han takka foreldrom sine* 'he thanked his parents (dat.)' vs *foreldra vart takka* 'the parents (nom.) were thanked'; *ho lova guta mat* 'she promised the boy (dat.) food' vs *guten vart lova mat* 'the boy (nom.) was promised food'. Apart from the case marking, there are no relevant syntactic differences between these conservative Scandinavian dialects and the modern standard mainland Scandinavian languages.

The Subject

In many languages, including Modern Scandinavian and English, the subject phrase can be shown to have a set of syntactic properties which helps to identify the subject among the argument phrases. In Old Scandinavian, the nominative phrase is not so clearly characterized by such properties; these properties become more evident at later stages and particularly in the modern period. We have already seen, for example, that the nominative subject is not the sole antecedent of a reflexive.

A main characteristic of the subject in the modern Scandinavian languages as opposed to the Old Scandinavian nominative, is its indispensability. In the modern languages every tensed sentence except imperative sentences needs a grammatical subject. In Old Scandinavian, as we have seen, nominative-less sentences are by no means unusual. Besides the examples already cited, such verbs as *vanta* 'lack', *dreyma* 'dream', *þyrsta* 'be thirsty', *fýsa* 'want, desire', etc. take an accusative phrase, and no nominative. Others have a dative phrase referring to the experiencer, such as *líka* 'like', where the source of the feeling is expressed in the accusative or nominative. Since the dative phrase with such a verb (almost) always denotes an animate being, it also tends to have a high degree of empathy and thereby be thematic. Therefore it would most often be topicalized and occur in first position. Such a definite, thematic noun phrase in first position could at some point be interpreted as the subject, and as case marking becomes structural rather than lexico-semantic, the experiencer phrase gets nominative case by virtue of its position. This way we get the modern construction with the experiencer as the subject of the verb 'like'.

In Old Scandinavian, the finite verb is found in first or second position in declarative main sentences (see below, pp. 64–6). The element preceding or immediately following the finite verb is often a nominative noun phrase, as in *Hálfdan hvítbein var konungr ríkr* 'Halfdan Whiteleg was a powerful king' and *hafið þit verit hér um hríð með mér* 'you have already stayed here with me for some time' (lit. 'have you been here for while with me'). However, we also find other case forms, so this position is not uniquely a nominative position: *var þeim gefinn dagverðr* (lit.) 'them (dat.) was given lunch (nom.)'. Thus if this position is reserved for a certain type of noun phrase, then that noun phrase cannot be defined only as being in the nominative. The constituent order in this example is, however, in accordance with the information structure: the dative phrase is an anaphoric pronoun and thus carries given information, whereas the nominative noun phrase carries new information and comes at the end of the sentence. What this seems to show, then, is that either the order of noun phrases has nothing to do with subjecthood at all, or that noun phrases other than nominative phrases can be subjects.

The main rule seems to be that only nominative phrases can trigger verb agreement. As it happens, however, nominative phrases that lack other subject-like properties do not always trigger verb agreement. In *í þann tíma fannsk í Danmǫrk kvernsteinar tveir* 'at that time there was two millstones in Denmark' (lit. 'at that time found (3 sg.)-themselves in Denmark two millstones (nom.)'), the nominative noun phrase fails to trigger verb agreement since it is rhematic and comes at the end of the sentence. The verb *þykkja*, past tense *þótti*, often does not agree with the nominative either; in *mér þótti vit vera í hellinum* 'I thought we were in the cave' (lit. 'me (dat.) seemed (3 sg.) we (nom.) be in the cave'), the most thematic element is the first person singular *mér*, rather than the dual *vit*. It is true that there is a high degree of correlation between nominative and verb agreement, but it is not absolute. Verb agreement has now practically vanished in mainland Scandinavian, and the kinds of examples we have just seen must have been the first steps in that direction.

When it comes to the possibility of subjects being missing from the sentence/clause, there is also a remarkable difference between the earlier and later stages of Scandinavian. As was shown above, the omissibility of nominative noun phrases in Old Scandinavian differs only minimally from that of other noun phrases.

There is, however, at least one clearly syntactic property whereby the Old Scandinavian nominative stands out from the other cases: it presupposes a finite verb. With non-finite verbs the nominative is regularly omitted, unless it is 'raised' into a higher clause: *hann heitr at gefa þeim bæði ríki ok fé* 'he promises to give them both power and wealth'; *opt hefi ek heyrt yðr þat mæla* 'I have often heard you (acc.) say that'.

The Passive

In Old Scandinavian, the passive is formed with the participle of the main verb and the auxiliary *vera* 'be' or *verða* 'become': *senn váru hafrar heim um reknir* 'soon the rams were driven home'; *af því varð bæn hans heyrð* 'therefore his prayer was heard'. The participles used in passive sentences are verbal adjectives, with a complete adjectival inflection. There is thus no syntactic difference between *bæn hans var heyrð* 'his prayer was heard' with a participle as a predicate, and *bœn hans var lǫng* 'his prayer was long' with a non-derived adjective.

Only those argument phrases that can be subjects of the copula verb can be subjects in the passive. Those always have the theme role, and thus correspond to accusative objects of active verbs. That is why the subject of passive sentences can only correspond to an accusative of the active counterpart. Other cases remain the same: *fjórir hleifar brauðs eru honum fœrðir hvern dag* 'four loaves (nom.) of bread are brought him (dat.) every day'; *þá er hefnt fǫður* 'then the father (gen.) is avenged'; *lesit er á bókum* 'one reads in books' (lit. 'read (part.) is in books'). Old Scandinavian lacks 'pseudo-passives', where the subject corresponds to the object of a preposition in the active. When the subject later was associated with a structural position rather than with a case form alone, underlying non-subject noun phrases could be moved into that position, and the modern 'pseudo-passives' became possible, such as the Norwegian *han må gjevast fire leivar brød* 'he must be given four loaves of bread', *bøkene vart lesne i* 'the books were read in', etc.

The Sentence
The sentence in Old Scandinavian is characterized by two interconnected properties: it has a 'flat' structure, where all the major constituents are represented at the same hierarchical level, and it has a relatively free word order, in the sense that the relative order of phrases in terms of grammatical function is variable. The order of elements in terms of discourse function, on the other hand, is rather fixed. From this it follows, for example, that a nominative phrase (the subject) may come at the beginning of the sentence and be topical, or it may come at the end and be focused. Sentences of the following kind are very common in Old Norse literature: *fyrst vil hann spyrja ef nǫkkur er fróðr maðr inni* 'first he will ask if there is a wise man (nom.) in there'; *hvernig óxu ættir þaðan* 'how grew families (nom.) out of it'; *en er han fell, þá hljóp svá mikit blóð* (nom.) *ór sárum hans* 'and when he fell, then so much blood (nom.) poured from his wounds'; *í honum miðjum liggr bruðr sá er Hvergelmir heitir* 'in the middle of it there is a well (nom.) which is called Hvergelmi'. This is in clear contrast to the situation at later stages of the language, where the subject is typically definite and carries given information. We see that there is a parallel development of syntactic and pragmatic properties of the subject as it becomes structurally rather than morphologically defined.

Constituent Structure
The lack of hierarchical structure and the entailed free word order shows up also in other ways. For one thing, the object may easily be separated from its governing verb: *felt hefir hon þá menn* 'she has slain those men' (lit. 'slain has she those men'); *sjá má ek þik* (lit.) 'see may I you'. This type of facts

may be interpreted in two ways: either we have discontinuous VPs, or there is no VP-node in Old Scandinavian. If a verb + its object is one constituent, we would expect at least in some instances to find them together in a position where only one constituent is permitted. Since this is a verb-second language, such a position would be in front of the finite verb. Sentences like the modern *Sjå deg må eg* 'see you I must', which are current in Modern Scandinavian, are, however, totally absent from Old Norse.

A most remarkable kind of discontinuity in Old Scandinavian is the separation of prepositions from their objects. When the preposition and its object are not adjacent, the object usually occurs in a position which is typical of a prepositional phrase, whereas the preposition itself is further to the left in the sentence, usually somewhere closer to the main verb. (This, then, has nothing to do with preposition stranding.) *hǫgg þú af tvær alnar hverju stórtré* (lit.) 'cut you off two ells (acc.) each bit-tree (dat.)'; *Snorri brá við skjótt orðsending Guðrúnar* 'Snorri got suddenly startled by the message from Gudrun' (lit. 'Snorri startled at suddenly message (dat.) Gudrun's'). The preposition may even be alone in the preverbal position: *á þykkir mér vera skuggi nǫkkur manninum* 'there seems to me to be some shadow over the man' (lit. 'on seems me (dat.) be shadow some the man (dat.)'). These facts seem to indicate that Old Scandinavian lacks prepositional phrases as well as verb phrases as syntactic constituents.

Constituent Order

Since major syntactic relations are not marked primarily by word order in Old Scandinavian, constituent order is available for other functions, such as pragmatic functions. This does not mean, however, that word order is totally determined by such functions.

In main sentences the finite verb is usually in second position. The position preceding the finite verb consists of at most one constituent, which can be an argument noun phrase: *Ólafr gekk til geitahúss* 'Olaf went to the goat-house', *fé þat alt gaf hann liðmǫnnum sínum* (lit.) 'all that property gave he to his followers'; it can be a predicate complement: *vitr var hann* (lit.) 'wise was he'; it can be an adverbial: *eigi hefir þú lit dauðra manna* 'you don't have the colour of dead men' (lit. 'not have you ...'); it can also be a non-finite verb: *þakka viljum vér yðr* 'we want to thank you' (lit. 'thank will we you'). Furthermore, the topic position can be empty: *hafi þit verit hér um hríð með mér* (lit.) 'have you been here for while with me'.

Sentence questions either have an empty topic position, *ætlar þú at hræða mik?* 'do you intend to frighten me?', or they are introduced by *hvárt*, which, when used in dependent questions (see below p. 68), can be glossed as 'whether', *hvárt eru allir menn í svefni á bænum?* 'are all men asleep on the farm?' Phrasal questions are introduced by a question word or phrase: *hverr var þessi hinn orðsnjalli maðr?* 'who was this eloquent man?', *hversu mikla frændsemi átt þú við Erling?* 'how close kinship do you have with Erling?'

The question word may also be part of a fronted prepositional phrase: *við hvat fœddisk kýrin?* 'on what did the cows feed?'

A post-verbal subject pronoun may often be a clitic, although it does not show in the spelling. Sometimes, however, the clitic status of the subject pronoun is reflected in the spelling: *áttu engis annars af ván* 'you have no other hope' (lit. 'have-you nothing else of hope'). Non-nominative pronouns may also be cliticized, and thus precede a full nominative noun phrase: *ekki hryggja mik hót þín* 'your threats do not distress me' (lit. 'not distress me your threats'). And there may be more than one pronoun: *máttir þú þat vita áðr* 'you were in a position to known that before' (lit. 'might you that know before'). Non-finite verbs regularly follow the subject, even when the subject is a full noun phrase and thus not cliticized to the finite verb. When the subject is not topicalized, it therefore intervenes between the two verb forms: *skulu vit brœðr vera búnir* 'we brothers shall be prepared' (lit. 'shall we brothers be prepared'). In the space between the finite and the (position of) the non-finite verb we also typically find sentence adverbials: *mun þér þó verða betra til vista en þeim* 'there will though be better conditions for you than for them' (lit. 'shall you (dat.) though become . . .') and time adverbials: *Arinbjǫrn hafði lengi fylgt málum Egils* 'Arinbjorn had long followed Egil's speech'.

Non-topical noun phrases, including nominative noun phrases, sub-categorized adverbials and other focused adverbials follow the (position of) the non-finite verb: *vér hǫfum fengit mikinn skaða* 'we have received great damage'; *var þeim gefinn dagverðr* (lit.) 'was them (dat.) given lunch'; *nú eru brúðir byrgðar í haugi* (lit.) 'now are brides shut up in a mound'.

Hence, the Old Scandinavian sentence can be divided into three parts, delimited by the verbal positions: the first part is the position in front of the finite verb, which contains at most one topical constituent; the second part starts with the finite verb and contains other topical noun phrases, such as subjects and clitic pronouns, sentence adverbials and time adverbials; the third part starts with the non-finite verb, and contains non-topical argument noun phrases and adverbials. This can be represented as in Figure 3.1, where the asterisk means that a category may be represented more than once.

The word order of Old Scandinavian main sentences exhibits two striking features, the verb-second constraint and the VO order, where V in the first instance means finite verb and in the second instance main verb. This is basically also the system of the Modern Scandinavian languages, the difference being that Modern Scandinavian is more consistent: whereas Old

Figure 3.1

Front	Middle	Final
Topic	V[+fin.] NP(nom.) Pron. SAdv.	V[–fin.] NP* Adv.*

Scandinavian allows empty topic positions, the topic position in the modern language is obligatorily filled in declarative sentences, making the V2 requirement absolute, and whereas the modern language always has objects and subcategorized adverbials after the main verb, Old Scandinavian has quite a few sentences with OV structure, as in *vér viljum ekki lof hans heyra* 'we do not want to hear his praise' (lit. '... praise his hear'). This latter pattern is a relic from an older stage where the language was basically OV. The oldest runic inscriptions in Ancient Scandinavian show verb-final order, as in the Danish Gallehus gold horn from *c.* AD 400: *ek hlewagastiz holtijaz horna tawido* (lit.) 'I Hlewagast of Holt horn made'. Auxiliaries would follow main verbs in final position, as in the Swedish Kalleby stone from the same period: *haitinaz was* 'was called'. However, in Old Scandinavian, only non-finite verbs occur in final position in main clauses.

Thus two word-order changes took place in the period from Ancient Scandinavian to Old Scandinavian: the finite verb moved from the final to the first or second position, and the object (and subcategorized adverbials) moved behind the main verb. The first of these changes is complete in classical Old Norse, whereas there are still plenty of exceptions to the second rule. It may be that Old Scandinavian is still underlyingly OV, where V stands for a non-finite verb, since the finite verb is in second (or first) position. All the VO surface structures are then either sentences with only one verb, or sentences where a rule applies to move elements to the right of the verb. Such a rule is easier to motivate on functional grounds, than one moving other elements in the opposite direction. It is also easier to motivate than a rule moving the verb in either direction, since the verb is sometimes found between other constituents, as in *hefir þú nǫkkura menn hitt í borginni?* (lit.) 'have you any men found in the castle?'

The verb-second constraint can be said to be absolute in Old Scandinavian if we count an empty topic position as a 'position', which would make a sentence-initial finite verb also 'second'. In the course of the fifteenth century, verb-initial sentences became more and more rare in Scandinavian, and at the same time we find the first occurrences of the expletive word *ther/der* 'there' or *det* 'it': *ther kom ey een tijl lande hiem* 'not one came back home to his country' (lit. 'there came not one to country home'). This is an expletive topic, not an expletive subject. Therefore it continues to appear only sentence initially for several centuries after this time. Still in eighteenth century Danish we find *derved er given Anledning til de vidløftige Reyser* (lit.) 'thereby is given opportunity for the extravagant journeys'. And it may co-occur with another subject in the sentence: *der har fire Mænd redet over Broen i dag* (lit.) 'there have four men ridden across the bridge today'. The noun phrase *fire Mænd* is between the two verbs, and must therefore be the subject. In Modern Scandinavian both of these sentences would be ungrammatical, since the expletive word is now clearly a subject. The origin of the expletive subject may be a reanalysis of the expletive topic as a subject.

The use of 'there' or 'it' as an expletive is geographically determined in Scandinavia; 'there' is used in Denmark and in southwestern Norway, 'it' in the rest of Norway and in Sweden. Thus we find *thet* in fifteenth-century Swedish: *thet war en man, ther hafdhe et ilt sar* 'there was a man who had a bad wound' (lit. 'it was ...').

Subordination

The word-order pattern of subordinate sentences is basically the same as that of main sentences: subordinate sentences obey the verb-second constraint, and the order is optionally VO or OV, *at ek muni eigi geta þessa konu* 'that I will not get that woman', *ef honum væri þat lofat* 'if that had been promised him' (lit. 'if him were that promised'). There are, however, some differences as to the frequency of various patterns. An empty pre-verbal position seems to be possible only when the subject is missing or when it is rhematic; the fronting of a non-subject in subordinate clauses is much rarer than in main clauses; and the OV order is more common in subordinate clauses. In addition there is at least one pattern that only occurs in subordinate clauses, the final position of a finite verb: *at þeir í verǫldu bornir váru* (lit.) 'that they in world born were'. This then is a relic of the original Germanic OV order, where V would stand for the finite verb. This is not very common in Old Scandinavian – it is found only in poetry – whereas a non-finite auxiliary in final position is quite common: *at skipit hafi sét verit* (lit.) 'that the ship has seen been'.

The subsequent development confirms the VO order in subordinate as in main sentences. But the verb-second order is abandoned in subordinate sentences: in the modern mainland Scandinavian languages finite and non-finite verbs are adjacent in subordinate sentences, and they can be preceded only by the subject and a sentence adverbial (and of course the complementizer). *ef honum væri þat lofat* can now only be expressed as the Norwegian *om det var lova honom* 'if that were promised him'. Sentences formed as sentence questions, without a complementizer and the verb first, can – then as now – be used as conditional clauses: *hefði hann lið slíkt, þá mundi hann optar sigr fá* 'had he such an army, then he would have victory more often'.

A constituent can be extracted from a subordinate sentence and placed in topic position of the matrix sentence, although this seems to be much less common than in the modern Scandinavian languages, *þau orð bað Ásta, at vit skyldim bera þér* 'those words Asta asked us to bring you' (lit. 'those words asked Asta that we should bring you'). A more remarkable kind of extraction is the placement of an adverbial in front of the complementizer of the sentence to which it belongs: *þat er sagt um sumarit, at einnhvern dag fór Sigmundr til eyjarinnar Dímun* 'that is said in the summer that some day Sigmund went to the island of Dimun'. This kind of extraction is found in Dano-Norwegian as late as the nineteenth century, but now it seems to have disappeared everywhere.

Nominal sentences are introduced by *at*: *eigi er undarligt, at þú sér kallaðr*

Ólafr digri 'it is no wonder that you are called Olaf the Stout', *hygg ek, at þú ljúgir* 'I think that you are lying', *sídan vil ek gefa lof til, at þú farir yfir land mitt* (lit.) 'then I will give permission that you travel over my land' (lit. '... permission to that you travel ...'). As shown above, clauses introduced by *at* are often appositive to a demonstrative pronoun: *ræð ek þat, at vér vindim segl várt* (lit.) 'suggest I that, that we hoist sail ours'. The clause may also be separated from the demonstrative: *er þat min vili, at svá gørir vér allir* 'that is my wish that we all do so' (lit. 'is that my will, that ...'). The word *þat* is also the neuter form of the unstressed personal pronoun, 'it'; thus it could be reinterpreted as an expletive subject, which has led to the modern extraposition constructions.

The demonstrative and the *at*-clause may be governed by a preposition, and thus function as an adverbial clause. A purpose clause may be introduced by *til þess at ...*, where *þess* is the genitive of *þat* governed by *til* 'to, for'; 'because' is expressed by the preposition *af* or *fyrir* + dative of *þat*, which is *því*, + *at* and the sentence.

Subordinate phrasal questions have the question word as its complementizer: *spurði Fjǫlnir brœðr sína, hvat þeir ætlaði honum af fé* 'Fjolnir asked his brothers what they had in mind for him in terms of money'. Dependent sentence questions are introduced by *hvárt*, which can be used also in independent questions (see above p. 64), or by *ef*: *þat skyldi svá reyna, hvárt Baldr var svá ástsæll sem sagt er* 'it would then be seen, whether Baldr was as popular as is said', *skal ek freista, ef ek mega þik drepa* 'I shall try if I can kill you'. Like its English cognate, *ef* is also used to introduce conditional clauses.

Classical Old Norse does not have relative pronouns; relative clauses are introduced by the complementizer *er*: *Visburr átti son, er Domaldi hét* 'Visbur had a son who was called Domaldi'. The head of the relative clause can also be an adverbial, in which case the relative construction has the function of an adverbial clause: *þá er Hrafnkell hafði land numit* 'when Hrafnkel had taken land'.

As we see from this brief survey, Old Norse does not really have adverbial complementizers. Most adverbial clauses are relative clauses introduced by *er*, with an adverbial head, or they are nominal clauses introduced by *at*, following a demonstrative governed by a suitable preposition. In many instances, however, the demonstrative or the head can be omitted, so that *at* or *er* acquires the meaning and function of an adverbial complementizer; besides the example with *þá er* above, we thus also find simply *er Hrafnkell kom heim* 'when Hrafnkel came home'. More importantly, in a diachronic perspective, the complementizer can also be omitted, leaving the demonstrative or the adverb with the complementizer function. Thus *fyrir því* has developed into the modern Norwegian *fordi* 'because', and *da* (< *þá*) is now both the adverb 'then' and the complementizer 'when'. As a consequence (or perhaps a cause) of this development, the complementizer *er* has disappeared from the language.

In relative clauses, *er* is gradually replaced by *sem*, originally a comparative particle 'as': *eptir því sem Eyvindr segir* 'after (= according to) that which Eyvind says'. By the fifteenth century, this has become the predominant relative complementizer, especially in mainland Scandinavian.

All nominal and most adverbial phrase types are accessible to relativization. Besides subjects and direct objects, indirect objects may be relativized: *Sigurðr, er brœðr mínir at bana urðu* 'Sigurd, whom my brothers killed' (lit. '. . . to death became'); objects of adjectives: *konu þá, er þeir hǫfðu enga sét jafnvæna* 'that woman (to) whom they had seen none equally beautiful'; objects of prepositions: *skip, er hann fór á yfir hǫf stór* 'a ship which he travelled in over big oceans'; instrumental dative: *mjǫðr sá, er hon fyllir skapker hvern dag* 'the mead (with) which she fills a vessel every day'; dative of comparison: *orð, er ek heyrði aldri in hnæfiligri* (lit.) 'words, (than) which I never heard the more taunting'; and of course adverbials, as we have seen already.

There are also non-finite complement clauses. Certain verbs take 'accusative with infinitive', that is complement clauses where the subject is 'raised' into an object position of the matrix verb and is therefore in the accusative, while the verb is in the infinitive: *opt hefi ek heyrt yðr þat mæla* 'I have often heard you say that'. Besides sensory verbs, such complements are also found with verbs of cognition and volition, and above all with *verba dicendi*. When the subject of the matrix clause and the infinitival complement are co-referent and in the third person, the reflexive pronoun is used: *kenni maðr sik svá hafa ást guðs* 'a man knows himself thus (to) have God's love'. Only nominative noun phrases become accusative. Subject-like dative noun phrases remain in the dative: *hann sagði sér enn þetta ofljóst þykkja* 'he said he still found this too clear' (lit. 'he said himself (dat.) still this too clear seem').

With *verba dicendi* the reflexive form of the verb is used instead of the reflexive pronoun: *þeir sǫgðusk eigi vilja gjalda tvennar skyldir* 'they said they did not want to pay double debt' (lit. 'they said-themselves not want pay two debts'). The ending *-sk* in *sǫgðusk* represents the subject of the infinitive *vilja* 'want'. When the suffix is used, a predicate adjective is in the nominative, agreeing with the matrix subject: *rammari hugðumk ǫllum vera* 'I thought myself to be stronger than all' (lit. 'stronger (nom.) thought-myself all (dat.) be'). Otherwise it agrees with a full reflexive pronoun: *hann sagði sik vera Ólaf* 'he said himself (to) be Olaf (acc.)'.

The subject of a complement clause may be 'raised' into subject position of the matrix verb. This then results in a 'nominative with infinitive' construction. This is typically found with the verb *þykkja* and its synonyms: *þótti honum hon vel hafa gert* 'it seemed to him that she had done well' (lit. 'seemed him (dat.) she well have done'). The dative phrase may be represented as the reflexive suffix on the verb if it is co-referent with the nominative: *þóttisk hann sjá í svefni mann einn standa þar* 'it seemed to him that he saw in his sleep a man standing there' (lit. 'seemed-himself he see . . .').

The accusative with infinitive constructions now have only a marginal status, and are used almost exclusively with sensory verbs. With other verbs they have been replaced by finite complements. The nominative with infinitive has also been replaced by finite clauses in most cases, and the dative of verbs like *þykkja* has become a nominative subject, as is the case with other subject-like datives. A sentence like *honum* (dat.) *þótti hon* (nom.) *vel hafa* (inf.) *gert* thus becomes modern Norwegian *han* (nom.) *tykte at ho* (nom.) *hadde* (past) *gjort vel* 'he thought that she had done well'.

3.5 Lexis

The major part of the Ancient Scandinavian vocabulary naturally belongs to the common Germanic stock. Some groups of words have, however, taken on specifically Scandinavian shapes, such as the words formed with the suffix *-n*: *bjǫrn* 'bear', *ǫrn* 'eagle' (Ger. *Aar*), *vatn* 'water', etc. More generally, a specifically Scandinavian vocabulary was created by means of productive derivations, such as the **-in* used to derive nouns from adjectives: *gleði* 'happiness, joy' from *glaðr* 'happy, glad', or **-nan* to derive inchoative verbs from adjectives: *blána* 'turn blue', etc. On the other hand, most common Germanic prefixes disappeared in Scandinavian, whereby certain words might become vague or ambiguous, as *lúka* 'close, open', corresponding to Old English *belūcan* 'close' and *onlūcan* 'open'. This was often remedied by the use of adverbial particles: *lúka upp* 'open up'. Some verbs became ambiguous between a causative/transitive and an intransitive meaning, such as *gráta* 'weep' or 'weep for, bemoan', through the loss of a transitivizing prefix *be-*. In some words the prefix remains in the form of a single consonant, which then just forms a cluster with the original initial consonant of the root: *granni* 'neighbour' (Go. *ga-razna*), *gnóg* 'enough' (Ger. *genug*).

The earliest loanwords that we know in Scandinavian are cultural loans from neighbouring languages that the Vikings and their predecessors were in contact with: *bátr* 'boat' from Frisian or Old English, *sekkr* 'sack' from Latin; some no doubt came via English, such as *stræti* 'street' (Lat. *strata*). The introduction of Christianity naturally led to an influx of new loanwords. Since the new religion came to Scandinavia via England and Germany, most Christian concepts are expressed by means of loans from or via those languages, such as *kirkja* 'church' and *dop* 'baptism'. Many of the new words are not loanwords in the strict sense, but rather loanshifts, where a native word has had its content modified to perform the same function as a corresponding foreign word; such words are *guð* 'God', *jól* 'Christmas', *dygð* 'virtue', etc.

Towards the end of the Middle Ages, during the last century before Reformation, the Scandinavian languages were above all influenced by Low German. This had great impacts, not only on the vocabulary, but on the whole structure of Scandinavian. For one thing, the great number of bilingual and foreign speakers of Scandinavian may have been one of the factors leading to a simplification in the morphology of Scandinavian during that period. Furthermore, some new grammatical words or function words were introduced, such as *men* 'but', and *bli(va)* 'become', which eventually took on the role of passive auxiliary, replacing the Scandinavian *verða* in many dialects.

Acknowledgements

I want to thank Jan Ragnar Hagland, Odd Einar Haugen and Trygve Skomedal for valuable suggestions and comments.

Further Reading

Dyvik, H. J. J. (1980) 'Har gammelnorsk passiv?', in E. Hovdhaugen (ed.), *The Nordic Languages and Modern Linguistics. Proceedings of the Fourth International Conference of Nordic and General Linguistics*, Oslo, Bergen and Tromsø: Universitetsforlaget, pp. 81–107.

Faarlund, J. T. (1975) 'Monoftongering i nordisk', *Maal og Minne*: 169–89.

—— (1980) 'Subject and nominative in Old Norse', *Scripta Islandica* 31: 65–73.

—— (1985) 'Pragmatics in diachronic syntax', *Studies in Language* 9: 361–93.

—— (1990) *Syntactic Change. Toward a Theory of Historical Syntax*, Berlin and New York: Mouton de Gruyter.

Falk, H. and Torp, A. (1900) *Dansk-norskens syntax i historisk fremstilling*, Kristiania: Aschehoug.

Hagland, J. R. (1978) 'A note on Old Norwegian vowel harmony', *Nordic Journal of Linguistics* 1: 141–7.

Haugen, E. (1976) *The Scandinavian Languages. An Introduction to Their History*, London: Faber and Faber.

Lødrup, H. (1983) 'Diskontinuitet i norrøne paratagmer', *Maal og Minne*: 29–38.

Noreen, A. (1923) *Altisländische und altnorwegische Grammatik*, Halle: Niemeyer.

Nygaard, M. (1906) *Norrøn syntax*, Kristiania: Aschehoug.

Platzack, C. (1985) 'Syntaktiska förändringar i svenskan under 1600-talet', *Svenskans beskrivning* 15: 401–15.

Sundman, M. (1985) 'Från *Mik angrar* till *Jag ångrar*. Om förhållandet mellan satsdelskategori och semantisk roll', *Folkmålsstudier* 29: 85–123.

4 Old and Middle Continental West Germanic

Marijke J. van der Wal and Aad Quak

4.1 Introduction

Old and Middle Continental West Germanic comprises four language areas: Dutch (Old Dutch and Middle Dutch), High German (Old High German and Middle High German), Low German (Old Saxon and Middle Low German) and Frisian (Old Frisian). Our focus will be on the earlier stages of Dutch and German. The description of Dutch will mainly concentrate on Middle Dutch, since little material is left from the Old Dutch period. Middle Dutch embraces the period of time which extends from the first Middle Dutch records about 1170 to 1500, after which Modern Dutch begins. In the German part of the survey both the High German language developments and the Low German data are discussed. Within the limits of this chapter choices have to be made: emphasis will be laid on the earliest stages, Old High German and Old Saxon, while both Middle High and Middle Low German will be dealt with in far less detail. Old High German and Old Saxon extend from the oldest texts of the eighth century to about 1100; Middle High German and Middle Low German are the common terms for the following period which is considered as ending either around 1400 or about 1500.

Sources differ in amount and genre as well as in time and place. The scarce Old Dutch (Old Low Franconian) material consists of glosses, a short verse line and a psalter translation, the fragmentary *Wachtendonck Psalms*. Apart from glosses and minor texts, the most important Old Saxon document is the *Heliand*, a lengthy biblical epic in alliterative verse. Translations and adaptations from Latin religious texts form the bulk of the Old High German records. The Middle Dutch, Middle High and Middle Low German sources are more abundant and show a greater diversity than those of the earlier period. Administrative and legal documents such as charters and laws abound and secular and religious literature, both in poetry and prose, is well preserved.

Old and Middle High German were spoken and written in central and southern Germany, south of the so-called Benrath line. Low German was the language of the north, i.e. the northern parts of Germany and the eastern provinces of the Netherlands. Both High and Low German cover a group of several dialects. The three major Old High German dialects are (Upper) Franconian, Bavarian and Alemannic. The common feature of those dialects is the second or Old High German sound shift. This shift probably occurred in the sixth century and divided the continental Germanic dialects into a High German and a Low German group. The last includes not only Low German, but also Dutch. Neither language was affected by the sound shift. Old Saxon differs from Old Dutch in a number of phonemic and morphological characteristics. It shares some of the so-called 'ingvaeonisms' with Old Frisian and Old English, e.g. *ôthar* 'other', *ûs* 'us', *fîf* 'five'. Dialect variation is also present in the subsequent period, although a tendency to avoid dialect characteristics can be observed. The Middle High German literary works from 1150 onwards were written in a language which is remarkably uniform. This supraregional tendency was lost when this courtly literature fell into decay (about 1250). Middle Low German was used from 1370 as the official language in all its correspondence by the Hansa, the important commercial league. This meant that Middle Low German became the international language of the Baltic, and as such it exercised a considerable impact on the Scandinavian languages. During the sixteenth century the importance of the Hansa waned and High German replaced Low German as the written language both in the cities and among the upper classes in northern Germany. Low German – or, as it later was called, *Platt* – was the lower-class language; it was banned from the schools, as it was considered to be vulgar.

For neither High nor Low German did a uniform standard language emerge during the Middle German period. The situation is similar for the early stages of Dutch. The major Middle Dutch dialects, used in the present-day area of the Netherlands (with the exception of Friesland and Groningen) and the northern parts of Belgium during the Middle Ages, are Brabantian, Flemish, Hollandish, the Limburg and the so-called eastern dialect. The last was the language of the northeastern provinces of the Netherlands which had several characteristics such as long vowel mutation (*quemen, weren* instead of *quamen, waren* 'came, were') and retention of the /1/-cluster (*solde, wolde* instead of *soude, woude* 'should, would'). The eastern dialect, covering the area from the River IJssel northeastwards, gradually passed into Low German, so that the linguistic borderline did not coincide with the present-day national frontier. The Limburg dialect shared several features with High German.

The German and Dutch dialectal variations will only occasionally be discussed in the following description of the major Old and Middle Continental West Germanic characteristics.

Old and Middle Dutch

4.2   Phonology

The earliest Dutch texts show phonological characteristics which differ from the corresponding ones in (High) German. The West Germanic consonant cluster /ft/ developed into /xt/ in Old Dutch (cf. Old Dutch *stihtan*, Modern Dutch *stichten* vs Modern German *stiften* 'to found'). Assimilation in the case of West Germanic /xs/ marks another important difference: /ss/ in Old Dutch *vusso* (gen. pl.), Modern Dutch *vossen* versus /xs/ (‹ch›, [ks]) in Modern German *Füchse*, 'foxes'. The Old Dutch cluster /ol/ + dental (from earlier /ol/, /ul/ and /al/ + dental) diphthongized to /ou/ + dental. Hence we find Middle Dutch *gout, schout, wout* but Middle High German (and Modern German) *Gold, Schuld, Wald* 'gold, guilt, forest'. The /l/-cluster was also retained in Low German and the Lower Saxon dialect.

An important Old Dutch development is the lengthening of short vowels in stressed open syllables. The operation of this sound law accounts for vowel differences between the singular and plural of Middle Dutch words, e.g.: *spĕl* : *spēle* 'game', *lŏt* : *lōte* 'lot', *văt* : *vāte* 'vessel', *smĭt* : *smēde* 'smith'. These vowel differences in the paradigm generally survive in Modern Dutch. Lengthening did not occur in closed syllables, hence e.g. *bed(de)* : *bedden* 'bed', *cop(pe)* : *coppen* 'cup', *lat(te)* : *latten* 'lath', *pit(te)* : *pitten* 'pith'.

As in all other Germanic languages, stress is initial (on the stem) in Old and Middle Dutch. In the long run initial stress caused weakening of unstressed syllables. In Old Dutch various vowels occurred in unstressed syllables (cf. *hebban* 'they have'; *vogala* 'birds'; *singit* 'sing!'; *namon* 'name'; *sulun* 'shall/ will'). In Middle Dutch, however, the weakening of such unstressed vowels became a rule, resulting in the vowel schwa, spelled ‹e› (cf. *hebben*; *vogele*; *singet*; *name(n)*; *sullen*). This phenomenon allows us to make a clear-cut division between the Old and Middle Dutch period. Further reduction of unstressed syllables took place in Middle Dutch and, consequently, most morphological endings were obscured and eventually disappeared. On the morphological level these phonetic changes resulted in the nearly complete erosion of case endings, a process almost completed by the end of the Middle Ages.

Middle Dutch orthography is inconsistent and phonetic or, at any rate, more phonetic than present-day Dutch orthography. Spelling conventions such as the principle of uniformity and that of analogy were not yet valid. Hence we meet such Middle Dutch phonetic spellings as *lant* 'land', *hi vint* 'he finds' as opposed to Modern Dutch *land* (pl. *landen*) and *hij vindt* (stem *vind* + *t*, cf. stem *woon* + *t*). Apart from this, Middle Dutch orthography reflects cliticization and phonetic reduction. Inconsistency is due not only to dialectical variations and chronological changes, but also to scribes with different spelling conventions. One should note, for instance, the three ways of representing a long vowel, particularly in closed syllables: by adding either an ‹e› to the sign of the short vowel, ‹ae, oe, ue, ee›, or an ‹i›, ‹ai, oi, ui, ei›, or by doubling the single vowel sign, ‹aa, oo, uu, ee›. Concerning the pronunciation of Middle Dutch, we only notice that ‹ue/ui/uu› on the one hand and ‹ij› on the other were both long monophthongs, as the diphthongization of these vowels took place mainly after the medieval period.

4.3 Morphology

The Nominal Group

Noun and Adjective

Middle Dutch nouns have a two-declension, four-case, three-gender system. The strong and the weak declensions are the two main declension classes. Nouns ending in a consonant mostly belong to the strong declension and nouns ending in -e generally belong to the weak declension. Middle Dutch distinguishes four cases: nominative, accusative, genitive and dative. These are signalled by inflectional endings on the noun, the adjective and the determiner. The gender distinctions in Middle Dutch are masculine, feminine and neuter. The number distinctions are singular and plural. Adjectives vary according to the case, gender and number of the noun with which they are combined. The Middle Dutch adjectives have only one paradigm. The former distinction between strong and weak adjectives is no longer found in Middle Dutch, but in genitive, singular masculine and neuter both *goets* and *goeden* occur. The declensions of the nominal group consisting of a definite article, an adjective (*goet* 'good') and a noun (*gast* 'guest', *mensche* 'man', *hof* 'garden, court', *herte* 'heart', *daet* 'action', *siele* 'soul') are given in Table 4.1. In the feminine singular strong and weak paradigm, genitive and dative *dade* and *sielen* are found alongside *daet* and *siele*. In origin the definite article is identical with the demonstrative pronoun *die*. The indefinite article has the same form as the numeral *een*.

Plural inflectional morphemes of the noun are -e (dative -en), marking the strong plurals, and -n, marking the weak ones. Apart from these, the markers -s and -er occur. Plural -s (of disputed origin) is to be found in loans (*pelgrims* 'pilgrims') and in words ending in -el, -en, -er (cf. *duvels* 'devils', *tekens* 'tokens', *cloosters* 'cloisters'). Only a few words, as *kint* 'child' – *kinder*; *ei* 'egg' – *eier*; *hoen* 'hen' – *hoender* (with inserted *d*), have the -er plural. These historically limited -er plurals were subject to accumulative pluralization: in Middle Dutch we find *kindere/kinderen/kinders* beside *kinder*, *eiere/eieren* beside *eier*, and *hoenders* beside *hoender*. Analogy also took place in the case of monosyllabic long-stemmed neuter words of which the plural form was identical to that of the singular (e.g. *been* 'leg', *dinc* 'thing', *jaer* 'year'). Apart from regular *been, dinc, jaer*, also *beene(n), dinghe(n), jaere(n)* appear in texts. Plural marker -n gained some ground from plural -e in Middle Dutch

Table 4.1 Strong and weak declensions of the nominal group

	Singular	Strong	Weak	Plural	Strong	Weak
Masculine						
Nom.	die goede	gast	mensche	die goede	gaste	menschen
Acc.	dien goeden	gast	mensche	die goede	gaste	menschen
Gen.	des goets/goeden	gast(e)s	menschen	der goeder	gaste	menschen
Dat.	dien goeden	gaste	mensche	dien goeden	gasten	menschen
Feminine						
Nom.	die goede	daet	siele	die goede	dade	sielen
Acc.	die goede	daet	siele	die goede	dade	sielen
Gen.	der goeder	daet/dade	siele(n)	der goeder	dade	sielen
Dat.	der goeder	daet/dade	siele(n)	dien goeden	daden	sielen
Neuter						
Nom.	dat goede	hof	herte	die goede	hove	herten
Acc.	dat goede	hof	herte	die goede	hove	herten
Gen.	des goets/goeden	hoves	herten	der goeder	hove	herten
Dat.	dien goeden	hove	herte	dien goeden	hoven	herten

and prevailed, alongside -s, as regular plural marker -en in Modern Dutch.

It should be noted that in predicative position the uninflected adjectival form appears: *goet* (*die coninc es goet* 'the king is good'). The adverb is usually formed by adding -e to the uninflected adjective (e.g. *diepe* 'deeply', *langhe* 'long', *stille* 'quietly'). The comparative and superlative of adjectives (and adverbs) are formed by adding the suffixes -er/-re (-der) and -(e)st to the positive: *scoen(d)er* 'more beautiful', *swaerre* 'heavier' and *scoenst* 'most beautiful', *swaerest* 'heaviest'. Some adjectives and adverbs have irregular comparison such as *goet* 'good' – *better* – *best, wel* 'well' – *bet/bat* – *best, clein* 'little' – *minre/minder* – *minst, groot* 'big' – *meere* – *meest*. Comparatives and superlatives as well as the possessive pronouns (*mijn* 'mine', *dijn* 'your', *sijn* 'his', *haer* 'her', *ons* 'our', *uw*, 'your', *haer* 'their') are declined like the adjective.

Pronouns

Some of the various pronoun types are dealt with here. The declension of the demonstrative pronoun *die* 'that' is, with a few exceptions, identical to the definite article forms in Table 4.1: *dies* instead of gen. sg. m./n. *des* and *dier* instead of gen. sg. f. and gen. pl. *der*. Other Middle Dutch demonstratives are *dese* 'this' and *ghene* 'that'. Apart from functioning as an article or a demonstrative pronoun, *die* may also play a role as relative pronoun. The relative pronoun varies according to the gender and number of its antecedent.

The declension of the personal pronouns is given in Table 4.2. The pronouns of address were *du* and *ghi, du* being originally used for the singular and *ghi* for the plural. In Middle Dutch the relationship between *du* and *ghi* is not a straightforward singular–plural one. In the singular *ghi* functions as a polite pronoun (owing to courtly fashions) and *du* as a pronoun of familiarity. This implies that *ghi* was used to mark respect, *du* being limited either to intimate contexts, or used in an asymmetric relationship. In the course of time the usage of pronouns of address has changed considerably. *Du* gradually fell into disuse and new pronouns such as *u* (polite pronoun singular and plural), *jij* (singular pronoun of familiarity) and *jullie* (plural pronoun of familiarity) arose. Since these developments took place after 1500, no further attention will be paid to them here. Both *du* and *ghi* may be used clitically: *slaepstu* (= *slaepes du* 'do you sleep?'), *wildi* (= *wilt ghi* 'do you want?'; -*i* is the clitic form of *ghi*). Third-person personal pronouns distinguish between full forms and clitics in all cases.

In Middle Dutch reflexivity is generally expressed through the personal pronoun. The personal pronoun forms *hem* (clitic -*em*, -*en*), *haer, hare* and *hen* were used as reflexives, for example: *God, die **hem** crucen liet* 'God who had himself be crucified'; *si rechte **haer** op* 'she raised herself'; *si wapenden **hem*** 'they armed themselves'. The reflexive pronoun *sich*, a High German loan serving for all genders and both numbers, occurs in fourteenth-century eastern Middle Dutch, but did not spread westward before the sixteenth century.

Table 4.2   Personal pronouns

	Nominative	Accusative	Genitive	Dative
1 sg.	ic	mi	mijns	mi
2 sg.fam.	du	di	dijns	di
pol.	ghi	u	uwer, uw(es)	u
3 sg.m.	hi, -i	hem, -ene, -ne, -en	sijns, -(e)s	hem, -em, -en
f.	si, -se	haer, -se	haer, -ere, -er, -re	haer, -ere, -er, -re
n.	het, -(e)t	het -(e)t	-(e)s	hem, -em
1 pl.	wi	ons	onser	ons
2 pl.	ghi	u	uwer, uw(es)	u
3 pl.	si, -se	hem, hen, -se	haer, -ere, -er, -re	hem, hen, -en

Some Remarks on Case Distinctions

The morphological case distinctions have syntactic functions. The nominative expresses the subject function. Possession and various other relationships are indicated by the genitive. The indirect object (or second object) has dative case, the direct object is in the accusative. Furthermore, some verbs may assign genitive case to their object: *Gods pleghen* 'to worship God'; *der ondaet loochenen* 'to deny the misdeed', others have a dative complement: *den kinderen slachten* 'to be like children'. Some adjectives assign genitive case (*werdich enechs prijs* 'worthy of some praise', *des wits voets girech* 'eager for the white foot [of a deer]') or dative case (*den kinderen vriendelic* 'kind to the children', *den wive gram* 'angry on the woman'). A preposition as head of a prepositional phrase may assign accusative (*up die vaert* 'on the trip'), dative (*met luder sprake* 'in a loud voice') and sometimes genitive case (*binnen huses* 'inside the house'). Some prepositions govern both dative and accusative (*in der zalen* 'in the hall', *tote in die zale* 'into the hall'), a choice which does not always involve a static–directional opposition.

The decline of the case system during the Middle Dutch period is obvious: distinct case endings collapse or disappear. Prepositional phrases take over functions previously performed by case endings. Possession, for instance, is indicated by the preposition *van* ('of') and verbs with genitival objects increasingly occur with accusative objects or prepositional phrases such as *gedinc van dinen quade* 'think of your wickedness'. Verbs which originally govern the dative may occur together with prepositional phrases (cf. *na den wolf slachten* 'to be like the wolf'). Thus, semantic and grammatical relationships originally marked by suffixed case morphemes were replaced by various prepositional syntagms.

The Verbal Group

The Germanic languages originally indicated person and number by suffixed person markers, a subject pronoun being a later development. In Old Dutch texts the subject pronoun is present in the majority of the instances. Mood, too, was marked by verbal morphology: the subjunctive and imperative endings differed from the indicative ones. There were two tenses: the present, indicating present and future time, and the preterite, indicating the past. The preterite and the past participle may be formed in two different ways: for the so-called strong verbs by vowel gradation (ablaut) and for the weak verbs by means of a dental suffix. Middle Dutch *keren* 'to turn' is an example of a weak verb, and *nemen* 'to take' of a strong one. Both strong and weak verbs share most of the endings. The conjugations given in Table 4.3 show that the differences between the indicative and the subjunctive have been considerably reduced due to weakening of the endings. Subjunctive markers are limited to the third-person singular present for both the weak and the strong verbs and to the first- and third-person singular preterite for only the strong verbs.

Table 4.3 Verbal conjugation

	Weak verbs *keren* 'to turn'		Strong verbs *nemen* 'to take'	
Present				
	Indicative	*Subjunctive*	*Indicative*	*Subjunctive*
1 sg.	ic kere	ic kere	ic neme	ic neme
2 sg.	du keers	du keers	du neems	du neems
3 sg.	hi keert	hi **kere**	hi neemt	hi **neme**
1 pl.	wi keren	wi keren	wi nemen	wi nemen
2 pl.	ghi keert	ghi keert	ghi neemt	ghi neemt
3 pl.	si keren	si keren	si nemen	si nemen
Preterite				
	Indicative	*Subjunctive*	*Indicative*	*Subjunctive*
1 sg.	ic keerde	ic keerde	ic nam	ic **name**
2 sg.	du keerdes	du keerdes	du naems	du naems
3 sg.	hi keerde	hi keerde	hi nam	hi **name**
1 pl.	wi keerden	wi keerden	wi namen	wi namen
2 pl.	ghi keerdet	ghi keerdet	ghi naemt	ghi naemt
3 pl.	si keerden	si keerden	si namen	si namen
Imperative				
Sg.	keer/kere		neem/neme	
Pl.	keert/keret		neemt/nemet	
Present participle				
	kerende		nemende	
Past participle				
	ghekeert		ghenomen	
Infinitive				
	keren		nemen	

The Middle Dutch subjunctive may indicate a wish: *God **hoede** dit ghesinde* 'God may save this company'; an incitement: *men **slaese** doot!* 'one must kill them'; or a supposition: *hadde mi yeman geleent sijn huus, in **ware** dus niet bereent* 'had anyone given me shelter, I would not have been so soaked'. The subjunctive is also found in various subordinated contexts: *Amelant waende dat hi doet **ware*** 'Amelant feared that he was dead', *hi sal hulpen der maget rike, dat si hare ere **behoude*** 'he will help the high-born maiden in order that she keeps her honour'. Except for a few stereotyped relics such as *leve de koningin* 'long live the queen' in Modern Dutch the subjunctive has become obsolete and is replaced by an indicative, if possible, or by the periphrastic combination of the verbs *mogen* 'may' or *moeten* 'must' with the infinitive.

The infinitive, a verbal noun, can be declined: cf. *hem begonste **slapens** lusten* 'he began to long to sleep'. The dative commonly occurs after the preposition *te*: *daer hi vele **te ligghene** plach* 'where he used to lie often'.

The weak preterite is formed by means of the suffixes *-de* (*keerde* 'turned') or *-te* (*maecte* 'made'), depending on the phonetic context. In the case of a voiceless final stem consonant, *-de* is assimilated to *-te*. The past participle consists of prefix *g(h)e-* + verbal stem + *-(e)t* (*ghekeert, ghemaect*). The past participle of strong verbs is formed by means of the prefix *g(h)e-*, the suffix *-en* and the verbal stem which generally has vowel change (*genomen* 'taken'). Most past participles take the prefix *g(h)e-*, the function of which originally was to indicate the completed action. Some verbs, e.g. *comen* 'to come', *vinden* 'to find', *brengen* 'to bring', *liden* 'to pass', which are by their very nature perfective, had prefixless participles, but through analogy they also adopted *g(h)e-*.

Vowel gradation (ablaut) in the strong verbs, a typically Germanic feature, falls into seven major patterns, all of which survive into Middle Dutch. All seven classes have four principal parts: infinitive, preterite singular, preterite plural and past participle.

Table 4.4   Strong verb classes

	Infinitive		Preterite Singular	Plural	Past participle
Class I	riden	'to ride'	reet	reden	gereden
Class II	gieten	'to pour'	goot	goten	gegoten
	stupen	'to steep'	stoop	stopen	gestopen
Class III	vinden	'to find'	vant	vonden	(ge)vonden
	werpen	'to throw'	warp	worpen	geworpen
Class IV	nemen	'to take'	nam	namen	genomen
Class V	meten	'to measure'	mat	maten	gemeten
Class VI	lachen	'to laugh'	loech	loechen	gelachen
Class VII	laten	'to let'	liet	lieten	gelaten

Table 4.4 shows that Middle Dutch still had two preterite forms, a singular and plural. The difference between the two was levelled in the course of time: for instance, *vant* became *vond*. This merger of two originally distinct forms also took place in German. In Dutch the plural vowel became predominant, whilst in German the singular form prevailed (cf. preterite *fand – fanden*).

Apart from the strong and weak verbs, some irregular verbs can also be found in Middle Dutch. The group of irregular verbs includes verbs with vowel gradation in the present tense (the so-called preterite-present verbs; e.g. *connen* 'to be able', *ic can, wi connen* 'I am able, we are able'; *moghen* 'to be allowed', *ic mach, wi moghen* 'I am allowed, we are allowed') and weak verbs with a deviant preterite (e.g. *brengen* 'to bring' – *bracht*; *denken* 'to think' – *dacht*). The verbs *sijn* 'to be' and *hebben* 'to have' also show several idiosyncratic features. The paradigms of these verbs, which are important in the formation of the compound tenses, are as follows: *sijn*: present indicative *ic bem (ben), du bist (best), hi es (is), wi sijn, ghi sijt, si sijn*; preterite indicative *ic was, du waers, hi was, wi waren, ghi waert, si waren*; present subjunctive *si*; preterite subjunctive *ware*. *Hebben*: present indicative *ic hebbe, du heves (heefst), hi hevet (heeft), wi hebben, ghi hebbet (hebt), si hebben*; preterite indicative *ic hadde*, etc.

4.4   Syntax

The Nominal Group

The structure of the noun phrase consisting of a noun, an adjective and a determiner (article or demonstrative) is generally determiner–adjective–noun in Middle Dutch, although postposition of the adjective and the possessive pronoun does occur, e.g. *Doen Elegast, die ridder goet, quam in des conincs sale* 'when Elegast, the excellent knight, came into the King's hall'. The word order of the elements noun and adjective, the position of the relative clause and many other word-order phenomena have been related to the basic word orders SOV and SVO in language typology research. In Middle Dutch attributive adjectives normally precede the noun with which they are collocated, a situation not uncommon in SOV languages. Possession is expressed by a genitive or a prepositional group. Both postposition (SOV) and preposition (SVO) of the genitive occur in Middle Dutch. A prepositional group generally follows the noun. In conclusion, the Middle Dutch word-order phenomena show both SOV and SVO characteristics. This observation fits in with the word order in the verbal group, as will be shown in the following section.

Extraposition of the prepositional phrase yields various uncommon types of word order, such as *so dat die bisscop staerf van der stede* 'so that the bishop of the town died'. Extraposition may also take place with a preposed genitive including a PP, as is shown by *sijn neve Jan, sGraven zone van*

Henegouwen 'his nephew Jan, the son of the count of Henegouwen'. The relative clause normally follows its antecedent, but there may be some distance between the two components, exemplified by the relative clause *die ... mede* with its antecedent *die hope*: *dus weert **die hope** van hem die doet, **die hem geeft troest ende coenheit mede*** 'thus the hope which gives him support and courage too, averts death from him'.

The Verbal Group

The West Germanic languages developed strong analytical tendencies and Dutch was no exception. The obligatory subject pronoun and the rise of periphrastic verbal patterns are typical of this development. In Middle Dutch the subject pronoun has become obligatory. Even in the Old Dutch material in the vast majority of instances, the subject pronoun is present for at least the first- and second-person pronouns. Observe the following Old Dutch example: *offran sal **ic** thi ohsson mit buckin* 'I will offer thee bullocks with goats'. As it had only two inflected tenses, present and preterite, Middle Dutch (and the other West Germanic languages) formed the perfect and the pluperfect with periphrastic combinations of the verbs *hebben* 'to have' and *sijn* 'to be' and the past participle. Only a few examples of periphrastic tenses show up in the earliest texts. Apart from the well-known Old Dutch sentence: ***hebban** olla vogala nestas **hagunnan*** 'all the birds have begun their nests', only one more Old Dutch example is attested, *faruuart heuit* 'has ruined'. The occurrence of periphrastic tenses with *hebben* and *sijn*, indicating the perfect and pluperfect, increases considerably in Middle Dutch. The rule which must have governed the use of the two verbs is as follows: *sijn* is used in the case of the unaccusatives, mutative intransitive verbs which express a change, while *hebben* appears in the case of transitive verbs and the other intransitive verbs. For instance: *si **sijn comen*** 'they have come', *hi vraechde wiet **gedaen hadde*** 'he asked who had done it', *hi **hadde gheslapen*** 'he had slept'.

The passive in particular illustrates the development from a synthetic to an analytic language. In Gothic a restricted synthetic passive is still present beside a periphrastic passive consisting of the past participle and the verbs *wisan* or *wairþan*. The West Germanic languages have a periphrastic passive and originally they all had the possibility of two auxiliaries in the present and preterite. In Middle Dutch the uncompleted passive event can be expressed by either *sijn* + past participle, or *werden* + past participle. This variation can be illustrated by the following examples: *hi **wart** gedragen* 'he was carried' and *een sward **was** gegeven* 'a sword was given'. In addition to these striking similarities in the imperfect tenses, the perfect tenses in Dutch and German were originally more alike than the present differences would suggest. In both languages the passive perfect consisted of *sijn* or *sein*, respectively, plus a past participle. Middle Dutch *had verbrant geworden* 'had been burnt down' and *mishandelt hadden geweest* 'had been ill treated', so-called tripartite constructions, and its German equivalents arose as a more recent development during the Middle Dutch and Middle High German period. The constructions with *geworden* and with *geweest* were both variants of the combination commonly used to refer to a perfect-tense event, namely *sijn* + past participle in e.g. *seyden dat dit slot **verbrant was** van viere* 'they said that this castle had been burnt down by fire'.

The situation just described, in which the interpretation of Middle Dutch *sijn* + past participle wavers ambiguously between an imperfect and a perfect tense, did not continue. Dutch kept *worden* to indicate the uncompleted event, while the earlier possibility of using *sijn* was no longer available. The change in favour of *worden* can be observed very clearly in the Middle Dutch period: the occurrence of the *sijn/werden* variation steadily decreases. The line of development is from a more frequent occurrence of *sijn* + past participle as compared with *werden* + past participle, through an increase of *werden* + past participle, to a higher occurrence of *werden* + past participle, expressing the uncompleted event, in fifteenth-century texts. As far as the perfect tenses are concerned, the development towards the tripartite construction was consolidated in High German and ousted the original combination *sein* + past participle. In Dutch the tripartite construction did not take the place of *zijn* + past participle. As a result Modern Dutch has the following system: the *worden*-combination for the imperfect tenses and the *zijn*-combination for the perfect tenses. Some ambiguity has been maintained, as *zijn* + past participle, not unlike Middle Dutch *sijn* + past participle, may also indicate a state.

In addition to the analytic constructions with a past participle, several combinations with the infinitive arose. The future was expressed by the present in the Germanic languages, but periphrasis with modal verbs + infinitive also occurred. In Old Dutch *sulon* + infinitive may indicate the future. In Middle Dutch the verbs *sullen, willen, moeten* play this role. Ultimately one of them, *zullen*, prevailed in present-day Dutch. As it became formally identical with the indicative, the subjunctive could no longer play an important part in the language. In Middle Dutch constructions with *mogen*, *moeten* and *sullen* gradually replace the subjunctive, in expressing volition, incitement or supposition.

As the above survey has shown, the development of a range of compound paradigms took place, involving a variety of auxiliaries in combination with either the past participle or the infinitive. Combinations of the verbs *werden*, *sijn* or *bliven* with the present participle, expressing either an ingressive (*werden*) or a durative aspect (*sijn, bliven*), also occurred, but never became consolidated patterns in later Dutch.

Grammatical Relations: The Passive and Impersonal Constructions

Two further points should be noted about the Middle Dutch passive. First, it permits the use of an agentive (prepositional) phrase which may vary. This is illustrated in *hoe Mariken seer schandelijcken toeghesproken wert **van haerder moeyen*** 'how Mariken was spoken to very disgracefully by her aunt' and *dat hi seide, dat desen brief bi hem alleene ware ghescreven* 'that he said that this letter was written all by himself'. The present-day agent indication by *door* 'through' arose after the medieval period and ousted the other possibilities completely. Apart from the usual passive pattern with a subject, Middle Dutch also knew subjectless passives. The handbooks occasionally label these passives as unreal or pseudo-passives. As far as the auxiliaries are concerned, the pseudo-passives show complete similarity with the passives. The *sijn/werden* variation occurs in the imperfect tenses, e.g. *menichwerff wart dair gecust* 'frequently kissing was done there' and *hem* (dat.) *was gedient wel utermaten* 'he was extremely well served'; and the auxiliary *sijn* is used for the perfect tenses, e.g. *hier van is nu ghenoech ghehoert* 'enough has been heard about this'.

Pseudo-passives are not the only type of subjectless sentences. A well-known phenomenon in this respect is the so-called 'impersonal construction', in which no subject in the nominative is available. A certain number of verbs, which seem to share some semantic core (they all indicate various types of experience), occurred in impersonal constructions. The option between personal and impersonal construction was associated with a difference in emphasis. The impersonal construction originally consisted of the third-person singular verb form (*lanct*), a dative element (*mi*) and a genitive element (*waters*), e.g. *mi lanct waters* 'I long for water'. However, the genitive object may be replaced by a prepositional phrase (*mi lanct na di* 'I long for you'), an infinitive (*mi lanct te comene* 'I long to come') or a *dat*-clause (*mi lanct dat ghi comt* 'I long for your coming'). In such sentences as the last, a provisional genitival object *des* may precede the *dat*-sentence: *mi lanct des dat ghi comt*. The impersonal construction became obsolete after the medieval period and disappeared in Dutch. Several hypotheses have been put forward to explain its disappearance. According to some linguists syntactic reinterpretation took place: after the inflectional ending was lost, the dative constituent was reinterpreted as the subject. Others maintain that the disappearance of the impersonal construction can be explained by the loss of inflection. Inflectional loss for the nouns and the reduction of the personal pronouns to only two forms, subject and oblique, made it impossible for the impersonal construction to survive. As the outcome, verbs with impersonal constructions only maintain their personal constructions, cf. Modern Dutch *ik verwonder me erover* 'I wonder at it' or *het verwondert mij* 'it surprises me' instead of Middle Dutch *mi wondert des* or *des wondert mi*. Unlike *mi lanct des dat ghi comt*, in which the provisional genitive object clarifies the nature of the following *dat*-clause, a clause such as *mi lanct dat ghi comt* may be interpreted as having either a genitive object or a subject. A further development is the requirement of the pronoun *het* which functions as a provisional subject, cf. Modern Dutch *het verwondert me dat hij komt* 'it surprises me that he comes'.

The Sentence

Word Order
In Middle Dutch various word-order patterns occur in main clauses and subordinate clauses. The constituent order in unmarked declarative sentences is SVO (Subject–Verb–Object or other complements), as in Modern Dutch and Modern German. In present-day Dutch and German the word order in subordinate clauses is SOV, although movement to a position behind the verb (*Ausklammerung* or exbraciation) is possible: extraposition of prepositional phrase, in the spoken language especially. The word order in Middle Dutch subordinate clauses with conjunction, relative pronoun, interrogative pronoun or relative/interrogative adverbs, shows more variety than does Modern Dutch. Verb-second word order such as in *ende dit doet hi/datmen **sal** weten verre ende bi/sine scalcheit ende sine quaethede* 'he does this in order that people far and near will know his malice and his wickedness', verb-final word order, e.g. *doe so bat heme Lanceloet/dat hi tote hem daer **quame*** 'then Lanceloet asked him to come to him there', and any word order in between, cf. *daer naer wart hi* [= the cup] *gegeven voert,/dat hi te Roeme **quam** in die poert* 'after that it was passed on, until it came within the city of Rome', are possible. The finite verb can take every position in the subordinate clause, except the first position, which is the subject position.

Further Main-clause Patterns and Subordinative Structures
Verb-second structures are a regular phenomenon in Middle Dutch. The finite verb immediately follows after one, and only one, preceding element, whether or not this is the subject. If a non-subject constituent takes the first position in a declarative sentence, inversion is entailed: the subject follows the finite verb which maintains its second position in the sentence, e.g. *ende **dit** doet hi* 'and this he does' and ***des margens** vor hi rechte vort* 'in the morning he went straightaway'. The verb-second rule enables us to distinguish main clauses from subordinate ones with initial ambiguous elements such as, for example, *die*, both demonstrative and relative pronoun, and *doe*, both temporal adverb and conjunction. It specifically provides a discriminating rule, important in a period when subordinate clauses do not yet have the verb-final position as a common feature.

Questions introduced by an interrogative element do not deviate from the word-order rules set out above. A verb-first pattern, VS(O), is found in yes/no questions. Imperative sentences show the same verb-first word-order structure, although they may be preceded by another constituent, e.g. ***wiset** mi dan den wech* 'show me the way' and ***nu leide** mi tote daer* 'now bring me there'.

Another word-order pattern, used for topicalization purposes, involves dislocation of a nominal element associated with the verb to the left or to the right of the core sentence: ***die coninc***, *hi seide* 'the king, he said'; *hi sprac vele, **die coninc*** 'he said much, the king'. Besides these examples with a personal pronoun, the construction also occurs with a demonstrative: *die ridder, die seide* (lit.) 'the knight, that one said'.

In addition to the subordinate clauses dealt with above, types of non-finite subordination and a subordinate verb-first structure occur. No special attention will be paid to non-finite subordination here. The verb-first structure may indicate a conditional relationship, as in the sentence: *ghiet mer eerst olye inne, hi blijfter langhe vet af binnen* 'if one pours oil in it [= the pot] first, it will stay greasy for a long time'.

Compound Sentences

Nothing special needs to be said about the word order of coordinate clauses. Subject and object clauses either precede or follow the main clause. A demonstrative or personal pronoun may be used as a provisional or repeating element, e.g. *laetti dit bliven onghewroken, dat u verde dus es tebroken* 'if you leave this unrevenged, that your peace has been disturbed in this way' and *dat die riddere swiget stille, dat doet hi dor minen wille* 'that the knight keeps silent, that he does for my sake'. Changes in word order become obvious in the case of fronted adverbial clauses, resulting in three different word-order patterns: (a) *alst evel wast, men soude het weeren int beghin* 'when evil grows, one ought to fight it from the start'; (b) *alst evel wast, so soude men het weeren int beghin* (lit) '... then one ought ...' and *alst evel wast, soude men het weeren int beghin* (lit.) '... ought one ...'. (a) represents the original pattern: the fronted adverbial clause, which does not occupy the forefield position, does not involve inversion. In (b) the adverb *so* repeats the fronted clause and occupies the forefield position. In due course a connection was made between this pattern and the preposed adverbial clause, hence inversion occurred even when the repeating element *so* was not available, as in (c). The preposed adverbial clause had become a part of the sentence, involving inversion as did any non-subject part. Consequently, the first pattern was bound to disappear. In Modern Dutch only the second and third patterns survive, but the correlative element was replaced by *dan*.

Additional Remarks

So far the most important word-order phenomena have been discussed. Some striking differences in usage emerge between Middle and Modern Dutch. For discourse-pragmatic purposes the object sometimes took the first place in main clauses and relative clauses. Owing to case endings, misinterpretation could generally be avoided in Middle Dutch. The accusative clarified the meaning of the sentence *dien carbonkel hadde in den voet een vogel* 'a bird had that carbuncle in its claw'. A similar instance in a relative clause is presented by the following sentence: *Van Job, den gheduldighen, dien nyemant en mochte beschuldighen* 'about the patient Hiob, whom nobody could accuse'. In present-day Dutch the former type tends to be avoided or, in the latter case, preference is given to the passive construction. The loss of case endings has limited the usage of certain word-order patterns in Modern Dutch.

Negation

Sentence negation has undergone important changes in Dutch as well as in the other West Germanic languages. The original sentence negation *ne* (*n, en*) with its position in front of the finite verb, is the only option in Old Dutch, e.g. *geuuigit got thie ne faruuarp gebet min* 'blessed be God, who did not turn away my prayer'. In Middle Dutch the pre-verbal negation element has a limited distribution: it occurs with certain verbs (e.g. *weten* 'to know', *roeken* 'to care', *mogen* 'to be able, may', *willen* 'to want', *connen* 'to be able') and in specific sentence patterns, e.g. *Die knape seide: 'Lieve here,/Van u en scedic nemmermere,/Ghi en geft mi ridders abijt'* 'The youth said: "Dear lord, I do not go away from you **unless** you give me the garments of a knight"'. The regular sentence negation for Middle Dutch was an embracing structure, in the main clause at least, consisting of the elements *ne/en* and *niet*: *hi en sprac niet* 'he did not speak'. *Niet* was a post-verbal element in the main clause. In subordinate clauses the word order was different: *dat hi niet en sprac* 'that he did not speak'. *Niet* was originally used in the case of constituent negation (cf. *ic ontsie u niet een haer* 'I fear you not a bit' (lit. 'not a hair'), *die zee was diep ende niet te wijt* 'the lake was deep but not too wide') and might have had reinforced the simplex sentence negation. After a period of free variation between *ne* and *en ... niet*, the latter became the regular sentence negation, the negation *ne* being exceptional. A similar development took place with respect to German *nicht*, English *not*, Frisian *nat*. 'Double' negation is also found with negative words, as *en ... niemen* 'nobody', *en ... nie* 'never', *en ... niewer* 'nowhere'.

A further development concerning negation started in Middle Dutch: single *niet* by itself may function as sentence negation. The following sentences give examples in which pre-verbal *en* is omitted: *lieghe ic niet, soe seg ic waer* 'if I don't lie, I say the truth', *want sonder u magic niet leven* 'for without you I can not live', *dat hem tcoude niet mochte deeren* 'that the cold could not harm him'. *Niet* has become the common sentence negator in Modern Dutch, a stage only reached in the second half of the seventeenth century.

In Middle Dutch, therefore, three forms of sentence negation were available: 'double' negation (the rule); pre-verbal negation *en* (the exception); and negation *niet*, the new pattern. The development of pre-verbal negation *ne/en* via double negation to post-verbal negation *niet* has been the subject of extensive scholarly debate. Some describe the process in terms of reinforcement by means of *niet* and subsequent redundancy and weakening of *ne*. Others refer to a stricter word order, which made it difficult to maintain pre-verbal *ne*. Even the change from a system of affix negation to a system of adverbial negation has been taken into consideration. The negation changes cannot be brought into direct relationship with changing basic word order, since the independent uninflected negator is pre-verbal in many languages, regardless of the basic word order.

In Middle Dutch multiple negation also occurs, that is, a collocation of several negation elements such as in *Daerne quam oec **nie geen** man* (lit.) 'no man never came there' and *In mijn huus dat gaen, dat comen, **dan** (= dat **en**) was **niewerinc noit** vernomen* (lit.) 'the going and coming in my house, that was nowhere never seen'. These negation elements reinforce the negative meaning of the sentences. In similar cases in Modern Dutch they neutralize each other, at least in the written language and in formal spoken styles, under the influence of prescriptive grammar, while the reinforcing usage of multiple negation remains a common feature of informal speech.

4.5 Lexis

Middle Dutch shares part of its lexicon with the other West Germanic languages. Even in the field of loans, striking similarities can be noticed which go back to a common past, such as the cultural influence of the Roman Empire and the spread of Christianity. An indication of the extent of borrowing during the Old and Middle Dutch period will be given here.

Extensive borrowing from Latin took place during the first centuries of our era. Words associated with the military system, trade, building and agriculture are conspicuously present. For example:

strate (via strata)	'street'
wal (vallum)	'rampart'
kerker (carcer)	'dungeon'
ketene (catena)	'chain'
pijl (pilum)	'arrow'
wijn (vinum)	'wine'
peper (piper)	'pepper'
pont/pond (pondus)	'pound'
munte (moneta)	'coin'
muur (murus)	'stone wall'
venstre (fenestra)	'window'
poorte (porta)	'gate'
solre (solarium)	'loft'
kelre (cellarium)	'cellar'
camer(e) (camera)	'chamber'
vrucht (fructus)	'fruit'
pere (pirum)	'pear'
cole (caulis)	'cabbage'

These form only a small selection from a great number of words which survived in more or less the same form in present-day Dutch.

Christianization is amply reflected in the lexicon as well. The main source of many specifically Christian words was Latin: Middle Dutch *kersten* 'Christian', *duvel* 'devil', *engel* 'angel', *cruce* 'cross', *pape* 'priest', *clerc* 'cleric', *leec* 'lay man', *capelle* 'chapel'; and the verbs *jubelen* 'to jubilate', *offeren* 'to sacrifice', *prediken* 'to preach', *vieren* 'to celebrate'. Both spoken and written medieval Latin may have played their roles in this process of borrowing. Introduction of new concepts and phenomena did not only take place through the borrowing of foreign words. Several Germanic words underwent a change of meaning during the spread of Christianity. *Boeten*, which originally meant 'to make something good/better, to compensate' acquired the Christian meaning of 'penance'; *doop* 'immersion', got the specific meaning of 'baptism'; *heilig* (originally full of *heil* 'welfare') obtained the religious meaning 'holy'. A third mainstream of loans passed into the language from Old French, owing to contacts in the border area of the German- and Romance-speaking parts in western Europe, in trade centres and in aristocratic circles. From the many French loan words, especially those belonging to the domain of courtly life and chivalry, only a few examples are given here: *cameriere/cameniere* 'servant', *bottelgier/bottelier* 'cupbearer' (= 'butler'!), *garsoen* 'squire', *tapijt* 'carpet', *faisaen* 'pheasant', *taerte* 'tart'. The profound influence of French is evidenced by the fact that loanwords are not confined to the domain of concrete objects but include words concerning inner life, e.g. *joye* and *jolijt* 'joy', *grief* and *vernooi* 'grief'. The extent of the influence of French is borne out further by the fact that French loan suffixes, e.g. *-ier*, *-age* and *-ie*, appear at an early stage in Middle Dutch words such as *herbergier(e)* 'landlord', *timmerage* 'carpentry', *schulage* 'hiding-place', *heerschappie* 'power' and *voghedie* 'guardianship'. This must be the result of analogical derivation modelled upon French loans with such suffixes, as *bottelier* 'cupbearer', *pelgrim-age* 'pilgrimage'.

In addition three points should be noted. First of all, it is not always possible to determine whether a loan was borrowed directly from Latin or indirectly via Old French. This indeterminancy applies in the cases of *creature* 'creature', *persone* 'person', *nature* 'nature', *purper* 'purple'. Second, dating the loan might be problematic. Occasionally, certain characteristics are indicative of the period of borrowing. For instance, Latin *altare* is to be found in Middle Dutch as *outaer* 'altar' which had been subject to the Old Dutch sound law *alt* > *olt* > *out*. Therefore, in an early stage, before or during that of Old Dutch, the word must have passed into the Dutch language. In Middle Dutch borrowing once more took place from Latin which is shown by the existence of the word *altare/altaar* in Middle and Modern Dutch. Third, new words may not just be borrowed, but modelled upon a foreign example. Middle Dutch *hovesch*, a derivation consisting of the noun *hof* 'court' and the suffix *-esch*, is a loan translation of French *courtois* 'courtly'.

Verrisenisse (*ver-* + verbal stem *ris-* 'to rise' + *-enisse*; Lat. *resurrectio* 'resurrection'), *bekeringe* (*be-* + verbal stem *ker-* 'to turn' + *-inge*; Lat. *conversio* 'conversion') and *almachtig* (*almachtig*; Lat. *omnipotens* 'almighty') are further examples of this phenomenon of loan translation or calque.

Old and Middle High German, Old Saxon and Middle Low German

4.6   Phonology

The Old High German and Old Saxon scribes adopted the Latin orthographical system. The difficulty in representing the German sounds caused spelling inconsistency. In the eleventh century some new signs were introduced to represent the sounds that resulted from vowel mutation, such as ‹æ› OHG *mâri* > MHG *mære* 'famous', ‹oe› OHG *hôren* > MHG *hoeren* 'to hear' and ‹iu› OHG *hûsir* > MHG *hiuser* 'houses'. In Middle Low German these graphemes could also represent long vowels.

Consonants

The most remarkable feature of Old High German is the so-called second sound shift. It still is uncertain whether or not this sound shift started in the south (in the Alemannic and Bavarian dialects) and subsequently spread to the north until it stopped at the Benrath line. According to some scholars the Franconian dialects had their own variant of this sound shift. This opinion is based on the Franconian form *hase* 'hate' which is found in an early eighth-century manuscript from Echternach.

The Old High German sound shift affected the voiceless plosives /p/ /t/ /k/ and the voiced plosives and fricatives /b/ /d/ /g/. The first group in particular had an almost complete shift, dependent on the position in the word and on the dialect. The initial /p/ /t/ /k/ developed into the corresponding affricates /pf/ /ts/ /kh/: cf. OSax. *pîl* vs OHG *pfîl* 'arrow'; OSax. *tîd* vs OHG *zît* 'time'; OSax. *kunni* vs OHG *chunni* 'gender'. The same occurred in post-consonantal position (OSax. *thorp* vs OHG *dor(p)f* 'village'; OSax. *kurt* vs OHG *kurz* 'short'; OSax. *werk* vs OHG *werch* 'work') and in the geminated plosives (OSax. *skeppian* vs OHG *skepfen* 'to create'; OSax. *sittian* vs OHG *sizzen* 'to sit; OSax. *wekkian* vs OHG *wecchen* 'to wake up'). In the other positions /p/ /t/ /k/ shifted to the corresponding fricatives /f/ /z/ /x/ e.g. OSax. *diop* vs OHG *tiof* 'deep', OSax. *lâtan* vs OHG *lâzzan* 'to let', OSax. *makon* vs OHG *mahhôn* 'to make'. The changes did not affect the Old High German dialects uniformly. The southern dialects (Bavarian and Alemannic) showed its most complete form. The sound shift became increasingly less complete towards the north.

The consonants /b/ /d/ /g/ developed into /p/ /t/ /k/: e.g. OSax. *beran* vs OHG *peran* 'to bear', OSax. *dag* vs OHG *tag* 'day', OSax. *geban* vs OHG *kepan* 'to give'. Here, too, the southern dialects show the complete shift. The forms *peran* and *kepan* appear in Bavarian and Alemannic texts, while Franconian texts keep /b/ and /g/, with the exception of the position in geminates. There all dialects show /pp/ /tt/ /kk/: OSax. *sibbia* vs OHG *sippa* 'kin', OSax. *weddian* vs OHG *wetten* 'to bet', OSax. *hruggi* vs OHG *rücki* 'back'.

In Old High German the Germanic fricatives /þ/ /v/ became plosives /d/ /b/ in all positions, e.g. OSax. *thing* vs OHG *ding* 'thing', OSax. *gevan* vs OHG *geban* 'to give' (or even *kepan* in Bavarian). In the consonant clusters /hr/, /hn/, /hl/, /hw/, /wr/, and /wl/ the /h/ or /w/ disappeared in initial position, e.g., OSax. *hring, hniosan, hlôpan, hwat, wrîvan* vs OHG *ring, niosan, loufen, waz, rîban* 'ring', 'sneeze', 'to run', 'what', 'to rub'.

In Middle High German and Middle Low German the voiced /b/ /d/ /g/ became voiceless /p/ /t/ /k/ in final position: MHG *lîp* vs *lîbes*, *nît* vs *nîdes*, *tac* vs *tages*; MLG *lîf* vs *lîves*, *nît* vs *nîdes*, *dach* vs *dages* 'life, body', 'hate, anger', 'day'. As in Old High German, initial /hl/, /hr/, /hw/ and /hn/ – still existing in Old Saxon – became /l/, /r/, /w/ and /n/ in Middle Low German.

Vowels

Several changes in the Old High German vowel system occurred. Short [a] was mutated to [e] under the influence of /i/ in the following syllable, e.g. sg. *gast*, pl. *gesti* 'guest(s)'. The same so-called *i*-mutation is found in Old Saxon. Other vowels were also subject to *i*-mutation, but the writing system of the Old High German and Old Saxon period had no means to express it. In the eleventh century forms like *hiute* (instead of *hûti*), plural of *hût* 'skin', show that *i*-mutation was no longer felt to be a variant form, but a phoneme. The /e/ before /i/, /j/, /u/ or /w/ in the next syllable changed into /i/ in Old High German and Old Saxon. Compare the present indicative of strong verbs like OHG *neman* 'to take': *ih nimu, dû nimis, er nimit* vs *wir nememes, ir nemet, sia nemant*. The /u/ before /a/, /e/ and /o/ in the next syllable became /o/ (so-called 'breaking'). This phenomenon appears in the past plural forms of certain strong verbs: e.g. OHG *wurfum*, OSax. *wurpun* 'we threw' – *giworfan, giworpan* 'thrown'.

Diphthongization in Old High German took place in /oː/ and /eː/. In the pre-Old High German period Germanic /oː/ already started to develop into /uo/. Germanic /e²/ was diphthongized to ‹ea›, ‹ia›, ‹ie› during the ninth century. The /e²/ (> ‹ia›, ‹ie›) is found in the past tense of strong verbs of class VII, e.g. *heizzan – hiaz – hiazzum – giheizzan* 'to order'.

The Germanic diphthongs /ai/, /au/, /eu/ also changed in Old High German and Old Saxon. The Germanic /ai/ became /eː/ before /r/, /h/ and /w/: OHG *mêro* 'more', *êht* 'possession'. In other positions /ai/ remained, written as ‹ei› or ‹ai›. Monophthongization probably started in the north, since Old Saxon has /eː/ in all positions, e.g. OHG *stein*, OSax. *stên* 'stone'. Germanic /au/ became /oː/ before /h/ and all dentals in Old High German, e.g. *hôh* 'high', *tôd* 'death'. Like the development of Germanic /ai/, this change occurred in the seventh and eighth centuries, beginning in the north. In all other positions /au/ remained, written as ‹ou› or ‹au›. In Old Saxon /au/ developed into /oː/ in all positions: OHG *boum* vs OSax. *bôm* 'tree'. In Old Saxon even the development of /au/ into /aː/ occurred, the common development for Old Frisian, e.g. OSax. *âst-* 'east' in place-names. From Germanic /eu/ two different diphthongs developed, depending on the vowel in the next syllable: Old High German and Old Saxon /eo/ (further developing into /io/) before /a/, /e/, /o/, e.g. OHG *beotan*, OSax. *biodan* 'to offer' and Old High German and Old Saxon /iu/ in all other positions, e.g. OHG *biutu*, OSax. *biudu* 'I offer'. In its complete form this development appears only in Old Saxon and Franconian texts. In Bavarian and Alemannic /eo/ and /io/ only resulted before dental consonants and before /x/.

The most striking feature of Middle High German and Middle Low German is the reduction of the vowels in the unstressed syllables. Only suffixes with secondary stress keep their vowel: *-bar*, *-dom*, *-heit*, *-unge*. The reduction to the vowel schwa, written ‹e›, e.g. OHG *salbon*, *faran* vs MHG *salben*, *faren* 'to anoint', 'to go', and OSax. *skriban* vs MLG *schriven* 'to write', implied conflation of the morphological endings in the declensions and conjugations. The relative richness of forms of the Old High German and Old Saxon period disappeared. The second most significant characteristic is the spread of *i*-mutation. In Old High German and Old Saxon only mutation of /a/ was expressed in orthography. During the tenth and eleventh centuries the differences between mutated and non-mutated vowels became significant and were also expressed. In Old High German and Old Saxon *i*-mutation had a complementary distribution according to the vowel in the following syllable. In Middle High German and Middle Low German the mutation gradually became a phonemic feature which was used in declensions and conjugations, e.g. to distinguish singular and plural forms such as *gast*, *geste* 'guest(s)'.

As in Middle Dutch the Middle Low German short vowels were lengthened in open syllables: OSax. *gripum*, MLG *wi grepen* 'we grasped'. This caused a difference between singular and plural of Middle Low German words like: *vat*, *vate* 'vessel(s)'. Lengthening did not take place in closed syllables: *osse*, *ossen* 'ox(en)'. In late Middle High German lengthening also occurred.

4.7 Morphology

The Nominal Group

Nouns
In Old High German and Old Saxon the old system of vocalic and consonantal declensions had deteriorated considerably. Some classes only have rest-forms and especially in the younger texts there can be considerable mixing of stems. Old High German and Old Saxon distinguish five cases: nominative, accusative, genitive, dative and instrumental. These are mainly signalled by inflectional endings of the noun, the adjective and the determiner. The three gender distinctions are masculine, feminine and neuter; and the number distinctions, singular and plural. The old dual forms have almost completely disappeared in Old High German, although remnants in Middle High German show that they existed in some dialects. Old Saxon has dual forms in the personal pronoun. Adjectives vary according to the case, gender and number of the noun with which they are collocated. In Old High German, Old Saxon, Middle High German and Middle Low German there still are two paradigms: a weak and a strong one. The former appears when a determiner is used. So, for example, there is a difference between *guot(êr) man* and *der guoto man*, cf. OSax. *gôd man* and *thie gôdo man* 'a (the) good man'.

The *a*-stems comprise masculine and neuter nouns (Table 4.5). The Old High German system no longer differentiated between long and short stems. The instrumental only appears in the singular.

The endings of Old Saxon *dag* and *word* are in most cases the same. The difference lies in nominative and accusative plural of masculine nouns, where *-os/-as* is the ending: *dagos, -as* 'days'. Endings with ⟨a⟩ in the unaccented syllable appear in genitive and dative singular of both masculine and neuter nouns: *dagas, daga*. The Old Saxon system still differentiated between long and short stems in the neuter forms, e.g. *graf* 'grave' and *hros(s)* 'horse'. Here the plural forms differ in the nominative and accusative: *gravu* 'graves' vs *hros* 'horses'.

Table 4.5   *a*-declension

	Masculine Singular		Plural		Neuter Singular		Plural	
Nom.	der	tag 'day'	dia	taga	daz	wort 'word'	diu	wort
Acc.	den	tag	dia	taga	daz	wort	diu	wort
Gen.	des	tages	dero	tago	des	wortes	dero	worto
Dat.	demo	tage	dem	tagum	demo	worte	dem	wortum
Instr.	diu	tagu			diu	wortu		

The so-called *iz/az*-stems are a special group. In the earliest texts forms like *kelbires* (gen. sg.; nom. sg. *kalb* 'calf') and *kelbire* (dat. sg.) are found. Generally in the singular these nouns have the case endings of the *a*-stems. In the plural they keep their original form together with the endings of the neuter *a*-stems: *kelbir – kelbir – kelbiro – kelbirum*. Originally, only a few words e.g. *(h)rint* 'cattle', *lamb* 'lamb' belonged to this group, but already in the Old High German period it extended to other neuter nouns e.g. *hûs* 'house', *feld* 'field'. In Old Saxon only a few representatives are found and there are no traces of other words joining this group.

To the *ô*-stems (Table 4.6) belong most feminine nouns. In some formulas and in adverbal use old endingless forms of the nominative survived e.g. *stunt* 'hour, time'. Feminine words in -*în*, such as *kuningîn* 'queen', also keep the endingless nominative. In Old Saxon essentially the same endings were used. Especially in later Old Saxon there is a tendency of the *ô*-stems to mix with feminine weak nouns (*n*-stems).

The *i*-stems include both masculine and feminine nouns. In the singular the masculine nouns had already merged with the *a*-stems. Cf. OHG *gast* 'guest' and *kraft* 'power' (Table 4.7).

Among the *u*-stems there is a strong tendency to converge with other declensions, especially *i*-stems. Only a few words retain historical forms and these appear only in the earliest texts.

The group of *n*-stems, or weak nouns, includes all genders. The endings differ in the various Old High German dialects: in masculine and neuter nouns

Table 4.6   *ô*-declension, *geba* 'gift'

	Singular		Plural	
Nom.	diu	geba	dio	gebâ
Acc.	dia	geba	dio	gebâ
Gen.	dera	geba	dero	gebôno
Dat.	deru	gebu	dem	gebôm

Table 4.7   *i*-declension

	Singular	Plural	Singular	Plural
Nom.	gast	gesti	kraft	krefti
Acc.	gast	gesti	kraft	krefti
Gen.	gastes	gestio, -o	krefti	kreftio
Dat.	gaste	gestim	krefti	kreftim
Instr.	gastiu, -u			

Table 4.8 *n*-declension

	Singular		Plural	
Masculine				
Nom.	der	hano	die	hanon, -un
Acc.	den	hanon, -un	die	hanon, -un
Gen.	des	hanen, -in	dero	hanôno
Dat.	demu	hanen, -in	dem	hanôm
Neuter				
Nom.	daz	herza	diu	herzun
Acc.	daz	herza	diu	herzun
Gen.	des	herzen, -in	dero	herzôno
Dat.	demu	herzen, -in	dem	herzôm
Feminine				
Nom.	diu	zunga	dio	zungûn, -on
Acc.	dia	zungûn, -on	dio	zungûn, -on
Gen.	dera	zungûn, -on	dero	zungôno
Dat.	deru	zungûn, -on	dem	zungôm

-en/-in and *-on/-un* in the singular; in the plural *-on/-un*. In feminine nouns the variation *-un/-on* occurs (Table 4.8). Like in the Old High German dialects, in Old Saxon the vocalism of the ending varies from text to text. In masculine and neuter words the ending *-an* appears, too, while in feminine words *-on* instead of *-un* is quite common.

The system of vocalic and consonantal stems as it existed in Old High German and Old Saxon continued into Middle High German and Middle Low German. In the course of the Middle High German and Middle Low German period the differences between the vocalic stems were further reduced. By then only a distinction between the strong (vocalic) declension and the weak (consonantal) declension could be made.

Adjectives

In Old High German and Old Saxon the adjective had two declensions, weak and strong. An adjective preceded by a determiner (i.e. possessives and demonstratives) is declined weak, otherwise it is declined strong. The weak declension corresponds to the endings of the *n*-stems (cf. Table 4.8). The strong declension has the endings of the vocalic stems and several pronominal endings which partly replaced the originally nominal ones. In Old High German both the nominal ending and the pronominal ending occur in the nominative singular of all genders; in Old Saxon only the nominal ending (cf. Table 4.9). The nominal ending usually appears in predicative use. Even in nominative and accusative plural endingless forms appear in predicative use.

Table 4.9   Strong declension of adjectives

	Old High German		Old Saxon		
Masculine					
Singular					
Nom.	blint, -êr	man	blind	man	'blind man'
Acc.	blintan	man	blindan	man	
Gen.	blintes	mannes	blindes	mannes	
Dat.	blintemu	manne	blindum	manne	
Instr.	blintu	mannu	blindu	mannu	
Plural					
Nom.	blinte	man	blinda	man	
Acc.	blinte	man	blinda	man	
Gen.	blintero	manno	blindero	manno	
Dat.	blintêm	mannum	blindun	mannum	
Feminine					
Singular					
Nom.	blint, -iu	frouwa	blind	quena	'blind woman'
Acc.	blinta	frouwûn	blinda	quenun	
Gen.	blintera	frouwûn	blindero	quenun	
Dat.	blinteru	frouwûn	blindaru	quenun	
Plural					
Nom.	blinto	frouwûn	blinda	quenun	
Acc.	blinto	frouwûn	blinda	quenun	
Gen.	blintero	frouwôno	blindaro	quenono	
Dat.	blintêm	frouwôm	blindun	quenun	
Neuter					
Singular					
Nom.	blint, -az	barn	blind	barn	'blind child'
Acc.	blint, -az	barn	blind	barn	
Gen.	blintes	barnes	blindes	barnes	
Dat.	blintemo	barne	blindum	barne	
Plural					
Nom.	blintiu	barn	blindiu	barn	
Acc.	blintiu	barn	blindiu	barn	
Gen.	blintero	barno	blindaro	barno	
Dat.	blintêm	barnum	blindun	barnum	

Table 4.10 Irregular comparative and superlative forms

Adjective Old High German	Old Saxon		Comparative Old High German	Old Saxon	Superlative Old High German	Old Saxon
guot	gôd	'good'	bezziro	betiro	bezzist	bezt
ubil	ubil	'evil'	wirsiro	wirsa	wirsist	
mihhil	mikil	'big'	mêro	mêro	meist	mêst
luzzil	luttil	'little'	minniro	minniro	minnist	minnisto

In Middle High German and Middle Low German the number of different forms was greatly reduced, because of vowel reduction in unstressed syllables. In the plural all genders had the same forms in Middle Low German. In Middle High German only the plural neuter forms were distinctive, as they kept *-iu* in the nominative and accusative. Probably due to Middle High German influence Middle Low German also had pronominal forms like *blinder* (m. nom. sg.) and *blinde* (f. nom. sg.).

Comparison of Adjectives
In Old High German and Old Saxon the comparative and superlative suffixes are *-ir/-ôr* and *-ist/-ôst*, respectively. Adjectives with more than one syllable tend to use the forms with *ô*, e.g. *sâligôro* 'more blessed'. The monosyllabic adjectives use both suffixes (e.g. *hôhiro, hôhôro* 'higher'), but the old *ja*-stems prefer forms with *-i-* such as *suoziro* 'sweeter'. The usage of the *i*-forms and *o*-forms in the superlative is roughly the same as in the comparative: *sâligôst* 'most blessed', *suozist* 'sweetest', *hôhist/hôhôst* 'highest'. The comparative only has a weak declension. The superlative has both the strong and the weak declension. Some adjectives derive their comparative and superlative from other roots, as shown in Table 4.10.

Adverbs
The regular adverbs in Old High German and Old Saxon are derived from adjectives with the suffix *-o*, such as *ubilo* 'badly'. This regards also *ja*-stems so that there is a difference between *scôni* 'beautiful' and *scôno* 'beautifully'. In Middle High German and Middle Low German a mutated vowel signifies this difference: *schône* vs *schoene*. The comparison of adverbs only has *-ôr* and *-ôst*, even if the adjective has *i*-forms, e.g. *altiro* 'older', *altôr* 'elderly'. Another possibility of constructing adverbs is the use of the suffix *-lîhho*, OSax. *-liko*.

Personal Pronouns
Old Saxon and Middle Low German shared the common Ingvaeonic convergence of dative and accusative forms of the personal pronoun. Another

Table 4.11 Personal pronouns

Old High German

First person

	sg.	pl.
Nom.	ih	wir
Acc.	mih	unsih
Gen.	mîn	unsêr
Dat.	mir	uns

Second person

	sg.	pl.
Nom.	dû	ir
Acc.	dih	iuwih
Gen.	dîn	iuwêr
Dat.	dir	iu

Third person

	sg. m.	sg. f.	sg. n.	pl. m.	pl. f.	pl. n.
Nom.	er	siu	iz	sie	sio	siu
Acc.	ina, in	sia	iz	sie	sio	siu
Gen.	sîn	ira	is	iro	iro	
Dat.	imu, -o	iru	imu, -o	iu	im	

Old Saxon

First person

	sg.	du.	pl.
Nom.	ik	wit	wî
Acc.	mî	unk	ûs
Gen.	mîn	unkaro	ûser
Dat.	mî	unk	ûs

Second person

	sg.	du.	pl.
Nom.	thû	git	gi
Acc.	thî	inc	iu
Gen.	thîn		iuwar
Dat.	thî	inc	iu

Third person

	sg. m.	sg. f.	sg. n.	pl. m.	pl. f.	pl. n.
Nom.	hê, hie	siu	it	sie,	sia	siu
Acc.	ina, in	sia	it	sie,	sia	siu
Gen.	is	iro, ira	is	iro	iro	
Dat.	im, imo	iru, iro	im, imu	iu	im	

special feature of Old Saxon is the existence of dual forms in the first and second person (Table 4.11). In Old High German the dual does not appear, in Middle High German there are a very few examples of it in some dialects.

In Middle High German and Middle Low German the number of different forms diminished as a result of the loss of the final vowels and of the development of /m/ to /n/.

Some Remarks on Other Pronouns

Old High German and Middle High German had reflexive pronouns in the accusative singular and plural of all genders: *sich*. In other cases the personal pronoun was used. Old Saxon and Middle Low German originally had no reflexive pronoun. The accusative personal pronoun was used instead. Under the influence of Old High German and Middle High German the dative and accusative form *sik/sek* is found in some texts.

In Old High German the following possessive pronouns appear: *mîn*, *dîn*, *unsêr*, *iuwêr* (OSax. *unsa*, *iuwa*). They are declined as strong adjectives. The possessive pronoun of the third person was taken from the reflexive pronoun: *sîn*. Because of this it relates only to masculine and neuter singular forms as a subject. For feminine singular and for the plural forms the genitive of the personal pronoun was used: OHG/OSax. *ira*, MHG/MLG *ir*. Being a genitive this pronoun could not be declined. During the Middle High German and Middle Low German period declined forms appear: *iren lîp* 'her life'.

The declension of the demonstrative pronoun is identical to that of the definite article forms. In the course of time a new demonstrative developed, formed with the particle -*se* that was added to the demonstrative forms: m. sg. nom. MHG *dise*, MLG *desse* and a great number of varying forms.

The interrogative pronoun is declined in the same way as the definite article. There are no plural forms and the same form is used for both masculine and feminine. Cf. m. f. nom. MHG *wer*, *wê*, MLG *wie*, *wi*, n. nom. MHG. *waz*, MLG *wat*.

The Verbal Group

In the Germanic languages person and number were originally indicated by suffixed person markers, but in Old High German the subject pronoun already appears in most instances. Mood, too, was marked by verbal morphology: the subjunctive and imperative endings differed from the indicative ones. There were two tenses: the present, indicating present and future time, and the preterite, indicating the past. The preterite and the past participle are formed in two different ways: for the strong verbs by vowel gradation, and for the weak verbs by means of a dental suffix. In Old High German there existed seven classes of strong verbs and three classes of weak verbs, besides some irregular verbs.

In Old High German and Old Saxon the subjunctive and indicative have different forms. Compare the present and preterite of the Old High German

Table 4.12   Verbal conjugation of OHG *helfan*

	Indicative			Subjunctive	
Present					
1 sg.	ih	hilfu		ih	helfe
2 sg.	dû	hilfis		dû	helfês
3 sg.	er	hilfit		er	helfe
1 pl.	wir	helfamês		wir	helfêm
2 pl.	ir	helfet		ir	helfêt
3 pl.	sia	helfant		sia	helfên
Preterite					
1 sg.	ih	half		ih	hulfi
2 sg.	dû	hulfi		dû	hulfîs
3 sg.	er	half		er	hulfi
1 pl.	wir	hulfum		wir	hulfîm
2 pl.	ir	hulfut		ir	hulfît
3 pl.	sia	hulfun		sia	hulfîn

strong verb *helfan* (Table 4.12). Another important difference between Old High German and Old Saxon – besides the High German sound shift – is the common plural form in Old Saxon: all three persons have the same form: pres. ind. *wi, gi, sia helpad*; pret. ind. *wi, gi, sia hulpun*. The nominal forms are: inf. *helfan* (OSax. *helpan*), pres. part. *helfanti* (OSax. *helpandi*), pp. *giholfan* (OSax. *giholpan*). The imperative forms are: sg. *hilf* (OSax. *hilp*), pl. *helfet* (OSax. *helpad*).

Vowel gradation in the strong verbs, as in all Germanic languages, follows definite patterns. In Old High German and Old Saxon seven main patterns are

Table 4.13   Strong verb classes

	Infinitive		*Preterite* Singular	Plural	*Past participle*
Class I	grîfan	'to grasp'	greif	grifum	gigrifan
Class II	biotan	'to offer'	bôt	butum	gibotan
	lûhhan	'to close'	lôh	luhhum	gilohhan
Class III	bintan	'to bind'	bant	buntum	gibuntan
	helfan	'to help'	half	hulfum	giholfan
Class IV	beran	'to bear'	bar	bârum	giboran
Class V	geban	'to give'	gab	gâbum	gigeban
Class VI	graban	'to dig'	gruob	gruobum	gigraban
Class VII	haltan	'to hold'	hialt	hialtum	gihaltan
	lâzzan	'to let'	liaz	liazzum	gilâzzan
	heizzan	'to order'	hiaz	hiazzum	giheizzan
	ruofan	'to cry'	riaf	riafum	giruofan

clearly discernible. As the Old High German examples in Table 4.13 show, all seven classes have four categories: infinitive, preterite singular, preterite plural and past participle.

The preterite of weak verbs in Old High German is formed by means of the suffix *-ta*. There are three classes of weak verbs, according to the final vowel of the infinitive ending: *-en* e.g. *hôren* 'to hear'; *-ôn*, e.g. *salbôn* 'to anoint'; *-ên* e.g. *habên* 'to have'. The first group takes *-i-* as its stem vowel, the second *-ô-* and the third *-ê-*. Hence the preterites *nerita, salbôta, habêta*. The endings of the three classes are the same, except for the first person present indicative: in the *-ên-* and *-ôn-* groups *-m* is found instead of *-u*, e.g. *ih suohhu* 'I seek' vs *ih salbôm, habêm* 'I anoint, have'.

The present indicative forms are: *ih suohhu – du suohhis – er suohhit – wir suohhemês – ir suohhet – sia suohhent*; the present subjunctive forms: *suohhe – suohhês – suohhe – suohhêm – suohhêt – suohhên*. The preterite of Class I weak verbs distinguishes between short and long stems. Long-stemmed verbs lost /i/ before the ending: *ih suohta* vs *ih nerita*. The endings of the past tense indicative are: *-ta, -tôs, -ta, -tum, -tut, -tun*. Thus: *suohta, nerita, salbôta, habêta*, etc. In the subjunctive the endings are: *-ti, -tîs, -ti, -tîm, -tît, -tîn*. Thus: *suohti, neriti, salbôti, habêti*, etc. In the imperative: sg. *suohhi, neri, salbo, habe*, pl. *suohhet, neriet, salbôt, habêt*. The infinitives are: *suohhen, nerien, salbôn, habên*, the present participles: *suohhenti, nerienti, salbônti, habênti*, and past participles: *gisuohhit, ginerit, gisalbôt, gihabêt*.

In Old Saxon the weak verbs appear in two classes: those with original *-ian* and those with *-ôn*. Traces of a third class are rare. The two classes differ in the same way as in Old High German. There is, however, one complication: long stems of the first class lose *-i-* in the preterite, e.g. *hôrean, hôrda* 'heard'. This could have consequences for the following dental consonant which was devoiced after a voiceless consonant, e.g. *lôsian, lôsda/lôsta* 'to release'.

Vowel reduction strongly reduced the number of forms in Middle High German and Middle Low German. Here only two groups of weak verbs existed: (1) weak verbs with *e* before the preterital suffix e.g. MLG *he makede*; (2) verbs without a vowel e.g. MHG *hôrte* 'heard', *dâhte* 'thought', MLG *he hôrde*. The seven classes of the strong verbs are still to be found in Middle High German and Middle Low German.

The anomalous verbs *sîn* 'to be', *tuon* 'to do', *gân/gên* 'to go' and *stân/stên* 'to stand' have special forms in the preterite and the past participle, both in Old High German and Old Saxon. Verbs with vowel gradation in the present tense belong also to the group of irregular verbs. All these verbs have been preserved in the Middle High and Middle Low German period.

4.8 Syntax

On the whole Old High German and Old Saxon manifest a development from a synthetic to an analytic language. This means that syntactic and semantic functions are no longer exclusively and clearly expressed by case endings, but by obligatory specifiers of the noun (article, preposition) and of the verb (personal pronouns, auxiliary verbs). The Old High German sentence *uuili mih dinu speru uuerpan* becomes *du willst mich mit deinem Speer werfen* 'you want to throw your spear at me' in Modern German. In Middle High German the use of the article became obligatory with count nouns.

Almost all Old High German texts are translations from a Latin source. Given this situation, it is highly probable that some characteristics, such as the use of participal constructions, betray Latin influence.

The Nominal Group

The word order in the early period was rather free, as the case endings were still discernible. There is a tendency to place the adjective before the noun, e.g. *dhese chisalbodo got* 'this anointed god'. The same applies to genitivals which are commonly put before the noun, even when the Latin source had a different word order: *widar mannes sune* 'against man's son'. Vowel reductions of vowels in the endings necessitated the use of personal and demonstrative pronouns to show the function of the nouns and verbs, e.g. *thô quad ín thér heilant: ir irrot ni uuizenti giscrib noh gotes megin* 'then the Saviour said to them: you err, neither knowing the scriptures nor God's power'.

Nouns

The nominative is the case of the subject and of the predicative noun referring to the subject. In Old High German and Old Saxon it also adopted the functions of the vocative.

The accusative is the case of the direct object; it is governed by a transitive verb. In some instances double accusatives existed: *lêrit iuuuih al uuâr* 'he teaches you the whole truth', cf. OSax. *lêrda thia liudi langsamana râd* 'he taught the people long during advice'. In its absolute use the accusative could signify place, e.g. *thô fuar er mit imo hôhe berga* 'then he went with him on high mountains', and duration of time, e.g. *wâron se allo worolti zi thir zeigônti* 'they have pointed to you throughout all ages'.

The genitive normally expresses possession: *mannes sune* 'man's son'. Besides this we very often find a partitive function. In this function it was also used after numerals, e.g. OHG *sumaro enti wintro sehstic* 'sixty summers and winters'; OSax. *twêntig wintro* 'twenty winters', and after nouns and adjectives denoting a measure or a quantity: OSax. *tehan embar honiges* 'ten buckets honey'. In both languages the genitive was also used after certain adjectives like *fruot, lôs*, cf. OHG *arbeo laosa* 'without heritance'; OSax. *barno lôs* 'without children'. In Old High German and Old Saxon, case forms still had the possibility of expressing circumstantial relations, e.g. OHG *se wara geloufan waldes odo weges odo heido* 'they run in the wood or along the path or over the heath'; *wârin mir mîne trâne brôt tages unde nahtes* 'my tears were bread to me day and night', *managero dingo* 'in manifold ways'. In Old Saxon we find e.g. *hie gibôd torhtaro têkno* 'he commanded with clear signs' (in this use we also find the dative or the instrumental).

The dative primarily is the case of the indirect object: *so imo se der chuning gap* 'as the king gave them to him'; *hilph mînan liutin* 'help my people'. Frequently used, especially with verbs of motion, is the ethic dative, in particular in Old Saxon: *tho geng im thanan* 'then he went away'. The dative is also used in combination with adjectives like *sêr, liob*, etc.: *imo was eo fehta ti leop* 'he always loved fighting too much'. In Old High German and Old Saxon the dative is often used in instrumental function, especially in plural forms. In the singular the earliest texts still had the instrumental: OHG *her fragên gistuont fôhem uuortum* 'he began to ask with few words'; OSax. *handon sluog* 'beat with his hands'.

In early Old High German and Old Saxon a number of masculine and neuter nouns preserve traces of the old instrumental in the singular, but even in the earliest texts *mit* or *mid* 'with' could be used with the instrumental: OHG *nu scal mih suâsat chind suertu hauwan,/bretton mit sînu billiu* 'now my own child shall hew me with the sword,/strike me down with his brand'; OSax. *awekid mit wînu* 'waked up with wine'. If the noun is accompanied by a qualifying word the dative is used: *mit drôstu* 'with comfort', *mit themo drôste* 'with the comfort'. In fact the instrumental was already redundant in the Old High German and Old Saxon period. After the eleventh century only traces of the instrumental are preserved, especially with pronouns: MHG *z(w)iu* 'wherefore?'. Up to this day OHG *hiutu* (< **hiu tagu*) and *hiuru* (< **hiu jâru*) – cf. OSax. *hiudu* (< **hiu dagu*) – have remained in use: Mod. Ger. *heute, heuer* 'today', 'this year'.

Adjectives

Originally in the Germanic languages the strong declension of adjectives was used both in definite and indefinite contexts. With the rise of the article in the Old High German period the strong declension was used for indefinite use and the weak declension for the definite one: *guot man* vs *thu guoto scalc*. Because of this the strong declension – unlike in Modern German – was also used after the indefinite article: e.g. *einemo diuremo merigrioze* 'an expensive pearl'. Both inflected and uninflected forms of the strong adjective were used without semantic difference in the Old High German and the Middle High German periods. In southern Germany the inflected forms were more frequent than in the north. Old Saxon did not have inflected forms in the nominative: OHG *arm(az) barn* vs OSax. *arm barn* 'poor child'. In postposition and in predicative use both inflected and uninflected forms were used: OHG *in einemo felde scônemo* 'in a fair field', *ther puzz ist filu diofêr* 'this well is very deep', *disiu buzza ist sô tiuf* 'this well is so deep'.

The weak declension referred to something definite. At first it was not necessary to have a definite article, e.g. *ni ist in kihuctin himiliskin gote* 'he is not in the mind of the heavenly Lord'. But already in Old High German and Old Saxon the definite marker was regularly used.

The Verbal Group

The analytical tendencies were strong in both Old High German and Old Saxon. The subject pronoun became increasingly obligatory during the period, e.g. (about 800) *suohhemes* 'we search', (about 1020) *dû habest mih kenómen* 'you have received me'. Originally both languages had only two tenses: the present and the preterite. The Latin future tense is normally translated by the present tense. Only rarely is the future expressed by an auxiliary, usually *sculan* 'shall'. In Old Saxon, it is quite commonly expressed with auxiliaries, also *sculan*, although the present is also used. In Old High German perfect and pluperfect can be expressed with the help of *sîn/wesen* 'to be' and *habên/eigan* 'to have', e.g. *intfangan eigut* 'you have received'. The rule governing the use of the verbs is the following: *sîn/wesan* is used in the case of ergative (unaccusative) verbs, i.e. verbs which express a change (*uuas erbolgan* 'was incensed'); *habên/eigan* is used in the case of transitive verbs and the other intransitive verbs: *eigun funtan* 'they have found'.

Like the other West Germanic languages Old High German, Middle High German, Old Saxon and Middle Low German had no synthetic passive, but an analytic one, consisting of the past participle with the auxiliaries *sîn/wesan* (MHG *sîn, wesen*) and *werdan/werthan* (MHG, MLG *werden*). The imperfect passive tenses are formed with the help of *sîn/wesan* 'to be' or *werdan* 'to become', e.g. *uuas gitragan* 'he was carried', *wirdu gitaufit* 'I am baptized', *mîn tohter ubilo fon themo tiuvale giweigit ist* 'my daughter is strongly vexed by the devil'. *werdan* + past participle may refer to future time: *thiz cunni diuuolo ni uuirdit aruuorfan noba thuruh gibet* 'this race of devils will not be driven out except by prayer'. *sîn/wesan* + past participle may indicate a state in Old High German (and Old Saxon): *bin gitruobit, bim gisentit* (lit.) 'I am one who has been sent'. This phenomenon is sometimes labelled 'stative passive' in the handbooks. Already at the close of the Old High German period the resultative construction with *sîn/wesan* was grammaticalized as a perfect and pluperfect (e.g. *ist/was gimachot*). Eventually this development implied a decreasing usage of the auxiliary *sîn/wesan* in the present and preterite, except in the imperative, as in Modern German: *sei gegrüßt. werden* remained as the only option: *Gothi wurten dannân vertriben fone Narsete patricio* 'the Goths were driven thence by Narses the Patrician'. During the Middle High German and Middle Low German period tripartite constructions came into use in the perfect tenses: ... *daz Gahmuret geprîset ... was worden* 'that Gahmuret has been praised'. They did not become common until after the Middle Ages.

Impersonal passives like *thes êr iu ward giwahanit* 'you were told before about that' deserve special mention. Impersonal (active) constructions have been used since the oldest times, above all with impersonal verbs, e.g. OHG *uuanta iz âbandêt* 'because it became evening'. In Middle High German the group of occasional impersonals arose: *den wîben ez durch diu ôren klanc* 'it sounded in the women's ears'. Another group that appears during the Middle High German period consists of constructions such as *ez troumte mir* or *mir troumte* 'I dreamed'.

The Sentence
Word order in Old High German and Old Saxon was rather free. The modern SVO or verb-second order in unmarked declarative sentences is by no means obligatory in the earliest texts: *fater meinida dhar sinan sun, dhuo ir chiminnan chneht nemnida* (lit.) 'the father meant his son by that, when he said beloved servant', but: *dhes martyrunga endi dodh uuir findemes* (lit.) 'of him the martyrdom and death we find' and: *quimit der brûtigomo* (lit.) 'comes the bridegroom'. In subordinate sentences SOV is possible but not necessary: *dhazs fater endi sunu endi heilac gheist got sii* (lit.) 'that Father and Son and Holy Spirit God is', but: *dat du habes heme* (lit.) 'that you have at home'.

Main Clause
In Old High German and Old Saxon asyndetic linking of main clauses regularly occurred: *gistirri záltun wir io, ni sáhun wir nan ér io* 'we used to count the stars, we never saw it before'. If clauses shared the subject, it was not necessary to repeat it: *denne varant engila upar dio marcha,/wechant deota, wîssant ze dinge* 'then angels fly over the lands, awaken the people, lead [them] to judgement'. Even in Middle High German this was quite common: *dô sâhen Bloedelînes man, ir herre lac erslagen* 'then Bloedelîn's men saw, [that] their lord was killed'. Interrogative sentences have the verb in initial position, if they are not introduced by an interrogative pronoun. The verb could also occupy the initial position in other sentence types: *garutun se iro gudhamun* 'they prepared their battle-dresses'.

Subordinate Clauses
Even in the earliest texts there are beginnings of compound sentences. Asyndetic linking was possible, especially in a conditional sense, of which the word order with an initial verb is a sufficient indication: *bistu Krist guato, sage uns iz gimuato* 'if you are the good Christ, please tell us so'. The earliest form also requires the use of the subjunctive to express subordination: *Hêrro, ih thicho ze dir: thaz wazzer gâbîst dû mir* 'Lord, I ask you, [that] you might give me that water'.

The next move is the use of conjunctions that clearly show the subordination. The most important conjunction in the early texts is OHG *daz*, OSax. *that*. Originally this was the accusative singular neuter of the demonstrative pronoun and used in the first clause to introduce the next: *joh gizálta in sar tház: thiu sálida untar ín was* 'and he quickly told them that: the salvation was among them'. The rhyme shows that *thaz* still is part of the first clause.

Normally, however, the pronoun was transferred to the second clause: *wánt er deta mári, thaz druhtin quéman wari* 'for he made known, that the Lord had come'. In Old High German, structures with more than one subordinate clause are quite rare. One example is found in the *Hildebrandlied*: *dat sagetun mi usere liuti, alte anti frote, dea erhina warun, dat Hiltibrant hætti min fater* ... 'Our people, old and wise, who lived for a long time, told me that, that Hildebrand was my father's name'. In Old Saxon much more complicated sentences were common. The *Heliand* has e.g. *manega uuâron, the sia iro môd gespôn,/... that sia begunnun uuord godes,/reckean that girûni, that thie rîceo Crist/undar mancunnea mârida gifrumida* 'there were many [people], whose mood caused them, that they began to relate the word of God, the secret that the mighty Christ wrought famous things among mankind'. It is, however, possible that the stylistic variation of the text caused these constructions to be used.

Other conjunctions already in use in Old High German and Old Saxon were: *thanne* 'then' in a conditional sense, e.g. *thanne ir betôt, duet iz kurzlîchaz* 'whenever you pray, make it brief' – in Middle High German this conjunction was replaced by *(s)wenne*: *die lûhten sô mit glanze,/ swenne er gie bî dem tanze* 'they [the buttons] shone with such brightness whenever he danced'; *thô* 'when' in a temporal sense: *tho thaz gihorta Herodes ther cuning, uuard gitruobit* 'when king Herod heard this, he was disturbed'; *wanda* 'for' in a causal sense: *ni uuolta sih fluobiren, uuanta sie ni uuârun* 'and she [Rachel] would not be consoled, for they [her sons] were not there'.

Even the relative clause could be asyndetic in the earliest texts: *in droume sie in zelitun then weg sie faran scoltun* 'in a dream they told them the way they should go'. The relative pronoun in Old High German and Old Saxon is formally identical to the demonstrative pronoun. The starting point for relative clauses probably was the Latin construction from the type *ego sum qui loquor tecum*. This was translated: *ih bin thê sprichu mit thir* originally: 'I am the one, I speak with you'. Demonstrative and relative pronoun are united in one word, cf. MHG *sie bienen die si wolten,/unt niht den si solten* 'they excommunicated those whom they wanted to and not him whom they should have'. Often the relative pronoun had the same case as the antecedent, even if that was not in accordance with its function in the subordinate clause: *thes thigit worolt ellu thes ih thir hiar nu zellu* 'for this all the world is pleading, which I am here now telling you'. In the first clause the genitive *thes* is correct, in the second clause it should have been the accusative. The tendency is, however, to take the case that is required in the subordinate clause. Even interrogative pronouns could develop into relatives. The connection between the two functions can be seen in: *inu ni lârut ir hwaz David teta?* 'have you not read what David did?'. An example for the use of an interrogative as a relative pronoun can be found in: *hérro, thu nu ni habes mit hiu scefes* 'Lord, you have nothing to draw with'. In Old High German and Old Saxon the interrogative pronoun in combination with *sô* could serve as indefinite relative pronoun: *sô uûer so fúrlaʒe sina quenun,* ... 'whoever leaves his wife ...'.

4.9 Lexis

Early Period

As a heritage from Old Germanic times Old High German and Old Saxon share the greater part of their lexicon with the other West Germanic languages. In the earliest instances of Old High German and in the Old Saxon biblical epics we even find words that probably belong to a common Germanic literary language, e.g. *ferah* 'life, people', cf. Go. *fairhvus*, OEng. *feorh*, OFris. *ferech*, ON *fjör*. The Roman occupation and the influence of Roman culture brought many loanwords to Old High German and, to a lesser extent, to Old Saxon. The periods of borrowing can in many cases clearly be distinguished, as loans from the earliest period went through the second sound shift, e.g. OHG *strazza* (< *via strata*) 'street', *phorza* (< *porta*) 'gate'. This suggests that also Old Saxon *strata, porta* originate from that period.

During and after the conversion many (Graeco-)Latin Christian loanwords came into use. Even here there is an old group of early loans that were borrowed before the High German sound shift: e.g. *kirihha* 'church', *phaffo* 'cleric' – cf. OSax. *kirika*, *Paping-* (in place-names) – and a younger group that lacks signs of the shift and probably were borrowed later (or lost those signs under the continuous influence of the Latin language).

An important feature of Old High German is the search for adequate translations of Latin words in religious literature. Many attempts were made to translate abstract words. As a large body of the surviving Old High German texts consists of glosses in Latin manuscripts there is a great number of hapaxes. As central an idea as Latin *resurrectio* 'resurrection' has no less than fifteen translations: *ur-stant, ur-rist, ur-stend-i, ur-rest-î, ur-stend-ida, ur-stend-idi, ur-stôd-ali, ar-stant-nessi, ar-stant-nunga, ir-stand-ini, ûf-er-stend-e, ûf-er-stand-unge, ûf-er-stand-en-keit, ûf-er-stent-nisse, ûf-er-stê-unge.* Only the last one survived: *Auferstehung.* It has to be assumed that part of the Old High German religious vocabulary never got farther than certain scriptoria or schools. As the amount of Old Saxon glosses is far less than that of the Old High German, it is difficult to assess whether Old Saxon showed a similar development. But it is highly probable that the situation there was the same.

Middle High German and Middle Low German Period

In the course of the eleventh and twelfth centuries Middle High German and to a lesser extent Middle Low German developed into a literary language. Old French exercised a strong influence on the language of the Middle High German courtly literature. Many words were introduced directly – or indirectly through Middle Dutch. In particular, the technical terms of courtly life were French: *aventiure* 'adventure', *tjostieren* 'fight in a tournament' etc. The meaning of other words was influenced by French equivalents, e.g. *hövesch* 'courtly'. The French influence went so far that even French suffixes like *-îe*, *-ieren* were attached to German words: *jegerîe* 'hunt', *stolzieren* 'to walk proudly'. After the decline of courtly literature most technical terms disappeared again, but the suffixes remained. In Middle Low German the influence of courtly literature was far less important. Here the urban vernacular remained quite free of foreign influences. The many translations from Middle Dutch resulted in a certain influence from that language, although the resemblance between these two languages makes it difficult to ascertain whether or not a word is a loan.

Further Reading

Bergman, R. (1987) *Althochdeutsch*, 2 vols, Heidelberg: Winter.

Braune, W. (1987) *Althochdeutsche Grammatik*, 14th edn revised by H. Eggers, Tübingen: Niemeyer.

Braune, W. and Helm, K. (1977) *Abriß der althochdeutschen Grammatik unter Berücksichtigung des Altsächsischen*, 14th edn revised by E. A. Ebbinghaus, Tübingen: Niemeyer.

Bree, C. van (1987) *Historische Grammatica van het Nederlands*, Dordrecht: Foris Publications.

Bremmer, R. H. and Quak, A. (eds) (1992) *Zur Phonologie und Morphologie des Altniederländischen*, Odense: Odense University Press.

Cordes, Gerhard (1973) *Altniederdeutsches Elementarbuch. Wort- und Lautlehre mit einem Kapitel 'Syntaktisches' von Ferdinand Holthausen*, Heidelberg: Winter.

Duinhoven, A. M. (1988) *Middelnederlandse Syntaxis, synchroon en diachroon. 1. De naamwoordgroep*, Leyden: Martinus Nijhoff.

Goossens, J. (1974) *Historische Phonologie des Niederländischen*, Tübingen, Niemeyer.

Holthausen, F. (1921) *Altsächsisches Elementarbuch*, 2nd edn, Heidelberg: Winter.

Horst, J. M. van der (1986) *Historische Grammatica en Taaltekens. Studies over de plaats van de persoonsvorm, samentrekking en de onpersoonlijke constructie in de geschiedenis van het Nederlands*, doctoral thesis, University of Amsterdam, Alblasserdam: private publication.

Lasch, A. (1974) *Mittelniederdeutsche Grammatik*, 2nd edn, Tübingen: Niemeyer.

Lockwood, W. B. (1968) *Historical German Syntax*, Oxford: Clarendon Press.

Loey, A. van (1966) *Middelnederlandse Spraakkunst, I. Vormleer*, 5th edn, Groningen/Antwerp: Wolters.

—— (1968) *Middelnederlandse Spraakkunst, II. Klankleer*, 5th edn, Groningen/Antwerp: Wolters-Noordhoff.

Michels, V. (1979) *Mittelhochdeutsches Elementarbuch*, Heidelberg: Winter.

Paul, H. (1989) *Mittelhochdeutsche Grammatik*, 23rd edn, revised by P. Wiehl and S. Grosse, Tübingen: Niemeyer.

Russ, C. (1978) *Historical German Phonology and Morphology*, Oxford: Clarendon Press.

Stoett, F. A. (1923) *Middelnederlandsche Spraakkunst. Syntaxis*, 3rd edn, The Hague: Martinus Nijhoff.

Wal, M. J. van der (1986) *Passiefproblemen in oudere taalfasen. Middelnederlands sijn/werden + participium praeteriti en de pendanten in het gotisch, het engels en het duits*, doctoral thesis, University of Leyden, Dordrecht: private publication.

5 Old and Middle English

Ans van Kemenade

5.1 Introduction

The terms Old English and Middle English refer to the vernacular language recorded in England in the period from *c*. AD 600 to *c*. AD 1500. Old English, or Anglo-Saxon, is the group of dialects imported by the immigrants from the continent in the fourth, fifth and sixth centuries, who drove back the native Romano-Celtic population to Cornwall, Wales and Scotland. The transition to Middle English is usually somewhat artificially marked by the date of the Norman Conquest of England as 1066.

For Old English, two main dialect groups are distinguished: West Saxon and Anglian (see Figure 5.1). West Saxon is the dialect in which the bulk of Old English manuscript material was written. West Saxon is very poorly documented until the literary activity of King Alfred in the late ninth century. In the literary tradition instigated by Alfred, 'early West Saxon' is represented in the Parker manuscript of the Anglo-Saxon Chronicle until 924 and the Alfredian translations of the *Orosius* and Pope Gregory's *Cura Pastoralis* (both *c*. 900). Late West Saxon is attested in the works of *Ælfric*, those of Wulfstan, the Abingdon manuscripts of the Anglo-Saxon *Chronicle* and the A manuscript of the Benedictine Rule. Apart from these, a number of texts that display more dialect mixture are still usually classified as West Saxon: the Old English translations of Bede's *Historia Ecclesiastica*, Pope Gregory's *Dialogues* and Boethius' *De Consolatione Philosophiae*, the *Blickling Homilies* and the D text of the Anglo-Saxon *Chronicle*. The Anglian dialect group is subdivided into two: Northumbrian and Mercian. The Northumbrian dialect is identified, above all, by rune inscriptions on Ruthwell Cross and further found in three eighth-century poems (*Caedmon's Hymn*, *Bede's Death Song* and the *Leiden Riddle*) and in three extensive tenth-century texts (the glosses on the *Lindisfarne Gospels*, part of the *Rushworth Gospels* and the *Durham Ritual*). In the Mercian dialect from before 900, there are charters from Mercian kings. Further, there is the ninth-century gloss of the *Vespasian Psalter*, the tenth-century partial gloss of the *Rushworth Gospels* and some

Figure 5.1   The dialects of Old English

Source: Baugh and Cable 1978: 53.
Note: Only the major dialect areas are indicated. That the Saxon settlements north of the
Thames had their own dialect features is apparent in Middle English.

minor glosses. Usually, a fourth Old English dialect is distinguished: Kentish. The material from Kentish is limited to the *Kentish Glosses*, and a few charters.

There is a good deal of beautiful poetry in Old English, in three main genres: heroic, elegiac and biblical. The bulk of the orally transmitted poetry is in four manuscripts: the *Beowulf* manuscript, the *Junius* manuscript, the *Exeter Book* and the *Vercelli Book*.

The only surviving original manuscript from the transition period from Old to Middle English is the relevant part of the E version of the Anglo-Saxon Chronicle, better known as the *Peterborough Chronicle*, with contemporary continuations up to 1154. This manuscript is therefore a very valuable source of information on this stage of the language, even if it represents only one dialect, that of the East Midlands.

For Middle English, a division into five dialects is customary: Northern, East Midlands, West Midlands, Kentish and Southern (see Figure 5.2). A few outstanding texts from the main dialect areas may be mentioned: from the Northern dialect there is the thirteenth-century *Cursor Mundi*, the thirteenth-century prose *Benedictine Rule*, the works of Richard Rolle (*c.* 1340) and the fifteenth-century York plays. The East Midlands/London have left us the *Peterborough Chronicle*, the *Ormulum* (*c.* 1200), *Havelok* from around the same date, Chaucer's works from the late fourteenth century and those of John Lydgate from the first half of the fifteenth century. From the West Midlands, we have the *Katherine group* (*c.* 1230), Langland's *Piers the Plowman* (*c.* 1375) and *Sir Gawain and the Green Knight*. From the Kentish area, there are the thirteenth-century *Kentish Sermons* and Dan Michel's fourteenth-century *Ayenbite of Inwit*. The South has left us the *Owl and the Nightingale* from the late twelfth century, the thirteenth-century *Laȝamon's Brut*, the *South English Legendary* and the late fourteenth-century works of Wycliffe.

In the transition from Old English to Middle English, English underwent a number of pervasive changes in the phonology, morphology, vocabulary and syntax. These changes have often been ascribed to French influence due to the Norman Conquest of England. It is doubtful whether this is correct, though. The Norman Conquest started in the south of the country, and left its imprint mainly in the top layers of society. It is clear that this caused a tremendous influx of Romance loanwords. There is little evidence, however, that French influence penetrated the language much deeper than that. The changes in the phonology of unaccented syllables (reduction of unstressed vowels to schwa) that had a domino effect in the morphology (reducing case endings) were already on the way in the north of England in the Old English period, before French influence could take effect. Recent work on the matter hypothesizes that it is the Viking conquest of the north and east of England in the ninth and tenth centuries that had the more profound influence, as it resulted in long-term settlement and assimilation of invading and native population. However

Figure 5.2   The dialects of Middle English

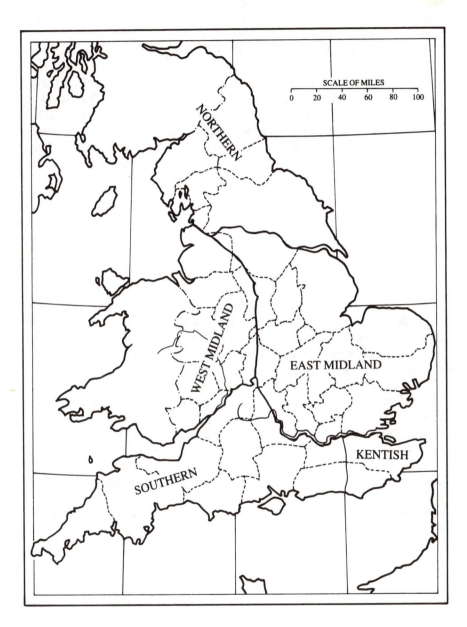

Source: Baugh and Cable 1978: 190.

plausible this is, we cannot verify it because the text material from the relevant period is in the Alfredian West Saxon literary tradition; since it was King Alfred's business to get the Vikings out of England, or at least to keep them at a distance, Scandinavian influence is not apparent there.

The West Saxon literary standard of the Old English period was broken by the Norman Conquest, and it was not before the second part of the fourteenth century that another one developed. The first new literary standard to arise was that apparent in the work of Wycliffe and his followers. The dialect of these works has proved difficult to localize precisely and appears to be based on the dialects of the central Midland counties. The clearest indication that it was a literary standard is the fact that it survived unchanged in written form until the late fifteenth century. There is good reason to assume that it was one of the major sources for the emerging modern standard norm.

5.2   Phonology

Vowels

Old English Vowel System
The system of Old English accented vowels can be represented as in Table 5.1, where the vowels are given in the standard spelling with presumed phonetic transcription added if the spelling is not transparent. There are eight pairs, distinguished by length only, and a central vowel [ə], spelled e.

Sound Change
The Old English vowel system evolved from the prehistoric system through a series of sound changes. The most conspicuous and pervasive of these is called *i*-umlaut. West Germanic had five canonical vowels /i, u, e, o, a/ which could be either short or long, plus a long /æ/. In stressed syllables preceding an unstressed syllable containing /i/ (syllabic or semivowel), back vowels developed a fronted allophone which had perhaps become phonologized by historic Old English times: /u/ > /y/, /o/ > /œ/, /a/ > /æ/. *i*-umlaut had a number of effects in the inflectional morphology of Old English, and led to important morphophonemic alternations.

Table 5.1   Vowels of Old English

	Front unround	Front round	Central	Back
High	i	y		u
Mid	e	œ/e	e	o
Low	æ		a	

i-umlaut was not the only source for Old English short /æ/. In prehistoric times, West Germanic short /a/ became Old English and Frisian /æ/ through the so-called Anglo-Frisian fronting.

Middle English

In the transition to Middle English, the accented vowels underwent a number of quantitative (conditioned) and qualitative (largely unconditioned) changes. The following is a summing up of the main developments. Changes in quantity: lengthening would take place when a vowel preceded a consonant cluster consisting of a nasal or liquid plus a homorganic voiced stop, e.g. ‹-nd, -mb, -ld, -rd, -ng›, as in *hand* > *hānd* 'hand', *climban* > *clīmben* 'climb', *cald* > *cāld* 'cold', *word* > *wōrd* 'word', *strang* > *strāng* 'strong'. This change did not apply to clusters with three consonants: the plural of 'child' remained *cildru* with short vowel, whereas the singular underwent lengthening: *cild* > *cīld*. Lengthening also took place in open syllables: *beran* > *bēren* 'bear', *mete* > *mēte* 'meat', *macian* > *māken* 'make', *hopian* > *hōpen* 'hope'. In all other environments, i.e. those involving consonant clusters other than the above, and double consonants, vowels were shortened: *sōfte* > *soft* 'soft', *fīftig* > *fiftig* 'fifty', also *cēpen* 'keep' vs past tense *cepte* 'kept', etc. Moreover, vowels were shortened in the first syllable of trisyllabic words: *crīstendōm* > *cristendōm* 'Christendom', *sūperne* > *superne* 'southern', etc. The changes in quality were largely unconditioned: short /æ/ regularly developed to /a/. In the course of the Middle English period, the rounded front vowels /y/ and /œ/, short or long, developed to /i/ and /e/ respectively. The vowels descending from the Old English long vowels underwent some

Table 5.2   Short vowels *c.* 1400

	Front	Central	Back
High	i		u
Mid	e	ə	o
Low	a		

Table 5.3   Long vowels *c.* 1400

	Front	Central	Back
High	iː		uː
High mid	eː		oː
Low mid	ɛː		ɔː
Low		aː	

unconditioned, yet fairly complex changes that will not be treated here. As a result of these developments, the late Middle English system of vowels can be represented as in Tables 5.2 and 5.3.

Vowels in Unstressed Syllables

The number of vowels occurring in unaccented syllables is considerably more limited than in accented syllables. The inventory includes a subset of the vowels in accented syllables: /u/, /a/, /œ/ (spelled ‹e›), and probably also /o/, though the rounded back vowel was always spelled ‹u›. The transition to Middle English was marked by a reduction of unstressed vowels; in Middle English the vowels of unaccented syllables are canonically spelled ‹e›, presumably reflecting a schwa-like quality. This reduction had massive consequences for the distinctiveness of inflexional endings, which will be dealt with in section 5.3.

Diphthongs

Old English had four diphthongs which could be either long or short: /ea/, /eo/, /ie/, /io/. The short versions of the diphthongs evolved out of West Germanic simple vowels through various diphthongization processes, of which the most important are *breaking* and *back umlaut*, both discussed below. Short /ie/ developed from short /ea/ and /io/ (by breaking) through *i*-umlaut. The long versions of the diphthongs arose in three ways: first, through the same processes as the short diphthongs; second, they were regular developments of Germanic diphthongs: */au/ > long /ēa/, */eu/ > long /ēo/, */iu/ > long /īo/ (long /ie/ arose through *i*-umlaut only); third, long /ēa/ and /ēo/ developed through coalescence resulting from the loss of intervocalic consonants, e.g. West Germanic *slaxan* > *slæxan* (Anglo-Frisian fronting) > *sleaxan* (breaking) > *sleaan* (loss of intervocalic /x/) > *slēan* 'hit' (coalescence and compensatory lengthening).

Breaking and Back Umlaut

Breaking and *back umlaut* both involve the same kind of diphthongization process, but are distinguished according to their conditioning environment: *breaking* is conditioned by following consonants, *back mutation* by unstressed *a* or *u* in the following syllable. Due to breaking, /æ/ > [ea], /e/ > [eo], /i/ > [io] (usually spelled ‹eo›) if it is followed by /x/ (spelled ‹h›), /l/ + consonant, or /r/ + consonant. For example, Go. *haldan* = OEng. *healdan* 'hold' (through fronting and breaking), OHG *kneht* = OEng. *cneoht* 'servant', Gmc *lirnōjan* > OEng. *liornian* 'to learn'. *Back umlaut* involves the same sort of process (though less regular in details in the various dialects) caused by a back vowel in the following syllable, with a single consonant intervening. Thus, OHG *ebur* = OEng. *eofor* etc.

The typical Old English diphthongs were all monophongized in the late Old English and early Middle English periods: long and short /ea/ became /æ/;

long and short /eo/ became /œ/ and /io/ shared this development; the /ie/ diphthongs developed to /y/.

Diphthongs in Middle English

In the course of the Middle English period a new series of diphthongs developed. The first set resulted from the vocalization after a vowel of the Old English voiced velar fricative /ɣ/ (spelled ‹g›). After a front vowel, /ɣ/ first developed to the palatal approximant [j] and subsequently became the second part of a front diphthong, thus: OEng. *dæg* > MEng. *dai* 'day'; OEng. *weg* > MEng. *wei* 'way'; OEng. *segl* > MEng. *sail* 'sail'; OEng. *ege* > MEng. *eie* 'eye'. After back vowels, /ɣ/ changed first to [w], then to the second part of a back diphthong: OEng. *lagu* > MEng. *lawe* 'law'; OEng. *agan* > MEng. *owen* 'own'; OEng. *boga* > MEng. *bowe* 'bow'; OEng. *plogas* > MEng. *plowes* 'ploughs'. The second set resulted later (late thirteenth, early fourteenth century) from the formation of a glide between a vowel and the voiceless velar fricative /x/ (spelled ‹h› or ‹gh›). After a back vowel, a back glide developed: MEng. *tahte* > MEng. *taughte* 'taught'; MEng. *dohter* > MEng. *doughter* 'daughter'; MEng. *lahter* > MEng. *laughter* 'laughter'. After a front vowel, a front glide developed: MEng. *eghte* > MEng. *eighte* 'eight'; MEng. *heh* > MEng. *heih* 'high'. The development is not so transparent to the Modern English ear/eye because in the course of the early Modern period the velar fricative itself disappeared and the diphthongs were affected by the Great Vowel Shift. The third set resulted from the vocalization of sequences of vowel followed by /w/: OEng. *blawan* > MEng. *blawen* 'blow'; OEng. *growan* > MEng. *growen* 'grow'; OEng. *feawe* > MEng. *few* 'few', etc.

Consonants

The consonants of Old English are represented in Table 5.4, in the standard orthography. It can be seen that each series of voiced and voiceless stops includes four members according to place of articulation; the voiceless and voiced fricatives have five members each.

Table 5.4 Consonants of Old English

	Labial	Dental	Alveolar	Palatal	Velar
Voiceless stops	p		t	c	c
Voiced stops	b		d	cg	g
Voiceless fricatives	f	þ/ð	s	sc	h
Voiced fricatives	f	þ/ð	s	g	g
Nasals	m		n		n
Liquids			l,r		
Approximants				j	w

It is evident from Table 5.4 that the orthographic symbols ‹f, þ/ð, s› do not reflect any voice opposition. The voice opposition for fricatives was presumably not phonemic in Old English, and the voiced/voiceless values were in complementary distribution as a result of a prehistoric sound change voicing fricatives in voiced environments. Thus, in all but these environments ‹f, þ/ð, s› represent [f, θ, s]. To illustrate, in *fōt* 'foot', *geaf* 'gave' and *sceaft* 'shaft', ‹f› represents [f]; in *drīfan* 'drive', *wulfas* 'wolves' and *hræfn* 'raven', ‹f› represents [v].

Similarly, the distinction between palatal and velar stops and fricatives was perhaps not phonemic: the palatal variants were the result of *palatalization*, a sound change affecting velar consonants in original (i.e. not the result of *i*-umlaut) front environments. To exemplify, *ceorl* 'churl', *cirice* 'church', *geard* 'yard', *georn* 'eager', *pic* 'pitch', *dæg* 'day', all with the palatal value vs *climban* 'climb', *cræft* 'craft', *cu* 'cow', *gold* 'gold', *boc* 'book', *plog* 'plow', all with the velar quality. The consonant spelled ‹sc› is an exception here, since it arose out of palatalization of *sk, and its palatalization became general, not limited to front environments: *sceolde* 'should', *scinan* 'shine', but also *scrud* 'shroud', all with palatal *sc*. Original Anglo-Saxon words with palatalized consonants may be contrasted with later Scandinavian loans that have the non-palatalized variant: native *shirt* vs Scandinavian *skirt*; native *yard* vs Scandinavian *garden*; native *eie* (dialectal) vs Scandinavian *egg*.

The most conspicuous consonant changes in the Middle English period are those already indicated in the section on diphthongs: the voiced velar fricative was vocalized when following a vowel. Similarly when following a liquid: OEng. *folgian* > MEng. *folȝen* later *folwen*; OEng. *morgen* > MEng. *morȝen* later *morwe* 'morrow'. Another conspicuous change involving velar fricatives that may be mentioned here, though it took place after the Middle English period, is the dual development of the voiceless velar fricative: it was noted above that in late Middle English a glide developed between a vowel and /x/. This glide was vocalized and incorporated in a diphthong as in *knight, height, though*. After a back vowel, there sometimes was an alternative development: the glide + /x/ developed to [f] as in *draught, laughter, enough*.

5.3 Morphology

In the stages of Germanic prior to Old English, it is feasible to look upon nouns and verbs as consisting of a root, a stem suffix determining the inflectional class, and an inflectional ending. Old English inflectional classes are still distinguished on this basis, though it is not clear to what extent the addition of the stem suffix constituted a productive process in Old English; in most cases the stem suffix itself has disappeared through phonological developments.

The Nominal Group

Nouns

Old English nouns are divided into stem classes distinguished on the basis of their original Proto-Germanic stem suffixes. If the original stem suffix ended in a vowel *a*, *ō*, *i*, *u*, the declension was strong; if the original stem suffix ended in *-n* preceded by *a*, *ō*, *i*, the declension was weak. In addition there are a few minor declensions with stems ending in *-nd* or *-r*, as well as athematic stems.

Gender in Old English is grammatical, not natural as in Modern English. Gender depends partly on the stem class: *a*-stems are masculine, feminine or neuter; *ō*-stems are feminine; *i*-stems are masculine, feminine or neuter; *u*-nouns are masculine or feminine. The gender of the weak stems is determined by the nature of the vowel preceding the *-n* as in the strong stems. The gender of the athematic stems is masculine or feminine; that of the *-nd* stems masculine or feminine; that of the *-r* stems masculine or feminine.

Nouns exhibit a two-term number contrast: singular and plural, and there are five cases: nominative, accusative, genitive, dative, instrumental. The last of these had already disappeared during the Old English period. Number and case together are expressed by one inflectional ending. There are thus at most eight different endings for any given noun. The genitive plural ending is always *a* and the dative plural *um*.

The inflectional paradigm of the very numerous *a*- nouns is exemplified in Table 5.5, where the main masculine and neuter declensions are given. There are a number of phonological variants due to sound changes. For instance, nouns ending in ‹-h› drop the ‹-h› when, due to an inflectional ending, it occurs in intervocalic position: nom. sg. *scōh* ‘shoe’, but nom. pl. *scōs* (**scōhas* > **scōas* (loss of x) > *scōs*). Table 5.6 contains some examples of the other strong nominal declensions, and shows that the endings of the masculine *i*-declension are the same as those of the *a*-declension. The difference between the two is that in the *i*-declension the stem vowel is frequently recorded as *-i* in early texts. Moreover, the original stem vowel invariably causes *i*-umlaut of the root vowel where this is possible. The weak declensions are exemplified in Table 5.7.

Table 5.5   Declension of *a*-stems

	Singular			Plural		
	m.	n.	n.	m.	n.	n.
	‘stone’	‘ship’	‘word’			
Nom.	stān	scip	word	stānas	scipu	word
Acc.	stān	scip	word	stānas	scipu	word
Gen.	stānes	scipes	wordes	stāna	scipa	worda
Dat.	stāne	scipe	worde	stānum	scipum	wordum

Table 5.6   Declension of o-stems, i-stems, u-stems

	o-stem Singular f. 'gift'	i-stem m. 'guest'	u-stem m. 'gift'	o-stem Plural f.	i-stem m.	u-stem m.
Nom.	giefu	giest	sunu	giefa	giestas	suna
Acc.	giefe	giest	sunu	giefa	giestas	suna
Gen.	giefe	giestes	suna	giefa	giesta	suna
Dat.	giefe	gieste	suna	giefum	giestum	sunum

Table 5.7   Weak declensions of nouns

	Singular m. 'man'	f. 'tongue'	n. 'eye'	Plural m.	f.	n.
Nom.	guma	tunge	ēage	guman	tungan	ēagan
Acc.	guman	tungan	ēage	guman	tungan	ēagan
Gen.	guman	tungan	ēagan	gumena	tungena	ēagena
Dat.	guman	tungan	ēagan	gumum	tungum	ēagum

In the transition to Middle English, case morphology was reduced drastically. This started as a sound change traditionally called 'reduction in unstressed syllables', which resulted in the weakening of distinctive vowel endings to schwa (spelled -e). It has been hypothesized that this levelling of inflectional endings was the result of the language-contact situation with Scandinavians in a large (northern and eastern) part of England. Language contact is generally known to be the cause for reduction of inflections, and this assumption is further supported in this case by the fact that the levelling began in the Northern texts; the first traces of it can be detected in the tenth-century Northern Lindisfarne gospels. As noted above, however, there is little linguistic evidence to support this conclusion. In a text as early as the *Peterborough Chronicle* (early twelfth century), two things about the reduction of noun endings stand out: first, the nominative and accusative plural of the older masculine and neuter a-stems is reduced to -es and extended to all the plurals (including dative) of *all* declensions. The dative case is lost completely, except in what seem to be some set phrases. Southern and Western texts at this stage or even later have not advanced quite so far, but the general trend is the same.

Table 5.8   Old English personal pronouns

	Nom.	Acc.	Gen.	Dat.
1 sg.	ic	mē	mīn	mē
2 sg.	þu	þē	þīn	þē
3 sg. m.	hē	hine	his	him
f.	hēo	hī	hire	hire
n.	hit	hit	his	him
1 pl.	wē	ūs	ūre	ūs
2 pl.	gē	ēow	ēower	ēow
3 pl.	hī	hī	hira	him

Pronouns

Personal pronouns
The set of personal pronouns in Old English is, in the standard spelling, as in Table 5.8. Number is distinguished as singular and plural, with the relatively infrequent dual form omitted. There are four cases. There is a gender distinction only in the third-person singular. The nominative–accusative distinction is made in all persons and numbers except the third-person singular neuter and the third-person plural. The dative–accusative distinction is made in the third-person paradigms, both singular and plural.

There are no clitic forms that are identifiable on a morphological basis, with the exception of some forms encliticized to a finite verb or a complementizer in glosses. Apart from this, what evidence there is for cliticization in Old English is syntactic in nature.

The personal-pronoun forms in Old English are used for pronominal reference, and for co-reference with or without emphatic *self*, thus: *ic bletsige me* 'I bless myself'. The personal pronouns are not the only pronouns used for pronominal reference; demonstrative pronouns can be used as well.

Demonstrative pronouns
Old English has two series of demonstrative pronouns, which are given in Table 5.9. The demonstrative series serves three functions. It is used for definite descriptions. It can also be used for pronominal reference, notably in those cases where personal pronouns are rarely used. For instance, if a pronoun serves as the antecedent of a relative clause, it will nearly always be a demonstrative pronoun. The third use is that of relative pronoun, with or without the relative complementizer *þe*.

Interrogative and indefinite pronouns
The Old English interrogative pronoun *hwā* 'who' has only masculine and neuter singular forms, which are declined for case. Two further interrogative

Table 5.9   Demonstrative pronouns

	Demonstrative Singular			Plural	Deictic Singular			Plural
	m.	f.	n.		m.	f.	n.	
Nom.	se	sēo	þæt	þā	þes	þēos	þis	þās
Acc.	þone	þā	þæt	þā	þisne	þās	þis	þās
Gen.	þæs	þǣre	þæs	þāra	þisses	þisse	þisses	þissa
Dat.	þǣm	þǣre	þǣm	þǣm	þissum	þisse	þissum	þissum

pronouns, *hwæðer* 'which (of two)' and *hwelc/hwylc* 'which (of many)' are declined as indefinite adjectives. In contrast to Modern English, the interrogative pronouns are not used as relative pronouns. All three interrogative pronouns could be used as indefinite pronouns or quantifiers: 'anyone', 'anything'. Many other forms of indefinite pronouns were built on the basis of these: *āhwā, āhwæðer, āhwelc* 'anyone, anything'; *gehwā, gehwylc* 'each one', etc. Other indefinite pronouns include *ælc* 'each'; *ænig* 'any'; *swelc* 'such'; *þyllic* 'such', all declined as indefinite adjectives.

Adjectives
In Old English pre-dating written records, adjectives were inflected as nouns, in agreement with the noun modified, and during the Old English period, the two main adjectival declensions can still be traced back to the main nominal declensions. The so-called strong declension or indefinite declension for the most part corresponds with strong nominal declensions. This declension is used when an adjective is used predicatively, or when it is a modifier of an indefinite noun phrase. The weak or definite declension corresponds with the weak nominal declensions (except for the genitive plural which has *-ra* instead of *-ena*) and is used when the attributive adjective follows a demonstrative pronoun.

Comparison
The regular formation of a comparative of Old English adjectives is by adding *-ra* to the stem. The comparative is declined according to the weak or definite declension. The superlative normally ends in *-ost* and may be declined both strong and weak. A number of adjectives which originally had different suffixes containing an *i*, have *i*-mutation of the root vowel in the comparative and the superlative. Some common examples are: *eald – ieldra – ieldest* 'old'; *sceort – scyrta – scyrtest* 'short'.

The Verbal Group
As in other Germanic languages, there is a distinction between weak and strong verbs. The weak verbs originally consisted of a root plus a stem suffix, and the past tense is expressed by adding a dental suffix to the stem suffix. The strong verbs have no stem suffix, and the past tense is expressed through ablaut alternations in the root. The tense system has only one opposition: preterite vs present.

Stem Classes

Weak verbs
For the distinction between the various classes of the weak verbs in Old English, two forms of stem suffixes are important: class I of the weak verbs originally had a stem suffix *i/j*; class II had a stem suffix *oi/oj*. In both classes a person ending would be added in the present forms, and a dental ending plus a person ending in the preterite forms. In class I, the *i/j* suffix was dropped except in the infinitive and the first person singular indicative of stems ending in *-r*, and left its mark in the form of *i*-umlaut of the root vowel, thus Gmc *framjan* > OEng. *fremman* 'do, perform'; Gmc *narjan* > OEng. *nerian* 'save'. In class II, the *i/j* suffix similarly disappeared. No *i*-umlaut took effect since the *o* suffix intervened. The latter is still found in the Old English preterite of class II, cf. the contrast between class I infinitive *fremman*, preterite first-person singular *fremede* and class II infinitive *lufian* 'love', preterite first-person singular *lufode*.

It is customary to distinguish a weak class III. This class consists of four rather irregular verbs with dental past endings: *habban* 'have'; *libban* 'live'; *secgan* 'say'; *hycgan* 'think'.

Strong verbs
The strong verbs form their past tenses by means of vowel ablaut. There are seven ablaut classes for the strong verbs. The ablaut patterns are listed in Table 5.10 with a sample verb typical of the class.

Table 5.10 Ablaut patterns in the strong verbs

	inf.		3 sg. pres.	1, 3 sg. pret.	pret. pl.	past part.
Class I	drīfan	'to drive'	drīfð	drāf	drifon	gedrifen
Class II	sēoþan	'to boil'	sýðð	sēað	sudon	gesoden
Class III	drincan	'to drink'	drincð	dranc	druncon	gedruncen
Class IV	cuman	'to come'	cymð	cōm	cōmon	gecumen
Class V	sprecan	'to speak'	spricð	spræc	sprǣcon	gesprecen
Class VI	faran	'to go'	færð	fōr	fōron	gefaren
Class VII	cnāwan	'to know'	cnǣwð	cnēow	cnēowon	gecnawen

In addition to the verb classes mentioned so far, there is a class of so-called preterite-present verbs: a number of very common verbs for which a new consonantal preterite developed in Germanic because the old vocalic preterite had acquired a present meaning. This class includes the modals *scæl* 'shall', *mæg* 'may', *cunn* 'can', *mōt* 'must', and a few more, some of them semi-modals: *witan* 'know', *þurfan* 'need', *durran* 'dare', *munan* 'remember', *dugan* 'avail', *agan* 'own'. Furthermore there is a small group of highly frequent, but very irregular verbs: *beon/wesan* 'be', *willan* 'wish, will', *don* 'do', *gan* 'go'.

Inflectional Categories

The inflections for the present tense
The stem is followed by an inflectional ending indicating first of all whether the verb is in a finite or non-finite form. The inflectional endings of finite forms indicate mood, number and person. There are three moods: indicative, subjunctive and imperative; and there are two numbers and three persons. The plural form of the verb is used also with dual subjects.

The infinitive is formed by adding *an* to the stem: *fremm + an > fremman* 'do, perform'; *lufi + an > lufian* 'love'. The present participle is formed by adding *ende* to the stem: *fremmende, lufiende*.

The present indicative singular generally has a first-person ending -*e*, a second-person ending -(*e*)*st*, a third-person ending -(*e*)*ð*, and a general plural ending -*að*. The second- and third-person singular in the strong verbs have an umlauted root vowel, since the ending originally contained an *i*. In weak class I, umlaut of the root vowel is general.

The inflections for the past
As we have seen, the first- and third-person singular indicative of the strong verbs have a separate stem. The stem receives no ending for the first and third persons, and -*e* for the second: *drāf, drife, drāf* 'drove'. For the indicative of the weak verbs, the endings are -*e* for the first- and third-person singular, -*est* for the second-person singular and -*edon* for the plural, thus class I sg. *fremede, fremedest*, pl. *fremedon*; class II sg. *lufode, lufodest*, pl. *lufodon*.

The past subjunctive singular ending is, like that of the indicative first- and third-person singular, -*e*; the plural ending is -*en*.

The past participle of the weak verbs has the dental suffix; that of the strong verbs an -*en* suffix attached to the past plural ablaut stem. All past participles have a prefix *ge*-, thus weak: *gefremed, gelufod*, strong: *gedrifen*.

It was observed above that the transition to Middle English for the nominal system was marked by rather drastic reduction of inflectional endings as a result of weakening in unstressed syllables. This is true for verb morphology as well, albeit with some qualifications. The distinct vowel endings were reduced, but we can see that verb endings are rich in consonants. These were retained, and as a result, the system of verb endings in early Middle English (subject to some dialectal variation) still made a distinction for three persons in the singular present indicative, two in the singular preterite indicative, and had a clearly marked number contrast in the present as well as the preterite. Further reductions that led to the Modern English system took place largely in the fourteenth and fifteenth centuries.

5.4   Syntax

The Nominal Group

The Structure of the Noun Phrase

Word order in Old English is freer than in Modern English, though not really what one might call free. For a number of aspects of word order, there are strong preferences. This is as true at the phrasal level as it is at the clausal level. For nominal phrases, the preferred situation is for all modifiers to precede the head noun, and the preferred order is not very different from that in Modern English: *quantifier, demonstrative pronoun/possessive pronoun, numeral, oþer, adjective* (one or more), *genitive noun, head.* Of course, noun phrases of this complexity are not attested; the ordering is illustrated by the following examples: *anum unwisum cyninges þegne* 'an unwise thane of the king', *ealle his leofan halgan* 'all his dear saints', *mænig oþer god man* 'many another good man'. It is easy to list exceptions: *monig* 'many' can follow a demonstrative pronoun as in *þara monegena gewinna* 'the many battles'; *oþer* can precede a quantifier, as in *oþre fela bisceopas* 'many other bishops', but the order mentioned above is a fairly safe guide for pre-modification. Post-modification by the same elements is also attested, though much more frequent in poetry than in prose. All the individual modifiers can follow the head: *þegne monegum* 'many thanes', *þa scipo alle* 'all the ships', *mægwine mine* 'my dear kinsman', *þa roda þreo* 'the three roods', *alle Cent eastwearde* 'all eastern Kent', *tamra deora unbebohtra syx hund* 'six hundred unsold tame animals'. Such examples are not very frequent and some of them are restricted to poetry. Slightly more frequent are examples with both demonstrative and modifying adjective in postposition. In these cases the demonstrative precedes the adjective: *cyle þone grymmestan* 'the grimmest cold'.

Certain constituents always follow the rest of the noun phrase: prepositional modifiers are an example of this: *ane boc be cyrclicum ðeawum* 'a book about ecclesiastical customs'. Another example is the relative clauses: *to þam ylcan campdome þe heora fæderas on wæron* 'to the same military service which their fathers had been in'. Conjoined pre-modifiers, with or without demonstrative or even a governing preposition, can also follow the head: *berenne kyrtel oððe yterenne* 'a garment of bearskin or otterskin'; *liflice onsægednysse and halige and Gode andfenge* 'living and holy sacrifice, and acceptable to God'.

In the Middle English period, noun-phrase internal word order becomes more restricted towards the Modern English norm, though exceptions of various sorts are still found. Quantifiers can precede the article: *þurh out **vch a** toune* 'throughout each (a) town' and *some þe messagers* 'some messengers'; determiners can be combined in a genitive relationship: *hare baðre luue* 'the love of both of them'; quantifier + personal pronoun are ordered more freely: *we alle* or *all we*; attributive adjectives following the nominal head become more clearly restricted to poetry: *oure othere goodes temporels* 'our other temporal goods', or *lyouns all white* 'lions which are all white'.

Apposition

Two nouns or noun phrases may enter into an appositive relation where one specifies or modifies the other. A frequently occurring type is that of an appellative in combination with a title: *Sidroc eorl se gioncga* 'the young earl Sidroc'. In Old English, the name usually precedes the title in such cases. Middle English displays more variation in this respect. It is possible in Old English to have several appositions within one group, as is evident from the following example: *heahfæderas, eawfæste and wuldorfulle weras on heora life, witegena fæderas, þæra gemynd ne bið forgiten* 'patriarchs, religious and glorious men in their lives, the fathers of the prophets, whose memory shall not be forgotten'. Pronouns are often modified by an appositive noun phrase: *he cwæð, se apostol Paulus* 'he said, the apostle Paul'; *se heora lareow* 'he, their teacher'.

Discontinuous phrases

Noun phrases may be discontinuous in Old English. Those elements that may occur as post-modifiers at the end of the noun phrase, may also be moved outside the noun phrase, to a position separated from the rest of it: *maran cyle ic geseah, and wyrsan* 'I have seen a greater and worse cold' (lit. 'greater cold I saw, and worse'). An example involving a relative clause: *forðan þe manegum wæron his wundra cuþe þe god worhte þurh hine* 'because the miracles that God wrought through him were known to many' (lit. 'because that to many were his miracles known that God performed through him').

Unexpressed Subjects

Old English, unlike Modern English, allows omission of a subject when that subject has no semantic (thematic) role. For example, in sentences with weather verbs, the subject can be left out: *and swa miclum sniwde swelce micel flys feolle* 'and it snowed so heavily, as if a lot of fleece were falling' (lit. 'and so heavily snowed as if much fleece fell'). Similarly in sentences with impersonal verbs it is possible, though by no means obligatory, to omit the subject: *hine* (acc.) *nanes þinges* (gen.) *ne lyste on þisse worulde* 'nothing in this world pleased him' (lit. 'him nothing not pleased in this world'). The option of leaving out a subject without semantic role continued through the

Middle English period into the fifteenth century, with differences between various types of predicates. With weather verbs, Old English already had predominantly an *it* subject, and examples without *it* are extremely sparse in Middle English. With impersonal verbs and other types of subjectless predicates, on the other hand, the construction without a subject remained productive into the fifteenth century. A Middle English example is: *him* (obj.) *wile sone longe parafter* 'he will soon long for that' (lit. 'him will soon long after that').

Omission of a subject is also allowed in conjoined sentences, when the identity of the subject is apparent from the first conjunct, and in narratives which describe a series of actions by the same person where the identity of the person is similarly clear from the context. An example of the latter is: *He swanc ða git swiðor. Wolde geswutelian his mihte* 'He laboured then even harder. Wanted to make clear his power'. Conjoined subject deletion, the first type mentioned, underwent no essential change between Old English and Modern English. The second type is still possible in colloquial Modern English, so perhaps there are no essential changes here either.

Reflexives and Reciprocals

Reflexivity in Old English is expressed by the accusative, dative and genitive forms of the personal pronoun. To the reflexive pronoun may be added the element *-self* for emphasis, but *-self* is not generally a reflexive marker. This is to a large extent the case in Middle English as well, though *-self* is more frequently used non-emphatically: OEng. *Simon to ðisum wordum hine gebealh* 'Simon got angry about these words' (lit. 'Simon at these words himself angered'). Apart from the form of the reflexive pronoun, there appear to be no significant independent differences in the syntax of reflexives between Old English and Modern English. The choice of a possible antecedent does not extend beyond the closest subject of a finite clause, contrary to what seems to be possible in some form in all the historical stages of the Scandinavian languages.

Similar remarks apply to the reciprocal relationship. In Old English it can be expressed by the plural form of the personal pronoun, optionally emphasized. An example of this is: *and hie æt Tharse þære byrig **hie** gemetton* 'and they met each other at the city of Tarsus' (lit. 'and they at Tarsus the city each other met'). In addition to this, there are a number of expressions that can all mean something more or less equivalent to Modern English *each other*: *ægðer, naþer, oþer, æghwylc, ælc, gehwa, gehwylc, ænig* used in combination with *oþer*. For example: *we sceolan andettan ure synna gelome, and ælc for oðerne gebiddan* 'we should frequently confess our sins, and pray for each other' (lit. 'each for other pray').

The Verbal Group

It is generally agreed that Modern English has a set of auxiliaries with more or less clearly defined properties. This does not hold for older stages of English. While perfective *have* and passive and progressive *be* were presumably auxiliaries in Old English, periphrastic *do* did not yet exist and modals were not so clearly auxiliaries. Some even claim that in Old English, modal verbs are ordinary main verbs. The latter is not tenable either, but it is clear that in Old English, and to a large extent in Middle English as well, modal verbs had a number of morphosyntactic properties that made them look more like main verbs than auxiliaries. In this section modal auxiliaries are discussed, followed by a consideration of the appearance and development of a number of periphrastic constructions expressing modality and aspect.

The Old English inflectional morphology of modals shows that they had some range of verb inflections, certainly more than the present/past distinction they have in Modern English: two different person endings in the present as well as the preterite; a singular/plural distinction in the present and preterite. The distinctions are consistent within the Old English class of preterite/present verbs, which has more verbs than modals alone. The modals do not, however, occur in participial forms, and the use of infinitival forms is very sparse indeed. The sparse use of infinitival forms indicates that we cannot consider them to be simply lexical verbs.

In the syntax, the same situation obtains: we find a wider range of properties typical of lexical verbs, alongside a number of usages typical of auxiliaries. One property which is like those of lexical verbs is that modal verbs can have their own agentive subject. Thus, the sentence: *cwæþ þæt he wolde his man beon* (lit. 'said that he would his vassal be') means 'he wanted to be his vassal' rather than 'he would (fut.) be his vassal'. In a similar way, modal verbs can occur without an accompanying infinitive and with a direct object or with a tensed clause complement: *þæt he geornor wolde sibbe wið hiene þonne gewinn* 'that he wanted peace rather than war with him' (lit. 'that he rather would peace with him than war'); *ic wolde þæt þa ongeaten þe . . . hwelc mildsung siþþan wæs, siþþan se cristendom wæs* 'I would want those who . . . to perceive what blessing there has been since the rise of Christianity' (lit. 'I would that they perceived who . . . what blessing since was, since the Christianity was'). Another property that seems to be characteristic of main-verb syntax is that modal verbs enter into verbal clusters similar to those of the modern continental West Germanic languages. Thus, verb orders such as the following are suggestive of verbal clustering of some sort at the end of the sentence: *ðæt he Saul ne dorste ofslean* 'that he didn't dare to murder Saul' (lit. 'that he Saul not dared murder'); *þeh hie æt þæm ærran gefeohte him ne* **mehten to cuman** 'though they could not get him at the earlier fight' (lit. 'though they at the earlier fight him not could to come' i.e. they could not penetrate through the battlefield and reach him). This verbal clustering in the West Germanic languages is usually analysed as a feature of main-verb syntax. We will deal with these constructions as a word-order phenomenon in the section on word order (pp. 135–7).

On the other hand, some uses of the modals indicate not lexical-verb properties, but typical auxiliary behaviour; for Modern English, the use of *shall* and *will* as future markers is often analysed as a typical auxiliary property. This use is already attested in Old English: *& hie him geheton þæt hie ðæt gefeoht ærest mid him selfum þurhteon **wolden*** 'and they promised him that they would first try out the fight among themselves' (lit. 'they him promised that they the fight first with themselves perform would'); *wenen and wilnian ðæt ge lange libban **scylan** her on worulde* 'think and want that you long live shall here on world: think and wish that you will live long in this world'.

Thus, it seems fair to conclude that in Old English, modals are a class with mixed properties. This situation continues into Middle English; the mixture of main-verb and auxiliary properties remains. Modals can still have their own agentive subject and can take direct objects and tensed clause complements: *wultu kastles and kinedomes?* 'Do you want castles and kingdoms?' (lit. 'will-you castles and kingdoms'); *ichulle þet ȝe speken selde* 'I want you to speak' (lit. 'I-will that you speak should'). Also, modals now evidence more infinitival forms and appear in longer clusters as in: *þatt I shall cunnen cwemenn Godd* 'that I will be able to please God' (lit. 'that I shall can please God'). On the other hand, there is a marked increase in the course of the Middle English period towards auxiliary uses. Perhaps this is to be viewed against the background of the general rise of periphrastic forms for modality and aspect that are discussed below. During the course of the Middle English period, and particularly in the fourteenth century, the system of verb endings became impoverished to such an extent that the distinctive endings for the subjunctive mood disappeared, and these functions were largely taken over by uses of the modals as auxiliaries: *may/might* expressing possibility; *can/could* expressing possibility; *must* expressing logical necessity. This development, in combination with a number of morphological ones as a result of which the modals lost their non-finite forms completely, accelerated in the late fifteenth and early sixteenth centuries: modals largely lost their main-verb properties, though with some exceptions (e.g. *can* retained main-verb properties into the nineteenth century).

Periphrastic Verbs
The Middle English period can be characterized as one that witnessed the development of a number of periphrastic verb forms to express modality and aspect. We shall first turn our attention to the so called *quasi-modals*, the set of periphrastic constructions complementing the core modals and occurring in main-verb contexts (i.e. they have regular tense oppositions and occur in non-finite forms): *be going to, be able to, have to*. In general, these three forms acquired some modal meanings during the Old English or early Middle

English period. This modal meaning was consolidated in the course of the Middle English period, so that the periphrases could be adopted in main-verb contexts when the core modals had developed as exclusive auxiliaries. *Be going to* originates in Old English *gangan* 'go'. It usually referred to movement in some direction, but it could also be followed by an infinitive or gerund of purpose, and in such contexts its meaning comes close to the Modern English futural meaning: *ic geongo to cunnanne ða ilca* 'I am going to find that out' (lit. 'I go to know the same'). This use was consolidated in the Middle English period, and was readily available for use in those contexts requiring a main verb to express modal future meaning. *Be able to* has been employed with a modal sense expressing ability from the time that it was borrowed from French. Examples of this use can be found from the fourteenth century, e.g. *feithful men, which schuln be also able to teche other men.* Although *have ... to* was predominantly possessive in Old English, it acquired a modal sense of obligation quite early, cf. *hæfst þu æceras to erigenne?* 'do you have fields to plough/have to plough fields' (lit. 'have you fields to plough'). Even in early Middle English, examples can be found where the meaning of obligation predominates: early thirteenth-century *þu a hest ... to witen hit* 'you always have to know it'. This use was consolidated in the course of the Middle English period, and made *have to* a prime candidate for expressing obligation in addition to *must*.

Another modal periphrasis to be mentioned here is *is/are/were to* in its modal meaning of obligation/destination. This development is similar to that of the quasi-modals: the seeds of modal meaning are there in Old English and develop more firmly in Middle English, cf. OEng. *se þearfa ... þe mid þe is to cumene to engla gebeorscipe* which has two possible meanings when translated, 'the poor one who is with you to come to the feast of the angels/ who is to come with you to the feast of the angels' (lit. 'the needy one who with you is to come to the angels' feast'); early MEng. *ic wot al þat to cumen is* 'I know all that is to come'; late MEng. *he wist what he was to do* 'he knew what he was to do'. *Is/are/were to* differs from the quasi-modals in one important respect: it came to be used as a finite verb only, like the core modals.

The progressive form

Old English does not have a fully grammaticalized aspectual contrast: progressive aspect was (optionally) expressed by means of a form of *be* followed by the present participle with *-ende*. During the late Old English period confusion arose between the present participle and the verbal noun then ending in *-ung*. The verbal noun came to be used with adverbial adjuncts. This use is consolidated in the Middle English period and replaced the older present participle in *-ende*, though unambiguous examples of gerunds with verbal properties are not found until the early fourteenth century, except perhaps for examples like *þe sonne rysyng* 'the sun rising' which go back to earlier constructions with a genitive. Throughout the Old English and Middle English periods the use of the present participle and later the gerund as a means of marking progressive aspect was optional. There were alternative constructions such as *he com ridan* 'he came riding' (lit. 'he came ride'), and *he wæs on huntunge* (lit.) 'he was ahunting'. Gradually, all these constructions were replaced by the *be + -ing* form. It was in the early Modern English period that the progressive was grammaticalized as an obligatory marker of progressive aspect. This was also when its frequency increased dramatically.

Periphrastic *do*
In Old English *do* was a lexical verb which occurred in such contexts as *uton ... don hine on þone ealdan pytt* 'let us do [put] him in the old well'. This use is often called factitive *do*. Already in Old English *do* could be used as a proform for verbs, as in *he miccle ma on his deaðe acwealde, ðonne he ær cucu dyde* 'he killed many more in death than he did before [when he was] alive' (lit. 'he many more in his death killed, than he earlier alive did'). And *do* was used as a causative verb as in *þe king þe maiden dede rise* 'the king did [i.e. made] the maiden rise'. It is more or less generally accepted that causative *do* is the precursor of periphrastic *do*. For one thing, this is *the* construction in which *do* is followed by an infinitive. Also *do + infinitive* in Middle English is often ambiguous between a causative and a non-causative interpretation, e.g. *a noble churche heo dude a-rere* is ambiguous between 'she built a noble church' and 'she had a noble church built'. It would take us into too much detail to trace the development from causative to periphrastic *do* precisely, not least because there seems to be much room for disagreement here. Like the other verbal periphrases, *do* was grammaticalized as such in the early Modern English period.

Phrasal Verbs
The verb–particle combinations of Old English differ in an interesting way from those of Modern English. The most striking characteristic of Old English verb–particle constructions is that the relative ordering of verb and particle differs sharply between matrix clauses and embedded clauses: in embedded clauses the particle usually immediately precedes the verb: *þa idlan word þe he ær unrihtlice ut forlet* 'the idle words to which he wickedly gave utterance before' (lit. 'the idle words that he before wickedly out let'). Where the particle follows the verb, there are severe limitations on the number and types of constituents that may intervene between verb and particle. In particular, no subject intervenes, except in a few cases with ergative verbs. In matrix clauses on the other hand, the particle nearly always follows the verb, with no clear restrictions on the number and type of constituents intervening, and subjects often intervene: *þa ahof Drihten hie up* 'then the Lord raised them up' (lit. 'then raised the Lord them up'); *aslat þa þa tunas ealle ymb þa burg onwæg* 'and then destroyed all the villages around the city' (lit. 'destroyed then the

villages all around the city away'). This asymmetry is best explained by assuming that Old English has a basic SOV order and a rule preposing the finite verb to second position in matrix clauses: the so-called verb-second (V2) rule to which we will come back in the section on word order. Since V2 applies in matrix clauses only, and usually leaves the particle behind in the base position of the verb, we get this curious discrepancy. We will come back to this below. The asymmetry is so clearly marked in Old English because the base position for the verb is at the end of the sentence: Old English is SOV. This base word order changed to Middle English SVO. The development of the position of particles in relation to the verb can be shown quite clearly to correlate with the change from SOV to SVO.

Grammatical Relations

Case Marking

Grammatical relations in Old English are encoded partly through word order, and partly by means of morphological case marking. As noted above, Old English is an SOV language. This might suggest a fixed SOV order, but this is not in fact the case. In the SOV order, the position of the subject is relatively fixed: the subject can almost always be recognized by its position, the exceptions being in the case of heavy subject postposing. Next to the subject noun phrase, it is plausible to recognize a verb phrase as one constituent in Old English. However, unlike in Modern English, there are no adjacency requirements for verb and noun phrase in Old English, and word order within the verb phrase is relatively free. Encoding occurs through morphological case marking. The objects can be marked for accusative, dative or genitive case: *hwi wolde God swa lytles þinges* (gen.) *him* (dat.) *forwyrnan* 'why would God deprive him of such a small thing?', *þæt nan mon ... ne offrode his Gode* (dat.) *nanne hlaf* (acc.) 'that no one offered his God any bread'. The Old English case endings still correspond fairly closely to specific semantic roles. Thus, the dative is regularly used for roles such as Goal: *þeos worold is on ofste, and hit nealæcð ðam ende* (dat.) 'this world is in haste and it approaches the end'; Recipient: *þa geafon þa cynegas ... þam halgan Birine* (dat.) ... *þa burh Dorcanceaster* 'then gave the kings the holy Birine the city of Dorchester'; Experiencer: *for ðon he him* (dat.) *cweman þohte* 'because he thought to please him'. A number of verbs take a genitive object. As in Old Scandinavian (Chapter 3) these verbs do not form a definable group on semantic grounds, yet most of them imply a *partitive* reading of the argument, where *partitive* must be understood in a wide sense. Some examples are: *hwi wolde God swa lytles þinges* (gen.) *him forwyrnan*? 'why would God deprive him of such a small thing', *nu ic þyses Alexandres* (gen.) *her gemyndgade* 'now I call to mind this Alexander'. The accusative generally expresses the Patient role: *þæt ic þas boc* (acc.) *of Ledenum gereorde to Engliscre spræce awende* 'that I translate this book from the Latin language to the English tongue', *maran cyððe* (acc.) *habbað englas to Gode þonne men* 'angels have more affinity to God than men'. The correlation with specific semantic roles is less clear in the case of accusatives; subjects of embedded non-finite clauses can be marked accusative: *se ealdormon sceal lætan hiene selfne* (acc.) *gelicne his hieremonnum* 'the ruler must put himself equal to his subjects'. Also, accusative can often be used instead of dative or genitive case. There is no correlation, however, between nominative case and semantic roles: nominative can be used for the Agent subject, but also for the Patient in a passive sentence; for the Experiencer in sentences with a psychological verb such as *lician* 'like', *hreowan* 'rue'.

When the predicate of a matrix sentence is an adjective, a copula verb must be used. The noun phrase of which the adjective is predicated can be said to have the semantic role *Theme*. Predicative adjectives can have noun-phrase complementation; in these cases the noun phrase appears in the dative or in the genitive case. The cases correspond roughly to the same semantic roles as with the verbs: dative for, for example, the Experiencer as in *þeah hit þam cynge* (dat.) *ungewill wære* 'though it was displeasing to the king'; genitive for a partitive reading as in *ðæt he bið dierneligres* (gen.) *scyldig* 'that he is guilty of adultery'.

As the system of morphological cases collapsed in the course of the early Middle English period, the correspondence between case endings and semantic roles went with it. In general, this meant that in the course of the thirteenth and fourteenth centuries, the earlier relation between verb or adjective and the dative or genitive object, came to be expressed by means of prepositions, very often *to* for the earlier dative and *of* for the genitive. As a result, case assignment by adjectives was lost altogether. The distinction between dative and accusative was lost: both came to appear as 'objective' case, cf. a number of constructions such as the double object construction (*I gave him a book*).

The Subject

In many languages, including Modern English, the subject phrase has a set of syntactic properties that serve to identify it as such. Among these are the following: the subject is nominative; the verb agrees with the subject; the subject acts as the antecedent for a reflexive. Such tests hold for Modern English, and they largely hold in the history of English. Even in Old English, the nominative subject is the antecedent of the reflexive, and in most cases the subject is nominative and the verb agrees with the subject. There is one notable set of constructions where this is not necessarily the case: constructions with so-called dative or quirky subjects. The phenomenon has been studied in detail from this perspective through the history of *like*. The Old English equivalent of *like*, *lician*, could be used with a nominative Cause argument (indicating the source of the pleasure) and a dative Experiencer argument, as in *ge* (nom.) *noldon Gode* (dat.) *lician* 'you would not please

God'. Since Old English was a verb-second language (see p. 132), the dative could also appear in first position, followed by the finite verb: *ac gode* (dat.) *ne licode na heora geleafleast* (nom.) 'but their faithlessness did not please God'. It turns out that in sentences with a preposed dative, it is the dative that has at least one subject property; a coordinate subject can be deleted under co-reference with the preposed dative in the first conjunct, whereas such deletion is otherwise only possible under co-reference with 'real' (i.e. nominative Agent) subjects. Thus, the sentence quoted above is expanded as follows: *ac gode* (dat.) *ne licode na heora geleafleast* (nom.) ... *ac asende him to fyr of heofonum* 'but their faithlessness did not please God, but (he) sent them fire from heaven'. This shows that the dative is interpreted as the subject. In the fifteenth century, the preposed dative was reinterpreted as a nominative, thus ousting the construction with the nominative Cause argument in initial position. Consequently, in earlier stages of English, in a construction without a semantic (Agent) subject, a preposed dative could have at least one subject property. Hence the notion 'subject' did not always correspond completely to the noun phrase in nominative case.

Throughout the development of English, the rule is that only nominative noun phrase can trigger verb agreement and that the nominative must trigger agreement. From this, together with the information about the preposed dative construction, it follows that nominative case presupposes the presence of a finite verb.

The Passive

In Old English, the passive is formed with the participle of a main verb and an auxiliary of the passive: *beon* 'be' or *weorðan* 'become'; *to bysmore* **synd** *getawode þas earman landleoda* 'the poor people of this land are brought to shame'; *se munuc pa Abbo ...* **wearð** *sona to abbode geset* 'this monk Abbo was soon appointed abbot'. It is plausible to suggest that passives in Old English are derived by a syntactic rule that moves a potentially accusative noun phrase to subject position. There is no passivization of indirect objects or prepositional objects. There is, however, impersonal passivization of datives, but in such cases the dative case is retained: **him** (dat.) *wæs swa forwyrnad ðæs inganges* 'he (him) was thus prohibited entry'. This is not 'true' passivization, in the sense in which an object becomes the subject and is marked for nominative case. There is no agreement relation between the dative noun phrase and the finite verb. The preposed dative, retaining its case marking, moves to the first constituent position in the sentence, a topic position preceding the finite verb, as we will see below in relation to the verb-second phenomenon. Preposing of the dative in such constructions is not obligatory, as is shown by: *swa wyrð eac gestyred* **ðæm gitsere** *ðæs reaflaces* 'thus the miser is also corrected of extortion' (lit. 'thus is also corrected the miser of extortion').

Passivization of an accusative object remained stable through the history of

English. Impersonal passivization remained an option until the fifteenth century, then died out. In the course of the Middle English period the scope of passivization was expanded to include indirect objects and prepositional objects. This is almost certainly a result of the breakdown of the Old English case system, in combination with the basic change from SOV to SVO. In early Middle English, sporadic examples of indirect and prepositional passives began to appear: *the duke Mylon was geven hys lyff* 'the duke M. was given his life'; *childere unarayede, unkepide, and noghte tente to as þam aughte for to be* 'children, undressed, unkept and not cared for as they ought to be'. From the middle of the fourteenth century such passives become firmly rooted.

The Sentence

Word Order

Several observations on word order have already been made above: the position of the subject in Old English is best characterized in structural terms; Old English word order is best analysed as basically SOV, with a rule of verb-second in matrix clauses. Old English has a verb phrase with relatively free verb-phrase internal, word order. The rule of verb second entails that some sentential constituent is preposed to first constituent position, and the finite verb is preposed to second constituent position. Good illustrations of this are given by the following examples: (matrix clause) *on twæm þingum hæfde God þæs mannes sawle gegodod* 'with two things God had (lit. 'had God') man's soul endowed'; (embedded clause) *þæt ic þas boc of Ledenum gereorde to Engliscre spræce awende* 'that I this book from the Latin language to the English tongue translate'. Thus, the order for matrix clauses is: constituent–Vfinite–subject–VP; the order for embedded clauses conjunction–subject–VP. A number of comments should be added to these basic observations. Fronting of the finite verb was not obligatory in main clauses, and second conjuncts introduced by *and* tended to have the verb at the back.

The first constituent position in matrix clauses can be left empty in lively narrative style: in a very lively passage of the Anglo-Saxon chronicle one finds several sentences like *wæs Hæsten þa þær cumen mid his herge* 'Hæsten had then come there (lit. 'was H. then there come') with his army'. The position can be filled with one constituent as illustrated above. That constituent can be the subject (very frequent), an object or an adverbial, but not a non-finite verb form. One also comes across sentences where more than one constituent precedes the finite verb.

There is a discrepancy between the relative positioning of finite verb and nominal subject and finite verb and pronominal subject in matrix clauses, interacting with the type of first constituent in the sentence. When the first constituent is not the subject and not a *wh*-question word, i.e. an ordinary topic, the nominal subject as a rule follows the finite verb, as illustrated above.

When the subject is a pronoun, however, it precedes the finite verb: *on ðisum wræcfullum life we sceolon earmra manna helpan* 'in this life of exile we should help poor people' (lit. 'poor people help'). When the first constituent is a *wh*-question word, or a negative element, or *þa* 'then', all types of subjects follow the finite verb: *hwæt wille we eow swiðor secgan be ðisum symbeldæge* 'what more shall we say to you (lit. 'what will we you more say') about this feast-day'.

The subject can be postposed when it is 'heavy': *ðone onwald mæg wel reccean se þe ægðer ge hiene habban con ge wiðwinnan* 'he who can both have it and resist it, can wield power well' (lit. 'power may well wield he who both it have can and resist').

Considering that the position of the subject can be so clearly defined in structural terms and separate from the VP, it seems reasonable to assume that Old English indeed has a VP. Word order within VP is comparatively free. Several examples have been quoted above of verb-final word order. But nominal objects and VP adverbials can occur easily to the right of the verb: *þæt we ure ælmessan* (acc.) *sellan earmum mannum* (dat.) 'that we give our alms (lit. 'our alms give') to poor people'; *þæt þu Drihtne* (dat.) *brohtest micel gestreon haligra sawla* (acc.) 'that you brought God (lit. 'God brought') a great treasure of holy souls'. In both preverbal and postverbal position inside the verb phrase, the relative order of the dative and accusative object is more or less free. Object pronouns are more restricted as far as position is concerned: they nearly always precede nominal objects, and indeed very often precede all other verb-phrase constituents, and when there are two pronominal objects the order is almost completely fixed as accusative–dative: *ic hit þe þonne wile getæcan* 'then I want to teach it to you' (lit. 'I it you then will teach'). The relatively fixed position for personal pronouns suggests that they have some clitic properties, though there is little phonological evidence for this.

There are some interesting peculiarities concerning the position of the verb inside the VP, notably when there is more than one verb. It must be borne in mind that in Old English there was no such thing as a fixed auxiliary position as there is in Modern English. We often find what looks like the verbal clustering that is so characteristic of Modern Dutch and Modern German: *ðæt he Saul ne dorste ofslean* 'that he didn't dare to murder Saul' (lit. 'that he Saul not dared murder'); *þæt hie gemong him mid sibbe sittan mosten* 'that they must settle in peace among themselves' (lit. 'they among themselves in peace settle must'). But there are more variant patterns which seem to suggest that the clustering can also include part of the (infinitival) verb phrase: *ðæt he wisdom mæge wið ofermetta æfre gemengan* 'that he may ever combine wisdom with pride' (lit. 'that he wisdom may with pride ever mingle'). Examples like the last are not very frequent; more frequent are sentences like *þæt he mehte his feorh generian* 'that he might save his life' (lit. 'that he might his life save'). The crucial difference is in the position of the finite verb: in the last example it immediately follows the subject, in the preceding one it follows some VP constituent. For the former case, verbal clustering appears to be plausible; for the latter case, there is cause for debate whether these represent movement of the finite verb to the left, similar to verb-second movement, or verbal clustering including VP constituents.

The transition to Middle English brought about a number of changes in the picture sketched above for Old English. The initial change was that, inside the verb phrase, VO patterns became absolutely predominant. Though OV word orders are found frequently until well into the Middle English period, we can see from the syntax in general that the typological shift from OV to VO was completed around 1200. This marked the advent of a syntax in which typical VO constructions such as prepositional passives could be introduced.

The second change that took place was that English lost its verb-second character. It was observed above that in Old English the first constituent position in matrix clauses is a topic position, followed by the preposed finite verb and the subject position. This verb-second character remained fairly stable through the Middle English period; until well into the fourteenth century, topicalization of a constituent other than the subject regularly led to subject–verb inversion of a nominal subject: *thus may thine instrument last perpetuel*. If the subject is a pronoun, inversion does not take place, as was observed above for Old English; *bi þis ypocrisie þei wolen bringe in. . . .* Verb second was lost at the close of the Middle English period. From the middle of the fourteenth century we can see that, with the exception of the work of Chaucer, nominal subjects increasingly behaved in the same way as pronominal subjects did: they preceded the finite verb, even if the topic was a non-subject. As a result, topicalization ceased to trigger fronting of the finite verb and the fairly regular verb-second character was lost. It remained only in sentences with a *wh-* question word or a negative element as the first constituent, as it still does nowadays. Another relic is sentences like *in came John, on the wall hung a picture*. Later on, in the early Modern English period, lexical verbs could no longer be preposed, and only auxiliaries could take part in subject–verb inversion.

Subordination

Finite clauses

There are many finite clauses in Old English for which it is unclear whether they are truly subordinate to (some element in) the matrix clause, i.e. whether they are 'hypotactic', to use the traditional term. Thus, there are many conjunctions for which it is unclear whether they are coordinating or subordinating, for example: *ær* 'before'; *siþþan* 'since'; *þonne* 'then'. But there is also a set of conjunctions which is quite clearly subordinating: *þæt* 'that' used for all sorts of finite embedded clauses, but not for relative clauses; *þe* 'that' for relative clauses; *gif* 'if' for conditionals. This by no means exhausts the list of elements and combinations that can be used as a subordinating conjunction. When the conjunction used is not conclusive as to the matrix or subordinate character of the clause, the word order sometimes helps: as observed above, matrix clauses usually have a preposed finite verb, and in subordinates, if they appear to have preposing, this preposing is recognizably of a different nature. Furthermore, the position of the infinitival verb in embedded clauses is very often at the end of the VP. But these criteria must be used with considerable caution, and they leave a host of undecidable examples. The traditional view that Old English had a considerable amount of parataxis (putting clauses next to each other without connecting them with conjunctions like *and* or *that*), which gradually came to be replaced by hypotaxis, appears to be well founded.

Noun clauses are introduced by the conjunction *þæt*: *ic wat þæt ðis Iudeisce folc micclum blissigan wile mines deaðes* 'I know that this Jewish people will rejoice greatly at my death'. Relative clauses are optionally introduced by the relative conjunction *þe*, optionally in combination with a relative (demonstrative) pronoun. This yields three types of (tensed) relatives, namely, with *þe* alone: *þæt gewrit þe hit on awriten wæs* 'the writ that it was written in'; with demonstrative pronoun + *þe* (the rarest of the three constructions): *se arwurða bisceop, ðone ðe God sylf geceas* 'the worthy bishop, whom (that) God himself chose'; with demonstrative pronoun: *Osric, ðone Paulinus ær gefullode* 'Osric, whom Paulinus earlier baptized'. It is also possible to relativize a constituent out of a clause further embedded: *syx dagas synd on ðam gebyrað ðæt man wyrce* 'there are six days on which it is fitting that one work'. Such examples are not attested for the *se þe* relative, but this is likely to be a coincidence. Note also that in the example of the *þe* relative quoted above the preposition is stranded (i.e. left behind next to the verb: *þæt gewrit þe hit on awriten wæs* 'the writ that it was written in'), a phenomenon restricted in Old English to relatives without an overt relative pronoun. In the Middle English period *þe* was replaced by *that* as a relative complementizer, and the *wh-* series ousted the demonstrative pronouns as relative pronouns. Preposition stranding was generalized to all relative (and interrogative) clauses in Middle English.

Non-finite clauses
There are two kinds of infinitives in Old English: the bare infinitive and the *to*-infinitive. There is no apparent correlation between marking the infinitive with *to* and the status of a particular clause, S or S′ in theoretical terms. (S or S′ constitutes the minimal clausal level that has its own tense domain.) This is evident from the fact that, apart from modals, causatives and perception verbs, no verb is followed canonically by either a bare infinitive or a *to*-infinitive. Rather, the correlation seems to depend on whether the infinitive is governed by the verb which selects it. Infinitives which are object clauses, i.e. which are governed by the verb that selects

them, are predominantly bare infinitives. An example is: *he ... þohte mid þam bigan ætberstan þam deaðe* 'he ... thought he might escape death by the doubling' (lit. 'he thought by the doubling escape the death'). Bare infinitives are not, however, canonical in object infinitives; *to*-infinitives are always possible, though a clear minority: *and ge ðencað to awendenne eowerne freond* 'and you plan to pervert your friend' (lit. 'and you think to pervert your friend'). Subject infinitives are predominantly *to*-infinitives, and infinitival complements of nouns and adjectives are canonically *to*-infinitives. In the course of the Middle English period we see a development from the older system towards the Modern English system where *to*-marking signals the clausal status (S or S′) of the infinitive complement, with concomitant semantic distinctions. This system is clearly emerging at the close of the Middle English period.

Negation
In Old English the negative adverb is commonly *ne* and it is in a position to the immediate left of the finite verb, whichever position the finite verb is in: *he ne andwyrde ðam wife æt fruman* 'he didn't answer the woman at first'. Very often it is cliticized on to the finite verb, yielding e.g. *nolde* (*ne wolde*) 'not wanted'; *he nolde beon cyning* 'he didn't want to be king' (lit. 'he not-wanted be king'). It is rare for negative adverbs other than *ne* to occur alone. Double (or even triple) negation is also possible in Old English: if another negative adverb is added, *ne* is maintained in its usual position: *heo ne geendað næfre* 'it never ends' (lit. 'she not ends never'); *for ðam ðe þa Iudeiscan noldon næfre brucan nanes þinges mid þam hæþenum* 'because the Jews never wanted to partake of anything with heathens' (lit. 'because that the Jews not-wanted never partake anything with the heathens'). Emphatic negation can be expressed by *ne* in combination with *na* or *naht* (both from *nawiht* 'nothing').

In Middle English the old emphatic combination rapidly loses its emphatic character and becomes the common form of negation. While *ne* retains its position on the left of the finite verb, the position of *naht/noht* is gradually fixed on the right of the finite verb: *ant þah nis inempnet her nawt of heouenliche luren* 'and though there is no mention here of heavenly losses' (lit. 'and though not-is mentioned here not of heavenly losses'). In the course of the Middle English and early Modern periods *ne* is dropped and *naht* or *noht* > *not* becomes the negation, to the immediate right of the finite verb.

5.5 Lexis
The major part of the Old English vocabulary is from common Germanic stock. Old English had a number of typically Germanic word-formation processes. Some of these have survived to the present day, e.g. prefixation by *un-* and suffixation by *-ness*. The suffix *-lic* '-ly' was not an adverb-forming

one in Old English, but became so later. Most of these processes lost their productivity and have left us some relics, such as *withstand* from the productive verbal prefixing process expressing 'against-V', cf. OEng. *wiþ cweþan* 'contradict' (lit. 'against-speak'). Further examples are remnants with *be-*, originally a transitivizing prefix, e.g. *bespeak, bemourn*. This prefix is still (or perhaps again) productive, it seems, in informal registers. But many of the Old English word-formation processes have left no trace in the standard language; French and Latin processes have taken their place, for example suffixation by *-ment, -ous, -able, -al, -ance, -ate, -ize, -ant*; prefixation by *circum-* (OEng. *ymb-*), *counter-* (OEng. *with-*), *dis-, mis-, inter-, mal-, pre-, post-, re-, semi-, sub-, vice-*. The list is far from complete. French loan formations are of course due to the influence of the French invaders after 1066; Latin loans during and after the Middle English are usually the result of prestige borrowing.

The earliest loanwords in Old English are loans from Latin, together with some examples such as Celtic, with which the Anglo-Saxons had contacts. The Scandinavian invasions of the ninth and tenth centuries have left their mark on the vocabulary. Some Scandinavian loanwords are recognizable from the velar consonants in environments in which native Anglo-Saxon words would have palatals: *bank, rig, skirt, scar, car, gate, crook, garden*, but consider also *fell, tarn*, etc. The Norman conquest led to a tremendous influx of loanwords from French, too numerous to attempt to indicate here.

Further Reading

Allen, C. (1986) 'Reconsidering the history of *like*', *Journal of Linguistics* 22: 375–409.

Baugh, A. C. and Cable, T. (1978) *A History of the English Language*, 3rd edn, London: Routledge and Kegan Paul.

Campbell, A. (1959) *Old English Grammar*, Oxford: Clarendon Press.

Denison, D. (1993) *English Historical Syntax*, London: Longman.

Elmer, W. (1981) *The History of the Old and Middle English Subjectless Constructions*, Linguistische Arbeiten 97, Tübingen: Niemeyer.

Fischer, O. C. M. (1990) *Syntactic Change and Causation*, Amsterdam Studies in Generative Grammar 2, Amsterdam: Amsterdam University.

Hiltunen, R. (1983) *The Decline of the Prefixes and the Beginnings of the English Phrasal Verb*, Turku: Turun Yliopisto.

Hogg, R. (ed.) (1992) *The Cambridge History of the English Language*, 7 vols, vol. 1, *Old English*, vol. 2, *Middle English*, Cambridge: Cambridge University Press, vols. III–VII, forthcoming.

Jordan, R. (1974) *Handbook of Middle English Grammar: Phonology*, trans. and rev. E. J. Crook. The Hague: Mouton.

Kemenade, A. van (1987) *Syntactic Case and Morphological Case in the History of English*, Dordrecht: Foris.

Koopman, W. (1990) *Word Order in Old English*, Amsterdam Studies in Generative Grammar 1, Amsterdam: Amsterdam University.

Lightfoot, D. W. (1981) 'The history of NP movement', in C. Baker and J. McCarthy (eds) *The Logical Problem of Language Acquisition*, Cambridge, Mass. and London: MIT Press, pp. 86–119.

Minkova, D. (1991) *The History of Final Vowels in English*, Topics in English Linguistics 4, Berlin: Mouton de Gruyter.

Mitchell, B. (1985) *Old English Syntax*, 2 vols, Oxford: Clarendon Press.

Visser, F. T. (1963–73) *An Historical Syntax of the English Language*, Leyden: E. J. Brill.

Warner, A. (1993) *English Auxiliaries: Structure and History*, Cambridge: Cambridge University Press.

6 *Icelandic*

Höskuldur Thráinsson

6.1 Introduction

Iceland was mainly settled in the late ninth and early tenth century and the majority of the settlers came from Norway. They spoke the language commonly referred to as Old Norse or Old Scandinavian. There probably were some dialectal differences in the Nordic language of the settlers. It is likely, however, that certain dialectal levelling took place after the settlement since it does not appear that the settlers speaking the same dialect formed any kind of dialectal colonies within Iceland. Yet it could be argued that West Nordic dialectal traits have prevailed in Iceland since Modern Icelandic is closest to Faroese and to the Norwegian dialects spoken in southwestern Norway.

It is customary to divide the history of the Icelandic language roughly into the Old Icelandic period (before 1540) and Modern Icelandic (after 1540), the dividing line being drawn at the year the first Icelandic translation of the New Testament was published. This is obviously a very coarse division, but we need not worry about it here. When Modern Icelandic is compared with the other modern Nordic languages on one hand and with Old Norse on the other, it is evident that it has changed less than the other Modern Scandinavian languages, at least with respect to morphology and syntax.

There are some dialectal differences in Modern Icelandic, but very minor ones compared with the situation in most Germanic languages. The best-known differences have to do with phonological variation (see p. 151). Since these differences are so minimal, it has not been necessary to define a particular standard or 'received pronunciation' or anything similar. Hence the announcers on radio and television, teachers in schools, etc. can, by and large, use their own dialect and they do.

6.2 Phonology

Since we will be using Icelandic spelling when giving examples below, we will begin by listing the Modern Icelandic alphabet. The symbols in parentheses have their place in the Icelandic alphabet but they are only used in words of foreign origin (c, q, w) and/or older versions of Icelandic spelling (z):

Table 6.1   Distinctive feature structure of Old Icelandic vowels

	Front Unrounded		Rounded		Back Unrounded		Rounded	
	short	long	short	long	short	long	short	long
High	i	iː	y	yː			u	uː
Mid	e	eː	ø	øː			o	oː
Low	(ɛ)	ɛː			a	aː	ɔ	ɔː
Diphthongs	au̯, ei̯, ey[1]							

Note: 1 The first part of this diphthong may have been rounded like the second.

a á b (c) d ð e é f g h i í j k l m n o ó p (q) r s t u ú v (w) x y ý (z) þ æ ö

The phonological system of Modern Icelandic has probably changed more, compared with Old Norse, than any other component of the language. This is especially true of the vowel system. We have an excellent description of the Old Icelandic sound system in the twelfth century, the so-called *First Grammatical Treatise*. This description indicates that twelfth-century Icelandic had 'nine qualitatively distinct vocalic units' (if we do not count nasality in vowels as 'quality') as shown in Table 6.1. The First Grammarian (FG, the author of the *First Grammatical Treatise*) shows by producing distinctive pairs that the *quantity distinction* was systematic throughout the Old Icelandic vowel system. In addition, it appears that the diphthongs corresponded to long vowels metrically. But the FG also shows, by giving pairs of oral vs nasal vowels for each of the nine different qualities, that the vowels could either be *oral* or *nasal*.

If one takes into account the fact that there does not seem to have been a distinction between short /e/ and /ę/ any more in the twelfth century, one could say that Old Icelandic had 26 different vowel phonemes (monophthongs) when the FG wrote his treatise. In Modern Icelandic, on the other hand, the corresponding number is 8, as we shall see in the next section, the main difference being that neither vowel quantity nor nasality are distinctive in Modern Icelandic.

The Vowel System
The vowel system of Modern Icelandic can be diagrammed as shown in Table 6.2. In addition to the five diphthongs shown in the table, it is frequently assumed that Modern Icelandic also has the diphthongs /ɣi̯/ and /ɔi̯/ in words like *hugi* 'thought' and *bogi* 'bow'. The vowels in these words are interpreted differently here.

The development that led to the present situation was quite complex. Since a good understanding of the modern vowel system and its relation to the older stages is essential for anyone who wants to study Icelandic, an attempt to sketch this relationship is made in Figures 6.1 and 6.2.

Table 6.2   Distinctive feature structure of Modern Icelandic vowels

| | Front | | Back | |
	Unrounded	Rounded	Unrounded	Rounded
High	i (í)			u (ú)
Mid	ɪ (i)	ʏ (u)		
Low	ɛ (e)	œ (ö)	a (a)	ɔ (o)
Diphthongs	eɪ̯ (ei, ey), œɪ̯ (au), aɪ̯ (æ), oʊ̯ (ó), aʊ̯ (á)			

Note: The phonetic quality of the vowels is indicated by phonetic transcription symbols, but their most common representation in the orthography is given in parentheses.

Figure 6.1   Development of the Old Icelandic short vowels

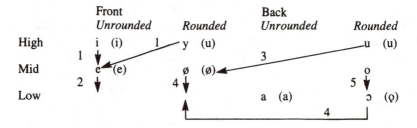

Key: 1 /y/ (y) merged with /i/ (i) which was lowered to [ɪ]. 2 /e/ (e) was lowered to [ɛ]. 3 /u/ (u) was fronted and lowered to [ʏ]. 4 /ɔ/ (ǫ) merged with /ø/ (ø) which was lowered to [œ]. 5 /o/ (o) was lowered to [ɔ].
Note: Symbols within parentheses indicate standard orthographic representations. The arrows indicate the qualitative changes that have occurred since Old Icelandic, i.e. lowering, fronting, loss of rounding etc.

Figure 6.2   Development of the Old Icelandic long vowels

	Front		Back	
	Unrounded	Rounded	Unrounded	Rounded
High	iː (í) ___1___	yː (ý)		uː (ú)
Mid	eː (é) _2_ [i̯ɛ]	øː (ǿ,œ)		oː (ó) _5_ [oʊ̯]
	ɛː (æ) _3_ [aɪ̯]		aː (á) _4_ [aʊ̯] _4_ ɔː(ǫ)

Key: 1 /yː/ (ý) merged with /iː/ (í). 2 /eː/ (é) was diphthongized to [i̯ɛ]. 3 /ɛː/ (æ, ę́) and /øː/ (ǿ,œ) merged and were diphthongized to [aɪ̯]. 4 /aː/ (á) and /ɔː/ (ǫ́) merged and were diphthongized to [aʊ̯]. 5 /oː/ (ó) was diphthongized to [oʊ̯].
Notes: Most of the long Icelandic vowels have been diphthongized. Symbols within parentheses indicate standard orthographic representations. The arrows indicate the qualitative changes that have occurred since Old Icelandic, i.e. lowering fronting, loss of rounding, etc.

Table 6.3   Old and Modern Icelandic vowel correspondences

| | Old Icelandic | | | Modern Icelandic | |
Vowel	Example	Phonetic transcription	Vowel	Example	Phonetic transcription
i (i)	sinn 'his (refl.)'	[sinː]	ɪ (i)	sinn 'his (refl.)'	[sɪnː]
				sin 'sinew'	[sɪːn]
iː (í)	síma 'thread'	[siːma]	i (í)	sími 'phone'	[siːmi]
				ríms 'rhyme (gen.)'	[rims]
e (e)	eða 'or'	[eða]	ɛ (e)	eða 'or'	[ɛːða]
				enn 'still'	[ɛnː]
eː (é)	él 'snow shower'	[eːl]	jɛ/jɛ (é)	él 'snow shower'	[jɛːl]
				éls 'snow shower (gen.)'	[jɛls]
ɛː (æ)	ær 'ewe'	[ɛːr]	ai̯ (æ)	ær 'ewe'	[ai̯ːr]
				æfri 'mad (dat. f.)'	[ai̯vrɪ]
y (y)	flyt 'move (1 sg.)'	[flyt]	ɪ (y)	flyt 'move (1 sg.)'	[flɪːt]
				þynnri 'thinner (comp.)'	[θɪnrɪ]
yː (ý)	flýt 'float (1 sg.)'	[flyːt]	i (ý)	flýt 'float (1 sg.)'	[fliːt]
				lýst 'described (pp.)'	[list]
ø (ø)	mølva 'break'	[mølva]	œ (ö)	mölva 'break'	[mœlva]
				kjör 'election'	[cʰœːr]
øː (ø, œ)	øði 'madness'	[øːði]	ai̯ (æ)	æði 'madness'	[ai̯ːðɪ]
				æðri 'of higher rank'	[ai̯ðrɪ]
a (a)	far 'ship'	[far]	a (a)	far 'ship'	[faːr]
				fars 'ship (gen.)'	[far̥s]
aː (á)	fár 'damage'	[faːr]	au̯ (á)	fár 'damage'	[fau̯ːr]
				fárs 'damage (gen.)'	[fau̯r̥s]

Table 6.3 *continued*

Old Icelandic			Modern Icelandic		
Vowel	*Example*	*Phonetic transcription*	*Vowel*	*Example*	*Phonetic transcription*
u (u)	þula 'long poem'	[θula]	ʏ (u)	þula 'long poem'	[θʏːla]
				þuls 'announcer (gen.)'	[θʏls]
uː (ú)	súla 'pillar'	[suːla]	u̞ (ú)	súla 'pillar'	[suːla]
				fúls 'sulky (gen.)'	[fuls]
o (o)	hol 'cavity'	[hol]	ɔ (o)	hol 'cavity'	[hɔːl]
				hols 'cavity (gen.)'	[hɔls]
oː (ó)	hól 'praise'	[hoːl]	ou̞ (ó)	hól 'praise'	[hou̞ːl]
				hóls 'praise (gen.)'	[hou̞ls]
ɔ (ǫ)	ǫr 'arrow'	[ɔr]	œ (ö)	ör 'arrow'	[œːr]
				örk 'ark'	[œɽk]
ɔː (ǿ)	ǫ́ss '(heathen) god'	[ɔːsː]	au̞ (á)	ás '(heathen) god'	[au̞ːs]
				áss 'god (gen.)'	[au̞sː]

Note: Long nasal /ɔ/ merged with long oral /o/ and not with long oral /a/ as its non-nasal counterpart.

The result of the development sketched in Figures 6.1 and 6.2 is illustrated in Table 6.3 (with the examples given in normalized Old Icelandic orthography vs Modern Icelandic orthography). Note in particular that an accent over a vowel indicates quantity in Old Icelandic orthography but a separate quality in the modern one (usually diphthongization). The quantity differences will be dealt with below. The phonetic transcription is slightly simplified. In the column 'vowel' we give a phonetic symbol for the vowel followed by the usual orthographic symbol (letter) in parentheses. It should be noted that the spelling has for the most part remained the same although the phonetic quality of the phonemes has changed in many cases. Note also that for each vowel there is only one Old Icelandic example whereas there are two for Modern Icelandic since all vowels can be either long or short in Modern Icelandic but vowel length was distinctive in Old Icelandic.

It should be fairly clear from this that there have been rather drastic changes in the vowel system from Old to Modern Icelandic. Loss of distinctive vowel length, distinctive nasality and the diphthongization of most of the Old Icelandic long vowels are the most important ones. (Although we have not classified /i/ and /u/ as diphthongs here, it is possible that they should be so classified. Similarly, the combination /je/, which developed from Old Icelandic /e:/, is possibly a rising diphthong, namely [i̯ɛ], indicated as a possibility in Table 6.3.)

The Consonant System

The Modern Icelandic consonant system is diagrammed in Table 6.4. The system represented here is not strictly phonemic in the classical sense nor is it the system of underlying segments in the generative sense since it contains a number of segments that are predictable (for the most part at least) in terms of their environment. This is true for the alternation between palatal and velar stops, on the one hand, and voiced and voiceless sonorants, on the other. We will return to these alternations in the section on consonantal processes below. The voiced fricatives are in general very 'weak' and hence possibly better classified as approximants. The /j/ may even be better classified as a glide, as /h/ is also sometimes classified. The short /r/ is also frequently a single flap rather than a trill. The palatal and velar nasals only occur before the palatal and velar stops, respectively.

Table 6.4 might suggest that the difference between the spelling and the phonetic/phonological representation of words is greater than it in fact is. There are a number of regular correspondences that are not evident from the

Table 6.4 The Modern Icelandic consonant system

	Bilabial/ labiodental	Dental/ alveolar	Palatal	Velar	Glottal
Aspirated stops	pʰ (p)	tʰ (t)	cʰ (k)	kʰ (k)	
Unaspirated stops	p (b)	t (d)	c (g)	k (g)	
Voiceless fricatives	f (f)	θ (þ)	ç (hj)	x (k, g)	h (h)
Voiced fricatives/ approximants	v (v)	ð (ð)	j (j)	ɣ (g)	
Voiceless sibilant		s (s)			
Voiceless nasals	m̥ (m)	n̥ (n)	ɲ̥ (n)	ŋ̥ (n)	
Voiced nasals	m (m)	n (n)	ɲ (n)	ŋ (n)	
Voiceless lateral		l̥ (l)			
Voiced lateral		l (l)			
Voiceless trill/flap		r̥/ɾ̥ (r)			
Voiced trill/flap		r/ɾ̥ (r)			

Note: Symbols in parentheses give the most common orthographic representations.

Table 6.5   A list of correspondences between spelling and sound

Letter	Phonetic realization	Example
p	[pʰ] in initial position	*par* 'pair'
	[p] after a voiceless sound	*spara* 'save'
b	[p]	*bar* 'bar'
t	[tʰ] in initial position	*tala* 'talk'
	[t] after a voiceless sound	*stela* 'steal'
d	[t]	*dalur* 'valley'
k	[cʰ] in initial position before a front unrounded vowel or /j/	*kerfi* 'system', *kjöt* 'meat'
	[c] between a voiceless sound and a front unrounded vowel or /j/	*skel* 'shell', *skjól* 'shelter'
	[kʰ] in initial position before other vowels and consonants	*kalla* 'call', *króna* 'crown'
	[k] between a voiceless sound and a vowel that is not front and unrounded or between a voiceless sound and a consonant	*skafa* 'scrape', *skrapa* 'scrape'
	[x] before /t/	*rakt* 'damp (n.)'
g	[c] in initial position before a front unrounded vowel or /j/	*gefa* 'give', *gjöf* 'gift'
	[k] in initial position before other vowels and consonants	*gata* 'street', *grafa* 'dig'
	[k] in medial position before /l, n/	*sigla* 'sail', *signa* 'bless'
	[j] between a vowel and /i/	*segi* 'say (1 sg.)'
	[ɣ] in medial position before vowels (other than /i/) and /ð, r/	*saga* 'saga', *sagði* 'said', *sigra* 'win'
	[x] before /t, s/	*sagt* 'said', *lags* 'tune (gen.)'
f	[f] in initial position and before /t/	*fara* 'go', *saft* 'juice'
	[v] in medial position between vowels and between a vowel and /ð, r, j/	*hafa* 'have', *hafði* 'had', *hafrar* 'oats', *hefja* 'begin'
	[p] in medial position between a vowel and /l, n/	*efla* 'strengthen', *hefna* 'revenge'

table. Some of the less obvious ones are listed in Table 6.5. This list is by no means complete but it will be useful for reference in the following sections.

Stress and Intonation

The major stress in Icelandic falls on the first syllable. This holds for loanwords too. There is also a tendency to put weak secondary stress on every second syllable after the stressed initial one. This can be seen in the following examples where ' before a syllable indicates the primary stress and ˌ the weak secondary one: *'hestur* 'horse', *'lektor* 'lecturer, assistant professor', *'hestuˌrinn* 'the horse', *'lektoˌrarnir* 'the lecturers', *'almaˌnakið,* 'the almanac'. In trisyllabic words this secondary stress is normally not noticeable on the third syllable if it is an inflectional ending but it becomes clearer if a fourth syllable is added (cf. *'lektorar* 'lecturers' vs *'lekto,rarnir* 'the lecturers'). Note also that this 'strong–weak–strong–weak' pattern can be broken up in compound words since there is also a tendency for compound words to carry weak secondary stress on their second part. Hence we get the following, for instance (where the * indicates an unacceptable stress pattern and # shows the word boundary in the compound): *'höfðingja#,vald/*'höfðin,gja#vald* 'power of chiefs'.

Finally, it should be noted that, unlike Norwegian or Swedish, Icelandic does not have lexical tones. Icelandic sentence intonation has not been studied carefully enough to yield any interesting results yet.

Quantity and Syllable Structure

The basic facts about vowel length in Modern Icelandic can be informally stated as follows:

Stressed vowels are long if no more than one consonant follows

The exception to this simple rule is that stressed vowels are also long before two consonants if the first one is a member of the set /p, t, k, s/ and the second of /j, v, r/. Hence the stressed (first) vowels in (a) in the following list are all long and so are the stressed vowels in (b) whereas the stressed vowels in (c) are short, as indicated:

a *búa* ['puːa] 'live', *tala* ['tʰaːla] 'talk', *lesa* ['lɛːsa] 'read'
b *nepja* ['nɛːpʰja] 'coldness', *kátra* ['kʰauːtʰra] 'happy (gen. pl.)', *flysja* ['flɪːsja] 'peel'
c *elda* ['ɛlta] 'cook', *andi* ['antɪ] 'spirit', *belja* ['pɛlja] 'bellow', *inni* ['ɪnːɪ] 'inside'

It is assumed here that long consonants are in fact geminates, or at least equivalent to double consonants phonologically, and that consonant length is basic or underlying in Icelandic and vowel length derived. It should also be noted here that the only vowels that occur in completely unstressed syllables in native Icelandic words are /i, a, u/. (Note that this does not hold for syllables that carry secondary stress, such as in words like *'asna,legur* (see the section on stress above, pp. 148–9).)

The consonant sets mentioned in the exception to the vowel quantity rule stated above (and exemplified in the (b) (vs (c)) examples in the list) suggest that syllable boundaries may play a role in vowel quantity since the members of the first and second sets are probably at the opposite ends of the sonority hierarchy for Icelandic consonants. The question is how to build this into the quantity rule.

It is a well-known fact for many languages that have positionally determined vowel length that vowels tend to be long in open syllables, i.e.

syllables that are not closed by consonants. Hence it would seem natural to assume that the syllable boundary in the words in the list is as follows: (a) *bú.a, ta.la, le.sa*; (b) *ne.pja, ká.tra, fly.sja*; (c) *el.da, an.di, bel.ja, in.ni*. As the reader may have noticed we have in fact been assuming a syllabification along similar lines above. This would mean that one intervocalic consonant always forms part of the second syllable, and given two intervocalic consonants the boundary varies depending on the sonority of the consonants (this would have to be spelled out in more detail). This would give open syllables in (a) and (b) but closed in (c). If this were correct, we could simply say that stressed vowels are long in open syllables in Icelandic.

The problem with this is the quantity in monosyllabic words that end in one consonant and hence would seem be closed syllables. There the vowel is long too. Examples include words like *tal* ['tʰaːl] 'speech', *les* ['lɛːs] '(I) read', *fit* ['fɪːtʰ] 'web'. There are various ways to solve this problem. One is to say that there is something special going on in monosyllables. Another is to say that the syllabification we have been assuming is wrong and should be like this: (a) *bú.a, tal.a, les.a*; (b) *nep.ja, kát.ra, flys.ja*; (c) *eld.a, and.i, belj.a, inn.i*. This could be called 'the final-maximalistic' syllabification, meaning that you let 'as many consonants as you can' follow the preceding vowel. Then you could say that the vowel in stressed syllables is long if at most one consonant follows.

The main motivation for this last analysis is the fact that it seems to allow us to have one rule for vowel quantity in monosyllables and polysyllables. That is desirable, of course. Unfortunately, it is not obvious that this works, however. The test case would be monosyllables that end in consonant clusters of the sort /p, t, k, s/ + /v, j, r/. These are very rare in the language but the few that can be formed certainly contain long vowels. In that respect the words in (a) differ from the ones in (b): (a) *snupr* ['sʰnʏːpr̥] 'scolding', *flysj* ['flɪːsç] 'peeling', *pukr* ['pʰʏːkr̥] 'secretiveness', *sötr* ['sœːtr̥] 'slurping'; (b) *kumr* ['kʰʏmr̥] 'bleating', *emj* ['ɛmj] 'wailing', *bölv* ['pœlv] 'cursing'. So either we need a more sophisticated theory of syllables, namely one that does not consider final consonants and certain final consonant clusters part of the preceding syllable in some sense, or the length of stressed vowels in Modern Icelandic does not depend on syllable boundaries.

Some Consonantal Processes
Whereas aspirated stops are very common in the world's languages, *pre-aspirated* ones seem to be rather rare, although they occur in some Scandinavian dialects. Icelandic pre-aspiration is illustrated in the following examples: (a) *tappi* [tʰahpɪ] 'cork', *kátt* [kʰaṳht] 'happy (n.)', *pakkar* [pʰahkar] 'parcels'; (b) *epli* [ɛhplɪ] 'apple', *rytmi* [rɪhtmɪ] 'rhythm', *vakna* [vahkna] 'wake up'. The stops /p, t, k/ are aspirated in initial position, for instance. Double (or geminate) consonants are normally long in Icelandic, as explained in the preceding section, but where we would expect long /pp, tt, kk/ on historical or synchronic grounds we get pre-aspirated stops instead.

This is illustrated in the (a) examples above (the example *kátt* involves synchronic alternation since it is the neuter form of the adjective *kátur* where the stem is *kát-* but the neuter is formed as usual, by adding a #-*t*#, see p. 155). In addition, /p, t, k/ are pre-aspirated when they precede /l, m, n/. This is illustrated in the (b) examples.

Devoicing of sonorants is also not very common in the world's languages, but it occurs in Icelandic (and in certain Scandinavian dialects too). The sonorants are not all equally susceptible to devoicing and there are some dialectal differences. In short, /r/ is devoiced before /p, t, k, s/ and in the most common dialect /l, m, n/ are also devoiced before /p, t, k/. This can be illustrated by the following examples: (a) nom. *far* [faːr] 'fare', gen. *fars* [fars̥]; (b) f. *fúl* [fuːl] 'sour', n. *fúlt* [ful̥t]; f. *fim* [fiːm] 'nimble', n. *fimt* [fim̥t]; f. *fín* [fiːn] 'fine', n. *fínt* [fin̥t]. Sonorants are also devoiced word-finally (or rather phrase-finally) after voiceless consonants (and optionally after voiced segments in phrase-final position): *vatn* [vahtn̥] 'water', *rusl* [rʏstl̥] 'garbage'. In addition, most speakers of the devoicing dialect also devoice /ð/ before /k/ (it does not occur before /p, t/). Note also that devoicing of sonorants before /p, t, k/ leads to *de-aspiration* of the stops. In general, Icelandic stops are not aspirated after voiceless consonants (see Table 6.5).

There are various types of alternations between stops and fricatives in Icelandic. Thus we have *fricativization* of /p, k/ between a vowel and /t/ as in f. adj. *tæp* [tʰaiːpʰ], n. *tæpt* [tʰai̯ft] 'uncertain'; f. adj. * rík* [riːkʰ], n. *ríkt* [rixt] 'rich'. Similarly, /p, t, k/ are sometimes realized as their homorganic fricatives between vowels and /s/, but this does not hold for all words and is usually only optional when it can apply: nom. *skip* [scɪːpʰ], gen. *skips* [scɪfs] 'ship'; acc. *bát* [pau̯ːtʰ], gen. *báts* [pau̯sː] 'boat'; nom. *þak* [θaːkʰ], gen. *þaks* [θaxs] 'roof'. On the other hand, the fricatives /v, ɣ/ show up as [p, k] before /l, n/. This 'stopping' occurs for instance when the appropriate environment is created by an ellipsis of unstressed vowels (actually, intervocalic [v] could either be analysed as /f/ or /v/ since there is no contrast between the two in that position): fem. sg. *grafin* [kraːvɪn], pl. *grafnar* [krapnar] 'buried'; nom. sg. *saga* [saːɣa], gen. pl. *sagna* [sakna] 'saga'; acc. sg. *hefil* [hɛːvɪl], nom. pl. *heflar* [hɛplar] 'grader'; f. sg. *þögul* [θœːɣʏl], pl. *þöglar* [θœklar] 'silent'. This process does not apply to /ð/ before /l, n/, however.

Homorganic (dental or alveolar) unaspirated *stops are inserted* between /rl/, /rn/, /sl/, /sn/. The proper environment can again be created by ellipsis of unstressed vowels: f. sg. *farin* [faːrɪn], pl. *farnar* [fartnar] 'gone'; f. sg. *lasin* [laːsɪn], pl. *lasnar* [lastnar] 'sick'; acc. sg. *feril* [fɛːrɪl], dat. sg. *ferli* [fɛrtlɪ] 'career'; acc. sg. *drýsil* [triːsɪl], dat. sg. *drýsli* [tristlɪ] 'devil'.

Vocalic Processes

The so-called *u*-umlaut is probably among the best known phonological rules of Modern Icelandic, although there has been considerable discussion as to whether it really is phonologically rather than morphologically conditioned.

Omitting all details one can say that it turns /a/ into /ö/ [œ] if there is an /u/ in the following syllable. These a/ö alternations are very common in the inflectional system: nom. *saga* [saːɣa], acc. *sögu* [sœːɣʏ] 'saga'; nom. pl. *dalir* [taːlɪr], dat. pl. *dölum* [tœːlʏm] 'valley'; 1 sg. *tala* [tʰaːla], 1 pl. *tölum* [tʰœːlʏm]. That this rule is alive and well can be seen from the fact that it applies in new words, (inflected) loanwords and even foreign names that are inflected, such as nom. *Randa*, acc. *Röndu*, etc. The picture is complicated by the fact, however, that we do have instances of /u/ that does not cause *u*-umlaut and we also appear to have *u*-umlaut in certain instances where there is no /u/ to condition it. Thus the nominative singular of 'valley' is *dalur* with no umlaut (the /u/ is arguably inserted during the derivation) and the nominative plural of *barn* 'child' is *börn* with umlaut but no /u/ (although there was one in Proto-Nordic times). Note also that the umlaut rule does not apply in loanwords where the /u/ is part of the same morpheme as the /a/, cf. *kaktus* (not *köktus*) 'cactus'.

The *u*-umlaut rule interacts with a 'weakening' rule that (optionally) turns /ö/ into [ʏ] in unstressed syllables in certain words: nom. sg. *banani*, dat. pl. #*banan+um*# 'banana', *u*-umlaut → #*banön+um*#, weakening → #*banun+um*#, u-umlaut → #*bönun+um*#, result = *bönunum* [pœːnʏnʏm]. There are lexical restrictions on the weakening rule and if it does not apply in words of this sort and the [œ] remains in the syllable following the /a/ in the initial syllable, the first /a/ will not be umlauted and we get *banönum* rather than *bönunum*. But if the /ö/ is weakened to /u/ then *u*-umlaut is obligatory in the initial syllable, i.e. *banunum* is not an acceptable form.

6.3   Morphology

The changes of the morphological system from Old to Modern Icelandic have been relatively minor. Modern Icelandic still has four distinct cases, three genders, rich person, number, tense and mood distinctions in the verbal morphology, etc.

Nominal and Adjectival Inflection

The Inflection of Nouns
All Icelandic nouns have *inherent gender*, i.e. they belong to one of the three gender classes: masculine, feminine or neuter. There is some semantic relationship between this grammatical gender classification and the sex of the individuals referred to by the noun, much as in German, for example. Words denoting things, concepts, etc., can be either masculine, feminine or neuter and this shows up in the form of the definite (suffixed) article, the form of adjectives agreeing with the nouns and in the selection of pronominal forms that refer to them. Thus we have for instance *penninn er fallegur ... **hann** er hér* (lit.) 'pen-the(m.) is beautiful ... he is here'; *bókin er falleg ... **hún** er hér* (lit.) 'book-the(f.) is beautiful ... she is here'; *blaðið er fallegt ...*

Table 6.6 Icelandic nouns

| | Strong inflection
Genitive singular ends in a consonant | | | | | | Weak inflection
All singular cases end in a vowel | | | | | |
| | *Masculine* | | *Feminine* | | *Neuter* | | *Masculine* | | *Feminine* | | *Neuter* | |
	Gen. Sg.	Nom. Pl.	Gen. Sg.	Nom. Pl.	Gen. Sg.	Nom. Pl.	Gen. Sg.	Nom. Pl.	Gen. Sg.	Nom. Pl.	Gen. Sg.	Nom. Pl.
I	-s,	-ar	-ar,	-ar	-s,	–	-a,	-ar	-u,	-ur	-a,	-u
II	-ar,	-ar	-ar,	-ir			-a,	-ir	-i,	-ar		
III	-s,	-ir	-ar,	-ur			-a,	-ur	-i,	-ir		
IV	-ar,	-ir	-ur,	-ur								
V	irregular		irregular									

Table 6.7 Inflectional paradigms of Icelandic nouns

| | Masculine | | Feminine | | Neuter | |
| | Strong I | Weak I | Strong I | Weak I | Strong | Weak |
	'horse'	'time'	'needle'	'tongue'	'table'	'eye'
Singular						
Nom.	hest-ur	tím-i	nál	tung-a	borð	aug-a
Acc.	hest	tím-a	nál	tung-u	borð	aug-a
Dat.	hest-i	tím-a	nál	tung-u	borð-i	aug-a
Gen.	hest-s	tím-a	nál-ar	tung-u	borð-s	aug-a
Plural						
Nom.	hest-ar	tím-ar	nál-ar	tung-ur	borð	aug-u
Acc.	hest-a	tím-a	nál-ar	tung-ur	borð	aug-u
Dat	hest-um	tím-um	nál-um	tung-um	borð-um	aug-um
Gen.	hest-a	tím-a	nál-a	tung-na	borð-a	aug-na

Note: The ordering of cases differs from that in most British texts for linguistic reasons – one reason being that accusative and dative are frequently identical in Icelandic, and this similarity is obscured by inserting the genitive case between them.

það er hér (lit.) 'newspaper-the(n.) is beautiful . . . it is here'. This would seem largely abitrary from a semantic point of view. But in addition to determining the gender of agreeing adjectives and pronouns, the gender classification plays a crucial role in the inflection of nouns.

It is a well-established tradition to divide Modern Icelandic nouns into a number of inflectional classes. The classification is based on the ending of the genitive singular (the first ending given in Table 6.6, e.g. #-s# in strong masculine class I), the gender of the noun and the ending of the nominative plural (the second ending given in the table, e.g. #-ar# in strong masculine class I). The classification would also seem to suggest that there are 16 different inflectional classes of Icelandic nouns, in addition to the irregular strong masculine and feminine nouns. But this misses a number of generalizations, as strict classifications of this kind tend to do. Some of these should be evident from the paradigms given in Table 6.7.

As already pointed out, the traditional classification exemplified in Table 6.7 is misleading in certain ways. First, the major division between the so-called strong and weak nouns is not arbitrary, as it were, but *predictable* on the basis of gender and the form of the nominative singular. Thus if a noun is masculine and ends in /i/ in the nominative singular we know that it has the weak declension and we do not have to learn that separately. Similarly, all feminine and neuter nouns that end in a vowel (/a,i/) in the nominative singular have the weak declension. As far as the different declension classes of the weak masculine nouns are concerned, the first one (*tími*) is the default class and the others are quite limited. The weak feminine nouns ending in /i/ in the nominative singular are also very few.

The division according to gender is clearly a more important one from a synchronic point of view. But a strict division into paradigms as in the preceding tables obscures the similarities between certain cases across the gender classes. Thus the dative plural marker is always #-um# and the genitive plural always ends in #-a# (with an extra /n/ before the genitive plural ending in weak neuter nouns and certain weak feminine ones).

In addition, other regularities can be predicted on the basis of the nominative singular form (the *basic form*) and/or the gender. Some are presented informally in the list below. Needless to say, these regularities may not hold for the irregular nouns and there are certain lexical or morphologically conditioned exceptions to them:

1   All nouns that have a consonantal nominative singular ending or have no ending in the nominative singular, are without ending in the accusative singular.
2   Masculine and neuter nouns that end in an #-r# or have no ending in the nominative singular get #-i# in the dative singular. (Actually, this depends on the phonological properties of the stem in the case of the masculine nouns (basically, the -i is deleted unless the stem ends in two consonants) but this is the general rule for neuter nouns.)
3   Neuter nouns that have no ending in nominative singular have #-s# in the genitive singular.
4   All neuter nouns have identical nominative and accusative in the singular and plural.
5   All feminine (regularly inflected) nouns that end in a consonant in the nominative singular have identical nominative, accusative and dative in the singular. (This does not hold for proper names, however.)
6   All feminine nouns have identical nominative and accusative in the plural.
7   For all regularly inflected masculine nouns (except the third weak class) the accusative plural is identical to the nominative plural minus the final /r/.

In addition, it turns out that some of the genitive singular and nominative plural endings in strong masculine and feminine nouns are less marked than others and are thus more likely to be generalized by children acquiring the language, for instance, but we cannot go into this here.

The Inflection of Adjectives and the Article

Icelandic adjectives have *gender* inflection. In addition, most adjectives can both have the so-called *strong* and the *weak* inflection (or indefinite vs definite). Finally, most adjectives are inflected for *comparison*, i.e. they can occur in the so-called positive, comparative and superlative form.

We do not, however, have as many different forms for each adjective as this might suggest (3 genders × 2 numbers × 4 cases × 3 degrees × 2 (strong and weak) would give 144 forms if all were different). First, the comparative only has weak inflection (to the extent that it has any inflection at all. Actually, it has one form for all cases in the neuter singular (e.g. *gulara* 'yellower') and another for all cases in the masculine and feminine singular and all plural forms (e.g. *gulari* 'yellower') so this 'weak' inflection is different from the weak inflection in the positive degree). In addition, the inflectional endings for the superlative are the same as for the positive degree. Thus we will get a pretty good idea of the most regular adjectival inflection by looking at the weak and strong inflection in the positive degree. This is shown in Table 6.8 for the adjective *gulur* 'yellow' where the basic schema is given. The strong form of the adjectives is used when they are modifying indefinite nouns or used predicatively but the weak form is used when the adjective is modifying a definite noun: *gulur hestur* 'a yellow horse', *þessi hestur er gulur* 'this horse is yellow', *guli hesturinn* 'the yellow horse'.

Table 6.8 Icelandic adjectival inflection

	Strong inflection			Weak inflection		
	Masculine	*Feminine*	*Neuter*	*Masculine*	*Feminine*	*Neuter*
Singular						
Nom.	gul-ur	gul	gul-t	gul-i	gul-a	gul-a
Acc.	gul-an	gul-a	gul-t	gul-a	gul-u	gul-a
Dat.	gul-um	gul-ri	gul-u	gul-a	gul-u	gul-a
Gen.	gul-s	gul-rar	gul-s	gul-a	gul-u	gul-a
Plural						
Nom.	gul-ir	gul-ar	gul	gul-u	gul-u	gul-u
Acc.	gul-a	gul-ar	gul	gul-u	gul-u	gul-u
Dat	gul-um	gul-um	gul-um	gul-u	gul-u	gul-u
Gen.	gul-ra	gul-ra	gul-ra	gul-u	gul-u	gul-u

Table 6.9   Comparison of adjectives

	Strong inflection			Weak inflection		
	Masculine	*Feminine*	*Neuter*	*Masculine*	*Feminine*	*Neuter*
1 The regular (default) pattern						
Positive	gul-ur	gul	gul-t	gul-i	gul-a	gul-a
Comparative				gular-i	gular-i	gular-a
Superlative	gulast-ur	gul*u*st	gulast	gulast-i	gulast-a	gulast-a
2 The *i*-umlaut pattern						
Positive	ung-ur	ung	ung-t	ung-i	ung-a	ung-a
Comparative				yngr-i	yngr-i	yngr-a
Superlative	yngst-ur	yngst	yngst	yngst-i	yngst-a	yngst-a

Table 6.10   Inflection of the definite article

	The free article			The suffixed article		
	Masculine	*Feminine*	*Neuter*	*Masculine*	*Feminine*	*Neuter*
Singular						
Nom.	hin-n	hin	hi-ð	hestur-inn	nál-in	borð-ið
Acc.	hin-n	hin-a	hi-ð	hest-inn	nál-ina	borð-ið
Dat.	hin-um	hin-ni	hin-u	hesti-num	nál-inni	borði-nu
Gen.	hin-s	hin-nar	hin-s	hests-ins	nálar-innar	borðs-ins
Plural						
Nom.	hin-ir	hin-ar	hin	hestar-nir	nálar-nar	borð-in
Acc.	hin-a	hin-ar	hin	hesta-na	nálar-nar	borð-in
Dat.	hin-um	hin-um	hin-um	hestu-num	nálu-num	borðu-num
Gen.	hin-na	hin-na	hin-na	hesta-nna	nála-nna	borða-nna

The formation of *comparative forms* is shown in Table 6.9. Most adjectives form the comparative and superlative by adding #-*ar*-# and #-*ast*-# to the stem as shown in pattern 1. There are only a few adjectives that use the shorter suffixes #-*r*-# and #-*st*-# for this purpose as shown in pattern 2 and here we usually find the *i*-umlaut whenever it is possible and lengthening of the /r/ after (tense) vowels: *hár* (stem *há*) – *hærri* – *hæstur* 'high', *þunnur* – *þynnri* – *þynnstur* 'thin'. Adjectives with the suffixes #-*leg*-# and #-*ug*-# and a few others form the comparative with the short form #-*r*-# but the superlative with the long form #-*ast*-#, e.g. *fallegur* – *fallegri* – *fallegastur* 'beautiful'. There are also familiar instances of irregular comparison (*gamall* – *eldri* – *elstur* 'old'). Indeclinable adjectives do not have comparative forms but the meaning can be conveyed by using *meira* 'more' and *mest* 'most': *ég var hugsi, hann meira hugsi og hún mest hugsi* 'I was pensive, he more pensive and she most pensive'. Certain adverbs also show comparison, usually with #-*ar*-# and

#-ast-#: *fallega – fallegar – fallegast* 'beautifully – more beautifully – most beautifully'.

There is *no indefinite article* in Icelandic and the inflection of the *definite article* is in many ways rather similar to that of the adjectives. As can be seen from Table 6.10, the main principle is that the noun and the suffixed article both inflect. In addition, certain alternations in the forms of the nouns and the articles show up when they are combined and these depend to some extent on their phonological make-up.

The Inflection of Pronouns and Numerals

The Icelandic personal pronouns exist in three different persons. In the third person there is the familiar three-way gender distinction. First- and second-person pronouns are unmarked for gender. The pronouns also inflect for case and we have the four cases and singular and plural of the personal pronouns in the modern language. In Old Icelandic there was a distinction between dual and plural in the first and second person. What has happened is that the old dual now serves as the unmarked plural whereas the original plural forms are only used as honorific forms. The first-person honorific form *vér* 'we' is only used with a plural meaning (to the extent it is used at all) but the second-person honorific form *þér* 'you' can be used to refer to an individual or a group of two or more but it always controls plural agreement on the verb (but not necessarily on predicative adjectives). The use of the honorific forms decreased rapidly around 1970 and these forms are now hardly used at all in spoken Icelandic (except by some individuals of the oldest generations). They can however still be found in the written language, for example in translations.

The inflection of the personal pronouns is quite irregular, as is common in the Germanic (and other) languages. There is no special reflexive pronoun for first and second person and the third-person reflexive pronoun is unmarked for number and gender. It only exists in the accusative, dative and genitive (there is no nominative form): acc. *sig*, dat. *sér*, gen. *sín* 'himself, herself, itself, themselves'. As will be noted in section 6.4, the form *sjálfur* 'self' is used in combination with the reflexive *sig* and the first- and second-person pronouns in certain contexts. It has gender distinctions and inflects like an adjective.

Words of other traditional pronominal classes also inflect for gender, number and case. These include demonstrative, possessive, indefinite and interrogative pronouns. There are no relative pronouns in Modern Icelandic, only the indeclinable relative particles (or complementizers) *sem* and *er*, the latter being restricted to the written language. As we will see in section 6.4, there is a reflexive possessive pronoun *sinn* 'his/her/its/their'. There is no separate non-reflexive possessive pronoun for third person. Instead, the genitive forms of the third-person personal pronouns are used: *bókin hans/ hennar/þess* 'his/her/its book'.

The first four *numerals* (cardinals) are inflected for case and gender, and the number *einn* 'one' is also inflected for number(!). The plural forms of *einn* are used with *pluralia tantum* and in the sense 'a pair of'. Thus we have *einir hanskar* 'one pair of gloves' vs *einn hanski* 'one glove', and also *einar buxur* 'one (pair of) pants' (plural only, as in English), etc. The *ordinal numbers* inflect like adjectives. The word for 'first' has both strong and weak inflection, 'second' only strong but other ordinal numbers have only weak inflection.

Verbal Inflection

The Inflectional Categories and the Basic Classification
The categories *tense, person, number* and *mood* are all reflected in the Icelandic verbal inflection. In addition there are systematic ways to express distinctions that are usually associated with *voice* and *aspect*, mainly through special syntactic constructions. In this section we will show how all these distinctions are expressed, beginning with the clearly inflectional (or morphological) ones.

There are *two morphologically distinct* tenses: present and past (or preterite). There are *three persons* (first, second, third), *two numbers* (singular and plural) and *three moods*: indicative, subjunctive and imperative (the imperative only existing as a special form for second-person singular). In addition there are special verbal forms for the *infinitive, past participle* and *present participle* and these are used in various verbal constructions. Some linguists have also maintained that it is necessary to distinguish the *supine* form (formally identical to the neuter form of the past participle) from the past participle and we will occasionally do so here.

The so-called *weak verbs* form the past tense by adding a *dental suffix* to the stem whereas the *strong verbs* do not have a special inflectional suffix for the past tense but exhibit the so-called vowel shift (or ablaut). As in other Germanic languages, the class of weak verbs is large and open but the strong verbs form a closed class. There seem to be only about 100–150 strong verbs that are commonly used in the modern language but some of these are very common.

The Basic Inflectional Patterns
Modern Icelandic weak verbs are traditionally divided into four conjugational classes. In the paradigms in Table 6.11 we give one example from each weak class and one strong verb. The material in the parentheses in the imperatives (/ðu/, /du/ or /tu/) is in fact the second-person singular pronoun *þú* which has been cliticized in a weakened form on to the imperative. The simple imperative forms are more formal.

In historical grammars the classes corresponding to weak I–IV are called *ja*-verbs, *ija*-verbs, *e*-verbs and *o*-verbs, based on phonological properties of their stems in Germanic. In synchronic grammars, the definitions of the classes typically are as follows:

Table 6.11 Inflectional paradigms of some verbs

		Weak 1	Weak 2	Weak 3	Weak 4	Strong
Infinitive		telj-a	dæm-a	dug-a	kalla	bíta
		'believe'	'judge'	'suffice'	'call'	'bite'
Present						
Indicative	1 sg.	tel	dæm-i	dug-i	kalla	bít
	2 sg.	tel-ur	dæm-ir	dug-ir	kalla-r	bít-ur
	3 sg.	tel-ur	dæm-ir	dug-ir	kalla-r	bít-ur
	1 pl.	telj-um	dæm-um	dug-um	köll-um	bít-um
	2 pl.	telj-ið	dæm-ið	dug-ið	kall-ið	bít-ið
	3 pl.	telj-a	dæm-a	dug-a	kall-a	bít-a
Subjunctive	1 sg.	telj-i	dæm-i	dug-i	kall-i	bít-i
	2 sg.	telj-ir	dæm-ir	dug-ir	kall-ir	bít-ir
	3 sg.	telj-i	dæm-i	dug-i	kall-i	bít-i
	1 pl.	telj-um	dæm-um	dug-um	köll-um	bít-um
	2 pl.	telj-ið	dæm-ið	dug-ið	kall-ið	bít-ið
	3 pl.	telj-i	dæm-i	dug-i	kall-i	bít-i
Preterite						
Indicative	1 sg.	tal-di	dæm-di	dug-ði	kalla-ði	beit
	2 sg.	tal-dir	dæm-dir	dug-ðir	kalla-ðir	bei-st
	3 sg.	tal-di	dæm-di	dug-ði	kalla-ði	beit
	1 pl.	töl-dum	dæm-dum	dug-ðum	köllu-ðum	bit-um
	2 pl.	töl-duð	dæm-duð	dug-ðuð	köllu-ðuð	bit-uð
	3 pl.	töl-du	dæm-du	dug-ðu	köllu-ðu	bit-u
Subjunctive	1 sg.	tel-di	dæm-di	dyg-ði	kalla-ði	bit-i
	2 sg.	tel-dir	dæm-dir	dyg-ðir	kalla-ðir	bit-ir
	3 sg.	tel-di	dæm-di	dyg-ði	kalla-ði	bit-i
	1 pl.	tel-dum	dæm-dum	dyg-ðum	köllu-ðum	bit-um
	2 pl.	tel-duð	dæm-duð	dyg-ðuð	köllu-ðuð	bit-uð
	3 pl.	tel-du	dæm-du	dyg-ðu	köllu-ðu	bit-u
Imperative	2 sg.	tel(du)	dæm(du)	dug(ðu)	kalla(ðu)	bít(tu)
Past participle		talinn	dæmdur		kallaður	bitinn
Supine		talið	dæmt	dugað	kallað	bitið
Present participle		teljandi	dæmandi	dugandi	kallandi	bítandi

1 The first-person present indicative singular is monosyllabic and shows *i*-umlaut in certain forms (but there is no *i*-umlaut in the preterite indicative). For most of these verbs the past participle ends in -*inn*.

2 The first-person present indicative singular is disyllabic with /i/ as the second vowel and the root vowel is *i*-umlauted if possible. The umlaut also shows up in the past tense.

3 The first-person present indicative singular is disyllabic with /i/ as the second vowel but the root is normally without *i*-umlaut.

4 The first-person present indicative singular is disyllabic with /a/ as the second vowel.

These 'definitions' are obviously descriptive generalizations that can then be used to predict the inflectional differences between the classes. This is usually expressed by saying that one has to know three basic forms (or principal parts) in order to know how a given weak verb inflects, namely the infinitive, the preterite indicative singular first person and the supine. But the differences between the classes are actually largely predictable. As in the case of the nominal inflection, we could express this by assuming that each inflected verb has a *basic* (or lexical look-up or default) form. The verb stems can be found by comparing the infinitive to (the short form of) the imperative, for instance. That way we see that the final /a/ in the infinitive of class IV verbs like *kalla* 'call' is a part of the stem. Assume that the basic forms of the verbs are roughly identical to the infinitives, i.e. #telj-a#, #dæm-a#, #dug-a# and #kalla# (the notation indicating that the final /a/ in *kalla* is a part of the stem and not an inflectional ending). We can then say, for instance, that verbs that have the basic form #X-a# where X is a stem that does not end in /j/ (i.e. verbs like *dæma* and *duga*) have an extra /i/ in the present indicative singular (cf. *ég tel/dæmi/dugi/kalla* 'I believe/judge/suffice/call', *þú telur/dæmir/dugir/ kallar* 'you believe/judge/suffice/call', etc). That way we can account for some of the observed differences.

There are different types (or sequences) of vowel shift in strong verbs. The main types are usually said to be at least six, in addition to some additional irregular ones. According to the tradition, there are four basic forms (principal parts) for each strong verb (vs three for the weak ones, see above). This is illustrated in the following chart:

	Preterite indicative				
	inf.	1 sg.	1 pl.	sup.	
1	bíta	beit	bitum	bitið	'bite'
2	bjóða	bauð	buðum	boðið	'invite'
3	bresta	brast	brustum	brostið	'burst'
4	stela	stal	stálum	stolið	'steal'
5	gefa	gaf	gáfum	gefið	'give'
6	fara	fór	fórum	farið	'go'

In addition to these types there is a group of verbs that originally formed their past tense with reduplication (e.g. *gráta* 'cry' (pret. *grét*)), which show quite varied stem alternations.

The most obvious differences in weak and strong verbal paradigms are:

1   Strong verbs have no inflectional ending in the first-person singular preterite indicative but the weak verbs do. The whole preterite indicative singular is monosyllabic in strong verbs (except in prefixed or compound ones) but disyllabic (or more) in weak verbs.

2   Strong verbs end in #-st# in the second-person singular preterite

indicative whereas corresponding weak forms end in #-*ðir*# (or #-*dir*#, #-*tir*#).

The so-called *preterite-present verbs* have monosyllabic present singular forms that are similar to the corresponding preterite forms of strong verbs (hence the name). On the other hand, the preterite of these verbs is more similar to that of weak verbs. This class includes certain common modal verbs such as *mega* 'may' (pres. *má*, pret. *mátti*, supine *mátt*) and the (defective) auxiliary *munu* 'will' (pres. *mun*). It should be noted that there do not seem to be any inflectable past participle forms of the preterite-present verbs and the verbs *munu* 'will' and *skulu* 'shall' do not even seem to have any supine forms. They are also reported to have had special preterite forms of the infinitive, together with the verb *vilja* 'want', namely *mundu*, *skyldu* and *vildu*, respectively. This is probably still true of *munu*, as indicated by the following contrasts: *hann telur þá munu koma þá* 'he believes them to be coming then' (lit. 'he believes them (acc.) will (pres.inf.) come then') vs *hann taldi þá mundu koma þá* 'he believed them to be coming then' (lit. 'he believed them would (pret.inf.) come then'). Here it seems natural to have the present form of the infinitive after the present form of *telja* 'believe' in the first example but the preterite form after the preterite form of 'believe' in the second (see the discussion of the rule of 'sequence of tenses' in section 6.4). It is more difficult to construct examples of this sort with the verbs *vilja* and *skulu*.

Finally, the inflection of the verb *vera* 'be' is highly irregular in Icelandic as in many other Germanic languages.

The So-called Middle Forms

Many traditional Icelandic grammars maintain that *middle voice* is a special inflectional category in Icelandic. It is said to be characterized by adding #-*st*# to the relevant form of the active voice. It turns out, however, that the verb forms so constructed have a variety of functions, so it is very difficult to maintain that they all represent a particular inflectional category. In most cases it seems more promising to look at the formation of -*st*-verbs as a special word-formation process. It does, however, have the special status of adding the suffix #-*st*# *after* the inflectional endings and that creates certain stem alternations. Some of these can be seen in Table 6.12. As indicated, the paradigm is partially defective. Part of the reason is probably semantic: since many -*st*-verbs have a passive-like reading (as indicated in the glosses, Table 6.12) they cannot occur in the imperative. (This is a general property of passives in Icelandic although not obviously so in English.) The imperative form *bjóðstu* is in fact only possible in the context *bjóðast til* 'offer to do something', not in the passive (or middle) sense 'be offered'. In general, the possibility of having imperative forms of -*st*-verbs seems to depend on their semantic properties. Thus there is nothing wrong with the imperative forms

Table 6.12 Some typical middle forms

Infinitive		telja-st 'be believed'	dæma-st 'be judged'	kalla-st 'be called'	bíta-st 'bite each other'	bjóða-st 'be offered'
Present Indicative	1 sg.	tel-st	dæmi-st	kalla-st	bí-st	býð-st
	2 sg.	tel-st	dæmi-st	kalla-st	bí-st	býð-st
	3 sg.	tel-st	dæmi-st	kalla-st	bí-st	býð-st
	1 pl.	teljum-st	dæmum-st	köllum-st	bítum-st	bjóðum-st
	2 pl.	telji-st	dæmi-st	kalli-st	bíti-st	bjóði-st
	3 pl.	telja-st	dæma-st	kalla-st	bíta-st	bjóða-st
Subjunctive	1 sg.	telji-st	dæmi-st	kalli-st	bíti-st	bjóði-st
	2 sg.	telji-st	dæmi-st	kalli-st	bíti-st	bjóði-st
	3 sg.	telji-st	dæmi-st	kalli-st	bíti-st	bjóði-st
	1 pl.	teljum-st	dæmum-st	köllum-st	bítum-st	bjóðum-st
	2 pl.	telji-st	dæmi-st	kalli-st	bíti-st	bjóði-st
	3 pl.	telji-st	dæmi-st	kalli-st	bíti-st	bjóði-st
Preterite Indicative	1 sg.	taldi-st	dæmdi-st	kallaði-st	bei-st	bauð-st
	2 sg.	taldi-st	dæmdi-st	kallaði-st	bei-st	bauð-st
	3 sg.	taldi-st	dæmdi-st	kallaði-st	bei-st	bauð-st
	1 pl.	töldum-st	dæmdum-st	kölluðum-st	bitum-st	buðum-st
	2 pl.	töldu-st	dæmdu-st	kölluðu-st	bitu-st	buðu-st
	3 pl.	töldu-st	dæmdu-st	kölluðu-st	bitu-st	buðu-st
Subjunctive	1 sg.	teldi-st	dæmdi-st	kallaði-st	biti-st	byði-st
	2 sg.	teldi-st	dæmdi-st	kallaði-st	biti-st	byði-st
	3 sg.	teldi-st	dæmdi-st	kallaði-st	biti-st	byði-st
	1 pl.	teldum-st	dæmdum-st	kölluðum-st	bitum-st	byðum-st
	2 pl.	teldu-st	dæmdu-st	kölluðu-st	bitu-st	byðu-st
	3 pl.	teldu-st	dæmdu-st	kölluðu-st	bitu-st	byðu-st
Imperative	2 sg.					bjóð-st(u)
Past participle						
Supine		tali-st	dæm-st	kalla-st	biti-st	boði-st
Present participle						

sestu 'sit down' or *klæðstu* 'dress' of the verbs *setjast* 'sit (oneself) down', *klæðast* 'dress (oneself)'. Note here that the enclitic form of the second-person personal pronoun follows the 'middle' #-*st*# whereas all inflectional endings precede it.

Auxiliaries and Verbal Complexes

There is no morphologically distinct class of auxiliaries in Icelandic, although some of the preterite present (or modal) verbs can be used in auxiliary constructions and these have certain inflectional peculiarities, as we have seen. The class of auxiliaries can be argued to have certain syntactic characteristics, however (see section 6.4).

The most important complex verbal constructions are listed in the chart below.

Some complex verbal constructions

Perfect aux. *hafa* 'have' + supine	ég hef farið	'I have gone'
Future aux. *munu* 'will' + bare inf.	hann mun fara	'he will go'
Progressive aux. *vera* 'be' + inf. with *að*	hún er að borða	'she is eating'
Inchoative aux. *fara* 'go' + inf. with *að*	hún fer að borða	'she's going to eat'
Completed action *vera búinn að* + inf.	hún er búin að borða	'she has finished eating'
Passive aux. *vera* 'be' + pp.	hann var bitinn	'he was bitten'

In traditional grammars the perfect and the future are usually considered parts of the tense system although that is debatable. Note, for instance, that sentences with *munu* have partially a modal meaning. This can be seen if they are compared with simple sentences with verbs in the present tense: *skipið kemur á morgun* 'the ship comes tomorrow' vs *skipið mun koma á morgun* 'the ship will [apparently] come tomorrow'. Note also that the verb *vera* 'be' can be used with the inflected past participle of intransitive verbs of motion with a sort of a perfective meaning. There is a subtle distinction between it and the normal perfective, however, in that the forms with *vera* are more stative or adjectival: *hann er kominn* 'he has arrived (and he is here)' vs *hann hefur komið* 'he has come (and he has left again)'. Not surprisingly the construction with *vera* takes purely adjectival participles, e.g. prefixed with *ó-* 'un-', whereas there is no such construction with *hafa*: *hann er ókominn* 'he hasn't arrived yet' (lit. 'he is uncome') vs **hann hefur ókomið*. What we have labelled here as progressive, inchoative and completed action are more closely related to aspectual systems, however.

Table 6.13   Examples of word formation by derivation

Basic word	Suffix	Derived word	
Formation of nouns			
From nouns			
Ísland 'Iceland'	-ing-	Íslend+ing-ur	'Icelander'
hass 'pot'	-ist-	hass+ist-i	'pot smoker'
strætisvagn 'bus'	-ó-	stræt+ó	'bus'
dóni 'boor'	-skap-	dóna+skap-ur	'rudeness'
trumba 'drum'	-il-	trymb+il-l	'drummer'
strákur 'boy'	-ling-	strák+ling-ur	'small boy'
From verbs			
nema 'study'	-and-	nem+and-i	'student'
kenna 'teach'	-ar-	kenn+ar-i	'teacher'
frysta 'freeze'	-i-	frysti+i-r	'freezer'
kynna 'introduce'	-ing-	kynn+ing	'introduction'
hanna 'design'	-un-	hönn+un	'design'
From adjectives			
sniðugur 'clever'	-heit-	sniðug+heit	'cleverness'
heilagur 'holy'	-leik-	heilag+leik-i	'holiness'
virkur 'active'	-ni-	virk+ni	'activity'
Formation of adjectives			
From nouns			
tröll 'giant'	-leg-	trölls+leg-ur	'gigantic'
Ísland 'Iceland'	-sk-	íslen+sk-ur	'Icelandic'
skítur 'dirt'	-ug-	skít+ug-ur	'dirty'
From verbs			
spyrja 'ask'	-ul-	spur+ul-l	'inquisitive'
bila 'break down'	-ð-	bila+ð-ur	'out of order'
hrífa 'enchant'	-and-	hríf+and-i	'enchanting'
ýta 'push'	-in-	ýt+in-n	'pushy'
From adjectives			
púkalegur 'tacky, dowdy'	-ó-	púkó	'tacky, dowdy'
Formation of verbs			
From nouns			
flipp 'foolish act'	-a-	flipp+a	'flip (out)'
sjarmi 'charm'	-era-	sjarm+era	'charm'
From adjectives			
blár 'blue'	-na-	blá+na	'become blue'

Some Productive Word-formation Processes

Derivation by Suffixes

Some word-formation suffixes are listed in Table 6.13. The list does not exclusively contain suffixes that are common in spontaneous word formation but also several suffixes that have been frequently used in 'learned' word formation (see section 6.5). The suffixes are divided into classes according to the type of basic word they can be attached to for the purposes of new word formation. In the new words the boundary between the basic word and the suffix is indicated by a plus (+) but the inflectional ending that sometimes follows is separated from the suffix by a hyphen (-).

The suffix #+*ist*# is one of the few borrowed suffixes in the language, together with #+*heit*# and the verbal suffix #+*era*#. The difference is, however, that #+*ist*# and #+*heit*# are obviously productive in the language whereas most of the verbs that end in #+*era*# may have been borrowed as a whole. Sometimes the sequence /ís/ (probably from Danish -*is-ere*, cf. also Eng. -*ize*), is part of such verbs, cf. *skandalísera* 'scandalize'.

When a suffix is added to a basic word, there are frequently minor adjustments of the vocalism or consonantism of the basic stem. Note, however, that the highly productive suffix -*legur* is added to the genitive form rather than to the stem of nouns to form adjectives, cf. *tröllslegur* 'gigantic'. Note also that word formation with (the slangy) #+*ó*# frequently involves a lot of truncation of the basic word, as should be evident from the pairs *strætisvagn/strætó* 'bus' and *púkalegur/púkó* 'tacky, dowdy' (Table 6.13).

Some Prefixes

A number of prefixes are found in Icelandic nouns, some of which can also be attached to verbs and adjectives. Icelandic prefixes include *einka-* 'private': *einkatölva* 'personal computer'; *endur-* 're-': *endurvinnsla* 'recycling'; *fjar-* 'remote': *fjarstýring* 'remote control'; *for-* 'pre': *forhita* 'prewarm'; *ó-* 'un-': *ólokinn* 'unfinished'; *ör-* 'micro-': *örgjörvi* 'microchip'. However, these are not all productive in the language. The prefix #*ó*+# is probably the most productive and transparent one, although it is also possible to find pairs where the semantic relationship is somewhat unpredictable. Consider *léttur* 'light' and *óléttur* 'pregnant', for instance.

Compounding

It is customary to speak of three types of compounding: *stem compounding* (or close compounding) where the first part of the compound is a stem; *genitive compounding* (or loose compounding) where the first part of a compound is in the genitive case; and *connective compounding* where a special connective sound (usually a vowel) that cannot be interpreted as a case ending connects the two parts. The difference can be seen in the following examples: (a) *snjóhús* 'snow house', *sólskin* 'sunshine'; (b) *barnaskóli* 'children's school', *barnslegur* 'childlike'; (c) *ráðunautur* 'adviser', *leikfimishús* 'gymnasium'.

It is difficult to formulate rules that predict when each of these types is used. Genitive compounding is often required when the first part of a compound is itself a compound. Thus we get pairs like *borðplata* 'table top' (stem compound) and *skrifborðsplata* 'writing desk top' (genitive compound).

Most compound words are nouns and noun+noun-compounding is the most common type by far although adjective+noun compounds are also quite common. Examples include words like *stórhýsi* 'a large house' (stem compounding) and *sjúkrahús* 'hospital' (genitive compounding). Compound adjectives can also be found, such as *nautsterkur* 'ox-strong, strong as an ox' and *rauðhærður* 'red-haired', whereas compound verbs are quite rare.

Inflection normally only affects the last part of a compound word (its head). Some compound place-names where the first part is a weak form of an adjective are exceptional in this respect. Thus the name of a street or a farm may be *Langahlíð* (lit. '(the) long slope') and it will be *Lönguhlíð* in the accusative and dative, and *Lönguhlíðar* in the genitive.

The elements of Icelandic compound words are not separated in writing. The stress pattern is also typical of single words (i.e. word-initial stress) rather than sequences of words (where each major class word carries some stress). Note also that whereas there are many noun+noun compounds in Icelandic where the first part has the genitive form, genitive complements of nouns normally follow their heads in Icelandic. Compare, for example, the compound word *læknishús* 'doctor's house' with the phrase *hús læknis* 'the house of a doctor'.

6.4   Syntax

Types of Noun Phrases

Modifiers of Nouns
Indefinite pronouns (including quantifiers), demonstrative pronouns, numerals and adjectives *precede the nouns* they modify, and in this order: *allir þessir fjórir frægu málfræðingar hafa borðað hákarl* 'all these four famous linguists have eaten shark'. Demonstrative pronouns, as well as the definite article, trigger the *weak inflection* of adjectives. This can be seen if the previous example is compared with the following two: *frægu málfræðingarnir hafa borðað hákarl* 'the famous linguists have eaten shark' (lit. 'famous linguists-the have eaten shark'); *frægir málfræðingar hafa borðað hákarl* 'famous linguists have eaten shark'. But although the selection of the weak vs the strong form of adjectives in noun phrases is thus normally totally dependent on the presence vs absence of definite determiners, it is possible to get near-minimal pairs: *þau horfðu lengi á blátt fjallið í fjarska* 'they looked for a long time at the blue mountain in the distance' vs *þau horfðu lengi á bláa fjallið* 'they looked for a long time at the blue mountain'. The difference between these two examples lies in the fact that in the second example the noun phrase containing the weak (or definite) form of the adjective is restrictive, whereas in the first example, the noun phrase is non-restrictive, i.e. implying 'the mountain in the distance happened to be blue'.

Pre-nominal modifiers agree with the noun in gender, number and case: *falleg stúlka sá ljótan hund* 'a beautiful (nom. sg. f.) girl saw an ugly (acc. sg. m.) dog'; *fallegt barn klappaði ljótum hundi* 'a beautiful (nom. sg. n.) child petted an ugly (dat. sg. m.) dog'; etc. Here the verbs *sjá* 'see' and *klappa* 'pet' govern accusative and dative, respectively, so we get different cases on the object. This affects the form of the modifying adjective, as does the gender and number of the noun in each sentence.

Genitive complements of nouns (including expressions of possession) normally *follow* their head but they can frequently be preposed for emphasis, although this depends to some extent on their nature. Thus it is virtually impossible to prepose a noun with modifiers, in contrast to a proper name: *hús Haraldar* vs **Haraldar** *hús* (*en ekki Jóns*) 'Harold's house' (lit. 'house Harold's') vs 'Harold's house (but not John's)' – but *dúkkur litlu stelpnanna* vs ?*litlu stelpnanna *dúkkur* lit. 'the little girls' dolls (lit. 'dolls the little girls'') vs ?*'the little girls' dolls'.

Personal pronouns can be used as modifiers with nouns. They then have a special stylistic function, somewhat similar to that of demonstrative pronouns in German in such contexts: *hann Haraldur gerir það ekki* 'Harold doesn't do that' (lit. 'he Harold does that not' – cf. Ger. *Der Harald tut das nicht*). Note, however, that the following type of construction is the most normal or neutral expression of possession in Icelandic: *húsið* **hans** *Haraldar* (vs **hús hans Haraldar*) 'Harold's house' (lit. 'house-the his (gen.) Harold's (* without the def. art.)). In this construction the noun (what is possessed) must have the definite article as indicated. This is also the unmarked option if possession is indicated by a possessive pronoun (or the genitive of a personal pronoun) rather than the genitive of a noun, although it is also possible to use the indefinite form of the noun: *húsið mitt er þarna* vs *hús mitt er þarna* 'my house is there' (lit. 'house-the my is there' vs 'house my is there'). Using the indefinite form of the noun is the marked option and lends a certain formal flavour to the construction in most cases. With nouns of family relationship, however, the article can normally not be used: *bróðirinn minn vs *bróðir minn* 'my brother' (lit. '*brother-the my' vs 'brother my'). The possessive pronoun follows the noun in these constructions. It may be preposed for the purpose of emphasis, but then it is impossible to use the definite form of the noun: **mitt** *hús* (*en ekki Jóns*) vs ***mitt** *húsið* ... 'my house (but not John's)' (lit. '*my* house (but not John's)' vs *my house-the ...).

Recall that there is no possessive pronoun for the third person. Instead the genitive of the relevant personal pronoun is used. The regular possessive pronouns agree in gender, number and case with the noun, just like other modifiers, but the genitive pronouns do not, of course: *þetta eru pennarnir þínir/hans, bókin þín/hans og borðið þitt/hans* 'these are your/his pens, your/his book and your/his table' (lit. 'these are pens-the your (nom. pl. m.)/his (gen. sg. m.), book-the your (nom. sg. f.)/his (gen. sg. m.) and table-the your (nom. sg. n.)/his (gen. sg. m.)').

Inalienable possession can be expressed by the dative within prepositional phrases of certain types but not otherwise. Observe the following: *hún stakk þessu í munn honum/hans* 'she put this in his mouth' (lit. 'she put this in mouth him (dat.)/his (gen.)') vs *þetta er munnur *honum/hans* 'this is his mouth' (lit. 'this is mouth *him (dat.)/his (gen.)'). But both of these constructions are quite formal in this context and the normal way to express inalienable possession of body parts the spoken language would be *í munninn á honum* (lit. 'in the mouth on him') and *munnurinn á honum* (lit. 'the mouth on him').

Relative clauses follow their heads. They are introduced by the relative particles *sem* and *er* (more formal), there being no relative pronouns in the modern language: *konan sem þú spurðir um býr ekki lengur hér* 'the woman that you asked about no longer lives here' (lit. '... lives no longer here').

Pronouns and Anaphora

Icelandic exhibits the following pattern of referential possibilities for personal pronouns: (a) *María$_i$ greiddi henni$_{*i/j}$* 'Mary combed her hair' (lit. '... combed her (dat.)') (co-reference impossible); (b) *María$_i$ skipaði mér að hjálpa henni$_{*i/j}$* 'Mary ordered me to help her' (co-reference impossible); (c) *María$_i$ heldur að ég elski hana$_{i/j}$* 'Mary believes that I love (subj.) her' (co-reference possible); (d) *þegar hún$_{?*i/j}$ kom heim var María$_i$ þreytt* 'when she came home Mary was tired' (co-reference almost impossible). Note that co-reference is impossible between the object in an infinitival clause and the matrix subject in (b). It should also be pointed out that for most speakers it seems virtually impossible to get co-reference between a pronoun in a preposed adverbial clause and the matrix subject in sentences like (d).

Unlike in Romance languages such as Spanish or Italian, in Modern Icelandic we do not find the free occurrence of referential null subjects. In the following examples [e] indicates an empty noun phrase-slot, without any theoretical claims about its nature implied: (a) *[e] er dauður* '(he) is dead (nom. sg. m.)'; (b) *María heldur að [e] hafi séð Harald* 'Mary believes that (she) has seen Harold'. By contrast, in the case of coordinated sentences, on the other hand, the subject of the second conjunct can be left out. In some cases it may seem plausible to analyse such constructions as instances of verb-phrase-coordination, or V'-coordination, or something of that sort. But there is no straightforward analysis of that type for sentences like the following, for reasons of agreement: (a) *þeir$_i$ sáu stúlkuna einir/*einum og [e] fannst/ *fundust hún álitleg* 'they (nom. pl. m.) saw (3 pl.) the girl (acc. sg. f.) alone (nom./*dat. pl. m.) and (they) found (3 sg./*pl.) her attractive' vs (b) *þeim$_i$ líkar maturinn og [e] kaupa/*kaupir hann einir/*einum* 'they (dat. pl.) like (3 sg.) the food and (they) buy (3 pl./*sg.) it alone (nom./*dat. pl. m.)'. In (a) we have a nominative subject in the first conjunct and the verb of that conjunct is agreeing with it in person and number and the indefinite pronoun *einir* agrees with it in case and number. In the second conjunct, on the other hand, the verb is in the default third-person singular form as if it had a non-nominative subject (cf. the section on marking of grammatical relations below, pp. 175–6). This is not what we would expect under a verb-phrase-conjunction analysis since then the nominative subject of the first conjunct would be serving as the subject for the second conjunct too. This is, however, compatible with a null-subject analysis, provided that the null subject has (dative) case. Conversely, in (b) we have a dative subject in the first conjunct and a non-agreeing (third-person singular) verb but agreement facts in the second conjunct point to the presence of a (null) nominative subject there (third person plural of the verb and nominative plural masculine of the indefinite pronoun *einir*).

As stated above, the referential null subjects need a linguistic antecedent in Modern Icelandic, and it has to be a subject: **ég sá myndina$_i$ og [e$_i$] gerði mig reiðan* 'I saw the movie and (it) made me angry'. This is different from Old Icelandic where it was possible to get referential null subjects with non-subject antecedents or even with no linguistic antecedents at all. Note also that it is not possible in Modern Icelandic to have a null subject in the second conjunct if something is topicalized there. Observe that it is normally possible to topicalize constituents in the second conjunct: (a) *Pétur$_i$ elskar Maríu og hann$_i$ dáir Önnu* 'Peter loves Mary and he adores Ann' vs (b) *Pétur$_i$ elskar Maríu og Önnu dáir hann$_i$* 'Peter loves Mary and Ann he adores' (lit. . . . 'and Ann he adores'). Here we could leave the subject out of the second conjunct in the (a) version (the non-topicalized version) but not in the (b) version: (a) *Pétur$_i$ elskar Maríu og [e$_i$] dáir Önnu* 'Peter loves Mary and (he) adores Ann' vs (b) **Pétur$_i$ elskar Maríu og Önnu dáir [e$_i$]* 'Peter loves Mary and Ann (he) adores'. This would seem to suggest that these zero subjects in Modern Icelandic are really zero topics. This does not seem to have been the case in Old Icelandic. In general it seems that the restrictions on leaving out noun phrases are much stricter in Modern Icelandic than in Old Icelandic. It is quite easy to find instances of null objects and prepositional objects in older Icelandic texts. The examples with null prepositional objects all seem to be bad in Modern Icelandic. It is, however, possible to find acceptable instances of null objects, although they are rather heavily restricted: *Jón$_i$ tók bók$_j$ úr hillunni og [e$_i$] gaf mér [e$_j$]* 'John took a book from the shelf and (he) gave me (it)'. These null objects can serve as antecedents for reflexive pronouns, as can be seen from the following comparison: (a) **ég hjálpaði honum$_i$ á fætur og fylgdi þér heim til sín$_i$* 'I helped him to his feet and followed you to his home' (lit. 'I helped him on feet and followed you home to him (refl.)') vs (b) *ég hjálpaði honum$_i$ á fætur og fylgdi [e$_i$] heim til sín$_i$* 'I helped him to his feet and followed (him) to his (refl.) home'. Note, however, that it is not possible to have a null object in a second conjunct if there is an overt subject in it: **Jón brenndi bókina$_i$ en Haraldur las [e$_i$]* 'John burned the book but Harold read (it)'. This apparently holds for Swedish and Norwegian too. Old Icelandic seems to have been less strict in this respect since there it is possible to find sentences with overt subjects and null objects.

With respect to non-referential or expletive NPs, Icelandic differs from its mainland Scandinavian relatives, as can be seen from the following examples: (a) *það rigndi í gær* 'it rained yesterday' vs *í gær rigndi (*það)* 'yesterday rained (*it)'; (b) *það eru mýs í baðkerinu* 'there are mice in the bathtub' vs *eru (*það) mýs í baðkerinu?* 'are (*there) mice in the bathtub?'; (c) *það hefur einhver étið hákarlinn* (lit. 'there has somebody eaten the shark' vs *hákarlinn hefur (*það) einhver étið* (lit. 'the shark has (*there) somebody eaten'; (d) *hann segir að það hafi verið dansað á skipinu* (lit. 'he says that there was danced on the ship' vs *hann segir að á skipinu hafi (*það) verið dansað* (lit. 'he says that on the ship (*there) was danced'. As these examples indicate, the expletive *það* 'it' is used with weather verbs, in existential sentences (also with transitive verbs) and in impersonal passives. But it can only occur in clause-initial position. As soon as something is preposed in the clause, or if the verb occurs clause-initially as in direct question (cf. (b)), the expletive *það* disappears.

Reflexives and Reciprocals
First, observe the following examples of Icelandic reflexives: (a) *Haraldur rakaði sig/sjálfan sig* 'Harold shaved REFL./self REFL. (complex emphatic)'; (b) *Haraldur mismælti sig/*sjálfan sig* 'Harold misspoke REFL./ *self REFL. (complex impossible)'; (c) *Haraldur talar við *sig/sjálfan sig* 'Harold talks to *REFL./self REFL. (simplex impossible)'. For each sentence two possibilities are indicated. Before the slash we have the morphologically simple reflexive *sig* and after the slash the *sig* is preceded by *sjálfan* which (in these cases) is accusative singular masculine of the word *sjálfur* which literally means 'self' (and it agrees in gender and number with the antecedent and in case with the following reflexive which is invariant for gender and number; see p. 157).

As the (a) example indicates, the simplex reflexive is the normal non-emphatic choice with verbs like *raka* 'shave' and the complex reflexive would be interpreted as emphatic. In (b) we see that with reflexive idioms like *mismæla sig* 'make a slip of the tongue' (where the reflexive object is not really a semantic argument of the verb), the complex reflexive is completely ungrammatical. The same is true of inherently reflexive verbs which describe actions that can only affect, or states that can only be true of, the subject, such as *haga sér* 'behave', *skammast sín* 'be ashamed'. Verbs like *tala við* 'talk to', on the other hand, describe actions that normally involve somebody other than just the subject. With verbs of this sort, the complex reflexive has to be used, the simplex reflexive being totally out as shown in the (c) example.

Now let us look in somewhat greater detail at the distribution of the simplex reflexive:

(a) María$_i$ greiddi sér$_{i/*j}$
    Mary combed REFL. (coref. necessary)
(b) *María$_i$ talaði við sig$_{i/j}$
    Mary talked to REFL. (simplex impossible, cf. above)
(c) Ég skilaði Maríu$_i$ bókinni sinni$_{i/*j}$
    I returned Mary REFL.'s new book (coref. necessary)
(d) *Ég talaði við Maríu$_i$ um bókina sína$_{i/j}$
    I talked to Mary about REFL.'s book (impossible)
(e) María$_i$ skipaði mér að hjálpa sér$_{i/*j}$
    Mary ordered me to help REFL. (coref. necessary)
(f) María$_i$ heldur að ég elski sig$_{i/*j}$
    Mary believes that I love (subj.) REFL. (coref. necessary)
(g) *María$_i$ veit að ég elska sig$_{i/j}$
    Mary knows that I love (ind.) REFL. (sentence impossible for most
    speakers)
(h) *María$_i$ var þreytt þegar bókin sín$_{i/j}$ kom út
    Mary was tired when REFL.'s book came out (sentence impossible)
(i) María$_i$ segir að bókin sín$_{i/*j}$ komi út á morgun
    Mary says that book REFL.'s come (subj.) out tomorrow (coref.
    necessary)
(j) Bókin sín$_i$ segir María$_i$ að komi út á morgun
    Book REFL.'s Mary says that come (subj.) out tomorrow (sentence
    possible)
(k) María$_i$ heldur að sig$_{i/*j}$ vanti peninga
    Mary believes that REFL. (acc.) need (subj.) money (coref. necessary)
(l) *Sig vantar peninga
    REFL. (acc.) wants money (sentence impossible)
(m) *Ég sagði Maríu$_i$ að þú elskaðir sig$_{i/j}$
    I told Mary that you loved REFL. (sentence impossible)
(n) Skoðun Maríu$_i$ er að sig$_{i/*j}$ vanti hæfileika
    Opinion Mary's is that REFL. lack (subj.) talent (coref. necessary)
(o) Skoðun Maríu$_i$ kom *sér$_i$/henni$_i$ í vandræði
    Opinion Mary's caused REFL./her trouble (refl. impossible)

The facts just illustrated can be summarized as follows:

1 In simple sentences the reflexive must have an antecedent. It is normally
   the subject but it is possible to find sentences where the object is an
   acceptable antecedent (c). Prepositional object is not an appropriate
   antecedent, however (d).
2 The antecedent of the simplex reflexive need not be within the same
   clause. Thus it is possible to have the reflexive within an infinitival clause
   or a subjunctive clause with the matrix subject as the antecedent (e)–(f).
   For most speakers, however, this does not hold for indicative clauses (g).

3   As (h) shows, a reflexive pronoun in an adverbial clause normally can not have an antecedent outside this clause (for exceptions see below). That the ungrammaticality of (h) is not due to the nominative of the reflexive is shown in (i) where we have a reflexive in subject position (the possessive reflexive having a nominative form although the non-possessive reflexive does not, as pointed out above, p. 157).

4   Reflexives normally follow their antecedents but they can be preposed under certain conditions, as shown in (j).

5   The non-possessive reflexive can occur in subject position of embedded clauses if the verb is in the subjunctive mood and is one that takes an non-nominative subject (k). But it cannot, of course, occur as the accusative subject of such verbs in simple sentences since then the antecedent would be missing (l).

6   The matrix object cannot serve as the antecedent of the so-called long-distance reflexive in Icelandic (m). But it is possible to find sentences where the antecedent is the genitive complement of a noun meaning 'opinion' or the like and the reflexive is in a subjunctive predicative clause describing the opinion, as in (n). In simple sentences a genitive complement cannot serve as the antecedent of a reflexive, as shown in (o).

The preceding examples contain a number of instances of the so-called long-distance reflexive in Modern Icelandic. There seem to be very few instances of this type of reflexive in Old Icelandic texts and some of the few that exist have the reflexive in an indicative clause. Note in addition that although all of the long-distance reflexives above have (and need) an antecedent in a preceding matrix clause (and this antecedent cannot be an object, for instance), it is possible to find examples of long-distance reflexives where no antecedent is explicitly mentioned in the preceding matrix clause: **hann**$_i$ lá andvaka í rúminu sínu$_i$ og hugsaði. Það var merkilegt hvað María$_i$ var alltaf andstyggileg. Þegar stelpurnar kæmu segði hún$_j$ **sér**$_i$ áreiðanlega að fara (lit.) 'he lay awake in his (refl.) bed thinking. It was strange how nasty Mary always was (ind.). When the girls would (subj.) come, she would certainly tell him (refl.) to leave'. This long-distance reflexive has a clear semantic antecedent although it is syntactically very distant and a part of another sentence. It can only be the individual whose thoughts are being represented in the narration.

The complex reflexive, on the other hand, is clause-bounded in the sense that it must find its antecedent in its own clause. This is illustrated in the following examples: (a) María$_i$ talar alltaf við sjálfa sig$_i$ 'Mary talks always to self REFL.'; (b) *María$_i$ skipaði mér að tala við sjálfa sig$_i$ 'Mary ordered me to talk to self REFL.'; (c) *María$_i$ segir að ég tali aldrei við sjálfa sig$_i$ 'Mary says that I talk never to self REFL.'

The reciprocal hvor/hver annan 'each other' is also clause bounded: (a)

strákarnir_i tala aldrei hvor við annan_i 'the boys never talk to each other' (lit.
'the boys talk never each to (the) other'); (b) **strákarnir_i skipuðu mér að tala*
hvor við annan_i 'the boys ordered me to talk to each other' (lit. 'the boys
ordered me to talk each to (the) other'); (c) **strákarnir_i segja að ég tali aldrei*
hvor við annan_i 'the boys say that I never talk to each other' (lit. 'the boys
say that I talk never each to (the) other'). Here we have used the version with
hvor rather than *hver*, the difference being that the former means 'each of
two', the latter 'each' in general, although this distinction may be on its
way out with the plural *hver* taking over. Note also that the 'each'-part (*hvor/
hver*) of the reciprocal agrees here with the subject (and is outside the
prepositional phrase) but many (perhaps most) speakers would say something
like *þeir töluðu við hvorn annan* 'they talked to each (acc.) other (acc.)' or
þær hjálpuðu hverri annarri 'they helped each (dat.) other (dat.)' with the
'each'-part agreeing with the 'other'-part (the object of the preposition or the
verb).

Quantifiers and Moving Modifiers
Quantifiers like *allir* 'all' modifying the subject can show up in various places
in the sentence: (a) **allir** *Íslendingar munu kyssa Annie* 'all (nom. pl. m.)
Icelanders (nom. pl. m.) will kiss Annie'; (b) *Íslendingar munu **allir** kyssa
Annie* 'Icelanders will all kiss Annie'; (c) ?**Íslendingar munu kyssa **allir***
Annie 'Icelanders will kiss all Annie'; (d) *Íslendingar munu kyssa Annie **allir***
'Icelanders will kiss Annie all'. As this shows, quantifiers can float around in
the sentence but not occur between the non-finite main verb and its object. If
there is no auxiliary verb, on the other hand, the floating quantifier can show
up between the (finite) main verb and its object: (a) **allir** *Íslendingar kysstu
Annie* 'all Icelanders kissed Annie'; (b) *Íslendingar kysstu **allir** Annie*
'Icelanders kissed all Annie'.

Auxiliaries and Main Verbs

Auxiliaries and Auxiliary-like Verbs
Most traditional Icelandic grammars and handbooks give a list of auxiliaries.
These lists vary slightly from one book to another but will include some or
all of the following:

1   With supine or past participle: *hafa* 'have', *vera* 'be', *geta* 'be able,
    may';
2   With the bare infinitive: *munu* 'will', *skulu* 'shall', *vilja* 'want', *mega*
    'may';
3   With *að* plus the infinitive: *eiga* 'ought', *kunna* 'know, may', *þurfa*
    'need', *verða* 'be, become, have to', *hljóta* 'must', *ætla* 'intend', *fara* 'go,
    be going', *vera* 'be', *byrja* 'begin', *hætta* 'stop'.

This is obviously a very heterogenous list from a semantic point of view and nobody has claimed that all these verbs are used to represent special grammatical categories although some of them are (cf. chart 'Some complex verbal constructions', p. 163 above). But they do have important syntactic characteristics in common. This can be seen by comparing the (putative) auxiliaries *hafa* 'have', *munu* 'will', and *kunna* 'may' with the verb *reyna* 'try' which takes an infinitival complement superficially similar to that of *kunna*. First, note the difference in behaviour with respect to the expletive *það*: (a) *það rignir í nótt* 'it rains tonight'; (b) *það hefur rignt í nótt* 'it has rained (sup.) tonight'; (c) *það mun rigna í nótt* 'it will rain (inf.) tonight'; (d) *það kann að rigna í nótt* 'it may rain tonight' (lit. 'it may to rain (inf.) tonight'); (e) **það reynir að rigna í nótt* (lit. 'it tries to rain tonight'). All these examples involve the weather verb *rigna* 'rain' which takes no thematic subject and can occur with the semantically empty expletive *það* 'it'. As shown in (b)–(d), it is also possible to have this semantically empty *það* in constructions with the putative auxiliaries *hafa*, *munu* and *kunna* preceding the main verb *rigna* but this is not possible if we put the verb *reyna* 'try' in the same position as in (e). Second, observe that we get a similar pattern with non-nominative subjects: (a) *mig langar í ís* 'I want ice cream' (lit. 'me (acc.) longs for ice'); (b) *mig hefur langað í ís* 'I have wanted ice cream' (lit. 'me (acc.) has longed for ice'); (c) *mig mun langa í ís* 'I will want ice cream' (lit. 'me (acc.) will long for ice'); (d) *mig kann að langa í ís* 'I may want ice cream' (lit. 'me (acc.) may to long for ice'); (e) **mig reynir að langa í ís* (lit. 'me (acc.) tries to long for ice'). Here we have the verb *langa* (*í*) 'long for want' which is one of the verbs taking a non-nominative subject (here accusative). The putative auxiliaries can have non-nominative subjects of this sort if the main verb requires one, as we see in (b)–(d), but this does not hold for non-auxiliary verbs like *reyna* as shown in (e). This does not hold either for modal verbs in the so-called root sense but only in the epistemic sense. Hence we may get minimal pairs like the following: (a) *ég kann að syngja* 'I know how to sing' or 'I may sing' vs (b) *mig kann að vanta peninga* 'I may lack money' (lit. 'me (acc.) may to lack money'). With the accusative subject in (b) we can only get the epistemic reading of *kunna*. The reason for this is presumably that epistemic modals are comparable to (other) auxiliaries in that they do not assign an independent thematic role to their subject and are thus 'transparent' to the thematic role of the 'main' (infinitive) verb.

Normally one does not get more than three auxiliary-like verbs in each clause. With multiple auxiliaries the order is quite fixed: *Haraldur mun hafa verið að borða* 'Harold has apparently been eating' (lit. 'Harold will (3 sg.) have (inf.) been (sup.) to eat (inf.)'). The auxiliary verbs *munu* and *skulu* never follow any other auxiliary verbs. No supine or participle form of these verbs exists (see p. 161), so one would not expect them to follow the auxiliary *hafa* which requires the supine form of the following verb. But since they have a special infinitival form, it is clear that there cannot be a morphological reason for their non-occurrence after infinitive-taking auxiliaries. After all, they are found in the so-called accusative-with-infinitive construction (see p. 161).

Phrasal Verbs

In Icelandic we find a familiar contrast between verbal particles and prepositions. First, observe the word-order possibilities in sentences with the particle verb *taka fram* 'take out': (a) *fjöldi manns tók fram bækurnar* 'a lot of people took out the books'; (b) **fram bækurnar tók fjöldi manns* 'out the books took a lot of people'; (c) *fjöldi manns tók bækurnar fram* 'a lot of people took the books out'; (d) *fjöldi manns tók þær fram/*fram þær* 'a lot of people took them out/*out them'. These sentences can be compared with sentences with the verb *horfa á* 'look at': (e) *fjöldi manns horfði á stúlkuna* 'a lot of people looked at the girl'; (f) *á stúlkuna horfði fjöldi manns* 'at the girl looked a lot of people'; (g) **fjöldi manns horfði stúlkuna á* 'a lot of people looked the girl at'; (h) *fjöldi manns horfði *hana á/á hana* 'a lot of people looked her at/at her'. In the first set of sentences (a–d) we see that the particle *fram* cannot move to the front of the clause with the object of the verb (b) but it can follow the object (c) and it must in fact do so if the object is a pronoun (d). In the second set (e–h), on the other hand, *á* has the properties of a preposition rather than a particle. Hence it can move to the front of the clause together with its object (f) but it cannot follow its object (g), not even if it is a pronoun (h).

Grammatical Relations and Agreement

Some Properties of Subjects and Objects

Recent research has established a set of typical subject properties, as opposed to objects and other noun phrases, and led to the conclusion that certain non-nominative noun phrases share most of the subject properties with the regular nominative subjects. The typical subject properties include the following: (i) the subject precedes the finite verb in neutral declarative word order; (ii) the subject immediately follows the finite verb in direct questions; (iii) in existential sentences it is possible to have the subject in initial position or the sentence can begin with the expletive *það* 'it, there' with the logical subject immediately following the finite verb or the sentential adverb if there is one; (iv) the subject can immediately precede the infinitival verb in the 'accusative-with-infinitive' construction (or 'exceptional case marking' construction); (v) subjects cannot serve as antecedents for personal pronouns in simple clauses, only for reflexives; (vi) subjects can serve as antecedents for non-clause bounded (or long-distance) reflexives whereas objects cannot; (vii) it is possible to have null subjects in the second conjunct in coordinated sentences if it has a co-referential subject antecedent.

Keeping these subject properties in mind, we can show the similarity between regular nominative subjects and non-nominative ones by looking at direct questions (a); clause bounded reflexives vs pronouns (b); non-clause bounded reflexives (c); and omission of subject in the second conjunct of coordinated structures (d): (a) *hefur strákurinn aldrei séð peninga?* 'has the boy (nom.) never seen money?' vs *hefur strákinn aldrei vantað peninga?* 'has the boy (acc.) never lacked money?'; (b) *strákurinn*$_i$ *þarf pelann* *hans$_j$/*sinn*$_i$ 'the boy (nom.) needs his (*non-refl./refl.) bottle' vs *strákinn*$_i$ *vantar pelann* *hans$_j$/*sinn*$_i$ 'the boy (acc.) lacks his (*non-refl./refl.) bottle' vs *ég rétti stráknum*$_i$ *pelann hans*$_j$/*sinn*$_i$ 'I handed the boy his (non-refl./refl.) bottle'; (c) *María*$_i$ *er leið yfir því að þú skulir aldrei heilsa sér*$_i$ 'Mary finds it depressing that you never greet her (refl.)' (lit. 'Mary (nom.) is depressed over it that you shall (subj.) never greet her (refl.)') vs *Maríu*$_i$ *leiðist að þú skulir aldrei heilsa sér*$_i$ 'it bothers Mary that you never greet her' (lit. 'Mary (dat.) it-bothers that you shall (subj.) never greet her (refl.)') vs *ég sagði Maríu$_i$ *að þú hefðir aldrei heilsað sér*$_i$ 'I told Mary that you had (subj.) never greeted her (refl.)'; (d) *Haraldur*$_i$ *gaf Maríu*$_j$ *hamstur og [e*$_i$*] bauð henni*$_j$ *svo í bíó* 'Harold gave Mary a hamster and (he) took her then to the cinema' vs *Haraldi*$_i$ *geðjast vel að Maríu og [e*$_i$*] býður henni oft í bíó* 'Harold (dat.) has a liking for Mary and takes her frequently to the cinema' vs *Haraldur$_i$ *gaf Maríu*$_j$ *hamstur og [e*$_j$*] bauð honum*$_i$ *svo í bíó* 'Harold gave Mary a hamster and (she) took him then to the cinema'. As these examples show, the non-nominative subjects pattern with the nominative ones except with respect to subject–verb agreement. There is thus no one-to-one relationship between morphological case marking and grammatical function. Subjects can have any of the four morphological cases and so can objects. This can be illustrated further for subjects (a) and for objects (b): (a) *stelpan þarf peninga* 'the girl (nom.) needs money' vs *stelpuna vantar peninga* 'the girl (acc.) lacks money' vs *stelpunni leiðist hér* 'the girl (dat.) is bored here' vs *vindsins gætir ekki mikið hér* 'the wind isn't very noticeable here' (lit. 'the wind (gen.) is-noticeable not much here'); and (b) *stelpunni ?líkar/líka hestarnir vel* 'the girl (dat.) likes (sg./pl.) the horses (nom.) fine' vs *stelpan sá strákinn* 'the girl saw the boy (acc.)' vs *stelpan hjálpaði stráknum* 'the girl helped the boy (dat.)' vs *stelpan saknar stráksins mikið* 'the girl misses the boy (gen.) much'. The unmarked option is that verbs take nominative subjects. Dative subjects are quite common too (at least 120 verbs take these) and accusative subjects not uncommon (about 70 verbs) whereas there are probably only about 2 verbs that take genitive subjects. All the non-nominative subjects are non-agentive. Accusative objects are the unmarked or default case whereas dative and genitive objects are more marked. Nominative objects only ocur with verbs that take dative subjects and there the verb usually agrees with the nominative object rather than occurring in the non-agreeing third-person singular form.

In addition, we have the traditionally well-known examples of (adverbial) accusatives of time and duration and instrumental datives: (a) *hún beið hans þar allan daginn* 'she waited (for) him there all day' (lit. 'she waited him (gen.) there all day (acc.)'); (b) *hún tók honum opnum örmum* 'she greeted him (dat.) (with) open arms (dat.)'.

A number of verbs take two objects in Icelandic. The following case marking patterns seem to occur. The numbers in parentheses are supposed to be approximate numbers of existing verbs of each type:

1   nom. – dat. – acc. (75+): *Ég sagði honum söguna* 'I (nom.) told him (dat.) the story (acc.)'
2   nom. – acc. – dat. (25): *hún leyndi mig því* 'she concealed it from me' (lit. 'she (nom.) concealed me (acc.) it (dat.)')
3   nom. – acc. – gen. (10): *við kröfðum þá þess* 'we demanded it from them' (lit. 'we (nom.) demanded them (acc.) it (gen.)')
4   nom. – dat. – dat. (10): *þær lofuðu mér því* 'they (nom.) promised me (dat.) it (dat.)'
5   nom. – dat. – gen. (15): *þeir óskuðu henni gleðilegra jóla* 'they (nom.) wished her (dat.) merry Christmas (gen.)'
6   nom. – acc. – acc. (2): *bíllinn kostaði mig mikla peninga* 'the car (nom.) cost me (acc.) much money (acc.)'

Passives, Agreement and Middles
Note the following typical passives: (a) *einhver barði strákana í skólanum* 'somebody (nom.) hit the boys (acc. pl.) in the school' vs *strákarnir voru barðir í skólanum* 'the boys (nom. pl. m.) were (3 pl.) hit (nom. pl. m.) in the school'; (b) *einhver hjálpaði strákunum með heimaverkefnið* 'somebody (nom.) helped the boys (dat. pl.) with the homework' vs *strákunum var hjálpað með heimaverkefnið* 'the boys (dat. pl.) was (3 sg.) helped (nom. sg. n.) with the homework'. In (a) we see that the accusative object in the active sentence corresponds to the nominative subject in the passive sentence. The passive auxiliary *vera* 'be' agrees in person and number and the past participle *barðir* 'hit' in case, number and gender with the nominative subject. In (b), on the other hand, we see that the dative object in the active sentence corresponds to the dative subject in the passive sentence. Since there is a close relationship between nominative and agreement, as we have already seen, the passive auxiliary verb *vera* no longer agrees with the subject nor does the past participle. Instead we get the unmarked third-person singular of the auxiliary and the unmarked nominative singular neuter form of the participle (which is identical to the supine form). The relation between genitive objects of active verbs, genitive subjects of passive verbs and (non-) agreement in passives follows the same pattern.

The agreement/non-agreement pattern observed here for passives is found in other types of sentences too, such as in predicative constructions like the following: *stelpurnar voru mjög kaldar* 'the girls (nom. pl. f.) were (3 pl.) very cool (nom. pl. f.)' vs *stelpunum var mjög kalt* 'the girls felt very cold' (lit. 'the girls (dat. pl. f.) was (3 sg.) very cold (nom. sg. n.)'). The generalization is this: dative and genitive objects of actives 'stay' dative and genitive in passives and they do not trigger any agreement and neither do other dative or genitive subjects (nor accusative subjects for that matter), as we have seen.

Verbs taking two objects vary with respect to passivizability. Verbs that take dative + accusative objects can sometimes have two types of passives, although the passivizability of a given object may depend to some extent on its semantic properties (human vs non-human, definite vs indefinite). Thus we have two possible passives of sentences with the verb *gefa* 'give' in cases like the following: *einhver hefur gefið konunginum þrælana* 'somebody has given the king (dat.) the slaves (acc. m.)' vs *konunginum hafa verið gefnir þrælarnir* 'the king has been given the slaves' (lit. 'the king (dat.) have (3 pl.) been given (pl. m.) the slaves (nom. pl. m.)') vs *þrælarnir hafa líklega verið gefnir konunginum* 'the slaves (nom.) have probably been given (pl. m.) (to) the king (dat.)'. In general, it is easier to passivize an object that refers to a person, for example, a Recipient, than a non-human object or concept. If the Recipient is left out, then the remaining object passivizes freely. Thus we can get the following pattern: *kennarinn hefur lengi kennt börnunum reikning* 'the teacher has long taught the kids (dat.) maths (acc.)' vs *börnunum hefur lengi verið kenndur reikningur* 'the kids (dat.) has (3 sg.) long been taught (nom. sg. m.) maths (nom. sg. m.)' vs *??reikningur hefur lengi verið kenndur börnunum* 'maths (nom. sg. m.) has long been taught (nom. sg. m.) (to) the children (dat.)' vs *reikningur hefur lengi verið kenndur í þessum skóla* 'maths (nom. sg. m.) has long been taught (nom. sg. m.) in this school'. With other types of ditransitive verbs it is apparently impossible to passivize the non-human object (Theme) if the human one (Recipient, Goal) is present but fine if it is left out: *einhver hefur leynt hana þessu* 'somebody has concealed this from her' (lit. 'somebody has concealed her (acc.) this (dat.)') vs *hún hefur verið leynd þessu* '(lit. she (nom.) has been concealed this (dat.)') vs **þessu hefur verið leynd/leynt hún/hana* (lit. 'this (dat.) has been concealed (f./sup.) she (nom./acc.)') vs *þessu hefur verið leynt* 'this (dat.) has been concealed (sup.)'.

Note that if we have a ditransitive verb taking dative and accusative objects and passivize the dative object, as in the example with *gefa* 'give' above, the (former) accusative object shows up in the nominative in the passive and we get agreement with it rather than with the dative subject. This gives rise to the same dative-nominative pattern as we saw in active sentences with the verb *líka* 'like' above (the only difference being that in the passive agreement with the nominative object is obligatory whereas non-agreement is sometimes a possibility in active dative-nominative sentences). The generalization seems to be that if the subject is idiosyncratically marked but the object is not, the object will show up in the nominative case rather than the expected accusative case.

Several types of verbs do not passivize at all. This holds for: (a) most -*st*-verbs: *margir hafa ásælst þessa peninga* 'many (nom.) have wanted this money (acc.)' vs **þessir peningar hafa verið ásælstir/ásældirst* ... 'this money has been wanted ...' (There may be a morphological reason for this, namely that no past participle exists for these verbs.); (b) inherently reflexive verbs: *María hefur alltaf hagað sér vel* 'Mary has always behaved herself well' vs **María segir að sér hafi alltaf verið hagað vel* 'Mary says that REFL. has always been behaved well' (This can be contrasted with: *María segir að sér hafi alltaf verið hjálpað* (lit.) 'Mary says that REFL. has always been helped'.); (c) various verbs that take non-agentive subjects in the active (and these usually cannot occur in the imperative either): *vagnarnir hafa alltaf tekið tuttuguogþrjá farþega* 'the buses have always taken twenty-three passengers (acc.)' vs **tuttuguogþrír farþegar hafa alltaf verið teknir ...* 'twenty-three passengers (nom.) have always been taken ...'; (d) verbs taking cognate objects: *margir sváfu værum svefni* 'many slept a sound sleep (dat.)' vs **værum svefni var sofið ...* 'a sound sleep was slept ...'

In the case of intransitive verbs, on the other hand, we get the so-called impersonal passive with the expletive *það* 'it', which has all the usual characteristics (only occurring in the position immediately preceding the finite verb): *margir hafa áreiðanlega dansað þá* 'many have certainly danced then' vs *það hefur áreiðanlega verið dansað þá* 'people have certainly danced then' (lit. 'there has certainly been danced (nom. sg. n.) then') vs *þá hefur (*það) áreiðanlega verið dansað* 'then people have certainly danced' (lit. 'then has (*there) certainly been danced'). It seems that it is typically verbs that take volitional agents as subjects that allow impersonal passivization. Thus the so-called unaccusative (or ergative) do not: *margir bátar hafa áreiðanlega sokkið þá* 'many boats have certainly sunk then' vs **það hefur áreiðanlega verið sokkið þá* 'there has certainly been sunk then'. Note also that impersonal passivization is impossible for most speakers with verbs that have any kind of NP-object whereas it is fine if the verb takes a prepositional object: (a) *einhver hefur barið hestinn* 'somebody has beaten the horse' vs **það hefur verið barið hestinn* ('lit. there/it has been beaten (sup.) horse-the') – but (b) *einhver hefur slökkt á tölvunni* 'somebody has turned off the computer' vs *það hefur verið slökkt á tölvunni* 'the computer has been turned off' (lit. 'there/it has been turned off computer-the'). It should be noted, however, that impersonal passives of transitive verbs (cf. **það hefur verið barið hestinn*) can frequently be heard in Modern Icelandic child language. It is not possible, on the other hand, to form a 'regular passive' (or pseudo-passive or prepositional passive) with verbs that take prepositional objects. Thus note the following set of sentences: *einhver hefur sofið í þessu rúmi* 'somebody has slept in this bed' vs *það hefur einhver sofið í þessu rúmi* 'there has somebody slept in this bed' vs *þessu rúmi hefur verið sofið í* 'this bed (dat.) has been slept in' vs **hefur þessu rúmi verið sofið í?* 'has this bed been slept in?' In the second example we have the type of impersonal passive we have already seen, whereas the third might look like a 'pseudo-passive' or prepositional passive where the object of a preposition has been passivized. In fact, however, it is an instance of topicalization of the prepositional object. The expletive *það* then disappears as always when something is fronted. We see that the dative *þessu rúmi* 'this bed' is a topicalized constituent rather than a subject from the fact that it cannot immediately follow the transitive verb in a direct question like the last example. It seems that pseudo-passives of the type *this bed has been slept in* do not exist in Icelandic whereas noun phrases can easily be moved out of many types of PPs by topicalization.

In all the examples of passives above the Agent has been left out. That is typical of Icelandic passives. It is much harder in Icelandic than in English, for instance, to find natural examples of passives with the Agent in a prepositional phrase although these exist: *dyrnar voru opnaðar (af dyraverðinum)* 'the doors (nom.) were opened (by the guard)'. The 'anti-causative middle' differs from the passive in this respect: *dyrnar opnuðust (*af dyraverðinum)* 'the door opened (*by the guard)'. In general, it seems that the difference between the passive and (this type of) the middle is that in the passive it is assumed that an Agent exists, and it can even be lexically expressed, whereas the middle implies the 'loss' or 'deletion' of the Agent role. It is, however, possible to find instances of 'middle verbs' (or -*st*-verbs) that have a real passive reading with an assumed Agent but these frequently have a marked stylistic value: (a) *fundurinn átti að haldast daginn eftir* 'the meeting was to be held the next day'; (b) *allar vörur staðgreiðist* 'all goods to-be-paid-for-by-cash'; (c) *bakist við vægan hita* 'to-be-baked at moderate temperature'.

Unaccusative or Ergative Features
Icelandic has two types of pairs of verbs where one is transitive, and the other intransitive and takes subjects that are identical to the objects of the transitive member of the pair. These can be called case-preserving and non-case-preserving. Thus in examples like (a) *María kitlaði mig* 'Mary tickled me (acc.)' vs *mig kitlar* 'me (acc.) tickles'; and (b) *þeir hvolfdu bátnum* 'they capsized the boat (dat.)' vs *bátnum hvolfdi* 'the boat (dat.) capsized', the subject of the intransitive member of the pair 'preserves' the case of the object of the transitive member. This does not hold for examples of the following type: (a) *þeir breikkuðu veginn* (lit.) 'the broadened the road (acc.)' vs *vegurinn breikkaði* 'the road (nom.) broadened' and (b) *þau sökktu bátnum* 'they sank the boat (dat.)' vs *báturinn sökk* 'the boat (nom.) sank'. It seems that when we have a non-case-preserving verb the inflection of the unaccusative (or ergative) verb is frequently strong whereas that of the transitive one is weak. This is by no means the rule, though. But we apparently never get this kind of difference in inflection if the pair is case-preserving.

The semantic relationship between active verbs and certain middle or -*st*-verbs is quite similar. The middle verbs, however, do not preserve case. Thus observe the relation between the following transitive verb and its middle (or anti-causative) counterpart: *þeir lokuðu herberginu (viljandi)* 'they closed the room (dat. (intentionally))' vs *herbergið lokaðist (*viljandi)* 'the room (nom.) closed (*intentionally)'. Note also the impossibility of having a volitional adverb with the middle form, since no agentivity is involved.

Word Order, Types of Sentences and Clauses

Word Order in Declarative Sentences

Icelandic exhibits the well-known Germanic verb-second (V2) phenomenon in declarative clauses. Thus if something is preposed or topicalized, the subject will follow the finite verb rather than precede it. Most constituents can be preposed (topicalized) in Icelandic, except the verb phrase: (a) *oft hefur María gefið Haraldi hring á jólunum* 'Mary has frequently given Harold a ring at Christmas' (lit. 'frequently has Mary given ...'); (b) *Haraldi hefur María oft gefið hring á jólunum* (lit. 'Harold (dat.) has Mary frequently given ...'); (c) *á jólunum hefur María oft gefið Haraldi hring* (lit. 'at Christmas has Mary frequently given ...'); (d) **gefið Haraldi hring hefur María...* (lit. '*given Harold ring has Mary...').

The discourse function of topicalization is apparently not always the same. In many instances topicalization just gives an already established discourse topic a more prominent (or thematic) position in the sentence. Hence it is frequently quite odd as an out of the blue discourse starter. It can also have a contrastive function and is then accompanied by a constrastive stress. But neither of these functions seems to explain the fact that adverbial phrases are typically very easy to topicalize.

The so-called narrative verb-initial order is an exception to the general verb-second pattern in Icelandic. It is basically a literary phenomenon not used in colloquial speech: *komu þeir þá að stórum helli* 'they came then to a big cave' (lit. 'came they then to big cave'). This type of word order has been referred to as 'narrative inversion' since it is particularly frequent in narrative style. It must be distinguished from two other types of non-interrogative verb-initial clauses, namely the one found in conditional clauses without a conjunction, and the type found in parentheticals of a certain type. These are illustrated in the following examples: (a) *ef hann kemur, fer ég* 'if he comes I go' (lit. '... go I') vs *komi hann, fer ég* (lit. 'come he, go I'); and (b) *Jón hefur, segir María, aldrei verið við kvenmann kenndur* 'John has, Mary says, never been associated with a woman' (lit. 'John has, says Mary, never been with a woman associated'). In the (a) examples we have a preposed conditional clause beginning with the conditional conjunction *ef* 'if'. The word order in the following clause is 'inverted' as always when something is preposed, as shown above. In the second version of that example the conjunction of the preposed conditional clause has been left out and the verb is clause-initial. The (b) example illustrates verb-initial order in a parenthetical clause.

Apparent verb-third order can also be found in main clauses when adverbs of a certain type occur between the subject and the finite verb rather than after the verb: (a) *ég hitti bara Harald svo sjaldan* 'I meet just Harold so infrequently' vs *ég bara hitti Harald svo sjaldan* 'I just meet Harold so infrequently'; and (b) *hann kann einfaldlega ekkert* 'he knows simply nothing' vs *hann einfaldlega **kann** ekkert* 'he simply knows nothing'. Here we see that the adverbs like *bara* 'just' and *einfaldlega* 'simply' can either follow the finite verb or precede it. Icelandic adverbs have considerable freedom of occurrence although this varies from one type to another. Thus it is apparently a rather restricted class of adverbs that can occur between the subject and the finite verb as in the examples just given. One possible account would be that these adverbs are cliticized onto the finite verb and thus do not count as separate constituents in these instances.

Some Non-declarative Sentence Types

Direct (*yes/no*) questions typically have verb-initial order in Icelandic and any finite verb can be sentence-initial. The subject then immediately follows the finite verb: (a) *hefur María aldrei gefið Haraldi hring?* 'has Mary never given Harold a ring?'; (b) *borðaði María brauðið?* 'did Mary eat the bread?' (lit. 'ate Mary bread-the?'). The position of the negation in questions follows the same rules as in declarative sentences: if the negation immediately follows the finite verb in a declarative sentence, the subject will intervene between the sentence-initial verb and the negation in the corresponding direct question. If the negation follows, say, the indirect object in a declarative sentence, it normally stays there in the corresponding direct question: (a) *Jón hefur ekki séð heilagan anda* 'John has not seen (the) Holy Ghost' vs *hefur Jón ekki séð heilagan anda?* 'has John not seen (the) Holy Ghost?'; (b) *María gaf Haraldi ekki jólagjöf í fyrra* (lit. 'Mary gave Harold not a Christmas present last year') vs *gaf María Haraldi ekki jólagjöf í fyrra?* (lit. 'gave Mary Harold not a Christmas present last year?'). It is also possible to 'cliticize' the negation on to the sentence-initial finite verb in interrogative sentences: (a) *hefur ekki Jón séð heilagan anda?* 'hasn't John seen (the) Holy Ghost?'; (b) *gaf ekki María Haraldi jólagjöf í fyrra?* 'didn't Mary give Harold a Christmas present last year?' (lit. 'gaven't Mary Harold a Christmas present last year?'). The meaning of these questions is roughly 'Isn't it the case that . . . ?'

Constituent questions are introduced by *hv*-words like *hver* 'who', *hvernig* 'how', *hvenær* 'when', etc. The verb-second order is observed so that if the *hv*-word is not the subject, the subject will immediately follow the finite verb: (a) *hver hefur sofið í rúminu mínu?* 'who has slept in my bed?' (lit. 'who has slept in bed-the my?'); (b) *hvern kyssti María í trjágöngunum?* 'who (acc.) did Mary (nom.) kiss in the alley?' (lit. 'whom kissed Mary . . . ?').

Imperative sentences are verb-initial like direct questions. The second-person singular pronoun *þú* 'you' is typically cliticized in a weakened form on to the imperative, as we have seen, but the full form of the second-person singular pronoun can also follow the imperative. Thus we get alternations like the following where the first is more formal: *far ?(þú) nú og gjör (þú) skyldu þína* 'go (imp.) now and do (imp.) your duty' (lit. 'go you now and do (you) duty your') vs *farðu nú og gerðu skyldu þína* (lit. 'go-you now and do-you now duty your'). It is quite unnatural to leave out the second-person singular pronoun in imperative sentences, except in a second conjunct in sentences like the first one. There is no special imperative verb form for the second-person plural but there it is also possible to use verb-initial sentences with the discourse function of orders or requests. The second-person plural pronoun can be left out: *reynið (þið) nú að gera þetta vel* 'try (2 pl.) now to do this well' (lit. 'try (you) now ...') vs *reyniði nú að gera þetta vel* (lit. 'try-you (pl.) now ...'). The colloquial form of the second-person plural imperative has a cliticized and reduced form of the second-person plural pronoun *þið* on the verb. We have tried to represent this in the second version of the sentence. For some reason, however, this cliticization of the plural pronoun is not represented in Modern Icelandic spelling although the comparable cliticization of the singular pronoun is.

Finite Subordinate Clauses

As illustrated in the section on reflexives, some Icelandic verbs select indicative complement clauses whereas others select subjunctive clauses. It is roughly non-factive verbs of saying, believing etc. that take subjuntive clauses whereas (semi-)factive verbs of knowing, seeing etc. require the indicative: (a) *Jón segir að tunglið sé/*er úr osti* 'John says that the moon is (subj./*ind.) made of cheese' (lit. 'John says that moon-the be (subj.) of cheese') vs (b) *Jón veit að tunglið *sé/er úr osti* 'John knows that the moon is (*subj./ind.) made of cheese'. Note also that in sentences with embedded subjunctive clauses we get the phenomenon known in traditional grammars as the 'sequence of tenses': the tense of the matrix verb determines the tense of the embedded subjunctive verb: (a) *Jón segir að tunglið sé/*væri úr osti* 'John says that the moon is (pres./*pret.) made of cheese' (lit. 'John says that the moon be/*were ...') vs (b) *Jón sagði að tunglið *sé/væri úr osti* 'John said that the moon is (*pres./pret.) made of cheese' (lit. 'John said that the moon *be/were ...'). This does not hold for subordinate indicative clauses: (a) *Jón veit að Haraldur er/var heima* 'John knows that Harold is/was at home' vs (b) *Jón vissi að Haraldur er/var heima* 'John knew that Harold is/was at home'.

With a few verbs or predicates it is possible to select either subjunctive or indicative in the complement clause: *Jón las það í blaðinu að María hafði/hefði komið heim* 'John read it in the paper that Mary had (ind./subj.) come home'. The two possibilities are not synonymous, however, since the truth of the indicative clause is presupposed whereas it is not if the subjunctive is selected. Hence one can continue with *en hún kom ekki heim* 'but she didn't come home' if the subjunctive is selected, but not if the indicative is.

Indirect questions are introduced by *hv*-words. The subjunctive is typically used in the complements of verbs of asking whereas the indicative is found in the complements of knowing, understanding, etc. In the subjunctive clauses we get the same phenomenon of sequence of tenses as illustrated for the *að*-clauses above, but not in the indicative clauses: (a) *María spurði hvort* *hákarlinn *sé/væri góður* 'Mary asked (pret.) whether the shark was (*pres./ pret./subj.) good' vs (b) *María veit ekki hver hefur/hafði sett músina í baðkerið* 'Mary doesn't know who has (pres./pret. ind.) put the mouse in the bathtub' (lit. 'Mary knows not who has . . .'). Note that it is not possible in indirect questions introduced by a *hv*-pronoun to add any sort of a complementizer or an extra element after the *hv*-word: *María veit ekki hver *að/*sem hefur gert þetta* (lit. 'Mary knows not who that has done this').

Relative clauses are introduced by the relative complementizers *sem* 'that' or *er* 'that', the latter being more formal and not used in colloquial speech. There is no regular relative pronoun in Modern Icelandic (see the section on the inflection of pronouns above, p. 157). Relative clauses contain a gap that normally cannot be filled with any kind of a (resumptive) pronoun: *þetta er konan sem ég talaði við (*hana) í gær* 'this is the woman that I spoke (ind.) to (*her) yesterday'. There are no special requirements as to tenses and moods in relative clauses as such. Note, however, that if the relative clause is a part of a subjunctive complement, we can get the subjunctive inside it: *Haraldur sagði að það væri María sem hefði gert þetta* 'Harold said that it was (pret. subj.) Mary that had (pret. subj.) done this'.

Finally, there are a number of adverbial clause types that can occur as adjuncts. These are customarily divided into semantically based classes such as temporal clauses, conditional clauses, etc., with each class having its typical set of conjunctions. Some of these conjunctions require a subjunctive in the adverbial clauses whereas others do not: (a) *Jón fer ekki ef þú ferð/ *farir líka* 'John doesn't go if you go (ind./*subj.) too' vs (b) *Jón fer ekki nema þú *ferð/farir líka* 'John doesn't go unless you go (*ind./subj.) too'.

The general rule is that the verb-second order is observed in embedded clauses in Icelandic (not counting the complementizer or the subordinating conjunction). In that respect there is no difference in word order between main clauses and subordinate clauses in Icelandic (as opposed to the mainland Scandinavian languages and German, for example): (a) *Haraldur hefur aldrei/*aldrei hefur borðað hákarl* 'Harold has never/*never has eaten shark' vs (b) *María segir að Haraldur hafi aldrei/*aldrei hafi borðað hákarl* 'Mary says that Harold has never/*never has eaten shark'. If we assume that the *hv*-word in indirect questions is 'outside' the clause itself, like a conjunction for instance, we can also say that the verb-second order holds in embedded questions in Icelandic: (a) *María spurði hvort Haraldur hefði aldrei borðað hákarl* 'Mary asked whether Harold had never eaten shark'; (b) *María spurði hvað Haraldur hefði aldrei borðað* 'Mary asked what Harold had never eaten'.

Topicalization is also possible within embedded clauses of various types. It varies from one type to another, however, being easiest in *að*-clauses and certain adverbial clauses (such as concessive clauses introduced by *þótt* 'although' and various adverbial clauses introduced by an adverb or PP + *að*) but being virtually impossible in relative clauses, temporal clauses introduced by *þegar* 'when' and indirect questions introduced by interrogative pronouns. Consider the following, for instance: *María segir að **Harald** elski hún mest* 'Mary says that Harold she loves the most'; *Stína sagði að bókin í heild væri frekar leiðinleg þótt **einstaka kafla** gæti hún hugsað sér að lesa aftur* 'Stína said that the book as a whole was rather boring although individual chapters she could think of reading again'; **hann sagðist eiga bíl sem **mér** gæti hann selt* (lit. 'he said that he had a car that me he could sell'; ?**Skúli ætlar að taka sér langt frí þegar **ritgerðinni** verður hann búinn að skila* (lit. 'Skúli intends to take a long vacation when the thesis he has turned in'); **ég spurði Stínu hverjum **þessa bók** hefðum við getað gefið* 'I asked Stína whom this book we could have given'. This indicates that structural properties of clauses are not sufficient to determine whether topicalization will be acceptable within them and that semantic or pragmatic aspects must play a role.

Now note that in embedded clauses that contain a subject gap, such as relative clauses or interrogative clauses or adverbial clauses with impersonal passives or where the (indefinite) logical subject is in non-initial position, etc., it is normally possible to prepose past participles, adjectives, adverbs or particles. This phenomenon is usually referred to as *stylistic fronting* since it is largely confined to literary style. It is even acceptable in the types of clauses where regular topicalization seems impossible, as illustrated in these examples (compare attempted topicalization above): *hann spurði hver **selt** hefði mér bílinn* 'he asked who had sold me the car' (lit. 'he asked who sold had me the car'); *það fór að rigna þegar **farið** var af stað* 'it began to rain when people left' (lit. 'it began to rain when gone was from place'); *þetta er keppandinn sem **líklegastur** er til að vinna* 'this is the contestant who is most likely to win' (lit. 'this is contestant-the who likeliest is to win'). Stylistic fronting also occurs in main clauses, most typically in news report style: *talið hefur verið að maðurinn sé njósnari* 'it has been believed that the man is a spy' (lit. 'believed has been that...'). It has been argued that there is an accessibility hierarchy involved here of roughly the following sort: *ekki* > predicate adjective > past participle/verbal particle. This means that if the relevant clause contains more than one preposable element the negation (*ekki* 'not') is selected over the other types, if there is no negation the predicate adjective is next in rank, etc.

It is in general easy to topicalize out of *að*-complement clauses, even the subjects of these. Topicalization is also possible out of (certain types of) interrogative clauses but in general impossible out of relative clauses and adverbial clauses: (a) *Haraldur held ég að hafi aldrei komið hingað* (lit. 'Harold (nom.) think I that has never been here'); (b) *Guðmund veit ég ekki hvort María hefur nokkurn tíma hitt* 'Gudmundur (acc.) I don't know whether Mary has ever met'; (c) **hringinn er þetta maðurinn sem María gaf* (lit. 'ring-the (acc.) is this man-the that Mary gave'); (d) **Guðmund var ég þar þegar þú hittir* (lit. 'Gudmundur (acc.) was I there when you met'). Note in connection with the (a) example that it is by no means necessary to leave out the *að*-complementizer, although the *að* can sometimes be left out in the complements of verbs, especially right after the finite matrix verb when a pronominal subject immediately follows the complementizer position: *ég held (að) þú megir fullyrða það* 'I think (that) you can claim that'; *hún veit (að) hann hefur gert þetta áður* 'she knows (that) he has done this before'.

Infinitival Constructions
Most modal verbs select infinitival complements. Some of these have the so-called infinitival marker *að*, even when they are used as auxiliaries, whereas others do not (see above, p. 173): *það mun rigna á morgun* 'it will rain tomorrow'; *það kann að rigna á morgun* 'it may rain tomorrow' (lit. 'it may to rain on morning'); *það vill oft rigna mikið í Reykjavík* 'it tends to rain a lot in Reykjavík' (lit. 'it wants frequently rain a lot ...'); *það hlýtur að rigna mikið á Amazonsvæðinu* 'it must rain a lot in the Amazon area'. Most of the modal verbs select *að*-infinitives (*munu* 'will', *skulu* 'shall', *mega* 'may', *vilja* 'want' are the exceptions) and so do 'aspectual' verbs like *vera* 'be (progressive)', *fara* 'be going to', *byrja* 'begin', *hætta* 'stop'. All of these have auxiliary-like properties in their epistemic sense but not in the root sense (see above, p. 174).

Typical control verbs, on the other hand, like *reyna* 'try', *lofa* 'promise', *hóta* 'threaten' and *skipa* 'order' for instance, do not have the auxiliary-like properties of modal verbs. They invariably select the *að*-infinitive. Interestingly, we find the same order of verb and sentence adverbial in the infinitival complements of these verbs as we find in finite complement clauses (i.e. with the verb preceding the sentence adverbial) but not in the complements of modal verbs (the definition of modal verb assumed here being 'a verb that has root sense and epistemic sense'): *ég lofa að berja aldrei konuna mína* 'I promise never to beat my wife' (lit. 'I promise to beat never wife-the my') vs **ég ætla að berja aldrei konuna mína* (lit. 'I intend to beat never wife-the my'). Also note that it is totally impossible in Icelandic to insert the adverb between the infinitival *að* and the verb, although comparable placement of adverbs is possible in some other Scandinavian languages: **ég lofa að aldrei berja konuna mína* (lit. 'I promise to never hit wife-the my').

The so-called 'Raising' (or Accusative with Infinitive (ACI) or Exceptional Case Marking (ECM) or NP-movement) infinitives, on the other hand, never have the infinitival marker: (a) *ég tel Harald (*að) hafa kysst Maríu of harkalega* 'I believe Harold (acc.) (*to) have kissed Mary too violently'; (b) *Haraldur virðist (*að) hafa kysst Maríu of harkalega* 'Harold (nom.) seems (*to) have kissed Mary too violently'. Note that in the subject-to-object (or exceptional case marking) example in (a), the logical subject of the infinitive, namely *Harald*, has the accusative case as if it were the object of the verb *telja* 'believe'. Note further that a matrix-oriented adverbial modifier can follow *Harald* in sentences of this sort, suggesting that *Harald* is in some sense part of the matrix clause: *Haraldur taldi mig í barnaskap sínum hafa étið* *hákarlinn* 'Harold believed me in his foolishness to have eaten the shark'.

Að-infinitives can also be complements of prepositions, as can finite clauses. Thus we have pairs like the following: *ég vonast til þess* 'I hope for that (gen.)' vs *ég vonast til að fá peninga á morgun* 'I hope to get money tomorrow' (lit. 'I hope for to get money on morning'); *hann er gráðugur í þetta* 'he is eager for this (acc.)' vs *hann er gráðugur í að fara* 'he is eager to go' (lit. 'he is eager for to go'); *hann var að hugsa um ferðina* 'he was thinking about the trip' vs *hann var að hugsa um að hann gæti farið* (lit.) 'he was thinking about (it) that he could go' vs *hann var að hugsa um að fara* 'he was thinking about going' (lit. 'he was thinking about to go'). The infinitive in the last example corresponds to a participial or gerundial construction in English, there being no gerunds in Icelandic.

Negation

The adverbial *ekki* 'not' is the normal negation in Icelandic. As a sentence negation it typically occupies the position right after the finite verb as many sentential adverbs do. If there is no auxiliary verb in the sentence the negation can, however, follow the object of the finite verb, especially if the verb is a ditransitive one. This holds for some other sentential adverbs too: (a) *María gaf ekki Haraldi/Haraldi ekki bókina* 'Mary didn't give Harold the book' (lit. 'Mary gave not Harold/Harold not the book'); (b) *hann sá ekki bílinn/bílinn ekki* 'he didn't see the car' (lit. 'he saw not car-the/car-the not'). The first order in example (a) seems to be more marked in the sense that it would probably mainly be used with a contrastive function: not Harold but somebody else (corrective negation). It is difficult to find any such difference between the two orders in example (b).

The word *neinn* '(not) any' is restricted to negative contexts whereas *enginn* 'no (one)' and *einhver* 'some' are used in positive or neutral contexts: *ég á engan/*neinn bíl* 'I have no/* any car' vs *ég á ekki neinn bíl* 'I don't have any car' vs *ég á ekki engan bíl* 'I do not have no car' (= 'It is not the case that I have no car'); *átt þú einhverjar/*neinar málfræðibækur?* 'do you have some/*not any linguistics books?' *nei, ég ekki *einhverjar/neinar* 'no, I do not have *some/any'.

As an affirmative answer to a negative question Icelandic uses the word *jú* whereas *nei* 'no' is a negative answer. The normal *já* 'yes' is used as an answer to positive questions. This system is rather similar to that found in German (*doch* vs *ja*) and the mainland Scandinavian languages (*jo* vs *ja*) but rather different from the Old Icelandic one.

6.5   Lexis

The Modern Icelandic lexicon is relatively free of unassimilated loanwords. Although this aspect is sometimes exaggerated in reports on Icelandic and the language contains a number of loanwords and slang expressions, it is nevertheless true that there is a strong and conscious effort to create new words from Icelandic material for new concepts, for example in science and technology. Many professional societies have their own language committees that meet regularly to discuss proposed neologisms in the field or to try to come up with new ones. These committees will then make word lists and even publish dictionaries, sometimes with the help of *Íslensk málnefnd* (The Icelandic Language Committee). Recent dictionaries of this kind include dictionaries of technical terms related to computers and data processing, psychology, medicine etc.

The methods used in coining new words include translation of the foreign word bit by bit, compounding of existing nouns, derivation by productive derivational suffixes, creation of new roots and assimilation of foreign words to the Icelandic sound and inflectional systems. Sometimes old words are also given new meanings.

Interestingly, only some of the inflectional classes accept new words. For nouns it is mainly these: (i) strong masculine nouns in #-r#, gen. sg. #-s#, nom. pl. #-ar#; (ii) weak masculine nouns in #-i#, nom. pl. #-ar# (quite common); (iii) strong feminine nouns without a nominative singular ending plural either #-ar# or #-ir# (rather infrequent); (iv) weak feminine nouns in #-a# (quite common); (v) strong neuter nouns (quite common). Almost all new verbs add /-a/ to the stem and thus join class 4 of weak verbs.

The following list will give some ideas of the kinds of new words (or new meanings to old words) introduced in the twentieth century: *sími* (m.) 'telephone' (< *síma* (n.) 'thread'); *tölva* (f.) 'computer' (< *tala* 'number'); *útvarp* (n.) 'radio' (*út-* meaning 'out', *-varp* being related to the verb *varpa* 'throw, cast'); *skjár* (m.) 'screen' (originally an old-fashioned window); *eyðni* (f.) 'AIDS' (based on the phonology of the international word but with reference to the Icelandic verb *eyða* 'deplete, destroy', hence the spelling).

The assimilation of foreign words to the Icelandic language invariably involves putting the stress on the first syllable. Thus familiar nouns like *stúdent* and *prófessor* have initial stress and plurals in #-ar#: *stúdentar*, *prófessorar*.

The colloquial language uses a lot of semantically vague 'modal' particles. They usually come immediately after the finite verb and before any sentential adverbs that might occur in the sentence. They can never be preposed or topicalized: (the position of the modal particle is indicated by X in the English translation when no obvious translation offered itself) *hann hefur **nú** aldrei séð Chomsky* 'he has X never seen Chomsky'; *ég ætla **sko** ekki að fara þangað aftur* 'I intend X never to go there again'; *þau hafa **víst** lengi búið saman* 'they have reportedly lived together for a long time'; *þeir verða **jú** áreiðanlega á* *móti þessu* 'they will X certainly be against this'. The last one may be a loan from Danish and hence it is frequently frowned upon by Icelandic language purists.

Finally, observe the following distinction between *þar* and *þarna*: *ég hef aldrei verið þar áður* 'I have never been there before' vs *sérðu stólinn þarna?* 'do you see the chair over there?'. Here the form *þar* 'there' refers to a place that has been mentioned before whereas *þarna* 'there' is used deictically. The form *þar* could not be so used. Among other pairs that show the same morphological distinction one could mention *hér – hérna* 'here', *svo – svona* 'so', *nú – núna* 'now' but here the semantic distinction is much less clear.

Further Reading

For reasons of space, this bibliography only lists books on Icelandic and not papers. For further references the reader is referred to bibliographies in these books, especially in Maling and Zaenen (1990).

Árnason, K. (1980) *Quantity in Historical Phonology: Icelandic and Related Cases*, Cambridge: Cambridge University Press.

Benediktsson, H. (1972) *The First Grammatical Treatise*, Reykjavík: Institute of Nordic Linguistics.

Chapman, K. G. (1962) *Icelandic-Norwegian Linguistic Relationships*, Oslo: Universitetsforlaget.

Einarsson, S. (1949) *Icelandic, Grammar, Texts, Glossary*, 2nd edn, Baltimore: Johns Hopkins Press.

Guðmundsson, H. (1972) *The Pronominal Dual in Icelandic*, Reykjavík: Institute of Nordic Linguistics.

Holmberg, A. (1986) *Word Order and Syntactic Features in the Scandinavian Languages and English*, doctoral thesis, Stockholm: University of Stockholm.

Kress, B. (1982) *Isländische Grammatik*, Munich: Hueber.

Magnússon, F. (1990) *Kjarnafærsla og það-innskot í aukasetningum í íslensku*, Reykjavík: Málvísindastofnun Háskóla Íslands.

Maling, J. and Zaenen, A. (eds) (1990) *Modern Icelandic Syntax*, Syntax and Semantics 24, San Diego: Academic Press.

Ottósson, K. G. (1992) *The Icelandic Middle Voice: The Morphological and Phonological Development*, doctoral thesis, Lund: University of Lund.

Pétursson, M. (1978) *Les Articulations de l'islandais à la lumière de la radio-cinématographie*, Paris: Klincksieck.

Rögnvaldsson, E. (1990) *Íslensk orðhlutafræði: Kennslukver handa nemendum á háskólastigi*, Reykjavík: Málvísindastofnun Háskóla Íslands.

Sigurðsson, H. Á. (1989) *Verbal Syntax and Case in Icelandic in a Comparative GB Approach*, doctoral thesis, Lund: University of Lund.

Thráinsson, H. (1979) *On Complementation in Icelandic*, New York: Garland.

Zaenen, A. (1985) *Extraction Rules in Icelandic*, New York: Garland.

7 Faroese

Michael P. Barnes, with Eivind Weyhe

7.1 Introduction

Faroese is derived from the language of Norse (probably mainly Norwegian) settlers who established themselves in the islands in the ninth century. Owing to the virtual absence of Viking Age and medieval sources, little is known about the development of this language in pre-Reformation times. After the Reformation and until 1948 Danish was the official medium, and nothing of substance was written in Faroese before the 1770s, by which time most of the features associated with the modern language must have developed. Lack of official status in the post-Reformation period has had a number of consequences for Faroese. Speech is for the most part dialectally based and is heavily influenced by Danish, especially at the lexical level. The written language, in contrast, is relatively homogeneous and very puristic. Its orthography, established in the middle of the nineteenth century, owes much to Old Norse and something to Icelandic, and these languages have also had a certain influence on the morphology, syntax and lexicon of written Faroese. As in Icelandic, the lexicon is replete with neologisms, but many of these are used only in writing, the spoken language preferring Danish-derived equivalents. Although virtually every Faroese village has its own characteristic form of speech, mutual comprehension is no problem, and the capital, Tórshavn, where a sizeable proportion of the population now lives, has become something of a linguistic melting pot. It is not impossible that with time a spoken standard will develop based on Tórshavn speech. For the present chapter, the wide degree of variation in Faroese has necessitated the adoption of a somewhat abstract approach: by and large the description is based on those forms and features which are perceived to have the widest currency.

7.2 Phonology

Faroese has the same syllabic structure as most other forms of Scandinavian except Danish. In lexical pronunciation stressed syllables are long (V:, V:C, VC: or VCC – note, however, the clusters /pl, pr, tr, kl, kr/, where the preceding vowel is long) and unstressed are short. In the majority of its features Faroese phonology is firmly West Scandinavian. Especially striking are developments in the vowel system. Following the quantity shift whereby all stressed syllables became long – which in Faroese mostly involved the lengthening of short vowels – nearly all the original long vowels and ultimately one of the lengthened short vowels were diphthongized. This parallels similar if on the whole less radical developments in Icelandic and west and central Norwegian dialects. The West Scandinavian character of Faroese phonology otherwise will be apparent from details in the following description.

Vowels

The vowel system of Faroese, based on the most common distinctions, is given in Table 7.1. Different analyses are possible. Attempts have been made to present length as allophonic, but the corollary seems to be that length in consonants must then be regarded as phonemic, so little is gained in the way of economy. Some have considered the eight diphthongs as manifestations of long vowel phonemes, which certainly simplifies the system, but entails a fair degree of abstraction. For present purposes, Table 7.1 on its own is already too abstract since it disguises the considerable difference in quality which exists between long and short monophthongs. This is remedied in Table 7.2, which presents the vowel system in a broadish phonetic transcription. To aid comprehension of the remainder of this section, the principal Old Norse sources of the tonic and post-tonic vowels are also indicated (the pre-tonic vowel qualities given here exist mainly in words of foreign origin).

There are a number of points to be noted about the Faroese vowel system. The long monophthongs [iː, uː, eː, øː, oː] are in free variation with a slightly diphthongal pronunciation, roughly [iːj, uːw, eːe, øːœ, oːo]. In words of foreign origin [aː] and [ʏː] may be found, e.g. *statur* 'state', *myta* 'myth', and these are regarded by some as allophones of /ea/ and /yu/ respectively. When followed immediately by post-tonic /a/, /ea/ is realized as [eː], [ẹː], [ɛː] or [ɛɪ], and /oa/ as [oː], [ọː], [ɔː] or [ɔu], e.g. *hagar* [hẹːar] 'hither', *fáa* [fọːa] '(to) get'. The sequences /ev/, /øv/, /ov/, /av/ tend to have diphthongal pronunciation before /n/, especially the last, e.g. *havn* [haun] 'harbour'. Neither /eː/ nor /oː/

Table 7.1 Vowel phonemes of Faroese

Tonic						Pre-tonic				Post-tonic		
iː	i		y	uː	u	i		u		i		u
	eː	e	øː	ø	oː	o	e	o				
				a				a			a	
ui	ei	oi	ai									
yu	ou	ea	oa									

Table 7.2   The vowels of Faroese in phonetic transcription together with their Old Norse sources

	Tonic		
iː (<i,y)			uː (<u)
ɪ (<i,y)		ʏ (<uː)	ʊ (<u)
eː (<e)		øː (<øː,ø,ɔ)	oː (<o)
ɛ (<e,au)		œ (<øː,ø,ɔ,oː)	ɔ (<o,aː,ɔː)
		a (<a,æː,eː)	
ʊɪ (<iː,yː)	ɔ^I (<øy)	ɔu (<oː)	
ʊ^I (<iː,yː)	aɪ (<ei)	ɛa (<a,æː,eː)	
ɛɪ (<au)	a^I (<ei)	ɔa (<aː,ɔː)	
ɔɪ (<øy)	ʉu (<uː)		

Pre-tonic			Post-tonic	
i		u	ɪ (<ɪ)	ʊ (<ʊ)
e	o			
a			a (<a)	

normally appears before post-tonic /a/, the pronunciation being [iː] and [uː] respectively, e.g. *mega* [miːja] 'must (pl.)', *noða* [nuːa] 'ball of yarn'. Neutralization of phonemic contrasts has been identified elsewhere too, but in most such cases it is hard to disentangle phonemic, morphophonemic, and historical considerations. A basically historical perspective is adopted for present purposes since it provides the clearest and most informative exposition. The short diphthongs [ʊ^I], [ɔ^I], and [a^I] are monophthongized before certain consonants: [ʊ^I] > [ʊ] before [ɟ], [ɽ], [ʂ], [ʃ], and, sometimes, [g] and [k], e.g. *lýggi* [lʊɟːɪ] 'scythe', *írskur* [ʊʂkʊr] 'Irish', *líknandi* [lʊknandɪ] 'similar'; [ɔ^I] > [ɔ] before [ɟ], [ɽ], and, sometimes, [g] and [k], e.g. *oyggj* [ɔɟː] 'island', *moyrkna* [mɔɽtna] '(to) rot', *roykti* [rɔktɪ] 'smoked (sg. past)'; [a^I] > [a] or [ɔ] (the variation is partly dialectal, partly free) before [ɟ], [ɲɟ], and [ɲc], e.g. *deiggj* [daɟː] 'dough', *eingin* [ɔɲɟɪn] 'no one'. Old Norse /a/ > /e/ before [ŋg], [ŋ̊k], [ɲɟ], and [ɲc], e.g. *langur* [lɛŋgʊr] 'long', *banki* [bɛɲcɪ] 'knock (1 sg. pres.)'; apart from the cases where [a^I] is monophthongized to [a], it is only in loanwords (usually of Danish origin) that we find the sequences [aŋg], [aŋ̊k], [aɲɟ], and [aɲc], e.g. *sangur* [saŋgʊr] 'song', *banki* [baɲcɪ] 'bank'. Old Norse /uː/ > /i/ and /oː/ > /e/ before (intercalated) /gv/, e.g. *kúgv* [kɪgv] 'cow', *gjógv* [ɟɛgv] 'rock-cleft'.

As is clear from Table 7.1, the pre-tonic and post-tonic vowel systems have far fewer contrasts than the tonic. The five-way pre-tonic system is realized as [i, u, e, o, a], e.g. *mirakul* [miˈrɛakʊl] 'miracle', *studentur* [stuˈdɛn̪tʊr] 'student', *metal* [meˈtaːl] 'metal', *politistur* [polɪˈtɪstʊr] 'policeman', *barbarur* [barˈbaːrʊr] 'barbarian'. The three-way post-tonic system, found in derivative suffixes and above all in inflectional endings, is in theory realized as [ɪ, ʊ, a], but the distribution of [ɪ] and [ʊ] varies greatly from dialect to dialect (nowhere does it follow the distribution of the written language). In some dialects post-tonic /i/ and /u/ have completely or almost completely coalesced, leading to considerable variety in their realization. In its treatment of the post-tonic vowels Faroese contrasts sharply with Icelandic, which, alone of all the Scandinavian languages, consistently maintains the three-way system of Old Norse.

Owing partly to the vowel variations caused by ablaut, mutation and breaking, and partly to the differentiation of the Old Norse vowel system, morphophonemic relations in Faroese can be extremely complex. As many as five phonemes (or phonemes and allophones) may be found in the root of some words, e.g. *kúgv* /kigv/ 'cow', nom./acc. pl. *kýr* /kuir/, def. dat. sg. *kúnni* /kyni/, def. dat. pl. *kúnum* /kyunun/; *dagur* /deavur/ 'day', gen. sg. *dags* /dags/, dat. sg. *degi* /deːji/, nom./acc. pl. *dagar* [dɛːar], dat. pl. *døgum* /døːvun/; *síggja* [suɟːa] '(to) see', 2 sg. pres. *sært* /sart/, 3 sg. pres. *sær* /sear/, 1 and 3 sg. past *sá* /soa/, pl. past *sóu* /souvu/.

Consonants

The consonant inventory of Faroese is given in Table 7.3. The following remarks outline the realization of these phonemes in various phonological environments. The plosives /p, t, k/ are unvoiced and tense; in lexical pronunciation they are aspirated before a stressed vowel and may also be so intervocalically. When preceded by /s/ they are unaspirated, as they often are intervocalically and in connected speech. /b, d, g/ are voiced, lax and unaspirated; however, the voicing is at best weak and sometimes absent (especially in word- or sentence-final position – but that is a characteristic of most voiced consonants). In connected speech the tense–lax distinction is often neutralized as well. A further complication is the fact that in the southern and northern extremities of the Faroes and to some extent in the Tórshavn area /p, t, k/ in intervocalic and post-vocalic position are realized as [b, d, g] or [b̥ d̥, g̊] in all cases. No wholly satisfactory account of the relationship between

Table 7.3 Consonant phonemes of Faroese

	Labial	Dental	Palatal	Velar	Glottal
Plosive	p b	t d		k g	
Fricative	f v	s	ʃ j		h
Affricate			c ɟ		
Nasal	m	n		ŋ	
Lateral		l			
Rolled		r			

these two series of plosives has yet been given. The status of /ŋ/ is not entirely clear. Mostly it appears before /g/ and is therefore regarded by many as an allophone of /n/; however, it may also be followed by other consonants, e.g. *longd* 'length', which is pronounced [lɔŋd̥] or [lɔŋᵍd̥]. Palatal allophones of /l/ and /n/ occur between diphthongs with a palatal second element and a consonant, and before /c/ and /ɟ/, e.g. *hvíld* [kvuˡʎd] 'rest', *tangi* [tɛɲɟɪ] 'tongue (of land)'. Where /t, d, s, n, l/ immediately follow /r/ they are often realized as retroflexes, as in central Swedish and Norwegian, e.g. *gjørdi* [ɟœrɖɪ] 'made (sg. past)', *mars* [maʂ] 'March'. The extent to which /r/ is realized as a separate segment in such cases varies, but the sequence /rs/ is usually [ʂ]. Sometimes retroflexion may affect more than one consonant, e.g. *menninir standa* [ˈmɛnːɪnɪˌʂʈanda] 'the men stand'. Faroese /r/ may be realized in a variety of ways from a full rolled [r] to a virtually frictionless continuant [ɹ]. The most common pronunciation in ordinary speech seems to be fricative [ɹ], but [r] is regularly heard before a stressed vowel, especially after /p, t, k/. In the phonetic transcription here, only [r] is used. Most voiced consonants may be unvoiced when immediately preceding or following an unvoiced sound, but the variation is regular for /g, m, n, ŋ, l, r, v/ between a vowel and /p, t, k, s, c/, and marginally /f/, in the same syllable. The distinction /k/ : /g/ and /f/ : /v/ is thus neutralized in this position. Examples are: *lagt* [lakt] 'laid (pp.)', *lampa* [lampa] 'lamp', *ansa* [aṇsa] '(to) look after', *banki* [bɛɲcɪ] 'knock (1 sg. pres.)', *banka* [bɛŋka] '(to) knock', *alt* [alt] 'all (nom./acc. n. sg.)', *heilsa* [haˡʎsa] '(to) greet', *lurta* [luɹʈa] '(to) listen', *skeivt* [skaˡft] 'wrong (nom./acc. n. sg.)'; note also *langt* [lɛŋkt], [lɛɲt] nominative/accusative neuter singular of *langur* [lɛŋgʊr] 'long'. Between vowels /v/ may be realized as [v], [ʋ], or [w]; the last occurs after /u, yu, ou/. In common with their Icelandic counterparts, Faroese [pː, tː, kː] are pre-aspirated; pre-aspiration also occurs before [cː] and sporadically before /p, t, k/

Figure 7.1   The development of Faroese palatalization

Note: 1 The front vowels concerned are specified in the text. Length, except in the source form, is left out of consideration.

+ certain consonants. Neither this nor post-aspiration is marked in the phonetic transcription used here.

Considerable changes (most of which can be paralleled in other forms of West Scandinavian) separate the consonant system of Modern Faroese from its Old Norse source. As in all the Scandinavian languages except Danish (where the process was reversed), there has been extensive palatalization. The velars /k(ː), g(ː)/ and the cluster /sk/ developed palatal variants before the high and mid front vowels /i/, /y/ (if this had not already coalesced with /i/), /e/ and the diphthong which developed from /au/ (Modern Faroese /ei/), and these gradually coalesced with other palatal clusters as depicted in Figure 7.1. The two affricates which resulted are found not just in initial position (as is the case with the products of palatalization in many other forms of Scandinavian, including standard Norwegian and Swedish), but also medially, and they are regularly triggered by inflexional endings or suffixes, e.g. nom. sg. *bak* [bɛak] : dat. sg. *baki* [bɛacɪ] 'back'; nom. sg. *veggur* [vɛɡːʊr] : dat. sg. *veggi* [vɛɟːɪ] 'wall'; *bók* [bɔuk] 'book' : *bókin* [bɔucɪn] 'the book'. The reflex of Old Norse /sk/ in such cases is [sc], e.g. *elska* [ɛl̩ska] '(to) love' : *elski* [ɛl̩scɪ] 'love (1 sg. pres.)'. A system of glides has developed to fill the hiatuses which existed in Old Norse or which arose through the loss of intervocalic [ð] and [ɣ]: /j/ is found in palatal environment and /v/ in labial, realized as [w] following /uː, yu, ou/ and [v] elsewhere. Examples are: *áir* [ɔajɪr] 'streams (nom./acc. pl.)', *deyður* [dɛɪjʊr] 'dead', *vegi* [veːjɪ] 'road (dat. sg.)', *bøur* [bøːvʊr] 'infield', *maður* [mɛavʊr] 'man', *lágum* [lɔavʊn] 'low (dat. pl.)', *sóu* [sɔuwʊ] 'saw (pl. past)', *góður* [ɡɔuwʊr] 'good', *dugir* [duːwɪr] 'manages'. Neither [ð] nor [ɣ] survived in Faroese: in final post-vocalic position as well as between mid and low vowels they were normally lost without trace or replacement; sometimes they were assimilated to immediately following consonants or changed their manner and place of articulation in another way, e.g. *kvøða* [kvøːa] '(to) chant', *eg* [eː] 'I', *maðkur* [makːʊr] 'grub (noun)', *veðrið* [vɛɡrɪ] 'the weather', *drignan* [drɪdnan] 'pulled (pp. acc. m. sg.)'. As universally in Scandinavian outside Icelandic [θ] > /t/; in certain pronouns and adverbs, and compounds with *Þór-* as the first element, [θ] > /h/, a development closely paralleled in several Scandinavian dialects including Orkney and Shetland Norn. Common to Faroese and Norn is also the change /m/ > /n/ in dative endings, e.g. *tveimum óm* /tvaimun oun/ 'two ewes', *søgunum* /søvunun/ 'the stories'. Several of the consonantal developments that affected Faroese are found in all or virtually all West Scandinavian dialects, including Icelandic (though the products may be realized in slightly different ways). This is the case with /hu/ > /kv/ and /lː/ > /dl/, to which there are few exceptions in Faroese, with /nː/ > /dn/, which occurs almost exclusively after /oi/ and /ai/, and with /rn/ > /dn/ and /rl/ > /dl/, to which there are numerous exceptions, most notably the definite nominative/accusative plural, where normally only /n/ is heard, and syncopated past participle forms, where the pronunciation is still /rn/, e.g. *bátarnir* /boatanir/ 'the boats', *farnir* /farnir/ 'gone (nom. m. pl.)'.

Stress and Related Matters

Phonologically there seems no reason to distinguish more than two degrees of stress, and in the above the terms 'stressed' and 'unstressed' have been used. Phonetically it is useful to distinguish four degrees: primary, strong secondary, weak secondary, and zero stress. Strong secondary stress is the norm in the first syllable of the second element of a compound. A four-syllable word like *fjallatindin* 'the mountain top (acc. sg.)' – a particularly common type – is pronounced ['fjadla,tındın] with zero stress on the second and weak secondary or zero stress on the final syllable. In most native words, primary stress falls on the initial syllable. In common with the mainland Scandinavian languages, however, but unlike Icelandic, Faroese does allow primary stress elsewhere, chiefly in words of foreign origin, where it is not restricted to any particular syllables, and in native words and Danish loans with certain prefixes, where it can be located in the second. Examples are: *politi* [polɪ'tiː] 'police', *studentur* [stu'dɛn̩tʊr] 'student', *ófatiligur* [ˌɔu'fɛatɪˌliːjʊr] 'incomprehensible', *forstanda* [fɔr'ʂtanda] '(to) understand'. Compound adverbs, of which there are many in Faroese, also regularly have primary stress on syllables other than the first, e.g. *framvið* [fram'viː] 'past', *afturfyri* [atʊr'fiːrı] 'in return'. Stress-linked tones, as found in many varieties of Norwegian and Swedish, do not occur in Faroese.

Other Phonological Points

A number of external sandhi forms are found in Faroese, most notably the retroflexion of /t, d, s, n, l/ when they follow final /r/, e.g. *ger so væl!* [ɟeːʂoːveal] 'here you are!', *ber neyðarrópini* [beːrɳɛɪjarɔupını] 'carries the cries of distress'; cf. also *ov mikið* ['ɔmːiːcɪ] 'too big (nom./acc. n. sg.)', *at gera við tað* [a'ɟeːra'vɪtːa] 'to do (something) about it'. Like virtually all forms of Scandinavian, Faroese does not easily tolerate large consonant clusters. Where such would otherwise arise, one of the consonants is usually lost, e.g. *fylgdi* 'followed (sg.)', *fygldi* 'caught birds (sg.)', both /fildi/, *myrkt* /mirt/ 'dark (nom./acc. n. sg.)'. In the (relatively rare) cases where four consonants might be juxtaposed, they are most often reduced to three, e.g. *sandflundra* [saɱflʊndra] 'plaice', *eingilskt* [aɲɟɪl̩st] 'English (nom./acc. n. sg.)', in special cases to two, e.g. *írskt* [ʊʂt] 'Irish (nom./acc. n. sg.)'. Where /t/ is added to the cluster /sk/ in monosyllables, metathesis normally results, giving /kst/, e.g. *danskt* /daŋkst/ 'Danish', *frískt* /frukst/ 'healthy', both nominative/accusative neuter singular. Length may be lost (a) in compounding; and (b) in connected speech where there is weakened stress, e.g. (a) *húskallur* ['hʏsˌkadlʊr] 'farm-hand' from *hús* [hʉus] 'house' + *kallur* [kadlʊr] 'man', *kinnklovi* ['cɪɱ̊ˌkloːvɪ] 'corner of the mouth' from *kinn* [cɪnː] 'cheek' + *klovi* [kloːvɪ] 'opening'; (b) *nú kunnu tey fara til Havnar* ['nʉukʊnətefaratl̩'haunar] 'now they can go to Tórshavn', with which the lexical forms [nʉu kʊnːʊ tɛɪ fɛara tɪl haunar] can be contrasted.

Orthography

The fact that Faroese orthography is based on Old Norse (in effect on etymological principles) and Icelandic means that the gap between the spoken and written form is considerable. The many new diphthongs are written as though they were still monophthongs, ‹i› is distinguished from ‹y› and ‹í› from ‹ý›, but there are no corresponding differences in speech, ‹ð› is still widely used although [ð] has long since dropped out of the language, ‹g› appears where Old Norse had [ɣ] but Faroese has zero or a glide, /kv/ may be written ‹kv› or ‹hv›, final /n/ regularly appears as ‹m› – and so on. In favour of the current orthography it has been argued first that it enables speakers of other Scandinavian languages to read Faroese more easily and second that it unites the many dialects in a common written form. When Modern Faroese was first written down, a quasi-phonetic approach was adopted, that is, people brought up with Danish (and to a lesser extent Latin and German) spelling habits wrote what they thought they heard. Once the etymological-Icelandic orthography was introduced in the 1840s and 1850s (subsequently refined), this kind of phonetic spelling was abandoned, though various attempts were made around the turn of the century to bring speech and writing into greater harmony. By way of exemplification two ballad stanzas are given, first in the original spelling, then in modern orthography. They are from the 1780s (1) and the 1820s (2) and represent different dialects.

(1)   Drikkjin drak tû Mirman   'Drykkin drakk tú, Mirman,
       aldri bujur tû Beût   aldri bíður tú bót,
       Feârin eer tujn fagri Litur   farin er tín fagri litur
       beâï eâv Hond o Feût   bæði av hond og fót.'

    '"You drank the drink, Mirman, you will never recover, your fair colour has gone both from [your] hand and foot."'

(2)   Hoon toug up ta siurtina   Hon tók upp ta skjúrtuna,
       ædl var uj blouvi drijin   øll var í blóði drigin:
       Heer skal tu sujdgja tej hærklajir 'Her skalt tú síggja tey herklæði,
       qvær uj tujn fajir er vijin   hvarí tín faðir er vigin.'

    'She took up that shirt [which] was all covered in blood: "Here you shall see that armour in which your father was killed."'

7.3 Morphology

Nouns

Faroese has simplified somewhat the inflectional system it inherited from Old Norse, but to nothing like the same degree as the mainland Scandinavian languages. In Old Norse nouns inflected according to stem class, and gender was very much an inherent category. Though inflection by stem class survives in Faroese, there has been a tendency for gender to be given more overt expression; thus most nouns will follow the pattern set out in Table 7.4. The four cases: nominative, accusative, genitive and dative are still distinguished, but nominative and accusative forms have become identical everywhere except in the singular of most masculine nouns and of one feminine stem class, and the genitive has been largely superseded by circumlocutions (see section 7.4). Many nouns have genitive forms only in the written language; the plural -a has all but disappeared as a spoken form and of the singulars only -s is at all common, though -ar may be heard in some set phrases. Where genitives are used in the spoken language, there is a tendency for -s to replace other endings, although in personal names and nouns used as such a new colloquial ending, -sa(r), has developed (see further, section 7.4). Number consists of a singular–plural opposition, as in all Scandinavian languages. In Old Norse most neuter nouns did not have distinct singular and plural forms in the nominative and accusative, but in spoken Faroese one class of this gender has adopted an analogical -r as a plural marker while another has added -r to an existing plural ending. Noun

Table 7.4   The basic noun inflections of Faroese

	Strong Masculine		Strong Feminine		Strong Neuter	
	sg.	pl.	sg.	pl.	sg.	pl.
Nom.	-ur	-Vr	-Ø	-Vr	-Ø	-Ø/-r
Acc.	-Ø	-Vr	-Ø	-Vr	-Ø	-Ø/-r
Gen.	-s/ (-ar)	(-a)	(-ar)	(-a)	-s	(-a)
Dat.	-i/-Ø	-um	-Ø	-um	-i/-Ø	-um

	Weak Masculine		Weak Feminine		Weak Neuter	
	sg.	pl.	sg.	pl.	sg.	pl.
Nom.	-i	-ar	-a	-ur	-a	(-u)/-ur
Acc.	-a	-ar	-u	-ur	-a	(-u)/-ur
Gen.	(-a)	(-a)	(-u)	(-a)	(-a)	(-na)
Dat.	-a	-um	-u	-um	-a	-um

Note: Brackets indicate that the form concerned is found chiefly or exclusively in the written language. V = vowel (i.e. i, u, or a, but see section 7.2, 'Vowels'). The distinction -s/-ar in the genitive masculine singular depends on stem class. The strong dative masculine and neuter -i ending is sometimes omitted, especially where the root of the noun ends in a vowel, and in personal names. Strong neuters ending in -i add no additional -i in the dative singular; like the weak neuters they have -r in the nominative/accusative plural in spoken and less formal kinds of written Faroese; in the genitive and dative plural of this class -i is deleted before -a or -um is added. The root vowel of many nouns changes in different parts of the paradigm according to fixed patterns.

derivation patterns do not differ greatly from those in Old Norse and Icelandic. Derivation by suffix and by compounding are both common (see also section 7.5).

Adjectives and Adverbs

Adjectival inflection too, while preserving the basics of the Old Norse system, has undergone some simplification (see Pronouns, Table 7.6). Adjectives still mostly agree in gender, number and case with the noun phrase they modify, both in attributive and predicative position, and there are still two sets of endings, 'weak' and 'strong' (the choice between which is largely determined by the definiteness or otherwise of the noun phrase, see section 7.4), but genitive forms are seldom found, even in writing, and certain endings have been modified on analogy with others. The strong neuter dative singular ending is now -*um*, just as the masculine, where Old Norse and Icelandic have -*u*; the strong masculine accusative plural is -*ar* (making final -*r* the norm for the nominative and accusative plural of masculine and feminine nouns and strong adjectives), Old Norse/Icelandic -*a*; the weak plural ending is -*u* throughout, as in Icelandic, whereas Old Norse had a weak dative plural in -*um*; of uncertain origin is the -*a*- in the strong feminine dative singular ending -*ari*, Old Norse -*ri*. Adjectives with root vowel -*a*- which end in -*aður* or -*in* (many of them past participles) do not follow the pattern of most others, which modify the -*a*- to -*ø*- or -*o*- in certain parts of the paradigm. One result of this is that the strong feminine nominative singular and strong neuter nominative/accusative singular and plural may have the same form: contrast Faroese *kastað* /kasta/ 'thrown' (the neuter nominative/accusative plural is most often *kastaði* /kastaji/ in the spoken language) with Old Norse *kǫstuð* (nom. f. sg. and nom./acc. n. pl.) and *kastat* (nom./acc. n. sg.) and with Faroese *gomul* 'old' (nom. f. sg. and nom./acc. n. pl.) and *gamalt* (nom./acc. n. sg.). New patterns of inflection have arisen in those adjectives with intercalated /ʝː/ or /gv/ in their roots, owing to the fact that these consonantal extensions have not spread to the forms where an original consonant immediately follows the root vowel, e.g. *nýggjur* 'new', *búgvin* 'ready', nom./acc. n. sg. *nýtt*, dat. m. sg. *búnum*.

Adjectival comparison is made chiefly through the addition of suffixes, -*ar* or -*r* for the comparative, -*ast* or -*st* for the superlative (the second of the two forms usually appears in conjunction with modification of the root vowel). Present participles and adjectives in -*s*, both of which are indeclinable, form their comparative and superlative analytically, as do certain compound adjectives, e.g. *meira fámæltur* 'quieter' (lit. 'more few-spoken'), *mest hóskandi* 'most suitable' (lit. 'most suiting'). Synthetic comparatives have no strong declension, the strong endings being replaced by an invariable -*i*; the weak forms are the same as in the positive. Synthetic superlatives have the normal strong and weak endings.

Adverbs are chiefly formed in Faroese in one of the following three ways: (a) by the addition of the suffix *-liga* to the root of the adjective, or by the changing of the adjectival suffix *-lig* to *-liga*, e.g. *stór-* 'big', *stórliga* 'greatly', *serlig-* 'special', *serliga* '(e)specially'; (b) through use of the strong neuter nominative/accusative singular form of the adjective, e.g. *skjótur* 'quick', *skjótt* 'quickly'; (c) by the addition of *-a* to the root of the adjective, e.g. *ill-* 'bad', *illa* 'badly'. The comparison of adverbs follows the same pattern as the comparison of adjectives. The synthetic forms are *-ari* or *-ri* (in a few words *-ur*), *-ast* or *-st*, e.g. *dúgligari* 'more capably', *tyngst* 'most heavily'.

Pronouns

Syntactically it may sometimes be useful to distinguish between pronouns and determiners in Faroese, but morphologically it makes little sense since all possessive, demonstrative, interrogative, and indefinite pronouns also function as determiners. Only the personal pronouns (third-person plural excepted) are solely pronominal; the relative is best regarded as a particle, since its function is that of complementizer rather than pronoun, but its form will be briefly mentioned here for completeness' sake.

Table 7.5   Personal pronouns

	1 sg.	2 sg.	3 sg. m.	f.	n.
Nom.	eg	tú	hann	hon	tað
Acc.	meg	teg	hann	hana	tað
Gen.	mín	tín	hansara	hennara	tess
Dat.	mær	tær	honum	henni	tí

	1 pl.	2 pl.	3 pl. m.	f.	n.
Nom.	vit	tit	teir	tær	tey
Acc.	okkum	tykkum	teir	tær	tey
Gen.	okkara	tykkara		teirra	
Dat.	okkum	tykkum		teimum	

	3 refl.	2 sg. pol.
Nom.	——	tygum
Acc.	seg	tygum
Gen.	sín	tygara
Dat.	sær	tygum

The personal pronouns alone of the Faroese nominals have retained the full four-case system of Old Norse. The paradigms are set out in Table 7.5. The first- and second-person plural go back to the Old Norse dual. The second-person singular polite form is based on the accusative/dative of the Old Norse second-person plural, *yðr*, with initial /t/ (< /θ/) from the nominative, but otherwise there is little trace in present-day Faroese of the old first- and second-person plurals. As in Old Norse, the third-person plural forms also function as demonstratives, determiners, and as the preposed definite article (see below), e.g. *tey av tykkum* 'those of you', *teir menninir* 'those men', *tær ungu kýrnar* 'the young cows'. If allowance is made for the sound changes that separate Faroese from Old Norse, the only noteworthy developments in the paradigms not so far mentioned are the spread of the pronominal and adjectival dative ending *-um* into the first- and second-person plurals and the third-person dative plural (ON *okkr, ykkr, þeim*), and the addition of *-a* (of uncertain origin) to the genitive forms in *-ar*, as well as the extension of this ending to the third-person masculine singular (ON *hans*). In unstressed position, personal pronouns undergo a number of changes, most notably the regular shortening of vowel or consonant and the frequent loss of initial /h/, e.g. *tað veit eg* [ta'vaɪte] 'I know it', *eg tók hann við* [eˌtɔukan'viː] 'I took him with (me)'. There seems no phonetic justification, however, for positing a class of clitics since the behaviour of these pronouns in connected speech is little different from that of the generality of words.

In common with other Scandinavian languages, Faroese makes no distinction in form between possessive pronouns and adjectives. The first- and second-person singular and the reflexive possessive (nom. m. sg. *mín, tín, sín*) are inflected according to the scheme in Table 7.6 (nom./acc. n. sg. *mítt, títt,*

Table 7.6 Schematic overview of pronoun (non-personal) and determiner inflections

	Singular			*Plural*		
	m.	f.	n.	m.	f.	n.
Nom.	-Ø	-Ø	-t(t)	-ir	-ar	-Ø/-i
Acc.	-Ø/-an	-a	-t(t)	-ar	-ar	-Ø/-i
Dat.	-um	-i/-ari	-um		-um	

Note: Individual pronouns and determiners may vary from this pattern in certain forms, especially the nominative/accusative neuter singular and plural. The nominative feminine singular, the nominative/accusative neuter plural, the dative masculine and neuter singular, and the dative plural may be marked by change of the root vowel (*a > ø* or *o*). Genitive forms of a few pronouns and determiners are occasionally found in writing: m. and n. sg. *-s*, f. sg. *-ar* (very rare), pl. *-a*. Apart from *-ur* in the nominative masculine singular as opposed to *-Ø*, this is the paradigm according to which strong adjectives by and large are inflected (acc. m. sg. *-an*, dat. f. sg. *-ari*, nom./acc. n. pl. *-Ø*).

sítt), the other possessives are invariable and take the same form as the genitive of the corresponding personal pronoun.

The principal demonstratives in Faroese are *tann* 'that', *hesin* 'this', *hasin* 'that', and *hin* 'the other'. The latter three are inflected more or less in accordance with the scheme in Table 7.6 (*hesin* and *hasin* have accusative masculine and nominative feminine singular *henda(n)*, *handa(n)* and nominative/accusative neuter singular *hetta(r)*, *hatta(r)*, the forms with the final consonant are colloquial); the plural of *tann* is set out in Table 7.5 (*teir*, etc.) and the singular is as follows: nom./acc. m. and nom. f. *tann*, acc. f. *ta*, nom./acc. n. *tað*, dat. all genders *tí*, although the dative feminine may also be *teirri*. The deictic sense of *tann* is somewhat weakened, possibly as a result of the availability of *hasin*, which has a strongly pointing function and is often reinforced by the addition of *har* 'there'. As well as being a demonstrative, *tann* also serves as the preposed definite article (as can *hin* in older written Faroese and in certain phrases in the spoken language), in which function it naturally loses its deictic sense altogether. Since *tann* is the preposed counterpart of the suffixed definite article and, like the other three demonstratives, regularly appears in conjunction with it (on the syntax of these and related phrases, see section 7.4), it is convenient to consider here both the forms of the article and its pattern of suffixation to the noun. Fundamentally it is like *hin* (of which it is probably the reflex) without initial /h/, and its inflections parallel those of the pronoun except in the nominative/accusative neuter singular where *hin* has the form *hitt*; however, those noun endings that are syllabic (except the strong nominative masculine singular) cause syncopation of the initial /i/. The forms are thus as given in Table 7.7.

Table 7.7   The suffixed definite article

	Singular			Plural		
	m.	f.	n.	m.	f.	n.
Nom.	-(i)n	-(i)n	-(i)ð	-nir	-nar	-(i)ni
Acc.	-(i)n	-(i)na	-(i)ð	-nar	-nar	-(i)ni
Gen.	-(i)ns	(-(i)nar)	-(i)ns		-nna	
Dat.	-num	-(i)ni	-num		-num	

Note: The genitive forms are little used, even in the written language, the feminine almost never; the genitive plural occurs in both spoken and written Faroese in a limited number of postpositional phrases involving *millum*, contrast *húsanna millum* with *millum húsini* 'between the houses'. The -*m* (/n/) of the dative plural is dropped from nouns when the definite article is added, e.g. *bátum* (/boatun/) 'boats', *bátunum* (/boatunun/) 'the boats'. In the spoken language there is a tendency for the nominative and accusative masculine plural of the definite article to coalesce, usually in favour of the nominative form.

The interrogative pronoun and adjective in Faroese is *hvør*. It inflects according to the scheme in Table 7.6, but with the following idiosyncrasies: the accusative masculine singular is *hvønn*, the nominative/accusative neuter singular *hvat*, and all endings that begin with a vowel are preceded by /j/.

The relative particle is *sum* or *ið*, between which there are a few slight differences of syntactic function; outside these, *sum* is by far the most common of the two in the spoken language. Literary Faroese sometimes uses *hvørs* (formally the masculine or neuter genitive singular of the interrogative *hvør*, *hvat*) in the sense 'whose'; this is probably in imitation of the corresponding Danish form *hvis*.

Indefinite pronouns and determiners include *nógvur* 'much, a lot', *hvør* 'each, every', *ein* 'one', *annar* 'another, other, the other, the one (of two)', *báðir* (pl.) 'both', *fáur* 'few', *eingin* 'no one, none, no', *hvørgin* 'neither', and *nakar*, *onkur*, *summur*, the latter three all in the range 'some/any(-one/-thing)', for which senses *ein* can also be employed. These words are all inflected according to the scheme in Table 7.6, though most exhibit some idiosyncrasies; *hvør* has exactly the same forms as the interrogative except for the nominative/accusative neuter singular, which is *hvørt*. The relationship between *nakar*, *onkur*, *summur*, and *ein* is subtle and complex, and not yet completely understood. It seems to involve such features as [± existence], [± specific], [± distributive], and while there is a considerable degree of overlap, there are many contexts in which only one or some of these pronouns or determiners are grammatical. To a certain extent Faroese parallels English, in that *nakar* is the preferred word in interrogative and negative clauses (see section 7.4), but *nakar* is also widely used in declaratives, especially when the required sense is [+specific], contrast: *nakrar dagar* '(for) some days (acc.)', *summar dagar* 'some (individual) days (acc.)', *hann hoyrdi nakað* 'he heard something (specific)', *hann hoyrdi okkurt* 'he heard something (or other)'. Synonymous with pronominal *ein* is *man* 'one' (from German via Danish), but this is not a word favoured by purists and it has the disadvantage that it can only be used when nominative is the appropriate case. As well as being an indefinite pronoun or determiner, *ein* also functions as the numeral 'one' and the indefinite article. In the latter two senses it may appear in the plural (a) when denoting a pair, e.g. *einir skógvar* 'one/a pair of shoes'; (b) when modifying a plural noun, e.g. *eini hjún* 'one/a married couple'; (c) when used to denote an approximate number, e.g. *einar fimm seks gentur* 'five or six girls'. The numeral also has weak forms, which occur when it is preceded by a determiner, e.g. *tann eini vinurin* 'the one friend (of many)'. In connection with numerals, it is worth mentioning (a) that as well as *ein*, *tveir* 'two' and *tríggir* 'three' are inflected for case and gender; (b) that in counting the unit usually precedes the ten, e.g. *ein og tjúgu* 'twenty-one'; and (c) that the words for the tens from 'fifty' to 'ninety' are normally *hálvtrýss*, *trýss*, *hálvfjerðs*, *fýrs*, *hálvfems*, these and their ordinal counterparts being based on the corresponding Danish forms *halvtreds(indstyve)* 'fifty', etc.

Verbs

Faroese verbs are inflected for person and/or number, and tense, according to a system greatly simplified in comparison with Old Norse or Icelandic. As in all Germanic languages, the finite forms are either present or past, and the two main conjugation types are 'weak' and 'strong'. The principal inflections are outlined in Table 7.8. The second-person singular -*t* and -*st* endings are often dropped in both the written and the spoken language, and there are tendencies locally for the past singular and plural to coalesce in certain weak verb classes, either because the singular form is extended to the plural or because post-tonic /i/ and /u/ are no longer distinguished, e.g. *vit elskaði* 'we loved', *nevndi-nevndu* 'mentioned', both [nɛundɪ], [nɛundə] (or some other unitary form). In strong verbs the past singular–plural distinction is still maintained by all speakers, e.g. *eg kom* [eˈkoːm] 'I came' : *vit komu* [vitˈkoːmɪ] 'we came'.

Finite inflections not included in Table 7.8 are those of the modal auxiliaries and, to a limited extent, of *vera* '(to) be' (for both see below), and the imperative and subjunctive forms. Faroese has a second-person singular imperative, which for most verbs consists simply of the root, but for one class of root + -*a*, and a second-person plural with the ending -*ið* (/i/), e.g. *kom!* 'come! (sg.)', *komið!* 'come! (pl.)', *kasta!* 'throw! (sg.)', *kastið!* 'throw! (pl.)'. Note that as in the mainland Scandinavian languages but unlike in Icelandic imperative constructions as a rule have no overt subject. In spoken Faroese the imperative singular form is often used even when more than one person is being addressed. In the absence of first-person imperative forms (found only in archaizing style), the imperative singular (rarely the plural in the spoken language) of *lata* '(to) let' is used followed by *meg* 'me' or *okkum* 'us' and the infinitive of the main verb, e.g. *lat okkum fara* 'let's go'. The residual subjunctive can sometimes act as a substitute for a third-person

Table 7.8 The principal verb inflections of Faroese

	Present	Past weak	Past strong
1 sg.	-i	-Di	-∅
2 sg.	-(V)r(t)	-Di	-(s)t
3 sg.	-(V)r	-Di	-∅
1 pl.	-a	-Du	-u
2 pl.	-a	-Du	-u
3 pl.	-a	-Du	-u

Note: V = vowel (i.e. *i*, *u*, or *a*, but see section 7.2, 'Vowels'). D = suffix, originally and still often dental. There may in addition to these endings be changes of root vowel between the second- and third-person singular present and the other present-tense forms (which preserve the vowel of the infinitive), between the present and past of strong verbs and of some weak verbs, and also between the singular past and plural past of many strong verbs.

imperative, but the use of the subjunctive is severely restricted in Faroese and it can hardly any longer be regarded as a productive verb form. It appears only in the present tense and almost exclusively in the third person, and has just the one ending: *-i*. Typically, it occurs in exclamations, e.g. *ólukka slái hann!* 'misfortune strike him!', *Harrin fylgi tær!* 'the Lord accompany you!', *verði ljós!* 'let there be light!' (lit. 'become light'), but in officialese instructions are also occasionally attested, e.g. *nýggir limir vendi sær til skrivaran* 'new members should apply to the secretary' (lit. 'new members turn themselves to . . .'). The unproductiveness of the subjunctive is revealed by the severe restrictions on the choice of subject and verb phrase in clauses of the type exemplified: *pápi hansara slái hann!* '(let) his father hit him!', *nýggir limir kvøði eitt ørindi* 'new members (should) recite a verse', for example, are pragmatically extremely odd.

To all the finite endings in Table 7.8 may be added *-st* (corresponding to the *-s* or *-st* of the other Scandinavian languages). The use of this suffix usually involves reflexive, reciprocal or passive meaning; it can be applied to the majority of Faroese verbs, but by no means all. Before *-st* the endings *-(u)r*, *-rt*, and *-st* are lost, e.g. *krevur* 'demands', *krevst* 'is demanded'.

The conjugation types of Faroese are many. Weak verbs can be divided into three classes, but irregularities abound. Class I has *-ar* in the second- and third-person singular present, *-aði/-aðu* (/aji/, /avu/) in the singular and plural past, and *-a* in the imperative singular. Class II has *-ir*, *-di/-du*, *-ti/-tu*, or *-ddi/-ddu*, and zero, class III *-ur*, *-di/-du* or *-ti/-tu* + vowel change, and zero in the corresponding forms. A small number of verbs with *-ar* in the present tense have *-di/-du*, *-ti/-tu*, or *-ddi/-ddu* in the past. Strong verbs exhibit many different vowel alternations; the number of classes to be distinguished depends on how big a 'miscellaneous' group one is prepared to tolerate. Common alternations in the present, past singular and past plural are: *í–ei–i*, *(j)ó/ý–ey–u*, and *e–a–u*. Five modal auxiliaries, *kunna* 'be able to', *mega/ muga* '(to) have to', *munna* 'be probable', *skula* 'be obliged to, intend', *vilja* '(to) want to', as well as *vita* '(to) know', have present-tense forms radically different from those of other verbs. The characteristics are: zero ending in the first- and third-person singular, *-t* or *-st* (depending on the verb) in the second person, and *-a* or *-u* (in part depending on the verb, in part on dialect) in the plural; apart from *vilja*, all have a different root vowel in the singular from in the infinitive and plural. Except for *mátti/máttu* 'had to' and *átti/áttu* 'ought' (from *eiga*, which has an ordinary present tense; cf. also *visti/vistu* 'knew'), the modals have a regular weak past tense, consisting of the root of the infinitive + *-di/-du* endings, e.g. *kundi* 'could (sg.)' (= *kun + di*). Note that the endings of *vera* '(to) be' except in the present plural are predictable, though the root is not; the forms are: present 1 sg. *eri*, 2 sg. *ert*, 3 sg. *er*, pl. *eru*, past 1 and 3 sg. *var*, 2 sg. *vart*, pl. *vóru*.

The non-finite forms of the Faroese verb are the infinitive, the present and past participles, and the supine. The infinitive ends in *a*, and this termination has been extended to those verbs which had monosyllabic infinitives in Old Norse, e.g. *fáa* '(to) get'. The present participle is formed through the addition of *-andi* to the verbal root, e.g. *komandi* 'coming'. It does not inflect. Apart from a straightforward adjectival function, it commonly has the modal and passive sense '-able, -ible', e.g. *etandi* 'edible', from *eta* '(to) eat', *óhugsandi* 'inconceivable', from *hugsa* '(to) think'. The form of the past participle depends on verb class, but can usually be predicted on the basis of past-tense endings. Weak verbs thus exhibit the following formations: class I *-aður* (*-dur, -tur, -ddur*), class II *-dur, -tur, -ddur*, class III *-dur, -tur* (with the same root vowel as the past tense); the past participles of strong verbs end in *-in*, and the root vowel is often different from either of those in the past tense, although mostly predictable (inf./pres. *í* gives pp. *i*, (*j*)*ó/ý* gives *o*, *e* gives *o* or *u*). The past participle inflects like an adjective and has both strong and weak endings. The supine is identical in form with the nominative/accusative neuter singular of the past participle, and is used after various auxiliaries in the formation of complex verb phrases. While not every verb has a past participle, virtually all have a supine. The *-st* ending discussed above (p. 205) does not occur in the present or past participle (except *lagstur* 'gone to bed', *setstur* 'seated', *vilstur* 'lost'), but may be added to the infinitive and the supine, whereupon the latter loses its final *-t* or (written) *-ð*, e.g. *hevur bart* 'has hit', *hava barst* 'have fought', *hevði fingið* (/finʤi/) 'had obtained', *hevði fingist* 'had been obtained'.

Complex verb phrases are best dealt with under syntax, but it may be noted here that *hava* '(to) have' combines with the supine and *vera* '(to) be' (in the case of 'change of state' intransitives) with the past participle to form the perfect, e.g. *hon hevur sungið* 'she has sung', *vatnið er runnið burtur* 'the water has run away' (lit. '... is run ...'); further, that *verða* or *blíva* '(to) become' (the latter mainly restricted to spoken Faroese) and *vera* function as passive auxiliaries, e.g. *tað verður gjørt* 'it is being done, it will be done', *tað er gjørt* 'it is done'.

7.4 Syntax

The Nominal Group

The primary division of the Faroese noun phrase is into indefinite and definite. Indefinite noun phrases are characterized first and foremost by strong adjective morphology, but also by the absence of demonstratives, definite articles, possessives, and genitive modifiers, and (often) by the presence of the indefinite article or indefinite determiners. The word order in such phrases is article/determiner + adjective + noun. Examples illustrating the different types are: *bátar* 'boats', *stórir bátar* 'big boats', *ein stórur bátur* 'a big boat', *nakrir stórir bátar* 'some big boats'. With determiners of similarity we may have article + determiner, e.g. *ein sovorðin stórur bátur* 'a big boat of that kind' (lit. 'a such big boat'). Definite noun phrases are characterized by weak adjective morphology and/or the presence of demonstratives, definite articles, possessives, and genitive modifiers. Here the word order and the structures are more complex. If we ignore possessives and genitives initially, the word order is: preposed definite article/demonstrative + adjective + noun + suffixed definite article. Examples are: *báturin* 'the boat', *hinir bátarnir* 'the other boats', *tann gamli báturin* 'the old boat'. Where definite noun phrases contain an adjective or a demonstrative, or both, Faroese prefers double definition, as illustrated by these examples, but single definition also occurs, and a noun phrase may be marked definite solely by the weak form of the adjective. The type adjective + noun + suffixed article, e.g. *gamli báturin* 'the old boat', occurs widely in written Faroese and is especially common in the press. In the spoken language it is mainly restricted to names or set phrases, e.g. *Heilagi Andin* 'the Holy Ghost', sometimes also with reverse word order: *Áin Mikla* 'the Big Stream' (lit. 'Stream-the Big'). Preposed article + adjective + noun, and demonstrative ± adjective + noun are constructions that can be found sporadically in spoken and written Faroese, most commonly where the adjective is an absolute superlative, e.g. *tann versti ránsmaður* 'a thoroughly wicked bandit' (lit. 'the worst bandit'), or where *tann* is part of a noun phrase modified by a relative clause, e.g. *í teirri oyggj, sum...* 'in that island which...'. The marking of definiteness by weak adjective morphology alone is mainly restricted to names, vocatives, qualified superlatives, and set phrases, e.g. *Svarti Deyði* 'the Black Death', *góðu fólk!* 'dear people!', *vit róðu yvir um longsta fjørð í Føroyum* 'we rowed across the longest firth in the Faroes', *aðru ferð* '(for) the second time (acc.)'. The phrase *longsta fjørð* unqualified by *í Føroyum* would tend to have the force of a place-name 'Longest Firth'; however, in poetic writing weak adjective + noun does not necessarily invite this interpretation, contrast *ígjøgnum Grønu Líð* 'across Green Slope' with *ígjøgnum grønu líð* 'across the green slope'.

Two further points concerning the indefinite and definite article need to be noted. In generic noun phrases there is usually no indefinite article, contrast *Páll er frálíkur lærari* 'Páll is (an) excellent teacher' with *vit hava fingið ein frálíkan lærara, sum eitur Páll* 'we have got an excellent teacher, who is called Páll'. The definite article is sometimes not used where a noun or noun phrase denotes a unique phenomenon or a phenomenon only one example of which is of immediate relevance, e.g. *kongur* 'the king', *prestur* 'the priest', *føroyskt mál* 'the Faroese language'.

The expression of possession in Faroese is complicated by the almost total loss of the genitive case for this purpose in the spoken language, and attempts by linguistic purists to resuscitate it. In Old Norse genitive modifiers followed their head word; in Faroese, to the extent they were used at all, they came for the most part to precede it. As a result, the resuscitated literary genitive may either precede or follow its head word, while such colloquial genitives as exist tend largely to precede it, e.g. *ríkisins ovasta umboð* or *ovasta umboð ríkisins* 'the kingdom's foremost representative', *Jógvansar bátur* (less commonly *bátur Jógvansar*) 'Jógvan's boat', *móti foreldurs ráðum* (**móti ráðum foreldurs*) 'against parents' advice' (the genitive ending -*sa(r)*, added to personal names or their equivalent, and the analogical plural -*s* both have their inspiration in the spoken language). Not even the literary genitive can regularly trigger agreement in modifiers since the necessary forms are mostly lacking. We may attest *hvørs manns* 'every man's', but in *nakað annað lands kvæði* 'the ballads of any other country' the -*s* is attached only to the head word since *nakar* and *annar* have no generally accepted formal means of indicating agreement with a genitive. On the other hand, Faroese does not normally exhibit constructions like those in mainland Scandinavian in which an -*s* is attached to the last word in a genitive phrase irrespective of whether it is the head word or not (cf., however, *Djóna í Geils gøta* (lit. 'Djóni's in Geil's Street'), a street-name in Tórshavn – the official name *Djóna í Geil gøta* is never used in the spoken language and is felt by most natives to be ungrammatical). The reasons for this are the almost universal replacement of the genitive (in all but certain preposition phrases) by prepositional circumlocutions and the difficulty, even if this had not been so, of attaching the genitive -*s* to existing case endings. Norwegian *mannen med det hvite hårets kontor* 'the man with the white hair's office' thus corresponds to Faroese *skrivstovan hjá manninum við tí hvíta hárinum* 'the office of the man with the white hair'. Personal relationships, for which the prepositions *at* 'at' or *til* 'to' are commonly used, e.g. *mamma til Kjartan* 'Kjartan's mother', may also be expressed by an accusative singular following the head word: *pápi drongin* 'the boy's father' (lit. 'father boy-the'), but this construction has been losing ground in the last 40 or 50 years (earlier it was not restricted to personal relationships). The possessive adjective normally follows the noun it modifies. Faroese differs from the other Scandinavian languages that have this order in that the noun always appears without a suffixed article: *drongur mín* 'my boy'. The reverse order, *mín drongur*, also occurs, but normally only when the sense is contrastive, '*my* boy'. Where an adjective is used in addition to the possessive, the latter may precede the noun without implying a contrast: *mín nýggi bátur* or *nýggi bátur mín* are alternative ways of saying 'my new boat', but '*my* new boat' would normally only be *mín nýggi bátur*. Just as the genitive has largely been superseded by preposition phrases, so noun + possessive adjective may be replaced by noun + suffixed article + *hjá* ('at, with') + personal pronoun, e.g. *hesturin hjá mær* 'my horse' (lit. 'horse-the at me'), and adjective + noun + possessive adjective by preposed article + adjective + noun + suffixed article + *hjá* + personal pronoun, e.g. *tann nýggi báturin hjá mær* 'my new boat' (lit. 'the new boat-the at me'). Unlike the genitive, however, possessive adjectives (and pronouns) are still very much part of modern spoken and written Faroese (the former especially when used to modify terms of relationship).

Since, in most respects, Faroese pronouns and anaphors behave exactly like their counterparts in other Scandinavian languages, we will limit our discussion of them to two points: the occurrence of zero elements and patterns of reflexivization, both of which in part distinguish Faroese (and Icelandic) from virtually all forms of mainland Scandinavian. Like its sister languages, Faroese, as we might expect, has zero anaphors as the underlying subjects of infinitives (so-called 'PRO'), e.g. *vit hava nóg mikið at gera* 'we have enough to do', and allows them in 'telegraphic style', e.g. *kom heim ígjár* 'came home yesterday'. Where it differs from Danish, Norwegian and Swedish is in regularly omitting expletive *tað* 'it' from non-clause-initial position. We find: *nú regnar* 'now it's raining' (lit. 'now rains'), *kalt er úti* 'it's cold out' (lit. 'cold is out'), *spurt varð, hvussu lá fyri* 'people asked what the situation was' (lit. 'asked was how lay before'), but, e.g., *tað regnar nú* 'it's raining now', where *tað* cannot be omitted since an ungrammatical clause-initial finite verb would result (see 'The sentence' below, pp. 214–16). In one important respect Faroese differs from Icelandic: expletive *tað* is *sometimes* found in other than clause-initial position – *regnaði tað ígjár?* 'did it rain yesterday?', for example, is a possible alternative to *regnaði ígjár?*

In matters of reflexivization, Faroese, like Icelandic, follows the basic Scandinavian pattern. In a sentence with just two noun phrases, a reflexive anaphor, whether non-possessive *seg* or possessive *sín* must (except in certain cases of long reflexivization, mentioned below) be co-referential with the subject, while a pronominal or name must not. The distribution of the simple reflexive and the complex *seg sjálvan* (reflexive + 'self') is also much as in the mainland Scandinavian languages, i.e. the complex form is used by and large contrastively or to disambiguate, e.g. *Jógvan er stoltur av sær sjálvum* 'Jógvan is proud of himself', *Mikkjal bað Pætur raka sær sjálvum* 'Mikkjal asked Pætur (to) shave himself'. Because complex reflexives are bound within the clause, the co-reference in the last example must be between *sær sjálvum* and *Pætur*; if we remove *sjálvum*, ambiguity results: *Mikkjal₍ᵢ₎ bað Pætur₍ⱼ₎ raka sær₍ᵢ/ⱼ₎.* Like other Scandinavian languages, Faroese allows object-controlled reflexivization within the clause, but only where the relation between object and reflexive phrase is that of subject and predicate, e.g. *eg sá Mortan á skrivstovu síni* 'I saw Mortan in his office', **eg bardi gentuna við dukku síni* 'I hit the girl with her doll'. Although long reflexivization – the ability of a reflexive in a tensed clause to find its antecedent in a higher clause – is found in mainland Scandinavian, it is a very marginal phenomenon in these languages (and frowned upon by normative grammarians). In Faroese, as in Icelandic, it is a regular, though entirely optional feature. Long reflexivization is largely an indirect speech phenomenon. It is important to note, however, that the governing category in which reflexives are bound may extend far beyond the sentence containing the matrix clause that introduces the indirect speech. Thus, *sær dámdi væl musikk* 'she liked music' (lit. 'herself (dat.) liked well music') may stand as an independent sentence, but it presupposes 'she said that ...' or the equivalent – either stated or implied – as an antecedent.

Long reflexivization thus has something of the force of the German subjunctive, which is doubtless why in Icelandic it appears to correlate with this mood – an impossibility in Faroese, which has no productive subjunctive (see section 7.3).

The Faroese quantifiers can be dealt with briefly since they show few syntactic features which are not widely paralleled in other Germanic languages. We may note the following. In general quantifiers follow determiners but precede adjectives: *hesir tríggir gomlu menninir* 'these three old men'; the pattern applies to *báðir* 'both' as well: *hesir báðir menninir* 'both these men', *teir báðir* 'both of them'. This notwithstanding, 'quantifier floating' is a widespread phenomenon in Faroese; note, e.g., the varying position of *allir* 'all' in the following sentences: *allir vóru teir komnir í land, teir vóru allir komnir í land, teir vóru komnir allir í land, teir vóru komnir í land allir* 'they had all come ashore'. In conjunction with many quantifiers nouns may appear both with and without the suffixed definite article. Often there is a difference in meaning, but sometimes only one of style, e.g. *allan dag* 'all day (today) (acc. m. sg., AdvP)', *allan dagin* 'all (of some) day (acc. m. sg., AdvP)', *eina nátt* 'one night (only) (acc. f. sg., AdvP)', *eina náttina* 'one (particular) night (acc. f. sg., AdvP)', but *nógv ár, nógv árini* 'many years (nom./acc. n. pl., NP or AdvP)' – *nógv árini* is more colloquial and has perhaps less emphasis on the quantifier. In some phrases the article is obligatory, e.g. *annar báturin* 'the one boat (of two)', *hin báturin* 'the other boat'. Where numerals are used in conjunction with the definite article in noun phrases a partitive sense results: *ein ærin er hvít* 'one of the ewes is white' (lit. 'one ewe-the . . .'), *ein tann besti lærarin* 'one of the best teachers' (lit. 'one the best teacher-the'). Three residual points are worth mentioning. In the senses 'barely' and 'just over' the plurals of *knappur* 'scarce' and *góður* 'good' can precede numerals greater than one: *knappar tvær vikur* 'barely two weeks', *góðar tvær vikur* 'just over two weeks'. The quantifier *mangur* is used in both singular and plural; in the singular it has the sense 'many a'. Where the reference is to age, numbers above one normally trigger the genitive plural of *ár* 'year': *hon er átta ára gomul* 'she is eight years old'.

The Verbal Group

There are no absolutely watertight formal criteria by which auxiliaries can be distinguished from lexical verbs in Faroese, and there are therefore a number of verbs which it is hard to classify. The principal criterion must be the ability to be followed by an infinitive, past participle or supine without an intervening *at* 'to', but *eiga* 'ought (inf.)' and *kunna* 'be able', which share characteristics with other modals, are always (*eiga*) or occasionally (*kunna*) followed by *at*, while *biðja* '(to) ask', which mostly behaves like a lexical verb, is often followed by a bare infinitive: *um menn kundu at skriva um tað* 'if men were able to write about it', *hann bað geva sær vatn* 'he asked (someone to) give him (lit. 'himself') water'. Other criteria include the very irregular conjugations of *kunna, mega, munna, skula, vilja* (cf. section 7.3) and the ability of these verbs and also *hava* '(to) have', *vera* '(to) be', *blíva* or *verða* '(to) be (passive)', *eiga, fáa* '(to) get', *duga* '(to) manage' to occur in elliptical responses, e.g. *ja, tað hava vit* 'yes, we have', *nei, tað vildi hann ikki* 'no, he didn't want to' (lit. 'no, that wanted he not'). The tendency in elliptical responses otherwise is to use the pro-verb *gera* '(to) do', e.g. *lær hann ofta? ja, tað ger hann* 'does he laugh often? yes, he does' (*ja, tað lær hann*); with some verbs, however, a dual response is possible, e.g. *minnist tú, hvaðani hon kom? nei, ikki minnist eg/nei, tað geri eg ikki* 'do you remember from where she came? no, I don't remember/no I don't' (lit. '... no, not remember I/no, that do I not').

In Faroese we often find a supine where in other Scandinavian languages an infinitive is used. This happens (a) where a supine has already occurred in the sentence, the second one being 'attracted' by the first; and (b) in connection with auxiliary verbs. Two typical examples will suffice to illustrate (a): *eg havi hoyrt hann sagt tað* 'I have heard him say it' (lit. '... said ... '), *tað hevði verið stuttligt at sæð hana* 'it would have been nice to see her' (lit. 'it had been nice to seen her'). In the first example an infinitive could be used although the supine is more common, in the second only the supine can occur. Past-tense auxiliary + supine has in many cases taken over the function of the past-tense subjunctive of the auxiliary + infinitive, and there is a minimal contrast with past-tense auxiliary + infinitive, e.g. *vit kundu rógva yvir um sundið* 'we were able to row (inf.) across the sound', *vit kundu róð yvir um sundið* 'we could row (sup.) across the sound (if ...)'. Note that the latter example is ambiguous between 'could row' and 'could have rowed'; it can be disambiguated by the addition of *havt* 'had (sup.)': *vit kundu havt róð yvir um sundið* 'we could have (sup.) rowed (sup.) ...'.

In matters of tense and aspect Faroese does not differ greatly from mainland Scandinavian. The uses of present, past and perfect parallel those in Danish, Norwegian and Swedish, and there are incipient progressive and inchoative constructions such as *vit sótu og prátaðu* 'we sat talking, we were talking' (lit. 'we sat and talked'), *hann sá menninar fáast við at seta gørn á vatninum* 'he saw the men putting fishing nets in the water' (lit. '... busy themselves with putting ...'), *hann er um at fara* 'he is about to go', *hon er farin at eldast* 'she has begun to grow old'. However, Faroese has nothing like the Icelandic aspectual system.

Three points concerning word order in the verbal group should be noted. Phrasal verbs that take objects may, as in Norwegian, have the object before or after the particle, but the former, e.g. *hann las brævið upp* 'he read the letter out' is more usual than the latter: *hann las upp brævið* (there are, however, deviations from the pattern, depending in part on the particular phrasal verb used and in part on dialect). Where a transitive verb and its object follow directly the auxiliary *lata* '(to) cause', the order is usually verb + object: *tey lótu mála húsini* 'they had the house painted' (lit. 'they let paint buildings-the'), although the reverse: *tey lótu húsini mála* is not unknown. Periphrastic verbs, like their phrasal counterparts, do not form an indivisible syntactic unit; just as *brævið* may intervene between *las* and *upp*, so too may the subject between the verb and noun of a periphrastic verb, e.g. *har bar politisturin eyga við hana* 'there the policeman caught sight of her' (lit. '... bore policeman-the eye with ...').

Grammatical Relations

Here we will be concerned primarily with the relationship between morphological case and word order, and between active and different types of passive. The retention of a morphologically distinct nominative, accusative and dative in nouns, pronouns and adjectives makes it possible to mark some grammatical relations by case. Thus the subject normally stands in the nominative, the direct object in the accusative and the indirect object in the dative. However, word order is probably more important in establishing grammatical relations since, providing it is unmarked, noun phrases with subject properties always occur leftmost, and in clauses with both direct and indirect objects, the latter precede the former. Furthermore, none of the three morphological cases can satisfactorily be used to define a particular syntactic function since they each have a variety of functions. Thus nominatives, for example, may appear as subject complements: *hann er lærari* 'he is a teacher', or as complements to the accusative in accusative and infinitive constructions: *hann segði seg vera bangin* 'he said he was afraid' (lit. 'he said himself (acc.) be afraid (nom.)'); accusatives are found in many adverb phrases: *vit hava arbeitt allan dag* 'we have worked all day'; and datives may be subjects and direct objects as well as indirect objects: *sum óviti dámdi mær ost* 'as a child I liked cheese' (lit. 'as child liked me (dat.) cheese'), *eg møtti teimum í býnum* 'I met them (dat.) in the town'.

The example *hann segði seg vera bangin*, in which the complement to the accusative stands in the nominative (the accusative is also used in such cases), illustrates the rather tenuous grip grammatical concord has on Faroese. As long as the relationship between the words where agreement is expected is clear-cut and they stand in close proximity, the traditional rules of concord are applied. Thus, attributive adjectives never fail to agree with the nouns they modify, nor, normally, do predicative adjectives, though superlatives in predicative position may be without ending, e.g. *Paulus er størst* (for *størstur*) 'Paul is greatest'. Consider, however, the following examples: *eg rokni við tí* 'I assume that (dat.)', *tað rokni eg við* 'that (acc.) I assume', *hann gongur við einum barnavogni, fullan við dukkum* 'he walks (around) with a pram (dat.), full (acc.) of dolls', *tey nokta seg sekan* 'they deny they are guilty' (lit. 'they (n. pl.) deny themselves guilty (acc. m. sg.)'). In the last example, *seg*, which is marked only for case, seems to have influenced the form of the following adjective, which is accusative, as we would expect, but does not agree with the subject in either gender or number. Observe also how in cleft sentences the focused constituent is attracted into the case of its counterpart in the corresponding simple clause: *tað eri eg, sum eri komin* 'it's me who's come' (lit. 'it am I who am come'), *tað er meg, tú sært* 'it's me you see'. Two further points about case marking in Faroese should be noted. First, personal names and titles (of books etc.) are often left uninflected. Second, idiosyncratic case is often reanalysed; thus, dative subjects alternate in many cases with nominatives, and nominative objects, common in Icelandic, are seldom found, e.g. *mær dámar/eg dámi ferskan fisk* 'me likes/I like fresh fish', *honum tókti skattin ov lítlan* 'he thought the tax was too small' (lit. 'him (dat.) thought tax-the (acc.) too small (acc.)') (cf. also the remarks on the passive below).

Present and past passives in Faroese are formed with the auxiliary *verða* (lit. 'become'; *verða* alternates with *blíva*, the latter being especially common in the spoken language) + past participle, and perfect passives with *er vorðin* (*er blivin*) (lit. 'is become') or, more usually, just *er* + past participle: *hetta verður broytt* 'this is being changed, this will be changed', *hetta er broytt* 'this is changed'; the first example corresponds to the active *tey broyta hetta* 'they are changing this, they will change this', the second to *tey hava broytt hetta* 'they have changed this'. The dative objects of active clauses usually become nominative subjects in the passive equivalents, e.g. *tey hjálptu honum* 'they helped him (dat.)' : *hann varð hjálptur* 'he (nom.) was helped'. Where the active clause contains both a direct and an indirect object, it is usual for the direct object to become subject in the passive equivalent, e.g. *hann seldi bóndanum kúnna* 'he sold the farmer the cow' : *kúgvin varð seld bóndanum* 'the cow was sold to the farmer', although where for reasons of focus the direct object cannot easily become subject, the indirect object takes its place; in such cases the subject remains in the dative and the object often, but not always, in the accusative, e.g. *tey ynsktu honum eina góða ferð* 'they wished him a good journey' : *honum varð ynskt eina góða ferð* 'he (dat.) was wished a good journey (acc.)'.

Passives in Faroese may also be formed with the *-st* suffix, which corresponds typologically but not always in function to the *-s(t)* of the other Scandinavian languages. The *-st* passive is particularly common in complex verb phrases consisting of modal auxiliary + infinitive, e.g. *alt má etast* 'everything must be eaten', but it also occurs regularly in the finite forms: *so sigst* 'so it is said', *nógv fekst fyri fiskin* 'much (money) was obtained for the fish'; perfect passives, where the *-st* is added to the supine, are distinctly uncommon. Apart from marking the passive, the *-st* suffix has a number of other functions, not all of which can easily be defined in broad terms. To certain verbs it imparts a reflexive sense, and may then sometimes alternate with the reflexive pronoun, e.g. *setast* or *seta seg* '(to) sit down' (lit. 'set oneself'); to other verbs, when used with a plural subject, it gives reciprocal meaning, and the appropriate form of *hvønn annan* 'each other' is occasionally a possible alternative, e.g. *kennast* or *kenna hvønn annan* '(to) know each other'. With some verbs the *-st* suffix has only one reading, but with others it may have two or more, and interpretation will depend on the make-up of the rest of the clause; thus, *kennast* may also be passive as in *ikki eitt livandi kendist* 'not a bite (from a fish) was felt' (lit. 'not anything living ...'), or combine with a preposition and become transitive, e.g. *kennast við* (+ object) '(to) recognize, (to) acknowledge'. Some *-st* forms on their own have a transitive reading, e.g. *minnast* '(to) remember', *óttast* '(to) fear', but the majority of those which are not passive, reflexive, or reciprocal tend towards an ergative sense, e.g. *opnast* '(to) open', *kvalast* '(to) suffocate' (both intransitive), *gerast* '(to) become' (cf. *gera ein ríkan* 'make someone rich'), and even – with a dative object – *nærkast* '(to) approach' (cf. the transitive *nærka* '(to) move closer'). With a number of verbs the finite *-st* form can have a generic passive reading indicating possibility, e.g. *tað fæst* 'it can be obtained, it is obtainable', *tað sást* 'it could be seen, it was evident'; an active equivalent of the first example might be *tað er at fáa* 'it is obtainable' (lit. 'it is to obtain'), or *tað ber til at fáa tað* 'it is possible to obtain it'. Ergativity is not restricted to *-st* forms; we find *halda* '(to) keep (intr.)', *krevja* '(to) be required', *selja* '(to) sell (intr.)' (a recent import from English via Danish), and also some relaxation of the strong form = intransitive–weak = transitive dichotomy (both this and ergative *selja* are frowned upon by purists). However, the norm in Faroese is for there to be a separate intransitive verb corresponding to the transitive, e.g. *bróta* '(to) break (tr.)', *brotna* '(to) break (intr.)'; there is some justification for seeing *-st* ergatives as part of this pattern and for classing, for example, *gerast* and *gera* as different lexical items.

The Sentence

The principal matter to be considered here is word order. One or two brief points will also be made about negation and subordination. Faroese, not unexpectedly, is a verb-second language, both in the Generative and the more traditional sense. Its basic word-order patterns for the most part parallel those in other Scandinavian languages, but it exhibits a few idiosyncrasies, mainly arising from its typological position between mainland Scandinavian and Icelandic. Fundamentally, there are seven slots in declarative and six in interrogative and embedded clauses. These may be filled as follows. Declarative clauses: (1) topic; (2) finite verb; (3) subject, pronouns (indirect object, object, or subject complement); (4) modal, negation, sentence, and certain other adverbs; (5) infinite verbs; (6) noun phrases (indirect object, object, subject complement, object complement); (7) adverbials, e.g. *her man fólk ongantíð hava fingið fisk fyrr* 'people have surely never caught fish here before' (lit. 'here will people never have caught ... '). Interrogative clauses: as declaratives, but without the topic position, e.g. *man fólk nakrantíð hava fingið fisk her?* 'have people ever caught fish here, I wonder?' (lit. 'will people ever have caught fish here?'). Embedded clauses (except verb-first conditionals, which have the same order as interrogatives): (1) subject; (2) modal, negation, sentence, and certain other adverbs; (3) finite verb; (4); (5); (6) as

(5); (6); (7) in declaratives; this is the pattern of embedded clause word order in mainland Scandinavian too, but in Faroese the position of (2) and (3) may be reversed, as is normally always the case in Icelandic, e.g. *(hóast) fólk ongantíð hevur fingið fisk her, (hóast) fólk hevur ongantíð fingið fisk her* '(although) people have never caught fish here'.

Unlike the mainland Scandinavian languages, Faroese allows a fair amount of deviation from this order, though the principal deviations are literary and lend an archaic or bookish flavour to the style. Four possibilities will be mentioned here, three affecting declaratives and one embedded clauses. Because expletive *tað* is often omitted when it is not needed as a clause-introducer, the subject may appear in position (6), e.g. *her hevur verið ein maður* 'there has been a man here' (lit. 'here has been a man'), although *her hevur ein maður verið* is perhaps more usual. After the conjunction *og* 'and' in narrative style the finite verb may precede the subject (so-called 'connective inversion'), e.g. *tollarar tustu umborð, og hevði skiparin úr at gera* 'customs officers rushed on board, and the skipper was extremely busy' (lit. '. . . and had skipper-the out-of to do'). In older Faroese verb-initial order was more common, but except after *og* (and occasionally after *men* 'but' in imitation of the *og* construction) it is no longer part of the living language. Occasionally we find verb-third in written Faroese, e.g. *vit hugdu trúliga, men onga sól vit sóu* 'we looked steadily but no sun we saw'. This appears to be deliberate alteration of the normal word order for stylistic effect, but it is not uncommon and does not strike native speakers as in any way ungrammatical. In embedded clauses Faroese shares with Icelandic the phenomenon called 'stylistic fronting'. Essentially this means the moving of some (virtually any) element from the right of the finite verb into an empty subject position, e.g. *meðan farið varð í kirkjuna* 'while people were going to church' (lit. 'while gone was into church-the'), *tað, ið allan munin ger* 'that which makes all the difference' (lit. '. . . all the difference makes'), *hann spurdi, hvussu til stóð* 'he asked how things were' (lit. '. . . how to stood').

We have seen that the normal position for negation is (4) in declarative, (3) in interrogative, and (2) or (3) in embedded clauses. This affects not just the adverb *ikki*, but other negatives such as *eingin* 'none, no one, nothing, no', e.g. *tí hevur hann onga eydnu havt* 'therefore he's had no luck', *hóast hann ongar pengar átti/hóast hann átti ongar pengar* 'though he had no money'. Negatives may however appear in other pre-infinite verb positions, and are especially common initially, where they are placed to achieve slight emphasis: *ikki var hann nakar oldingur* 'he (certainly) wasn't an old man', *onga hevði hann eydnuna* 'he had no luck (at all)'; or to frame marked negative interrogatives: *ikki er hann ræddur fyri mær?* 'he isn't afraid of me, is he?' (the positive equivalent uses the tag *ikki sannheit?* 'not truth?', e.g. *hann var heima ígjár, ikki sannheit?* 'he was home yesterday, wasn't he?'). Because of the inability of negatives to appear after the infinite-verb position, *eingin* is often replaced by *ikki nakar* 'not any(one/thing)', e.g. *hann hevur ikki havt nakra eydnu* 'he hasn't had any luck'. As pointed out in section 7.3, *nakar* is not interchangeable with *onkur* 'some(one/thing)' in negative clauses. This is part of a wider distinction, paralleled in other Germanic languages, between non-assertive and assertive forms, the choice between which is determined by whether or not they come within the scope of a negation. Non-assertive *nakrastaðni* 'anywhere', *nakrantíð* 'ever', *heldur* 'either', *longur* 'any longer', *enn* 'yet', etc., thus contrast with assertive *onkustaðni* 'somewhere', *onkuntíð* 'sometime (or other)', *eisini* 'also', *enn* 'still', *longu* 'already', etc. Two final points about negation are worth recording. First, Faroese has no regular cases of multiple negation. Second, there is an optional construction involving focusing negation: *ikki ... men* 'not ... but' is sometimes replaced by *ikki ... uttan* 'not ... but (rather)'.

Subordination in Faroese is both finite and non-finite. Apart from the usual range of subordinating conjunctions introducing finite clauses, there are a few which may be followed by an infinitive or supine clause, e.g. *uttan at missa andlit* 'without losing face', *fyri at stýra hesum viðurskiftum* 'in order to control these affairs', *við at gjørt stýrið føroyskt* 'by making (sup.) the management Faroese'. In addition to this type of non-finite subordination, accusative or nominative + infinitive constructions are commonplace. Accusative + infinitive is found where there is an active verb in the matrix clause, e.g. *eg sá hann fara* 'I saw him go', *hann hevði sagt seg verið kokkur* 'he had said he was a cook' (lit. '... said himself been cook'), *teir hildu hana liggja deyð á gólvinum* 'they thought she was lying dead on the floor'. Nominative + infinitive occurs with a passive matrix verb and involves subject-to-subject raising, e.g. *ikki er hann sagdur at vera vitugur maður* 'he is not said to be an intelligent man', *dansurin hoyrdist ganga lystiliga* 'the dance was heard going merrily'.

7.5   Lexis

The vocabulary of written Faroese derives mainly from the Old Norse of the ninth-century settlers, that of spoken Faroese from the same source and from Danish. It is in the lexicon that the wide gulf between the written and the spoken language can be most clearly seen. While the claim that almost any Danish lexical item can be used in Faroese is probably exaggerated, it is certainly true that vast numbers of everyday words are Danish loans. Purists have fought an energetic and protracted battle against Danicisms in Faroese and have in large measure succeeded in eradicating them from the written language or preventing their appearance there at all. A number of obvious Danicisms can be found in the language of journalism, but there are few in other forms of writing and very few indeed in the works of lexicographers. This means that many of the most common words on people's lips cannot be found in any dictionary. An instructive example is the Faroese for 'ticket'. The word almost all native speakers use when talking is *billett*, from French via

Danish, but what they write, officially at least, and what one finds in dictionaries is *ferðaseðil* (lit.) 'journey note'. To discover the gender and inflections of *billett* one must make enquiries of a native speaker. Certain neologisms have been gaining ground in the spoken language recently owing to their prevalence on radio and television, and it may be that many Danicisms will eventually be displaced. Neologisms are chiefly formed (a) by the coining of new words through the use of derivative suffixes; (b) by extending the meaning of existing words; or (c) by compounding, e.g. (a) *telda* 'computer' (cf. *tal* 'number', *telja* '(to) count'); (b) *góðska* 'quality' (original meaning 'goodness'); (c) *orðaskifti* 'debate' (lit. 'word-exchange'). Many Faroese neologisms are borrowed from Icelandic, either directly, e.g. *mentan* 'culture', or indirectly, e.g. *fólkaræði* 'democracy' (cf. Icelandic *lýðræði*, *lýður* 'people' is hardly known in Faroese).

In spite of the policy of purism, a number of 'international' terms have entered Faroese vocabulary and seem likely to be permanent fixtures, e.g. *telefon* 'telephone', *politi* 'police', *tomat* 'tomato'. One does not however see the great influx of English words and phrases that has taken place in the mainland Scandinavian languages, although Faroese is not immune from the pressure of Anglo-Saxon culture; it is only a few years, for example, since banks were able to inform their customers that they were 'on line'. On the whole, though, the influence of English on Faroese has tended to be of a different kind – longer-term but gentler – than on mainland Scandinavian. Because of its geographical situation, natives of the British Isles have found their way up to the archipelago in small numbers throughout its recorded history. This has given Faroese loans not found in other Scandinavian languages, e.g. *fittur* 'nice' (Eng. *fit*), *trupul* 'difficult' (Eng. *trouble*, but cf. also Icelandic *trufla* '(to) disturb'), *fokkaður* 'knackered' (Eng. *fuck*), and the now archaic *batlari* (Eng. *bottle*). Long before the English speakers there were visitors and settlers familiar with *Q*-Celtic, and they too left their mark on Faroese vocabulary, e.g. *kjadlámur* 'the left hand' (Gaelic *làmh chearr*), *korki* 'lichen' (from which purple dye is made) (Ir. *corcra* 'purple (dye)'), *sornur* 'device for drying corn' (Ir. *sorn* 'kiln'), *dunna* '(tame) duck' (Gaelic *tunnag*). Nor can the existence in Faroese of *Q*-Celtic modes of expression be ruled out: *tað er ótti á mær* 'I am afraid' (lit. 'there is fear on me') has no counterpart in other Scandinavian languages, but matches perfectly Irish *tá eagla orm* (lit. 'is fear on-me').

Further Reading

Barnes, M. P. (1986) 'Reflexivisation in Faroese – a preliminary survey', *Arkiv för nordisk filologi* 101: 95–126.
—— (1986) 'Subject, nominative and oblique case in Faroese', *Scripta Islandica* 37: 13–46.
—— (1987) 'Some remarks on subordinate-clause word-order in Faroese', *Scripta Islandica* 38: 3–35.

—— (1992) 'Faroese syntax – achievements, goals and problems', in J. Louis-Jensen and J. H. W. Poulsen (eds), *The Nordic Languages and Modern Linguistics* 7, 2 vols, Tórshavn: Føroya fróðskaparfelag.

Clausén, U. (1978) *Nyord i färöiskan*, Stockholm Studies in Scandinavian Philology, New Series 14, Stockholm: Almqvist & Wiksell.

Djupedal, R. (1964) 'Litt om framvoksteren av det færøyske skriftmålet', in A. Hellevik and E. Lundeby (eds), *Skriftspråk i utvikling* (Norsk språknemnd, skrifter 3), Oslo: Cappelen, pp. 144–86.

Hagström, B. (1967) *Ändelsevokalerna i färöiskan*, Stockholm Studies in Scandinavian Philology, New Series 6, Stockholm: Almqvist & Wiksell.

—— (1984) 'Language contact in the Faroes', in P. S. Ureland and I. Clarkson (eds), *Scandinavian Language Contacts*, Cambridge: Cambridge University Press, pp. 171–89.

Hansson, Å. (1983) 'Phonemic history of Faroese', in K.-H. Dahlstedt, Å. Hansson, R. Hedquist, and B. Lindblom (eds), *From Sounds to Words. Essays in Honor of Claes-Christian Elert 23 December 1983*, Acta Universitatis Umensis 60, Stockholm: Almqvist & Wiksell, pp. 127–58.

Hægstad, M. (1917) 'Færøymaal', in *Vestnorske maalføre fyre 1350* II, 2, second section, Videnskapsselskapets skrifter II, Hist.-filos. klasse, 1916, No. 41, Kristiania, pp. 63–190 + 5 facsimiles.

Lockwood, W. B. (1977) *An Introduction to Modern Faroese*, 3rd printing, Tórshavn: Føroya skúlabókagrunnur.

Sandqvist, C. (1980) *Studier över meningsbyggnaden i färöiskt skriftspråk*, Lundastudier i nordisk språkvetenskap A 32, Lund: Ekstrand.

Sandøy, H. (1992) 'Indefinite pronouns in Faroese', in J. Louis-Jensen and J. H. W. Poulsen (eds), *The Nordic Languages and Modern Linguistics* 7, 2 vols, Tórshavn: Føroya fróðskaparfelag, pp. 547–54.

Werner, O. (1964) 'Die Erforschung der färingischen Sprache', *Orbis* 13: 481–544.

—— (1965) 'Nachtrag zu: Die Erforschung der färingischen Sprache', *Orbis* 14: 75–87.

Weyhe, E. (1987) 'Dialekt og standard i færøsk', in M. P. Barnes and R. D. S. Allan (eds), *Proceedings of the Seventh Biennial Conference of Teachers of Scandinavian Studies in Great Britain and Northern Ireland*, London: University College London, pp. 298–312.

8 Norwegian

John Ole Askedal

8.1 Introduction

Norwegian is the only modern Germanic language of which two officially recognized literary varieties exist. These are *Bokmål* ('book language'; BM) and *Nynorsk* ('New Norwegian'; NN). The reasons for the existence of the two varieties are to be found in the political and cultural history of the country. In 1380 Norway entered a political union with Denmark which was to last until 1814, when the country became affiliated with Sweden through a union with the Swedish king as head of state. This union was dissolved in 1905.

In 1814 the Norwegian linguistic situation was a kind of functional diglossia. As early as the sixteenth century, the traditional Norwegian literary language was supplanted by written Danish. However, the development of the spoken language followed its own course, yielding a large variety of different dialects. There even existed a Norwegian pronunciation of written Danish which is estimated to have been used by approximately 1 per cent of the population. This situation was not altogether as unnatural as it might seem at first glance. Both Norwegian and Danish had undergone a highly similar morphosyntactic restructuring since the classical Old Norse (ON) and Old Danish period. The syntactic patterning of the two languages was to a large extent the same, and so were even the main inflectional categories. The differences between the two languages mainly concerned the phonological system and the morphological (allomorphic) manifestation of inflectional categories, i.e. areas where many languages tolerate considerable discrepancies between their written and spoken forms.

The political and cultural renaissance after 1814 engendered a wish for a more genuinely Norwegian standard language. An evolutionary approach was advocated by Knud Knudsen (1812–95) who sought to transform the Danish standard by integrating into it specifically Norwegian elements from the colloquial speech of the educated classes in urban areas. On the other hand, the linguistic revolutionary Ivar Aasen (1813–96) created an altogether new variety of written Norwegian based on those – predominantly western – dialects that were most similar to Old Norse. This was simply called 'Norwegian', or '*landsmål*' 'the language of the countryside/realm'. Ivar

Aasen's new brand of Norwegian found favour with nationalist intellectuals and politicians. In 1885 Parliament agreed on an address to the government that New Norwegian and Dano-Norwegian should be considered languages of equal standing for official and educational purposes. This became the basis of all future language policy and language planning in Norway.

At that time, the usual designation for traditional Dano-Norwegian was *det almindelige Bogsprog* 'the common literary language'. Later the term *riksmål* 'the language of the realm' came into use. The present official terms *Bokmål* and *Nynorsk* were adopted in 1929. *Riksmål* (RM) is now being used in a restricted fashion with reference to a more conservative, traditional form of what was originally Dano-Norwegian.

Norwegian linguistic development in the twentieth century is above all characterized by several spelling reforms, the two overall objectives and main results of which have been a reduction of the specifically Danish traits of *Bokmål/Riksmål* orthography and morphology, and a levelling of differences between *Bokmål* and New Norwegian. The two reforms of 1907 and 1917 together replaced a large number of specifically Danish word forms with more orthophonic Norwegian ones and also introduced a number of properly Norwegian inflectional endings. As regards New Norwegian, a certain amount of morphological simplification was carried through and provision was made for a greater influx of widespread (South-)East Norwegian ((S)EN) word forms.

In 1938, this general line of development was carried still further to a point where quite a number of people felt the cultural identity of the two standard languages to be threatened. The 1938 reform brought with it a classification of all word forms of both official varieties in five classes which is still in use in officially authorized dictionaries and language manuals: (a) obligatory in all written language; (b) obligatory in text books for use in schools, but not in other forms of written language; (c) equivalent (and optional) alternatives in all written language, including school books (indicated by a slash between the alternatives); (d) subsidiary forms allowed in most written language including pupils' exercises, but not in school books (indicated by square brackets); (e) not allowed in any form of official written language, including pupils' school exercises.

This classificatory system implies that the concept of 'standard language' is, in the case of Norwegian, a rather tenuous one.

In 1938 a great number of words and word forms that were alien to traditional usage, but which were widely used in spoken Norwegian, were included in the (a) and (b) parts of the vocabulary, whereas certain traditional forms with a high frequency of occurrence in literary language were allocated to the (e) category. After the war, the prospect of a *samnorsk* 'Common Norwegian' as an eventual merger of *Bokmål* and New Norwegian emerged as a political issue. This caused the debate to harden during the fifties and early sixties, but the decision to establish a *Norsk språkråd* ('Norwegian

Language Council') in 1966 with its concomitant recommendation of a less rigorous enforcement of radical measures has brought about a fair degree of 'language peace' within the linguistic community. The last reform so far was carried through in 1981 and concerned *Bokmål* only. It brought about the reintroduction of a great number of commonly used Dano-Norwegian forms, i.e. their transfer from the (e) to the (d) or (c) categories in the above taxonomy.

At present, 83 per cent of the population receive their primary education in *Bokmål* and 17 per cent in New Norwegian. At higher educational levels, in the armed forces, and in publishing, the New Norwegian percentage is greatly reduced. The strongholds of New Norwegian are certain rural districts in the interior of southern Norway and above all in the less centralized coastal districts in west Norway.

All Norwegian dialects are mutually intelligible. For *Bokmål/Riksmål* a Southeast Norwegian pronunciation based mainly on the spoken language of the capital Oslo and the surrounding area is the most prestigious standard, but there also exist regional standards (e.g. in Bergen and Trondheim). For New Norwegian, no such standard pronunciation exists. New Norwegian is in general spoken with whatever dialectal pronunciation a person happens to have acquired.

8.2   Phonology

Segmental Phonology
The phonemic inventories of Norwegian dialects are highly diverse. The following exposition is based on the Southeast Norwegian system which is the predominant standard pronunciation of *Bokmål* and which is also by and large acceptable in eastern varieties of New Norwegian.

Vowels
The subsystem of monophthongs is set out in Table 8.1. All the vowels in Table 8.1 may be either short or long. With one debatable exception (short [e, æ]), they contrast phonemically. [æ] is usual before [r], where it may be considered an allophone of /e/. Minimal pairs are rare, but cf. *hesje* [heʂe] 'dry hay on a rack' vs *herse* [hæʂe] 'pester', and English loanwords like *bag* /bæg/. Unstressed central [ə] is naturally considered an allophone of /e/.

In addition, Norwegian also possesses the diphthongs / ei, øy, oi, ai, aʉ /. /ai/ and /oi/ occur mainly in loan words. Phonetically, /au/ is [æʉ] or [œʉ]. Diphthongs are in general subject to the same morpheme-structure rules as long vowels (but short diphthongs occur in many dialects).

Table 8.1 Norwegian vowel phonemes

	Fronted Non-rounded	Rounded	Back Non-rounded	Rounded
Close	i	y ʉ		u
Mid	e	ø		o
Open	æ		a	

Consonants

The Southeast Norwegian system of consonantal phonemes is given in Table 8.2. Except after /s/, the unvoiced plosives are aspirated. (Dialectal) Southeast Norwegian /ʈ/ either corresponds to etymological /l/, as in *sol* 'sun' /suːʈ/ vs standard /suːl/, or to standard /r/ from the Old Norse cluster /rð/, as in *gård* 'farm' as SEN /goːʈ/ vs standard /goːr/. Still, many words retain spoken /rd/, e.g. *herde* 'harden'. To Southeast Norwegian /ʈ, ɳ, ʂ/ correspond the graphematic renderings ‹rt, rn, rs› and the corresponding phoneme sequences in non-Eastern dialects. The Southeast Norwegian retroflex sounds occur in lexical stems, cf. *hjort* /juʈ/ 'deer', *barn* /baːɳ/ 'child', but they also arise from productive morphophonemic processes, cf. the infinitive *høre* /høːre/ 'hear' vs the preterite *hørte* /hø(ː)ʈe/ 'heard' and *gård* /goːr/ or /goːʈ/ 'farm' vs *gården* /goːren/ or /goːɳ/ 'the farm'. Another source of /ʈ, ɳ/ are sequences with /ʈ/ corresponding to /lt, ln/, cf. *gul*, m. sg., *gult*, n. sg. 'yellow', *gulne* 'turn yellow' as /gʉːl/, /gʉːlt/, /gʉːlne/ or /gʉːʈ/, /gʉːʈ/, /gʉːɳe/, respectively. Similarly, /ɖ/ occurs in lexemes like *ferdig* /fæːɖi/ 'ready' or as the result of an optional sandhi attraction in word sequences, cf. *gjør det!* 'do it!' as /jøːr de/ or /jøɖːe/. On account of these dialectal correspondences and morphophonemic rules, the phonemic status of the retroflex sounds as monophonematic units or as surface manifestations of biphonematic sequences is a moot question. Current analyses tend to favour the monophonematic interpretation or a combined solution.

Table 8.2 Norwegian consonant phonemes

	Plosive		Fricative		Lateral approximant	Trill	Flap	Nasal
	Unvoiced	Voiced	Unvoiced	Voiced		Voiced		
Labial	p	b	f	v				m
Alveolar	t	d	s		l	r		n
Retroflex	ʈ	ɖ	ʂ		ɭ		ɽ	ɳ
Dorsal	k	g	ç	j				ŋ
Glottal			h					

Only syllables with main or secondary stress show phonetic length. Postvocalic consonants are short after long vowels and diphthongs, and long after short vowels, thus yielding the two canonic and complementary phonetic syllable types V:C and VC:, cf. *tak* [taːk] 'roof, ceiling' vs *takk* [takː] 'thanks'. Length is in general only considered phonemic with vowels. Consonant clusters appear to be equivalent to long consonants with respect to syllable formation, thus rendering the assumption of VC:C sequences as a special case systematically superfluous. On the other hand, certain inflectional endings are appended to stem syllables of the form V:C, yielding V:CC, cf. the infinitive *mase* /maːse/ 'be very persistent' and the corresponding participle *mast* /maːst/ and *fint* /fiːnt/, n. sg. of *fin* /fiːn/ 'fine'.

Syllable Structure and Morphophonemic Rules

The overwhelming majority of monosyllabic lexical stems belong to one of the following syllable structures: (1) V *i* 'in'; (2) CV *ta* 'take'; (3) VC *av* 'of'; (4) CCV *fri* 'free'; (5) VCC *øks* 'axe'; (6) CCCV *skru* 'screw'; (7) VCCC *angst* 'fear'; (8) CVC *til* 'to'; (9) CCVC *bråk* 'noise'; (10) CCCVC *skrik* 'scream'; (11) CVCC *heks* 'witch'; (12) CVCCC *vekst* 'growth'; (13) CCVCC *slekt* 'family'; (14) CCCVCC *skrift* 'writing'; (15) CCVCCC *blomst* 'flower'; (16) CCCVCCC *sprelsk* 'boisterous'.

With the exception of /h/, which only occurs word-initially, all consonants are possible as the single consonantal element in initial and final position in lexical stems. The quantity of a syllable-final single consonant stands in inverse relation to the quantity of the preceding vowel. In stem-final position, /v/ almost always occurs after long vowels where it is short. The phonotactic rules allow for the (a) stem-initial and (b) stem-final consonantal clusters indicated by italics in Table 8.3. Some further cases of stem-final clusters are formed by adding an inflectional *t*-suffix or a derivational *sk*- suffix to lexical stems with a final cluster, cf. *kvalmt* from *kvalm* 'nauseated', *skarpt* from *skarp* 'sharp', *habsburgsk* from *Habsburg*. Clusters consisting of or containing *rn*, *rs*, *rt* in western dialects correspond to retroflex sounds or clusters with retroflex sounds in Southeast Norwegian. Secondary clusters with syllabic /l, r, n/ arise through the optional deletion of /e/ [ə] in unstressed syllables, yielding, e.g. *handel* [handl̩] 'commerce', *våpen* [voːpn̩] 'arms', *maten* [maːtn̩] 'the food', and even *mannen* [manː̩] 'the man'.

The Relation of the Phonemic System to Orthography

The graphematic rendering of most vowels appears fairly unproblematic from a European point of view, cf. /i(ː)/ as ‹i› (*finn* 'find!', *fin* 'fine'), /e(ː)/ as ‹e› (*venn* 'friend', *ven* 'nice'), /a(ː)/ as ‹a› (*tall* 'number', *tal* 'speak!'), /ø(ː)/ as ‹ø› (*føll* 'foal', *føl* 'feel!'), and /y(ː)/ as ‹y› (*tynn* 'thin', *tyn* 'torment!'. /æ(ː)/ is regularly written ‹æ›, but appears as ‹e› in front of /r/ and in a few other cases, cf. *hær* 'army' and *her* 'here', both /hæːr/. With the other vowel

Table 8.3 Norwegian consonantal clusters

(a) Stem-initial consonantal clusters

språk		*splid*		*spjåk*			
strøm				*stjerne*			
skrue		*sklie*				*skvett*	
pris	*bris*	*plog*	*blind*	*pjatt*	*Bjørn*		
tru	*driv*			*tjene*	*djerv*	*tvang*	*dvask*
krig	*gris*	*klang*	*glans*	*fjern*		*kvinne*	*(Gvarv)*
frisk	*vri*	*flink*		*sjø*		*svak*	
spak	*slank*						
stil							
skall			*gni*	*mjølk*	*(Rjukan)*		
kna				*(Njål)*			
fnugg							
snu							
små							

(b) Stem-final consonantal clusters

løpsk	vekst									surl
hatsk	blomst									
	kunst							korps		
uhumsk	helst									
svensk	verst									
trolsk	angst[ŋst]									
morsk	verft			hugst	mulkt					
vers	vert	verd	verk	arg	verp	smurf	arv	arm	ørn	
hals	velt		kalk	elg	valp	alv	kalv	halm	(Køln)	
hems	tomt	sømd	hank[ŋk]		kamp				hamn	
hans	vant									
finans[ŋs]	lengt[ŋt]									
	hest		fisk		visp					
tufs	tuft	hevd							hevn	
øks	økt	bygd						vatn	rogn[ŋn]	avl
veps										

Note: Italicized letters indicate consonantal clusters. Phonetic transcriptions are given in a few cases where the phonetic nature of the cluster is not clearly indicated in the orthography. Proper nouns showing clusters not found elsewhere in the vocabulary are given in parentheses.

phonemes certain discrepancies resulting from the North Scandinavian vowel shift of the late Middle Ages should be noted. /oː/ is most often written ‹å›, cf. *bål* 'bonfire', *få* 'few', and, correspondingly, /o/ as ‹å›, cf. *åtte* 'eight' and, with shortened /oː/, *tålmodig* 'patient' (cf. *tåle* 'endure'). However, ‹o› is also used for /oː/ in certain words in front of ‹g›, ‹v›, cf. *doven* 'lazy', *svoger* 'brother-in-law', and New Norwegian participles like *brote* 'broken', *krope* 'crept'. ‹o› is also used for /o/, cf. *topp* 'top', *holde* 'hold', *toll* 'customs'. /uː/ is rendered as ‹o›, cf. *skog* 'forest', *stor* 'great', and /u/ as ‹o›, cf. *ost* 'cheese', or ‹u› as in *lukke* 'close', *tung* 'heavy'. /ʉ(ː)/ is uniformly written ‹u›, cf. *full* 'full', *ful* 'cunning'.

Vowel length is indicated in a way which mirrors the quantity relationship between vowels and consonants within stressed syllables. Long vowels are followed by a single consonant grapheme, and short vowels by a geminated consonant or a cluster. Consonants in clusters are only written as geminates in a restricted number of lexemes for the purpose of distinguishing vowel length within the syllable, cf. *visst* 'known' vs *vist* 'shown', *fullt* 'fully' vs *fult* 'cunningly'.

The rendering of the consonantal phonemes /p, t, k, b, d, g, f, v, s, h/ by means of corresponding graphemes poses no special problems. /m/ follows the usual rules with the exception that it is never geminated finally, cf. *dom* – *dommen* '(the) verdict'. [lː] and [nː] are variously written ‹ll›, ‹nn› or ‹ld›, ‹nd› according to etymological origin, cf. *kall* 'vocation' vs *kald* 'cold' and *henne* 'her' vs *hende* 'happen'. Similarly, /r/ is occasionally rendered as ‹rd› for etymological reasons as in *gjorde* 'did', *hard* 'hard'. In *Bokmål*, initial /v/ is written etymologically as ‹hv› in interrogative words: *hva* 'what', *hvem* 'who', *hvorfor* 'why' and in a few other cases: *hval* 'whale', *hvit* 'white'. Somewhat more complicated is the – largely etymological – orthographic rendering of the three remaining continuants /ʂ, ç, j/. /ʂ/ is written ‹sj› in words with Proto-Nordic 'breaking' and more recent loanwords: *sjø* 'sea', *bagasje* 'luggage'; or ‹sk› in front of ‹i, y, ei, øy›: *ski* 'ski', *sky* 'cloud', *skei* 'spoon', *skøyte* 'skate'; or ‹sk› in front of other vowels: *skje* 'spoon', *skjære* 'cut', *skjule* 'hide'. /ç/ is ‹k› in front of ‹i, y, ei, øy›: *kinn* 'cheek', *kyss* 'kiss', *keiser* 'emperor', NN *køyra* 'drive'; ‹kj› in front of other vowels: *kjele* 'kettle', *kjære* 'dear'; and ‹tj› in a few other cases: *tjern* 'small lake', *tjære* 'tar'. /j/ is ‹j›: *jeg* 'I', *jakt* 'hunting'; or ‹g› in front of ‹i, y, ei, øy›: *gild* 'dashing', *gyllen* 'golden', *geit* 'goat', NN *gøyma* 'hide'; or ‹hj› or ‹gj› in front of other vowels: *hjerne* 'brain' vs *gjerne* 'gladly', *hjelpe* 'help', *gjøre* 'do'.

Orthographical differences between *Bokmål* and New Norwegian do exist, but in general they reflect differences of pronunciation rather than different spelling conventions. One instance of a purely orthographic difference is that between *Bokmål* ‹å› and New Norwegian ‹o› for /oː/, cf. BM *åpen* and NN *open* 'open', BM *skåret* and NN *skore* 'cut'. Here, New Norwegian ‹o› reflects Old Norse spelling.

Prosodic Phenomena

In the greater part of the vocabulary, which is of Common Germanic origin, main stress is assigned to the first syllable of the word. Composite words, like *'samfunns,liv* 'social life', *'om,vende* 'convert (verb)', *'hår,fin* 'very subtle', have rather strong secondary stress under which the syllabic quantity distinction between V:C and VC: is preserved, cf. *vintap* ['vi:n,ta:p] 'loss of wine' vs *vintapp* [vi:n,tap:] 'wine plug'. The stress falls on the second syllable in many common loanwords with the originally (Low) German prefixes *be-*, *er-*, *for-*, e.g. *be'tale* 'pay', *erk'lære* 'declare', *fork'lare* 'explain', and their derived nominals, cf. *be'taling, erk'læring, fork'laring*. In imitation of German, some adjectives also carry stress on the second syllable, cf. *rett'ferdig* 'righteous', *u'mulig* 'impossible'. Penultimate stress is found in more recent non-German loans with certain nominal suffixes, cf. *refe'ranse, materi'ale, sosial'isme, me'tode, tra'gedie, pro'fessor*, and in the numerous verbs ending in *-ere*, cf. *repa'rere* 'repair'. More recent French loanwords retain their original stress on the last syllable, cf. *poli'tikk, nasjo'nal, universi'tet, insti'tutt, sta'sjon*. Associated derivations often exhibit a stress shift, either backwards: *tra'gedie* vs *'tragisk, poli'tikk* vs *po'litisk*; or to the following syllable in the case of the plural of nouns with the *-or-* suffix: *pro'fessor* vs *profes'sorer*. The general rules seems to be that stress is assigned to the rightermost syllable of the canonical form V:C or VC: (excluding derivational affixes). Southeast Norwegian dialects strongly tend to generalize the indigenous Germanic pattern with main stress on the first syllable of all words, but this is not accepted as standard pronunciation.

Norwegian exhibits a tonal opposition which manifests itself in connection with main stress in bi- and polysyllabic words and word forms. Thus the word form written *tanken* when pronounced with tone 1 means 'the tank', but with tone 2 it means 'the thought'. Phonetically, the opposition is in Southeast Norwegian one between steadily rising tone (pitch) and delayed rise of tone. In the speech of the Oslo area it manifests itself in the two different tonal contours diagrammatically depicted in Figure 8.1.

Monosyllables are neutral with regard to the tonal opposition. But as Southeast Norwegian stress is associated with low tone, tone 1 may be interpreted as the polysyllabic continuation of the basic monosyllabic stress–pitch correlation. Tone 2 is naturally considered the marked member of the opposition as it is phonetically more complex and also subject to lexical restrictions, being largely excluded from words of German and Romance origin. In the linguistic literature the tonal opposition is indicated by a variety of notations that reflect the markedness relationship or the phonetic difference, cf. for 'the tank' and 'the thought', respectively: ^{1}*tanken* vs ^{2}*tanken*; *'tanken* vs *''tanken* or *ˇtanken*; *'tanken* vs *`tanken* or *'tan,ken*; *tan'ken* vs *tan'ken* or *tanke'n*.

The basic distributional rule is commonly stated in etymological terms: modern words and word forms which in (possibly early) Old Norse were

Figure 8.1 Tonal contours in Southeast Norwegian

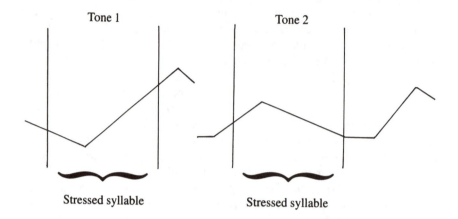

Tone 1   Tone 2

Stressed syllable   Stressed syllable

monosyllabic, or syntactic phrases without internal word coherence, have tone 1, and words that derive from Old Norse bi- and polysyllables have tone 2. It follows that polysyllables with tone 1 are either later borrowings, cf. e.g. ʼhandel, ʼkloster, ʼorden, or are secondarily developed by vowel epenthesis, such as the present-tense form of (originally) strong verbs: ON *bítr* > BM ʼbiter; the plural of root nouns: ON *geitr* > ʼgeiter; and certain lexical stems: ON *akr* > ʼaker, BM ʼåker 'field'.

Synchronically, the tonal opposition is functionally connected with grammatical and derivational morphemes, which may for this reason be classified as either tone-inducing or tonally transparent. For instance, the verb suffix *-ere* and stressed verbal prefixes like *ut-*, *gjen-*, *på-*, *til-* induce tone 1: BM ʼutgjøre 'consist in, of', ʼgjenta 'repeat', ʼpåkalle 'invoke', ʼtilkjenne 'grant'. Tone 2 is induced by final *-e* in most of its inflectional or stem-forming uses (but not as a definiteness suffix in the neuter singular, written *-et*). The same goes for the common derivational suffixes *-inne* (ven ˇninne 'female friend'), *-lig* (ˇfarlig 'dangerous'), *-dom* (ˇrikdom 'wealth'). The definiteness suffix in the singular is tonally transparent: *gutt* – ʼgutten '(the) boy', ˇherre– ˇherren '(the) gentleman', *elv* – ʼelva '(the) river', ˇjente – ˇjenta '(the) girl', *hus* – ʼhuset '(the) house', as is the derivational suffix BM *-het*: (ʼfrihet 'freedom'). In inflectional paradigms tone is associated with word forms rather than with lexemes as such, due to the tone-inducing character of certain suffixes, cf. for example, ˇsitte – ʼsitter – ˇsittet 'sit (etc.)'. Tonal pairs are invariably connected with a difference in lexical or stem formation or in grammatical morpheme, cf. (*tank* –) ʼtanken vs (ˇtanke –) ˇtanken, (ˇbonde –) ʼbønder 'peasants' vs (ˇbønne –) ˇbønner 'beans', (*rev* –) ʼreven 'the fox' vs (ˇrive 'tear' –) ˇreven 'torn'. It is estimated that several hundred or as many as two thousand word pairs are phonologically distinct only through the tonal opposition. This is mainly due to the functional diversity of the ending *-er* in *Bokmål*, which occurs as a plural suffix, as the finite verb ending in the present tense of most verbs, as a derivational suffix of agent nouns, and as the unstressed final syllable of many non-decomposable lexical stems. Mainly because New Norwegian strong verbs normally have no present-tense ending *-er*, and the usual agent noun formation in New Norwegian has the suffix *-ar*, which is also a common plural ending, the number of tonal opposition pairs is less in New Norwegian than in *Bokmål*.

In Southeast Norwegian the use of tone 2 is extended to syntactic phrases. Outside of the East Norwegian area, verb particles of adverbial or prepositional origin carry monosyllabic stress, but in East Norwegian they form one stress and tone group together with the immediately preceding verb form, cf. non-EN, *'han 'tenkte 'ut en 'plan* vs EN *'han 'tenkte-ut en 'plan* 'he devised a plan', non-EN *'været slo 'om* vs EN *'været 'slo-om* 'the weather changed'. The last example shows that even monosyllabic verb forms partake of this phenomenon. True prepositions are not accessible to the stress and tone shift in question. Thus there is a clear difference between e.g. EN *'ta på 'noe* 'touch something' and EN *'ta-på 'noe* 'put on something'.

Specific intonation patterns are identifiable on the sentence level. In contrast to most other European languages, Southeast Norwegian declarative sentences expressing statements end on a rising melody, and in these cases the last stressed syllable is likely to receive the strongest stress. Interrogative sentences are amenable to basically the same characterization, with the difference that the rise in pitch in the last stressed syllable is stronger than in declaratives. When, however, the sentence initial constituent is focused or given emphatic stress, sentence-final stress is largely suspended and the sentence ends on a falling melody, cf. for example, *i dag kommer hun* 'today she'll be here' and *når kommer hun?* 'when will she be here?' as opposed to *hun kommer i dag* 'she comes today' and *hvem kommer i dag?* 'who comes today?', respectively.

8.3 Morphology

The Nominal Group

Nouns
The inflectional categories of Norwegian nouns are gender, definiteness and number (but not case; see below on the genitive), which are given cumulative expression in portmanteau suffixes. Word-internal inflectional marking (umlaut, vowel gradation) is only of marginal importance in Modern Norwegian.

Both *Bokmål* and New Norwegian have masculine, feminine and neuter gender, but the feminine is not of equal standing in the two varieties. It is

Table 8.4 Types of plural formation in Norwegian

New Norwegian		Bokmål	
Masculine		**Masculine**	
1 -ar/-ane	(gut-) gutar/-ane '(the) boys'	1 -er/-ene	(gutt-) gutter/-ene
2 -er	(søknad-) søknader/-ene '(the) applications'	2 -er*/-ene*	(fot-) føtter/-ene '(foot-) (the) feet'
3 -er/ene [-ar/-ane]	(bekk-) bekker/-ene [bekkar/-ane] '(the) brooks'	3 -e/-ne	(lærer-) lærere/-ne '(the) teachers'
4 -ar*/-ane*	(far-) fedrar/-ane '(the) fathers'	4 -e*/ene*	(far-) fedre/-ene
5 -er*/-ene*	(fot-) føter/-ene	5 -r/-rne*	(sko-) skor/-rne '(the) shoes'
6 -r/-rne	(sko-) skor/-rne	6 -r*/-rne*	(tå-) tær/-rne '(the) toes'
7 -Ø*/-ne*	(bror-) brør/-ne '(the) brothers'		
Feminine		**Feminine**	
1 -er/-ene	(bygd-) bygder/-ene '(the) rural communities'	1 -(e)r/-(e)ne	(bygd-) bygder/-ene (vise-) viser/-ene
2 -r [-or]/-ne [-one]	(vise-) viser [visene] [visor/visone] '(the) songs'	2 -er*/-ene*	(hånd-) hender '(the) hands'
3 -er*/-ene*	(hand-) hender/-ene	3 -e*/-ene*	(datter-) døtre/-ene '(the) daughters'
4 -ar [-er]/-ane [-ene]	(elv-) elvar/-ane [elver/-ene] '(the) rivers'	4 -r*/-rne*	(ku-) kyr/-rne '(the) cows'
5 -ar/-ane	(kjerring-) kjerringar/-ane '(the) wives/hags'		
6 -r*/-rne*	(ku-) kyr/-rne		
Neuter		**Neuter**	
1 -Ø/-a [-i]	(hus-) hus/-a[-i] '(the) houses'	1 -Ø/-ene, -a	(hus-) husene/-a
2 -Ø*/-a [-i]*	(barn-) born/-a [-i] '(the) children'	2 -er/-ene	(skrift-) skrifter/-ene '(the) publications'
3 -o/-o	(auga-) augo/augo '(the) eyes'	3 -e/-ene, -a	(under-) undre/-ene, -a '(the) wonders' (øye-) øyne/-ene '(the) eyes'
		4 -r*/-rne*	(tre-) trær/-rne* '(the) trees'

Note: Indefinite plural forms and corresponding forms with the definiteness suffix are separated by a virgule. Umlaut is indicated by an asterisk *. The singular forms from which the plural forms are derived are given in parentheses.

firmly rooted in New Norwegian due to its general presence in the dialects. Dano-Norwegian, on the other hand, had no feminine gender, but a common gender resulting from the merger of the old masculine and feminine. Feminine gender was reintroduced into *Bokmål* through the language reforms of this century. With many words the feminine is the more colloquial, and the common gender the more literary option (*ei bok – boka* vs *en bok – boken* '(a/the) book'. There is thus in *Bokmål* a certain competition between the more indigenous three-gender system and the traditional Dano-Norwegian two-gender system. The latter is more strongly favoured in the unofficial *Riksmål* variety.

Whereas definiteness is marked by a suffixal morpheme, indefiniteness in the singular is either marked by the prenominal indefinite article (BM *en gutt*, NN *ein gut* 'a boy') or, in certain cases, left morphologically unmarked (*det var god vin* 'that's a good wine'). In the plural, indefiniteness is part of a morphological opposition between a definite and an indefinite form of the plural morpheme (which in certain cases may be zero).

The main inflectional differences between New Norwegian and *Bokmål* clearly pertain to plural morphology. Masculine and feminine nouns are subject to somewhat more allomorphic variation in New Norwegian than in *Bokmål*, whereas the reverse is true with regard to the neuter. *Bokmål* plural formation is restricted to suffixes with an *-e-*. New Norwegian has both *-er* and *-ar*, but *-er* predominates with feminine and *-ar* with masculine nouns. On the whole, *Bokmål* shows more levelling of gender distinctions than does New Norwegian even in the domain of plural morphology.

The main declensional classes are given in Table 8.4. In the singular the definiteness morpheme is *-en* in the masculine (including *Bokmål* common gender), *-a* in the feminine, and *-et* in the neuter in both *Bokmål* and New Norwegian. In addition, New Norwegian has *-i* as a subsidiary option with feminine consonantal stems (*jorda* [*jordi*] 'the earth').

The only remnant of morphological case inflection is the suffixal *-s-* genitive whose main function is to mark a subordinate nominal constituent in complex noun phrases, cf. NN *den gamle mannens bil* 'the old man's car'. It is also used elliptically with noun-phrase functions, as in BM *den andre bilen var den gamle mannens* 'the other car was the old man's'. The *-s-* morpheme is not subject to declensional variation, and its status as a case suffix is dubious for the further reason that it may be adjoined to the last constituent of a complex noun phrase regardless of syntactic rank: BM *tusener av drepte menneskers blod* 'the blood of thousands of killed people', BM *ungene i gatas eget hus* 'the children in the street's own house'.

A number of productive suffixal derivations exist for the formation of nouns from other word classes. The suffix *-ing* (feminine, in *Bokmål* also common gender) is used freely to derive from verbs nouns denoting processes, e.g. *blomstring* 'flowering', *venting* 'waiting', *matlaging* 'cooking'. Only *Bokmål* also has *-ning*, as in (*ned*)*rivning* 'demolition'. Infinitival constructions are a productive means for the nominal expression of action or event rather than processual meaning, either on their own or as a complement to the neuter pronoun *det* as head of a complex noun phrase: BM (*det*) *å leve i en storby er ikke lett* 'living in a large city is not easy'. Typically *Bokmål* are verbal nouns with the suffix *-else*, e.g. *stadfestelse* 'confirmation' which is avoided in New Norwegian on account of alleged Low German origin. Abstract nouns with the suffix *-nad* are typical of New Norwegian, e.g. *freistnad* 'attempt', but some of them are common in *Bokmål* also, e.g. *søknad* 'application'. The common suffix for agent nouns, including terms for the performer of an occupation and for various nationalities, is BM *-er*, NN *-ar*: *arbeider, arbeidar* 'worker', *tysker, tyskar* 'German'. The corresponding female terms in *-ske* (*arbeiderske* 'female worker') and *-inne* (*skuespillerinne* 'actress') are not used in New Norwegian, and they are also not productive in *Bokmål*.

The suffix *-het* is freely used in *Bokmål* for deriving nouns from adjectives, as in *snillhet* 'kindness'. Due to its Middle Low German origin, it is officially shunned in New Norwegian. Instead New Norwegian employs a variety of suffixes: *-leik* (BM *nærhet* vs NN *nærleik* 'vicinity', *-dom* (BM *frihet* vs NN *fridom* 'freedom'), *-skap* (BM *likhet* vs NN *likskap* 'similarity') and certain other formations (BM *ensomhet* vs NN *einsemd* 'loneliness', BM *arbeidsløshet* vs NN *arbeidsløyse* 'unemployment').

Pronouns

The personal pronouns are the only nominal category of Modern Norwegian to exhibit a morphological case distinction between a subject ('nominative') and a non-subject ('accusative' or 'oblique') form, but this distinction is not made consistently in all persons in the singular and the plural. The non-subject form does service as a direct as well as an indirect object. In *Bokmål* it is also used as a predicative: BM *det er ham* 'it is him'. The corresponding possessives constitute a 'split' system, in which certain personal pronouns have associated with them inflected adjectival possessive pronouns, whereas others form a regular or irregular uninflected (*-s-*) genitive.

Table 8.5 shows that the personal pronouns are subdivided into the following declension classes: (1) subject and oblique form in combination with inflected possessives (1 sg., 2 sg., 1 pl.); (2) subject and oblique form in combination with the genitive (2 pl. in NN, 3 pl. in BM, and BM 3 sg. m., f. as the favoured alternative, but optionally in NN 3 sg. m.); (3) no distinction between subject and oblique form, in combination with the genitive (2 pl. in BM, 3 pl. in NN, optionally NN, BM 3 sg. m. and NN f., and in the subsidiary option BM 3 sg. f. *ho* – *hennes*), BM 3 sg. common gender and n.; (4) no distinction between subject and oblique form, and no genitive (NN 3 sg. common gender).

The formation of the genitive is to a certain extent irregular in both New Norwegian and *Bokmål*, but more so in New Norwegian. The reflexive

Table 8.5   Personal, reflexive, and possessive pronouns in Norwegian

	Subject form	Oblique form	Inflected adjectival possessive (m. sg., f. sg., n. sg., com. sg., pl.)	s-genitive
Singular				
1	NN eg	NN meg /meːg/	NN, BM min,	——
	BM jeg	BM meg /mei/	mi, mitt, mine	
2	NN, BM du	NN deg /deːg/		
		BM deg /dei/	NN, BM din, di, ditt, dine	——
3 m.	NN, BM han	NN han/honom	——	NN, BM hans
		BM ham/han		
f.	NN ho	NN ho/henne	——	NN hennar
	BM hun [ho]	BM henne [ho]		[hennes] BM hennes
com.	NN, BM den	NN, BM den	——	NN—— BM dens
n.	NN, BM det /de(ː)/	NN, BM det /de(ː)/	——	NN dess (rare) BM dets
Plural				
1	NN vi/me, BM vi	NN, BM oss	NN, BM vår, vårt, våre	——
2	NN de /deː/ BM dere	NN dykk BM dere	——	NN dykkar BM deres
3	NN dei BM de /diː/	NN dei BM dem	——	NN deira [deires] BM deres
Reflexive				
3 sg./pl.	——	NN seg /seːg/ BM seg /sei/	NN, BM sin, si, sitt, sine	——

pronoun in the third-person singular and plural lacks a subject form but apart from this inflects according to declension class 1 above (*seg* as BM [sei], NN [seːg] – *sin* m., *si* f., *sitt* n., *sine* pl.).

As a means of formal address *Bokmål* uses the third-person plural forms: *De – Dem – Deres*, which are restricted to addressing one person only; and New Norwegian the second-person plural: *De – Dykk – Dykkar*. The formal/non-formal opposition is thus in fact neutralized in the plural. On the whole, non-formal singular *du* is, however, the predominant unmarked form used in most social circumstances.

Enclitization of subject or object pronouns is widespread in colloquial speech, e.g. SEN *nå er'n borte* 'now he's gone', *har'u sett'n?* 'have you seen him?' But Southeast Norwegian *'a* (from ON accusative *hana*) for both *hun* and *henne* is the only clitic form which is not readily explainable as a case of phonetic stem reduction, e.g. *nå er'a her* 'she is here now', *har'u sett'a?* 'have you seen her?'. Enclitization of pronouns is as a rule not reflected in the written language.

As a pronoun with non-specific personal reference *Bokmål* has *man* and *en* (the former with subject function only), New Norwegian has *ein*, but even the third-person plural *dei* and the noun *folk* 'people' are used in a similar fashion.

The interrogative pronouns show a basic distinction between human (animate) BM *hvem*, NN *kven* and non-human (inanimate) BM *hva*, NN *kva*. *Bokmål* also has a literary genitive form *hvis* and an interrogative adjective *hvilken*, both of which are lacking New Norwegian counterparts. For the latter, New Norwegian uses *kva for (ein)*, which corresponds to *Bokmål hva for (en)* as the somewhat more colloquial option.

Norwegian has no inflecting relative pronoun, but only the invariant relative particle *som*. In *Bokmål hva* is used in restrictive relative clauses as an alternative to *det (som)*, e.g. *det (som)/hva han tidligere hadde sagt, kunne ikke være sant* 'what he had said earlier could not be true'. In non-restrictive relative clauses *hva* and the still more literary neuter form *hvilket* of the interrogative adjective refer to propositional content as alternatives to *noe (som)*, NN *noko (som)*: *han måtte gi opp, hva/hvilket/noe (som) alle hadde forutsett* 'he had to give in, as everyone had foreseen'.

Among the so-called 'indefinite' pronouns we find a number of quantifying words which share the property that they occur both as main phrases and as attributive modifiers (determiners) of nouns. They differ as to the extent to which they partake of the gender and number distinctions of the strong declension of adjectives (see below). See Table 8.6 for details.

Adjectives

Adjectives have two inflectional paradigms that are differentiated by the number and phonological shape of the endings involved:

A   The strong declension, comprising four declensional subclasses according to the number of morphological oppositions:

1   Four endings (as the possible maximum): NN [BM] *eigen* m., *eiga* f., *eige* n., *eigne* pl.; NN *open* m., *open* [*opi*] f., *ope/opi* [*opi*] n., *opne* pl.;
2   Three endings: BM/NN *stor* m./f., *stort* n., *store* pl., BM *åpen* m./f., *åpent* n., *åpne* pl.;
3   Two endings: BM/NN *viktig* m./f./n., *viktige* pl.;
4   Some adjectives and adjectival forms, most of them ending in a vowel, do not inflect. Among these we find all present participles (BM *lysende*, NN *lysande* 'shining'), the weak past participles ending in *-a* (*kasta*

Table 8.6 Indefinite pronouns and quantifiers in Norwegian

		Singular			Plural
		nokon [noen] (m.)	noka [noen] (f.)	noko [noe] (n.)	nokre 'some', nokon 'any' [noen]
1 Singular – plural opposition; gender distinctions in the singular					
'Some, any'	NN	nokon [noen] (m.)	noka [noen] (f.)	noko [noe] (n.)	nokre 'some', nokon 'any' [noen]
	BM	noen (com.)		noe (n.)	noen 'some, any'
'None, nothing'	NN	ingen (m.)	inga [ingi] (f.)	inkje (n.)	ingen
	BM	ingen (com.)	inga (f.)	intet, ingenting (n.)	ingen
'All'	NN/BM	all (com.)		alt (n.)	alle
2 Only singular, with gender distinction					
'Some(one)'	NN	einkvan (m.)	eikor (f.)	eitkvart (n.)	—
	NN	ein eller annan (m.)	ei eller anna (f.)	eit(t) eller anna (n.)	—
	BM	en eller annen (com.)	ei eller anna (f.)	et eller annet (n.)	—
3 Only singular; gender distinction common–neuter					
'Each, every'	NN	kvar (com.)		kvart (n.)	—
	BM	hver (com.)		hvert (n.)	—
'Anyone'	BM	enhver (com.)		ethvert (n.)	—
4 Singular–plural opposition; one singular (neuter) form with mass-noun meaning					
'Much – many'	NN			mykje (n.)	mange
	BM			mye (n.)	mange
'Little – few'	NN/BM			lite (n.)	få
'Some'	NN/BM			somt (n.)	somme
5 Only plural					
'Both'	NN			—	båe/begge
	BM			—	begge

'thrown'), adjectives with a final *-e*, *-a*, *-u*, *-o* (*moderne*, *bra* 'good', *slu* 'cunning', BM *tro* 'faithful') and final *-s* (*nymotens* 'modish', *avsides* 'remote').

Of these, type 1 is by far the least, and type 2 the most common one. With minor lexical exceptions, *Bokmål* has generalized *-t* in the neuter singular where New Norwegian has stem-class alternation between *-t* and *-e/-i*.

The strong declension is used in those syntactic environments where agreement in gender and number is required, i.e.: (a) prenominally when no determiner is present (BM *gammelt brød* 'old bread', NN *dyre bilar* 'expensive cars'); (b) prenominally after the indefinite article and the homophonous numeral 'one' (NN *eit/eitt stort hus* 'a large house'); (c) even as a postnominal appositional attribute (BM/NN *dette gamle huset, stort og dyrt* 'this old house, large and expensive'); (d) in predicative position (*det huset er dyrt* 'that house is expensive', NN *desse husa er dyre* 'these houses are expensive'), including the use as a so-called free predicative without a copula verb (NN *dei kom rike og mektige attende frå Amerika* 'they returned from America rich and powerful'). Complement clauses and infinitives are generally treated as being of neuter gender, hence also when they function as subjects with which the neuter form of the adjective agrees: BM *å være hjemme/at vi endelig er hjemme, er godt* 'to be home/that we are finally at home is good'. The neuter form is even found with non-neuter subjects when a propositional reading is inferrable: *erter er godt* '(eating) peas is/are good'.

B The weak declension has a generalized *-e*- ending in all genders and both numbers in *Bokmål* as well as in New Norwegian. Invariant adjectives (type 4 above) retain their strong form. This declension is found after determiners, such as the preposed definite article and all possessives including the *-s*- genitives: *det store huset* 'the large house', *hans/mitt/foreldrenes store hus* 'his/my/the parents' large house', and in vocatives: *kjære mor!* 'dear mother', *gode Gud!* 'good God!'

Comparative and superlative forms are formed with the suffixes BM *-er*-, NN *-ar*- and BM *-est*-, NN *-ast*-, respectively, e.g. BM *vakrere – vakrest(e)*, NN *vakrare – vakrast(e)*. A few suppletive formations have an *-r*- and *-st*- suffix: *god –* BM *bedre*, NN *betre – best*. There also exist analytic formations with BM *mer*, NN *meir* in the comparative and *mest* in the superlative. These are obligatory with participial forms BM *mer/mest* levende 'more/most alive' and in a few other cases (NN *meir/mest framand* 'more/most foreign'), but more often it is optional (BM *lykkeligere/mer lykkelig* 'happier'). Suffixal comparatives and superlatives have a defective paradigm, being restricted to the weak declension. In addition, the superlative does not inflect when used predicatively: BM/NN *bilen/huset/bøkene var billigst* 'the car/house/books was/were cheapest'.

A few fairly productive derivational suffixes exist, such as *-sk*, *-isk* (*spotsk* 'scornful', *samisk* 'Lappish') and a number of suffixes that have different phonological shape in *Bokmål* and New Norwegian; cf. BM *-lig*, NN *-leg* (*folkelig, folkeleg* 'popular'), BM *-som*, NN *-sam* (*morsom, morosam* 'funny'), BM *-løs*, NN *laus* (*arbeidsløs, arbeidslaus* 'unemployed'), BM *-et(e)*, NN *-ut/-ete* (*krokete, krokut* 'bent'). Certain *Bokmål* suffixes are avoided in New Norwegian due to their foreign, (Low) German origin, such as *-aktig* (*narraktig* 'conceited'), *-messig* (*bymessig* 'citylike') and *-bar* (BM *kostbar*, NN *kostesam* 'costly'). When BM *-bar*-adjectives derived from verbs have passive meaning, New Norwegian instead uses the present participle: BM *kniven var ikke brukbar*, NN *kniven var ikkje brukande* 'the knife could not be used'.

Determiners

The various morphemes and lexemes traditionally designated as 'articles' and 'determiners' are clearly related from a functional point of view. Still, they constitute no unitary morphosyntactic class. The so-called 'definite article' is a bound inflectional morpheme where definiteness is always expressed together with a value on the number and gender parameters: *gutten* 'the boy', *jenta* 'the girl', *barnet* 'the child', *jentene* 'the girls'. The 'indefinite article' is, on the other hand, a prenominal adjectival modifier which is lexematically restricted to singular expressions: BM *en gutt* 'a boy', *ei jente* 'a girl', NN *eit barn* 'a child', *jenter* 'girls'. To the bound definiteness morpheme there corresponds a preposed definiteness determiner when a prenominal adjective is also present: *den store mannen* 'the big man', *den store jenta* 'the big girl', *det store huset* 'the big house', BM *de store jentene* 'the big girls'. When stressed, *den, det, de/dei* retain their original deictic meaning and may then enter into an opposition with the proximal *denne* m./f. sg., *dette* n. sg., BM *disse*, NN *desse* pl. 'this', as expressing a relatively distal meaning 'that'. The old distal demonstrative *hin* m./f., NN *hi* f., *hitt* n., *hine* pl. is virtually extinct in *Bokmål* but still used to a certain extent in New Norwegian.

The quantifiers set out in Table 8.6 also have prenominal determiner function. They all inflect according to the strong declension of adjectives. The identifying determiner BM *selv/sjøl*, NN *sjølv* belongs, however, to the weak declension when prenominal (BM *selve faren* 'the father himself'). Postnominally, it is not inflected in *Bokmål* (*barnet selv* 'the child itself', *foreldrene selv* 'the parents themselves'), whereas in New Norwegian it is optionally inflected in accordance with the weak adjective declension (*foreldra sjølv(e)*). BM *samme*, NN *same* 'same' inflects like a weak adjective and is only used prenominally. In *Bokmål* it most often occurs in connection with the prenominal article (*den samme mannen* 'the same man'), which is expendable in New Norwegian (*same mannen*). BM/NN *slik*, BM *sånn*, NN *såvoren*, NN *dilik* 'such' inflect like regular adjectives.

The Verbal Group

Morphosyntactic Categories and Conjugation Types
The finite verb forms show a morphological opposition between present and preterite (simple past), cf. *lever – levde* 'live(s) – lived', BM *går – gikk*, NN *gjeng, går – gjekk* 'go(es) – went'. Norwegian present- and past-tense forms are not morphematically marked for person, number, mood or aspect. An optative ending *-e* is vestigially present in a small number of more or less phraseological locutions like *leve Kongen!, Kongen leve!*. In *Bokmål*, this form is always homophonous with the infinitive. In New Norwegian it is in principle morphologically independent of the infinitive, being restricted to the *-e-* ending, whereas New Norwegian infinitives end in *-e* or *-a*.

As a special kind of finite verb form one may also consider the imperative. In *Bokmål* it is in general formed by omitting any infinitive ending: *arbeid flittig!* 'work diligently!' The usual New Norwegian imperative is formed in the same way and is in like manner neutral with regard to the singular–plural opposition. In addition, New Norwegian weak verbs of the *kaste/kasta* class (see below) allow for an imperative homophonous with the infinitive (*kaste!/ kasta!* 'throw!'). A special New Norwegian plural imperative obligatorily ending in *-e* is also in principle available (*køyre!* 'drive!').

On account of the relative paucity of Norwegian finite verb morphology the finite verb forms have a number of functions in addition to that of indicating present or past time reference. The present is often used to denote future time, and the preterite may express hypothetical or counterfactual meaning: BM *jeg gjorde det nok hvis jeg var deg* 'I'd probably do it if I were you'; or even a kind of emotionally tinged present; *det var bra at du kom!* 'it's good that you've come!' The verb morphology also provides no formal means to distinguish auctorial and reported speech acts. In indirect speech, the principle of *consecutio temporum* is applied: BM *Per sa: 'Jeg gjør det'* → *Per sa at han gjorde det* 'Per said, "I do it."' → 'Per said that he did it'.

The infinite verb forms comprise the infinitive(s) and the so-called past and present participles.

There are two kinds of infinitive formations: (a) a small class of suffixless verb stem infinitives like *gå* 'go', *tru* 'believe'; and (b) infinitives with a suffixal morpheme, which is in *Bokmål -e*. In New Norwegian it is optionally *-e* (*vere* 'be', *kaste* 'throw') or *-a* (*vera, kasta*). Besides, both New Norwegian and *Bokmål* allow for a so-called 'split' infinitive formation where *-e* and *-a* are distributed in accordance with Old Norse stem length (*vera, kaste*). Due to differences of syntactic distribution infinitives occur either with or without a preposed particle *å* (henceforth: *å-* vs ∅-infinitive). This particle is ambiguous between a verbal prefix and a subjunctional element. Very often it precedes the verb form directly: BM *han hadde klart ikke å gjøre noen feil* 'he had managed not to make any mistakes', but a restricted set of adverbial elements, in particular the sentence negation BM *ikke*, NN *ikkje*, may intervene: NN *han hadde klara å ikkje gjera nokon feilar*. In coordinate structures, the second instance of *å* is often left out: BM *han lærte å lese og skrive* 'he learnt to read and write'.

The present participle is in all cases formed by adding BM *-ende*, NN *-ande* to the verb stem (BM *lysende*, NN *lysande* 'shining'). The formation of the past participle depends on the declension class of the verb. There is a general difference between *Bokmål* and New Norwegian to the effect that in New Norwegian many participles are in certain constructions inflected according to the agreement rules and declensional class system of adjectives, whereas all *Bokmål* verb constructions have an invariant supine form (see below). *Bokmål* participial forms showing adjectival agreement are only possible with a restricted number of verbs and are then mainly used in attributive position: BM *de nylig ankomme gjestene* 'the guests who had recently arrived', *Ibsens samlede verker* 'the collected works of Ibsen'.

With regard to strong verbs, the *Bokmål* inflectional paradigms are characterized by more analogical levelling and a certain influx of Danish forms as compared with the somewhat greater transparency of the Old Norse declensional system in New Norwegian. See Table 8.7. The greater regularity of the *Bokmål* paradigms derive from the following facts. First, the present tense ending *-(e)r* has been generalized in *Bokmål*, cf. BM *skyter* 'shoots', *finner* 'finds' vs NN *skyt, finn*. (The subsidiary NN *-er-* forms are seldom used.) Second, New Norwegian still has some cases with vowel alternation in the present tense (NN *søv* 'sleeps', *held* 'holds' vs BM *sover, holder*). Third, New Norwegian has in many cases inflecting participles as against invariant *Bokmål* supine forms. In the latter connection it should be noted that the neuter form of the New Norwegian past participle has lost its final *-t* which is retained in the corresponding *Bokmål* supine, and that *Bokmål* supine forms like *sovet* 'slept', *sunget* 'sung', coincide with respect to the *-et*-ending with the supine of the most productive class of weak verbs in traditional *Bokmål* (e.g. *kastet* 'thrown'). Moreover, forms like *tatt* 'taken', *sett*, NN *sedd* 'seen' are examples of participle formations originating with weak verbs (see below). This tendency is far stronger in *Bokmål* than in New Norwegian, as is indicated by the numerous *Bokmål* supine forms like *bitt* 'bitten', *brutt* 'broken'. *grått* 'cried' vs NN *bite/biti, brote/broti, gråte/gråti*. On the whole, more originally strong verbs have become weak in *Bokmål* than in New Norwegian, cf. the New Norwegian preterites *drap* 'killed', *las* 'read', *bles* 'blew', *togg* 'chewed' vs BM *drepte, leste, blåste, tygde* (RM even *tygget*), (but BM *hjalp* 'helped', *traff* 'met' vs NN *hjelpte, trefte*). However, a supine system is now, as a subsidiary option, accepted even in New Norwegian due to its widespread use in the dialects: NN *breva er skrivne* [*skrive*] 'the letters have been written'.

The weak verbs inflect in accordance with the following main declension classes:

Table 8.7 Classes of strong verbs in Norwegian

	Infinitive	Present	Preterite	Participle/Supine pp. com. sg.	pp. f. sg.	pp. n. sg./sup.	pp. pl.
1	NN bita/e 'bite' BB bite	bit[er] biter	beit bet/beit	biten	[biti]	bite/biti bitt	bitne
	NN driva/e 'drive' BM drive	driv[er] driver	dreiv drev/dreiv	driven	[drivi]	drive/drivi drevet	drivne
2	NN bryta/e 'break' BM bryte	bryt[er] bryter	braut brøt/braut	broten	[broti]	brote/broti brutt	brotne
	NN fyka/e 'blow' BM fyke	fyk[er] fyker	fauk føk/fauk	føken	[foki]	foke/foki føket	fokne
3	NN drikka/e 'drink' BM drikke	drikk[er] drikker	drakk drakk	drukken	[drukki]	drukke/drukki drukket	drukne
	NN syngja/e, synga/e 'sing' BM synge	syng[er] synger	song sang	sungen	[sungi]	sunge/sungi sunget	sungne
4	NN bera/e 'carry' BM bære	ber[er]/ber bærer	bar bar	boren	[bori]	bore/bori båret	borne
5	NN beda/be 'ask' BM be/bede 'pray'	bed[er]/ber ber	bad bad [ba]	beden	[bedi]	bede/bedi/bedt/bedd bedt	bedne
	NN liggja/e, ligga/e 'lie' BM ligge	ligg ligger	låg lå			lege/legi ligget	

NN sjå 'see'	ser	såg	sedd		sett	sedde
BM se	ser	så			sett	
6 NN taka/e, ta 'take'	tek [tar, teker]	tok	teken	[teki]	teke/teki [tatt]	tekne
BM ta	tar	tok			tatt	
7 NN gråta/e 'weep'	græt	gret			gråte/gråti	
BM gråte	gråter	gråt			grått	
NN sova/e 'sleep'	søv[er]	sov			sove/sovi	
BM sove	sover	sov			sovet	
NN hogga/e 'art'	høgg[er]	hogg	hoggen	[hoggi]	hogge/hoggi	hogne
BM hogge, hugge	hogger, hugger	hogg			hogd, hugd	

1 NN infinitive ending *-ja/-je*, no present tense suffix, *-de* as past tense suffix vs BM absence of *-j*-stem formation, suffix *-er* in the present tense, *-te* as past tense suffix, with or without vowel alternation, e.g.: NN *telja* (inf.) 'count' – *tel* (pres.) – *talde* [*talte*] (past) – *tald* [*talt*] (pp. sg. m./f.), *talt* (pp. sg. n. and sup.) – *talde* (pp. pl.) vs BM *telle* (inf.) – *teller* (pres.) – *talte*/*telte* (past) – *talt*/*telt* (sup.), NN *selja* (inf.) 'sell' – *sel* (pres.) – *selde* [*selte*] (past) – *seld* [*selt*] (pp. sg. m. f.), *selt* (pp. sg. n) – *selde* (pp. pl.) vs BM *selge* (inf.) – *selger* (pres.) – *solgte* (past) – *solgt* (sup.).

2 Consonantal stems with past tense ending *-de* or *-te* according to morphophonemic or lexical rules: NN *byggja* [*bygga*] (inf.) 'build' – *byggjer* [*bygger*] (pres.) – *bygde* (pret.) – *bygd* (pp. sg. m./f.), *bygt*/*bygd* (pp. sg. n. and sup.) [*bygd*] (sup.), *bygde* (pp. pl.) vs BM *bygge* (inf.) – *bygger* (pres.) – *bygde* (pret.) – *bygd* (sup.), NN *dømma* [*døma*] (inf.) 'judge' – *dømmer* [*dømer*] (pres.) – *dømde* [*dømte*] (pret.) – *dømd* [*dømt*] (pp. sg. m./f.), *dømt* (pp. sg. n. and sup.) [*dømd*/*dømt*] (sup.), *dømde* (pp. pl.), NN *senda* (inf.) 'send' – *sender* (pres.) – *sende* [*sendte*] (pret.) – *send* (pp. sg. m./f.), *sendt* (pp. n. and sup.), [*send*/*sendt*] (sup.), *sende* (pp. pl.) vs BM *sende* (inf.) – *sender* (pres.) – *sendte* (pret.) – *sendt* (supine), NN *lysa* (inf.) 'shine' – *lyser* (pres.) – *lyste* (pret.) – *lyst* (pp. sg. and sup.), *lyste* (pp. pl.) vs BM *lyse* (inf.) – *lyser* (pres.) – *lyste* (pret.) – *lyst* (sup.).

3 Vowel stems with past tense ending *-dde*: NN *nå* (inf.) 'reach' – *når* (pres.) – *nådde* (pret.) – *nådd* (pp. sg. m./f.), *nått*/*nådd* (pp. sg. n. and sup.), *nådde* (pp. pl.) vs BM *nå* (inf.) – *når* (pres.) – *nådde* (pret.) – *nådd* (sup.).

4 Past tense and participle (supine) ending NN *-a*, BM *-et/-a*: NN *kasta* (inf.) 'throw' – *kastar* (pres.) – *kasta* (pret.) – *kasta* (pp. and sup.) vs BM *kaste* (inf.) – *kaster* (pres.) – *kastet*/*kasta* (pret.) – *kastet*/*kasta* (sup.).

Again, New Norwegian has more morphological variation than NN. For instance, in the present tense of weak verbs New Norwegian has the endings *-Ø* in Class I, *-er* in Class II, *-r* in Class III, and *-ar* in Class IV, whereas *Bokmål* with a couple of insignificant exceptions (*spør* 'asks', *gjør* 'does') has generalized *-er/-r*. As with strong verbs, the use of invariant supine forms is now accepted in New Norwegian.

Lexical equivalents in New Norwegian and *Bokmål* do not always belong to the same declensional class. *Bokmål* (and even more so *Riksmål*) tends to have as members of the most productive Class IV certain verbs which in New Norwegian belong to Class II, e.g. *festa/feste* 'fasten'. As a rule, new verbs inflect according to Class IV, the only exception to this being verbs with the affix *-ere/-era* (*galvanisere*) which belong to Class II. Class IV is the only class where New Norwegian has neither a dental ending nor morphological variation with regard to number or gender agreement in the participle.

A few verbs constitute exceptions to the inflectional patterns described so far. To these 'irregular' verbs belong the four main modals *kunne* 'can'; *måtte* 'must'; *skulle* 'shall'; BM *ville*, NN *vilja* 'will'. These have a Ø-ending in the present (*kan*, *må*, *skal*, *vil*) and a past tense without a dental suffix, but with an -*e*-ending, and they are thus homophonous with the corresponding *Bokmål* infinitives. The past participle in *Bokmål* is formed with the -*et*-ending of weak verbs of Class IV (*kunnet* etc.), whereas New Norwegian has -*a* (*kunna* etc.).

Morphologically reflexive verbs constitute an inflectional class of their own. The reflexive suffix in New Norwegian is -*st* [-*s*], which entails the -*a*-ending of the infinitive, and in *Bokmål* -*s*. The -*r* of the present-tense ending is deleted, thus yielding the following regular patterns: BM *møtes* – *møtes* – *møttes* – *møttes* 'meet' vs NN *møtast* – *møtest* – *møttest* – *møtst*. Special morphophonemic rules give rise to *Bokmål* forms like *undres* (inf., pres., pp.) 'wonder' and *undredes* (past). Reflexive verbs with the -*s*(*t*)-suffix are in general lexicalized, the productive reflexive formation being the construction with a reflexive pronoun: NN *eg vaskar meg, du vaskar deg, han/ ho vaskar seg* 'I/you/he/she wash(es)'. The -*s*(*t*)-verbs form no unitary semantic class, some being reciprocal, like NN *møtast*/BM *møtes*, others rather 'medial', cf. BM *undres* 'wonder', and still others have a lexicalized passive meaning, like BM *kalles* 'be called'.

Apart from its occurrence in lexicalized reflexive verbs, the *s*(*t*)-suffix also functions as a verbal passive morpheme. It is then inflectionally defective in the modern language. In New Norwegian it is generally only used with infinitives in construction with modals: NN *borna må hentast før klokka tre* 'the children will have to be picked up before three o'clock'. *Bokmål* also has present-tense forms which most often express frequentative aspectual meaning: BM *hver dag hentes barna klokken tre* 'every day the children are picked up at three o'clock'.

In the domain of verb derivation both prefixal and post-verbal particle formations are to a certain extent productive. *Bokmål* and New Norwegian have prefixal verbs with indigenous prefixes, cf. *mislike* 'dislike', *samarbeide* 'cooperate', NN *vanvørda* 'dishonour'. More specifically in *Bokmål* there are a large number of verbs with originally German prefixes, like *forstå* 'understand', *betale* 'pay', *forekomme* 'occur', *bifalle* 'applaud', *anmelde* 'report', *unnskylde* 'excuse', *anerkjenne* 'recognize'. Traditionally, such verbs have for puristic reasons been disallowed in New Norwegian, but a fair number of them, especially verbs with *for-* and *be-*, are now fully integrated elements of New Norwegian vocabulary. Likewise, most composite verbs with a prefixed Norwegian preposition or adverb are translation loans of German verbs with a prefix, e.g. *overleve* 'survive', *etterforske* 'investigate', *inneholde* 'contain'. Traditional New Norwegian reluctance towards such formations seems to be on the wane. More typically and indigenously Norwegian are composite verbs with a prefixed noun or adjective, e.g.

saumfare 'scrutinize', *lovfeste* 'establish by law', *saksøke* 'sue'. The most productive verbal lexeme formation pattern is presumably the combination of a verb and a post-verbal adverbial or prepositional particle, e.g. *gi bort* 'give away', *holde ut* 'endure', *legge sammen* 'add', *ta til* 'begin', *bære over (med)* 'be patient (with)', *gå med (på)* 'consent (to)'. Occasionally, a prefixal and a post-verbal particle formation with the same lexical element coexist. Often there is then hardly any semantic difference between the two formations, cf. *inndele : dele inn* 'classify', *utgi : gi ut* 'issue', *uttenke : tenke ut* 'devise'. The particle formation is preferred in New Norwegian cf.: BM *de fremsatte/satte fram et forslag* vs NN *dei sette fram eit forslag* 'they made a proposal'. In some verb couplets of this kind the prefixal and the post-verbal particle formation differ semantically, the latter having a more basic and the former a more abstract or metaphorical meaning, e.g. *kalle fram* 'summon' – *framkalle* 'produce', *bryte av* 'break off' – *avbryte* 'interrupt'. New Norwegian has fewer such couplets than *Bokmål/Riksmål*, but compare, for example, BM/NN *vende (seg) om* 'turn around' – *omvende* 'convert', *føre ut* 'lead outside' – *utføre* 'export/carry through'.

Auxiliaries and Periphrastic Constructions

The non-finite verb forms partake of a variety of verbal constructions consisting of a governing finite (or non-finite) verb and a governed non-finite verb form. The present participle occurs only in a small number of rather special cases, and the *å*-infinitive is in general part of a complementation system with governing verbs not having the specialized semantic and grammatical functions of traditional auxiliaries. The past participle and the Ø-infinitive are, on the other hand, predominantly found in auxiliary constructions.

Temporal Auxiliaries

The perfect and pluperfect are formed with the present and past, respectively, of *ha* 'have' or BM *være*, NN *vera* 'be'. *Ha* is universally possible, whereas *være*, *vera* is used optionally with verbs indicating change of state or location: BM *han har kjøpt boken* 'he has bought the book', *de hadde danset lenge* 'they had been dancing for a long time', NN *dei var nett komne/hadde nett kome til staden* 'they had only recently arrived in town'. *Bokmål* has the uninflected supine in all perfect constructions. In New Norwegian the perfect with *vera* is formed with inflecting participles agreeing in gender or number with the subject of the sentence (but the supine is a subsidiary option even here). Just like its counterpart in English, the Norwegian perfect cannot be used for narration and is thus in clear opposition to the past tense. Hence it is in general not combined with adverbials denoting past-tense reference: BM **jeg har gjort det for to uker siden* (lit.) ***'I've done it two weeks ago'. It is also the natural expression for combined past- and present-tense reference: NN *eg har butt her sidan i fjor* 'I've been living here since last year'.

Futurity is often expressed by the present tense: NN *han kjem nok i morgon* 'he'll probably come tomorrow', BM *den boken kjøper vi senere* 'we'll buy that book later'. Auxiliary constructions with the largely desemanticized modals *skulle* 'shall' and *ville* 'will' are equally common: *du vil like denne boka* 'you'll like this book', NN *eg skal gjera det seinare* 'I'll do it later'. In addition, the deictic verb *komme* 'come' with the directional prepositional particle *til* and the *å*-infinitive is an unequivocal, non-modal expression of futurity: NN *heile familien kjem til å emigrera til Amerika* 'the whole family is going to emigrate to America'. The notion of completion in the future may be expressed by the perfect: NN *han har nok skrive brevet før du kjem* 'he'll have written the letter before you arrive'; or by means of *få* 'get' with the past participle: BM *han får gjort det til i morgen* 'he'll have it done by tomorrow'; or by the preterite of desemanticized *skulle/ville* with the infinitive perfect: BM *jeg skal/han vil ha ordnet alt før neste uke* 'I/he'll have it all arranged before next week'; or by corresponding constructions with the present of *komme* 'come': NN *han kjem til å ha/få gjort arbeidet ferdig før neste uke* 'he'll have the work completed before next week'. Past future is expressed by the preterite of *skulle/ville* with the infinitive: BM *han sa at han skulle/ville tenke på det* 'he said he'd think about it'. In non-embedded sentences only *skulle* is used with a prospective sense: *det skulle gå mange år før han kom* 'many years were to pass before he came'. In *oratio tecta*, *få* is used: NN *han fekk gjera det seinare* 'he'd have to do it later'.

Modality

The traditional modals govern the Ø-infinitive. Constructions with the infinitive perfect are semantically diverse. With the present tense of the modal, they carry an epistemic (or in the case of *skulle*, reportive) meaning: *han må/skal ha gjort det* 'he must/is assumed to have done it'; but when the modal is in the preterite, the meaning switches to deontic counterfactuality: *han skulle ha gjort det* 'he ought to have done it'. Whereas *skulle* in counterfactual expressions still retains its basic meaning of obligation, *ville* is a modally desemanticized marker of counterfactuality: BM *det ville ha vært fint* 'that would have been fine'. Contrary to what is the case in constructions with the present tense of modals and the perfect infinitive, deletion of the auxiliary *ha* is not only possible, but even highly usual in counterfactual constructions: *han skulle (ha) reist dit* 'he should have gone there'.

The counterfactual use of the simple preterite with the infinitive present, e.g. BM *hadde jeg vinger, skulle jeg fly* 'if I had wings, I'd fly', is restricted to present or rather non-past time reference. To express past counterfactuality, the pluperfect or the preterite of a modal in combination with the infinitive perfect or the past participle is used: BM *hvis jeg hadde hatt vinger, skulle jeg (ha) fløyet*. It is worth noting that the latter are also freely used with non-past (present or future) time reference.

Modal *få* 'get' with the Ø-infinitive vacillates between permissive and obligative deontic meaning: BM *han får slippe den prøven* 'he'll have to be exempted from that test', *han får gjøre brevet ferdig* 'he shall have to finish the letter'. BM *behøve, trenge*, NN *trenga, turva* with the Ø- or å- infinitive function as the negative counterpart of *måtte* 'must': BM *du behøver ikke (å) gjøre det*, NN *du tarv ikkje gjera det* 'you needn't do it'.

Passive Auxiliaries

The usual actional passive auxiliary is *bli* and in New Norwegian also *verta*: *bilen blir vaska* 'the car is being washed', NN *huset vart/blei selt* 'the house was sold'. The statal passive with BM *være*, NN *vera* denotes (the result of) a completed action: NN *huset er selt* 'the house is sold'. The present-tense statal passive is often understood to be temporally equivalent to the perfect active. The distinction between the statal passive and the perfect/pluperfect of the actional passive is also in many cases less than clear-cut: BM *han er (blitt) valgt til stortingsmann* 'he has been elected a member of parliament'. The *Bokmål* passive is formed with the invariant supine form: *de ble kjørt hjem*, but New Norwegian has a participle agreeing in gender or number with the subject: *dei vart køyrde heim* 'they were driven home' (with the supine construction as a subsidiary option).

Another kind of passive construction is formed with *få* 'get' and the supine or past participle: BM *han fikk tilsendt bøkene* 'the books were sent to him', or, with another word order which betrays the syntactic origin of the non-finite verb form as a predicative to the object: *han fikk bøkene tilsendt*. New Norwegian in addition makes a distinction between the supine: *han fekk tilsendt bøkene*, and the participle: *han fekk bøkene tilsende*, in accordance with the distributional variation.

New Norwegian also has a passive use of the present participle which is not paralleled in *Bokmål*, and for which a variety of *Bokmål* counterparts have to be used: compare for example, NN *han er ventande heim* 'he is expected home' vs BM *han er ventet hjem*; NN *vegen er ikkje gåande* 'the road is not fit for walking' vs BM *veien er ikke til å gå på*; NN *vatnet er drikkande* 'the water is fit for consumption' vs BM *vannet er drikkelig*.

Aspectuality

Aspectuality is only of marginal importance in the grammar. However, note should be taken of a common aspectual periphrasis where *drive* 'drift around' or one of the basic dimensionality verbs *gå* 'go', *stå* 'stand', *ligge* 'lie' is coordinated with another, preferably imperfective verb: NN *han dreiv og las* 'he was reading', BM *hun stod og tenkte* 'she stood there thinking'. When coordinate structures of this kind are combined with ingressive *bli*, NN *verta*, only the first verb appears as a present participle and the second verb is shifted into the infinitive, whereas *og* 'and' is retained: BM *han ble gående og tenke* 'he kept walking around thinking'.

Pro-verb
The pro-verb BM *gjøre*, NN *gjera* 'do' is used when a lexical verb is topicalized. A finite lexical verb is then either turned into an infinitive: BM *synge gjør han alltid*; or simply retained in finite form: *synger gjør han alltid* 'he is always singing'. Correspondingly, even infinitives may optionally change into past participles in accordance with the participle of the pro-verb in the perfect tense: BM *synge/sunget har han alltid gjort*.

8.4 Syntax

The Nominal Group

The Structure of Noun Phrases
The contrast between the lexematic indefinite article and the affixal definite article (definiteness suffix) correlates with certain specific traits of the composition of noun phrases. The indefinite article is strictly pre-nominal and precedes all attributive adjectives: BM *en hyggelig gammel mann* 'a nice old man', NN *eit vent andlet* 'a nice face'. It is itself only preceded by a small number of indeclinable quantifying elements: BM *mang(en) en ung forfatter* 'many a young author', *nok en dårlig ny bok* 'another bad new book', and the inflecting identifying determiners *slik, sånn*: BM *sånt et rot* 'such a mess'. Apart from this, the indefinite article forms part of a larger paradigmatic class of quantifying determiners (see Table 8.6 for details).

Nouns with the definiteness suffix may be followed by an inflecting possessive pronoun or a syntagmatically and paradigmatically equivalent pronominal genitive: *boka mi* 'my book', *boka hennes* 'her book'. Non-pronominal genitives are, on the other hand, restricted to prenominal determiner position: BM *mannens bok* 'the man's book' vs **boken/boka mannens*. Inflecting and genitive pronominal possessives are also used prenominally, in which case the definiteness suffix is no longer possible: *min/mi/hennes bok(*a/*en)* 'my/her book'.

When a prenominal adjective is also present in a definite noun phrase, a further unstressed lexematic pre-adjectival determiner is added, which for this reason is often called 'the adjective article': *den gamle mannen* 'the old man', *den gode boka* 'the good book', *det vesle barnet* 'the small child', *de store husa* 'the large houses'. Definite and indefinite noun phrases containing pre-nominal adjectives differ with respect to head-noun pronominalization. Indefinite noun phrases like *ei gammel kjerring* 'an old hag' allow for the pronominalized version *ei gammel ei* 'an old one'. In the plural, BM *noen gamle biler* 'some old cars' is even colloquially rendered as *noen gamle noen* 'some old ones'. In definite noun phrases, on the other hand, the head noun is simply omitted, whereby, for example, *den gamle bilen* 'the old car' is reduced to *den gamle*.

The 'definiteness doubling' in *den gamle bilen* etc., is applied more consistently in New Norwegian than in *Bokmål* and, in particular, *Riksmål*, where, in accordance with Danish usage, the definiteness suffix is often omitted. In *Bokmål* the suffixal article is often dispensed with before various kinds of post-nominal modifiers, such as complement clauses: BM *det tvilsomme syn at alt er tillatt* 'the dubious point of view that everything is permitted', and restrictive relative clauses: *de vanskeligheter som nå var overvunnet* 'the difficulties that were now surmounted'. In most other circumstances, current *Bokmål* noun phrases with pre-nominal modifiers, but lacking the definiteness suffix, are most often set phrases: *det norske folk* 'the Norwegian people', *den hellige skrift* 'the Holy Writ', or they are felt to be more or less bookish (reflecting Danish influence).

Expressions of Possession and Other Modifiers

The inflecting possessive pronouns and the pronominal genitive possessives are the only determiners to occur post-nominally after the definiteness suffix. All possessive pronouns and genitives may function syntactically as elliptical noun phrases: BM *min/hans/den andre guttens var bedre* 'mine/his/the other boy's was better'.

Prenominal genitives are fairly usual in *Bokmål*, but in New Norwegian they are more often than not avoided. This leaves the question of fully acceptable equivalents of BM *mannens bil* 'the man's car', as, according to a general rule, non-pronominal genitives only occur pre-nominally. Here, post-nominal prepositional phrases with possessive meaning are used instead. The most usual prepositions are BM/NN *til* 'to' and NN *åt* 'to', which are also the prepositions found in benefactive prepositioned phrases alternating with indirect objects: compare for example, NN *han gav kona si ei ny bok* 'he gave his wife a new book' – *han gav ei ny bok til/åt kona si* – *den nye boka til/åt kona hans* 'his wife's new book'.

Norwegian dialects possess two common periphrastic possessive constructions that are to a certain extent also used in standardized New Norwegian. The first comprises the inflecting reflexive possessive pronoun and obeys the general rule requiring prenominal position of non-pronominal genitives: *engelskmannen sin båt* 'the Englishman's boat'; cf. *engelskmannens båt*, *båten til engelskmannen*. Being originally a loan from Low German, this construction has traditionally been typical of West and North Norwegian usage, but it is at present gaining ground and is making its way into spoken East Norwegian, including that of the Oslo area. The other composite possessive construction comprises a pronominal genitive in the usual post-nominal position and an uninflected proper name or a noun with similar meaning: *huset hans Ola/far* 'Ola's/father's house'.

The Old Germanic possessive dative is in Modern Norwegian only vestigially present in a few set phrases: BM *det ligger ham i blodet* 'it's in his blood'. Elsewhere it has been replaced by prepositional phrases in particular with the preposition *på* 'on, at': BM *ordet glapp ut av munnen på ham* 'the word just escaped him', or by regular attributive possessive expressions: NN *han kyste handa hennar* 'he kissed her hand'.

With the exception of the usual kind of adjectival phrases consisting of an adverbial modifier and a modified adjectival head (BM *meget uvitende*, NN *mykje fåkunnig* 'very ignorant'), prenominal modifiers on the whole tend not to be syntagmatically complex. Adjectives can be modified by complements or adverbial adjuncts as constituents of a complex adjectival phrase: BM *dette i mange henseender særdeles pålitelige dokument* 'this in many respects extraordinarily reliable document'; but such constructions have a distinct stylistic flavour as being literary, or even artificial-sounding officialese. The same goes for present participles used as a prenominal attribute: BM *en leende pike* 'a laughing girl', where the further addition of dependent elements often results in stilted 'Danish'- or 'German'-sounding expressions: BM *en høyt leende pike* 'a loudly laughing girl'. The present participle is typically used with a quasi-adjectival, characterizing meaning.

In accordance with Old Germanic participle formation and semantic interpretation rules, past participles of perfective intransitive verbs denoting change of state or location are used attributively with active meaning: BM *de nylig ankomne flyktningene* 'the recently arrived refugees'. The past participle of transitive verbs has passive meaning in this position: BM *de etterlyste rømlingene* 'the wanted runaways'. As in the case of present participles, syntagmatic expandability is heavily constrained. When complements are added in accordance with the valency requirements of the verbs in question, the result is stylistically marked or even deviant: BM *de av politiet etterlyste rømlingene* 'the refugees wanted by the police'. Both in New Norwegian and in *Bokmål*, postnominal relative clauses are normally used instead: *ei jente som ler/lo høgt*, NN *rømlingane som var etterlyste av politiet* 'the runaways who were wanted by the police'.

The syntactic constitution of Norwegian noun phrases thus displays both operator–operand and operand–operator order. Outside the domain of quantifiers, including the indefinite article, and of adjectival modification there is a noticeable overall tendency towards operand–operator order. This tendency manifests itself with the suffixal definite article, in pronominal possessive constructions, in the position of relative clauses, and even in the noticeably restricted expandability of prenominal modifiers, and it is even more pronounced in New Norwegian than in *Bokmål* or *Riksmål*.

Pronominalization and Quantifiers

Anaphora and Quantifiers

Gender distinctions are absent in the personal pronoun in the plural, cf.: *guttene* m. 'the boys'/*jentene* f. 'the girls'/*borda* n. 'the tables' → *de*. In the singular, the personal pronouns obey different agreement rules in New

Norwegian and *Bokmål*. The New Norwegian agreement system is, in principle, based on grammatical gender, whereby *han* m., *ho* f., *det* n. refer to full noun phrases in the masculine, feminine or neuter, respectively, irrespective of natural gender (sex): NN *guten* 'the boy', *stolen* 'the chair' → *han*; *jenta* 'the girl', *grana* 'the spruce' → *ho*; *barnet* 'the child', *bordet* 'the table' → *det*. As most nouns denoting males and females belong to the masculine and feminine gender, respectively, this system displays a partial fit between grammatical and natural gender.

In *Bokmål* the pronominalization rules are sensitive to animacy, with natural gender as a further specifying feature within the class of animate nouns (noun phrases): compare *gutten* 'the boy' m. and animate → *han* vs *stolen* 'the chair' m. and inanimate → *den*; *jenta* 'the girl' f. and animate, *piken* 'the girl' com. and animate → *hun* vs *feiringa* 'the celebration' f. and inanimate, *feiringen* com. and inanimate → *den*; but both *barnet* 'the child' n. and animate, and *bordet* 'the table' n. and inanimate → *det*.

Both in New Norwegian and *Bokmål* natural gender and notional plurality tend to override grammatical gender and number requirements when there is a conflict as in, for example, *kvinnfolket* n. sg. 'the woman' → *hun/ho* f. sg.; *politiet* n. sg. 'the police' → *de* pl.

In addition to its co-referential uses the neuter singular form *det* is also found as a merely formal subject in so-called 'impersonal' constructions: *det snødde i går* 'yesterday it was snowing', BM *nå kommer det an på deg* 'now it's up to you'; in the impersonal passive: NN *det vart kjempa til siste stund* 'there was fighting going on until the last moment'; and in existential sentences: BM *med ett kom det til syne en person foran døren* 'suddenly a person appeared in front of the door'. *Det* is also used as an 'anticipatory' element in sentences with a postposed subject or, far less often, object clause: NN *det er ille at dei vil gje opp sjølvråderetten* 'it is terrible that they are willing to relinquish their autonomy', BM *hun finner det inspirerende å arbeide om natten* 'she finds it inspiring to work at night'. A co-referential *det* may be stressed and also allows for 'right copying': BM *han betraktet den gamle villaen. Det var et fint hus, det* 'he was looking at the old mansion. It was really a beautiful house'; NN *faren var nett komen heim. Det var morosamt for borna, det* 'the father had just come home. It was very pleasant for the children'. On the other hand, the non-co-referential *det*, including the anticipatory *det*, does not allow for right copying: *det snør, det; NN *det vart kjempa til siste stund, det; NN *det er ille at dei vil gje opp sjølvråderetten, det.

Reflexives and Reciprocals

Non-reflexive personal pronouns, on one hand, and reflexive and reciprocal pronouns, on the other hand, are in principle in complementary distribution with regard to the extra- and intra-sentential position of the antecedent. Non-reflexive personal pronouns refer to an antecedent not located in the same clause: BM *Mannen$_i$ snakket med naboen$_j$. Han$_{i/j}$ sa til ham$_{i/j}$ at han$_{i/j}$ måtte klippe plenen* 'the man talked with his neighbour. He told him that he ought to mow the lawn'. Reflexive and reciprocal pronouns refer to an antecedent located in the same clause which is also normally the subject of that clause. With a number of verbs the reflexive pronoun is a non-substitutable lexically required element: BM *han skammet seg/*sin bror* 'he was ashamed', whereas in other cases there is paradigmatic opposition to other non-reflexive elements: NN *ho vaska seg/barnet lenge* 'she kept washing herself/the child for a long time'.

The reflexive lexeme BM *selv, sjøl*, NN *sjølv* (with the optional plural *sjølve*) is only possible with not inherently reflexive verbs: BM **han skammet seg selv*. In other cases it may be added for contrast: NN *dei vaska seg sjølve* 'they washed themselves'. The reflexive lexeme is also regularly used in connection with actions which are not in the normal course of events directed towards oneself: BM *hun elsker seg selv* 'she loves herself', NN *presidenten gav seg sjølv ei utmerking* 'the president awarded himself a distinction'.

Reflexive pronouns are not only found as sentence elements, but also in attributive prepositional phrases. Here the antecedent may be the subject of the sentence: BM *Han$_i$ viste sin$_i$ kone$_j$ et gammelt bilde av seg selv$_i$* 'he showed his wife an old picture of himself' (but: . . . *av henne selv$_j$/henne$_{j/k}$*), or even a prenominal genitive with an appropriate semantic role function: NN *Petter$_i$ si$_i$ skryting av seg sjølv$_i$ vart etter kvart noko keisam* 'Peter's bragging about himself eventually became somewhat boring'.

Infinitival complements to verbs are not ordinarily topologically independent clause constructions and hence do not constitute independent binding domains for pronouns. Thus, a reflexive pronoun may refer to the subject argument of a higher predicate in the complex sentence structure: BM *hun$_i$ lovet sin$_i$ mor$_j$ å vaske seg$_i$ ordentlig* 'she promised her mother to wash properly'(but: . . . *å hjelpe henne$_j$/seg selv$_i$* '. . . to help her/herself'). Even higher-clause objects act as the antecedent of lower-clause reflexives, in which case the reflexive lexeme *selv, sjøl, sjølv* may narrow down the range of possible interpretations: NN *Jon$_i$ freista å få henne$_j$ til å tala vent om seg$_{i/j}$/seg sjølv$_j$* 'John tried to make her say something nice about herself/himself', BM *han$_i$ ba dem$_j$ vise ham$_{i/k}$ et bedre bilde av seg$_{i/j}$/seg selv$_j$/ham selv$_{i/k}$* 'he asked them to show him a better picture of himself/themselves'. The last example shows that the interplay between personal and reflexive pronouns engenders binding problems of its own.

The reciprocal pronoun is BM *hverandre*, NN *einannan, kvarandre*. The traditional number and gender inflection of NN *kvarannan* m./f., *kvartanna* n., *kvarandre* pl. now appears to be obsolete. Like personal pronouns, the reciprocal pronoun is sensitive to notional plurality: NN *tynna fell frå kvarandre* 'the barrel fell apart'. Like reflexives, the reciprocal pronouns are bound by an antecedent in the same tensed clause, which may, however, be the subject or object argument of a higher predicate: BM *de$_i$ lovet sin$_i$ mor$_j$*

å respektere hverandre$_i$ 'they promised their mother to respect each other', NN *mora$_i$ bad dei$_j$ å respektera kvarandre$_j$* 'their mother asked them to respect each other'.

Quantifiers

The main quantifiers are listed in Table 8.6. They are all used as prenominal – and preadjectival – determiners in noun phrases, e.g.: BM *ingen avgjørelse*, NN *inga [ingi] avgjerd* 'no decision'. *Begge*, NN *både* usually occurs with a definite noun: BM *begge problemene*. *All(e)*, NN *einkvan* 'some(one)' and NN *kvar* 'each, every' allow for nouns with or without the definiteness suffix: BM *all mat* 'all food' (non-specific), *all maten* 'all the food' (specific), NN *einkvan gut(en)* 'some boy or other', NN *kvar skilling(en)* 'every penny'. The rest are combined with indefinite nouns only: BM *hver måned* 'every month', NN *nokre gamle menneske* 'some old people'.

With the exception of *hver, kvar* and the singular form *all*, the quantifiers are also employed as noun phrases in argument position: BM *alle hadde sagt sitt* 'everyone had had his say', NN *ingen hadde sett noko* 'nobody had seen anything'. For *hver, kvar* the lexically reinforced forms BM *hver og en*, NN *kvar og ein* are used: NN *kvar og ein hadde høyrt noko* 'everyone had heard something'.

Only the quantifiers *alle, alt, begge, både* and *hver, kvar* are 'floated' and are then bound by the syntactic subject. The quantifiers so used tend to be lexically reinforced as BM *alle sammen*, NN *alt saman*, BM/NN *begge to*, NN *både to* and BM *hver og en*, NN *kvar og en*. Such reinforcement is not necessary when the floated quantifiers *alle, alt* and *begge, både* are sentence-initial or placed in the central (nexus) field: BM *alle (sammen) hadde de kjørt av veien* 'they had all of them driven off the road'. But it is at least highly usual when the quantifier is floated to clause-final adverbial position: NN *dei hadde køyrt av vegen begge to*. Similar rules pertain to BM *hver (og en)*, NN *kvar (og ein)*: BM *de hadde tatt sin del hver og en* 'each had taken his share'. Non-reinforced BM *hver*, NN *kvar* has distributive meaning: BM *de tok en hver* 'they took one each'.

Basic Sentence Structures and their Syntagmatic Variations

The Basic Topological Patterning of Sentences

Due to the paucity of morphological marking of noun phrases basic syntactic relations are encoded topologically by means of restrictions on linear order. Therefore an overview of Norwegian sentence topology appears to be both a practical and a theoretical prerequisite for a discussion of the syntax of the language.

The serialization patterns of Norwegian are amenable to a description in terms of a sequence of 'topological fields', consisting of categorically defined 'positions', which may comprise one or more elements of the same morphosyntactic category, see Table 8.8. For example:

Main clause (example in BM)

IE	v	n	a_1	a_2	V_1	V_2	N_1	N_2	A
Denne gangen	hadde	han	dess- verre	ikke	villet	sende	de andre utvalgsmedlem- mene	sakspapi- rene	før møtet.

Subordinate clause (example in NN)

IE/ Comp	n	a_1	a_2	a_3	v	V_1	V_2	N	A_1	A_2
(...) av di	han	denne gongen	diverre	ikkje	hadde	villa	senda	saks- papira	til dei andre utvalsmedle- mene	før møtet.

'(because) this time he had unfortunately not wanted to send the documents to the other committee members before the meeting'

Key: **IE** = initial element; **Comp** = complementizer; **v** = finite verb; **V** = non-finite verb; **n, N** = nominal element; **a, A** = adverbial element.

Table 8.8   Field and position analysis of Norwegian clause and sentence structure

Sentence/Clause Fields	Initial Field	Nexus Field	Content Field
Positions	MC: Initial Element	v n_1–n_n a_1–a_n	
			V_1–V_n N_1–N_n A_1–A_n
	SC: Initial Element/ Complementizer	n_1–n_n a_1–a_n v	

Key: **MC** = main clause; **SC** = subordinate clause; **v** = finite verb; **V** = non-finite verb; **n, N** = nominal element, **a, A** = adverbial element.

Encoding of Grammatical Relations
When syntactic subjects are conceived of as a class of elements with which specific syntactic rule properties are associated (infinitive and imperative formation, passive and certain agreement rules, etc.), the defining encoding position of nominal subjects is n_1, since it is the elements occurring here that display the syntactic properties in question: BM *etterpå hadde han gitt sin kone blomster* 'afterwards he had given his wife flowers', NN *etter krangelen hadde dei freista å vera hyggelege mot kvarandre* 'after the quarrel they had tried to be nice to each other'. Sentence-initial position cannot be regarded as the subject-encoding position in Norwegian on account of its availability to all kinds of syntactic categories.

When not topicalized, non-pronominal direct and indirect objects are placed in the content field after the sentence negation BM *ikke*, NN *ikkje* and any non-finite verb forms. The position in the nexus field in front of the sentence negation is available to pronominal objects on the condition that the lexical verb is finite: BM *han ga henne den ikke* 'he didn't give it to her' vs *han hadde ikke gitt henne den.*

The indirect and the direct object are not linearly interchangeable: BM **da ga han den henne ikke*; NN **etterpå hadde han gjeve blomar kona si.* Instead a benefactive element eligible for indirect-object function (and position) may appear in a prepositional phrase in the adverbial position of the content field for purposes of rhematization and focusing: BM *etterpå hadde han gitt blomster til sin kone.*

The nominal position in the content field is also the locus of various 'small clause' constructions which involve a direct object in construction with some predicative or quasi-predicative element: BM *hun kalte sine fiender løgnere* 'she called her enemies liars', NN *maten gjorde han sjuk* 'the food made him sick', NN *dei fann ho heime* 'they found her at home', BM *de fant ham sovende* 'they found him asleep'. In connection with the passive construction with *få* 'get' and the past participle, mention has been made of a certain vacillation between a 'small clause' construction: BM *han fikk pengene tilsendt*; and the auxiliary construction: BM *han fikk tilsendt pengene*. A similar alternation is also found in certain cases with the present participle: BM *hun hadde flere hester stående på stallen/stående flere hester på stallen* 'she had several horses standing in the stables'.

It is a moot question whether the term 'indirect object' should be restricted to the first of two nominal objects. Occasionally it is also extended to objects governed by predicative adjectives or noun phrases: BM *hun var ham kjær* 'she was dear to him', BM *det er meg en glede å ønske Dem velkommen* 'it is a pleasure for me to wish you welcome'; and to noun phrases in construction with a particle or an adverbial element in set phrases: BM *det kommer ikke deg ved* 'it's no concern of yours', BM *det gjør meg vondt* 'it hurts me'.

The Distribution of Adverbials and Negation Markers

The various kinds of adverbial elements differ with regard to linear distribution in the sense of field availability, the nexus field and the content field being the two subclassifying fields.

Sentence modifiers, including in particular modal particles and the sentence negation BM *ikke*, NN *ikkje*, are restricted to the adverbial position in the nexus field: NN *ho hadde jo kan hende ikkje kjøpt boka ennå* 'she had after all perhaps not as yet bought the book'. The order of such elements reflects semantic scope. Modal particles (like *jo* 'after all') come first, and the sentence negation stands last in the sequence with grading adverbials of various semantic designations in between.

The sentence negation is normally preceded by the pronominal subject: BM *da lo han ikke lenger* 'then he didn't laugh any longer'; and pronominal objects when there is no non-finite verb present: NN *nå såg han henne ikkje* 'now he didn't see her' vs NN *nå hadde han ikkje sett henne* 'now he hadn't seen her'. The order negation element–pronominal subject is also found on occasion: BM *hvis ikke det er sant...* 'if it isn't true...'. This latter position of the negation element directly after the finite verb in main clauses and after the complementizer in subordinate clauses is normal with non-pronominal subjects, cf.: CM *den dagen var ikke fru Hansen hjemme* 'on that day, Mrs Hansen was not at home', NN *... tilhøve som ikkje domstolane kunne vurdera* '... circumstances that the courts of law were in no position to assess'. The 'negation hopping' to the position in front of a subject cannot take place when more adverbials are present in the nexus field: BM *den dagen var fru Hansen jo likevel ikke hjemme* 'on that day Mrs Hansen was after all not at home' – **den dagen var ikke fru Hansen jo likevel hjemme*. It thus rather appears that it is the first of a series, or even the whole series, of adverbial elements that may be so moved: BM *den dagen var jo fru Hansen likevel ikke hjemme – den dagen var jo likevel ikke fru Hansen hjemme*. In the spoken language the sentence negation is, partly on the basis of the movement rule in question, often cliticized to the finite verb: NN *har'kje nokon gjort noko?* 'hasn't anybody done anything?', SEN *jeg ha'kke gjort det* 'I haven't done it'.

The sentence negation is either used as an independent word form in combination with the indefinite pronoun (quantifier) BM/NN *noen, noe*, NN *nokon, noko*, or the semantic components of negativity and indefiniteness are incorporated into one single word form as *ingen* 'no one, nobody', *ingenting* 'nothing'. Although BM *ikke noe(n)*, NN *ikkje noko(n)* are certainly possible, *ingen* and *ingenting* are commonly used as a syntactic subject regardless of the composition of the verbal predicate: *det hadde ingen visst* 'no one had known that', *ingenting var bra nok* 'nothing was good enough'. With objects, however, the choice between incorporated and unincorporated negation depends on the composition of the verbal predicate. On account of the general constraint against content-field position of the sentence negation, forms with incorporated negation cannot occur in object position after a non-finite verb form: NN *dei hadde ikkje sett nokon* 'they had not seen anyone' – **dei hadde sett ingen*. Object forms with incorporated negation are acceptable in the nexus field, where the positional constraint in question is not violated: BM *de hadde ingenting sett* 'they had seen nothing'; but this usage feels awkward (and archaic) on account of a conflict with the usual distribution rules requiring non-pronominal objects to be content-field elements. In the absence of a non-finite verb, forms with or without negation incorporation are equally possible: BM *de så ikke noen/ingen* 'they saw no one'.

Ikke/ikkje also functions as focusing negation in contrastive contexts: BM *han elsket ikke datteren, men hennes vakre mor* 'he did not love the daughter, but her beautiful mother'. Here the same adversative conjunction *men* 'but' is used as in the case of non-negated contrastivity: BM *de var fattige, men lykkelige* 'they were poor, but happy'. *Ikke/ikkje* is also, when heavily stressed, available to a limited extent for use as constituent negation: BM *ikke vi ønsker dette* 'we are not the ones to wish for this'. This usage is, however, more often than not avoided. Instead, negated cleft constructions are commonly used: BM *det er ikke vi som ønsker dette*.

Adverbials and prepositional complements that subcategorize the main lexical verb occupy the adverbial position in the content field and are excluded from the nexus field: BM *han hadde tenkt på henne hele tiden* 'he had been thinking of her all the time' – **han hadde på henne tenkt hele tiden*, NN *den vesle jenta hadde sunge særs vent* 'the small girl had sung beautifully' – **den vesle jenta hadde særs vente sunge*. Local or temporal adverbial adjuncts occur both in the content field and the nexus field: BM *han hadde arbeidet med den nye boken under et opphold i utlandet* 'he had been working on the new book during a stay abroad' – *han hadde under et opphold i utlandet arbeidet med den nye boken*. In clause-final adverbial position prepositional complements regularly precede the adverbial adjuncts due to their closer semantic affinity with the governing lexical verb. In the case of adverbial adjuncts, the adverbial position in the nexus field is often used for the purpose of thematization, compare: NN *ho hadde kjøpt ein ny kjole i Paris* 'she had bought a new dress in Paris' – *ho hadde i Paris kjøpt ein ny kjole* 'in Paris she had bought a new dress'.

The extent to which the adverbial subclasses partake of the categorially open sentence-initial position varies greatly. Adverbial adjuncts are often naturally placed sentence-initially as mediators of text or discourse coherence: BM *i forrige uke hadde hun likevel kjøpt enda en ny kjole* 'last week she had, however, bought still another new dress'. Adverbial complements in this position have some sort of specific communicative motivation and therefore regularly receive emphatic stress: NN *vent sang ho ikkje* 'she did not sing well at all', BM *i Paris hadde hun bodd lenge* 'as for Paris, she had been living there for a long time'. The sentence negation marker only appears sentence-initially in a special contrastive environment: BM *ikke var han fornøyd med de andre bøkene heller* 'he was not satisfied with the other books either'. Modal particles are in general exempt from this position: NN *han hadde jo lese boka* 'he had after all read the book' – **jo hadde han lese boka*.

Modal particles and certain sentence-modifying adverbials are in the spoken language often placed at the rightmost end of the sentence: BM *nå må dere gå, da!* 'now you'll have to go, then!', BM *det var hyggelig, vel!* 'that was nice, wasn't it?', NN *det går betre neste gong, kan hende* 'perhaps it will turn out better next time', including the reply particles *ja* 'yes', *jo* '(in answer to negative questions) yes', *nei* 'no': *den boka var god, ja* 'that book was really good'. As there is a clear intonational break between the particle and the preceding sentence structure in most cases, the position in question cannot be conflated with the regular sentence-final adverbial position. Still, the overall semantico-pragmatic effect is that the adverbial elements with the lowest degree of semantic predicate affinity are here also treated linearly as the most predicate-remote argument.

The negation marker BM *ikke*, NN *ikkje* cannot be used sentence-finally in this way. Instead the negative reply word *nei* appears: BM *det var ikke bra, nei* 'that was not good, I dare say'.

'Ergative' Features and Passive Constructions

There is a certain semantic parallelism between the subjects of intransitive verbs and the (direct) objects of transitive verbs to the effect that in both cases the interpretation varies with the type of argument they select: compare *han går til byen* 'he walks to town' – *klokka går godt* 'the watch functions well' – *det går bra* 'things are fine'; and BM *han tok et eple fra treet* 'he picked an apple from the tree' – NN *han tok ein lur* 'he had a nap'; and also: BM *menneskene/*mannen myldret fram* 'the people were/*the man was swarming forth' – NN *ho talde sølvskeiene sine/*sølvskeia si* 'she counted her silver spoons/*her silver spoon'. In Norwegian, both subjects of intransitive verbs and various kinds of objects partake of relation-changing rules which are, in the two cases, significantly different.

Subjects of intransitive verbs undergo a demotion rule which places them in what is topologically the direct-object position of the content field in so-called 'existential-presentative' constructions, for example: NN *ein katt hadde seti på taket heile dagen* 'a cat had been sitting on the roof all day long' – *det hadde seti ein katt på taket heile dagen* 'there had been sitting a cat on the roof all day long'; NN *mange innvandrarar var komne til den vesle fjellbygda* 'many immigrants had arrived in the small mountain community' – *det hadde kome mange innvandrarar til den vesle fjellbygda*; BM *en stor arv ventet ham* 'a large inheritance was waiting for him' – *det ventet ham en stor arv*. In these constructions, a formal subject *det* is in general obligatory, and definite, or rather specific, NPs are as a rule excluded: **det hadde seti katten på taket.... Hence these constructions are naturally considered grammaticalized means of rhematization.

The constructions in question are called 'ergative' in current linguistic parlance. As the logical subject of intransitive verbs is here encoded topologically in the same manner as the direct object of transitive verbs, they are more properly termed 'absolutive'. It has been suggested that the absolutive construction in question should be considered the primary lexical option with intransitive verbs not occurring in the passive. In that case, a distinction would have to be made between 'primary absolutives', as with *komme* 'come': NN **det vart kome heim*; and, on the other hand, 'derived absolutives' as, for example, *hoppe* 'jump': BM *noen hoppet av toget i full fart* (active) 'someone jumped off the train at full speed' – *det hoppet noen av toget i full fart* (existential-presentative) – *det ble hoppet av toget i full fart* (impersonal passive), where both the existential-presentative and the impersonal passive constructions are indeed possible.

Absolutive and passive constructions, to which we now turn, have in common that the subject for which the verb is, or may be, subcategorized does not appear in surface subject position ('subject demotion').

Strongly similar to the absolutive constructions are the impersonal passive constructions with a retained indefinite direct object: BM *elevene spiste epler hele tiden* 'the students were eating apples all the time' (active) – *det ble (av elevene) spist epler/*eplene hele tiden* (impersonal passive of transitive verb with direct object).

A further structural variety is the objectless impersonal passive: NN *dei åt til seint på kveld* (active) 'they were eating until late in the evening' – *det vart ete til seint på kveld*.

In the so-called 'personal passive', subject demotion is compensated for by the promotion of some other syntactic element to surface subject function. Norwegian allows for a morphosyntactically wide range of candidates for surface subjecthood, including, of course, direct objects: BM *presidenten overrakte ham ordenen* 'the president presented him with the decoration' – *ordenen ble overrakt ham (av presidenten)*; indirect objects: BM *han ble overrakt ordenen (av presidenten)*; the noun-phrase constituent of a prepositional object: NN *foreldra passa på borna* 'the parents were looking after the children' – *borna vart passa på (av foreldra)*; and even the noun-phrase constituent of certain purely adverbial prepositional phrases: *noen hadde skåret kjøtt med kniven* 'someone had been cutting meat with the knife' – *kniven var blitt skåret kjøtt med*. The general requirement seems to be valency dependence or at least close semantic affiliation with the verb. However, not all adverbial elements so describable are eligible as subjects in the passive: BM *mange reiste til Tromsø på den tiden* 'lots of people travelled to Tromsø at that time' – **på den tiden ble det reist til Tromsø (av mange)*. Whereas impersonal passives with a retained direct object obey the (in)definiteness constraint, their counterparts with a prepositional complement are exempt from it: NN *det vart passa godt på borna* 'the children were well cared for'.

A number of composite passive constructions show in principle the same demotion and promotion processes as the *bli-* and *s-* passives considered so far, but they comprise two lexical verbs, the first and superordinate of which is characterized by an extension of the basic selectional requirements, for example: BM *han antas å komme i morgen* 'he is supposed to arrive tomorrow', where the passive form of *anta* 'suppose' has an animate subject, although the direct object in the active is an expression for propositional content. Even more intriguing are the so-called 'double passives' where the first, governing lexical verb is in the *-s-* or *bli-*passive, and the second main lexical verb occurs in the form of the passive participle also found in *bli-*passive constructions: BM *sykkel ønskes kjøpt* 'a bicycle is wanted for purchase', *postkontoret ble vedtatt nedlagt* 'it was decided that the post office should be closed down', *mannen var begjært fengslet* 'a request had been made for the man's imprisonment'; and impersonal: BM *det ble vedtatt nedlagt flere gamle postkontorer* 'it was decided that more old post offices be closed down'.

The passive construction with *få* 'get' and the past participle mentioned earlier applies to the indirect not the direct object of corresponding active constructions: BM *man overrakte ham ordenen* 'they gave him a decoration' – *han fikk overrakt ordenen*. In addition, in certain cases, the subject of this construction corresponds to a prepositional phrase in the active: BM *banken finansierte prosjektet for ham* 'the bank financed the project for him' – *han fikk prosjektet finansiert/finansiert prosjektet av banken*. Occasionally, a reflexive pronoun that is co-referential with the subject of *få* is added: BM *han fikk seg forelagt planen/planen forelagt seg* 'he was presented with the plan'. The *få*-periphrases in question tend to be used with verbs where the usual kind of *bli-/s*-passive is either outright ungrammatical or would feel awkward.

Relationally Neutral Topological Variation Patterns (Movement Rules)
The discussion in the preceding sections has shown that certain cases of topological variability do affect syntactic relations, whereas others do not. Apart from the particular rules pertaining to pronominal objects, change of position from the nexus field to the content field or vice versa is of relational relevance in the case of subjects and objects (noun phrases), but not in the case of adverbials (which are mostly adverbs or prepositional phrases). In addition, in a topological system where serialization serves as a means for encoding syntactic relations and semantic dependence, it is only to be expected that clause- and field-internal linear variability is restricted. However, objects and adverbials in the content field occasionally change places for reasons of stylistic focusing or simply morphophonemic weight: BM *han hadde invitert til sin fødselsdag alle de gamle vennene sine* 'he had invited to his birthday all his old friends'. Most of the remaining relationally neutral, topological variation patterns (movement rules) pertain to the initial field and to the extrapositional field(s) that does (do) not form part of the basic field schema in Table 8.8, i.e. to the 'outer' regions of the clause or sentence structure.

The forefield serves the twofold purpose of (primary) discourse connecting and (secondary) focusing. In the former case, syntactic subjects, being 'grammaticalized topics', are the statistically dominant, unmarked option, but other sentence elements are equally possible. Even the noun phrase constituent of prepositional phrases is so topicalized (the marking ____ indicates the position within the prepositional phrase from which a noun phrase has been extracted): BM *den fyren kan vi ikke stole på* ____ 'that fellow we cannot trust'; including cases where the prepositional phrase from which the noun phrase is extracted is, relationally, an attributive modifier of a noun: BM *disse problemene hadde de ikke sett halvparten av* ____ *ennå* 'they had not seen half of these problems yet'. As a rule, the constituent occupying the forefield is in such cases definite and receives no special stress. In the case of focusing, the preposed constituent receives emphatic stress and is often an indefinite noun phrase: NN *lærar ville han ikkje bli* 'he did not at all want to become a teacher', or some other kind of constituent like, for example, a complex verb phrase: BM *reise til Tromsø nå vil jeg ikke* 'I will not go to Tromsø now' (vs *reise vil jeg ikke til Tromsø nå*). The movement rule in question has equally general application in all main and subordinate clause types whose forefield consists of a categorial variable, such as interrogative clauses: BM *hvem så du på gaten?* 'whom did you see on the street?'; NN *ho spurde kven han hadde gjeve den pakken til* ____ 'she asked whom he had given that package to'; and relative clauses: BM *den personen som hun hadden sett på gaten* 'the person whom she had seen on the street'. In the other kinds of subordinate clause, the initial position (the forefield) is occupied by an invariant complementizer which precludes the application of variable topicalization, for example: BM *til fødselsdagen hadde hun fått en kunstbok* 'for her birthday she had received a book on art' vs *hun fortalte at til fødselsdagen hun hadde fått en kunstbok* (lit.) 'she told that for her birthday she had got a book on art'. However, topicalization is possible in *at*-clauses with main clause word order, in which case a secondary forefield is introduced adjacent to the complementizer *at*: BM *hun fortalte at til fødselsdagen hadde hun fått en kunstbok*.

It is often assumed that sentence-final position of infinitival and tensed clauses is due to a syntactic rule or pattern of extraposition; compare the following alleged subject clauses: BM *det var morsomt å gå på auksjon* 'it was fun going to auction sales', NN *det er godt at du er komen heim att* 'it is good that you have come home again'; and the object clauses in: BM *han hadde foreslått for henne at de skulle gå på kino* 'he had suggested to her that they go to the movies', NN *han fann det vanskeleg å tru henne* 'he found it difficult to believe her'. Here the allegedly 'anticipatory' *det* behaves more like formal subjects and objects in so far as it is not normally stressed and cannot, for example, be subjected to right copying (see above). Even the distributional evidence is not unequivocal, as subject infinitives may be followed by adverbials that have in their scope the content of the matrix clause: BM *det var mer morsomt å gå på auksjon i gamle dager* 'in the old days, it was more fun going to auction sales'.

As shown earlier, sentence adverbs and modal particles are in the spoken language often placed clause-finally in intonationally delimited extraposition. The frequency of this position is in actual usage further enhanced by the rule of right copying which applies to modal particles: BM *du er vel ikke sint, vel?* 'you aren't angry, are you?', certain adverbs: *nå må vi raske på, nå* 'now we'll have to hurry up', and, in particular, personal pronouns: BM *jeg går hjem nå, jeg* 'as for me, I'm going home now', NN *det var guten sin, det!* 'atta boy!'

Verb Order and Verb Constructions

Verb Order and Clause Types
Three clause types are distinguishable according to the position of the finite
verb. Subordinate clauses have the finite verb in third position (after the
complementizer): BM (*han sa*) *at hun ikke var kommet hjem ennå* '(he said)
that she had not come home yet'. Omission of the complementizer effects no
change of this pattern: BM (*han sa*) *hun ikke var kommet hjem ennå*.
Declarative word order with the finite verb in second position is occasionally
used as well, particularly in reported speech: BM (*han sa*) (*at*) *hun var ikke
kommet hjem ennå*.

Main clauses have the finite verb in second or first position. In declaratives
and in constituent questions, the finite verb comes second: NN *ho er ikkje
heime* 'she is not at home', NN *kva tid kjem ho heim?* 'when will she be
home?' Even sentence questions may be verb-second when appropriately
stressed: BM *hun er ikke kommet hjem ennå?* 'she has not come home yet?';
but in this case the finite verb normally comes first, i.e. there is no forefield:
NN *er ho ikkje komi heim ennå?* 'has she still not come home?' In addition,
conditional clauses lacking a complementizer are also verb-first: BM *kommer
hun ikke hjem snart,* (*så*) *får hun heller ingen aftensmat* 'if she does not come
home soon, she will not get any supper'.

Imperatives are analyzable as clause constructions lacking a forefield and
an overt subject in the nexus field. The sentence negation is either preposed
as in subordinate clauses: BM *ikke forsøk å vri dere unna nå!* 'don't try to get
away with it!'; or it is placed after the finite verb, as in main clauses: BM
forsøk ikke å vri dere unna nå! A periphrastic construction with the imperative
of the causative verb *la*, NN *lata* 'let' is also used: BM *la meg/ham/oss/dem
gjøre det!* 'let me/him/us/them do it!', which may be considered the pragmatic
equivalent of imperatives for the first- and third-person singular and plural.

In the morphologically and pragmatically highly restricted optative mood
both verb-second and verb-first constructions occur: BM *Gud velsigne deg!*
'God bless you!', *leve Kongen!* 'may the King live!'

Norwegian verb chains consisting of a maximally governing finite or non-
finite verb and one or more governed non-finite verb forms are unidirec-
tionally right-branching and may attain considerable length: BM *han
burde[1]ha[2]kunnet[3]forsøke[4]å lære[5]å utføre[6]arbeidet noe raskere* 'he ought to
have been able to try to learn to do the work more quickly'. Within the
topological field framework all non-finite auxiliaries and the first lexical verb
can be assumed to belong in the verb (V) position of the content field.
However, in the traditional *accusativus cum infinitivo* construction, and with
other three-place predicates governing an infinitive as a direct object, the
infinitive is regularly preceded by a nominal object in the content field, and
may therefore be assumed to occupy a nominal (N) position: BM *de hadde
latt ham gå uten flere spørsmål* 'they had let him go without further

questioning', NN *dei hadde tilbode han å køyra han heim* (lit.) 'they had offered him to drive him home'; or even an adverbial (A) position in the content field: BM *hun overtalte vennene til å bli over helgen* 'she persuaded her friends to stay over the weekend'. Seen from this perspective, the nominal and adverbial positions of the content field, being the locus of non-finite V-embedding, *ipso facto* function as the point of departure for right-expanding content-field recursion in accordance with valency and further collocation properties of the main lexical verb. Hence constructions like the following may be derived: BM *hun hadde [ᵥ overtalt ham [ₐ/ᵥ til å anbefale sine venner [ₙ/ᵥ å tilby kollegene [ₙ/ᵥ å kjøpe billig reinsdyrkjøtt av hennes onkel til jul]]]]* 'she had persuaded him to recommend his friends to offer their colleagues to buy cheap reindeer-meat from her uncle for Christmas'. Infinitival constructions introduced by V-recursion do not present barriers to permutation of constituents into higher clauses: BM *billig reinsdyrkjøtt hadde hun overtalt ham til å anbefale sine venner å tilby kollegene å kjøpe ___ av hennes onkel til jul.*

Phrasal Verbs

A number of composite verbal expressions exist whose constituent parts form tone groups in Southeast Norwegian. Some of these, like *komme ut* 'appear', *ta til* 'begin', are one-place predicates. Occasionally, a prefixal formation is also possible: BM *boken utkommer i neste uke*, NN *boka kjem ut i neste veke* 'the book is going to appear next week' – NN *boka er nett utkomen* 'the book has appeared quite recently'. The corresponding two-place constructions with true particles are topologically distinct from verbs with prepositional complements. Particles precede non-pronominal object noun phrases, but are themselves preceded by pronominal objects: BM *han gav bort boken – han gav den bort/*bort den* 'he gave away the book/it away' vs *han ventet på sin kone/på henne/*henne på* 'he was waiting for his wife/her'. Sequences of the sentence negation and a true particle behave in the same fashion with regard to objects as do particles alone: NN *han gav ikkje bort boka – han gav ho ikkje bort* 'he didn't give the book/it away'. In other respects the two-place phrasal-verb constructions are syntactically diverse. The main cases are: (1) The particle is an adverb, e.g. *kreve inn* 'collect', *stille ut* 'exhibit', *legge fram* 'present'. In certain cases a semantically equivalent prefixal formation is also found: BM *innkreve, framlegge*, or, as in New Norwegian, it is required in the participle (supine) and in deverbal nouns: BM *lære opp* 'train' – *lært opp/ opplært – opplæring*; NN *dei la ned fabrikken* 'they closed down the factory' – *fabrikken vart nedlagd – den nedlagde fabrikken*. (2) The particle is homonymous with a preposition, but has the distributional properties of a true post-verbal particle: NN *leggja ved ein sjekk – leggja han ved* 'enclose a cheque/it'. (3) In Southeast Norwegian, with a fairly large number of verbs, the preposition has the same intonational characteristics, but not the same distributional properties as in the preceding cases: BM *legge på prisen/på* *den/*den på* 'raise the price/it', NN *taka etter far sin/etter han/*han etter* 'become similar to one's father/him'. To this group belong the cases where a prepositional complement is dependent on a phrasal-verb group containing a true adverbial particle (which may also be homonymous with a preposition): NN *gå med på eit krav/på det/*det på* 'comply with a demand/it'. In this context, mention should also be made of the numerous constructions where a verb and a non-referential noun together form a complex semantic unit with a dependent prepositional complement: *ha råd til* 'be able to afford', BM *ha mulighet for* 'be in a position to', NN *taka omsyn til* 'take into consideration', where the same distributional restrictions obtain: NN *ho hadde ikkje råd til den største bilen/han* 'she could not afford the largest car/it'.

Subordination

Relative Clauses

Norwegian does not have relative pronouns proper showing gender or number agreement with their antecedents. Instead the invariant particle *som* acts as a complementizer in initial position in the relative clause. Both subjects and all kinds of objects are relativized, as is also the noun phrase constituent of prepositional phrases for which verbs, adjectives, or even nouns are subcategorized: BM *saken (som) de hadde kjempet for ____ så lenge* 'the cause for which they had been fighting so long', NN *noko (som) vi ikkje har høve til ____ nett nå* 'something which we have no opportunity to do right now'. The relative particle *som* is generally deletable in restrictive relative clauses when it is not a subject, and when the antecedent and the relative clause form one continuous noun phrase. On the other hand, *som* cannot be deleted when the relative clause is extraposed: NN *eg såg den jenta i går *(som) du har tala så vent om* 'I saw the girl yesterday whom you have praised so highly'; or in non-restrictive relative clauses: *bankdirektøren, som de alle hadde kjent i årevis, var likevel ikke til å stole på* 'the bank manager, whom they had all known for years, was after all not trustworthy'.

To a limited extent *som* also combines with adverbial antecedent head expressions: NN *der (som) du står nå* (BM: *der (hvor) du står nå*) 'where you now stand'; and: BM *samme dagen (som) dette hendte* (lit.) 'the same day (that) this happened'; but more often complementizers of the kind introducing regular adverbial clauses are used: NN *alle dei åra (då) eg var utanlands* 'all those years when I was abroad'. Deletion of the relative complementizer then occurs as in relative clauses with *som*, whereas the complementizers in question are non-deletable in adverbial clauses: NN *eg lengdest til Noreg *(då) eg var utanlands* 'I was yearning for Norway when I was abroad'.

A special kind of relative clause formation is the cleft sentence construction, where some sentence element is made the predicative of a higher matrix clause with an unstressed formal subject *det* for its subject. Again, the formation rules have wide categorial application: BM *Per hadde gitt henne en bok for en uke siden* 'Per had given her a book a week ago' – *det var henne* (*som*) *Per hadde gitt en bok for en uke siden* (clefting of indirect object) – *det var for en uke siden* (*at*) *Per hadde gitt henne en bok* (clefting of time adverbial). The morphological form of the clefted constituent in the matrix clause corresponds to its syntactic function in the relative clause. The rules for the deletion or non-deletion of *som* are in principle as in other relative clauses, but a non-subject *som* is more frequently omitted in practice. When the clefted element is not a referring nominal expression, but some kind of adverbial element, the complementizer *at* is used instead of *som*.

Cleft constructions are of considerable functional importance and hence of frequent occurrence. Due to relationally conditioned constraints on topological variation and to the unmarked exploitation of the forefield for discourse-connecting purposes, the cleft construction is the main grammatical strategy for the focusing of constituents. In addition constituent questions are often rendered as cleft constructions: BM *hvem kommer?* 'who is coming', but also frequently: BM *hvem er det som kommer?*; and BM *når kommer hun?* 'when will she come?' – *når er det hun kommer?* Here a non-subject *som* (or *at*) is regularly omitted.

Bokmål also employs interrogative pronouns in indefinite (non-specific) relative clauses: BM *hva du ikke vet, har du ikke vondt av* 'what you don't know causes you no harm'; in concessive clauses derivable therefrom: *hva han enn gjorde, så var ingen fornøyd* 'whatever he did, nobody was satisfied'; and in relative clauses with a sentential antecedent: *det var en ulykke, hva/ hvilket vi alle vet* 'it was an accident, as we all know'. *Bokmål hva* is used as an alternative to *som* after the quantifier *alt*: BM *han solgte alt* (*som/hva*) *han eide* 'he sold everything (that) he owned'.

Complement Clauses

Embedded declaratives are introduced by the complementizer *at* which is often deleted both in subject and object clauses: BM *det er bra* (*at*) *dere kommer nå* 'it's fine that you arrive now'; NN *ho sa* (*at*) *ho hadde gløymt boka heime* 'she said that she had forgotten the book at home'. *At*-deletion is not possible when the *at*-clause occupies the forefield: NN *at ho hadde gløymt boka heime, sa ho med ein gong*; or is governed by a preposition: BM *han klaget over at ingenting var blitt gjort* 'he complained that nothing had been done'; or when the *at*-clause has main-clause word order (see above).

Embedded sentence interrogatives are introduced by *om* which is under no circumstances deletable: NN *ho spurde om han ville vera med* 'she asked if he would come along'. Embedded constituent questions are introduced by the interrogative pronouns and adverbs also used in main clauses: BM *han spurte hvem hun var/når hun kom* 'he asked who she was/when she would be coming'. When the question-word corresponds to the subject of the interrogative clause, the particle *som* is added: NN *dei visste ikkje kven som kom* 'they did not know who came'. Like the corresponding main-clause interrogatives, even embedded constituent questions frequently appear as cleft constructions: BM *han spurte hva det var hun hadde sett* 'he asked what she had seen'.

Adverbial Clauses

The majority of temporal complementizers are homonymous with corresponding prepositions: *til* 'until', *før* 'before', BM *fra*, NN *frå* 'since', BM *siden*, NN *sidan* 'since'; or adverbs: *da*, *når* 'when'. There is also a number of sequential, analytic formations such as temporal *etter at* 'after', causal NN *av di*, *med di* (cf. also BM/NN *fordi*) 'because', conditional (including counterfactual) *i fall* 'in case', NN *så framt* (but *dersom*, BM *hvis*, BM *bare*, NN *berre*) 'if', final *for at*, *slik at* 'in order that', concessive *trass i at*, BM *til tross for at*, NN *jamvel om*, BM *selv om* (but also *enda*) 'although, even though'. The comparative complementizers are *som* 'as' and *enn* 'than'.

Adverbial clauses are most often sentence-final, but when stating a precondition of the main clause or expressing presupposed information they are placed in the forefield or in the adverbial position of the nexus field: BM *han måtte reise hjem da han ikke hadde mer penger igjen* 'he had to return home when/because he had no money left' – *da han ikke hadde mer penger igjen, måtte han reise hjem* – *han måtte, da han ikke hadde mer penger igjen, reise hjem.*

Just as participial constructions only very infrequently substitute for relative clauses in stylistically neutral *Bokmål* and New Norwegian, participial clauses also very infrequently occur as the equivalent of adverbial clauses. Rather marginally, present participles without further complements or adjuncts are used as 'free predicatives' referring to and characterizing the subject: BM *hun forlot værelset smilende* 'she left the room smiling'.

Extractability of Sentence Elements from Embedded Clauses

Infinitival constructions do not in general provide barriers against the permutation (extraction) of constituents into a higher clause. To a considerable extent, Norwegian also allows for the extraction of constituents from tensed clauses with a finite verb.

Extraction from a subordinate clause dependent on some head constituent is by and large prohibited. Compare (the extraction site is marked by ____ in the Norwegian sentences and by parentheses in their English renderings) BM *det innrømte Ola at han hadde sagt* ____ (lit.) 'that Ola admitted that he had said (that)' vs **det innrømte Ola den kjensgjerning at han hadde sagt* (lit.) 'that Ola admitted the fact that he had said (that)'. However, when the verb and a noun together form a semantico-syntactic unit, this constraint may be invalidated: BM *den stillingen regnet mange med muligheten av at han ville søke* ____ (lit.) 'that position many people reckoned with the possibility that he would apply for (that position)'. Extraction from relative clauses is uncommon, but not generally prohibited: NN *det embetet kjenner* *eg mange som har søkt* ____ (lit.) 'that office I know many people who have applied for (that office)'.

Extraction is felt to be most natural in the case of embedded complement clauses without an overt complementizer (*at*): BM *i morgen håper jeg alt skal være i orden* ____ (lit.) 'tomorrow I hope everything will be all right (tomorrow)', NN *han trur eg nok eg kjenner* ____ (lit.) 'him I believe I know (him)'; but it is not generally prevented in the presence of a complementizer, including *at*: BM *henne vet jeg at du kan stole på* ____ (lit.) 'her I know you can trust (her)', NN *venene mine tåler eg ikkje at du plagar* ____ (lit.) 'my friends I do not tolerate that you pester (my friends)'; interrogative pronouns: BM *det vet vi alle hvem som har gjort* ____ (lit.) 'that we all know who has done (that)'; and complementizers introducing conditional clauses: NN *den jenta vert eg sjalu dersom du kysser* ____ (lit.) 'that girl I shall be jealous if you kiss (that girl)', BM *her ville jeg bli skrullete hvis jeg skulle bo* ____ (lit.) 'here I would turn crazy if I were to live (here)'. However, sentences like the last two examples have a colloquial flavour and are not likely to occur in the written language.

The extracted element is most often a non-subject, but subjects are by no means excluded: BM *han tror jeg nok* (*at*) ____ *kan klare det* (lit.) 'he I am certain that (he) can make it', NN *det der venta me alle på at* ____ *skulle henda* (lit.) 'that we all expected that (that) would happen'.

The examples adduced so far illustrate extraction as topicalization into the forefield of the superordinate declarative main clause. But main- and subordinate-clause interrogative formation is also usual: BM *hvem mente hun* (*at*) *hun hadde sett* ____ *på gaten?* 'whom did she think that she had seen on the street?', NN *dei spurde henne kven ho trudde at ho hadde sett* ____ *på gata* 'they asked her whom she thought that she had seen on the street'; as is of course also relativization: BM *den kvinnen som du vet at han elsker* ____ *så høyt* 'that woman whom, as you know, he loves so dearly', NN *denne staden som han alltid hadde ynskt at han kunne reisa til* ____ 'this place to which he had always wanted to travel'.

Extraction most often operates on the lower-most clause in the sentence structure. There is, in principle, no limit to 'structural depth', nor is there a quantitative restriction to the extraction of one clause element only: BM *disse bøkene$_i$ er det ikke mange kolleger$_j$ (som$_j$) Tarald kan snakke med* ____ $_j$ *om* ____ $_i$ (lit.) 'these books there are not many colleagues with whom Tarald can talk about (these books)'.

In all the cases of extraction in question, Norwegian generally does without resumptive pronouns. As far as the governing verbs are concerned, the above examples are typical in that the verbal predicate has evidential or speech-act referring meaning, i.e. propositional scope.

8.5 Lexis

Extent of Borrowing and Foreign Influence on the Lexicon

The greater part of present-day Norwegian vocabulary can be traced back to Old Norse origins, and from there to Common Germanic lexical sources. Still, the cultural contacts with western Europe since the Iron Age have left their indelible imprint on the modern language. With respect to the acceptance and assimilation of linguistic borrowings of a grammatical or lexical nature, the standardized versions of *Bokmål* (and *Riksmål*), on one hand, and New Norwegian, on the other, exhibit obvious differences. In keeping with its supranational origin as Dano-Norwegian, the vocabulary of modern *Bokmål/Riksmål* bears abundant testimony to the manifold cultural and linguistic influences to which Norway and the Norwegian language have been exposed in the course of the long political union with Denmark.

In spite of the various spelling reforms of this century, traditional *Bokmål/Riksmål* still has a large number of word forms whose graphematic and phonological shape betray their Danish origin, for example, *lav* (NN *låg*) 'low', *lov* (also NN) 'law', and, in particular, words with monophthongs where most Norwegian dialects have diphthongs such as *løv* (NN/BM *lauv*) 'leaves', *ren* (also *rein*) 'clean', *høre* (NN *høyra*) 'hear', and words with Danish voiced vs Norwegian unvoiced consonants like *begredelig* 'mournful' (cf. *gråte* 'weep'), *skudd* (NN *skot*) 'shot'. A number of words have a Danish stem vowel, cf. *hull* (NN/BM *hol*) 'hole', RM *hugge* (BM/NN *hogge*) 'cut, carve'.

Part of the *Bokmål* inflectional endings also reflect Danish influence. Although East and South Norwegian have also undergone a process of vowel weakening in unstressed syllables, the predominance of the unstressed vowel *-e*(-) in modern *Bokmål* inflectional morphology clearly has to be seen in the context of Danish influence.

A conspicuous trait of traditional New Norwegian is the wholesale rejection of entire classes of *Bokmål* words which by virtue of specific affixes can be traced back to Danish or German origins. New Norwegian was created in the culturally highly formative and self-conscious period of Norwegian national romanticism which developed in the aftermath of the political restoration of 1814. The general New Norwegian attitude became one of selective purism. According to this view, New Norwegian should incorporate such lexical items as bear witness to cultural developments of a truly international nature, above all loanwords of Greek and Roman, but to a certain extent even French, English or Dutch origin. On the other hand, words and word forms which reflected dependence on former political and economical masters were felt to be nationally disgraceful and hence to be shunned. (By contrast, proponents of Dano-Norwegian and later on *Riksmål* have emphasized the value of a shared cultural heritage.) In addition, there was a declared intention to restore to literary usage old Norwegian words and word forms which had survived in the dialects. In practice this amounted to the programmatic exclusion from New Norwegian of a large number of lexical elements that were recognizably Danish or German. These derive from three main historical sources:

1   During the late Middle Ages, the activities of the Hanseatic League had a tremendous impact on Norwegian trade and economy, and the linguistic influence of Middle Low German on the Norwegian vocabulary was to acquire equal proportions;
2   After the protestant reformation of 1536, High German became, through Danish, an important source of lexical innovation;
3   As early as about 1500, Norwegian was virtually extinct as a written language. For all administrative and literary purposes it had been replaced by Danish.

The selective purism resulting from a desire to combat the consequences of this rather massive lexical influence has, in practice, had more a structural than a strictly etymological bent. Loanwords which conform to indigenous Norwegian phonotactic and derivational patterns which are naturally heir to Old Norse formations are accepted quite easily. To these belong such common words as BM/NN *rykte* 'rumour, reputation', BM *middel*, NN *medel* 'means', BM/NN *ære* 'honour', BM/NN *alvor* 'earnest', BM *fremmed*, NN *framand* 'foreign', BM/NN *krig* 'war', BM/NN *bruke* 'use', BM/NN *reise* 'travel', BM/NN *selskap* 'party, company', etc. On the other hand, New Norwegian has to some extent pursued the policy of creating translation loans to replace *Riksmål/Bokmål* formations of actual or alleged foreign provenance: compare NN *sjølvstende* (BM *selvstendighet*) 'independence', NN *takksemd* (BM *takknemlighet*) 'gratitude', NN/BM *tiltak* 'initiative', NN/BM *ordskifte* 'discussion', NN/BM *samrå seg med* 'confer, discuss with'. However, present-day New Norwegian usage seems to indicate a certain weakening of former puristic positions. In particular, a large number of common *Bokmål* words with the originally German prefixes *be-* and *for-* are now being admitted into New Norwegian.

Aspects of Lexicalization

The specific lexicalization patterns of a language are, at least from a heuristic point of view, presumably best established by comparison with other languages. From this perspective, it seems reasonable to assume that Norwegian does not possess the wealth of, in particular, abstract words found in English. Hence, certain semantic distinctions are less prone to be lexicalized in Norwegian than in English: BM *mulighet* vs English *possibility, opportunity, option*. Norwegian is also able to dispense with certain 'logical' distinctions which are lexicalized in, for example, English. Thus, the *some–any* distinction is only vestigially present in NN *nokre* vs *nokon*, and with regard to the *each–every* distinction, Norwegian conflates 'each' and 'every' as BM *hver*, NN *kvar*. On the other hand, Norwegian has definitely more modal particles than English, but less than German and Russian. For example, the highly frequent sentence-final particle BM *da*, NN *då* does service as the equivalent of the three clause-internal German particles *schon, denn, mal* in the following different sentence types: German *nun seid ihr schon verlobt* – BM *nå er dere forlovet, da* 'now you are engaged, then' vs German *wie sah denn der Wagen aus?* – NN *korleis såg bilen ut, då?* 'what did the car look like?' vs German *laß mal hören!* – BM *få høre, da!* 'let's hear then!'

When comparing Norwegian and German, it is evident that the latter language has a far richer system than Norwegian in the domain of prefixal formations. In particular, Norwegian counterparts to the important subsystem of verbs with a deictic prefix consisting of *hin-*, *her-* and a preposition are lacking entirely. Furthermore, Norwegian often has one lexical verb where German has two or more syntactically and semantically distinct verbs with different prefixes, cf. BM *true*, NN *truga* 'threaten' vs German *drohen, bedrohen, androhen*; BM *høre*, NN *høyra* 'hear, listen' vs German *hören, (sich) anhören, zuhören*; BM *spørre*, NN *spørja* 'ask' vs German *fragen, befragen, erfragen, anfragen*.

By contrast, phrasal-verb constructions constitute a productive lexical pattern in Modern Norwegian. They appear to be syntactically characteristic in two important respects. First, they display the kind of operand–operator ((S)VO) serialization which is typical of other constituent domains also, above all the (v–)V–N–A(–Sentence–final Particle) patterns of the verbal part (VP) of sentences and clauses, the post-adjectival part of noun phrases, and the positioning of prepositions and complementizers before the remainder of the prepositional phrases and clauses they introduce. Second, phrasal verbs appear to be another instance of a pervasive tendency to give separate lexical expression to semantic units and relations, so that semantic complexity of content is iconically reflected as syntagmatic complexity of expression. The following verbatim quote from a radio interview with an important Norwegian government official would seem to be a rather extreme, but not altogether untypical example of a more general semantic strategy of this kind: BM *vi får nok se til å legge litt mer jobb i å få orden på dette*. The following is a literal translation into English (with some grammatical comments added): 'we get (aux. with modal obligational meaning) enough (modal particle roughly corresponding to English *then*) look to (phrasal verb with particle of prepositional origin) to (inf. particle) lay a little (quantifier) more (comparative quantifier) job (i.e. 'work, effort') in (prep. dependent on the preceding phrasal-verb expression) to (inf. particle) get order on (prep. dependent on phrasal-verb expression) this here (deictic adverb specifying the preceding demonstrative)'. A more appropriate English translation in official style would rather seem to be something like: 'we must increase our efforts to rectify this'. It appears to be a not too controversial suggestion that this analytic tendency constitutes a semantic analogue to the morphosyntactic analyticity which manifests itself in the categorial paucity and the comparatively regular affixal character of the Norwegian, in particular *Bokmål*, inflectional-marking system.

Further Reading

Comprehensive bibliographies are found in the anthologies by Jahr and Lorentz indicated below.

Coward, G. (1986) *Riksmålsgrammatikk. Med en sproghistorisk innledning og en rettskrivningslære*, Oslo: Dreyer.

Golden, A., MacDonald, K. and Ryen, E. (eds) (1988) *Norsk som fremmedspråk. Grammatikk*, Oslo: Universitetsforlaget.

Haugen, E. (1966) *Language Conflict and Language Planning: The Case of Modern Norwegian*, Cambridge, Mass.: Harvard University Press.

Jahr, E. H. and Lorentz, O. (eds) (1981) *Fonologi/Phonology*, Oslo: Novus.

—— (eds) (1983) *Prosodi/Prosody*, Oslo: Novus.

—— (eds) (1985) *Morfologi/Morphology*, Oslo: Novus.

—— (eds) (1989) *Syntaks/Syntax*, Oslo: Novus.

Johnsen, E. B. (ed.) (1987) *Vårt eget språk 1–3*, Oslo: Aschehoug.

Næs, O. (1972) *Norsk grammatikk. Elementære strukturer og syntaks*, 3rd edn, Oslo: Fabritius.

Sandøy, H. (1991) *Norsk dialektkunnskap*, 2nd edn, Oslo: Novus.

Skard, V. (1967–79) *Norsk språkhistorie*, vols 1–4, Oslo, Bergen and Tromsø: Universitetsforlaget, vol. 1, 1967; vol. 2, 1972; vol. 3, 1976; vol. 4, 1979.

Venås, K. (1990) *Norsk grammatikk. Nynorsk*, Oslo: Universitetsforlaget.

Vinje, F.-E. (1987) *Moderne norsk. Råd og regler for praktisk språkbruk*, 4th edn, Oslo, Bergen, Stavanger and Tromsø: Universitetsforlaget.

9 Swedish

Erik Andersson

9.1 Introduction

Swedish is spoken by more than 8 million native speakers. Most of them live in Sweden, but there is also a Swedish population of 300,000 native speakers in Finland. In addition, there are Swedish-speaking persons in other countries, for instance, descendants of about 1,400,000 Swedish emigrants from the turn of the century onwards (1870–1930), mostly in the United States and Canada, but very few of them have Swedish as their first language today. Swedish populations have existed in Estonia on some of the islands and the Ukraine (Gammalsvenskby), but they are now almost extinct. Swedish is to some extent studied abroad as a foreign language, especially in Finland, where all pupils in the comprehensive schools learn some Swedish. Finland belonged to the Swedish kingdom before 1809 and is still officially bilingual between Finnish and Swedish. The Swedish population (6 per cent, with roots from the twelfth century) lives along the southern and western coast, and has strong minority rights in the constitution.

Sweden used to be an almost monolingual country until some decades ago, the main exceptions being 40,000 Finns living mostly along the Finnish border in Tornedalen in the north, and 7,000 people in the Saami population closer to the Norwegian border. Now there are about 750,000 immigrants in Sweden, half of them with Swedish citizenship, speaking Finnish, Spanish, Arabic, Polish, Serbian or Croatian, Persian, English, Turkish, German, Greek, Danish, Hungarian, etc. The number of bilingual speakers in these groups exceeds 1 million, if children of immigrants are included. So far, the immigration wave has not influenced the Swedish language to any greater degree, but there is linguistic borrowing from international languages, mainly English, but also French and German.

Old dialects are still spoken in rural areas, especially in northern Sweden, including Dalecarlia, in Gotland and in Finland, but most dialects have been levelled out to a considerable degree. There are also urban dialects, closer to the central standard. However, regional variation is a conspicuous trait in the Swedish-speaking area, more important, maybe, than social variation.

There are regional variants, especially for pronunciation, although a central

SWEDISH

super-regional norm originally found in the Stockholm area has had the strongest social status, and has spread to other areas at least in formal contexts. A deviant regional variant is used at all levels of communication in Finland. Another fairly strong regional norm is used in southern Sweden (Skåne, Halland and Blekinge), an area which belonged to Denmark before 1658. Western Swedish is pretty close to Southern Swedish, while Northern Swedish is less uniform. On the other hand, stylistic differences have tended to diminish during the twentieth century, resulting in a fairly uniform standard language in both written and spoken discourse. Generally, an informal style has spread to more formal contexts, and spelling tends to influence pronunciation.

9.2 Phonology

In Swedish, there are 9 vowel phonemes (18, if short and long vowels are counted separately) and at least 18 consonant phonemes.

Vowels

The Swedish vowels are given in Table 9.1. Short and long vowels are generally pronounced with different vowel quality, the short variants being more centred and lax – unstressed /e/ generally has a schwa-pronunciation. Short /a/ has a front pronunciation, and long /a/ a back pronunciation with a weak rounding. Long /ɯ/ has a front pronunciation with a characteristic closed rounding, which means that Swedish uses two different types of rounding in front vowels, outward rounding in /y, ø/, and inward rounding in /ɯ/. Short /ɯ/ has a close-mid pronunciation. Long high vowels end in a glide phonetically, [ij, yj, ɯw, uw]. However, almost none of these remarks applies to Finland Swedish, which fits in with the second variant of Table 9.1 only, with central /ʉ/ and /a/.

In most variants, including Finland Swedish, /ø/ has two very distinct allophones, an open pronunciation being used in front of /r/, e.g. hö [hø:] 'hay', hör [hœːr] 'hears'. The same is true for /ɛ/, which normally has a mid pronunciation, but an open pronunciation in front of /r/. In many central and

Table 9.1 Swedish vowel phonemes

	Front	Back	or	Front	Central	Back
Close	i, **y, ɯ** ‹u›	**u** ‹o›		i, **y**	**ʉ** ‹u›	**u** ‹o›
Close-mid	e, **ø** ‹ö›	**o** ‹å›		e, **ø** ‹ö›		**o** ‹å›
Open-mid	ɛ ‹ä›			ɛ ‹ä›		
Open		a				a

Note: Rounded vowels are given in bold; normal spellings are in angular brackets.

eastern areas, the mid variant of /ɛ/ has merged with /e/, especially the short vowel, Many speakers, therefore, have a merger in *hetta* 'heat' and *hätta* 'cap', while others do not even distinguish between *veta* 'know' and *väta* 'moisten', with long vowels. But all speakers distinguish between e.g. [beːr] 'asks' and [bæːr] 'carries'. The /e–ɛ/ distinction is also neutralized in unstressed syllables, likewise the distinction between /u/ and /o/.

Consonants

The Swedish consonants are given in Table 9.2. Voiceless stops are generally aspirated, which has permitted voiced stops to start devoicing next to a pause or a voiceless segment, e.g. *bar* 'bare', *fadd* 'stale', *snabbt* 'rapidly', *utgå* 'expire, emanate'. Somewhat similar devoicing processes apply to other voiced segments. Therefore, the distinction between fortis and lenis stops could be described as a difference in aspiration rather than voice. On the other hand, voiceless stops are deaspirated after /s/ in the same morpheme, e.g. *stå* 'stand', before voiceless segments, e.g. *bets* 'stain', *makt* 'power', and non-initially before an unstressed syllable, e.g. *leka* 'play', *hampa* 'hamp'. Aspiration and to some extent loss of voice are still almost lacking in Finland Swedish.

The pronunciation of the palatal and velar spirants varies. Often, /ʃ/ is pronounced dorsally, further back than the apico-alveolar /ç/, and it can even have a velar pronunciation [x], especially in young speakers and in the west. It may also be a velarized labiodental or an apico-alveolar sound. In Finland, both /ʃ/ and /ç/ have an apico-alveolar pronunciation, but the latter is realized as an affricate [tʃ].

Dental /r/ has an apico-alveolar pronunciation, but uvular /r/ is used in southern Sweden up to a line drawn by Kalmar – Jönköping – Falkenberg, and, in initial position and as a geminate further north. Dental /r/ is sometimes pronounced as a tap with one closing only, and often has a fricative rather than a tremulant pronunciation, particularly in the central region – this is very common in word-final position. In many regional or dialectal variants, /l/ can be a retroflex flap in certain positions, especially after or before a labial or velar consonant, e.g. *glad* 'glad', *valp* 'puppy', or after a long non-palatal

Table 9.2 Swedish consonants

	Labial	Labiodental	Dental	Palatal	Velar	Laryngeal
Stops	p, b		t, d		k, g	
Nasals	m		n		ŋ	
Spirants		f, v	s	ç, j	ʃ	h
Tremulants				r		
Laterals			l			

vowel, e.g. *kal* 'bare', *påle* 'pole'. The fricatives /v/ and /j/ are pronounced with relatively weak friction and are phonotactically similar to /r/ and /l/.

Retroflex Sounds

Combinations of /r/ and a following dental consonant are generally contracted into single retroflex sounds, which are sometimes regarded as separate phonemes: the dental is somewhat retracted in *barn* /baːɳ/ 'child', *bort* /botʈ/ 'away', *hård* /hoːɖ/ 'hard', *mars* /maʂː/ 'March', *arla* /aːɭa/ 'early'. The retroflexes are not used in southern Sweden, where /r/ has a uvular pronunciation, nor in standard Finland Swedish.

Dental consonants also have a retroflex pronunciation after other retroflex sounds, e.g. *först* [fœʂʈ] 'first'. Retroflex sounds are used also over morpheme and word boundaries as in *barnstuga* [baːɳʂʈɯːga] 'children's cottage', *har du* [haːɖə] 'do you have'.

Syllable Structure

Syllables with primary or secondary stress must be long, i.e. either contain a long vowel, or a short vowel followed by a long consonant or a consonant cluster, e.g. *å* ['oː] 'stream', *ås* ['oːs] 'ridge', *oss* ['osː] 'us', *ask* ['ask] 'box'. Stressed short syllables only occur in Finland Swedish colloquial language, e.g. *bara* ['bara] 'only'. Nor can a stressed syllable have double length, i.e. simultaneously contain a long vowel and end in a long consonant. However, some consonant clusters, for instance those corresponding to retroflex sounds, can be preceded by a stressed long vowel, e.g. *färd* ['fæːɖ] 'trip', *aln* ['aːln] 'ell'. Long vowels also occur before many clusters containing a morpheme boundary, e.g. *råds* ['roːds] 'council's', although the vowel is shortened in some words like *Guds* ['gøts] 'God's', *till havs* [til'hafs] 'at sea'. Before /rt/, there is variation between words and between speakers, e.g. *fart* ['faːʈ] 'speed', *svart* ['svaʈː] 'black', but *port* ['puːʈ/'puʈː] 'gate'. Unstressed syllables do not contain long sounds, the possible exception being syllables with a reduced tertiary stress, cf. derivations with primary stress on the affix as in the minimal pair *säteri* [sɛːtər'iː] 'main estate exempt from dues to the crown' : *sätteri* [sɛtːər'iː] 'composing-room'.

Tonal Accent

There is a distinction between two tonal word accents, except in Finland Swedish. The acute accent (accent 1) is, roughly speaking, used in monosyllables and words with stress on the last syllable, also in their longer definite forms, e.g. ´and-en 'the duck', ´steg-en 'the steps', ´bur-en 'the cage', universi´tet-et 'the university'. The gravis (accent 2) is used in polysyllables with initial stress, e.g. `ande-n 'the spirit', `stege-n 'the ladder', `buren 'carried'. However, many two-syllable words corresponding to monosyllabic words in runic Swedish have the acute accent, e.g. ´fågel 'bird', ´vatten 'water', ´finger 'finger'.

The realization of the accents varies in different areas, but their distribution in the lexicon is fairly stable. In the central area, the gravis accent is realized with two peaks, i.e. as a temporary fall in the word tone at the end of the first syllable. Further south, in the Göta region, the peaks are somewhat delayed, especially the peak in accent 1 words. Still further south, both accents have one peak, early (accent 1) or late (accent 2) in the first syllable. Gotland and Dalecarlia have a similar system, but again, the peaks are delayed.

Polysyllables with acute accent include: (a) all present-tense forms in -er (originally strong verbs only), e.g. *'spring-er* 'runs', *'lek-er* 'plays'; (b) definite forms of nouns with acute accent, e.g. *'bit-en* 'the piece', *ka'fé-et* 'the café'; (c) some plurals in -er of monosyllable nouns, e.g. *'böck-er* 'books'; (d) comparatives with the ending -re, e.g. *'stör-re* 'bigger'; (e) most words with non-initial and non-final stress, e.g. *be'tala* 'pay', *för'sörja* 'provide for', *deko'rera* 'decorate'; (f) many words of foreign descent, including foreign names, e.g. *'ångest* 'agony', *'känga* 'boot', *'atlas* 'atlas', *'Afrika*, *'Belgrad*, *'Indien*; (g) at least optionally or regionally, compound words, which are in the process of losing their compound character, e.g. *'trädgård* 'garden', *'söndag* 'Sunday'; (h) optionally or regionally, many names, e.g. *'Erik*, *'Hilda*, *'Lundberg*, *'Halmstad*.

Polysyllables with gravis accent include most plurals, e.g. *`alm-ar* 'elm trees', most forms of verbs and adjectives, e.g. *`skämta-de* 'joked', *`stark-ast* 'strongest', and most compounds and compound-like derivations, e.g. *`ord-bok* 'dictionary', *`barn-dom* 'childhood'.

Phonotactics
Native words have a restricted phonotactic structure. There are no diphthongs, and a typical root morpheme contains only one syllable with a single vowel, possibly preceded and/or followed by up to three consonants. Unstressed syllables are generally much simpler. Dissyllabic stems have a simple second syllable, typically ending in a vowel or /l, n, r/. Derivational and inflectional endings can complicate medial and final clusters considerably, e.g. *skälmskt* 'roguishly'.

Possible initial clusters are given in Figure 9.1. Two connected elements in the figure (but not three) can be combined as indicated, e.g. *spl, dv, vr*, with the exception of the combinations in the filter.

Impossible initial clusters still occurring in the orthography are ‹stj, skj, sj›, all pronounced [ʃ]; ‹tj, kj›, pronounced [ç]; ‹gj, lj, hj›, pronounced [j]. The cluster ‹dj›, too, is often simplified to [j]. In addition, initial ‹k› is often pronounced [ç], ‹sk› [ʃ], and ‹g› [j] before front vowels, but this phonotactic restriction has been removed, so that [k, sk, g] + front vowel can occur again word-initially.

Some orthographic clusters containing ‹g› have a deviant pronunciation in final and generally also in medial position: ‹rg› [rj]; ‹lg› [lj]; ‹ng› [ŋ]; and ‹gn› [ŋn].

Figure 9.1   Possible initial clusters

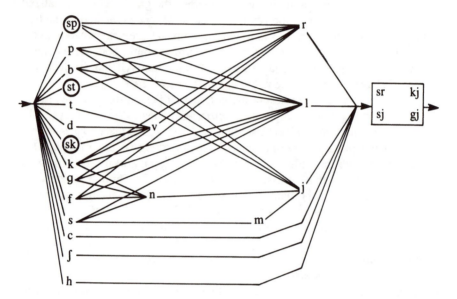

Source: Sigurd 1970: 41.

Words felt to have a foreign origin can have a more complex phonotactic structure. But even here, diphthongs are avoided, sometimes being replaced by a vowel–consonant combination or split on two syllables, e.g. *farmaceut* [farma'seft] 'pharmaceutist', *paus* 'pause', and consonant combinations are often simplified, e.g. *psalm* [salm] 'hymn'.

Stress Placement

Stress is normally placed on the first syllable in non-derived native words. In words felt to have a foreign origin, the stress is sometimes on the first syllable, e.g. *'tivoli* 'place of amusement', but often on the last syllable, or one syllable before the end, e.g. *ma'net* 'jelly-fish', *ben'gali*. Weak tertiary stresses can be put on the first syllable, e.g. *indi'vid* 'individual', *peri'od* 'period', *gut-ta'perka* 'gutta-percha'. In derivations and inflections with unstressed endings, the stress can be placed even further away from the end of a foreign word, e.g. *peri'od-isk-a*. On the other hand, many derivational endings are stressed and remove the stress from the stem, often leaving behind a weak tertiary stress, e.g. *individu'ell* 'individual (adj.)', *individuali'tet* 'individuality'. Some derivations are similar to compounds and have secondary stress on the suffix, e.g. *'broder,skap* 'brotherhood', or perhaps a tertiary stress, e.g. *'positiv* 'positive'. In the latter case, there is sometimes a variation, e.g. in *feminin* 'feminine', where either the first or the last syllable can carry the primary stress. Some false compounds are stressed as if they were compounds, although it is hard to recognize an internal morpheme structure, e.g. *'ar₁bete* 'work'. (See Morphology, section 9.3.)

9.3 Morphology

Compounding

New words can be created either by compounding or by derivation, especially nouns, adjectives and, to some extent, verbs. These processes are less productive for pronouns, adverbs, prepositions and conjunctions.

Compounding can be either modifying, e.g. *husbåt* 'house boat', or copulative, i.e. similar to conjoining, *matematisk-naturvetenskaplig* 'for mathematics and science'. Modifying compounds consist of two elements, the first being the modifying element, but copulative compounds often consist of several parallel elements, e.g. *svensk-norsk-dansk* 'Swedish-Norwegian-Danish'. Compounds are written in one word, but especially in copulative compounds and after proper names hyphens are often used to make the structure clear, e.g. *Kurosawa-film* 'Kurosawa movie'.

Special linking morphemes, an *-s-* or a vowel, are sometimes attached to the first element, e.g. *land-s-ting* 'county council', *läs-e-bok* 'textbook', *kvinn-o-arbete* 'women's work'. In some cases, there are special allomorphs of the first element to be used in compounds, e.g. *lant-bruk* 'agriculture' from *land* 'land'. The use of linking morphemes is lexically marked, and the same first element can take an *-s-* in some compounds and be used alone in others, e.g. *dag-s-inkomst* 'daily income', *dag-tid* 'day time'. The *-s-* is also used when the first element of the compound is complex in itself (compound or derived), e.g. *talspråk-s-data* 'data on spoken language', *avgift-s-fri* 'free of charge', *parkering-s-förbud* 'parking prohibition'. The main exceptions to this rule are first elements ending in /s, ʃ/ or a cluster containing one of these phonemes, e.g. *sjukhus-byggnad* 'hospital building', *uppmarsch-order* 'deployment order', *humanist-överskott* 'humanist surplus', or ending in a vowel or in an unstressed vowel + /r, l, n/, e.g. *stortå-nagel* 'big-toe nail', *försommar-natt* 'night in early summer'.

Typical compounds have primary stress on the first element and secondary stress on the second element, even if the second element is semantically and syntactically the head of the compound, e.g. *'blod₁röd* 'blood red', *'upp₁ställa* 'put up'.

Sometimes, the primary stress is on the last element: (a) in contracted phrases, e.g. *förgätmig'ej* 'forget-me-not' (and here the first element can be the head element, e.g. *kryp'in* 'cosy corner'); (b) in additive numerals, e.g. *trettio'fem* '35'; (c) in compounds consisting of three or more constituents, e.g. *OEC'D-länderna* 'the OECD countries'. But in the last case all elements often have equal stress, e.g. *norskt-danskt-svenskt samarbete* 'Norwegian-Danish-Swedish cooperation'.

Nouns and participles are more easily compounded than verbs, cf. *tomgång* 'idle running' – *gå på tomgång* 'run idle', *snabbgående* 'fast' – *gå snabbt* 'go fast'.

Phrases do not normally occur within word formations. If they do, hyphens are often used between the words inside the word, or at least after the phrase, e.g. *ta det lugnt-attityd* '(lit.) take it easy-attitude'. The phrase can also be reformulated into a compound, e.g. *ordhållig* 'keeping one's word' from *hålla ord*, *tremotorig* 'with three motors', cf. *med tre motorer*.

Inflectional endings can occur inside a compound in a few cases only, e.g. the neuter *-t* in copulative compounds, or a plural ending in compounds with a numeral in the first element like *femdagarsvecka* 'five-day week'.

Derivation

New nouns, adjectives and verbs are easily formed by derivation. Most derivational affixes are suffixes, but some prefixes are used. The last element (stem or suffix) determines the word class of the derivation. Some derivational affixes are unstressed, while others carry a secondary stress, like the last element of a typical compound. Still others carry the main stress of the word, thereby removing the stress from the stem.

Prefixing: *be-'lägga* 'cover', *för-'tala* 'defame', *'o-₁rädd* 'fearless', *'miss-₁tag* 'mistake'. It is often hard to draw a borderline between prefixing and compounding, e.g. *'kvasi-popu₁lär*, *'mini-₁räknare* 'mini-calculator'.

Noun formation with suffixes: *sök-ande* 'search', *bo-ende* 'living', *överför-ing* 'transport', *läs-ning* 'reading', *bak-else* 'pastry', *frukt-an* 'fear', *realis-a'tion* 'sale', *brygg-e'ri* 'brewery', *'vag-₁het* 'vagueness', *'kär-₁lek* 'love', *'rike-₁dom* 'richness', *'moder-₁skap* 'motherhood', *individual-i'tet* 'individuality', *modern-'ism* 'modernism'. *löp-are* 'runner', *spekul-'ant* 'prospective buyer', *kontrah-'ent* 'party', *komment-'ator* 'commentator', *dans-'ör* 'dancer', *sol-'ist* 'soloist', *vek-ling* 'weakling', *hård-ing* 'tough guy', *feg-is* 'coward', *sömm-erska* 'dress-maker', *fin-ska* 'Finnish woman/language', *prost-'inna* 'dean's wife'.

Adjective formation with suffixes: *ljud-lig* 'loud', *lust-ig* 'funny', *själv-isk* 'selfish', *syn-sk* 'para-normal', *minim-'al* 'minimal', *individ-u'ell* 'individual', *represent-a'tiv* 'representative', *nerv-'ös* 'nervous', *enarm-ad* 'one-armed', *'stånds-₁mässig* 'conformable', *'trä-₁aktig* 'wooden-like', *'spar-₁sam* 'economical', *'efter₁häng-sen* 'clinging', *'del-₁bar* 'divisible', *diskut-'abel* 'debatable'.

Verb formation with suffixes: *såg-a* 'saw', *telefon-'era* 'telephone', *legal-is'era* 'legalize'.

Noun Inflection

The noun is inflected for number (singular and plural), definiteness (bare and definite form) and case (basic case and genitive), the endings coming in that order (cf. The noun phrase, pp. 287–90), e.g. *bil-ar-na-s* 'of the cars'. Only count nouns are inflected for all three categories, mass nouns and other uncountables are normally inflected for definiteness and case, e.g. *ull-en-s* 'of the wool', and proper nouns for case only e.g. *Sverige-s*.

Declensions

Nouns can be classified into declensions according to the form of the plural ending, and into two genders (utrum and neutrum) according to the singular definiteness ending. There is a correlation between gender and declension: generally, nouns in declensions (a–d) have gender utrum, and nouns in declensions (e–f) gender neutrum.

a Plural in *-or*. Utrum words ending in unstressed /a/ belong here, and a few words ending in a consonant, e.g. *(flicka)/flick-or* 'girls', *(näsa)/näs-or* 'noses', *våg-or* 'waves'. The /a/ is dropped in the plural and could also be treated as a singular ending.

b Plural in *-ar*. Most utrum words ending in unstressed /e/ belong here, but also many other utrum words, e.g. *(pojke)/pojk-ar* 'boys', *våg-ar* 'scales', *by-ar* 'villages'. The /e/ is dropped in the plural and could be regarded as a singular ending.

c Plural in *-er*. Many utrum nouns belong here, e.g. *min-er* 'facial expressions', *vy-er* 'views', *idé-er* 'ideas', but also some neuters, e.g. *(land)/länd-er* 'countries', especially polysyllabics ending in a stressed vowel, e.g. *part'i-er* 'portions', and some original mass nouns, e.g. *vin-er* 'wines'.

d Plural in *-r*. Some old monosyllabic words ending in a vowel belong here, e.g. *sko-r* 'shoes'. The ending is more productive for words ending in an unstressed /e/, but less common after unstressed /o/, cf. *aktie-r* 'shares', seldom *radio-r* 'radios'.

e Plural in *-n*. Most neutrum nouns ending in a vowel belong here, e.g. *bi-n* 'bees', *buande-n* 'booings'.

f Plural without ending. Neutrum nouns ending in a consonant belong here, e.g. *hus* 'houses', *vad* 'bets', but also utrum nouns with reference to persons and ending in *-are*, *-ande*, *-iker*, and some others, e.g. *lärare* 'teachers', *ordförande* 'chairmen', *magiker* 'magicians', *(man)/män* 'men'.

g Plural in *-s*, *-i*, *-ta* (borrowed endings). Some loanwords can be inflected with foreign endings, especially English *-s*, but parallel forms according to one of the declensions (a–f) are now preferred, e.g. *schlager-s/schlagr-ar* 'hits', *trick-s/trick*, *(tempo)/temp-i/tempo-n*, *schema-ta/schema-n* 'schedules', *(pronomen)/pronomina/pronomen* 'pronouns'. Some other nouns, too, vary between two different declensions, e.g. (*prisma*)/*prism-or*/*prism-er* 'prisms'.

For some words in declensions (b), (c), and (f), the plural form has undergone vowel shift (umlaut), e.g. (*dotter*)/*döttr-ar* 'daughters', (*son*)/ *söner* 'sons', (*tång*)/*täng-er* 'tongs', (*man*)/*män* 'men'. Other changes can co-occur, such as accent shift or quantity shift, e.g. (*fader*)/*fäder* 'fathers' (accent 2 in sg. and accent 1 in pl.), (*mus*)/*möss* 'mice', (*gås* [goːs])/*gäss* [jæːs] 'geese'.

Before a syllabic plural ending, an unstressed syllable loses its vowel, e.g. (*cykel*)/*cykl-ar* 'bicycles', (*finger*)/*fingr-ar* (also *finger*) 'fingers', (*sägen* [sɛːgən])/*sägner*, [sɛŋnər] 'tales'. Also, /-um/ is lost between a vowel and a plural or definite ending, and could be regarded as a singular ending, e.g. (*muse-um*)/*muse-er* 'museums'. (*obligatorium*)/*obligatori-er* 'obligatories', cf. *album-ar* 'albums'. Words ending in unstressed /-or/ undergo stress shift in the plural, e.g. ('*doktor*)/*dokt'orer* 'doctors'.

Gender

Swedish nouns have either of two genders, although in some words there is variation, often regional, cf. *en penni – ett penni* 'a penny'.

1 Utrum: the singular definite ending is *-en*, generally *-n* after any vowel and after an unstressed vowel + /l, r/, e.g. *stol-en* 'the chair', *by-n* 'the village', *flicka-n* 'the girl', *lärar(e)-n* 'the teacher', *akademi-n* 'the academy' (*akademi-en* is archaic), *cykel-n* 'the bicycle', *cider-n* 'the cider'.

2 Neutrum: the singular definite ending is *-et*, and *-t* after an unstressed vowel (only colloquially after a stressed vowel), e.g. *hus-et* 'the house', *bi-et* 'the bee', *part'i-(e)t* 'the party', *ghetto-t* 'the ghetto'.

In the plural, the definite ending is generally *-na*, but *-a* after /n/ and *-en* after the zero plural ending, although *-na* is often optionally used after a stem in /r/, e.g. *flick-or-na, pojk-ar-na, sko-r-na, bi-n-a, hus-en, mönstr-en/mönster-na* 'the patterns'.

Before *-en*, the unstressed syllable /-en/ in the stem loses its vowel, e.g. *sägen/sägnen*. Before *-et*, the vowel in /-el/ or /-er/ is lost as well, as before plural *-en*, e.g. *segel/segl-et, lager/lagr-et, mönster/mönstr-en*. Stem final /-um/ is lost as before the plural ending, e.g. *muse-et* 'the museum'.

Case

The genitive ending is always *-s*, except after /s/, where the ending is assimilated and only occasionally signalled in the orthography with an apostrophe, e.g. *Bush-s, pojke-s/pojken-s/pojkar-s/pojkarna-s, hus/huset-s/hus/husen-s, Sibelius(') symfonier* 'the symphonies of Sibelius'.

Adjective Inflection

Adjectives, including past participles, are inflected for number, definiteness and gender. The form is determined by agreement with a head noun or a predicative base. The adjective is also inflected for case when it functions as the head of a noun phrase. Gradable adjectives can normally be compared (having positive, comparative and superlative forms).

In the positive, the plural ending is -*a*, or -*e* after an unstressed syllable with the vowel /a/, e.g. *stor-a, kastad-e*. The same form is also used as a singular definite form, e.g. *den gaml-a stugan* 'the old cottage', but here a form in -*e* is often used for masculine referents, e.g. *den gaml-e mannen* 'the old man', obligatorily when the adjective is the head of the noun phrase, e.g. *den gaml-e* 'the old man'. In the indefinite singular, the base form is used without an ending in agreement with utrum nouns, e.g. *en gammal man*, and with the ending -*t* otherwise, i.e. in agreement with neutrum nouns and when agreement is lacking, e.g. *ett gammal-t hus* 'an old house' *att du kom var trevlig-t* 'it was nice that you came'.

Adjectives can be divided into three comparation classes, according to what endings they take.

1   Comparative ending -*are*, superlative ending -*ast*, in the long form -*aste*, e.g. *fin* 'fine' *finare/finast/finaste*.
2   Comparative ending -*re*, superlative ending -*st*, in the long form: -*sta/ste*, e.g. *stor* 'big' *större/störst/största/störste*, *lång* 'long' *längre/längst*. These endings are often accompanied by umlaut and shortening, if possible. Only a few common adjectives belong to this class. Some of them are irregular in the stem or use suppletive stems, e.g. *bra* 'good' *bättre/bäst*, *liten* 'small' *mindre/minst*.
3   Comparative ending -*re*, superlative ending -*erst*, in the long form: -*ersta/-erste*. For these forms, the positive is not an adjective, but an adverb, e.g. *bort* 'away', *bortre* 'more distant (of two)' *borterst/bortersta* 'most distant'. (The superlative could perhaps be analysed as containing both a comparative and a superlative ending.)

The comparative form is never inflected, like any adjective ending in a vowel. The superlative long form is for many speakers predominantly a definite form as in the positive, e.g. *den godaste glassen* 'the most delicious ice-cream', but for other speakers a form generally used attributively, as in *en sista hälsning* 'a last greeting'. The short form is always used for predicative adjectives, e.g. *glasstrutar är godast* 'ice-cream cones are most delicious', but is, for many speakers, common in certain attributive uses, too, e.g. *Lisa lagar godast glass* 'Lisa makes the most delicious ice-cream'.

A stem final /n/ in an unstressed syllable is lost before -*t*, e.g. *öppen/öppet*. Stressed final vowels are shortened before -*t*, which is lengthened and assimilates a final /d/, e.g. *fri/fritt* [fri:, frit:], *röd/rött* [rø:d, røt:]. The unstressed syllables /-er, -en, -al/ lose their vowel before syllabic endings, e.g. *vacker* 'beautiful' *vackr-a/vackr-are/vackr-ast*, *öppen* 'open' *öppn-a/öppn-are/öppn-ast*, *gammal* 'old' *gaml-a*.

Pronoun Inflection

Pronouns can be subdivided into nominal pronouns, determiners and adjectival pronouns.

Nominal pronouns can function as noun phrases. Some of them can take complements typical to the noun, e.g. *hon som står där* 'she who is standing there', *du med vit skjorta* 'you in the white shirt', *ni där borta* 'you over there', *vem annan* 'who else', cf. *man* 'one', but they can combine with adjectives or nouns in a few marginal cases only, e.g. *lilla jag* 'little me', *han stackare* 'poor man'.

Determiners can function as noun phrases and take complements like nominal pronouns, but can also be combined with adjectives and/or nouns to form a noun phrase, e.g. *denna bil* 'this car', *min älskade* 'my beloved', *två långa dagar* 'two long days'.

Adjectival pronouns must generally be preceded by a determiner in the noun phrase and function very much like adjectives, e.g. *annan* 'other', *likadan* 'similar'. However, since a determiner is obligatory in individuative singular noun phrases only, the distinction between determiners and adjectival pronouns is often neutralized, especially for inherently plural pronouns.

Nominal pronouns are not inflected for number or definiteness, but possess themselves a certain number and definiteness, and sometimes semantic gender. They are inflected for case, although suppletive forms are often used, and personal pronouns have a specific accusative form in addition to the genitive, e.g. *han* 'he', *honom*, *hans*; *hon* 'she', *henne*, *hennes*.

The determiners generally possess number and gender, and may also be inflected for case, when they are used like nominal pronouns e.g. *denna(s)*, *detta(s)*, *dessa(s)* '(of) this/these', *vilken(s)*, *vilket(s)*, *vilka(s)* '(of) which', *någon(s)*, *något(s)*, *några(s)* '(of) some'.

The adjectival pronouns are generally inflected for number, definiteness, gender, and sometimes case, like normal adjectives, e.g. *likadan*, *likadant*, *likadana* 'similar'.

Nominal pronouns and determiners can be divided into definite, interrogative and indefinite pronouns. Definite pronouns can be divided into six groups:

1 Relative pronouns, i.e. *vilken(s)*, *vilket(s)*, *vilka(s)*, genitive also *vars*. (*Som* can be analysed as a subordinating conjunction rather than a nominal relative pronoun.) The nominal *vad* has no genitive and can be used in free relatives, preceded only by *allt*.

2 Reciprocal (or distributive) nominal pronouns, referring back to the subject

referents of the clause, *varandra(s)* '(of) each other'.

3 First- and second-person nominal pronouns. Instead of a genitive form, possessive pronouns are used.

	Nominative	Accusative	Possessive pronoun
1 sg.	jag	mig	min, mitt, mina
2 sg.	du	dig	din, ditt, dina
1 pl.	vi	oss	vår, vårt, våra
2 pl.	ni	er	er, ert, era

The possessive forms function as determiners and can marginally take the genitive ending, when they form a noun phrase on their own, e.g. *dina kusiners bil är dyrare än minas sommarstuga* 'Your cousins' car is more expensive than my cousins' summer cottage'.

4 Reflexive nominal pronouns, referring to the subject referent of the clause, *sig*. Instead of a genitive form, a possessive pronoun is used, *sin, sitt, sina*.

5 Third-person singular nominal pronouns, referring to other persons than the speaker or hearer, masculine, *han, honom, hans*, or feminine, *hon, henne, hennes*.

6 Demonstrative third-person determiners, referring to prominent inanimate or animate referents, *den(s), det, de*, in the genitive normally *dess, deras*. In spoken language, *dom* is widely used both for *de* (nom. pl) and *dem* (acc. pl.). *Denna(s), detta(s), dessa(s)* are more emphatic forms, which suggest a recent shift in prominence, by situational deixis (pointing) or by mentioning. The prominence can also be marked as distal, *den/det/de där(s)*, or proximal, *den/det/de här(s)*.

Interrogative pronouns are the nominal impersonal *vad* and personal *vem(s)*, and the determiner *vilken(s), vilket(s), vilka(s)*. *Hurdan* 'what sort of', *hurdant, hurdana* (archaic forms *hurudan*, etc.) may be adjectival, although the determiner *en* is normally deleted before it.

Indefinite pronouns are either nominal, e.g. *man* 'you, one, people' or determiners, e.g. *en/ett* 'a(n), one', *någon/något/några* 'some', *mången, månget, många* 'many', or adjectival, e.g. *sådan* 'such'. The difference between the latter categories is hard to tell for pronouns generally occurring in the plural only, like numerals and other quantifiers, e.g. *två* '2', *tusen* '1000', *få* 'few'. Strictly speaking, many indefinite pronouns are unmarked for definiteness, since they can occur in definite noun phrases as well as indefinite ones, e.g. *många bilar* 'many cars', *de många bilarna* 'the many cars'. A number of pronouns like *följande* 'following', *nästa* 'next', *ifrågavarande* 'in question', *sagda* 'mentioned', *respektive* 'respective' have a definite meaning and need not be combined with a definite article, although they are very similar to adjectives, e.g. *ovannämnda kommitté, den ovannämnda kommittén* 'the committee mentioned above.'

Verb Inflection

The verb is inflected for tense–mood and voice. The five tense–mood categories of Swedish have traditionally been grouped under three mood categories, indicative, subjunctive and imperative, with a tense distinction between present and past (preterite) in the first two. Here they are treated separately, but are called tenses when they have a temporal meaning and moods when they have a modal meaning.

The present tense is a neutral form which is used when no other form is motivated. It is generally used when the action takes place at the moment of speech (factive) or could take place at that time (potential). The ending is *-er*, but *-r* after a vowel, e.g. *läs-er* 'reads', *spring-er* 'runs', *kasta-r* 'throws', *sy-r* 'sews'. No ending is used after /r/ and in a few modal verbs, e.g. *lär* 'teaches, learns', *kan* 'can'.

The past form is used when the action is either a past event or state (past tense), or imagined at the moment of speech (modal past). The past tense therefore functions as a subjunctive for the weak verbs and can replace the subjunctive of the strong verbs, too. The ending is *-de* for weak verbs, but *-te* after voiceless consonant and sometimes after /-n/, and *-dde* after a stressed vowel, which is shortened, e.g. *kasta-de* 'threw', *väv-de* 'weaved', *läs-te* 'read', *rön-te* 'experienced', *sy-dde* 'sewed'. The same shortening takes place when the stem ends in a dental, e.g. *vät-a* 'moisten', *vät-te*, *led-a* 'lead', *led-de*. Strong verbs form their past tense by vowel shifts, which are only partly predictable from the present stem, e.g. *spring-a/sprang* 'run'.

The subjunctive mood of strong verbs is used when the action is imagined (either potential or unreal). The ending *-e* is added to a special subjunctive stem, formed by vowel shift, e.g. *få* 'get' *fing-e*, *spring-a* 'run' *sprung-e*, *bli* 'become' *blev-e*.

The optative mood (or present subjunctive) occurs mostly in lexicalized expressions and in archaic language. It is used to express wishes by the speaker, but also has a flavour of declaration or magic formula. The ending *-e* is added to the present stem, e.g. *lev-e* 'live'.

The imperative mood is used for ordering the listener to perform the action of the sentence, and the action is normally both potential and desired by the speaker. The form has no ending and consists of the present stem, e.g. *kasta* 'throw', *spring* 'run'.

Non-finite Verb Forms

The infinitive is used as a nominal constituent, and the supine in connection with the temporal auxiliary *ha*.

The infinitive has the ending -*a* after a consonant, and no ending after a vowel, e.g. *läs-a* 'read', *sy* 'sew'. In the first conjugation, the final /a/ can be analysed as a derivational element rather than as an infinitival ending, e.g. *hopp-a* 'jump', *fri-a* 'proposed marriage'.

The supine form has the ending -*t*, -*tt* for weak verbs, e.g. *väv-t* 'woven', *ro-tt* 'rowed', and -*it* for strong verbs, e.g. *riv-it* 'torn'. It was grammatically separated from the neutrum past participle in the eighteenth century, although there is a difference for strong verbs only, e.g. *skrivit* (sup.) 'written', *skrivet* (part.).

Voice

There are two verbal voice categories of non-finite as well as finite verb forms, i.e. the active and the passive (*s*-form). Voice inflection changes the valency of the verb, i.e. the rules for choice of subject and object.

S-forms are constructed by adding -*s* to the corresponding active form, except in the present tense, where the tense ending disappears, e.g. *kasta-s* 'be thrown', *kasta-s* 'is thrown', *kastade-s* 'was thrown', *kastat-s* 'been thrown', *riva-s* 'be torn', *riv-s*, *rev-s*, *rivit-s*. In the present tense, the voice ending is -*es* after a stem ending in /s/, and optionally in formal style after other consonants, e.g. *läs-es* 'is read', *riv-es*.

Instead of single voice forms, phrasal voice expressions are often used, combinations of a copula and a past participle. The copula *bli* is used with perfective verbs, and *vara* (sometimes alternatively *bli*) with imperfective verbs, e.g. *boken **blev** förstörd/förstördes* 'the book was (being) destroyed', *han **var** ansedd/blev ansedd/ansågs som en hederlig man* 'he was regarded as an honest man'. With perfective verbs, *vara* corresponds to a perfect-tense form, e.g. *boken **var** förstörd/hade förstörts* 'the book had been destroyed'.

Conjugations

The Swedish verbs can be grouped into weak verbs, strong verbs and a small residual group, mainly according to the type of ending in the past tense. Weak verbs take a dental suffix, strong verbs undergo vowel shift. Weak paradigms are given in Table 9.3, strong paradigms in Table 9.4. The forms in the weak paradigms given below are the infinitive, the imperative, the present, the past, and the supine. For the strong verbs, the subjunctive, too, is given after the preterite.

For Class I verbs, the thematic -*a* is present in all inflectional forms. This is the productive conjugation, where the majority of verbs belong. For Class II verbs, the stem ends in a voiced or a voiceless consonant; and for Class III verbs the stem ends in a stressed vowel.

Class IV verbs (strong verbs, see Table 9.4) form their past, subjunctive and supine forms partly by vowel shift. The stems therefore occur in four different variants, but two or more of them are always identical.

Table 9.3 Weak verbs

	Infinitive	Imperative	Present	Past	Supine
Class I	kasta 'to throw'	kasta	kasta-r	kasta-de	kasta-t
Class II	väv-a 'to weave'	väv	väv-er	väv-de	väv-t [vɛːft]
	löp-a 'to run'	löp	löp-er	löp-te	löp-t
Class III	sy 'to sow'	sy	sy-r	sy-dde	sy-tt

Table 9.4 Strong verbs

	Infinitive	Imperative	Present	Past	Subjunctive	Supine
Class IV	spring-a 'to run'	spring	spring-er	sprang	sprung-e	sprung-it
	bär-a 'to carry'	bär	bär	bar	bur-e	bur-it
	flyt-a 'to flow'	flyt	flyt-er	flöt	flöt-e	flut-it
	skriv-a 'to write'	skriv	skriv-er	skrev	skrev-e	skriv-it
	komm-a 'to come'	kom	komm-er	kom	komm-e	komm-it
	le 'to smile'	le	le-r	log	log-e	le-tt
	gå 'to go'	gå	gå-r	gick	ging-e	gå-tt

1 If there is a different supine stem, it is normally also used in the subjunctive, e.g. *springa, bära*.

2 If the present stem contains /y/, the past stem is used in the subjunctive, e.g. *flyta*.

3 If the present stem is used in the supine, the past stem is normally used in the subjunctive, e.g. *skriva*.

4 Only a few strong verbs have the same vowel in all forms, e.g. *komma*.

5 If the present stem ends in a vowel, the supine is formed as for weak verbs. The past stem ends in a consonant, but is often so irregular that it can be regarded as suppletive, e.g. *le, gå*.

Table 9.5 Residual verbs

Infinitive	Imperative	Present	Past	Supine
kunn-a 'to be able'	——	kan	kun-de	kunna-t
vilj-a 'to want'	——	vill	vill-e	vela-t
(skol-a) 'to be going to'	——	ska(ll)	skull-e	(skolat)
vet-a 'to know'	vet	vet	viss-te	veta-t

Residual verbs (see Table 9.5): a few irregular weak verbs have no ending, but possibly vowel shift in the present tense and a thematic -*a* in the supine.

Modal auxiliaries are found in several conjugations and are hard to distinguish from main verbs syntactically.

Vowel shift (umlaut) can sometimes occur in the weak conjugations. The past and supine forms have no umlaut, but often loss of stem final /j/ and sometimes lengthening of the vowel:

Infinitive	Imperative	Present	Past	Supine
välj-a 'to choose'	välj	välj-er	val-de	val-t
gläd(j)-a 'to give pleasure'	gläd	gläd-er	glad-de	glat-t

Some frequent verbs normally lose the final consonant in their present stem, which means that parallel forms exist like *taga/ta* 'take', *tag/ta*, *tager/tar*, *tog*, *tagit/?tatt*, *bliva/bli* 'become', *bliv/bli*, *bliver/blir*, *blev*, *blivit/?blitt*. The long forms are archaic, except in the supine.

Participles
The present participle is formed by adding -(*a*)*nde* to the present stem, -*ende* after a stressed vowel, e.g. *kasta-nde*, *läs-ande*, *skriv-ande*, *sy-ende*. Verbs with shortened stem forms use the longer form in the present participle, e.g. *givande* 'giving', *tagande* 'taking', *glädjande* 'satisfactory'.

The past participle is formed with the ending -*d*, -*t*, -*dd* for weak verbs, and the ending -*en* for strong verbs, e.g. *kasta-d*, *läs-t*, *sy-dd*, *skriv-en*.

9.4   Syntax

The Noun Phrase
The noun phrase typically contains a nominal pronoun or a determiner and/or a noun, but when these elements are missing, even an adjective can function as a noun phrase. There is no reason to distinguish between true noun phrases, containing a noun, and other noun phrases, since they have similar syntactic behaviour. Even infinitives and nominal clauses could be classified as noun phrases, but here all three categories are subsumed under the label nominal phrases. Typical noun phrase structures are the following:

Nominal pronoun or determiner: *hon* 'she', *alla därinne* 'everybody in there'
Proper noun: *Kalle (från Stockholm)*
   with determiner: *den oförsiktige Eriksson* 'the uncautious Eriksson'
Common or plural noun: *ylle* 'wool', *åkrar* 'fields', *bördiga åkrar med sädeskärvar* 'fertile fields with sheaves'
   with determiner: *denna dag* 'this day', *varje tung bok på hyllan* 'every heavy book on the shelf'

Adjective: *blinda* 'blind people'
  with determiner: *en blind* 'a blind person', *det enda goda med saken* 'the only positive thing in the matter'

When the noun phrase contains a noun, that word is generally regarded as the head of the phrase, but it would also be possible to give that role to the determiner.

Definiteness

There are three definiteness categories for the noun phrase: definite, indefinite and bare noun phrases. However, 'bare' could also be regarded as a variant of indefinite, since mass nouns and plurals can be bare when they function as indefinite expressions.

  definite: *den edsvurna translatorn* 'the certified translator'
  indefinite: *en edsvuren translator* 'a certified translator'
  bare: *edsvuren translator*

Definite noun phrases typically refer to uniquely identifiable referents and are marked with a definite pronoun, definite form of adjectival modifiers and definite form of the noun (although one or several markers may be missing), e.g. *den här nytvättad-e fin-a ull-en* 'this newly washed fine wool'.
  There is no definite pronoun in the following cases:

1   If there are no preposed modifiers, the definite ending of the noun is the only definiteness marker, e.g. *ullen* 'the wool', *häftet med blå pärmar* 'the booklet with blue covers'. *Hela* does not count as a preposed modifier in this respect, e.g. *hela (den långa) dagen* 'all day (long)'.
2   In lexicalized names, e.g. *Långa bron* 'the Long bridge', *Svarta havet* 'the Black Sea'.
3   Sometimes before a superlative, e.g. *Kalle var yngsta deltagaren* 'Kalle was the youngest participant'.

  The noun has no definiteness ending:

1   After genitival or possessive attributes, e.g. *barnens gamla kläder* 'the old clothes of the children', *min första läsebok* 'my first reader'.
2   After *denna, samma*, e.g. *detta bekymmersfria levnadssätt* 'this untroubled way of living', *samma trasiga hatt* 'the same ragged hat'.
3   Optionally after *den*, when a restrictive relative clause follows, especially in formal style, e.g. *vi satt i det nyrenoverade rum som låg genast till vänster* 'we were sitting in the newly renovated room that was right to the left'.
4   After an absolute superlative, e.g. *där satt den allra sötaste lilla apunge*

'there was the sweetest little monkey baby'.
5   In exclamations and vocatives with personal pronouns, e.g. *jag arma stackare!* 'poor me!' *du mäktige konung!* 'you mighty king!'

Both pronoun and definite ending is missing:

1   Optionally in noun phrases with *nästa, följande, motsvarande, ifrågavarande, vänster, höger*, e.g. *nästa beräknade solförmörkelse* 'next predicted solar eclipse', *ifrågavarande hårda omdöme* 'the hard judgement in question', *på vänster sida* 'on the left side'.
2   Sometimes after a superlative, e.g. *yngsta aktiva deltagare var Kalle* 'the youngest active participant was Kalle'.
3   In vocatives, e.g. *bästa bror!* 'dear brother!' *ärade åhörare!* 'honoured listener(s)!'

Adjectival marking and definiteness ending is missing after *varje, var*, e.g. *varje ny morgon* 'every new morning', *var tredje ditrest(a) turist* (lit.) 'every third arrived tourist'. After *all/allt/alla* and *båda, bägge*, either a definite or indefinite noun phrase can follow, e.g. *alla tjocka böcker – alla de tjocka böckerna* 'all (the) thick books', *allt annat skräp – allt det andra skräpet* 'all other garbish', *på båda håll – på båda hållen* 'on both sides'.

Case
Case categories are three, nominative, accusative and genitive, although the nominative–accusative distinction is valid for personal pronouns only. For other noun phrases, these two cases are merged into one basic case. The nominative is used in isolated words, in subjects, and in predicative complements, the exception being reflexive predicative complements, which must occur in the accusative, cf. *pojken med glasögon är jag* 'the boy with spectacles is me', *jag är inte mig själv i dag* 'I am not my real self today'. The accusative is also used in objects and after prepositions.

The genitive ending -*s* is attached to the final head of the noun phrase, generally a noun, but possibly an adjective or a pronoun. When the head has postposed complements, the genitive is avoided. However, it is possible to attach the genitive ending to such a head in formal style, especially in names, e.g. *Stiftelsens för Åbo Akademi forskningsinstitut* 'The Research Institute of the Åbo Academy Foundation', and to place the ending last in the entire noun phrase in colloquial style (group genitive), e.g. *mannen på gatans åsikter* 'the opinions of the man on the street'.

The genitive covers a wide range of meanings. Possessive genitive can express almost any affiliation: owner, user, location or located element, super- or subordinated element, source, result, etc. Partitive genitive expresses the whole of a part, e.g. *föreningens medlemmar* 'the members of the association'. Nexus genitive is either subjective, objective or temporal, e.g. *fiendens anfall* 'the attack of the enemy', *pjäsens framförande* 'the performance of the play', *dagens anfall* 'today's attack'. Genitives for measure and property occur in indefinite phrases, e.g. *en tre kilometers asfalterad raksträcka* 'a straight paved road of three kilometres', *ett smutsigt tredje klassens hotell* 'a dirty third-class hotel'. Other meanings are emphasis and identity. In the last case, Nordic place-names ending in a vowel have a genitive without ending inside fixed expressions functioning as names, e.g. *Åbo stad* 'the city of Turku', cf. *Stockholms stad*.

In many of these cases the genitive can be replaced by a prepositional phrase, an adjective, or a part of a compound. But this possibility does not apply to a genitive for owner or user, or a subjective genitive.

Attributive Modifiers

Attributive modifiers are either preposed or postposed (complements), and modify pronouns, nouns or independent adjectives.

Pronominal modifiers are normally preposed in the following order:

totality	demonstration	possession	quantity	selection	comparison	noun
båda	dessa	mina	två	andra	likadana	böcker
'both'	'these'	'my'	'two'	'other'	'similar'	'books'

Genitival modifiers occur in the possession slot in the above schema, (although they do not combine with a definite article in the demonstrative slot), e.g. *alla dessa Kalles otaliga böcker* 'all these innumerable books of Kalle's'

Adjectival modifiers, including participial ones, are normally preposed, following pronominal and genitival modifiers, but can be postposed, if they have modifiers of their own or form a coordinate structure, e.g. *en annan mycket tjock bok* 'another very thick book', cf. *en annan bok, mycket tjock*; *den lilla men naggande goda bakelsen – bakelsen, liten men naggande god* 'the pastry, little but very delicious'.

Prepositional and adverbial attributive complements are postposed, e.g. *huset på stranden* 'the house on the beach', *vägen hem* 'the way home'. When adverbs are preposed they can be reinterpreted as adjectives, e.g. *en gratis glass* 'a free ice-cream'.

Infinitival and sentential complements are postposed, e.g. *konsten att skriva* 'the art of writing', *frågan hur vi skulle forsätta* 'the question how to continue'.

The Prepositional Phrase

Prepositional phrases consist of a preposition and a nominal phrase, i.e. a noun phrase, an infinitive phrase, or a clause, e.g. *utan dig* 'without you', *hos blinda* 'in blind people'; *genom att springa* 'by running', *för att du skall må bra* 'in order for you to feel well'.

Some prepositions can be used as postpositions, especially in fixed phrases, e.g. *oss emellan* 'between us', *året runt* 'around the year'. There are also a few circumpositions in Swedish, e.g. *för en vecka sedan* 'a week ago', *för hennes skull* 'for her sake'.

The Adjective Phrase

Adjectives (including participles) can take other adjectives, adverbs, prepositional phrases and in some cases even nominal phrases as modifiers. The modifiers can be either preposed, e.g. *mycket stor* 'very big', *med svårigheter förtrogen* 'acquainted with difficulties', or postposed, e.g. *van med oljud* 'used to noise', *van (med) att svälta* 'used to starving'. When the adjective itself functions as a preposed modifier (to a noun), it cannot take postposed modifiers. However, in archaic style, modifiers which are normally postposed can be preposed, e.g. *alla i stadsmiljö boende medborgare* 'all citizens living in a city area', *en i alla avseenden lyckad kväll* 'an evening, successful in every respect'. But it is also possible to postpose the entire modifier: *alla medborgare boende i stadsmiljö, en kväll lyckad i alla avseenden.*

The adverb phrase can have a similar structure.

Subjects

Swedish is a subject-prominent language, which means that all clauses except imperative and some elliptical clauses must have an overt subject. The subject is marked by its position in the clause and, for personal pronouns, by nominative case.

The subject of subordinate clauses is generally placed clause-initially, immediately before preposed adverbials in the predicate and before the finite verb, e.g. *jag tror att **jag** inte kan komma i kväll* 'I think I cannot come tonight'. In main clauses, the finite verb is generally moved to pre-subject position, but since the subject in declarative sentences can be moved to clause-initial position, it is often placed right before the finite verb here, too, e.g. *i kväll kan **jag** inte komma, **jag** kan inte komma i kväll.*

The subject plays a role in many syntactic processes in a way that distinguishes it from other parts of the clause. However, in some cases objects exhibit similar properties.

1   The subject triggers tense–mood inflection in its predicate. If the subject is deleted, the finite verb may be reduced to an infinitive, which is often governed by the subject of the higher clause. Cf. *jag hoppas att jag klarar mig bra* 'I hope to manage well' *jag hoppas klara mig bra.*

2   The subject triggers number and gender agreement in predicative adjectives, and number agreement in predicative noun phrases, Cf. *flickan blev förvånad. Barnet blev förvånat. Kvinnorna blev förvånade,* 'the girl/ the child was astonished. The women were astonished' *mina farbröder är bönder* 'my uncles are farmers'.

3   The subject governs reflexive and reciprocal pronouns in the same clause,
     e.g. *han gav städerskan sin lön* 'he gave the cleaning maid his salary', *de
     gav eleverna varandras böcker* 'they gave the pupils each other's books.'
4   The subject can be raised to object or subject position in a superordinate
     clause with certain verbs, e.g. *jag såg henne springa bort* 'I saw her
     running away', *hon tycktes flyga över marken* 'she seemed to fly over the
     ground'.

Expletive Subject

If there is no semantic subject in normal subject position, an expletive subject
det is used. Especially in archaic or regional style, an adverbial like *här* 'here'
or *där* 'there', sometimes even a more complex adverbial, can fill the subject
position in the cases of impersonal clauses and existential clauses.

Impersonal Clauses

A semantic subject is lacking, or what could have been expressed by a subject
is expressed by an adverbial, e.g. *det regnar* 'it is raining', *det susar i skogen*,
cf. *skogen susar* 'the wood is whispering', *här är kallt* 'it is cold here', *trots
detta blev där allt trängre och hetare* 'in spite of this, it became more and
more crowded and hot' *?i vissa områden plöjs och harvas på hösten* 'in some
areas, they plough and cultivate the soil in the autumn'.

Existential Clauses

An indefinite subject noun phrase can be placed in postverbal (object)
position in many intransitive sentences. A locative adverbial is often present.
A lot of verbs allow for this existential construction, e.g. *det brukar sitta en
pojke på trappan* 'there is usually a boy sitting on the stairs'.

The requirements on indefiniteness are very high in more formal style. It
is not enough that the subject refers to an indefinite subclass of a definite class,
as in ??*det brukar sitta en av pojkarna på trappan* 'there is usually one of the
boys sitting on the stairs'.

In passive sentences the constituent placed in object position can be
regarded as either subject or object, as in *det dansades vals hela natten* 'they
danced walzes all night'.

Cleft Sentences

Almost any constituent in a sentence can be clefted, i.e. promoted to form a
higher clause together with the expletive subject *det* and a copula. The
original sentence is constructed as a subordinate clause introduced by *som*,
e.g. *det var Kalles bror som kom* 'it was Kalle's brother that came', *det är/blir
i morgon som allting skall ske* 'it is tomorrow that everything will happen',
det var doktor som han var 'he was a doctor'.

The clefted element is marked for case as if it were part of the subordinate clause, e.g. *det var mig som du såg* 'it was me that you saw', *det var hon som hjälpte mig* 'it was she who helped me'.

The matrix clause can include sentence adverbials and auxiliaries, e.g. *det var tyvärr inte Kalles bror som kom* 'unfortunately, it wasn't Kalle's brother who came', *det brukade vara på lördagarna som vi reste till landet* 'it was usually on Saturdays that we went into the countryside'.

Extraposition

An infinitival or sentential subject is normally placed at the end of the clause, which triggers an expletive subject, e.g. *naturligtvis är det roligt att skriva limerickar* 'of course, it is fun to write limericks', *det är möjligt att jag kommer* 'it is possible that I shall come'.

Extraposition is almost obligatory in subordinate clauses. In main clauses, it is possible to place the infinitival or sentential subject initially without an expletive subject, e.g. *att skriva limerickar är roligt/*naturligtvis är att skriva limerickar roligt/*jag vill veta om att skriva limerickar är roligt* 'I want to know whether it is fun to write limericks'.

Objects

An object is a nominal complement of a verb, normally expressing a referent undergoing a change or being created, a cause, a patient, an instrument, even a place or a time for the action, e.g. *Eva band en bukett av blommorna* 'Eva tied a bouquet of the flowers', *detta förvånade oss* 'this astonished us', *vi hörde att du kom* 'we heard that you came', *vi använde hammare* 'we used a hammer', *staketet omgav tomten på alla sidor* 'the fence surrounded the lot on all sides', *vi tillbringade ett år i utlandet* 'we spent a year abroad'. There are often alternative object choices, cf. *Eva band blommorna till en bukett*.

Objects are normally placed immediately after the head verb, but can also be placed initially, where they are sometimes hard to distinguish from subjects, e.g. *Hasse krossade äpplena till mos/äpplena krossade Hasse till mos* 'Hasse mashed the apples/the apples mashed Hasse'. Sentential objects are generally extraposed, e.g. *jag fick veta först i går att du skulle komma* 'I learned only yesterday that you would come'. In colloquial speech, personal object pronouns can be clitics, e.g. *jag såg'na inte* 'I didn't see her'.

The object can function as controller of predicative complements and adverbials, reflexives and infinitives, sometimes almost like subjects, e.g. *vi målade huset rött* 'we painted the house red', *han lade boken på sin plats* 'he put the book on its/his place', *hon skickade barnen utomlands för att lära sig svenska* 'she sent the children abroad for them to learn Swedish'.

A prepositional object (preposition and nominal phrase) is more freely placed, e.g. *jag hade prenumererat **på** DN i ett halvår/i ett halvår på DN* 'I had subscribed to *DN* for half a year'. It is not unusual that it is promoted to subject in a passive clause, e.g. *DN kan prenumereras (på) halvårsvis* '*DN* can be subscribed to by the half-year'.

Ditransitive verbs have two objects. The indirect object, expressing a receiver or experiencer, a person taking advantage of or suffering from the action, precedes the direct object, expressing a typical object role, e.g. *visa chefen din boksamling* 'show the boss your book collection'. Either object can normally be promoted to subject in a passive clause.

In many cases, the indirect object can be paraphrased with an adverbial prepositional phrase. But sometimes only an indirect object, sometimes only an adverbial is possible, cf. *visa din boksamling för chefen!* 'show your book collection to the boss!' *Allt detta gav **mig grå hår**/*grå hår åt mig* 'All this made me desperate (lit. gave me grey hairs)'. *Jag uträttade **ett ärende åt min bror**/*min bror ett ärende* 'I did an errand for my brother'.

Sometimes, an object in the topic position expresses a type of referent, while an object in normal object position expresses quantity, quality, or even identification (split or double object), e.g. *bilar har vi flera stycken* 'we have several cars', *ost köpte jag två kilo* 'I bought two kilograms of cheese', *pappershanddukar använde de bara oblekta* 'they used unbleached paper towels only', *mittfältare har dom bara Kenta och Lasse* 'in the centre field, they have only Kenta and Lasse'. This construction also occurs with existential subjects, e.g. *prydnadsväxter finns det både ettåriga och perenna* 'there are both annual and perennial decorative plants'.

The expletive object *det* is used in clauses with an objective predicative complement, when the object is missing or extraposed, e.g. *vi har det bra här* 'we are just fine here', *de ansåg det omotiverat att resa* 'they considered it unmotivated to go'. Cf. *de ansåg resan omotiverad* 'they considered the trip unmotivated'.

Predicative Complements

A predicative complement (noun phrase or adjective) to a verb agrees with a controller (subject or object), e.g. *vattnet är kallt* 'the water is cold', *vi drack saften kall* 'we drank the juice cold'. In many cases, it is preceded by a preposition like *som*, e.g. *som föräldrar har vi ett speciellt ansvar* 'as parents, we have a special responsibility'.

Obligatory nominal predicative complements occur with the verbs *vara*, *bli*, *heta*, *kalla(s)*, but adjectival and prepositional predicative complements occur with a wider range of verbs. Optional predicative complements in principle occur with any verb.

Nominal predicative complements often lack an article. This is true especially of complements expressing a conventional classification, e.g. nationality, religion, occupation, or function, e.g. *hon är amerikanska/ professor* 'she is an American/a professor', *Hr Johansson är katolik/ ordförande* 'Mr Johansson is catholic/the chairman'.

Adjectival predicative complements agree with the controller in number and gender, nominal predicative complements in number only. Sometimes there is no agreement, which means that the borderline between objects and adverbials is unclear, e.g. *mina kusiner satt barnvakt(er)* 'my cousins were baby-sitters', *vi använder dem som modell(er)* 'we used them as models.'

Quantifier floating: a predicative complement, rather than a noun phrase modifier, can specify the number of the subject or object, especially when the controller is a personal pronoun, e.g. *alla har vi varit små, vi har alla varit små* 'we have all been children'; *vi satt tre stycken vid bordet* 'we were (sitting) three at the table', *vi såg dem på teatern båda två* 'we saw them at the theatre, both of us/them'.

Adverbials

Adverbials are modifiers to verbs, adjectives or adverbs, expressing various circumstances:

Time

    identification (possibly together with duration): *klockan sex* 'at six o'clock', *år 1991* 'in 1991', *i fjol* 'last year', *under senaste krig* 'during the last war', *på natten* 'in the night', *efter middagen* 'after dinner', *före jul* 'before Christmas', *sedan sin födelse* 'since his/her birth', *mellan påsk och pingst* 'between Easter and Pentecost';

    duration: imperfective: *(sova) i en timme* '(sleep) for an hour': perfective: *(somna) på en timme* '(fall asleep) in an hour';

    iteration: *två gånger* 'twice';

    frequency: *varje dag* 'every day', *ofta* 'often';

    order in sequence: *för tredje gången* 'for the third time'.

Place:

    identification: *i staden* 'in the town', *på golvet* 'on the floor';

    source: *från väggen* 'from the wall', *ur säcken* 'out of the sack';

    goal: *till dörren* 'to the door', *in i rummet* 'into the room';

    path: *genom skogen* 'through the woods', *via stan* 'by the town'.

Cause: *vi gick av en annan orsak/på befallning* 'we left for another reason/on order'.

Agent: *huset köptes av en svensk* 'the house was bought by a Swede'.

Consequence: *bilarna kör så (att) huset skakar* 'the cars are running so that the house is shaking'.

Condition: *i så fall är du välkommen* 'in that case, you are welcome'.

Manner: *hon sprang fortare genom att gå på styltor* 'she ran faster by walking on stilts'.

Degree: *jag fryser en aning* 'I am a little cold':

Concomitance: *hon kom med sin syster* 'she came with her sister'.

Adverbials to verbs are normally postposed, but many of them can also be preposed (placed in mid-adverbial position), especially short-time adverbials. Sentence adverbials are placed as preposed verbal modifiers, but semantically modify the entire clause. They can be either modal or commenting, e.g. *säkert* 'certainly', *tråkigt nog* 'unfortunately'.

An adverbial specification of time or measure can often be expressed by a noun phrase, e.g. *jag besökte Rom våren 1990* 'I visited Rome in the spring of 1990', *Linda sprang (i) en halv timme* 'Linda ran for half an hour', *Kimmo kastade spjutet 90 meter* 'Kimmo threw the spear 90 metres'. Some specifications are more object-like, e.g. *gäddan vägde 2,5 kilo* 'the pike was 2.5 kilograms', *mötet varade två timmar* 'the meeting took two hours'.

Postposed adverbials to transitive verbs are normally placed after the object, but some short, stressed adverbials, closely related to the verb both semantically and prosodically, are placed before the object. Such adverbial particles are either short adverbs or prepositions, or prepositional phrases lexicalized as adverbs or containing an unstressed personal pronoun, e.g. *vi kastar bort alla lådor* 'we throw away all the boxes', *jag måste skriva om hela brevet* 'I have to rewrite the entire letter', *vi måste sätta igång tryckpressarna* 'we have to start the printing-machines', *han klädde på sig överrocken* 'he put on his overcoat'. In the last example, *sig* can also be analysed as indirect object. When the adverbial particle is further modified by a prepositional phrase, it is often placed after the object, e.g. *han lade **ner boken/boken ner** i väskan* 'he put the book in the bag'. But compare: *han kastade ner stenar från toppen* 'he threw stones down from the top'.

Focus particles can be placed before almost any constituent (even before a noun, if the noun functions as a noun phrase), e.g. *hon till och med skrattade åt oss* 'she even laughed at us', *jag kan äta bara gröt* 'I can eat only porridge'. Especially in colloquial style, they can also follow their sister constituent, e.g. *jag sov en liten stund bara* 'I slept just for a while'. Their semantic focus can be restricted to a part of their sister constituent, and they are often placed in typical mid-adverbial position, e.g. *jag kan bara äta gröt*. Compare *det där kan lyckas i åtminstone ett fall* 'that can be successful in at least one case', *det där kan lyckas åtminstone i ett fall, det där kan åtminstone lyckas i ett fall*.

Negation

The neutral negation adverbial is *inte*, with the rather formal variants *ej, icke*, and the emphatic *ingalunda*. Emphasis can also be added by the negative polarity adverb *alls*. The negation is typically placed in mid-adverbial position, but in emphatic sentences it can also be placed sentence-initially (more often so in Finland Swedish), e.g. *du vet att jag tyvärr inte (alls) kan komma* 'you know that I, unfortunately, cannot come (at all)', *jag vet inte någonting om det* 'I don't know anything about that', *inte vet jag någonting om det!*

The negations can also be used as constituent negations, especially in topic, subject or mid-adverbial position. Here, the negative determiner *ingen/inget/ inga* is often used instead of *inte någon/något/några*, e.g. **inte någon/ingen** hade varit där 'no one had been there', *där hade **inte någon/ingen** varit*, **inte i något fall/i inget fall** kan vi tillåta detta, vi kan **inte i något fall/i inget fall** *tillåta detta* 'we can allow this under no circumstances', *vi kan tillåta detta *inte i något fall/??i inget fall*. *Aldrig* 'never' and *ingenstans* 'nowhere' behave like constituent negations.

When an object contains a constituent negation, it must be placed as a mid-adverbial, before the verb, or as a topic, e.g. *vi hade inga bilar sett* 'we hadn't seen any cars', *inga bilar/?inte några bilar hade vi sett*. Constituent negation can marginally occur postverbally in free adverbials, at least in lexicalized emphatic expressions, e.g. *han hade rest bort av ingen orsak alls* 'he had gone away for no reason at all'.

Some elements of the clause, especially subjects, topics and free adverbials, can be outside the scope of the negation, e.g. *en kanin fanns inte i buren* 'there was a rabbit that was not in the cage', *en vecka sov jag inte* 'there was a week when I did not sleep' (but also: 'I did not sleep for a week'). Existential subjects are always inside the scope of the negation, and normally indirect and direct objects, too, e.g. *det fanns inte en kanin i buren* 'there was no rabbit in the cage', *han hade inte givit en student möjlighet att tentera* 'he had not given a single student a possibility to take the examination', *han gav inte studenten en/någon bok* 'he did not give the student any book'.

Double negation does not exist in the standard language, but the combination *inte aldrig* can occasionally be heard in dialectal speech.

There are a number of adverbial negative polarity items, which only occur is non-assertive contexts, e.g. *jag har knappt ens sett henne* 'I have hardly even seen her', cf. *jag har till och med sett henne*; *vi hade inte heller köpt biljett* 'we hadn't bought tickets, either', cf. *också* 'too'; *har du någonsin varit i Rom?* 'have you ever been in Rome?', cf. *ibland* 'sometimes', *en gång* 'once'.

In assertive contexts, *en* is the natural pronoun, while *någon* implies that the speaker does not care about the identity (cf. English *some*). In non-assertive contexts, *någon* is the neutral pronoun (cf. English *any*), while *en* is used to give emphasis to the number (or when the pronoun is outside the scope of the negation), e.g. *han köpte en/någon bok* 'he bought a/some book', *jag såg inte en (enda)/någon skylt* 'I didn't see a single/any sign'.

Sentence Types

There are at least seven sentence types in Swedish that can be distinguished from each other syntactically. The type markers include the preposing of the finite verb, constituent preposing or wh-preposing, and the use of a special mood. Some sentence types therefore have a special main-clause word order due to finite verb preposing, while others are more similar to subordinate clauses. As a rule, sentences with main-clause word order are more typically used in communicative interaction than sentences with subordinate-clause word order. The former require a response from the addressee, the latter often express a proposition that the speaker has not yet decided on.

1 In declarative sentences, almost any constituent can occupy initial position and function as topic [t] (called *fundament* by the influential Danish linguist Paul Diderichsen). The finite verb [v] is always placed in second position, e.g. *I dag har jag inte* [v] *kunnat sova middag hemma* [t], 'today I have not been able to take my dinner nap at home.' (The brackets indicate the places of the preposed elements in a corresponding subordinate clause, with different letters for different types of preposing.)

2 Interrogative sentences are of two types. In alternative questions (including yes/no questions), the finite verb is placed in initial position, e.g. *kommer du* [v] *med mig eller stannar du* [v] *hemma?* 'are you coming with me or are you staying at home?', *vill du* [v] *äta middag?* 'do you want to have dinner?'
In wh-questions, the constituent containing the question word [q] is preposed before the finite verb, e.g. *vem har* [q][v] *lagat middagen?* 'who has prepared dinner?', *vad vill du* [v] *äta* [q]? 'What do you want to eat?' This preposing also occurs in corresponding subordinate clauses.

3 Imperative sentences are introduced by the finite verb in the imperative mood, and have the same word order as yes/no questions. The subject includes a second-person pronoun, but is often missing. If it is present, the sentence can be interpreted as an advice or a threat, e.g. *kasta* (*du din lymmel*) [v] *in handduken bara!* 'just give in (lit. throw in the towel), you rascal!'

4 Optative sentences express a wish that is almost a magic formula or an enactment. The optative finite verb is preposed, and possibly preceded by an optional topic, e.g. *leve han! han leve!* 'may he live!' *gud give/give gud att ni kommer hem helskinnade!* 'God give that you come home unscathed!', *må ni alltid vara lika lyckliga!* 'may you always be as happy!', *vare nu nog talat om detta!* 'say no more!' The sentence type is archaic and mostly consists of lexicalized expressions, sometimes without an overt subject.

5 Desiderative sentences express a wish and have the structure of yes/no questions or of subordinate clauses introduced by (*tänk*) *om*. The finite verb is in the past tense or the subjunctive. Often an adverbial like *ändå* or *bara* is included, e.g. *hade jag ändå* [v] *fått sova lite till!* 'if I only had been able to sleep a little longer!', (*tänk*) *om jag ändå* (*hade*) *fått sova lite till!*; *Vore han bara* [v] *lite vänligare!* 'if he only would be a little kinder!', *om han bara vore lite vänligare!*

6 Suppositive sentences are similar to desiderative sentences, but express a hypothesis. The finite verb is normally in the indicative mood. When they are structured as main clauses, they cannot be distinguished from yes/no questions, e.g. *har jag kanske tappat den?* 'have I possibly lost it?', *tänk om jag har tappat den?*

7 In exclamative sentences (as well as in exclamative subordinate clauses), an exclamative phrase is the first constituent, and the rest of the sentence is constructed as a subordinate clause, which must be introduced by *som* if the exclamative phrase is the subject of the clause, e.g. *vilka/vad/så snygga stövlar du har* [e]*!* 'such beautiful boots you have!', *en sådan idiot som* [e] *redan har kastat bort lådan!* 'such an idiot to have thrown away the box already!' The exclamative can also be formed as a subordinate *att*-clause, e.g. *att du inte skäms!* 'Be ashamed!'

8 Echo-questions and statements have the form of subordinate clauses with the subjunctions *om* and *att*, respectively, e.g. *är du intresserad? – att/om jag är intresserad? det kan du lita på!/det kan jag inte påstå.* 'are you interested? – (lit.) that/whether I am interested? you can rely on that!/I cannot say so.'

9 Finite adverbs. In sentences containing the adverb *kanske* or *månne*, the adverb can be affected by finite verb preposing instead of the finite verb, e.g. *han kanske inte vill komma* 'maybe he does not want to come', cf. *han vill kanske inte komma, månne han vill komma?* 'does he want to come?', cf. *vill han månne komma?. Kanske* can also be placed initially with or without preposing of the finite verb, e.g. *kanske vill han inte komma; kanske han inte vill komma.*

10 Some sentence fragments lack a finite verb but nevertheless have a subject–predicate structure, e.g. *och han till att springa, och jag efter!* 'and he began to run, and I followed!', *vem där?* 'who's there?', *vad göra?* 'what should we do?', *vackra blommor i den här vasen!* 'beautiful flowers in this vase!'

There are also situationally elliptical sentences with a more unitary structure, e.g. *Intresserad?* 'interested?', *ruggigt väder* 'rough weather'; *vilka vackra blommor!* 'such beautiful flowers!'

Sentential topics in non-declaratives: questions, imperatives and desideratives are normally introduced by the verb, but this can be preceded by a subordinate clause (loose topic or, optionally, initial extraposition later referred to by *då*), e.g. *men om Lotta tänker komma, har hon (då) packat allting?* 'but if Lotta is planning to come, has she (then) packed everything?'; *när det börjar regna, var skall vi (då) söka skydd?* 'when it starts raining, where should we seek shelter?; *eftersom du ändå står där, kasta hit handduken!* 'since you are standing there anyway, toss me the handkerchief!'

Subordinate Clauses
Subordinate clauses can be classified according to their syntactic properties into nominal, adverbial and relative clauses. Subordinate clauses can also be structurally classified according to their initial constituent, which can be either

a subjunction or a clause constituent (sometimes both or neither of these elements). They can also be classified semantically.

Nominal *att*-clauses are neutral as to the factivity of their proposition, but are taken as factive if nothing else is implied by the context. They can be combined with a preposition, although the preposition is deleted more often than before noun phrases. Sometimes, it is possible to delete *att*, e.g. *jag tror (inte) (att) hon kommer.* 'I (don't) think she is coming', *vi är rädda (för) att han inte vet det* 'we are afraid that he doesn't know that'; cf. *vi är rädda för det* 'we are afraid of that'.

One type of interrogative nominal clauses are introduced by the subjunction *om* or *huruvida*. They are non-factive, but need not express a question, e.g. *vi hörde oss för om/(om) huruvida hon kunde komma* 'we asked (about) whether she could come.'

Wh-interrogative nominal clauses are introduced by a question word or a noun phrase or prepositional phrase containing a question word. They presuppose an open proposition associated with the clause, but are non-factive as far as the question word is concerned, e.g. *det beror på i hur många elevers väskor du måste leta* (lit.) 'that depends on in how many pupils' bags you have to look.' When the preposed *wh*-constituent is the subject of the subordinate clause, it should be followed by the subjunction *som*, e.g. *jag vet inte vilka gäster som har tackat ja* 'I don't know which guests have accepted.'

Free relative clauses are nominal, too, and can be introduced by *vad*, followed by *som* if the subject is relativized, e.g. *vad som förvånade mig var hans snabbhet* 'what surprised me was swiftness'.

Adverbial clauses are generally introduced by subjunctions or by word groups that can be analysed as complex subjunctions.

1　Temporal clauses start in *när*, *då* 'when', *medan* 'while', *förrän*, *innan* 'before', *tills* 'until', *sedan* 'since', *efter (det) att* 'after', e.g. *vi slutade inte förrän det började regna* 'we didn't stop until it started to rain.' *Då*- and *när*- clauses also function as relative clauses.

2　Locative clauses start in *där*, *dit*, *därifrån*. They normally function as relative clauses, and even when they function as adverbials they can be analysed as free relatives, e.g. *jag bor (i det hus) där du bor* 'I live (in the house) where you live'; *jag har en gång varit (till den stad) dit du reste* 'I have once been (in the town) where you travelled.' *Varifrån* replaces *därifrån* in non-free relative clauses. Compare: *hon kommer därifrån du har hämtat din fru* 'she comes from where you have taken your wife', *hon kommer från den plats varifrån du har hämtat din fru.*

3　Conditional clauses start in *om*, *ifall*, *i den händelse att*, e.g. *jag kan gå, om du vill* 'I can go, if you want me to.'

4　Concessives and concessive conditionals are introduced by *fastän*, *även om*, e.g. *fastän jag är sjuk, tänker jag gå* 'although I am sick, I will go';

även om jag vore sjuk, skulle jag gå 'even if I were sick, I would go.'

A special type is introduced by a *wh*-constituent. It can also have a nominal function, e.g. *vem som än kommer tänker jag strunta i (honom)* 'whoever comes, I am going to ignore (him).'

5 Causal clauses start in *eftersom, emedan, därför att, för att*, e.g. *jag kom eftersom du bad mig* 'I came, because you asked me to.'

6 Consecutive clauses start in *så (att)*, etc., e.g. *hon stannade, så att vi kunde hinna fatt* 'she stopped so that we could reach her'.

7 Purposive clauses start in *för att, så (att)*, e.g. *hon stannade så att vi skulle hinna fatt* 'she stopped in order for us to reach her'.

8 Comparative clauses start in *som* or *än*, e.g. *Kim går fortare än jag springer* 'Kim walks faster than I run'; *jag är en lika stor idiot som du (är)* 'I am as big an idiot as you are'. When the clause is reduced to a comparative phrase, the old subject can take the accusative in colloquial style, e.g. *jag är tröttare än du/dig* 'I am more tired than you'.

Relative clauses are normally introduced by the subjunction *som* or, particularly in formal style, by a constituent containing a relative word, *vilken, vilket, vilka, vars, där, dit, varifrån, varmed*, etc. These expressions correspond to a gap later in the relative clause. Any extractable constituent of the clause can be relativized, including prepositional phrases and complements in comparative constructions, e.g. *här är en bil där/i vilken baksätena är borttagna* 'here is a car where the back seats are removed'; *han var en kung som ingen var maktlösare än* 'he was such a king that nobody had less power than he'.

A preposition can be preposed with the relative pronoun or left behind (cf. constituent preposing), e.g. *här är en bil som baksätena är borttagna i*. A nominal head of the genitive *vilkens, vars* is preposed with the pronoun, but a nominal head of non-genitival *vilken* is preposed only in archaic style, e.g. *den kvinna i vilkens/vars sällskap jag satt, . . .* 'the woman, in whose company I was sitting, . . .'; *jag sände dem i ordningen a, d, b, i vilken ordning de också anlände till mötesplatsen* 'I sent them in the order a, d, b, in which order they also arrived at the meeting-place'.

The subjunction *som* can normally be deleted in restrictive relative clauses, if the subject position of the relative clause is filled, e.g. *jag tar den (som) du har i vänster hand* 'I take the one that you have in your left hand'. *Som*-clauses can have a special causal interpretation, e.g. *jag var dum som gick* 'I was foolish to go'.

Relative clauses are normally attributive, but may also modify a verb phrase or an entire clause, like an adverbial. Here, the pronoun *vilket* is always used, e.g. *Lisa skrev en sonett, vilket jag inte lyckades göra* 'Lisa wrote a sonnet, which I didn't manage to do'. Correspondingly, attributive clauses are typically relative, but they can also be either nominal or adverbial, e.g. *frågan om vi måste sluta* 'the question about our having to stop', *jublet efter att han gått i mål* 'the shouts of joy after he had reached the goal'.

Main Clause and Subordinate Clause Word Order

The word order in main clauses is more varied than in subordinate clauses. Most of the variation can be described by postulating two extra positions in main clauses, the topic and the position of the finite verb, which can also be seen as identical to the position of the subjunction (complementizer) in subordinate clauses. The topic position is filled in declarative sentences and *wh*-questions, but can also be filled in some other sentence types.

Both main and subordinate word order can be summarized in a single table (Table 9.6). As seen from the table, all positions can be filled in clauses containing *kanske*. But normally, main clauses have an empty finite verb position (if that position is kept separate from the non-finite verb position), and many subordinate clauses have an empty topic position.

Main clause word order can occur in some subordinate clauses as follows:

1   Initial conditional clauses can optionally be constructed as yes/no questions with verb preposing, e.g. *Vill du simma/Om du vill simma, (så) måste du ha baddräkt* 'if you want to swim, you must wear a bathing-suit'.

2   Comparative conditional clauses can also be constructed as yes/no questions with verb preposing, e.g. *han skrek som vore han galen/(om) han vore galen* 'he screamed as if he were crazy'.

3   *Att*-clauses can be constructed as declaratives, especially when the speaker agrees with the statement of the clause and when there is a need to prepose a constituent within the *att*-clause, e.g. *jag tror att i det fallet har du rätt* 'I think you are right in that respect', **jag tror inte att i det fallet har du rätt* 'I don't think ...'

4   Concessive, causal and consecutive clauses sometimes optionally take main-clause word order (possibly with a small shift in the semantic relation), at least in colloquial style. However, they can then be classified as conjoined clauses, rather than subordinate ones, e.g. *hon kom nog*

Table 9.6 Word order in main and subordinate clauses

Topic	Comp.	Subject	Mid-adv.	Finite	Non-Finite	Object/Pred	Final adv.
i går	ville	Lotta	inte	—	läsa	tidningen	
Lotta	ville	—	inte	—	vara	ensam	i går
Lotta	kanske	—	redan	har	träffat	dig	i dag
—	att	Lotta	inte	ville	koka	kaffe	i dag
vem	som	—	redan	har	druckit	kaffe	

*med, fast hon **inte** var/var **inte** så intresserad* 'she did come, although she wasn't very interested'; *Lisa får inte komma, därför att hon **inte** har/har **inte** beställt biljett* 'Lisa must not come, since she hasn't ordered a ticket'; *vi stängde dörren, så (att) katten **inte** kunde/kunde **inte** rymma* 'we closed the door, so the cat could not escape'.

5   Nominal subordinate clauses can be constructed as main clauses in initial position, especially if they function as objects, e.g. *det blir kallt i morgon, har väderleksrapporten sagt* 'it will be cold tomorrow, according to the weather forecast'; *det är faktiskt några kvar, ser det ut som* (lit.) 'there are indeed some left, it looks like'.

Non-initial indirect questions sometimes take main clause word order in colloquial speech (although they could also be taken as quoted direct questions, where deictic elements such as tense and pronouns have been changed to conform to the new speech situation), e.g. *?Han undrade, vem kunde möjligen hjälpa honom?* 'he wondered, who could possibly help him?', *han undrade vem som möjligen kunde hjälpa honom.*

Constituent Preposing

Almost any constituent can be placed initially as a topic in declarative main clauses, e.g. *jag* (su.) *har inte ätit morötter i dag* 'I haven't been eating carrots today', *i dag* (adverbial) *har jag inte ätit morötter, morötter* (obj.) *har jag inte ätit i dag*; *någon post* (existential su.) *hade det inte kommit* 'no mail had arrived'; *henne* (indir. obj.) *har jag inte gett lov att komma* 'I haven't permitted her to come', *glad* (pred. compl.) *blev hon* 'she became glad'. Auxiliaries, adverbial particles and some sentence adverbials are not preposed.

The noun phrase of a prepositional phrase can often leave its preposition behind. This is common for prepositional objects, but less natural for free adverbials, e.g. *dig har jag väntat på i biblioteket i en timme* 'I have been waiting for you in the library for an hour', *??biblioteket har jag väntat på dig i, *en timme har jag väntat på dig i*; cf. *i en timme har jag väntat.*

When a verb phrase is preposed, the dummy verb *göra* normally occupies the verb position, e.g. *åka skidor i Alperna brukar jag (göra) varje år* (lit.) 'go skiing in the Alps I use to do every year'. If the preposed verb phrase is finite, *göra* is obligatory with a redundant tense ending, and undergoes verb preposing, e.g. *åker skidor i Alperna gör jag varje år* (lit.) 'go skiing in the Alps I do every year'.

Noun phrases and subordinate clauses function as islands, which do not allow extraction of their parts. Compare, *jag såg en kalv med två huvuden i går* 'I saw a calf with two heads yesterday', *med två huvuden såg jag en kalv i går*, *??en kalv såg jag med två huvuden i går*. The extraction of heads is more acceptable than the extraction of noun phrase complements, since the complement can often be analysed as extraposed or parenthetic, e.g. *en kalv såg jag i går, (en) med två huvuden.*

Some noun phrases, including those with picture nouns, are weak islands and allow extraction of a complement or head, e.g. *Mona-Lisa ville jag måla ett porträtt av. Ett porträtt ville jag måla av Mona-Lisa. Ett porträtt av Mona-Lisa ville jag måla* 'I wanted to paint a portrait of Mona-Lisa'. Sometimes it is unclear whether there is a noun phrase complement or whether it has been reanalysed as a verb complement. In that case, the two parts of the noun phrase can both be placed non-initially in the sentence, e.g. *från att-satser är utflyttningen accepterad* 'the extraction from that-clauses is accepted'; cf. *Antagligen är utflyttningen helt accepterad från att-satser* 'probably the extraction is totally accepted from that-clauses'; *importen ökade betydligt från Tyskland* 'the imports from Germany increased considerably'.

Extraction from clausal islands is very common in colloquial style. The acceptability of the extraction is dependent on the type of the subordinate clause and the verb of the main clause. There is also regional variation, extraction being more acceptable in the western area.

Extraction from *att*-clauses functioning as objects to cognitive verbs is quite natural, e.g. *den här kakan vet/tror jag att du gillar*[t] 'this cake I know/ believe that you like'. Extraction is also acceptable from *att*-clauses functioning as objects to other verbs and from interrogative clauses, e.g. *den chokladen är jag verkligen förvånad över att du äter*[t] (lit.) 'that chocolate I am really surprised that you eat'; *några verkliga chanser undrar jag faktiskt om du har*[t] 'I really wonder whether you have any substantial chances'; *den här boken vet jag inte vem som har skrivit*[t] 'I don't know who has written this book'.

Extraction from adverbial clauses is marginal, but not infrequent, e.g. *?vissa exempel skrattade jag eftersom jag hade sett*[t] (lit.) 'some examples, I laughed since I had seen'; *?den här metoden sände de mig utomlands för att jag skulle lära mig*[t] 'they sent me abroad in order to learn this method'.

Extraction from relative clauses is marginal, but more acceptable when the preposed constituent could function semantically as a constituent in the matrix clause, although there is no syntactic position for it there, e.g. *??det här har jag träffat en lingvist som har förklarat*[t] *för mig* 'I have met a linguist who has explained this to me'; *?de här blommorna såg jag en man som vattnade*[t] 'I saw a man watering these flowers'. Compare also the grammatical extraction from an object-with-infinitive construction, e.g. *de här blommorna såg jag en man vattna*.

Since infinitival phrases are not islands, extraction is normally possible, e.g. *det här instrumentet är jag mycket stolt över att kunna spela på*[t] 'this instrument I am very proud of being able to play'. However, free infinitival adverbials behave like clausal adverbials, e.g. *?den här boken klarade jag tentamen genom att läsa*[t] 'I passed the course by reading this book'; *?den här väskan gick jag in i rummet utan att hitta*[t] 'I went into the room without finding this bag'.

Free adverbials allow for extraction, if the preposed constituent corresponds to a gap in the matrix clause as well as a gap in the infinitive. The latter 'parasitic' gap can also be filled with an anaphoric pronoun, e.g. *den här boken måste du läsa*[t] *grundligt för att hitta i* [t]/*den* 'as to this book, you have to read it thoroughly to be able to find things in it'; *den här väskan gick jag förbi*[t] *utan att plocka upp* [t]/*den* 'as to this bag, I passed by it without picking it up'.

Extraction is normally not permitted from conjoined structures unless an element is extracted simultaneously from all conjuncts. This can be regarded as a special instance of parasitic gaps, e.g. *korven skar Britta upp*[t] *och satte*[t] *i kylskåpet* 'the sausage, Britta sliced and put in the refrigerator'; compare ?*korven skar Britta upp*[t] *och gjorde en smörgås* (lit.) 'the sausage, Britta sliced and made a sandwich', **en smörgås skar Britta upp korven och gjorde* [t]. However, finite-verb preposing in main clauses easily affects only the first verb of a coordinated verb phrase, e.g. *därför tog jag* [v] *korven och satte en stekpanna på spisen* 'therefore, I took the sausage and put a frying-pan on the stove'.

Even the extraction of a subject from a subordinate clause is allowed in the standard language, if the subjunction is deleted. This is often possible for *att*, but not for *om*, e.g. *den här tror jag blir bra* 'this I think will do', **den här undrar jag om blir bra* (lit.) 'this I wonder whether will do'. In Finland Swedish, *att* need not be deleted, e.g. *den här tror jag att blir bra*.

The extraction of subjects is possible even after a subjunction in colloquial style, if an anaphoric pronoun fills the gap, e.g. *den här undrar jag faktiskt om den passar* 'as to this, I really wonder whether it will fit'. Such a resumptive pronoun can also be used marginally in other cases where the extraction is somewhat unnatural, e.g. ?*den här grammatikboken blev jag verkligen glad när jag såg en elev som läste* (*den*) (lit.) 'this grammar book, I was really glad when I saw a pupil reading it'.

Tense, Mood and Aktionsart (Mode of Action)

Tense inflection expresses the relation between the moment of speech and reference time, i.e. a time when the action either takes place or has some consequences. The speaker or the subject referent may also consider the truth value of the proposition at reference time, or wish to have it true. Inflected tenses are the present tense, e.g. *kastar* 'throws', and the past, e.g. *kastade* 'threw'. In addition, the auxiliaries *ha* and *skola* or *komma* are used to express the temporal relation between reference time and the time of action, if they are different. Thereby, eight tenses are formed in the following way.

Swedish Tenses

Present	kastar spjutet	'throws the spear'
Past	kastade spjutet	
Perfect	har kastat spjutet	
Pluperfect	hade kastat spjutet	

Future	skall (komma att) kasta spjutet, kommer att kasta spjutet
Past future	skulle (komma att) kasta spjutet
Future perfect	skall (komma att) ha kastat spjutet, kommer att ha kastat spjutet
Past future perfect	skulle (komma att) ha kastat spjutet

The present tense is used when the time of the relation includes the moment of speech, e.g. *i dag lyser solen* 'today the sun is shining', or when the action is timeless (general present).

When an act of communication is reported, the present tense can express that the message is perceived at the moment of speech, or the past or perfect can express that the sending has occurred in the past, e.g. *Newton **förklarar för oss**/förklarade/har förklarat planeternas rörelser* 'Newton explains to us/explained/has explained the movements of the planets'.

For a future action, it is not necessary to use a future auxiliary, especially if the action is momentary or if there is a time adverbial referring to future time, e.g. *akta dig, krukan går sönder!* 'beware, the jug will break!' *i morgon regnar det säkert* 'tomorrow, it will certainly rain'. Such a future present is regularly used in temporal and conditional clauses identifying a future time, e.g. *när jag **reser**/*kommer att resa hem i morgon*, ... 'when I go home tomorrow, ...'.

The past tense is used when the action takes place before the moment of speech, e.g. *jag var där i går* 'I was there yesterday.' The past is also used of an imagined event, e.g. *om jag nu var i dina kläder*... 'if I were in your shoes (lit. clothes) now, ...' This modal meaning is often clarified by the auxiliaries *skola* or *ha*, which signify potential and unreal action, respectively, e.g. *om han skulle vara hemma nu, vilket han ju kan vara*, ... 'if he were at home now, which he may be, ...'. *om jag hade varit hemma nu, vilket jag ju inte är*, ...' if I had been at home now, which I am not, ...'.

Skola is often used to express a potential but somewhat unexpected action. However, it is seldom used when the main clause also contains *skola*. Present tense can be used instead, e.g. *om han är hemma nu*, ... Strong verbs have a subjunctive form, which can be used instead of the past tense in the modal function.

The past can also be used in emotive exclamations and some almost lexicalized modest questions, proposals etc., e.g. *det var en väldigt god kaka*: 'this is a very tasty cake'; *hur var namnet?* 'what is your name?'

The past is used when an action is described as taking place at a certain time in the past, and the perfect is used when an action is described as taking place before the moment of speech. One reason for using perfect tense is that the past action has consequences for, or is relevant in some way to the situation at the time of speech, e.g. *jag har tagit sjuksköterskeexamen, så jag är behörig för tjänsten* 'I have taken a nursing examination, so I am qualified for the job'; *låset har varit sönder, men har blivit lagat* 'the lock has been out of order, but has been repaired'.

If the time of the action is specified exactly, this moment is so prominent that the past has to be used, e.g. *låset blev lagat i går* 'the lock was repaired yesterday'; cf. *låset har blivit lagat en gång* 'the lock has been repaired once'. However, if there is a temporal frame for the action, a potential time span including the moment of speech, the perfect tense can be used with an exact time specification, e.g. *i dag har jag ätit middag kl. 17* 'today I have had dinner at 5 p.m.' If the past is used here, it signals that the action cannot take place any more, cf. *jag har ätit några päron* 'I have eaten some pears (and I could eat some more)'; *jag åt några päron* 'I ate some pears (but now the party is over)'.

Aktionsart (Mode of Action)

The two main aktionsarts in Swedish are imperfective (unbounded) and perfective (bounded). These categories can be attributed to verbs, verb phrases or entire sentences.

Imperfective expressions refer to actions without a natural end point and perfective expressions refer to actions with a natural end point. Some verbs are inherently imperfective, e.g. *sitta* 'sit', *sova* 'sleep', while other verbs are inherently perfective, e.g. *försvinna* 'disappear', *sluta* 'end'. Many verbs, however, can be taken as referring to either unbounded processes or to bounded events, e.g. *andas* 'breathe', *äta* 'eat'. Imperfective expressions take duration adverbials formed by the preposition *i*, while perfective expressions take adverbials formed by the preposition *på*, cf. *springa i en timme* 'run for an hour', *nå målet på en timme* 'reach the goal in an hour'.

Past participles always refer to a state. For imperfective verbs, such participles have a present-tense meaning, referring to the same state as the verb, but past participles of perfective verbs refer to the state which the event of the verb leads up to, and therefore have a perfect meaning, e.g. **en älskad** monark – *en monark som älskas* 'a king who is loved', *en* **upphittad** *ring* – *en ring som har upphittats* 'a ring which has been found', *en* **försvunnen** *hund* – *en hund som har försvunnit* 'a dog that has disappeared'.

Voice and Subject Choice

The *s*-form of a verb can have five different functions: true passive, medium, reflexive, reciprocal and absolute function. Sometimes a reflexive construction is more common, i.e. the object *sig* is used instead of the ending -*s*. In many cases, either construction can be used.

The true passive is related to the active voice in such a way that the subject participant of the active verb is left without expression or is expressed by an adverbial with the preposition *av*, although the participant is felt to be present in the semantic interpretation (subject degradation). In addition, the indirect or direct object of the active verb is often constructed as the passive subject (object promotion), although the subject may also be the expletive *det*, e.g. *Diktatorn* **hatades/var hatad** (*av folket*) 'the dictator was hated (by the people)'; cf. *folket hatade diktatorn*; *hon tilldelades Nobelpriset (av Akademien)* 'she was awarded the Nobel prize (by the Academy)' *Nobelpriset tilldelades henne (av Akademien)*, cf. *Akademien tilldelade henne Nobelpriset*; *det dansades hela natten* 'it was danced all night'.

The medium function is lexicalized for certain verbs and less productive than the passive. The normal subject participant of the active verb is omitted totally from the semantic interpretation, and the action is viewed as happening by itself. The direct object of the active verb functions as subject of the medium verb, e.g. *himlen förändrades inför våra ögon* 'the sky changed before our eyes'. Many deponential verbs, which can occur in the *s*-form only, could be regarded as having medium voice, e.g. *Peter kallsvettades* 'Peter was in a cold sweat'. For some verbs, the form without *-s* can have a medium interpretation, e.g. *bollen rullade över golvet* 'the ball rolled over the floor', cf. *Kalle rullade bollen över golvet*.

It is hard to draw a sharp line between passive and medium function, since an Instrument can normally be constructed as subject instead of the Agent, e.g. *ett åskmoln förmörkade himlen* 'a thundercloud darkened the sky'. When such a sentence is passivized, e.g. *Himlen* **förmörkades/blev förmörkad** (*av ett åskmoln*) 'the sky (was) darkened (by a thundercloud)', classifying the verb as having medium function seems appropriate at least when the adverbial is missing.

Periphrastic passives can be used with medium interpretation especially when the past participle has been lexicalized as an adjective. A reflexive construction (an active verb with a reflexive object) is often used with medium interpretation, e.g. *stenen rörde sig inte* 'the stone didn't move'.

The reflexive interpretation of the *s*-form is restricted to a few lexicalized verbs. Normally the reflexive construction is used to express that the subject referent has two semantic roles, such as Agent and Patient. The *s*-form weakens the agent interpretation, e.g. *folket* **förvånade sig/förvånades/var förvånat** *över sin nyvunna självständighet* 'the people was astonished at its new independence'.

The reciprocal function is restricted to some lexicalized *s*-forms with a plural subject, e.g. *vi träffas snart igen* 'we'll soon meet again', cf. *Kalle träffade snart Lisa igen* 'Kalle soon met Lisa again'. Some reciprocal deponential verbs take the *s*-form non-reciprocally, too, e.g. *pojkarna slåss* 'the boys are fighting'; *Kalle slåss med Olle* 'Kalle is fighting with Olle'. There are also reciprocal constructions without the *s*-form, e.g. *pojkarna liknar varandra* 'the boys are similar'; *lastbilen och godståget kolliderade (med varandra)* 'the truck and the freight train collided', cf. *lastbilen kolliderade med godståget*.

A passive form with absolute function takes the same subject as the corresponding active verb, but the object is omitted, e.g. *nässlor bränns* (lit.)

'nettles burn (anybody)'. The omission of the object is often connected to a durative or generic meaning: since the total action consists of a tendency to specific singular actions, the identity of object referents can vary or be less important. The plain active verb can often be used instead, especially when the subject is not a person, e.g. *nässlor bränner*.

Agreement

Agreement mostly affects noun phrases, predicative complements, and anaphoric pronouns. It can be governed by grammatical, lexical classifications, or by semantic properties of referents.

Within the noun phrase, determiners and attributive adjectives agree with the noun in number, definiteness and gender, but gender agreement is neutralized in the plural. For adjectives, the definiteness agreement also is neutralized in the plural, and the gender agreement in definite noun phrases. Instead, there is an optional semantic gender agreement: the ending *-e* can be used for singular masculine referents.

A predicative complement agrees with its controller in number and gender, again, gender agreement being neutralized in the plural. However, there is a strong tendency towards a semantic gender agreement, when the controller is a person. Nominal predicatives agree in number only.

Predicative complements controlled by infinitives or clauses are inflected for neutral gender. Neutrum can be seen as the unmarked form, which should be used when no other form is motivated by agreement, as when an adjective is used as an adverbial complement, e.g. *hon sjunger vackert* 'she sings beautifully'.

Neutrum is also used when the controller is not treated as an individual or a group of individuals, but rather as a general phenomenon, similar to a mass noun, cf. *en ny statminister vore inte så dum* 'a new prime minister would not be that stupid', *en ny statminister vore inte så dumt* 'it wouldn't be too bad to get a new prime minister'. This is especially frequent when the controller is a bare noun phrase, e.g. *biologi är valfritt* 'biology is optional', cf. *biologin är valfri*; *ärter är gott* 'peas are delicious', *ärterna är goda* 'the peas are delicious'. For plural controllers, the neutral form is often optional, e.g. *långskaftade stövlar är modernt/moderna* 'high boots are fashionable'.

A predicative complement preceding its controller is often in the neutral form. On the other hand, it is often unclear which element is the predicative and which the controller, e.g. *karaktäristiskt/karaktäristiska för skotskan är de rullande r-en* 'characteristic of Scottish are the rolling r's'; *jag fick avklarat läxorna* 'I got my homework done', *jag fick läxorna avklarade*.

Anaphoric pronouns agree with their antecedent in number and gender. Here, too, the semantic properties of the referent are often more important than the lexical properties, cf. *dumt folk* (sg), 'stupid people' – *folk är så dumma, de tror* ... 'people are so stupid, they believe ...'. Individuals in the third-person singular are normally referred to by the personal pronouns *han*, *hon*, regardless of the gender of the antecedent, e.g. *statsrådet är medveten/ *medvetet om saken*; *han/hon/*det kommer att ta upp saken i regeringen* 'the cabinet minister is conscious of the matter; he/she will take it up in the cabinet'. But compare *vittnet är ?jävig/jävigt, han/hon/det kan således inte få vittna*. 'The witness is challengeable, therefore, he/she cannot testify'; *barnet är *sjuk/sjukt, ?han/?hon/det har hög feber* 'the child is ill, it has high fever'.

The Use of Reflexive Pronouns

Special reflexive pronouns are used in the third-person. They are normally co-referent with the subject of their own clause. Non-reflexive pronouns are used of referents mentioned in non-subject position or in earlier sentences, e.g. *professorn$_i$ kände docenten$_j$ från sina$_i$/hennes$_j$ föreläsningar* 'the professor knew the lecturer from his/her lectures'.

A reflexive pronoun can also be co-referent to the 'subject' of a clause equivalent. A syntactic unit can be more or less equivalent to a clause. Appositions consisting of at least two parts are always clause equivalents, e.g. *läraren reste utomlands med Lotta, då hans/*sitt enda barn* 'the teacher travelled abroad with Lotta, at that time his only child', cf. *Läraren$_i$ reste utomlands med Lotta$_j$, primus i hans$_i$/sin$_j$ klass* 'the teacher travelled abroad with Lotta, the top pupil of his/her class'.

The object-with-infinitive construction can be regarded either as a separate clause equivalent or as a part of its main clause, e.g. *Gunnar lät Hallgerd tvinna en bågsträng av sitt hår* 'Gunnar had Hallgerd twine a bowstring of her/his hair'. In the first case, *sitt* refers back to the 'subject' of the clause equivalent, Hallgerd, in the second case, to the subject of the entire sentence, Gunnar. *Hans* can also be used here to refer to Gunnar's hair, but *hennes* cannot be used to refer to Hallgerd's hair.

In nominalizations, a reflexive pronoun can refer to the referent of a genitival modifier corresponding to a subject, e.g. *Siri upphörde aldrig att förvånas över Strindbergs tro på sig själv* 'Siri never ceased to be astonished by Strindberg's faith in himself'. A similar interpretation can occur when the noun refers to a product and the genitive to the producer, e.g. *Siri gillade inte Strindbergs bok om sin barndom* 'Siri didn't like Strindberg's book on his/her childhood'.

Predicative adverbials, semantically specifying the object, can contain a reflexive pronoun referring to this object, e.g. *Lisa satte boken på sin plats i hyllan* 'Lisa put the book on its/her place on the shelf'.

The reciprocal pronouns *varandra, varandras* obey the same rules as the reflexive pronouns. However, their use may be somewhat broader, probably because there is no alternative to *varandra* in the way that *hans, hennes, deras* are alternatives to *sin*. *Varandra* in an object can marginally be co-referent even with the indirect object, e.g. *han råkade ge flickorna varandras böcker* 'he happened to give the girls each other's books', cf. *vi måste ge hembiträdet* *hennes/*sin lön* 'we must give the servant her wages'.

Ellipsis

Only a few elliptical constructions can be treated here. In a coordinated structure, identical elements can be deleted. When the first occurrence is sentence-final, it is deleted, otherwise the second occurrence is deleted, e.g. *Kalle älskar, men Lisa hatar gröt* 'Kalle loves, but Lisa hates porridge'; *flygplanet anländer till Åbo kl. 18.30, och bilfärjan kl. 20.15* 'the aeroplane arrives at Turku at 6.30p.m., and the ferry at 8.15p.m.'.

In noun phrases, the deletion rule is freer. Either the first or, preferably, the second element can be deleted, and the identity need not cover number. A singular element is deleted rather than a plural, e.g. *några engelska böcker och en svensk* 'some English books and a Swedish one', *en svensk bok och några engelska, en svensk och några engelska böcker*, ?*några engelska och en svensk bok.*

In interrogative main or subordinate clauses, everything except the question word can be deleted, e.g. *vi kunde anställa någon, men vem (skall vi anställa)?* 'we could hire somebody, but whom?'; *någons far har varit här, men jag vet inte vems* 'somebody's father has been here, but I don't know whose'.

In yes/no questions, a construction with the pronoun (*göra*) *det* is normally preferred, e.g. *jag är nöjd med mitt resultat, är du (det)?* 'I am satisfied with my result, are you?'; *jag har slutat röka, men jag tror inte att Olle har ((gjort) det).* 'I have stopped smoking, but I don't think that Olle has'.

In formal style, a concessive subordinate clause with a copula and a subject identical to the subject of the main clause can be reduced to a predicative complement preceded by a subjunction, e.g. *fastän (han var) sjuk, gick han på festen* 'although he was ill, he went to the party'. Ellipsis of the finite verb does not occur in other subordinate clauses, e.g. **vägen är hal när våt* 'the road is slippery when wet'; **de visste inte vad göra* 'they did not know what to do'; cf. *vad göra?* 'what should we do?'

9.5.   Lexis

The Swedish vocabulary can be divided on phonotactic grounds into a native and a foreign vocabulary (see Phonology, section 9.2). These systems are normally also kept apart in word derivation, although many foreign affixes can be combined with native stems, and vice versa, e.g. *läck-age* 'leakage', *run-olog* 'runologist', *kommend-er-ing* 'appointment'.

The great majority of words are loanwords. Since the early Middle Ages, there has been an almost constant borrowing of originally Latin or Greek words, e.g. *präst* 'clergyman', *tema* 'theme', *psyke* 'psyche'. There is still a Latin productivity in word formation. The influence of Low German was extremely powerful towards the end of the Middle Ages due to the trade of the Hansa, but the resulting loans have been totally assimilated to the native vocabulary, e.g. *jägare* 'hunter', *fara* 'danger'. After the Reformation, the Low German influence turned into a High German influence. In the eighteenth century, many French words were borrowed, e.g. *etapp* 'stage', *hotell* 'hotel'. There are also Italian loans, e.g. *sopran* 'soprano', and a few Finnish loans, e.g. *pojke* 'boy', *känga* 'boot'. Today, the English influence is noticeable, e.g. *poster, make-up, briefing*. Occasionally there has been a purist tendency to revive old Scandinavian words or to replace the borrowings with native compounds and derivations, but today the main tendency is to use translation loans if possible, e.g. *mjukvara* 'software', and make the orthography and inflection more Swedish when loan words are becoming more frequent, e.g. *schampo* 'shampoo', *tejp* 'tape'. New technical and administrative terms are often introduced on a common Scandinavian basis.

Further Reading

Andersson, E. (1993) *Grammatik från grunden. En koncentrerad svensk satslära*, Ord och stil 24, Uppsala: Hallgren and Fallgren.

Elert, C.-C. (1981) *Ljud och ord i svenskan*, Umeå and Stockholm: Almquist and Wiksell.

Engdahl, E. and Ejerhed, E. (eds) (1982) *Readings on Unbounded Dependencies in Scandinavian Languages*, Umeå: Almquist and Wiksell.

Garlén, C. (1988) *Svenskans fonologi*, Lund: Studentlitteratur.

Haugen, E. (ed.) (1974) *A bibliography of Scandinavian Languages and Linguistics 1900–1970*, Oslo: Universitetsforlaget.

Hellquist, E. (1929–32) *Det svenska ordförrådets ålder och ursprung I–III*, Lund: Gleerups.

Holm, L. and Westroth, H. (1987) *Svensk grammatisk bibliografi*, Stockholm: Svenska Akademiens grammatik.

Loman, B. (1967) 'Synpunkter på svenskans fonotaktiska struktur', *Arkiv för Nordisk Filologi* 82: 1–100.

McClean, R. J. (1947) *Swedish. A Grammar of the Modern Language*, London.

Sigurd, B. (1965) *Phonotactic Structures in Swedish*, Lund: Uniskol.

—— (1970) *Språkstruktur*, Stockholm: Wahlström and Widstrand.

Thorell, O. (1973) *Svensk grammatik*, Stockholm: Esselte.

—— (1981) *Svensk ordbildningslära*, Stockholm: Esselte.

10 Danish

Hartmut Haberland

10.1 Introduction

Danish is spoken by about 5 million speakers. It has developed as a standardized written language with a long tradition. The first law texts in Danish are from around 1200, and in the late fourteenth century, Queen Margaret I decided to change the language of administration from Latin to Danish. As a language of literature it has been used since the fifteenth century. Today speakers of Danish are mostly to be found within the present area of the Kingdom of Denmark, but there is a Danish minority in the Flensburg area in Germany (adjacent to the present Danish–German border), most of whose members are bilingual, very often with German as the dominant language. Until the mid-seventeenth century Danish was used in the Danish provinces of Skåne, Halland and Blekinge which became Swedish in 1658. After that, Swedish became the written language of these provinces, while spoken Danish lingered on for much longer and traces of it can still be found in the dialects of Skåne. During the union with Norway (1389–1814), Danish became increasingly important as a written language in Norway. Danish is still spoken to some extent in the former Danish North Atlantic colonies (Greenland, Faroe Islands), and (to a much lesser degree) it is still retained by Danish emigrants to the United States and Argentine.

Although the area in which Danish is spoken is rather small, the classical dialect picture (corresponding to the situation around the year 1900) shows distinct dialect differences. Perhaps the most striking phonological isogloss runs in an East–West direction. In the area north of this isogloss, speakers contrast 'normal' vowels and voiced consonants with those produced with a specific articulation known as *stød* (literally 'thrust' or 'push'; on *stød* see below). South of this isogloss, the *stød* articulation is not known (see Figure 10.1). A number of morphological-syntactic isoglosses run in a North–South direction. Thus there is a three-gender system for nouns in the East, namely, on the islands (masculine, feminine, neuter), a two-gender system in the Middle, namely the eastern part of the Jutish mainland (common vs neuter gender), and a system without gender contrast in the West (Western and Southern Jutland) (see Figure 10.2). Although the distinctions between the classical Danish dialects are of considerable linguistic and historical interest,

Figure 10.1   The *stød* isogloss

Source: Adapted from Ringgaard 1973.
Note: *Stød* does not occur in the shaded area.

it should be noted that the number of classical dialect speakers today is much smaller than in 1900. It has been estimated that there are at most 500,000 dialect speakers today. Dialects have been retained to a different degree in different areas, and very little is known about the extent of dialect/standard bilingualism especially among the younger generations. Although Danish dialects in principle are mutually intelligible, Copenhageners especially can have difficulties in coping with Western and Southern Jutish dialects.

Figure 10.2   Gender isoglosses in Danish

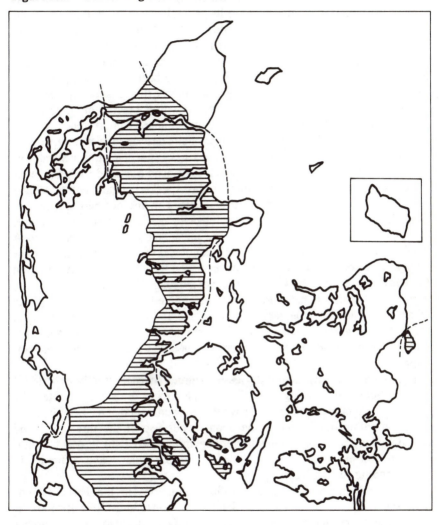

Source: Adapted from Ringgaard 1973.
Note: Dialects in the shaded area have the same gender system as Standard Danish (common gender vs neuter). Dialects to the East have a three-gender system (masculine, feminine, neuter), dialects to the West have no gender difference, but classify nouns as countables vs non-countables.

The written language is fairly standardized. Until recently, some people still used the 'old' spelling from before the last spelling reform in 1948, when the letter ‹å› was introduced as replacement for ‹aa›, and the use of initial capital letters for nouns was abandoned.

There is also a spoken standard, called *rigsdansk*, which has noticeable regional variation. Its name refers to its general acceptability throughout the whole of Denmark. (Danish *rige* means 'kingdom'.) The real extent of standardization in Denmark during the last generations, that is, how uniform Danish pronunciation has become after the relative decline of the classical dialects, is disputed. The regional variants have been under strong phonetic influence from the different Copenhagen sociolects; this influence spreads very fast and sometimes reaches Northern Jutland within a period of 10 years. By contrast, many syntactic innovations in the standard can be traced back to influence from the classical dialects. In phonetic descriptions, a variety called 'Advanced Standard Copenhagen' (ASC) has gained a quite central role without actually being a prestige dialect. Advanced Standard Copenhagen is Danish as it is spoken by educated middle-class speakers of the generation that is now between age 45 and 55, born and raised in the northern suburbs of Copenhagen. There is considerable sociolectal variation, which is best studied for Copenhagen, as well as generally quite considerable age-group variation. A detailed and comprehensive study of phonological variation and change in the Copenhagen sociolects of the last 150 years, conducted by Lars Brink and Jørn Lund in the 1970s, has shown that the rate of language change for Danish is very high, at least on the phonetic side. It has been pointed out that even the language of newsreels and documentary films from the 1950s is clearly recognizable today as belonging to an earlier linguistic stage; the general (but quite erroneous) impression is that in those days people used a spelling pronunciation.

Norwegians and (to a slightly lesser degree) Swedes usually experience little difficulty in reading Danish. The phonetics of Danish creates, by contrast, a significant obstacle in what has been called inter-Scandinavian semi-communication, namely, the spontaneous use of the three mainland Scandinavian languages (Danish, Norwegian and Swedish) in oral communication between their speakers. Swedes, in particular, have difficulty in understanding spoken Danish.

Outside Denmark, Danish has official functions in the Faroe Islands alongside with Faroese, and in Greenland in addition to Inuit (Kalaallisooq). Its teaching as a foreign language in school is largely restricted to Iceland, another former Danish colony. In Iceland, Danish is taught from primary school on. In the bilingual area in Germany near the Danish border Danish is a subject and teaching medium in the education system of the Danish minority. In this area, it is also offered by some majority schools as an optional subject. Danish is an official and working language of the European Community, and in terms of numbers of speakers it is the smallest of these languages.

10.2 Phonology

The variety of Danish described here is Advanced Standard Copenhagen.

Table 10.1 Comparison of three phonetic transcription systems for Danish

IPA	*Basbøll-Wagner*	*Dania*	
[miːlə]	[miːlə]	*mi'lə*	mile
[me̝ːlə]	[meːlə]	*me'lə*	mele
[me̞ːlə]	[mɛːlə]	*mæ'lə*	mæle
[mɛːlə]	[mæːlə]	*mȧ'lə*	male

There are other standard varieties, especially of Jutlandic origin, which sometimes are preferred in linguistic descriptions since they are allegedly easier for foreigners to master. The language described here (although originally defined as the speech of middle-aged middle-class Copenhageners) can be heard on the radio and on television, and in many types of relaxed or semi-formal speech occasions.

When transcribing Danish words, one is immediately faced with a dilemma. Ordinary IPA, not supplemented by diacritics, is simply too broad a transcription for the notation of Danish vowel qualities. In Danish, there are contrasts like *lidt* [lid̥] 'suffered' vs *lidt* [le̝d̥] 'little' vs *let* [le̞d̥] 'easy'. There is furthermore a vowel quality [ɛ] as in *ret* [ʁɛd̥] 'right', which does not contrast with [e̞]. Correspondingly there are four phonemically distinct long vowels: *mile* [miːlə] 'charcoal stack' vs *mele* [me̝ːlə] 'to flour' vs *mæle* [me̞ːlə] 'to utter' vs *male* [mɛːlə] 'to grind'. It is common practice (not only in Danish) to avoid the use of diacritics for the notation of phonemic contrasts and to use simple symbols as much as possible. Examples for this practice are the system used by Basbøll and Wagner (1985), and the traditional Dania system as shown in Table 10.1.

Still, this practice – although endorsed by the very principles of the IPA – has its disadvantages. Apart from the possible proliferation of symbols, it makes it difficult to compare phonetic systems across languages and even between different analyses of the same language. Thus, while following the analysis by Basbøll-Wagner, I do not introduce any new symbols, but use narrow IPA diacritics where they are necessary to distinguish phonological contrast rather than phonetic detail. But I write [ɔ] and [ʌ] rather than [ɔ̝$^{+c}$] and [ʌ$^{+ɔ}$], although [ɔ] and [ʌ] are not distinguished by their degree of rounding alone; there is also a significant difference of height. I also write [a] rather than [a̝], although the quality of Danish [a] is quite audibly raised as compared with German or French [a]-sounds.

The *Stød* Phenomenon

In Danish phonology, there is one phenomenon that, although maybe not uniquely Danish, is very unusual among the languages of Europe, namely, *stød* (literally 'thrust' or 'push'). Impressionistically, *stød* resembles a glottal stop without complete closure that occurs with long vowels and sonorants under certain conditions. Nevertheless it should not be considered as a segmental feature, but rather as a prosodic feature of the syllable. The supposed 'glottal stop' does not occur *after*, but *within* the affected vowels and sonorants. A syllable must have a so-called *stød* base in order to be able to carry *stød*, and it is only in syllables with a *stød* base that *stød* and non-*stød* can contrast. In the standard language, this *stød* base is either a long vowel or a sonorant after a short vowel. Vowels with *stød* have about 85 per cent of the length of a *stød*-less long vowel. Thus *stød* occurs at a rather constant temporal distance from the onset of the affected syllable. As notation for *stød* I use [ˀ] in connection with vowels, and simply ['] in connection with consonants and semivowels. The [.] in [ˀ] suggests the length or half-length of the vowel with *stød*. *Stød* is associated with stress and can only occur in stressed syllables; if a syllable loses its stress for morphological reasons (as in compound words), syntactic reasons (as in noun incorporation) or discourse prosodic reasons (as when it does not constitute the kernel of a prosodic stress group), it will not carry *stød*. *Stød* is not articulated in song, except as a stylistic feature in certain cabaret-type chansons.

Stød was originally a redundant feature of stressed monosyllables with either long vowel or final voiced consonant (like *hus* [huˀs] 'house', *land* [lanˀ] 'land'), and occurs in words etymologically related to Norwegian and Swedish words with tone 1 (the 'simple' tone). But this association with monosyllables does not hold synchronically any more. On the one hand, phonological change has created new monosyllables without *stød* (like *mor* [moːɐ] 'mother' (contracted from earlier disyllabic *moder* ['moːðɐ]) vs *mord* [moˀɐ] 'murder'). On the other, some morpheme boundaries are relevant, some are not, for *stød* assignment. The nominal definite inflection suffix (originally a separate word) does not exclude *stød* from the nominal stem (like in *huset* ['huˀsəð] 'the house'), while plural suffixes do (*huse* ['huːsə] 'houses'). In loans, *stød* is regularly found in polysyllables: loans with final stress on a long vowel, or ending on a sonorant after stressed vowel, will usually have *stød*: *information* [ɛnfɒmaˈʃoˀn]. The original association of *stød* with monosyllables has in these words been reanalysed as an association with final stress. (In the part of the Danish vocabulary that is originally Germanic, and disregarding compounds, final stress would only occur in monosyllables.) Loans have *stød* on stressed antepenultimates as well (as in *Akropolis* [aˈkʁoˀpolis] 'Acropolis'), but never on the penultimate. Even some polysyllabic present finite forms of verbs, like *synger* ['søŋˀɐ] 'sings', have *stød*.

Vowels

The Danish vowel system in stressed syllables is presented in Table 10.2. All the sounds in Table 10.2 with the possible exception of short [o], whose distribution is highly restricted, can be considered phonemic. ([o] is largely,

Table 10.2   The Danish vowel system in stressed syllables

	Unrounded		*Front* Rounded		*Back*	
high	iː	i	yː	y	uː	u
	eː	e	øː	ø	oː	o
	ẹː	ẹ	ọ̈ː	ọ̈	ɔː	ɔ
	ɛː					ʌ
		a				
low	ɑː	ɑ			ɒː	ɒ

but not completely, in complementary distribution with [ɔ].) Some vowel qualities historically have been conditioned by the surrounding consonants, which thus affected their phonemic status. Thus [a] and [ɑ] originally were in complementary distribution, [a] occurring finally and before dentals and alveolars, and [ɑ] occurring before other stops. A preceding [ʁ] conditions [ɑ] as well. This original, neat complementary distribution has now been superseded by [ɑ] sounds that originally were conditioned by a following [ʁ] (not necessarily in immediate contact with [ɑ], but always within the same morpheme). These [ʁ]s are still represented by ‹r› in writing, but have disappeared phonetically, which is why the occurrence of [ɑ] rather than [a] is not phonetically conditioned any more. Thus [a] and [ɑ] enter into minimal pairs now, both word-finally as in *kan* [ka] '(I) can' vs *kar* [kɑ] 'vessel' and word-internally as in (*de to*) *Anners* ['anɐs] gen. pl. '(of the two) Anns' vs *Anders* ['ɑnɐs] 'Anders'.

There are two schwa sounds that only occur in unstressed syllables, [ə] and [ɐ]. The only other vowels that can occur in unstressed syllables (except in loans) are [e] e.g. *madding* ['maðeŋ] 'bait', and [i] e.g. *dydig* ['dy̬ːði] 'virtuous'; both occur also in stressed syllables.

Since /ə/ is only defined as a neutral, central vowel with a great variability as far as place of articulation and degree of rounding are concerned, it is, especially in less distinct styles, easily affected by assimilation to an adjacent vowel or sonorant, as in *pige* ['piːə], less distinct: [piːi] 'girl', *inde* ['ẹnə], less distinct: ['ẹnṇ] 'inside', or is absorbed into a syllabic semivowel like in *gade* ['gɛːðə], less distinct: ['gɛːð̩] 'street'. This is a very striking feature of relaxed everyday Danish.

With the two schwa phonemes, and counting /o/ as a phoneme, Danish has 27 vowel phonemes. Even without counting allophonic variants, this must be considered a very high number of vowel phonemes for a language. Allophonic variants occur in particular in the environment before and after /ʁ/, or in the first part of diphthongs.

Diphthongs

The Danish phonetic system does not only show a high number of phonemic vowel distinctions, it also shows a quite exceptional number of diphthongs, all of them falling. These diphthongs are one of the most important stumbling blocks for the foreigner who wants to acquire a decent pronunciation of Danish, since they are phonetically very similar but still form contrasts. There are at least the following 19 diphthongs with a short first element, and with [i̯], [u̯] or [ɐ̯] as second element: *mig* [mɑi̯] 'me', *møg* [mʌi̯] 'dirt', *stiv* [sḍiu̯'] 'stiff', *peber* ['pe̞u̯ɐ̯] 'pepper', *levn* [le̞u̯'n] 'leftover', *hav* [hɑu̯] 'sea', *syv* [syu̯'] 'seven', *øvrig* ['øu̯ʁi] 'other', *støvle* ['sḍøu̯lə] 'boot', *tov* [tʌu̯] 'rope', *fog* [fɔu̯] 'snow drift', *hirse* ['hiɐ̯sə] 'millet', *Per* [pe̞ɐ̯] 'Per', *bær* [be̞ɐ̯] 'berries', *styrte* ['sḍyɐ̯də] 'fall down', *kørte* ['køɐ̯də] 'drove', *smør* [smøɐ̯] 'butter', *purk* [puɐ̯g] 'little boy' and *sort* [soɐ̯ḍ] 'black'. They cannot be considered phonemic, since the first parts of them commute.

There are also 19 combinations of long vowels with non-syllabic [i̯], [u̯] and [ɐ̯]. A few examples of these are: *bøg* [bø̞'i̯] 'beech', *borg* [bɒ'u̯] and *ord* [o'ɐ̯] 'word'.

Consonants

While the number of vowels (and certainly the number of diphthongs) is greater than in many other languages, the Danish consonant inventory is rather simple. There is a set of stops, all of them are unvoiced. [p, t, k] are aspirated and [b̥, ḍ, g̊] are non-aspirated. Strictly speaking, [p, t, k] should be transcribed as [b̥ʰ, ḍʰ, g̊ʰ], or, for younger speakers, as [b̥ʰ, ḍsʰ, g̊ʰ]. There are the following fricatives: [f, s, ʃ, h, v, j, ʁ]. Of these [f, s, ʃ, h] are voiceless, and [v, j, ʁ] voiced. There are three nasal stops [n, m, ŋ], and a lateral liquid [l]. And there are four semivowels: apart from the set of three, [i̯, u̯, ɐ̯], which we have encountered above in our discussion of the formation of diphthongs, one also has to count [ð], the 'soft d' as in *mad* [mað] 'food', as a semivowel. It is normally associated with obstruents like those written as ‹th› in English *this* or *there* or as ‹ð› in Icelandic *maður* 'man', but the English and Icelandic sounds are dental fricatives, while Danish [ð] is phonetically quite different: it is an alveolar voiced sonorant. Its auditive impression is quite close to [l] and it is often confused with it by non-native learners of Danish.

It should be noticed that a voiced/voiceless contrast is almost totally absent from the Danish consonant system. The contrast between [p, t, k] and [b̥, ḍ, g̊] really is one of aspiration vs non-aspiration, as is made clear by the narrower transcription [b̥ʰ, ḍʰ, g̊ʰ] vs [b̥, ḍ, g̊]. Although there are voiced fricatives and sonorants, none of them has a voiceless opposite number except for [v] that contrasts with [f], but this is rather a lenis–fortis contrast than one of voice.

Word Structure and Stress

The totality of the Danish vocabulary is made up of inherited Danish words (the bulk of the non-compound vocabulary), on the one hand, and loans, on the other. The main difference between these two groups of words is that the second group shows some phonological structures that are not found in the first. Non-compound inherited Danish words are either monosyllabic (*hus* [huˀs] 'house', *rod* [ʁoˀð] 'root', *vand* [vanˀ] 'water') or disyllabic with stress on the first syllable and an unstressed /ə/ in the second (*bakke* ['b̥ag̊ə] 'hill', *tidsel* ['tisəl] 'thistle'). Both types occur, of course, in loans aswell, like in *sky* [sg̊yˀ] 'gravy' < French *jus*, or *mode* ['moːðə] 'fashion' < Ger. *Mode*, and these loans cannot be distinguished phonologically from inherited Danish words. (*Sky* is phonetically identical to *sky* [sg̊yˀ] 'cloud'.) But loans exhibit phonological patterns not found in inherited Danish words, such as non-schwa vowels in unstressed syllables of what at least synchronically are non-compounds: *kursus* ['kuʁsus] 'course', *karma* ['kɑːma] 'karma', or polysyllables with stress on other than the first syllable, like *naiv* [na'iˀu̯] 'naive', *habil* [ha'biˀl] 'able', *konservativ* [kʌn'sɛʁvatiu̯] 'conservative'.

Compounds normally bear stress on the first element, if they are of the type free morpheme + free morpheme (*banegård* ['b̥ɛːnə,g̊ɒˀ] 'railway station', (lit.) 'rail+yard') or free morpheme + bound morpheme (*venlig* ['venli] 'friend+ly'). Compounds of bound morpheme + free morpheme or bound morpheme + free morpheme + bound morpheme can either carry stress on the first element (*undgå* ['ɔn,g̊ɒˀ] 'to avoid', *uhygge* ['u,hyg̊ə] 'eeriness', (lit.) 'un+cosiness'), or on the second (*fortryde* [fɒ'tʁyˀðə] 'regret', *uhyggelig* [u'hyg̊ə,li] 'uncanny'). Some verbal prefixes which are loans from Low German never carry word stress, like *betale* [be'tɛˀlə] 'pay' or *fortælle* [fɒ'tɛl'ə] 'tell'.

For compounds of three elements, there is a tendency to stress (A+'B)+C even where the compound of the first two elements is stressed 'A+B: although the part of town west of Copenhagen Central station is called 'Vester₁bro, the name of its main thoroughfare is stressed ₁Vester'brogade.

A peculiarity is the accent pattern of some compound adjectives where the first part does not express so much a specification as a degree. These adjectives carry two main stresses in one word. Thus there is a contrast between 'brand₁farlig 'dangerous as to fire' (i.e. 'inflammable'), and 'brand'farlig 'dangerous like fire' (i.e. 'very dangerous').

Spelling

Danish uses the Latin alphabet with three letters added: ⟨Æ æ⟩, ⟨Ø ø⟩, and ⟨Å å⟩ (before 1948, ⟨Aa⟩ and ⟨aa⟩ were used instead of ⟨Å å⟩). The relationship between phonemes and graphemes is not one to one, especially for short vowel phonemes; thus ⟨i⟩ is used for writing both /i/ and /e̜/. While ⟨e⟩ also is used to write /e̜/, mostly in loans, its main function is to write /e̜/, for which there is also a separate letter, ‹æ›. Danish spelling follows to a high degree the Principle of Greatest Similarity in the spelling of the same morpheme: even where the phonetic shape of a morpheme differs considerably in different contexts, identical, or similar, spelling is retained. Thus the morpheme *sag* 'thing, case' is spelled the same both where it occurs as an independent word with the pronunciation [sɛˀj], and as the first part of a compound like *sagfører* 'lawyer' (lit. '(s)he who leads your case'), where it is pronounced [sɑu̯]; similarly for present finite *sælge* ['sɛljə] 'sell' vs past finite *solgte* [sʌlḍə] 'sold'. Sometimes graphemic distinctions which in themselves are not phonemically significant are introduced to compensate for lacking graphemic distinctions in some other part of the word. Thus the only distinction between the verbs *spilde* [sbilə] 'to spill' and *spille* [sbelə] 'to play' is in the stem vowel which is represented by ‹i› in both words; the distinction is maintained by using the graphemes ‹ld› and ‹ll› for the same phoneme /l/. (A similar case is the above mentioned example of *mor* 'mother' vs *mord* 'murder', where the phonological distinction is non-*stød* vs *stød*, while the graphemic distinction is ‹r› vs ‹rd›.) In the case of different morphemes which have identical sounds (homophones), one can see a different principle at work which could be called the Principle of Greatest Dissimilarity of different morphemes. Here graphemic distinctions are introduced which do not correspond to some phonemic distinction in some other part of the word, but which have the sole function of distinguishing between phonemically identical morphemes or words, cf. *tigge* 'to beg' vs *tikke* 'to tick', both ['teğə], or *løg* 'onion' and *løj* 'lied', both [lʌi̯ˀ]. There are some cases where one phonetic sequence can be represented orthographically in several ways with distinct associated meanings. ['tiːɐ] can thus be *tiger* '(a) tiger', *tigre* 'tigers', *tier* 'keeps one's tongue' (or '(a) tenner'), and ['muːɐ] can be *muher* 'moos (of cows)', *murer* 'does masonry work' (or '(a) mason'), *murere* 'masons', and *muger* 'mucks out'. Homographs which are not homophones occur, though, cf. *steg* which can be [sdɑi̯ˀ] '(a) roast' or 'fry!' or [sdei̯ˀ] '(s/he) climbed'. There are also quite a number of homophones which also are homographs, like *frø* [fʁøːˀ] 'seed' and 'frog'.

Clause Prosody

The study of the suprasegmental features of the Danish clause is only in its early stages, but some results have already emerged. The most general overall feature is that sentence types are characterized by consistent patterns of fundamental frequency (F_0) contours. In syntactically unmarked questions, i.e. main clauses with declarative constituent order used as interrogatives (usually echo-questions), the pitch contour is level. In terminal declarative statements, the fundamental frequencies of successive stress groups fall steadily towards the end of the sentence. In syntactically marked questions (both *wh*-questions and yes/no questions) as well as non-final declarative and interrogative clauses, the frequency contour formed by the stressed syllables will still fall steadily towards the end of the sentence, but not nearly as much as in terminal declarative statements. This means that as far as clause types in Danish are marked by pitch contour, they are marked globally, in the entire clause, and not (like in other Germanic languages like English and German) by a typical contour in the last part of the clause only. This means that Danish has no sentence accent: in neutral sentences without contrast or focus accent, there is no particular stress group that is more prominent than others. In this Danish is different even from a closely related language like Swedish.

10.3 Morphology

The Nominal Group

Nouns
Nouns are inflected for number and definiteness. Case inflection is only found in pronouns; what looks like a genitive (*mandens* 'the man's') has synchronically become a phrasal affix attached to the whole noun phrase.

Gender
There are three regular classes of plural formation and a few irregular plurals. Nouns belong also either to the neuter or the non-neuter class. These classes select inflectional forms of attributive and predicative adjectives, and corresponding pronouns, as well as (in the singular) different definiteness affixes: *-et* for neuter and *-en* for non-neuter. These classes are considered as a grammatical gender system. In some Danish dialects, there is still a three-gender system similar to German, *nynorsk* and the Atlantic Scandinavian languages, and the standard Danish system can be considered as a development of this system where masculine and feminine have been conflated into one category non-neuter (which, accordingly, also is called common gender or *utrum*). The relationship of standard Danish grammatical gender categories to biological sex is mostly historical and remote and, therefore, the semantic content of these categories is vague. The non-neuter gender comprises (as one would expect on the background of the other Germanic languages with a gender system) both nouns denoting physical objects and abstract concepts (like *sko* 'shoe', *å* 'river', *glæde* 'joy') and nouns denoting (male or female) persons (like *ven* 'friend', *far* 'father', *datter* 'daughter'). Neuter nouns denote physical objects or abstract concepts (*bord* 'table', *tab* 'loss'), animals (*får* 'sheep') or young humans (*barn* 'child'). This is common in Germanic languages, but in Danish there are also a few neuter nouns that denote persons (*vidne* 'witness', *postbud* 'post(wo)man', *gidsel* 'hostage', *offer* 'victim'), which is less common. On the other hand, Danish has a gender system semantically based on biological sex in the personal pronouns *han* 'he' and *hun* 'she' (as opposed to *den*

'it [non-neuter]' and *det* 'it [neuter]'), which is discussed below.

The Danish gender system can be called covert since gender is not formally marked on the nouns and shows up only in the different inflectional forms for definiteness in the singular, and in the selection of gender in attributive and predicative adjectives, as well as the selection of gender-specific anaphoric pronouns. There are a number of gender related derivational suffixes. A number of them denote biological sex (for example *-inde*, *-ske* '-ess'), others trigger grammatical gender. Thus nouns with the agent suffix *-er* are non-neuter, as are abstract nouns from adjectives with *-hed*. Abstract nouns derived from verbs by the zero suffix are neuter (for example *beløb* 'amount' from *at beløbe sig* 'to amount').

It should be noted that in the dialects spoken in the west of Jutland, a different, semantically non-arbitrary two-way classification exists. In these dialects, definiteness is not marked by a suffix as elsewhere, but by a preposed definite article (usually spelled æ). The article does not distinguish between genders, but attributive demonstratives (*den*, *det*) and anaphorical pronouns do. This gender system is semantically motivated in the sense that one gender (accompanied by *den* 'this') is used for countables, while the other (accompanied by *det* 'this') is used for non-countables, thus *den fisk a fanget i søndags* 'the fish I caught last Sunday' as opposed to *a fik al det fisk a ku spis* 'I got all the fish I could eat'.

Properly speaking this is not a gender system since these demonstratives and pronouns do not categorize nouns lexically in gender classes but classify occurrences of nouns semantically as countable or non-countable. A similar tendency can be observed in the standard language, too. The noun *øl* 'beer' means 'type, brand of beer' when it selects neuter demonstratives and pronouns, as in *Hof er det øl jeg bedst kan lide* 'Hof is the beer I like best'. When it selects non-neuter elements, it means 'glass, bottle of beer', as in *drik så den øl!* 'come on and finish your (lit. this) beer!'

Definiteness

As in the other Scandinavian languages, nouns are inflected for definiteness: they have a 'bare' indefinite form like *hus* 'house', which, among other functions, combines with the indefinite article: *et hus* 'a house'; and they have a definite form *huset* 'the house'. In the singular, neuter and non-neuter nouns select different suffixes in the definite form (*-en* and *-et*), whereas there is no gender difference in the plural.

Lack of Case Marking

Whereas there is a distinction in pronouns (see below) between a non-oblique (nominative, subject) and an oblique (accusative, non-subject) case, there are no corresponding traces of the historical inflectional system of nouns.

Even the suffix *-s* attached to nouns represents a group genitive, not a genitive case. 'My father's house' is *min fars hus* in Danish which might make one think that there is a genitive form *fars* 'father's' of *far* 'father'. On closer inspection this turns out to be a misunderstanding. Not only can the possessive marker be attached to a whole noun phrase, as in *Kongen af Danmarks bolsjefabrik* 'the King of Denmark's candy factory', which corresponds to the structure of English 'the King of England's daughter'; it is also actually impossible to attach this marker to a noun if there is a post-nominal modifier in the same noun phrase, as in **kongens af Danmark*, while in colloquial language, this marker *-s* can even be attached to non-nominal morphemes such as stranded prepositions, as *med* 'with' in *det er pigen Uffe bor sammen meds datter* 'that's the daughter of the girl Uffe lives with'. This does not mean that the possessive marker can always be attached to the last word in the post-nominal modifier; thus neither **fuglens på taget vinger* 'the bird's on the roof wings' nor **fuglen på tagets vinger* 'the bird on the roof's wings' are possible. In many cases one prefers the use of a prepositional phrase for denoting possession anyway, like *vingerne på fuglen* 'the wings on the bird'.

The *-s*-affix originated of course as a genitive ending (originally only with strong *a*-stems in the singular). It can still be seen as a genitive in fossilized expressions with preposition + genitive: *til søs* 'at sea'. Other fossilized genitives are harder to recognize as such, like the plural genitive *fædrene* in *mine fædrene hus* 'my (fore)fathers' house'.

Number
Regular noun plurals are formed according to one of the following three processes:

Class 1, plural in *-er* (indefinite), *-erne* (definite):

måned 'month'	*måneder* 'months'	*månederne* 'the months'
ske 'spoon'	*skeer* 'spoons'	*skeerne* 'the spoons'
uge 'week'	*uger* 'weeks'	*ugerne* 'the weeks'

Notice that the *e* of the ending is dropped (leaving *-r* as the plural ending) after *e* like in *uger*. This goes, of course, only for written ‹e› when it represents the schwa vowel [ə]; after long [e̞ː] or [e̞ˑ] as in *ske* [sɡ̊e̞ˑ], the *e* of the ending is not dropped: *skeer, skeerne* 'spoons, the spoons'.

Class 2, plural in *-e* (indefinite), *-ene* (definite)

dag 'day'	*dage* 'days'	*dagene* 'the days'

Class 3, plural in Ø (indefinite), *-ene* (definite)

år 'year'	*år* 'years'	*årene* 'the years'
forsøg 'attempt'	*forsøg* 'attempts'	*forsøgene* 'the attempts'

There is no correlation between gender and plural formation, although most members of class 3 are neuter nouns that are either monosyllabic or denote abstract concepts (often derived from verbs). There are, of course, counter-examples: *mus* 'mouse' is non-neuter with a definite form *musen* 'the mouse', but it has a -Ø plural: *mus* 'mice' – *musene* 'the mice'.

There are a number of irregular plural formations outside these classes. Some nouns form the plural with umlaut (*mand* 'male person' – *mænd* – *mændene*, *fod* 'foot' – *fødder* – *fødderne*) or completely irregularly (*øje* 'eye' – *øjne* – *øjnene*, actually an old dual).

A few loans use plural forms calqued on the plural forms of the loan-giving language: *en konto* 'account' – *konti* 'accounts'. Loans from Latin ending in -*um* (and some loans from Italian in -*o*) take the Danish plural affix -*er*, but drop this ending before the affix, thus *et studium* 'study' – *studier* 'studies'. There is a tendency to eliminate these irregularities, though; one hears *kontoer* 'accounts' and *kontoerne*; from the plural *studier* a new singular *et studie* has developed.

Pronouns

Personal Pronouns

Personal pronouns are deictic elements that refer to speech-act participants: in the singular, the first-person pronoun refers to the speaker (*jeg*), the second-person pronoun to the hearer (*du*), and third-person pronouns (*han*, *hun*, *den*, *det*) to persons as well as physical and abstract objects talked about in the speech act. Only third-person pronouns are pro-nouns in a proper sense, since they – over and above this deictic use – can also be used anaphorically and thus stand for (Latin: *pro*) a noun, or more precisely, a noun phrase.

Danish follows a common European pattern in not distinguishing between different kinds of first and second persons (inclusive vs not inclusive, etc.) in the plural: the first-person plural personal pronoun (*vi*) does not distinguish between 'we (several speakers)', 'we (I, the speaker, and you, the hearer(s))', and 'we (I, the speaker, and my associates – not necessarily present)'. Similarly, the second-person plural pronoun (*I*) is used both in the sense of 'you (several hearers)' and 'you (you, the hearer, and your associates – not necessarily present)'. The plural form of the third-person personal pronoun is *de*.

POLITENESS LEVELS

In the second-person pronouns, Danish distinguishes two levels of politeness both in the singular and the plural, a familiar form and a polite form:

	Familiar	Polite
Singular	du	De
Plural	I	De

The use of the polite form is more marked than in either Dutch or German. The familiar form is used not only between friends and family, but also at most places of work at least in the public sector (although some private companies seem to develop a distinctive corporate culture involving the use of *De* among personnel and with customers), between politicians, by journalists and in teaching situations. In recent years, the use of the polite form has been gaining some, though not much, ground again.

GENDER AND SEX

Gender with Danish pronouns is only relevant for third-person pronouns in the singular, and it carves out two distinct subsystems of the third-person singular pronoun system.

One subsystem consists of the pronouns *han* 'he' and *hun* 'she' used for people; these pronouns are semantically distinguished by the natural sex of the person referred to. These pronouns can be used both deictically (referring to people present in the speech situation) and anaphorically (referring to people mentioned in the context). The other subsystem consists of the pronouns *den* and *det* which are distinguished by grammatical gender: *den* is used anaphorically for noun phrases with common gender heads, *det* for noun phrases with neuter heads. Both *den* and *det* (which both can be rendered by 'it') can only refer to physical and abstract objects, not to persons. The pronouns for deictic use referring to physical and abstract objects are written the same way as anaphorical *den* and *det*, but there is a difference in pronunciation. Anaphorical *den* and *det* are usually unstressed and therefore subject to phonological reduction, whereas deictic *den* and *det* usually bear stress. *Den* carries *stød* when used deictically ([dɛn']), while neuter *det* [dɛ] lacks a *stød* base and can therefore not carry *stød* even when used deictically and, therefore, stressed.

In anaphorical usage, we thus get the following set of examples:

Det er min kusine. Hun hedder Emma. (feminine, singular)
'This is my cousin. She's called Emma.'

Det er min fætter. Han hedder Kurt. (masculine, singular)
'This is my cousin. He's called Kurt.'

Det er min ny bil. Den har ikke været billig. (non-neuter, singular)
'This is my new car. It hasn't been cheap.'

Det er vores ny hus. Det er lige blevet malet. (neuter, singular)
'This is our new house. It has just been painted.'

Det er vores nye plader. De er faktisk ret gode. (plural)
'These are our new records. They are actually quite good.'

Table 10.3 The case system for Danish personal pronouns

		Singular Non-oblique	Oblique	*Plural* Non-oblique	Oblique
1st person		jeg	mig	vi	os
2nd person		du	dig	I	jer
3rd person [+ human]	m.	han	ham	}	
	f.	hun	hende	} de [di]	dem
[– human]	non n.	den	den	}	
	n.	det	det	}	

It should be noted that when reference is made to the type or brand of something, not to the individual, there is no gender anaphora: *Det er min ny bil. Det er en Toyota* 'this is my new car. It is a Toyota' uses *det*, not *den* to refer to the car in the second sentence.

In recent years, the attempt to avoid sexist language use has led to the creation of new pronouns like *han eller hun* 'he or she', while the 'unmarked' use of *han* referring to a person of unspecified or unknown sex is strongly avoided. In the 1970s, it had been suggested that one should create a new pronoun *høn* 's/he' after the model of gender-unspecific Finnish *hän* 's/he', [ø] being the phonetic middle between [a] and [u], but this suggestion has not caught on.

CASE

Pronouns retain two case forms (as summarized in Table 10.3), sometimes called nominative and accusative, since they typically express subjects and objects, as in *jeg elsker dig* 'I love you' vs *han kysser hende* 'he is kissing her', or in the plural: *I keder os* 'you (pl.) bore us'. The term accusative is misleading, though, since apart from the function of expressing direct and indirect objects, the oblique form has a number of other functions as well, like in prepositional phrases (*jeg stoler på dig* 'I trust (in) you'), predicatively (*det er ham* 'it's him'), and in comparisons (*jeg er større end dig* 'I am bigger than you').

Possessive Pronouns

Adjectival pronouns are possessives and demonstratives. The set of possessive pronouns is slightly heterogeneous (the forms are summarized in Table 10.4). There are two types: one type is inflected similarly to adjectives, and consists of *min* 'my', *din* 'your (sg.)', *vor* 'our', *eder* 'your (pl.)' and *sin* 'his/her/its (refl.)'. (For the usage of *sin*, see below.) The other consists of invariable forms, that is *hans* 'his', *hendes* 'her', *vores* 'our', *jeres* 'your (pl.)' and *deres* 'their' (along with *Deres* 'your (polite)'). The latter all end in -*s* and go back to old genitives. The distribution between the two types is

Table 10.4   Summary of forms of Danish adjectival pronouns

		Inflectable Singular	Plural	*Invariable* Singular	Plural
1st person		min	vor		vores
2nd person		din	(eder)		jeres
3rd person					
[+ human]	m.	} sin		hans	
	f.			hendes	} deres
[– human]	non-n.			dens	
	n.			dets	

asymmetrical, though. In some persons and numbers only one form exists (inflectable in the first- and second-person singular, invariable in the second- and third-person plural), whereas there is competition between *vor* and *vores* whose stylistic values differ in an intricate way. (The inflectable second-person plural form *eder* is obsolete.) The inflectable possessives have neuter and plural forms (like *mit, vort*; *mine, vore*).

Demonstratives
Among demonstrative pronouns, Danish originally had a proximity correlation between *denne* 'this' and *hin* 'that', but *hin* is all but obsolete today and survives only in archaic or jocular language, as well as in some fixed phrases like *dette og hint* 'this and that'. In the written language, one distinguishes between two demonstrative adjectives, *den* and *denne*. Both are only inflected for gender (*den* and *denne* are the non-neuter forms, the neuter being *det* and *dette*) and number (*de* and *disse* are the plural forms; gender distinctions as elsewhere are neutralized in the plural). There are no relics of a case inflection, especially no oblique form, although *denne, dette, disse* of course can carry the *-s* of the group genitive when they form noun phrases of their own. *Den* is usually identified with the so-called 'adjective article' (see below), although it occurs without adjectives, e.g. as a correlate of a relative clause like in *det brød som jeg købte i går* ... 'the bread that I bought yesterday ...'.

In the spoken language, the situation is somewhat more complicated. In a way similar to the two forms of the third-person pronoun *den*, attributive *den* also can be distinguished as to whether it has *stød* or not. (Neuter *det* and plural *de* have no *stød* base and cannot carry *stød* for this reason. Plural oblique *dem* has a *stød* base, but is not lexically marked for *stød*.) *Stød*-less *den* is anaphorical and *den* with *stød* is used deictically.

Unstressed *den, det* and *de* are also used as the so-called 'adjective article' (which is discussed below in connection with the definiteness inflection of adjectives).

Reflexive Pronouns

There are two sets of personal reflexive pronouns (*sig* and *mig selv*, etc.), and one reflexive possessive adjective (*sin*). The personal reflexive pronouns only have an oblique form, for obvious reasons. The first set consists only of the special oblique form *sig* which is used indiscriminately for persons and physical as well as abstract objects in the singular and the plural, that is, it functions as the reflexive oblique of *han*, *hun*, *den*, *det* and *de*. The second set consists of all the oblique forms of personal pronouns (but with *sig* substituting for *ham*, *hende*, *den* and *det*) with *selv* 'self' appended.

The difference between these two sets is the following: *sig* is only used with true reflexive verbs, that is, those where *at* V *sig* does not imply *to* V *somebody or something*. To begin with, these are those verbs that can only be used reflexively, like *at brokke sig* 'to complain', *at blære sig* 'to boast', *at skamme sig* 'to be ashamed'. But *sig* also occurs with verbs that can be used transitively, but which have an at least slightly modified meaning when used reflexively, like *at more sig* 'to have fun' (as opposed to *at more nogen* 'to amuse somebody') or *at kede sig* 'to be bored' (as opposed to *at kede nogen* 'to bore somebody'). On the other hand, *mig selv*, *sig selv*, etc. are used with ordinary transitive verbs under referential identity of subject and object: *jeg spørger mig selv* 'I'm asking myself', *hun hader sig selv* 'she hates herself'.

It should be noted that the reflexive of plural *de* is *sig* or *sig selv*, while the reflexive of the polite second-person singular and plural pronoun either is *Dem* and *Dem selv* or *sig* and *sig selv*.

The possessive adjective *sin* is only used for singular possessor referents, thus *han har glemt sin hat* 'he forgot his hat'. In the plural, *deres* is used: *de glemte deres barn* (not **sit barn*) 'they forgot their child'.

Adjectives

Strong and Weak Forms

Danish adjectives come in two forms, 'strong' and 'weak'. The strong form is inflected for number and gender (the distinction non-neuter vs neuter is neutralized in the plural, though). There is no inflection for case, as one by now would suspect. The suffix of the weak form is invariably *-e*. It occurs after the adjective article and possessive pronouns, and before proper names: *den lange march* 'the long march', *det grådige barn* 'the greedy child', *de gamle dage* 'the old days', *gamle Tobias* 'old Tobias'. Unlike in the other mainland Scandinavian languages, adjectives cannot be combined with a definite noun. If a definite noun phrase contains an adjective, the adjective is in the weak form preceded by the so-called adjective article. Proper names can either take the article before a weak adjective or leave it out: *den gamle Ole* '[the] old Ole' vs *gamle Tobias* 'old Tobias', also with geographical names: *det nye London* 'the new London' vs *dejlige København* 'wonderful Copenhagen'. Geographical names which are inherently definite like *Tyrkiet*

'Turkey', *Østen* 'the East', *Sovjetunionen* 'the Soviet Union', take the neuter adjective article even when their definiteness ending is non-neuter -*en*: *det forhenværende Sovjetunionen* 'the former Soviet Union', *det fjerne Østen* 'the Far East'.

Strong forms are used when the adjective is used predicatively, after the indefinite article, and when the noun phrase is non-definite and has no article: *mine børn er syge* 'my children are ill', *et sygt forslag* 'a sick proposal', *stort besvær* 'big trouble'.

The suffixes are:

	Singular	*Plural*
Non-neuter	-Ø	
Neuter	-*t*	-*e*

There are a number of adjectives that show irregular features. *Lille* 'small' has only one form (strong and weak, non-neuter and neuter) in the singular and has the suppletive plural *små*. Most adjectives ending in a vowel like *blå* 'blue', *grå* 'grey', *ublu* 'shameless' do not take the suffix -*e*, although *ny* 'new' sometimes does. Adjectives in -*t*, -*sk* and unstressed -*e* do not take the strong neuter suffix -*t*. Some adjectives in -*d* or stressed vowel take the strong neuter suffix (e.g. *godt* [g̊ɒd] from *god* [g̊oˀ] 'good', *blåt* [b̥lɒd̥] from *blå* [b̥lɔˀ] 'blue'), some do not (e.g. *glad* 'happy', *snu* 'smart').

Comparison

Comparison of adjectives is by adding the suffix -(*e*)*re* for the comparative and -(*e*)*st* for the superlative. A number of adjectives have suppletive forms like *god* 'good' – *bedre* 'better' – *bedst* 'best', and three adjectives have umlaut in their otherwise regular comparative and superlative: *stor* 'big' – *større* – *størst*, *ung* 'young' – *yngre* – *yngst*, and *lang* 'long' – *længere* – *længst*. Some adjectives (those that have unstressed *e* in the last syllable, like *rusten* 'rusty' or *fælles* 'common', and those formed with the suffix -(*i*)*sk* '-ish') do not have inflected comparatives and superlatives but have periphrastic forms instead: *mere rusten, mest rusten*.

Verbs

Danish verbs have relatively few inflectional categories. There is no marking of number or person, although the distinction between singular and plural forms of the verb was maintained in the written language until the last century (although even the first Danish grammarians in the sixteenth century had noticed that the spoken language did not make this distinction any more). There is a tense opposition between a non-past (commonly called present) and a past, over and above which forms which usually are considered compound tenses exist as well. There is a synthetic and an analytic passive; some verbs also form a middle form similar to, but not identical with, the synthetic passive. There are only two moods, a non-marked mood (indicative) and an imperative; in some fossilized expressions, remnants of an old optative can be found. Finite forms (of which there are only two, non-past and past) combine with subjects; the infinitive takes objects, but no subjects. There are two participial forms. The first (for example *leende* 'laughing') is either used as a verbal adjective with the meaning of an active present participle or joins certain verbs in an auxiliary construction, for example *de kom marcherende* 'they came marching'. The second functions both as an adjectival form (and is inflected in this case) and as a supine. The adjectival form is usually only formed from perfective transitive verbs and has a past passive meaning (for example *stegte ænder* 'fried ducks'). From the supine the compound tenses of the perfect system are formed (for example, *spist* 'eaten' in *har spist* 'has eaten').

Danish verbs are usually quoted in the infinitive with the infinitive marker which is written *at*, but (except in the most distinct pronunciation) pronounced *å* [ɒ], like *at svømme* 'to swim'.

Morphological Verb Classes

Danish verbs can be divided into a number of morphological classes on the basis of the formation of the present finite form and the past finite form.

Formation of the present finite form divides the bulk of verbs into two: those with the ending -*(e)r* and those without an ending. The former group is by far the biggest and comprises all verbs with the exception of a group of 'core' modal verbs (e.g. *at kunne*, *jeg kan* 'I can') and the verb *at vide* 'to know', *jeg ved* 'I know' which can be considered preterite-presents. Not all verbs that syntactically have properties of modal verbs (such as taking infinitives without *at*) belong to the latter morphological class. This group of verbs form their past tense in a number of ways, most of which involve a dental element similar to that of weak verbs (*jeg vidste* 'I knew', *jeg burde* 'I should have', *jeg måtte* 'I had to'), while with others, the dental element is either only present orthographically (*jeg turde* [toːɐ̯] 'I dared') or has been discarded even in writing (*jeg skulle* 'I should', which was written *skulde* in the pre-1948 spelling).

The group that marks its present finite with -*(e)r* can be subdivided according to the formation of past finite form. The first subgroup are strong verbs that form the past with ablaut, as *jeg giver* 'I give' : *jeg gav* 'I gave'. The second subgroup forms the past finite with some dental element, either -*ede* (the unmarked and only productive subgroup), as in *jeg husker* 'I remember' : *jeg huskede* 'I remembered', or -*te* as in *jeg glemmer* 'I forget' : *jeg glemte* 'I forgot'. Past formation with -*te* sometimes combines with vowel changes, too: *jeg sælger* 'I sell' : *jeg solgte* 'I sold'. Somewhat apart from these group stand the only two modestly irregular verbs *at være* 'to be' and *at have* 'to have', both of which also are used as auxiliaries, and which have some suppletive forms.

Verbs ending on a stressed vowel in the infinitive like *at bo* 'to live (dwell)', *at sy* 'to sow', *at betro* 'to confide', *at bestå* 'to consist of' have some phonetically conditioned peculiarities; they do not take *-er* as a present finite ending, but *-r*. Apart from that, they do not form a consistent morphological class; some of them take dental suffixes in the past tense (*boede, syede, betroede*) while some have strong past forms (*bestod*).

Tense

Like many other Germanic languages, Danish only has a structural opposition between two tenses: a present and a past. The present tense is really a non-past, since it also is the most common way of referring to the future: *jeg kommer i morgen* 'I'm coming tomorrow', *jeg går nu* 'I'm going now'. The past is the narrative tense (*der var engang* ... 'there was one time ...'), but it is also used in general for specific (as opposed to existential) past time reference.

The past tense does not necessarily have past time reference. It is also used in the protasis of counterfactual conditionals: *hvis jeg vandt i lotto, ville jeg købe dig en Mazda* 'if I won in the pools, I'd buy you a Mazda'.

There are additional compound forms that can be used for time reference. The modals *skal* and *vil*, which normally have the full meaning of obligation and volition, can be used with an extremely attenuated modal sense which makes *skal* (or *vil*) + infinitive come close in meaning to a future tense. Thus, a newspaper headline like *Argentina vil vinde i aften* 'Argentine will win tonight' is irresolvably ambiguous between a modal reading 'Argentine wants to win tonight' and a temporal reading 'Argentine is going to win tonight'. However, there is a difference between the latter and the pure future time reference of the non-past: *Argentina vinder i aften* 'Argentine is winning tonight'. The expression using the non-past conveys much more certainty than the modal expression.

It should be noted that this modal expression of future time reference sometimes is expressed by the modal verb alone: *jeg skal i biffen i aften* (lit.) 'I shall into the cinema tonight' (i.e. 'I'm going to the movies tonight') or *jeg vil af* (lit.) 'I want off' (i.e. 'I want to get off') are very common.

Danish has a compound form similar to the other Germanic perfects, which occurs both in a present (perfect) and past (pluperfect) form. It consists of one of the auxiliaries *at have* or *at være* and the non-inflected past participle (supine). The choice of the auxiliary is determined by a basic rule that *at være* is used with perfective intransitive verbs and *at have* with the rest. It should be noted that perfectivity here is not an inherent property of the verb stem (as in German), but can vary according to context. A verb like *at gå* 'to go' can therefore both form a perfect with *at være*: *jeg er gået* 'I'm gone' and with *at have*: *jeg har gået i en time* 'I've been walking for an hour'.

The difference between past reference by the simple past tense and the present perfect is basically that the perfect does not refer to some specific point of time (as in a narrative chain, or like a point specified by some time adverbial or just by shared knowledge of speaker and hearer about a past course of events), but just to some unspecified point in the past. Thus *har du set Casablanca?* (perfect) 'have you seen Casablanca?' asks if the hearer ever has seen Michael Curtiz' film (at some point of time), while *så du Casablanca?* (past) 'did you see Casablanca?' inquires about watching the film at some established point of time (such as when it was on TV last night).

The perfect is also used when the time span referred to begins in the past but extends to, and includes, the moment of utterance. *hvor længe har I ventet her?* corresponds to English 'how long have you been waiting here?' (with perfect), but German 'wie lange wartet ihr hier (schon)?' (with present).

Aspect

There is no synthetic verbal expression of aspect in Danish, but there are a number of fairly systematic ways of marking aspectual distinctions.

The expression *at være ved at* + infinitive takes on two distinct meanings depending on the *aktionsart* of the verb. With durative verbs, it has a progressive meaning 'to be doing something', as in *han var ved at skrive et brev* 'he was writing a letter'. With perfective verbs it has an ingressive meaning 'to be about to do something' as in *han var ved at dø* 'he was about to die' (*not* 'he was dying').

An alternative to the *at være ved at* + infinitive construction is the combination of a verb of position or movement like *gå* 'walk', *sidde* 'sit', *gå rundt* 'go around', *ligge* 'to lie' followed by *og* 'and' and a verb: *han sad og læste et brev* (lit.) 'he sat and read a letter', 'he was reading a letter'.

Mood

The only mood contrast in Danish is the contrast between the indicative and the imperative. The imperative has one form, which is the same for singular and plural, for example *syng* from *synge* 'to sing'. In some formulae like *længe leve dronningen!* 'long live the queen!', *man tage tre skefuld hjortetaksalt* ... (lit.) 'take (lit. one should take) three teaspoonfuls of potassium chloride ...', and a couple of oaths like *kraft æde mig!* 'cancer may eat me!', an optative survives. Modality is expressed by modal verbs and (as in counterfactual conditionals) by the past tense.

Voice

Danish has two passive voices: a synthetic passive ending in *-s*, and an analytic one with the auxiliary *at blive*; thus *den avis læses af tusinder af mennesker* 'this newspaper is read by thousands of people' vs *avisen blev læst straks efter den var kommet* 'the paper was read right after it had arrived'. The synthetic passive usually refers to generalized or objectively known facts, whereas the analytic passive refers to single specific events, usually within the speaker's experience. Accordingly, the two forms of passive trigger different readings (usually epistemic vs non-epistemic) of modal verbs with multiple readings: *dette æg kan ikke spises* 'this egg cannot be eaten (i.e. is not edible)' (non-epistemic) as opposed to *dette æg kan ikke blive spist* 'this egg cannot be eaten (i.e. it is inconceivable that it will be eaten)' (epistemic).

Some verbs form a middle which is often spelled like the synthetic passive but is pronounced with a shortened vowel or loss of [ə]. This form has usually a special meaning (sometimes without an associated active), as in: *bilen skal synes* [syːnəs] 'the car has to be inspected' vs *jeg synes* [syn's] *du har ret* 'I think (i.e. it appears to me) you are right', or it is a reflexive/reciprocal: *vi skilles* [vi sg̊ələs] 'we are being separated' vs *vi skilles* [vi sg̊el's] 'we part ways', *vi slås* [vi slɔːs] *altid* 'we always lose (lit. are beaten)' vs *vi slås* [vi slɒs] *altid* 'we always fight'.

The past (and the even rarer compound tenses) of the *-s* form is almost invariably the past of the middle: *vi syntes* 'we thought', but not **bilerne synedes hvert andet år* 'the cars were inspected every second year'.

Summary of Forms

The Danish verb does not have many distinct inflectional forms. The verb *at slå* 'to hit' has the following eight forms; it should be noticed that there are only six orthographically distinct forms and seven phonetically distinct forms:

Infinitive (= Optative)	*slå* [slɔ']
Present Finite	*slår* [slʌ']
Imperative	*slå* [slʌ']
Past Finite	*slog* [sloˑ]
Present Participle	*slående* ['slɔənə] (less distinct: ['slɔɔnə])
Passive	*slås* [slɔ's]
Middle	*slås* [slɒs]
Past Particle	*slået* [slɔːð]

In the case of *slå*, infinitive and imperative are written identically, which is not the case with all verbs (cf. *komme* 'to come' vs *kom* 'come!'). On the other hand, not all verbs have all these forms (the middle is only formed by a handful of verbs), and for some verbs there are even more systematic syncretisms. Thus for many verbs whose stem ends in *-r*, the present finite, infinitive and imperative forms are identical: *kører, køre* and *kør!* all are [kø̞ɐ̯]. (The infinitive *køre* 'drive' also has a stylistically marked, more formal variant [køːʁə].)

Adjectival adverbs are identical to the neuter singular form of the strong adjective: *hun synger dejligt* 'she sings beautifully', where *dejligt* is identical to the neuter form of the adjective *dejlig* like in *et dejligt hus* 'a beautiful house'.

Adverbs

Adverbs can themselves form comparatives and superlatives very much like adjectives where this makes sense, like *ofte* 'often' – *oftere* – *oftest*. Some adverbs (like *nede* 'down') form adjectival comparatives and superlatives (*nedre* 'lower' and *nederst* 'lowest').

There is, finally, a systematic correlation between static and dynamic adverbs of place that sometimes has been considered a type of inflection. Thus to dynamic *op* 'up(wards)' corresponds static *oppe* 'on top'. Similarly *han gik ud* 'he went out' vs *han var ude* 'he was out'.

10.4   Syntax

Danish belongs to the type of language commonly known as 'verb second', a term that is derived from the placement of the finite verb in the standard constituent order of declarative main clauses.

'Main Clause' Word Order and Constituent Functions

A minimal Danish main clause consists of a subject (which is obligatory in all finite clauses, except in those whose finite verb is in the imperative), and a finite verb: *pigen lo* 'the girl laughed'. The finite verb takes the second position in the clause, i.e. it is (topologically) the second constituent. If the verb consists of a finite and an infinite part, the finite verb (the auxiliary) remains in second position and the non-finite verb follows: *pigen er gået* 'the girl has left'. In a maximal main clause, there are two more positions between the finite and non-finite verb, as well as two positions following the non-finite verb. Adding a '0' position preceding the first constituent, we get as the maximal topological structure of a Danish sentence the following:

Og	ham	havde	Per	ikke	skænket	en tanke	i årevis.
(0)	(1)	(2)	(3)	(4)	(5)	(6)	(7)

'And him Per hadn't given a thought for years.'

The first position, (0), is external to the clause proper and can only be filled by connectors. Position (1) can be filled by most (though not all) phrases that can form clause constituents. If the subject is not in (1), its only alternative placement is in position (3), as in the above sentence. Position (3), in its turn, can only be filled by subjects. Position (4) is the position of certain classes of adverbials, mostly sentence adverbials, and of negation. Position (5) is the position of the non-finite verb. Position (6) is the position for indirect and direct objects. Finally, position (7) is another position for adverbials, so-called 'content' adverbials.

Strictly speaking, positions (6) and (7) are sequences of positions. They can be multiply filled and there is at least a partial ordering between different types of potential fillers. For example, indirect objects precede direct objects in (6).

Principles of Danish Main-clause Topology

There are four principles that govern the topology of the Danish declarative main clause. The first principle is that some elements only can occur in fixed positions. For those elements, topological position and grammatical function are directly tied to each other. This is the case with connectors in position (0), finite verbs in position (2), and elements that modify the whole predication rather than the predicate and that can only occur in position (4). (These include focus particles and adverbials that express polarity and degrees of certainty.) In particular, these elements can never occur in position (1).

The second principle is that for some positions, the position determines which grammatical relation the element in this position carries to the sentence, while the element itself can occur in several positions and, accordingly, can carry different grammatical relations. Noun phrases can occur in a number of positions: (1), (3), (4), (6) and (7). Apart from noun phrases in position (1), the grammatical function of the noun phrase is determined by the position it occurs in: a noun phrase in position (3) is a subject. A noun phrase in position (6) is a direct or indirect object. A noun phrase in positions (4) or (7) is an adverbial.

The third principle is that topological position also can mark pragmatic functions. An element that is placed in position (1) rather than (3), (4), (5), (6) or (7), is marked for certain discourse-pragmatic functions.

Finally, as a fourth principle, stress can disambiguate pragmatic functions. (Remember that Danish has no sentence stress; we are talking about emphatic or contrastive stress here.) Thus an unstressed noun phrase in position (1) would usually be a given topic, while a stressed noun phrase in the same position would be a contrasted focus.

These four principles are in part crossed by a principle of a different kind, sometimes referred to as the 'weight principle' which states that under certain conditions, 'light' constituents can occur in a position further to the left from the position they would occur in, according to the principles mentioned before, whereas 'heavy' constituents (most often long subordinate clauses) can occur in extraposition to the right of position (7). The light constituents affected by the weight principle are unstressed pronouns (*ham* 'him') or deictic adverbs (*her* 'here') which can be attached clitically to a finite main verb: *jeg 'kender ham ikke* 'I don't *know* him' as opposed to *jeg kender ikke 'ham* 'I don't know *him*'. Similarly some sentence adverbs which never can carry stress like *jo* (Ger. *ja*), *nok* 'probably', and others, can occur between a finite verb in position (2) and a subject in position (3), if the latter is not an unstressed pronoun.

Syntactic and Pragmatic Function Assignment

The assignment of syntactic and pragmatic functions is not unambiguous, though. On the one hand, in a topologically not maximally filled clause, some positions are indistinguishable. In *han husker hele dagen* 'he remembers the whole day', *hele dagen* 'the whole day; all day' is an object and thus in position (6); in *han synger hele dagen* 'he sings all day', it is an adverb and thus in position (7). When only one of the two positions (6) and (7) is filled, they are not distinguishable topologically (since their only topological difference is their relative order). Therefore, it is not the placement of *hele dagen* that unambiguously determines its grammatical function as adverbial or object. If more positions in the sentence are filled, positions become more easily distinguishable. Neither in

Han	har	arbejdet	på en løsning	hele dagen.
(1)	(2)	(5)	(7^1)	(7^2)

'He has been working on a solution all day.'

nor in

Han	har	hele dagen	arbejdet	på en løsning.
(1)	(2)	(4)	(5)	(7)

(lit.) 'He has all day worked on a solution.'

is it possible for *hele dagen* to be object: in the first case, because it follows a constituent occupying another subposition of position (7) (thus cannot be in position (6), the position for objects), and in the second case, because it is in position (4) which cannot be filled by objects.

On the other hand, since position (1) basically allows itself to be filled by all kinds of constituents that can be marked pragmatically (to the exclusion only of connectors, the finite verb itself which is fixed in position (2), and certain elements otherwise in position (4) that do not allow for pragmatic marking), placement in position (1) neutralizes all markings of grammatical relations:

Hele dagen	var	ødelagt.
(1)	(2)	(5)

'The whole day was destroyed.'

Hele dagen	tænker	han	på dig.
(1)	(2)	(3)	(7)

'The whole day he is thinking of you.'

Hele dagen	huskede	jeg	ikke.
(1)	(2)	(3)	(4)

'The whole day I didn't remember.'

All have *helen dagen* in position (1), while this noun phrase is subject, adverbial and direct object, respectively.

Since position (1), which marks its constituents for pragmatic functions, neutralizes grammatical functions, it is only by other than by topological means that grammatical functions of elements in position (1) can be determined. Infinite verbs are, of course, always recognizable as such, also in position (1). Personal pronouns have special non-subject forms, and since these forms mark a pronoun as object even when they occur in position (1), a pronoun can be unambiguously object even in position (1), as in *ham husker jeg* 'him I remember' as distinguished from *han husker mig* 'he remembers me'. (Strictly speaking, they are marked as non-subjects, and it is the verb and the type of argument it takes that single out these non-subjects as objects rather than, for example, predicatives.) This disambiguation is not possible with non-pronominal noun phrases. *Min tante husker min bedstemor* is ambiguous between 'my aunt remembers my grandmother' and 'my grandmother remembers my aunt'. (In isolation, one would always assume that this sentence could only have the first reading, but this is far from the case in connected discourse.)

Objects and Adverbials

Danish verbs can take two objects as in *han gav hende kurven* 'he gave her the basket' which can be distinguished as indirect and direct object (in that order), although there is no morphological marking on either of them. They are topologically distinguished by internal ordering within position (6), and of course by the different ways in which the two kinds of objects relate to other constructions (passive, etc.). There is also a kind of dative shift since *han gav kurven til hende* 'he gave the basket to her' is possible, too. It is disputed, though, whether *til hende* 'to her' is an adverbial or a prepositional object. Prepositional phrases like *på perronen* 'on the platform' can, in principle, stand in two different kinds of grammatical relations. They can be arguments of the verb, like in *Lars venter på toget* 'Lars is waiting for the train' and they can be non-argument modifiers of the whole clause of the verb like in *Lars venter på perronen* 'Lars is waiting on the platform'. In the latter, *på* has its full meaning of 'on, touching a surface from above', and is in contrast with prepositions denoting other spatial relationships like *i tunnellen* 'in the tunnel' or *ved billetlugen* 'at the ticket counter'. In the former, *på* it is governed by the verb of which it is an argument, hence the verb selects the preposition; *på* is in contrast with zero: *Lars venter toget* 'Lars is expecting the train'.

It is doubtful, though, if a sentence like *Lars venter på toget* can be said to contain a prepositional object. At least topologically we cannot consider *på toget* an object, since it has all the topological properties of a true adverbial. If *på ham* 'for him' in a sentence like *han har ventet på ham hele dagen* 'he has been waiting for him all day' were an object, one could assume that it is in position (6), followed by *hele dagen* 'all day' in position (7). That this is not possible is demonstrated by the same sentence with an added adverbial like *utålmodigt* 'impatiently'. *utålmodigt* is placed before *på ham*, and since an adverb like *utålmodigt* only can occur in positions (4) or (7), *på ham* must be an adverbial too, since it occurs after an element in position (7), thus having to be in position (7) itself.

Han	har	ventet	utålmodigt	på ham	hele dagen.
(1)	(2)	(5)	(7^1)	(7^2)	(7^3)

Semantically, and as far as government of the preposition is concerned, there is of course a significant difference between *på toget* 'for the train' in *Lars venter på toget* and *på perronen* 'on the platform' in *Lars venter på perronen* because of the difference in the argument status of the constituent. This semantic difference has indirect topological consequences. Prepositional phrases whose preposition is governed by the verb usually 'strand' their preposition when they are pragmatically marked by placement in position (1): thus it is usually *på perronen ventede Lars* 'on the platform, Lars was waiting', but *toget ventede Lars på* 'the train, Lars was waiting for'. These prepositional phrases can hardly occur in position (4) either, although many other prepositional phrases can: *det har han under ingen omstændigheder tænkt sig at gøre* (lit.) 'this he has under no circumstances thought of doing'.

A bare noun phrase functioning as an object is in its expected place, namely, position (6), like *ham* in the following sentence:

Han	har	ventet	ham	utålmodigt	hele dagen.
(1)	(2)	(5)	(6)	(7^1)	(7^2)

'He was expecting him impatiently all day.'

The contrast between zero in this sentence and a preposition (as in the sentence quoted above) is generally used to express *aktionsart* differences, cf. *hun skød pianisten* 'she shot the piano player' (telic) vs *hun skød på pianisten* 'she shot at the piano player' (atelic); or *han skrev en bog* 'he wrote a book' (telic) vs *han skrev på en bog* 'he was writing a book' (atelic).

'Non-declarative' and 'Subordinate Clause' Word Order

The topological schema sketched so far is traditionally associated with declarative main clauses. There is a variant of this topological schema, which is associated with non-declarative main clauses, and a different schema associated with subordinate clauses.

The traditional subordinate clause schema distinguishes itself from the schema discussed so far on three counts. First, the connector position can be filled by both coordinating and subordinating connectors, in that order. Second, pragmatic marking by placement of other elements than subjects into field (1) is excluded. Third, the adverbials placed in position (4) in the schema above are placed before the finite verb. This results in a new schema:

og	at	han	ikke	havde	set	ham	i går
(0^1)	(0^2)	(1)	(2)	(3)	(5)	(6)	(7)

(lit.) 'and that he hadn't seen him yesterday'

What is problematic with the traditional view that associates this second schema with subordinate clauses and the first one with main clauses is not only that the unrestricted main clause schema only applies to some main clauses (declaratives and *wh*-questions), while other main clauses (imperatives and yes/no questions) block the filling of position (1) which has to be empty. (In declarative main clauses, position (1) has to be filled obligatorily. In *wh*-questions, it is the *wh*-word that fills the position.) The problem is rather that the first schema also occurs in subordinate clauses (complement clauses introduced with *at* 'that'), while its variant with empty position (1) appears in conditional clauses without connector: *kommer han, går jeg* 'if he comes, I'll leave'. To complicate things further, there is a class of emotional and exclamatory main clauses that has subordinate clause topology as in:

Bare	hun	ikke	taber	den.
(0)	(1)	(2)	(3)	(4)

'If only she doesn't lose it.'

These sentences all have some connector; sentence adverbs like *måske* 'maybe', or frozen verbal elements like *sæt* 'given [that]' in position (1) but negation as well as other sentence adverbs are placed before the finite verb as in subordinate clauses. (Some sentence adverbs like *desværre* 'regrettably' or *næppe* 'hardly' which only occur with declarative sentence mood and whose occurrence in subordinate clauses is restricted, do not appear in this type of main clause either.)

Keeping in mind that both 'main clause' topology (both with and without filled position (1)) and 'subordinate' clause topology can be found both in independent and dependent clauses, we can chart the possible combinations as in Table 10.5. The traditional view is justified by the fact that the two clause types marked in bold are by far the most common ones. Examples like these fit with the traditional assumption that typological schemata code syntactic clause types (root vs constituent clauses). But the other types exist, too. To talk about main-clause and subordinate-clause topology is therefore a misnomer and it is more appropriate to ask what functions the three topological schemata A^1, A^2 and B have, if they do not code syntactic clause types. It appears that type A^2 and B have in common that they represent non-declarative sentence moods: the imperative, the interrogative, and the emotive/exclamatory in main clauses. Type A^1, on the other hand, represents (in main clauses) either a straightforward declarative, or a *wh*-interrogative. Subordinate clauses do not have independent illocutionary force, so it would be natural to expect them to have sentence types A^2 or B, but after certain verbs of assertion like *sige* 'say', or evidence expressions *det er tydeligt* 'it's clear', *det viser sig* 'it emerges', the illocutionary force of the main clause carries over to the subordinate clause which motivates the use of the declarative schema A^1 also in subordinate clauses.

The open question is why *wh*-questions, although non-declarative, follow topological schema A^1. If one doesn't consider it accidental that *wh*-questions share their topological model with declaratives (in which case the topological schemata did not represent sentence moods, but were assigned to syntactic and semantic sentence types in a random fashion), one could argue that there is at least one illocutionary property that declaratives share with *wh*-interrogatives. *Wh*-interrogatives presuppose the truth of some open clause for some variable assignment; they do not question the truth of the clause but demand a variable assignment for a clause whose truth is presupposed under some assignment. In this sense they share some sentence

Table 10.5 Danish clause types and topological patterns

	A^1 'Main clause' topology	A^2 'Main clause' topology without position (1)	B 'Subordinate clause' topology
Main clauses	Declarative: **Klaus er ikke kommet**. 'Klaus has not come'	Imperative: *Kom ikke hjem!* 'Don't come home!'	Emotive-exclamatory: *Gid Klaus ikke var kommet!* 'I wish Klaus hadn't come!'
	Wh-questions: *Hvem er ikke kommet?* 'Who has not come?'	Yes/no question: *Kommer han ikke?* 'Is he not coming?'	
Subordinate clauses	Complements of declarative verbs: *(Hun sagde) at han er ikke kommet i dag.* '(She said) that he hasn't come today'	Conditional: *Er han ikke kommet, (bliver jeg sur.)* 'If he hasn't come, I'll turn sour'	Complement: *(Han tror) at Klaus ikke er kommet i dag.* '(He thinks) that Klaus hasn't come today'
			Adverbial: *Når Klaus ikke er kommet, plejer han at være syg.* 'When Klaus hasn't come, he is usually ill'

mood with declaratives. Of course there is no reason why a language has to treat declaratives and *wh*-questions alike; but if it does (as Danish does) it makes sense.

Another question is what the motivation is for a different treatment of topological patterns A^2 and B, namely, whether they can be assigned to two distinguishable, but internally consistent classes of sentence mood. This does not seem to be the case. But it has to be noted that type B is a relatively new development. Superficially, the placement of negation and certain adverbials in a different position from clauses with assertive mood could remind one of the finite-verb-final (SOV) pattern in subordinate clauses in Dutch, German and Old English. But apart from not being exclusively associated with subordination at all, this pattern is not a remnant of an older, more general topological pattern that has survived in subordinate clauses alone. On the contrary, it is a relatively new development. In this sense, schemata A^2 and B could be said to represent historically different stages of language development (B being younger than A^2) and not a mood distinction within the non-declarative illocutionary class. Historically, A^2 occurred not only (as today) with the imperative, but also with other, now obsolete, inflectional characterizations of mood, like the optative.

Pragmatic Marking in Pre-verbal Position

Previously it was said that position (1) has the function of pragmatic marking. 'Marking' is to be understood both as low pragmatic prominence and as high pragmatic prominence; placement in position (1) can indeed have both functions. Low pragmatic prominence is typical for discourse-induced, i.e. given topics, and very often these topics are found in position (1), such as anaphoric pronouns, time and place adverbials denoting a 'setting', temporal adverbial clauses, and conditionals: *men han kunne ikke huske det* 'but he couldn't remember that', *i går var hun syg* 'yesterday, she was ill', *i Odense drikkes der Albani* 'in Odense Albani is drunk', *når jeg ringer, er hun nok klar* 'when I ring, she's probably ready', *hvis han husker det, skriver han nok* 'if he remembers to, he'll write'. In combination with marked stress, position (1) is for contrast: *Peter så jeg ikke, men Hans* 'Peter I didn't see, but Hans', *Japan er et ørige, men det er Korea ikke* 'Japan is an island empire, but Korea isn't'. Only in the latter case – which resembles the 'external topics' talked about in Functional grammar – does placement in position (1) resemble English topicalization.

By contrast, position (1) is not the place for another kind of pragmatically marked constituents, namely, focus constituents. In *jeg har vundet i lotto* 'I won in the pools', *i lotto* 'in the pools' is pragmatically marked as focus, but a placement in position (1) would sound awkward, *i lotto har jeg vundet*, unless some continuation follows (that is, unless some contrast is involved). The only focus elements allowed in position (1) are *wh*-words in *wh*-questions.

Dummy der *in Pre-verbal Position*

There are clauses that do not contain pragmatically marked (i.e. given or contrasted) elements. If these clauses are in the declarative sentence mood, they have to follow topological pattern A^1 and therefore have to have a filled position (1) lest they be reinterpreted as non-declaratives. In some of these cases, namely, in intransitive main clauses with indefinite subjects, a dummy *der* [dɒ] (phonetically reduced from the distal deictic adverb *der* [dę̇ːʁ] 'there') is introduced in position (1) of the clause. This is the case in sentences that contain only non-presupposed material, i.e. so-called all-new sentences, for example: *der kom en pige ind i huset* 'a girl came into the house' (lit. 'there came a girl into the house'), or in presentative existentials like *der findes mange smitsomme sygdomme* 'there are many contagious diseases'. The dummy *der* can not be used as a position (1) filler in transitive clauses nor in clauses with definite subjects.

Subordinate-clause Constituents Raised to Pre-verbal Position

What is placed in position (1) of a main clause can be a constituent of a subordinate clause, as long as it is not the subject of that clause since a subject cannot be removed from a finite clause. Thus *ham ved jeg du stoler på* 'him I know you trust' shows the following topological patterns for main and subordinate clause:

	Ham$_i$	ved	jeg	du	stoler	på e$_i$.
A^1	(1)	(2)	(3)	(6)		
B				(1)	(2)	(7)

That extraction in Danish works in a less limited fashion than in English (not to speak of languages like Dutch and German) has been noted and discussed by linguists.

Subordination

From what just has been said it has become clear that there is no particular pattern of clause topology that distinguishes main and subordinate clauses except for the lack of possibilities for the pragmatic marking of constituents (which is a consequence of the lack of independent illocutionary force rather than of subordination *per se*), and the presence of subordination markers. Finite subordination markers are the usual set of adverbial clause-introducing connectors like *når* '(always) when', *hvis* 'if', *da* '(then) when' (Ger. *als*), *fordi* 'because', *selv om* 'even though', as well as the complementizers *at* 'that' and *om* 'whether'. Infinite subordination markers are the infinitive marker *at* 'to' as well as a number of complex subordinators of the type preposition + *at*, e.g. *uden at* 'without' and *for at* 'in order to'. It should be noted that the finite complementizer *at* and the infinitive marker *at* are spelled the same but are pronounced differently: the former is [að̩, a] while the latter is [ʌ] and thus phonetically identical with a reduced (not stressed) form of the coordinating connector *og* [ʌu̯, ʌ] 'and'.

It was mentioned above that *wh*-words like *hvem* 'who', *hvor* 'where' or *hvorfor* 'why' are the only focus elements that can be placed into position (1) in sentence schema A^1. In subordinate clauses, position (1) is the subject position and not a position for pragmatically marked material. Accordingly, *wh*-words in indirect questions are placed in the connector position (0). This goes even for *wh*-words that are subjects, which leaves an open position (1) to be filled by the dummy *der*:

	De	vidste	ikke	hvem	der	var	kommet
A^1	(1)	(2)	(4)	(6)			
B				(0)	(1)	(3)	(4)

'They didn't know who had come.'

Thus one can distinguish between *de spurgte hvem Peter var* 'they asked who Peter was' where *hvem* 'who' is predicative and *Peter* 'Peter' subject, and *de spurgte hvem der var Peter* 'they asked which (of them) was Peter', where *hvem* is subject but not in subject position and has to be followed by a dummy *der* in position (1).

Relative Clauses

Relative clauses are introduced by the relative particle *som*: *jeg kender en mand som du ville elske at møde* 'I know a man that you would love to meet', *jeg kender en mand som hans søster har været gift med* 'I know a man that his sister has been married to'. If the subject is the target of the relative clause, *som* can take its place: *jeg kender en mand som bor i Helsingør* 'I know a man that lives in Elsinore'. There are also *som*-less relative clauses: *jeg kender en mand du ville elske at møde* 'I know a man you would love to meet', *jeg kender en mand hans søster har været gift med* 'I know a man his sister has been married to'. In their case, the subject position has to be filled with *der*: *jeg kender en mand der bor i Helsingør* 'I know a man that lives in Elsinore'. (Sometimes this *der* is reanalysed as a relative particle, although it is not different from the usual dummy *der* that fills otherwise empty subject positions.)

This applies at least to the written language. In the spoken language and especially in the dialects, *som* can be followed by *der*, where *som* is the subordinator in position (0) and *der* the subject dummy in position (1). Furthermore, like all clauses that follow schema B, relative clauses can contain a pleonastic marker *at* which only occurs with non-declarative sentence mood, as in *jeg kender en karl, som at der har tjent hos ham i fjor* 'I know a farmhand that worked for him last year'. This marker can stand alone as a relative marker as well, as in this example in Bornholm dialect: *brygjninjen va et arbeaj a kvinjfolken skulle passa* (lit.) 'brewing was a work that women should mind'.

This pleonastic *at* occurs in all examples of non-declarative sentence mood, such as in temporal clauses (with *ad* as the pleonastic marker; the dialect is from Skåne): *å då når ad lannsväjjen ble makadamiserad, så ble dänn rättad* ... 'and then when the road was macadamized, then it was straightened ...' or in exclamatory main clauses: *mon ikke at 'vi kunne få startet en slags indsamlingskomité?* 'perhaps we could start a kind of money collecting committee?'

10.5   Lexis

Structure of the Lexicon

It is assumed that Danish has about 2,000 non-compound words inherited from common Indo-European most of which are still in common use in Modern Danish; of these about 1,200 are nouns, 180 adjectives, more than 500 verbs and about 100 words belonging to other word classes. An additional 1,200 words, the lion's share of which are nouns, can be traced back to the common North Germanic period, and about 300 to East North Germanic.

Throughout history, this core stock has been supplemented by compounding, derivation and loans. The first wave of loans came with Christianity from Greek and Latin, usually by way of the languages of the missionaries (Old English, Old Frisian, Old Saxon), and the first loan translations (like the names of most days of the week, cf. *torsdag* 'Thor's day' from Latin *dies iovis*). During the Middle Ages, more Latin loans came into Danish, most of them by way of Middle Low German which also was the major source of loans during this period. Among these loans there was not only a number of nouns that were imported together with new cultural artifacts and institutions like *mur* 'wall' (from Lat. *murus*), *bukser* 'trousers' (from MLG *buxe*) and *krig* 'war' (from MLG *krich*), but also particles and adverbs like *dog* 'though', *ganske* 'quite' and *jo* 'after all'. In older Modern Danish (1500–1700) loans came mostly from High German and French, but in specific areas also from other languages (like words for sea travel from Dutch and Low German or for banking from Italian). After 1700 the first purist attempts can be noted, which very often replace French, Latin and Greek words by loan translations from German (an area in case is grammatical terminology). English loans are rare before 1870, but have become very common in the twentieth century. Their number is still not very big compared with the totality of older loans from Low German and French, but they are extremely visible since many of them, in contradistinction to practically all other loans, are not integrated phonetically and morphologically. As far as spelling is concerned, the degree of integration is low, far lower than e.g. in Norwegian. Norwegian spellings like *sjåfør* 'driver' where Danish has *chauffør* provoke smiles from Danes, and a heated debate in 1986 known as the 'Mayonnaise War' concerning the spelling of loans showed that a large part of the Danish public still considers the foreign spelling of loans as part and parcel of erudition and refinement.

Compounds and derivations make up the rest of the vocabulary. Compounding is very productive and structurally quite unrestricted; multiple compounds are construed freely especially in administrative language like *Kildeskattedirektoratet* 'Internal Revenue Service', (lit. 'source tax directorate'). Compared with other Germanic languages, it should be noted that often where, for example, Dutch would use derivational processes, Danish has compounds, cf. Danish *velsmagende* 'tasty' (lit. 'well tasting') as opposed to Dutch *smakelijk*, or Danish *småkager* 'cookies' (lit. 'little cakes') as opposed to Dutch *koekjes*. Actually, there is no bound diminutive morpheme in Danish, while *små* 'little', a free form, can form compounds not only with nouns, but also with adjectives (*småskør* 'a little bit crazy'), participles (*småfornærmet* 'slightly insulted') and verbs (*småfnise* 'to snicker' (lit. 'to grin a bit')). Derivative morphology is rich but only a few bound forms are truly productive like the Agent suffix *-er* (possibly itself a loan from Latin *-arius*) in *arbejder* 'worker' < *arbejde* 'to work'. Other bound morphemes like *-me/-ne* that form intransitive verbs from adjectives as in *rødme* 'blush' < *rød* 'red', or *-se* that forms transitive verbs as in *rense* 'to clean' < *ren* 'clean', are no longer productive.

Numerals

Finally, Danish numerals are worth mentioning in a chapter about the lexicon. They are puzzling to all non-Danish Scandinavians and create problems for non-Danes in inter-Scandinavian semi-communication.

Danish numerals up to, but not including, 50 follow a very common pattern in which inherited Germanic roots figure with only modest irregularities:

en, et	'one'
to	'two'
tre	'three'
. . .	
elleve	'eleven'
tolv	'twelve'
tretten	'thirteen'
fjorten	'fourteen'
. . .	
tyve	'twenty'
enogtyve	'twenty-one'
. . .	
tredive	'thirty'
fyrre	'forty'

It does not come as a surprise that the number one has two distinct forms for common and neuter gender; in phone numbers, etc. both forms are used, while counting is usually *en, to, tre.* . . . It is the tens from 50 on that are difficult for non-Danes. Here Danish has replaced the common North Germanic numerals by a vigesimal system, but unlike the French system that actually counts in twenties for numbers above 60, the Danish system counts in tens constructed from a base of twenty by multiplication with elements of the type known from German *anderthalb* '1½' and (obsolete) *dritthalb* '2½'. Thus 50 is *halvtredsindstyve* from *halv tredje sinde tyve* (lit.) 'half-third times twenty', 60 is *tresindstyve* (lit.) 'three times twenty', 70 is *halvfjerdsindstyve* (lit.) 'half-fourth times twenty', 80 is *firsindstyve* 'four times twenty' and finally 90, *halvfemsindstyve* 'half-fifth times twenty'. Except for the construction of ordinals like *halvfjersindstyvende* '70th', the cardinals are now usually shortened to *halvtreds, tres, halvfjerds, firs, halvfems,* a practice that arose at the end of the last century, originally in quoting prices: *to kroner halvfjerdsindstyve øre* '2 kroner 70 øre' > *to kroner halvfjerds,* and has spread from there. Ordinals, which have no short form, are usually avoided. Thus one would say *halvfjerdsårsfødselsdag* '70 years' birthday' rather than *halvfjersindstyvende fødselsdag* '70th birthday'. In some contexts (but mostly restricted to the writing out of amounts on personal cheques) 'Scandinavian' numerals are used like *otti* '80', *niti* '90', and even *toti* '20'.

Further Reading

Basbøll, H. and Wagner, J. (1985) *Kontrastive Phonologie des Deutschen und Dänischen. Segmentale Wortphonologie und -phonetik*, Tübingen: Niemeyer.

Brink, L. and Lund, J. (1975) *Dansk Rigsmål*, 2 vols, Copenhagen: Gyldendal.

Diderichsen, P. (1946) *Elementær dansk grammatik*, Copenhagen: Gyldendal.

—— (1964) *Essentials of Danish grammar*, Copenhagen: Akademisk Forlag.

Grønnum, N. (1992) *The Groundworks of Danish Intonation: An Introduction*, Copenhagen: Museum Tusculanum Press.

Hansen, Aa. (1967) *Moderne dansk*, 3 vols, Copenhagen: Grafisk Forlag.

Hansen, E. and Heltoft, L. (in preparation) *Grammatik over det danske sprog*, Copenhagen: Munksgaard.

Hansen, E. and Riemann, N. (1979) *Bibliografi over moderne dansk rigssprog 1850–1978*, Copenhagen: Gjellerup.

Mikkelsen, K. (1911) *Dansk Ordföjningslære*. Copenhagen: Lehmann & Stage, repr. Copenhagen: Hans Reitzel, 1975.

Ringgaard, K. (1973) *Danske dialekter. En kortfattet oversigt*, 2nd edn, Copenhagen: Akademisk Forlag.

Skautrup, P. (1944–70) *Det danske sprogs historie*, 4 vols plus index volume, Copenhagen: Gyldendal.

Spore, P. (1965) *La langue danoise. Phonétique et grammaire contemporaines*, Copenhagen: Akademisk Forlag.

Wivel, H. G. (1901) *Synspunkter for dansk sproglære*, Copenhagen: Det Nordiske Forlag.

11 German

Peter Eisenberg

11.1 Introduction

Modern German is the supra-regional standard of a connected language area in Central Europe. It has evolved as a written language. The so-called standard pronunciation is and has always been strongly influenced by the written standard. All users of German can understand the standard pronunciation, the vast majority of them can write and read standard orthography, but only a minority uses the standard pronunciation in everyday speech.

The main isoglosses in the German language area run from west to east, dividing it into three main dialect areas called – going from north to south – Low German, Central German and Upper German. The basis for this classification is the extent to which the dialects followed the Old High German Consonant Shift, which led to the separation of Old High German (sixth to eleventh century) from the other Germanic languages. It changed the voiceless stops [p, t, k] depending on the context either to the affricates (p͡f, t͡s, k͡x] or to the fricatives [f, s, ç–x]. The voiced stops [b, d, g] became devoiced to [p, t, k]. According to the traditional theory, the Consonant Shift reached completion in the Upper German dialects, it occurred only partly in the Central German dialects, whereas the Low German dialects in the north did not follow it at all. The modern standard is said to be based mainly on a dialect of East Central German (*Meißner Deutsch*).

German is the official language or one of the official languages in Austria, Germany, Liechtenstein, Luxembourg and Switzerland. In these countries it has approximately 90 million users. Another 2 million live in western European countries (Belgium, Alsace-Lorraine/France, South Tyrol/Italy), and the same number is found in Eastern Europe (Poland, Czech Republic, Slovakia, Hungary, Croatia, Slovenia, Rumania, and in the republics of the former Soviet Union). Outside Europe we have to mention the minorities in the Americas and in Australia, formed by immigrants mainly during the nineteenth and twentieth century, and some remainders from the colonial epoch in Namibia and South Africa.

As a foreign language, German is learned worldwide by an estimated 18 million people, in most cases as second foreign language competing with

349

French, Spanish, Russian and Chinese. The biggest groups of learners are found in Russia, France, Japan, South Korea, and in several East European countries. Since the unification of both Germanies the number of people learning the language has been growing steadily.

11.2   Phonology

In what follows we will concentrate on the central phonological system, i.e. on the sound structure of native words. It makes a considerable difference whether one takes into account the whole range of structural phenomena appearing in non-native words. For the sake of clarity, we will restrict ourselves to some indication of how non-native words are related to the central system. Most problems to be discussed have to do with the interaction of phonology in the narrower sense of the term (distinctiveness) and phonetics (variation of sounds). To avoid confusion, we normally use the more neutral phonetic notation ([ ]). Phonological notation (/ /) is restricted to discussions of allophony.

Vowels

German vowels are divided into two main classes depending on whether they can or cannot occur in stressed syllables. In articulated speech, the latter class comprises only schwa ([ə]). Phonetically schwa is a central mid lax vowel in unstressed syllables. Being restricted to this position, it does not stand in opposition to any other vowel. The vowels which occur in stressed as well as in unstressed syllables exhibit the full range of distinctive features only in stressed syllables. According to their distributional and inherent properties, they again have to be divided into two classes, namely tense vowels and lax vowels.

Tense Vowels

These vowels occur in open syllables as in [fʀoː] (*froh*, 'glad'), [ʃuː] (*Schuh*, 'shoe') as well as in syllables with one consonant in the coda (henceforth 'simple coda') as in [ʃʀoːt] (*Schrot*, 'grist'), [huːt] (*Hut*, 'hat'). There are only very few simplex words with a tense vowel and a complex coda like, for instance, [moːnt] (*Mond*, 'moon'). If a tense vowel occurs in a stressed syllable, it is phonetically long.

Table 11.1 presents the system of tense vowels, giving one example for every position of the chart. The system distinguishes two categories of backness and three categories of height. Rounding is only distinctive for front vowels ([i – y], [e – ø]). Back vowels are differentiated by both tongue height and rounding.

There is a special relation between the rounded back and the rounded front vowels. A rounded front vowel is called the umlaut of its back counterpart. So [y] is the umlaut of [u], and [ø] is the umlaut of [o]. Umlaut has to be

Table 11.1   The system of tense vowels

	Front Unrounded	Rounded	Back
High	i *Vieh* [fiː] 'cattle'	y *früh* [fʀyː] 'early'	u *Schuh* [ʃuː] 'shoe'
Mid	e *Schnee* [ʃneː] 'snow'	ø *Bö* [bøː] 'squall'	o *froh* [fʀoː] 'glad'
Low			ɑ *nah* [nɑː] 'near'

understood as a morphophonemic term. It plays an important role in inflectional morphology (e.g. [floː] 'flea' – [fløːə] 'fleas'; [kuː] 'cow' – [kyːə] 'cows') as well as in derivations ([fʀoː] 'glad' – [fʀøːliç] 'glad'; [natuːʀ] 'nature' – [natyːʀliç] 'natural'). Yet it has to be emphasized that [ø] and [y] also occur independently of their function as umlaut. There are many words like [ʃøːn] (*schön* 'beautiful') or [fʀyː] (*früh* 'early') which are no longer related to units like [ʃoːn] and [fʀuː]. In Old High German, the umlaut vowels always had a morphonological basis. In Modern German this is not the case though the special relationship between such pairs is still reflected in the writing system (‹u – ü›, ‹o – ö›).

Most phonological descriptions of German have one more tense vowel, namely [æ]. This vowel is situated in height between [e] and [ɑ], so it can be integrated into the system by distinguishing four instead of three degrees of height. We do not accept [æ] as a vowel of the phonological system proper, however, because its occurrence in standard pronunciation is highly restricted. It has a functional load in pairs like [seːə – sæːə]; [geːbə – gæːbə]; [neːmə – næːmə], orthographically ‹sehe – sähe›, ‹gebe – gäbe›, ‹nehme – nähme›. The first member of these pairs is a form of the present indicative of the verbs *sehen* 'to see', *geben* 'to give' and *nehmen* 'to take' respectively, the second member is a form of the preterite subjunctive. [æ] is used here to differentiate the forms in question, i.e. it bears morphological information.

Many phonologists suppose that [æ] occurs also as umlaut of [ɑ] in pairs like *Hahn* 'rooster' – *Hähne* 'roosters' or *Gefahr* 'danger' – *gefährlich* 'dangerous'. This supposition seems to be induced by the spellings of these words. It is true that the grapheme ‹ä› has been introduced into the writing system to mark the umlaut, but the difference between [æ] and [e] has never been established. The pronunciation [hæːnə], [gɛfæːʀliç] is still favoured by normative pronunciation dictionaries. Yet a realistically conducted pair test reveals that even in cases like *Beeren* 'berries' – *Bären* 'bears' or *Ehre* 'honour' – *Ähre* 'ear' the average speaker's pronunciation is [beːʀən; eːʀə]. This point is of some importance since the systems of tense vowels and lax vowels turn out to be parallel only if [æ] is not recognized as an element of the phonological system proper.

Table 11.2   The system of lax vowels

	Front Unrounded	Rounded	Back
High	ɪ *Kind* [kɪnt] 'child'	ʏ *hübsch* [hʏpʃ] 'pretty'	ʊ *Burg* [bʊʀk] 'castle'
Mid	ɛ *Geld* [gɛlt] 'money'	œ *Mönch* [mœnç] 'monk'	ɔ *Gold* [gɔlt] 'gold'
Low		a *Wand* [vant] 'wall'	

Lax Vowels

Lax vowels occur in syllables with simple and complex coda. They never appear in open, stressed syllables. The system of lax vowels is represented in Table 11.2. The only real structural difference with respect to the system of tense vowels is the position of the [a].

It is uncontroversial that the German vowels constitute two systems which are at least approximately parallel. Yet there is an old and ongoing discussion as to whether the two systems have to be distinguished by tenseness or by length. In stressed syllables, a tense vowel is long while a lax vowel is short, so that either pair of features could be taken as distinctive. The long–short distinction permits a direct and natural correlation of syllable weight and vowel length: the long vowel as nucleus combines only with an empty or a short (i.e. simple) coda, while the short vowel can also combine with long (i.e. complex) codas. Nucleus and coda tend to complement each other in length. On the other hand, the long–short distinction can only be made in stressed syllables, while the tense–lax distinction carries over also to unstressed ones. In polysyllabic non-native words in particular we often find short tense besides short lax vowels. For example the first syllables in [modɛrn] (*modern*), [motiːf] (*Motiv*) have a short tense vowel while in [mɔnɑːdə] (*Monade*), [mɔnaʊʀɑːl] (*monaural*) they have a short lax vowel. The problem is that in all these cases tenseness is not really distinctive, i.e. we can say, and in fact do sometimes say, [mɔdɛrn], [mɔtiːf] without changing anything semantically or even producing a really marked pronunciation. We cannot go further into this difficult problem here and have decided to make use of the tense–lax distinction in this chapter.

Schwa

Schwa is the only vowel restricted to unstressed syllables, i.e. schwa never occurs in monosyllabic words. In simplicia, its prototypical occurrence is as nucleus of the last syllable in bisyllabic words, e.g. [ʃuːlə] (*Schule* 'school'), [haməʀ] (*Hammer* 'hammer'), [ʃtiːfəl] (*Stiefel* 'boot'), [knoːtən] (*Knoten* 'knot'), [aːtəm] (*Atem* 'breath'). In this type of word, the syllable with schwa never has a complex coda. The coda is either empty or it consists of a single consonant, which is a nasal or a liquid ([ʀ, l, n, m]). The consonant preceding schwa is in most cases of lower sonority than the one in the coda, therefore these two consonants could never be connected to form a coda by themselves ([mʀ], [fl], [tn], [tm] in our examples). For this reason, schwa has been understood as epenthetic.

Consonants

There is no position in German words in which every consonant can occur. To reconstruct the system of consonants, we have to consider at least two positions: (1) word-initially before vowel as in [bax] (*Bach* 'brook') and (2) word-internally between lax vowel and schwa as in [tʀɛpə] (*Treppe* 'staircase'). Of the 20 consonants, 17 show up in position (1) and 15 in position (2). The overlap is 12 (see Table 11.3). From data like these, the system of consonants can be reconstructed as in Table 11.4.

Most phonological descriptions of German make use of features referring to places of articulation (bilabial, dental/alveolar, palatal, velar, glottal) instead of those referring to articulators. We do not intend to make this a major issue but would simply like to point out that for all phonological rules it is sufficient to have four instead of the usual five categories and that nearly all theories about 'feature geometry' operate with categories referring to articulators.

Table 11.3   The inventory of consonants

Position 1	Position 2
[pʊŋkt] *Punkt* 'point'	[lapən] *Lappen* 'rag'
[taːk] *Tag* 'day'	[latə] *Latte* 'lath'
[kint] *Kind* 'child'	[bakə] *Backe* 'cheek'
[ʔuːʀ] *Uhr* 'clock'	——
[bal] *Ball* 'ball'	[ɛbə] *Ebbe* 'ebb'
[dax] *Dach* 'roof'	[vɪdəʀ] *Widder* 'ram'
[gɪʃt] *Gischt* 'foam'	[ʀɔgən] *Roggen* 'rye'
[fɪʃ] *Fisch* 'fish'	[afə] *Affe* 'monkey'
——	[vasəʀ] *Wasser* 'water'
[ʃaːl] *Schal* 'scarf'	[aʃə] *Asche* 'ash'
——	[zɪçəl] *Sichel* 'sickle'
[huːt] *Hut* 'hut'	——
[vant] *Wand* 'wall'	——
[zant] *Sand* 'sand'	——
[jaːkt] *Jagd* 'hunt'	——
[man] *Mann* 'man'	[haməʀ] *Hammer* 'hammer'
[naxt] *Nacht* 'night'	[kanə] *Kanne* 'can'
——	[lʊŋə] *Lunge* 'lungs'
[lʊft] *Luft* 'air'	[hœlə] *Hölle* 'hell'
[ʀɪŋ] *Ring* 'ring'	[kʀalə] *Kralle* 'claw'

			Labial	Coronal	Dorsal	Glottal
obstruent {	plosive {	voiceless	p	t	k	?
		voiced	b	d	g	
	fricative {	voiceless	f	s, ʃ	ç, x	h
		voiced	v	z	j	
sonorant {		nasal	m	n	ŋ	
		oral		l	ʀ	

Presented as in Table 11.4, the system of consonants appears to be fairly balanced. Most gaps can be directly related to articulatory facts. To separate the voiceless coronal fricatives [s] and [ʃ], we need one more pair of features, for instance the *SPE*-feature [± distributive].

There are, of course, many debatable points concerning the consonant system, only some of which will be raised here.

/ç, x/

The voiceless back (dorsal or palatal) fricative [ç] has a positional variant [x]. [x] occurs after low and back vowels, [ç] after consonants and all other vowels. So we have [kʀax] (*Krach* 'noise'), [buːx] (*Buch* 'book') but [pɛç] (*Pech* 'pitch'), [ʃtɪç] (*Stich* 'sting') and [dɔlç] (*Dolch* 'dagger'). Neither [ç] nor [x] occurs in word-initial position in the native vocabulary. [ç] and [x] can be understood as allophones of each other in the classical sense. There is still a controversy about which of the two is unmarked, whether they really are in complementary distribution, and whether other sounds like [h] or [k] have to be regarded as variants of one or both of them.

Semivowels and Glides

In Standard German we have three closing diphthongs which can best be represented as consisting of a vowel proper followed by a 'non-syllabic vowel': [taɪ̯ç] (*Teich* 'pool'), [baʊ̯x] (*Bauch* 'belly'), [frɔɪ̯nt] (*Freund* 'friend'). Distinguishing vowels as non-syllabic means that they are not part of the nucleus. From a phonotactic point of view the second element of a diphthong is in the position of a consonantal element since it is part of the coda.

A coronal glide appears in non-native words like *Nation*, transcribed as [natsjoːn] according to the IPA. Since the IPA does not distinguish this glide from the respective fricative, it is perhaps more appropriate to use a transcription like [natsi̯on]. A bilabial glide (more or less rounded) appears in non-native words like [leːgwan] (*Leguan*). The same glide probably occurs in second position in the onset of the syllable like in [kwɑːl] (*Oual* 'pain'). Another glide [ɐ] can appear as realization of /R/ (see below).

Articulation of /R/

The question of how the ʀ-sounds are best described phonologically is not yet settled. For a realistic and phonetically sound analysis, we have to distinguish two sets of contexts. The first set comprises /R/ in the onset and in internuclear position. Here it can be either a coronal sonorant [r] (rolled or flapped) or an uvular sonorant [ʀ] (equally rolled or flapped). These variants are supposed to stand in free variation, so we have [roːt]/[ʀoːt] (*rot* 'red') and [eːrə]/[eːʀə] (*Ehre* 'honour'). The second set of contexts comprises /R/ in pre-consonantal and in word-final position following schwa. In pre-consonantal position we normally have so-called vocalic /R/, which can be represented as [ɐ], e.g. [vɪɐt] (*Wirt* 'host'), [vʊɐf] (*Wurf* 'throw'). In word-final position we also have [ɐ], but here it is vocalic, derived from schwa + [ʀ] as in [ʀuːdəʀ], [ʀuːdɐ] (*Ruder* 'scull'). Note that word final [ɐ] stands in opposition to schwa, so we have minimal pairs like [faːzə – faːzɐ] (*Phase* 'phase' – *Faser* 'fibre').

Affricates

Sequences of plosives and homorganic fricatives like [t͡s], [p͡f] and sometimes [t͡ʃ] are analysed as monosegmental by some authors. Besides phonetic considerations, there are in principle two types of arguments for deciding this question. First, we can ask whether the affricates behave phonotactically like one consonant or like two, and second, we can ask whether it is possible to separate the parts of the affricates by the familiar procedures of segmentation. Both lines of reasoning lead to different results for each of the clusters in different positions.

Syllable Structure and Syllabic Structure

Syllable Structure

The syllable in German can be rather complex. If we restrict ourselves to monosyllabic words without internal morphological boundaries, we find syllables with three consonants in the onset and up to four consonants in the coda.

The onset is built up of one, two, or three consonants. Figure 11.1 shows the combinatorial possibilities of the onset with two consonants (obstruent plus sonorant).

Two different types can be distinguished for the onset with three consonants. The first consists of affricate plus sonorant like in [p͡flɪçt] (*pflicht* 'duty') or [t͡svɛk] (*Zweck* 'purpose'). The second type begins with [ʃ] plus plosive like in [ʃplɪtəʀ] (*Splitter* 'shiver') and [ʃtʀɪç] (*Strich* 'stroke'). The coda is more complex than the onset and shows some significant structural differences. As we have already seen, the coda interacts with the nucleus with

Figure 11.1 Onset with two consonants

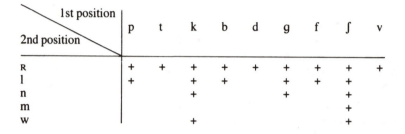

1st position / 2nd position	p	t	k	b	d	g	f	ʃ	v
R	+	+	+	+	+	+	+	+	+
l	+		+	+		+	+	+	
n			+			+		+	
m								+	
w			+					+	

respect to length, whereas the onset does not. The coda with two consonants does not show the combinatorial restrictions of the corresponding onset. Instead, every consonant in the first position of the coda also occurs in its second position. The best-known property of the coda in German is that it can not contain any voiced obstruent. The consequence of this restriction is a considerable amount of allomorphic variation called 'final devoicing' (*Auslautverhärtung*). So we have the form [hʊndə] (*Hunde* 'dogs') besides the form [hʊnt] (*Hund* 'dog'). That final devoicing indeed affects the whole coda and not just its final position can be seen in cases like [zaːgən – zaːkst] (*sagen* 'to say' – *sagst* 'you say').

The overall syllable schema of German can be represented as in Figure 11.2.

Syllabic Structure
The syllabic structure of a phonological word is its segmentation into syllables. The syllabic structure of a phonological word is given with the syllable boundaries contained by it.

In simplex words, syllabification in German conforms to the universally

Figure 11.2 Syllable schema of German

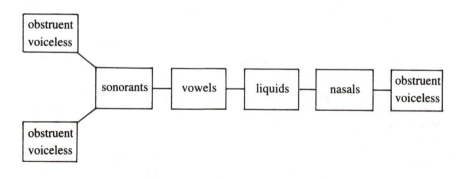

preferred syllable contact law: if there are several internuclear consonants, the one with the lowest sonority is the first element of the second syllable. This rule gives us the correct syllabification for words like [boː.dən], [fal.tə], [kan.tə], [kaʀ.pfən]. This general rule has to be complemented by a language-specific one, which states that a stressed syllable with a lax vowel cannot have an empty coda. From this it follows that the internuclear consonant in words like [halə], [kanə], [mʊtəʀ], [bagəʀ] belongs to both syllables: [halə], [kanə], [mʊtəʀ], bagəʀ]. The 'ambisyllabic consonant' after lax vowels is a widespread phenomenon in German.

Word Accent

Word accent in German is mainly determined by the syllabic structure and by the morphological structure of the word. For phonetic reasons we do not operate with more than two levels of accent, which we call 'primary' (´) and 'secondary' (`) accent. Syllables with schwa as nucleus can never be stressed.

Non-derived Words

In non-derived words with more than one syllable the accent is placed on the last syllable which can be stressed, but never on the last syllable of the word. Within a paradigm (set of inflected word forms) the accent never changes its position.

Let us consider some examples. In bisyllabic words like *Régen* 'rain', *Léiter* 'ladder', *Núdel* 'noodle' the first syllable has to be stressed of course. The same holds for inflected forms of monosyllabic base forms like *Kínd* 'child' – *Kínder* 'children' or *stárk* 'strong' – *stárker* 'stronger'. It also follows directly from the rules stated above that in words with bisyllabic base forms like *Héring* 'herring' and *Árbeit* 'work' the first syllable is stressed (though the last does not have schwa as nucleus). Consequently, the tri-syllabic inflected forms of these words have two unstressed syllables (*Héringe, Árbeiten*). In three-syllable base forms like *Forélle* 'trout' and *Holúnder* 'elder' the penultimate has to be stressed, since the last syllable has schwa as nucleus.

These statements can be generalized in the following way. The over-whelming majority of the word forms belonging to the central (i.e. native) part of the vocabulary have one of two accent patterns, namely $\acute{-}\,-$ or $\acute{-}\,-\,-$. The reason is that inflected forms of nouns, adjectives and verbs tend to be bisyllabic or tri-syllabic in such a way that only the first syllable can be stressed (see section 11.3 for further explication). No word form of the central, non-derived part of the vocabulary has a secondary accent.

Derived Words

In the literature on word accent in German we often find a partition of the derivational suffixes as to whether they are stressed or unstressed. Stressed suffixes are mostly non-native, e.g. *-ieren* (*kommandíeren*) or *-ie* (*Infamíe*).

Let us concentrate on the other set of suffixes, whose members are mostly native and generally unstressed.

A word like *fréundlich* 'friendly' has of course the accent on the first syllable, i.e. the suffix *-lich* is unstressed. The stress pattern is ´--. If we go on and build *Fréundlichkeit* (with *-keit* as nominalization suffix), we have two unstressed suffixes, the pattern is ´---. The plural form of this is *Fréundlich-kèiten* with the pattern ´--`-. Here we clearly have a secondary accent on the so-called 'unstressed' suffix *-keit*. Due to limitations of space we cannot elaborate this line of reasoning, so we simply state our thesis: derivational suffixes of the type discussed can be stressed or unstressed, depending on their position in the word. Derived words are completely broken up into stress patterns, one with two steps and the other with three steps. These two patterns are sufficient to handle all suffix-derived words with respect to their primary and secondary accents.

Compound Words

The basic rule for primary accent is that compounds with two constituents have primary stress on the first constituent. So we have *Héringsschwarm* 'shoal of herrings' because we have *Héring*. In compounds with three constituents, we basically have to distinguish two cases. In left-branching structures ((A B) C), the primary accent goes to the left constituent (and within this constituent again to the left subconstituent). So we have ((*Áußenhandels*) *gesellschaft*) 'foreign trade company' with primary accent on the leftmost constituent. In right-branching structures (A (B C)), the primary accent goes to the right constituent. This is due to the so-called Compound Stress Rule which says that a right constituent is 'strong' (i.e. it takes an accent), if it is branching. So we have (*Welt*(*áußenhandel*)) 'world foreign trade' with primary accent on the left subconstituent of the right part of the compound.

Orthography

The orthography of German can be characterized as highly systematic and as well integrated into the overall system of the language. Its basis is a phonographic correlation which maps the set of phonemes nearly one to one into the set of graphemes and vice versa. Graphemes can be single letters as well as certain sequences of letters like ‹sch› for /ʃ/ and ‹ng› for /ŋ/. Taking the graphemes as starting point, we have to mention a major deviance from the one-to-one mapping only for the vowels. More precisely, there is only one grapheme for every pair consisting of a tense vowel and its lax counterpart, So /a/ and /ɑ/ are both written as ‹a›, /u/ and /ʊ/ are both written as ‹u›, etc. This peculiarity can be explained by the fact that tense vowels and lax vowels differ systematically in distribution. As we have seen in section 11.2, the tenseness of a vowel is in most cases determined by the structure of the syllable in which it occurs. So the ‹a› in *laden* represents a tense vowel since it stands in an open, stressed syllable, whereas the ‹a› in *Land* represents a lax vowel since it is followed by a complex coda.

Apart from the phonographic component there is a strong syllabic as well as a strong morphological component in the orthography. We will give one example of either of them. Every ambisyllabic consonant is represented in writing by a geminate. So we write *Butter* 'butter' for [buṭəʀ] and *Tasse* 'cup' for [taṣə]. This is to say that every geminate follows a grapheme which is to be read as a lax vowel. As to morphology, the most significant property of German orthography is what has been called the Principle of Greatest Similarity of Morphemes. Whereas in the spoken language there is much allomorphic variation, in written language every morpheme tends to have one and only one form. Take for instance final devoicing. We say [kint] – [kindəʀ], but we write *Kind – Kinder*. Or take the morphological rule for gemination. If there is a form in the paradigm which causes gemination as in [ʃnɛḷəʀ] (*schneller* 'faster'), then all the forms in this paradigm preserve the geminate, no matter whether or not the consonant in question is ambisyllabic. Therefore we write *schnell* with double ‹l›.

11.3 Morphology

There is a rich inflectional system, both for nominals (pronouns, nouns, articles, adjectives) and for verbs. Moreover, the major lexical classes (nouns, verbs, adverbs, adjectives, prepositions) are interconnected by a complex network of word-formation rules. In a normal text, only a small percentage of the word forms can be regarded as strictly morphologically simple.

Nominals

We use the term 'nominal' as comprising those units which are inflected for number and case.

Pronouns

The pronominal inflection belongs to the inflection type called stem inflection. Every form in the paradigm consists of a stem plus a suffix. There are no suffixless forms.

Table 11.5 presents the inflection paradigm for the demonstrative pronoun *dieser* 'this'. Table 11.5a uses the form of presentation which we find in most grammars of German. We see that in the singular there is a differentiation with respect to case and gender. There is no gender in the plural. This holds for all nominals. All suffixes consist of schwa alone or schwa plus [ʀ], [n], [m], [s]. This can also be generalized to all nominals. No other phonetic material is used in declension suffixes than these five elements.

In Table 11.5b the suffixes are arranged in such a way that identical forms are put together as far as possible. This shows that the genitive and the dative are still relatively well distinguished from the nominative, and accusative. The

Table 11.5 Pronominal inflection

	Masculine	Feminine	Neuter	Plural
(a) Standard presentation				
Nom. dies	-er	-e	-es	-e
Gen.	-es	-er	-es	-er
Dat.	-em	-er	-em	-en
Acc.	-en	-e	-es	-e
(b) Fields of syncretism				
Nom.	-er	-e	-es	-e
Acc.	-en	-e	-es	-e
Dat.	-em	-er	-em	-en
Gen.	-es	-er	-es	-er

latter two cases have identical forms except for the masculine. This differentiation carries over at least in principle to the full noun phrase, consisting for instance of article, adjective and noun. It can be explained by the fact that case in German basically serves to indicate the syntactic function of noun phrases and pronouns. So the indirect object is marked as dative; the direct object as accusative. Since the two objects appear side by side in either of two sequences in sentences with three-place verbs, they have to be different in form. The genitive is the case of the attribute, i.e. the genitive appears with nouns in all cases. This keeps the genitive stable in the system and formally separated from the other cases. Similar arguments can be given for the prepositional phrase. Prepositions govern case (genitive, dative, accusative, but not nominative). Many prepositions govern both the dative as well as the accusative, so these cases have to be formally distinguishable. These remarks can only indicate how the functional load of the case forms has to be understood. It is, of course, a complex and difficult task to explain fully how the system is motivated.

Pronominal inflection is applied to pronouns from different classes as far as they are used in the full range of syntactic functions of nominals. This is the case for most demonstratives (*dieser* 'this', *jener* 'that', *solcher* 'such', and with further specifications *der*); for possessives (*meiner* 'my', *deiner* 'your', *seiner* 'his'); for some indefinites (*einer* 'one', *keiner* 'no', *jeder* 'each', *mancher* 'many (a)', *einiger* 'some', *weniger* 'few', *vieler* 'much') and for the interrogative pronoun *welcher* 'which'.

Many other pronouns are restricted in form and function. There is an interrogative *wer* 'who', which has only masculine and neuter forms in the singular, and there are numerous indefinites which have only one form in the paradigm like *etwas* 'some', *nichts* 'nothing', *mancherlei*, *allerlei* 'all kinds (of)' *vielerlei* 'many kinds (of)'.

Table 11.6   Personal pronoun

	Nom.	Gen.	Dat.	Acc.
1 sg.	ich	meiner	mir	mich
pl.	wir	unser	uns	uns
2 sg.	du	deiner	dir	dich
pl.	ihr	euer	euch	euch
3 m.	er	seiner	ihm	ihn
f.	sie	ihrer	ihr	sie
n.	es	seiner	ihm	es
pl.	sie	ihrer	ihnen	sie

There is no separate relative pronoun in German. The most commonly used relative pronoun is *der*. It has the same forms in its paradigm as the demonstrative *der*, from which it is derived. *Welcher* can also be used as relative pronoun, but it is stylistically marked. The third and syntactically very restricted relative pronoun is *wer*.

It is of some interest to consider, albeit briefly, the personal pronoun. Though the paradigm (Table 11.6) is highly suppletive, it has some interesting structural characteristics. The fact that the first person and the second person are not differentiated with respect to gender, whereas the third person is, can be explained by the deictic function of the personal pronoun. The differentiation for case is for the third person similar to the one we know from the other pronouns, but it is different for the first and second person. This can be explained by the fact that only the third person has a separate reflexive pronoun (*sich*), whereas the 'normal' pronoun has to be used for reflexivization in the first and second person (see below, section 11.4). All genitives are taken from the possessive pronoun. The genitive of the personal pronoun is excluded from the syntactic function of attribute (which otherwise is the most common function of the genitive). We do not say **das Haus seiner* '*the house of his' but *sein Haus* 'his house' with the possessive article *sein* (see again section 11.4).

Nouns

Like pronouns, nouns are inflected for case and number, but, of course, not for gender. So the status of gender is different for the two categories. For pronouns, gender categories are inflectional categories whereas each noun is classified either as masculine, e.g. *der Baum* 'the tree'; feminine, e.g. *die Bank* 'the bank'; or neuter, e.g. *das Haus* 'the house'.

Nouns are inflected according to several declension types. There is little agreement in grammars as to how these declension types have to be defined. We will first set out our views on the basic declension system for underived nouns, ignoring exceptions and marginal classes. We will then show how the system works for derived nouns.

Noun inflection is a type of 'base-form inflection' (*Grundformflexion*). The unmarked form (nominative singular) never has an inflectional suffix. All other forms can be marked by a suffix and by an umlaut (which we are not going to discuss here). The best marked forms are the plural and the genitive singular. Therefore, most classifications are based on these two forms. Whenever this is admitted by the phonological context, the dative plural is marked by *n*. The inflection of a noun is in part determined by its gender. Taking this into account, we can establish three main declension types.

Type 1

Type 1 comprises nearly all neuter nouns as well as those masculine nouns which do not belong to Type 2 (see below). Following the traditional terminology (which goes back to Jacob Grimm), we call type 1 nouns 'strong'. A paradigm case is given in Table 11.7. The genitive of strong nouns has -(*e*)*s*. Whether a noun takes -*es* or -*s* is determined exclusively by morphophonemic regularities. So in *Regen – Regens* 'rain' and *Schnabel – Schnabels* 'bill, beak' we have -*s*, since there is already a syllable with schwa in the stem. No noun with schwa in the last syllable can ever get another such syllable through inflection *Baum – Baumes* 'tree', *Hut – Hutes* 'hat', *Bein – Beines* 'leg' are examples with the 'normal' genitive -*es*. Of course schwa can be omitted here in the spoken language (baɥms, huts, baɪns]). The dative singular of strong nouns is optionally marked by schwa. This suffix is obsolete in the sense that it is scarcely found in the spoken language.

The unmarked form of the plural for Type 1 nouns is *e* (*Baum – Bäume, Hut – Hüte, Bein – Beine*). This again does not hold for nouns with schwa in the last syllable. These have a plural without suffix (*Schnabel – Schnäbel, Wagen – Wagen* 'carriage', *Eimer – Eimer* 'pail'). There are some neuter nouns with *er*-plural (*Kind – Kinder, Haus – Häuser*). This subtype is irregular in the sense of isolated. We do not regard it as part of the central system.

Table 11.7   Paradigms for noun declension

	Strong (Type 1)	sg.	pl.	Weak (Type 2)	sg.	pl.	Feminine (Type 3)	sg.	pl.
Nom.	Bein 'leg'	——	-e	Mensch 'man'	——	-en	Burg 'castle'	——	-en
Gen.		-es	-e		-en	-en		——	-en
Dat.		-(e)	-en		-(en)	-en		——	-en
Acc.		——	-e		-(en)	-en		——	-en

Type 2

These are nouns with the semantic feature [+animate]. In the present context they are perhaps best characterized in terms of grammatical and natural gender. Grammatically they are masculine. As will also be shown below for derived nouns, the masculine is the unmarked gender with respect to the male–female distinction. In nearly all cases where a noun designates a class of beings whose members can be either male or female (i.e. persons and animals), the noun is masculine. Let us call these nouns generic. Examples are: *Franzose* 'frenchman', *Löwe* 'lion', *Affe* 'monkey', *Mensch* 'man', *Kunde* 'client', *Zeuge* 'witness'. When these nouns belong to inflection Type 2, they are called 'weak'. Weak nouns have -(*e*)*n* in the genitive singular and in the plural. In the dative singular and accusative singular -(*e*)*n* is optional, i.e. archaic like the -*e* in the dative singular of Type 1.

Type 3

The third type comprises the feminine nouns. For this type the plural is always overtly marked, but there are no case endings. Most feminine nouns mark the plural by using -(*e*)*n*, as for *Burg* – *Burgen* 'castle', *Frau* – *Frauen* 'woman' and *Quelle* – *Quellen* 'source'. Only some of them take -*e* (*Stadt* – *Städte* 'town').

Figure 11.3 gives a summary of the basic declension system of German nouns as it has just been outlined. It should be noted that the morphonological condition 'only one syllable with schwa' always has priority. Many so-called subtypes like the 'zero plural' of strong nouns and the -*n*-plural of weak nouns are a consequence of this condition.

There is one other declension type which should also be mentioned. A growing set of nouns takes -*s* in the genitive singular and in the plural (e.g. *Echo* – *Echos*, *Balkon* – *Balkons*). Until recently this type comprised only proper names and some other marked nouns. It is now very productive because it is in use for large parts of the non-native vocabulary such as trade names, abbreviations and loanwords.

For derived nouns, the grammatical gender as well as the declension type is strictly fixed. Each derivational suffix leads to exactly one gender and one

Figure 11.3 The basic declension of nouns

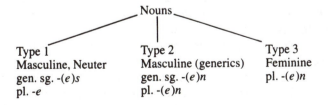

Nouns

Type 1
Masculine, Neuter
gen. sg. -(*e*)*s*
pl. -*e*

Type 2
Masculine (generics)
gen. sg. -(*e*)*n*
pl. -(*e*)*n*

Type 3
Feminine
pl. -(*e*)*n*

declension type. For the most productive nominal suffixes, we have the following assignments:

Masculine

-*ling*: de-adjectival personal noun; declension Type 1 e.g. *feige* 'cowardly' – *Feigling* 'coward'

-*er*: de-verbal agentive noun; declension Type 1 e.g. *schreiben* 'to write' – *Schreiber* 'writer'

There are also several specific suffixes for the derivation of non-native personal nouns like *Katholik, Astronom, Optimist, Demonstrant*. They are all generic and belong to declension Type 2.

Feminine

-*in*: de-nominal motion suffix; declension Type 3; *Schreiber* (m.) – *Schreiberin* (f.). Nouns with -*in* are marked as [+female], whereas their base nouns are normally generic.

-*ung*: most productive action noun; declension Type 3; e.g. *brefreien* 'to liberate' – *Befreiung* 'liberation'

-*heit* and *keit*: de-adjectival state nouns; declension Type 3; e.g. *echt* 'genuine' – *Echtheit* 'genuineness', *sauber* 'clean' – *Sauberkeit* 'cleanness'

Neuter

-*nis*: de-verbal noun which designates an act or its result; declension Type 1; e.g. *erleben* 'to experience' – *Erlebnis* 'experience'. By changing its meaning from action noun to 'resultative noun', -*nis* has changed the grammatical gender from feminine to neuter. There are still many feminine nouns like *Erlaubnis* 'permission', *Besorgnis* 'apprehension', which take declension Type 3.

-*chen*: de-nominal diminutive noun; declension Type 1; e.g. *Mann* 'man' – *Männchen* 'little man'

As the examples show, there is a clear tendency for derivational suffixes to select the gender according to their meaning. The feminine is selected if there is no semantic motivation for the masculine or the neuter.

Many of the specific properties of derived nouns are also valid for compound nouns. For instance *Heimatstadt* 'home town' is feminine and takes declension Type 3, since *Stadt* is feminine and takes declension Type 3. Moreover, the paradigmatic compound noun is the so-called *Determinativkompositum* ('determinative compound'), which internally shows an attribute–head-construction with the second constituent as head. So a *Heimatstadt* is a *Stadt* and a *Lehrbuch* 'textbook' is a *Buch*. This structure can be found in all types of compound nouns, no matter whether the first constituent is an adjective (*Kleinkind* 'little child, infant'), a verb (*Gießkanne* 'watering-can'), some kind of particle (*Unterarm* 'forearm'), or another noun. Since the rules for composition can be applied recursively, compound nouns can have a very complex structure. Composition is regarded as the most productive type of word formation in German.

Articles

Like pronouns, articles are inflected not only for case, but also for gender. For the definite articles we have the forms *der* (m.), *die* (f.) and *das* (n.). The gender of the article is governed by the adjacent noun, so we have *der Baum* 'the tree' *die Straße* 'the road' *das Buch* 'the book'.

Most pronouns can be used with nouns in one way or the other, cf. *dieser Baum* 'this tree', *jener Baum* 'that tree', *manche Bäume* 'some trees', *alle Bäume* 'all trees'. It is therefore not clear how to separate pronouns from articles. Traditionally, only two articles are recognized: the definite article *der* and the indefinite article *ein*. All other words in adnominal position are called 'article words', 'determiners' or the like.

Yet a closer look reveals that articles can be separated from pronouns on the basis of their inflectional behaviour.

The definite article is shown in Table 11.8. The differentiation of forms is almost the same as in pronominal inflection (Table 11.5) yet the paradigm of the article *der* is not identical with the paradigm of the demonstrative pronoun *der*. The genitive singular of the pronoun is *dessen* (m.), *deren* (f.), *dessen* (n.); the genitive plural is *deren* and the dative plural is *denen*. These differences in form can be explained by the restriction of the article to adnominal position. What we propose then is to restrict the notion of article in German to those units which only occur in adnominal position. By this criterion we get three more articles. The possessive article *mein* (as opposed to the pronoun *meiner*), the negation article *kein* (pronoun *keiner*) and the indefinite article *ein* (pronoun *einer*). All of these follow

Table 11.8 Inflection of articles

		Masculine	Feminine	Neuter	Plural
Definite article					
Nom.		der	die	das	die
Gen.		des	der	des	der
Dat.		dem	der	dem	den
Acc.		den	die	das	die
Other articles					
Nom.	*kein* 'no'	——	e	——	e
Gen.		es	er	es	er
Dat.		em	er	em	en
Acc.		en	e	——	e

the declension scheme for other articles in Table 11.7, except that *ein* has no plural form.

Adjectives

The inflectional behaviour of adjectives is determined by syntactic factors even more directly than the other nominal categories. In predicative position (*dieses Auto ist billig* 'this car is cheap') the adjective is uninflected: it appears in the so-called 'short form'. In attributive position (*dieses billige Auto* 'this cheap car') the adjective is inflected for gender, number and case according to several inflection types. Most grammars recognize three inflection types (strong, weak, mixed). Apart from morphophonological variation, all adjectives are inflected in the same way. Unlike for nouns and articles, there are no different declension types for adjectives.

The most interesting fact about the inflection of adjectives is its dependence on other elements within the noun phrase. How this works can be shown by considering the syntactic minimum of the prototypical noun phrase into which an adjective can be inserted. Two basic cases have to be distinguished. In the first case, the noun phrase consists of a single noun as frequently occurs with mass nouns e.g. *Suppe schmeckt gut* 'soup tastes good'. A noun of this type does not have any case endings (declension Type 3), and there are, as we have seen, many nouns which do not even have a plural suffix. If we add an attributive adjective as in *heiße Suppe schmeckt gut* 'hot soup tastes good', this adjective appears in the first position of the noun phrase. It occupies the position of the determiner and it has to do the syntactic work of the determiner by marking the noun phrase for case. Consequently, the adjective in this position is inflected according to what we have called the pronominal inflection (Table 11.4). Thus we get in the nominative singular *heißer Tee* (m.), *heiße Suppe* (f.), *heißes Wasser* (n.). The forms of all other cases in the singular and the plural can be constructed from the pronominal paradigm. To avoid terminological confusion, it is perhaps better not to speak of pronominal inflection of the adjective, but to use again the traditional term 'strong inflection'.

In the second case, the minimal noun phrase consists of a determiner and a noun. If the determiner is inflected according to the pronominal inflection, as it is the case of *dieser* or the definite article *der*, then there is little work for the adjective to do. The adjective takes schwa in the nominative singular for all genders and the accusative singular for the feminine and neuter, and *-en* for all other forms. This is the 'weak' inflection of the adjective, e.g. *dieser heiße Tee* 'this hot tea', *diese heiße Suppe* 'this hot soup', *dieses heiße Wasser* 'this hot water' for the nominative singular and *diese heißen Suppen* 'these hot soups' for the nominative plural.

There are three determiners which constitute their own inflection type. The articles *kein*, *mein* and *ein* do not take a suffix in the nominative singular masculine and neuter, and the accusative singular neuter (see Table 11.8).

Consequently, the adjective takes strong forms in these cases, cf. *kein heißer Tee* (nom. sg. m.), *kein heißes Wasser* (nom./acc. sg. nt.). All other forms of the adjective are, of course, weak. This is called the 'mixed inflection' of the adjective.

As can be seen from our discussion, it is somewhat artificial and clumsy to speak of three inflection types for the attributive adjective. The inflectional behaviour of the attributive adjective is governed by one single principle: the adjective marks the noun phrase for case, number and gender according to the pronominal inflection if no other constituent of the noun phrase does so.

The system of comparatives is highly regular although there are some irregular cases. A regular adjective like *klein* 'small' has the comparative *kleiner* and the superlative *kleinst*. On all three levels the adjective exhibits the usual inflection for gender, number and case.

Verbs

As for many other languages, the term 'verbal paradigm' is not used as a purely morphological term in most German grammars. Instead, the verbal paradigm is analysed as comprising many periphrastic forms such as the forms of the perfect tense or the forms of the passive. Since we are dealing with morphology in this section, we will restrict ourselves to synthetic forms within the paradigm and postpone the treatment of analytic forms.

Regular Main Verbs

The regular verb ('weak verb') has finite forms in the singular and plural of the present tense and the past tense. Table 11.9 shows the conjugation pattern for a verb without any morphonological peculiarities (*legen* 'to lay').

There is a syncretism between the first and third person in the past tense, whereas this syncretism is restricted to the plural in the present. It is very difficult to interpret this syncretism from a functional point of view, and it is even more difficult to really understand why the third-person singular present is marked the way it is. We cannot go into these problems here. What we want to point out is merely that the third-person singular present is the unmarked

Table 11.9 Conjugation of weak verbs, *legen* 'to lay'

	Present	Past
1 sg.	lege	legte
2 sg.	legst	legtest
3 sg.	legt	legte
1 pl.	legen	legten
2 pl.	legt	legtet
3 pl.	legen	legten

form of the verb in the semantic sense (deictic function) as well as in the syntactic sense of the word (agreement with the subject, see below, pp. 377–8). So in German as in many other languages the third-person singular present plays a special role within the verbal paradigm.

The regular verbs are called weak verbs because they 'need' a segmental morpheme for the past tense. Thanks to their ablaut, the strong verbs do not need a segmental morpheme of this kind (see below, pp. 370–1).

There is a special problem for the weak verbs with respect to mood. The verbal paradigm is normally seen as having subjunctive forms besides indicative forms in the present as well as in the past tense. In the present, the subjunctive looks like the indicative of the past without the -t-, so it has the forms *lege, legest, lege, legen, leget, legen*. This subjunctive is not in all forms separated from the indicative, but it is in the most frequently used forms (by far the highest frequence in use has the third-person singular). In the past, all forms of the subjunctive are identical with the forms of the indicative. Strictly speaking, we do not even know whether there is a past subjunctive for the regular verbs. All we can do is to conclude by analogy from the subjunctive forms of the strong verbs that some forms of the past of weak verbs have to be interpreted as subjunctives. There are also certain periphrastic forms which are often considered to be 'substitutes' for the synthetic subjunctives. Thus most grammarians say that *ich würde legen* 'I would lay' stands for *ich legte* (subj.). The whole question of the functional load of the subjunctive and the place of the forms with *würde* in the verbal paradigm cannot be settled within the traditional structure of the paradigm. Furthermore, in many cases it is difficult to decide whether a form is used for reasons of normative prescription or whether it has in fact to be considered as standard.

As can be expected, the imperative is marked with respect to number. In the singular we have the stem without suffix or stem plus optional schwa (*leg* or *lege*). In the plural the imperative has the form of the second-person plural (*legt*).

There are two synthetic non-finite verb forms in the paradigm, the infinitive (*legen*) and the participle (*gelegt*). For morphologically simple verbs, the participle consists of *ge*+stem+*t*, in other words, *ge*+past stem. For verbs with prefix, the participle does not take *ge*-, for instance *verlegen* 'to misplace' – *verlegt*, *zerlegen* 'to take apart' – *zerlegt*. If the prefix is separable (as is the case for most prepositional prefixes), then *ge*- is placed in front of the root. So we have *ablegen* 'to lay down' – *ich lege ab* – *abgelegt*, *vorlegen* – *ich lege vor* – *vorgelegt*. It is sometimes said that there is a third simple non-finite verb form *legend* which is called participle I or present participle. This form exists for all verbs, but it never occurs in periphrastic verb forms. Its normal (though not exclusive) use is that of an adjective. It is therefore questionable whether it should be considered as a form within the verbal paradigm.

Figure 11.4 gives an overview on the paradigm of the verb as it has just been outlined. The non-imperative forms are put under a scheme of

Figure 11.4   Structure of the inflectional paradigm of the verb

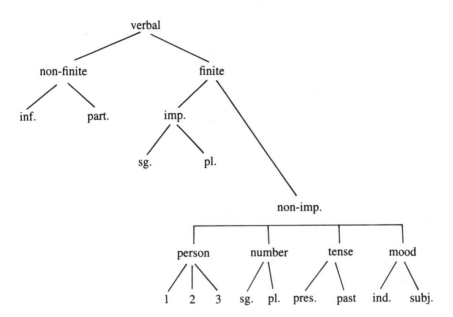

simultaneous categorizations, i.e. every form is classified by exactly one category from every categorization. So *lege* in *ich lege* is classified as first-person singular present indicative. The scheme of Table 11.10 is valid for all verbs, no matter whether they are main verbs, auxiliaries, or modals.

Irregular Main Verbs
Present day German has about 170 irregular main verbs ('strong verbs'). This class is decreasing in number, but it still comprises many verbs of the basic vocabulary. The most characteristic property of strong verbs is ablaut. If we take the infinitive, the first-person singular past, and the participle as stem forms, we get vowel gradations like *finden – fand – gefunden* [i – a – ʊ] 'to find', *schreiben – schrieb – geschrieben* [aɪ, iː, iː] 'to write', *streiten – stritt – gestritten* [aɪ, ɪ, ɪ] 'to fight'. There are more than 30 different sequences of ablaut, which have to be learned word by word. The most frequent of these sequences are the ones just mentioned. Each of them is selected by about 20 verbs.

The inflectional behaviour of strong verbs is presented in Table 11.10. As can be seen, the structure of the paradigm is the same as for weak verbs.

Both classes have the same suffixes in the present and identical syncretisms in the past. The participle of strong verbs takes the form *ge*+stem+*en* (*gefunden*), and *ge*- behaves as with weak verbs. There is, furthermore, no difference in the forms of the subjunctive present, see e.g. *schreibe –*

Table 11.10   Conjugation of strong verbs, *schreiben* 'to write'

	Present	Past
1 sg.	schreibe	schrieb
2 sg.	schreibst	schriebst
3 sg.	schreibt	schrieb
1 pl.	schreiben	schrieben
2 pl.	schreibt	schriebt
3 pl.	schreiben	schrieben

schreibest – schreibe – schreiben – schreibet – schreiben, but there is a difference in the past. Here the subjunctive is formed by the past stem and the suffixes of the subjunctive present: *schriebe, schriebest, schriebe, schrieben, schriebet, schrieben*. Except for *schrieben*, these forms are different from the relevant forms in the indicative.

As a prototype, strong verbs take the umlaut for the second- and third-person singular present indicative (*fahren – du fährst – er fährt* 'to drive'), and they take the umlaut for all forms of the subjunctive past (*ich fuhr – ich führe*).

Since many verbs are becoming more and more regular, we find pairs of forms like *buk – backte* (from *backen* 'to bake'), *gor – gärte* (from *gären* 'to ferment'), *scholl – schallte* (from *schallen* 'to sound'). In some cases this doubling leads to semantic differentiation. So we have *hängen – hing* 'to hang' as intransitive and *hängen – hängte* as transitive verb.

Auxiliary and Modal Verbs

If we consider auxiliaries to be those verbs which occur as constituents of periphrastic verb forms together with a non-finite form of a main verb, we have three auxiliaries in German: *sein* 'to be', *haben* 'to have', *werden* 'to be, to will, to become'. As will be shown below (pp. 378–80) there are some additional verbs which tend to be used as auxiliaries in some constructions.

With respect to their inflectional behaviour, auxiliaries are irregular to a different degree. The most irregular auxiliary is *sein*. *Sein* has no regular stem morpheme. For some forms it is difficult to separate a stem and a suffix, and some of its forms even have to be considered as suppletive (see Table 11.11).

If we look at the paradigm as a whole it appears to be pretty much regular in the sense that it has the same syncretisms as the regular verbs. The subjunctive is completely regular for both tenses. In the present it is derived from the infinitive (*ich sei, du seist*, etc.) and in the past it is derived in the usual way from the past stem with umlaut (*ich wäre, du wärest*, etc.).

Most grammars list six modal verbs: *wollen* 'will', *dürfen* 'may', *können* 'can', *müssen* 'must', *mögen* 'like', *sollen* 'shall'. There are additional

Table 11.11   Paradigm of *sein*

	Present	Past
1 sg.	bin	war
2 sg.	bist	warst
3 sg.	ist	war
1 pl.	sind	waren
2 pl.	seid	wart
3 pl.	sind	waren

candidates for such an analysis, such as *möchten* 'want', *brauchen* 'need', *lassen* 'let', *werden* 'become', which pose different problems and would have to be discussed in detail. For *werden* there is an intensive discussion of whether it is to be considered as a modal, as auxiliary or both. As in other Germanic languages, modals in German take the inflectional endings of the preterite for the present tense.

11.4   Syntax

The Noun Phrase
The basic structure of the noun phrase is given in Figure 11.5. The head noun *Kind* is preceded by a determiner and an adjectival attribute. All other types of attributes are found in postnominal position. Their relative order is fixed. In the position adjacent to the head noun we first have the genitive construction, then the prepositional phrase and after that the relative clause. With respect to the main constituents of the sentence German has relatively free word order. This does not hold for the noun phrase. Here the order of the elements is fixed.

Figure 11.5 is not meant to make any claim about the syntactic hierarchy of the noun phrase. For a description of its basic typological and language-specific characteristics, we only have to know which elements can occur in which order.

The sequence of all specifiers in a wide sense of the word (i.e. determiners and attributes) is determined by the universal principle of Heaviness Hierarchy which is known in traditional German grammar as *Gesetz der wachsenden Glieder* ('law of growing elements'). The heavier (i.e. longer and internally more complex) the prototype of a syntactic class, the later it appears in the sequence of elements. In German, the noun phrase conforms strictly to this principle. The principle may be motivated by such needs of the language-processing apparatus as relief of short-term memory. If this is so, one is tempted to establish a relation to another characteristic property of the noun

Figure 11.5   Basic structure of the noun phrase

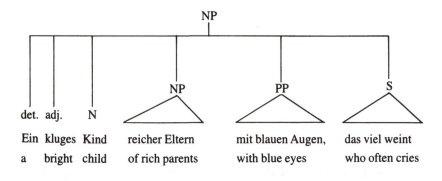

phrase. Its left part including the positions of the determiner, the adjective and the head noun, forms a block whose parts are highly interconnected by syntagmatic relations. The head noun governs the gender of the determiner and the adjective and agrees with both in number and case. Therefore many grammars speak of this part of the noun phrase as being bracketed by the determiner and the head noun (*Nominalklammer*).

It is much more difficult to interpret the position of the head noun typologically. According to one theory, the positions of the head in different categories are interrelated by a preference principle of Cross-category Harmony, and the reference point for the application of this principle is given by the position of the verb in the sentence. In the main clause the order is SVO, which seems to indicate that there is indeed a topological parallelism between the sentence and the noun phrase. But there are also good reasons to question this thesis. German is generally considered to be SOV, or at least, tending towards SOV. However, no such tendency is found in the noun phrase. And even if it is accepted that SVO is basic, then the intended parallel is not unconditionally clear. Is the determiner to be counted as a separate position or not? Is SVO to be understood as verb second or as verb central? We will come back to this later.

Let us now have a closer look at the relation between the different types of attributes and the head noun. The simple adjectival attribute can be replaced by complex constructions of different kinds. One possibility is syndetic and asyndetic coordination which would have the bracketing as in [*das* [*große gelbe*] *Haus*] 'the big yellow house'. On the other hand there are phrases which clearly seem to be right-branching, as, for example, *das* [*neue* [*technische Konzept*]] 'the new technical conception'. Here the adjectives are not interchangeable. Both constructions can be further extended and are recursive in this sense.

Another expansion of the simple adjectival attribute is the attachment of a complement. In predicative position, adjectives can be subclassified like verbs with respect to the complements they take (subjects and objects in a broad sense, see below). So we have *dieser Wein ist alten Menschen bekömmlich*, 'this wine is wholesome for old people' with a dative as complement of *bekömmlich*. This dative can also appear in attributive use, cf. *dieser alten Menschen bekömmliche Wein*. In fact all nominal and prepositional complements of an adjective apart from its subject can be used this way. This leads to constructions of considerable complexity, especially for participles, since there can be several complements. So from a sentence like *das Auto wurde meiner Frau von einem Engländer angeboten* 'the car was offered to my wife by an Englishman' we can derive *das meiner Frau von einem Engländer angebotene Auto*. Such structures are scarcely found in spoken language.

The attribute immediately following the head noun is the genitive construction. Except for the so-called Saxon genitive, which strongly resembles the relevant construction in English (e.g. *Chomskys Meinung* 'Chomsky's opinion'), the genitive is always restricted to this position and it always modifies the noun preceding it. In consequence, the head noun can have one and only one genitive following it as attribute. Since the construction is right-branching with a clear hierarchical order, there can be chains of genitives of considerable length which do not cause any difficulties for the syntactic processor (*der Hund des Bruders der Freundin des Bürgermeisters* 'the dog of the brother of the friend of the mayor').

For large classes of de-verbal nouns, the genitive has to be interpreted as one of the verb's thematic roles: an Agent noun derived from a transitive verb like *Lehrer* 'teacher' takes an *genitivus obiectivus*, i.e. the genitive is interpreted as the direct object of the verb whenever this is semantically possible. *Der Lehrer Meiner Kinder* is to be read like *lehrt meine Kinder* 'teaches my children'. A noun like *Schlaf* 'sleep' derived from the intransitive verb *schlafen* by contrast takes a *genitivus subiectivus*. *Der Schlaf meiner Kinder* has an interpretation parallel to *Meine Kinder schlafen*.

The prepositional attribute has much in common with the genitive. It is a right-branching, endocentric construction. (There are very few occurrences in prenominal position in the spoken language). Like the genitive, the prepositional attribute of de-verbal nouns has to be regularly interpreted as the prepositional object of the base verb, if it has the relevant form (e.g. *der Gedanke an Paul* < *denken an Paul* 'think of Paul'). The prepositional attribute is different from the genitive and does not have to be attached directly to the head. This has two consequences. First, a head noun can have more than one prepositional attribute, no matter whether there is a genitive or not. Second, if a prepositional attribute follows a genitive or another prepositional attribute, it normally can be related to several nouns as its head. So *mit blauen Augen* can be attributed to *Eltern* as well as to *Kind* in Figure 11.5. This construction is the source of a considerable amount of syntactic ambiguity.

So far, we have discussed some characteristics of those positions within the noun phrase which are normally called attributive. In a structure like that in Figure 11.5 all attributes are optional, that is they do not belong to the syntactic minimum of the noun phrase. The syntactic minimum comprises in most cases only the head noun and an element in the leftmost position, which we have called the position of the determiner. Yet these so-called determiners in no way constitute a homogeneous class, either from a syntactic or from a semantic point of view. Semantically, the main distinction is that between determination and quantification. Whereas determination relates to the definite–indefinite distinction, quantification is concerned with the specification of absolute or relative quantities of something specified in the rest of the noun phrase. In German, the main syntactic difference between determiners in the narrow sense and quantifiers is often seen in the greater mobility of the quantifiers. Thus we have *die drei großen Häuser* 'the three big houses' as well as *drei große Häuser*. And *all die großen Häuser* is possible besides *die großen Häuser alle*.

An important aspect of the mobility of quantifiers is known as quantifier floating: *Wasser habe ich keins bekommen* 'I did not get any water'. Since this construction is not restricted to quantifiers but also occurs with adjectives, it has been proposed to use the less-specific term *Distanzstellung* ('distance position'). To handle these cases, one could either think of a floating operation which moves the quantifier out of the noun phrase, or of a movement of the noun phrase (topicalization) which leaves the quantifier behind. Both suggestions are faced with the problem that the quantifier in distance position is a pronoun, i.e. it generally cannot be integrated into the noun phrase, cf. **keins Wasser, *die alle Häuser*.

Judged by their inflectional properties, quantifiers behave in part like adjectives and in part like pronouns. It is a question of principle whether one tries to establish a syntactic class of quantifiers or tries to understand the behaviour of these elements on the basis of established categories. The problem arises in this specific form because German still has a rich inflectional morphology. As we have seen, this morphology fulfils in part purely semantic functions; on the other hand, it is in part clearly motivated syntactically. If there is a syntactic motivation, it seems to be natural to establish syntactic classes on the basis of the inflectional behaviour of the elements at least to the extent that there is morphological encoding of syntactic functions.

We can find other interesting problems of this kind in the syntax of the noun phrase. So it seems to be unproblematic to distinguish a head noun from an adjectival attribute. But consider expressions like *Beratungsstelle für Abhängige* 'welfare centre for addicts', *die Integration Abhängiger* 'the integration of addicts', *ein Abhängiger berichtet* 'an addict reports', *alle anwesenden Abhängigen erzählten* 'all addicts present reported', *der Abhängige sucht Hilfe* 'the addict looks for help', *die Probleme eines Abhängigen* 'the problems of an addict' (examples due to Sue Olsen). Most grammars consider *Abhängiger* 'addict' as a nominalized adjective with the function of a head noun in all these expressions. Yet *Abhängiger* is inflected like an adjective here. It takes exactly the form of weak vs strong inflection which can be predicted by the context. Moreover, nouns of this type are inflected for gender. We have *der Alte* 'the old', *die Alte, das Alte*, and it is not possible to consider these expressions as elliptical.

Let us take up once more the difference in status between the syntactic features of case, on the one hand, and of gender and number on the other. The difference mentioned is not only relevant for the noun phrase itself, but also for its role as antecedent for anaphora and pronouns.

If an anaphoric pronoun is related to a noun phrase, both then normally agree in gender and number. If the pronoun is related to a sentence, it takes the form of the neuter singular: *Paul schläft. Das freut mich* 'Paul is sleeping. That makes me happy'. An anaphoric pronoun cannot be bound within its clause. In *Paul$_i$ sieht ihn$_j$, weil er$_{i,j}$ einen grauen Mantel trägt* 'Paul sees him because he is wearing a grey coat' *ihn* cannot be co-referential with the subject *Paul*, whereas *er* can be co-referential with either *Paul* or with *ihn*. Since the features of gender and number have to be seen as indicators of the meaning of a pronoun, these features are not strictly bound by anaphoric relations. We can have *Das Mädchen* (n.) *lachte. Sie* (f.) *schloß die Tür* 'The girl laughed. She closed the door'; or *Das Paar* (sg.) *fuhr ab. Sie* (pl.) *wollten nach Spanien* 'The couple left. They wanted to go to Spain'.

There is a rather strict functional and distributional separation between pronouns and anaphors (reflexives and reciprocals). German has the reflexive pronoun *sich* which occurs obligatorily with some 'reflexive' verbs like *sich schämen* 'to feel ashamed' or *sich freuen* 'to be glad'. These cases are not of interest here. In its genuinely reflexive use, *sich* stands in the position of a dative or an accusative. It then has the function of an indirect object, e.g. *Paula hilft sich* 'Paula helps herself'; of a direct object, e.g. *Paula wäscht sich* 'Paula washes (herself)'; or as part of a prepositional object e.g. *Paula denkt an sich* 'Paula takes good care of herself'. In each of these cases, *sich* refers back to the subject. Even though there are still some verbs with object in the genitive, this genitive can never be replaced by *sich*. Therefore in *Er gedenkt seiner* 'He thinks of him(self)', the genitive *seiner* is ambiguous. It can refer back to the subject, but this is not the only possible reading.

In three-place verbs, *sich* can refer back from the indirect object to the direct object, e.g. *Paula überläßt ihn sich* 'Paula leaves him to himself'; and even the other way round, e.g. *Paula empfiehlt ihm sich* 'Paula recommends him to himself'. Similar cases exist with prepositional objects. This use of *sich* is restricted in various respects, which we cannot discuss here.

The domain of reflexivization is the clause. The reflexive pronoun can only be bound by *Hans* in: *Paul glaubt, daß Hans sich verbessert* 'Paul believes that Hans will improve'; and by *Paul* in: *Paul glaubt, daß er sich verbessert*.

As is shown by *Paul glaubt, sich zu verbessern*, the reflexive can be bound from outside in an infinitival complement. This holds at least for those causes in which the infinitive is controlled in a clear-cut way.

The Verb Phrase and the Structure of Simple Sentences

The term 'verb phrase' is understood in a similar way as the term noun phrase as above. In this sense the verb phrase is the phrase with a verbal head. Its syntax is primarily concerned with the behaviour of the verbal complements.

The verb takes as complement different kinds of objects and possibly some types of adverbials. For reasons of space we will not consider any adverbials. The main types of objects in German are the accusative (direct object), the dative (indirect object), and the prepositional object. Although some verbs still take the genitive, this will not be discussed here.

The first question is whether the subject has to be counted as complement. If so, there will be at least some types of verb phrases which are sentences. There are many subject–object assymmetries in German. But it is questionable whether they 'prove' that the sentence has to be broken down into the main constituents of subject and verb phrase, the latter consisting of the predicate and the objects. There are clear syntactic differences between the different types of objects and there are also important similarities, between, for example, the direct object and the subject. Apart from this, there is the strong syntactic relation of agreement between the subject and the predicate which is often assumed to show that subject and predicate are bound together syntactically more tightly than the objects and the predicate. So, how this question is answered depends to a great extent on ideological commitments. Both positions are widespread in German grammaticography.

In what follows, we will concentrate on the strict subcategorization of the verb with respect to the subject and the direct object. This gives us the basic forms of sentences with two-place transitive verbs. In doing so, we presuppose that the verb is also subcategorized for the subject. Indeed, I would like to make this claim, though I do not deny that there are strong arguments for the 'existence' of a verb phrase (verb plus objects) in German.

The position of the direct object can be occupied by expressions of very different form. In addition to the accusative we find several types of sentential and infinitival complements. The main types of sentential complements are subordinate clauses with *daß* 'that', *ob* 'whether', or interrogative pronouns like *wer* 'who', *wie* 'how', *wann* 'when' as complementizers. The complementizers can be classified as we have listed them. *Daß* constitutes one class, *ob* another one, and the so-called *wh*-words a third one. The reason for classifying them this way is that they combine with different verbs. There are many transitive verbs which do not take any sentential complement in object position. Those which do are subcategorized into four classes. The first class takes only *daß*, e.g. *Paul behauptet, daß Helga schläft* 'Paul claims that Helga is sleeping'. The second takes *daß* and *wh*, e.g. *Paul bedauert, daß/wie Helga schläft* 'Paul is sorry...'. The third takes *ob* and *wh*, e.g. *Paul überlegt, ob/wie Helga schläft* 'Paul reflects...'. The fourth takes *daß*, *ob*, and *wh*, e.g. *Paul vergißt, daß/ob/wie Helga schläft* 'Paul forgets...'. Each of these classes comprises a great number of verbs. The classes also constitute relevant categories in so far as each class has its semantic characteristics. The *ob/wh*-class consists of a certain kind of question verbs, *daß/wh* and *daß/ob/wh* consists of factive verbs, whereas the *daß*-verbs are never factive.

There is another set of complements which could be called 'secondary'. They can be seen as closely related to the *daß*-complements. Most of them contribute to a further subclassification of the *daß*-verbs.

Similar to English, most *daß*-complements can be replaced by infinitivals. The infinitival complement with *zu* as in *Paul behauptet, Helga zu kennen* 'Paul claims to know Helga' has the same meaning as the *daß*-complement with a suitable subject. We do not want to go very far into the problems of the control relation, but we would like to mention two small classes of verbs which may be of interest here. The first consists of 'intentional verbs'. They take an infinitival complement but no *daß*-complement, e.g. *versuchen* 'to try', *zögern* 'to hesitate', *sich weigern* 'to refuse', *wagen* 'to dare', and a few others. The second class consists of verbs which do take *daß*-complements but do not permit infinitivals with *zu*. Instead they take the *accusativus cum infinitivo* (ACI, 'subject-to-object raising', 'exceptional case marking'). Semantically, this class is restricted to perceptual verbs like *sehen* 'to see', *hören* 'to hear', *fühlen* 'to feel', *riechen* 'to smell' in their basic meaning, as in *ich höre dich kommen* 'I hear that you are coming'.

The last type of complement to be mentioned is the one exemplified in *Ich höre, du seist gekommen*. Here *hören* is to be analysed as a cognitive verb. The complement is a sentence without complementizer. Contrary to the 'normal' subordinate clause, the finite verb is not found in final but in second position here. Moreover, it has to be a form of the subjunctive. This type of complement occurs with cognitive verbs and with *verba dicendi* as one form of reported speech.

Even our very rudimentary presentation of the facts with respect to the complements in object position shows that there is an unidirectional syntagmatic relation here. It is the verb which governs the object with respect to its form. For the subject this is different as far as agreement is concerned. If the subject is a personal pronoun, the verb agrees in number and person (*ich bleibe* 'I stay' – *du bleibst* 'you stay' – *wir bleiben* 'we stay'). If the subject is a noun phrase, the verb agrees in number and takes the form of the third person (*das Kind lacht* 'the child laughs' – *die Kinder lachen* 'the children laugh'). If the subject is a sentence or an infinitival clause, then the verb takes the form of the third-person singular: *daß du schläfst, ärgert Paul* 'that you are sleeping makes Paul angry'. There is no 'agreement' in this case but a relation of government. It is the subject which determines the form of the verb.

On the other hand, the subject position may be occupied by the same types of sentential complements as the direct object. There is, for instance, the large class of psychological verbs, whose prototype takes an animate dative (*das gefällt ihm* 'he is pleased with it') or an animate accusative (*das ärgert ihn* 'this makes him angry'). Most of these verbs can take sentential subjects. Moreover, they have to be subcategorized in a similar way to that of the direct object. So *vorschweben* 'to have something in mind/to think of' is a *daß*-verb, *erstaunen* 'to astonish' is a *daß/wh*-verb, and *interessieren* 'to interest' is a *daß/ob/w*-verb: *mir schwebt vor, daß du uns besuchst* 'I am thinking of your visit'/'I desire ...' *mich erstaunt, daß/wie du uns besuchst* 'I am astonished about your visit', *mich interessiert, daß/ob/wie du uns besuchst* 'I am interested in your visit'.

Much more could be said about the variety of expressions in subject position, for example, about the distribution of infinitival complements and their control relation. In all of this, the subject is not that different from the direct object, whereas both differ fundamentally from the indirect object. We do not find any sentential complement in this position.

Grammatical Relations and Diathesis

In the core grammar there are two main types of passive which can be called the *werden*-passive and the *bekommen*-passive. Both passives are very much alike in structure. The *werden*-passive (*Hans liest den Brief – der Brief wird von Hans gelesen* 'Hans reads the letter' – 'The letter is read by Hans') changes the direct object (*den Brief*) into the subject of the passive sentence (*der Brief*). We call this 'object conversion'. The subject of the active sentence (*Hans*) is changed into the *von*-phrase ('subject conversion'). For the paradigm of this passive the auxiliary is *werden*. The passive with *werden* manifests the highest degree of grammaticalization and is therefore considered to be 'the' passive of German.

The *bekommen*-passive (*Hans hilft dem Kind – das Kind bekommt von Hans geholfen* 'Hans helps the child ...') changes an indirect object (*dem Kind* (dat.)) into the subject of the passive sentence (*das Kind*). The subject is treated as in the *werden*-passive. The auxiliary *bekommen* (or *erhalten* in written language, *kriegen* in spoken language) is still on its way towards becoming established in this function besides its function as main verb. The main verb *bekommen* 'to receive, to get' takes an accusative (*Hans bekommt einen Brief* 'Hans gets a letter'). It is used frequently, but it is not a typical transitive verb because it does not take a *werden*-passive.

In order to describe the systematicity of the diatheses mentioned, it is best to characterize the conversion of the nominative, accusative and dative separately and then to have a look at their interaction. In doing so we will also accomplish a fairly general explication of what can be said to be a subject, a direct object, and an indirect object in German.

The conversion of the subject is highly grammaticalized, especially for the *werden*-passive. If the *werden*-passive is possible for a verb, then it goes with the conversion of the subject, i.e. only subject conversion is necessary for the *werden*-passive. The subject is regularly converted into a *von*-phrase. The prepositional phrase is optional for the *werden*-passive as for the *bekommen*-passive.

There seems to be no syntactic restriction for subject conversion in the *werden*-passive, but there seems to be a heavy semantic restriction. The subject can be converted, if it has the thematic role of Agent. Correlation between syntax and semantics is strict here, even for weak cases. Thus *ärgen* 'to annoy' takes *werden*-passive whereas *freuen* 'to be glad to' does not. We have *das ärgert/freut mich* and *er ärgert mich*, but we do not have **er freut mich*. As a consequence, every passive sentence of this type may appear with or without an Agent.

Subject conversion occurs with all kinds of verbs, no matter what number and what kind of objects they take. In particular, it occurs with verbs which do not take a direct object and therefore no subject in the *werden*-passive. An active sentence like *die Kinder tanzen heute* 'the children dance today' yields *von den Kindern wird heute getanzt* (lit.) 'by the children is today danced' which is called the 'impersonal' (i.e. subjectless) passive. Of course the impersonal passive does not need an Agent, so we get *heute wird getanzt* (lit. 'today is danced'). On the other hand it can have a formal subject *es* (impersonal *es*) like *es wird heute getanzt* (lit. 'it is today danced'). Yet this is not possible in subordinate clauses, which have to be subjectless for non-accusative verbs (*daß (*es) heute getanzt wird*) and which can be reduced to the absolute minimum of the verbal form itself (*daß getanzt wird*). All these reductions are quite normal for the *werden*-passive. They manifest the high degree of grammaticalization acquired by this construction.

For the subject there is an area of strict correspondence between syntax and semantics. Only if the subject is marked for agentivity it can be converted into a prepositional phrase. But as a grammatical function subject is grammaticalized far beyond this area. The logical reason for this might be seen in the fact that the subject is the goal of the conversion of other functional categories like the direct and the indirect object. In other words, the grammatical subject must be capable of bearing the semantic roles which are typical for the direct and the indirect object. Naturally, if this analysis is correct, it has some consequences for how the other grammatical functions are to be understood. The most striking difference between the subject and the direct object would be that 'subject' is a grammatical function in its own right, whereas 'direct object' is not.

An accusative complement (active) can be converted into a nominative one (passive) only if the nominative (active) is convertible into a *von*-phrase (passive). It would be in accordance with traditional terminology to restrict the term 'direct object' to those accusatives which can be converted into a subject. Traditional grammar uses the notion 'transitive' verb exactly in this sense: a transitive verb in German takes an accusative complement and has the *werden*-passive.

Seen from this point of view, the direct object becomes dependent on the semantics of the subject. The subject is convertible only if it is agentive, and consequently the accusative is convertible only if the subject is agentive. This might have the consequence that there is no uniform semantic correlate to the semantic function of direct object. Semantically, a direct object might be everything that goes with an agentive subject. Here we have a possible explanation for the peculiar difficulties in finding a notional characterization for the semantic role of the direct object. The traditional term 'Patient' is beside the point, and the term 'objective' of Case Grammar is as unspecific as the term 'Theme' used by generative grammarians.

What we propose, then, is to understand the notion of direct object, at least for German, in such a way that it is restricted by the semantic role of the subject. Since this semantic role has a syntactic correlate, 'direct object' remains of course a purely syntactic notion. Within its semantically restricted domain the direct object is highly grammaticalized. As has been mentioned, it can only have certain syntactic forms. Its defining syntactic property is its convertibility into a subject.

The status of the indirect object is again different. First, the notion 'indirect object' cannot be restricted to those datives which are convertible to the subject of the *bekommen*-passive. There are many verbs which clearly subcategorize for the dative but which do not allow the *bekommen*-passive, e.g. *widerstreben* 'to be reluctant to', *unterstehen* 'to be subordinate to', *angehören* 'to belong to', *entfliehen* 'to escape'. All grammars of German agree that it is very difficult to define the notion 'indirect object' syntactically. The reason is that one does not find a set of syntactic properties which define a homogenous class of datives. Due to the notorious problem of the so-called free datives, it is not possible to base 'indirect object' on the dative alone. There are dozens of verbs which accept a dative but which cannot be said to syntactically subcategorize for it e.g. *er kocht ihr Tee* 'he is preparing tea for her'; *das klingt ihr unwahrscheinlich* 'this sounds unlikely to her'. Furthermore, in some areas the dative is in keen competition with analytic constructions. Many verbs combine both with the dative and with a prepositional phrase: *ich schreibe ihm – ich schreibe an ihn* 'I write to him'. Overall, the dative as the case of a verbal complement is less grammaticalized than the accusative. In stating this, we confirm, in part, the hierarchy of syntactic relations known as NP Accessibility Hierarchy 'subject–direct object–indirect object–prepositional object'.

As a complement the dative is however clearly more specific than the accusative if one looks at its meaning. Most datives are animate. In the grammars they are characterized semantically with different terms like 'Recipient', 'Affected', 'Benefactive' or simply as 'Semi-agentive'. So, with respect to animacy, the indirect object clearly has to be put between the subject and the direct object. The animacy hierarchy is valid for German complements in the form subject–indirect object–direct object–prepositional object. It plays an important role in different parts of the grammar, e.g. for word order (see below pp. 381–4).

What has been said about the indirect object in general seems to be an *a fortiori* for dative conversion. Dative conversion occurs only if the dative is a Recipient. Furthermore, it occurs only if there is also a convertible subject. In other words the *bekommen*-passive depends on the semantics of the subject and that of the indirect object, whereas the *werden*-passive depends on the semantics of the subject alone. This difference might explain the fact that we have so many dative verbs which do not have a *bekommen*-passive.

Both the *werden*- and the *bekommen*-passive confirm the status of German as a nominative language in the typological sense of 'nominative'. In both diatheses we have sentence patterns with a grammatical subject, but without direct or indirect object. What is found as ergative structures in this language is marginal.

Sentence Type and Word Order

With respect to word order, German is considered to be of special interest for typologists. The topological system is counted as one of the most conservative within the Germanic language group. Word order is still relatively free, and there is a complex system of braces, dividing the main constituent types into strictly separated fields.

It is uncontroversial that the basic order of nominal complements is subject–object. Relative to the sequence SO, the verb can have every possible position. We have VSO (*schreibt Hans den Brief?* 'does Hans write a letter?') as well as SVO (*wer schreibt einen Brief?* 'who writes a letter?') and SOV (*wir wissen, daß Hans einen Brief schreibt* 'we know that Hans writes a letter').

But the variability of the position of the verb has nothing to do with free word order. As far as the basic sentence types are concerned, word order is distinctive. With a suitable intonation pattern, VSO is a yes/no-question or an imperative sentence e.g. *schreib einen Brief.* The SVO pattern can be a *wh*-question or a declarative sentence: *Hans schreibt einen Brief.* The function of SOV is different in nature. It is purely syntactic. SOV occurs in standard type subordinate clauses which have a characteristic initial element, be it a conjunction, a *wh*-word or a relative pronoun.

If one takes more complex sentences into account, SVO turns out not to be verb-central but verb-second, cf. *Hans schreibt seinen Freunden einen Brief* 'Hans writes a letter to his friends'. The question then arises whether German is basically verb-initial, verb-second, or verb-final. Verb-initial can be ruled out for many reasons, be it only the secondary communicative function of the relevant sentences (question, imperative). Verb-second is treated as basic by many grammars mainly because it is the pattern of the declarative main clause. Within language typology German is regarded as basically verb-final by a clear majority. In generative linguistics too, most authors decide on verb-final as basic word order. There are internal arguments for this view, such as the cohesion of the verbal group in final position, and there are external arguments from language acquisition and language disorders ('patholinguistics').

The characterization of the main clause as verb-second is an abstraction for most sentences. On the surface, verb-second is found only if the form of the verb is synthetic. A periphrastic verb form is always divided into a finite part in second position and a non-finite part in final position. So from *Hans schreibt einen Brief* we get *Hans hat einen Brief geschrieben* with the periphrastic form *hat geschrieben*. The parts of the periphrastic form are considered to constitute braces or a frame. Most grammars call this type of discontinuous constituent 'verbal braces' (*Verbalklammer*) or 'sentence frame' (*Satzrahmen*). The first part of the braces can be whatever may appear as an inflected (i.e. finite) verb form, be it the form of a main verb, of an auxiliary, or a modal verb. The second part of the braces is empty for synthetic verb forms. It might consist of a simple or complex non-finite form, of a verbal particle or a particle plus non-finite form.

In Figure 11.6 the braces divide the sentence into different sections, called 'topological fields'. The word-order regularities of German are mostly formulated in terms of these fields. For the main clause we get the forefield preceding the finite verb form, the middle field within the braces, and the final field following the non-finite part of the verb form. Co-occurrence restrictions differ considerably for these fields.

The forefield is regularly occupied by exactly one major constituent of the sentence, i.e. by the subject, by an object, or by an adverbial. If the forefield is occupied by the non-finite verb form, then the objects and the adverbials can go with the verb as indicated in the following sentences.

Figure 11.7 shows one of the many examples of pied-piping structures in German. It should be mentioned that the subject can never enter the forefield together with the non-finite verb, except in the case of some intransitive verbs as in *eine Lösung eingefallen ist mir heute* 'a solution has come to me today' ('ergative verb' in generative terminology).

The most striking difference between the forefield and the final field can be seen in the fact that there is no need to fill the final field at all. The final field

Figure 11.6

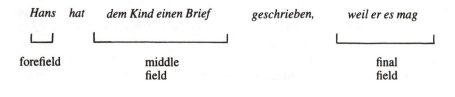

Figure 11.7

Hans hat heute einem Freund einen Brief geschrieben
(lit.) 'Hans has today to a friend a letter written'

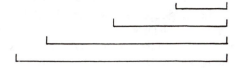

Geschrieben hat Hans heute einem Freund einen Brief
L_____I

Einen Brief geschrieben hat Hans heute einem Freund
L_____I

Einem Freund einen Brief geschrieben hat Hans heute
L_____I

Heute einem Freund einen Brief geschrieben hat Hans
L_____I

can be occupied by adverbials and in some cases even by an object, but whether this is possible or not is scarcely expressible in purely syntactic terms. There is a general tendency that a constituent is the more likely to appear in the final field, the heavier it is. By the 'weight' of a constituent is meant both its length, and also certain intonation features.

The filling of the final field is fully grammaticized only for subordinate clauses, cf. *Hans hat einem Freund geschrieben, daß er kommt*. Except for relative clauses, subordinate clauses are excluded from the middle field: **Hans hat einem Freund, daß er kommt, geschrieben*.

The most extended and complex part of the sentence is the middle field. There are no restrictions on the number and almost no restrictions on the type of constituent which can appear in the middle field. Furthermore, there are virtually no syntactic restrictions on the serialization of these elements. All one can do is to find out what has to be considered the unmarked order of subject, objects and adverbials in this part of the sentence.

The difficulty in doing so arises from the diversity of parameters determining the acceptability and pragmatic function of constituent order. For personal pronouns the unmarked and even grammaticalized order is subject–direct object–indirect object. For adverbials there seem to hold certain semantic restrictions saying that local–temporal is the unmarked order against temporal–local. Other criteria frequently discussed are definite before indefinite, short before long, subject before object, known before new, and unstressed before stressed.

A detailed examination of these parameters through systematic variation reveals that for the main types of complements there is no unmarked syntactic order valid for the language as a whole. What has to be considered as unmarked order is not determined syntactically, but semantically by the animacy hierarchy. So for a three-place verb from the semantic field of *geben* 'to give', the unmarked order is subject – indirect object – direct object – prepositional object, cf. *heute hat Hans seinem Freund einen Brief geschrieben* with *schreiben* 'to write'. The same relative order holds of course for two-place verbs as long as there is the normal descent of animacy from the subject to the object. Otherwise the unmarked order is syntactisized differently.

For a dative verb like *fehlen* 'to be missing', the order indirect object – subject is unmarked compared to subject – indirect object: *bis heute hat den Europäern das Selbsbewußtsein gefehlt*. For an accusative verb like *begeistern* 'to inspire', things are not so clear. But there is no doubt that the sequence direct object – subject is much more acceptable for a *begeistern*-type verb than it is for the paradigmatic transitive verb with an agentive subject like *behindern* 'to hamper': *bis heute hat keinen Europäer die Zollunion begeistert* is clearly less marked than *bis heute hat keinen Europäer die Zollunion behindert*.

11.5 Lexis

The vocabulary of Modern Standard German naturally shares most of its structural characteristics with the vocabularies of the neighbouring languages like French, Dutch, Polish, Danish or English. Since there is no developed methodology for comparing the overall vocabularies of closely related languages, I would like to mention very briefly two points with respect to which German might be different at least from some of its neighbours.

The first point concerns the distinction of a native and a non-native part of the vocabulary. With this distinction one normally refers to structural properties of words, rather than to etymological ones. It is widely agreed that one should make this distinction with respect to phonology as well as morphology. We will illustrate what is meant here by a few examples.

In segmental phonology, the [ʒ] is often regarded as being restricted to non-native words. First, it appears in non-native suffixes like [aːʒə] (*Blamage, Garage, Massage*), and second, it appears in phonotactically marked combinations as in [dʒ] (*Dschungel* 'jungle', *Dschunke* 'junk'). There are no combinations of voiced stop + fricative in the onset of syllables in native words. On the other hand, [ʒ] very easily finds its place in the system of consonants since it has a voiceless counterpart [ʃ]. Without [ʒ], there would be a gap in the system.

One of the main areas of non-native structural properties is found in the prosodic and syllabic structure of words and morphemes. Thus suffixes without influence on the accentuation of the stem are regarded as native, whereas stressed suffixes count as non-native. Oddly enough, the latter class seems to be even bigger than the former. It comprises suffixes like *-ieren* (*kuríeren* 'to cure' *garantíeren* 'to guarantee'), *-eur* (*Ingeniéur*, 'engineer', *Doptéur* 'farmer'), *-ion* (*Revolutión, Inspektión*), *-ist* (*Sozialíst, Romaníst*) and many others. With regard to the stem it is often held that the simple native stem is monosyllabic whereas polysyllabic stems are non-native. This criterion plays an important role in discussions of the peculiarities of non-native words in word formation. First, it is often very difficult to decide whether a stem is a simplex or not. There are for instance many words with stem final [oː] like *Manko* 'deficiency', *Lasso* 'lasso', *Photo, Ghetto, Porto* 'postage'. They have certain properties in common which show that they are marked (e.g. they take [s] as the plural morpheme). Moreover, [oː] cannot be separated by the stems in most cases, but these words do have more internal structure than say monosyllabic native ones like *Baum* or *Stuhl*. It is equally difficult to distinguish the basic types of word formation in the non-native part of the vocabulary. There are of course some native semi-affixes like *-los* (*friedlos* 'peaceless'), *-mäßig* (*schulmäßig* 'orthodox'), and *-frei* (*schulfrei* 'free from school/no school'). But such elements have a much wider range in non-native words. Morphemes like *poly-, mini-, makro-, bio-, zero-, mono-, extra- semi-, inter-, deko-, contra-, auto-, retro-* are clearly neither real prefixes nor first components of compounds in the relevant words.

German has been influenced by other languages in a very specific way. The influence may be thought of as coming in waves, first from Latin (from the Roman occupation up to the Renaissance), then from French (from the Middle Ages up to the French Revolution), and then from English. It could well be that this kind of steady and strong influence from different but relatively few sources has had its specific consequences.

As a second point I would like to call attention to the notion of univerbation, which is a key notion in most textbooks on German word formation. On the basis of its 'normal' word-formation regularities, German forms new words either by combining stems and affixes (approximately 250 affixes and 3,000 to 4,000 simplex stems) or by composition. The extensive use of compounds, especially of compound nouns, is often seen as one of the most characteristic features of the vocabulary. The latest edition of the orthographic dictionary of the former German Democratic Republic comprised about 75,000 entries (Duden 1985), the one of the Federal Republic of Germany about 110,000 (Duden 1986). The vast majority of the difference consists of compound nouns, showing how difficult it is to decide what has to be considered as being lexicalized.

One source of the numerous patterns of composition is univerbation. Syntactic phrases or parts of them are put together into one word. Some randomly selected examples are given in Figure 11.8. All of these examples

Figure 11.8

Mutters Sprache 'mother tongue' > *Muttersprache*
noun+noun   noun

kleines Kind 'litle child' > *Kleinkind*
adjective+noun   noun

auf dem Grund 'on the basis' > *aufgrund*
preposition+noun   preposition

legen auf 'to put on' > *auflegen*
verb+preposition   participle verb

fahre Auto 'drive a car' > *autofahren*
verb+noun   particle verb

Durst stillend 'thirst quenching' > *durststillend*
noun+partic.adjective   partic.adjective

manifest possible transitions from syntactic units to morphological units. Some of them have led to productive composition patterns which have become independent of their respective syntactic sources, yet there remains a close relation between the structure of complex morphological and syntactic units. A close relation of this kind seems to be typical of a major part of the complex words of German.

Further Reading

Basbøll, H. and Wagner, J. (1985) *Kontrastive Phonologie des Deutschen und Dänischen*, Tübingen: Niemeyer.
Duden (1985) *Der große Duden. Wörterbuch und Leitfaden der deutschen Rechtschreibung*, 18th edn, Leipzig: Enzyklopädie.
—— (1986) *Duden. Rechtschreibung der deutschen Sprache und der Fremdwörter*, 19th edn, Mannheim: Bibliographisches Institut.
Eisenberg, P. (1994) *Grundriß der deutschen Grammatik*, 3rd edn, Stuttgart: Metzler.
Fleischer, W. and Barz, J. (1992) *Wortbildung der deutschen Gegenwartssprache*, Tübingen: Niemeyer.
Grewendorf, G. (1988) *Aspekte der deutschen Syntax*, Tübingen: Narr.
Hawkins, J. (1986) *A Comparative Typology of English and German*. London: Croom Helm.
Heidolph, K. E., Flämig, W. and Motsch, W. (1981) *Grundzüge einer deutschen Grammatik*, Berlin: Akademie.
Helbig, G. and Buscha, J. (1991) *Deutsche Grammatik*, 14th edn, Berlin: Langenscheidt.
Lessen Kloeke, W. van (1982) *Deutsche Phonologie und Morphologie*, Tübingen: Niemeyer.
Olsen, S. (1986) *Wortbildung im Deutschen. Eine Einführung in die Theorie der Wortstruktur*, Stuttgart: Kröner.

Russ, C. T. (ed.) (1990) *The Dialects of Modern German. A Linguistic Survey,* London: Routledge.

Stechow, A. von and Sternefeld, W. (1988) *Bausteine syntaktischen Wissens,* Opladen: Westdeutscher Verlag.

Vennemann, T. (1982) 'Zur Silbenstruktur der deutschen Standardsprache', in T. Vennemann (ed.), *Silben, Segmente, Akzente,* Tübingen: Niemeyer, pp. 261–305.

Wegener, H. (1985) *Der Dativ im heutigen Deutsch,* Tübingen: Narr.

Wiese, R. (1988) *Silbische und lexikalische Phonologie. Studien zum Chinesischen und Deutschen,* Tübingen: Niemeyer.

Wurzel, W. U. (1971) *Studien zur deutschen Lautstruktur,* Berlin: Akademie.

12 Yiddish

Neil G. Jacobs, Ellen F. Prince and Johan van der Auwera

12.1 Introduction

Of all the Germanic languages, Yiddish looks least Germanic: it uses a Hebrew alphabet and is read from right to left, and its grammar and lexicon have undergone considerable influence not only from Hebrew and Aramaic (HA), but also from various Slavic languages. Today Yiddish exists as an international minority language of an older generation of Jews whose sons and daughters have largely assimilated themselves to English, Hebrew, Russian, French or whatever other language is spoken by the co-territorial majority, as well as of Orthodox Jewish communities that decide against assimiliation and keep Yiddish as a part of their identity. Both groups have their origin in the Jewish population of Eastern Europe, especially Poland and the western parts of the former Soviet Union. The drastic decline of the Yiddish speech community is due to a combination of the Nazi genocide, assimilation, and massive migration, caused by persecution, poverty or Zionism. That East European Jews spoke a Germanic language, amidst speakers of Slavic and Baltic, was again due to assimilation and migration, for their forebears had come from Germany (from the twelfth century onwards), where they had created Yiddish from Middle High German – in particular from the Southeast dialects – and a Semitic, primarily Hebrew, substratum and adstratum. East European Yiddish developed more in isolation from High German than the Yiddish of the Jews that had stayed in German lands and it was further influenced by co-territorial Slavic languages. This led to the emergence of two dialect groups, Western Yiddish (WYid.) and Eastern Yiddish (EYid.). From the end of the eighteenth century most Jews in the West began assimilating to their German linguistic environment and Western Yiddish has now virtually died out. Modern Yiddish, therefore, is Eastern Yiddish, even though it may now be spoken in the West again.

According to phonological and other criteria, the main Modern Eastern dialects are: Central Yiddish (CYid.; often called 'Polish' Yiddish), Northeastern Yiddish (NEYid.; 'Lithuanian', though encompassing large parts of Byelorussian territory as well), and Southeastern Yiddish (SEYid.;

Map 1   Classification of Yiddish Dialects (based on Landau and Wachstein 1911)

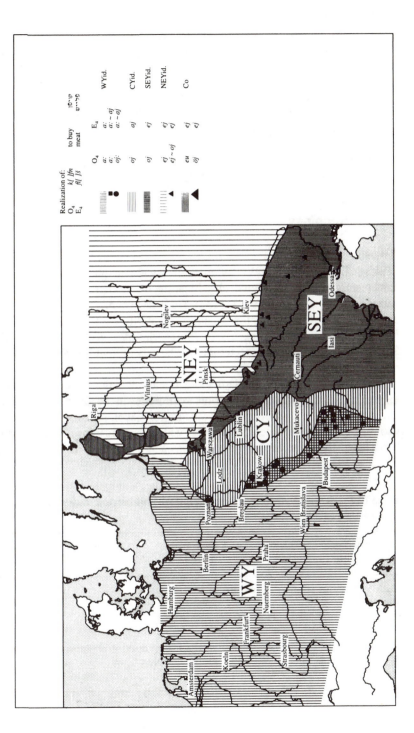

'Ukrainian' Yiddish). Modern Standard Yiddish (StYid.) is the variety that conforms to modern reference manuals, especially the ones associated with the YIVO (*yidisher visnshaftlekher institut*) Institute of Jewish Research (New York). While the pronunciation is inspired by Northeastern dialects, the grammar draws more on Southern dialects. German, too, contributed to the standardization, especially under the influence of those that regarded Yiddish as a corruption of German. Yet this German-based purism had an inverse effect as well, as it triggered an anti-German purism, successfully banning many of the German-inspired (*daytshmerish*) features, typical of some written Yiddish of the second half of the nineteenth century. Discussion will concern Standard Yiddish, unless otherwise noted.

12.2 Phonology

Vowels

Yiddish dialects differ radically in their vocalism, but minimally in their consonantism. The traditional classification of Modern Yiddish dialects is based on the realizations of Proto-Yiddish (PYid.) */ei/ and */ou/, as exemplified in the words for 'meat' (StYid. /flejʃ/) and 'to buy' (StYid. /kojfn/), respectively. Thus, CYid. /flajʃ/, /kojfn/; NEYid. /flejʃ/, /kejfn/; SEYid. /flejʃ/, /kojfn/. (Characteristic for largely extinct Western Yiddish are /flaːʃ/, /kaːfn/.)

The vowel systems of Standard Yiddish and the major dialects are given in Table 12.1. Underlying the synchronic symmetries in the given vowel systems are a number of dialect-specific diachronic developments. For example, varieties of Yiddish which have preserved phonemic vowel-length distinctions have filled the /aː/ gap (from Proto-Yiddish times) in different ways:

Table 12.1 Stressed vowel systems: Standard Yiddish and major dialects (one variant each)

	Standard Yiddish		Western Yiddish		Central Yiddish		Southeastern Yiddish		Northeastern Yiddish	
High	i	u	i–iː	u–uː	i–iː	u–uː	i–ɨ	u	i	u
Mid	e	o	e–eː	o–oː	e–—	o–—	e	o	e	o
Low	a		a– aː		a– aː		a		a	
	ej	oj	ej	ou (~ au)	ej	oj, ou	ej	oj	ej	oj
		aj		aj		aj		aj		aj

CYid. /aː/ < PYid. */aj/ (CYid. /haːnt/ < */hajnt/ 'today'); WYid. /aː/ < PYid. */ei/, */ou/ (WYid. /flaːʃ/ < */fleiʃ/ 'meat'; /kaːfn/ < */koufn/ 'buy').

The stressed-vowel system of Standard Yiddish is – historically – a simplified one, with mergers occurring at every point in the system except Proto-Yiddish */aj/ (cognate MHG /iː/). Standard Yiddish has a basic five-vowel system: /i, e, a, o, u/, plus the three diphthongs /ej, aj, oj/ (and is thus identical – synchronically, though not in terms of historical development – with one variety of Northeastern Yiddish). Distinctive vowel length has been lost; Proto-Yiddish long monophthongs are realized in Standard Yiddish either as diphthongized (PYid. */eː/, */oː/ as StYid. /ej/, /oj/), or shortened (PYid. */iː/, */uː/, */ɛː/, */ɔː/ as StYid. /i/, /u/, /e/, /o/, merging with existing diphthongs or short monophthongs. The cognates of Middle High German ⟨î⟩, ⟨û⟩ are Standard Yiddish diphthongs /aj/ and /oj/ (the latter merging with other /oj/ [< PYid. */ou/], and */oː/).

Yiddish shows general unrounding of cognate Middle High German front rounded vowels; cf. StGer. *schön, Löcher, müde, Häuser*, StYid. /ʃejn/, /lexər/, /mid/, /hajzər/ 'pretty', 'holes', 'tired', 'houses'. Regional Yiddish instances of front roundedness (e.g., [y] in Brajnsk; [øy] in Courland) are later innovations.

The issue of vowel length is crucial in Yiddish dialectology. Using a rough, geographically based generalization, it may be said that the westernmost dialects – Western Yiddish and Central Yiddish (an Eastern Yiddish dialect) – have distinctive vowel length, whereas the geographically easternmost dialects – Northeastern Yiddish, Southeastern Yiddish – lack this feature. However, the dialectal divisions are not as clear-cut in fact as this rough geographical classification implies. In Western Yiddish, the system of phonemic vowel length is quite fully entrenched and exploited. In Central Yiddish, it is arguably limited to the peripheral vowel qualities, /iː/, /aː/, /uː/. The system breaks down successively in the geographic sweep across Central Yiddish from west to east, as it approaches the Southeastern Yiddish territory. In Southeastern Yiddish, loss of length occurred relatively late, historically, and it may be argued that a length distinction remains marginally for at least one vowel quality: /i/ (either as /iː/ vs /i/, or via the qualitative distintion /i/ vs /i/). Loss of distinctive vowel length is considered a primary change in the development of Northeastern Yiddish, yet even here some vowel length survived into the twentieth century in certain conservative subregions of the Northeastern territory, notably, Courland, and (less) in adjacent areas.

Glides typically pose a challenge for classification (as consonant or vowel). In Yiddish dialects, there is an important positive correlation between the presence of phonemic vowel length and the presence of the [w] (= non-syllabic [u]) glide. Whereas Proto-Yiddish (which had distinctive vowel length) is reconstructed as having both unround [j] and round [w], lengthless Standard Yiddish shows only the unround glide [j]. Length-preserving Central Yiddish and Western Yiddish have [j] and [w]. Non-length dialects

Northeastern Yiddish and Southeastern Yiddish generally lack a [w] glide. In the conservative Courland subregion of Northeastern Yiddish, which has preserved phonemic vowel length (though with rapid collapse of length distinctions in the twentieth century under the influence of Standard Yiddish), the [w] glide is found. While both glides – [w] and [j] – may be associated (in Yiddish dialects) with long vowels/diphthongs, only [j] has independent consonantal function; cf. StYid. /ojx/ 'also' vs /jojx/ 'broth'; but not /**wojx/. (The double asterisks are used to show non-occurring or non-grammatical forms.) For Standard Yiddish, at least, there is little or no synchronic justification for deriving surface [v] (e.g. /ven/ 'when') from an underlying phoneme **/w/.

A situation of vocalic overlength (three morae) is found in Central Yiddish *breaking* and *drawl*. In both processes, [ə] is inserted between certain long vowels or diphthongs and a tautosyllabic consonant, resulting in overlong vocalic sequences. In Central Yiddish *breaking*, [ə] is inserted between any long vowel/diphthong (possible exception: /aː/) and tautosyllabic velar fricative /x/, /r/ (= [ɣ]); thus, compare forms with breaking (/r/ in syllable rime undergoes later vocalization and loss): /biːx/ 'book', /fiːr/ '(I) lead', /fuːr/ '(I) travel', /hojx/ 'high', /boux/ 'belly, stomach', /fiːrst/ '(you) lead' → [biːəx], [fiːə], [hojəx], [bouəst], [fiːəst], versus forms without breaking ($ = syllable boundary): [fiː $ rŋ] 'to lead', [biː $ xə] 'books', etc. Central Yiddish *drawl* appears to be an analogical partial extension of breaking to other (non-labial/velar) tautosyllabic consonants. Here, however, the vowels/diphthongs eligible are generally more limited to those with second mora [u]; thus: /buːd/ 'bath', /hout/ 'skin' → drawled [buːət], [houət], while remaining undrawled are: [buː $ dn] 'to bathe' ([d] not tautosyllabic and /brojt/ 'bread' (second mora of vowel ≠ [u]). Central Yiddish breaking is an obligatory rule, whereas drawl is an ongoing and incomplete change with optional application. In the eastern part of the Central Yiddish area drawl has been analogically extended phonologically to include the high front vowel /iː/. Also, in eastern Central Yiddish, breaking has been extended (though not uniformly) to environments where the velar fricative is not tautosyllabic: /fiː $ rn/ 'to lead', /biːxər/ 'books' → [fiːə $ rŋ], [biːə $ xə].

Unstressed Vowels

In dealing with unstressed vowels (at the word level) it is best to make two distinctions: (a) pre-tonic vs post-tonic position; and (b) underlying versus derived schwa. Because Germanic word stress overwhelmingly falls on the initial root syllable, pre-tonic syllables in Germanic tend to be habitually unstressed inseparable prefixes, with a greatly reduced inventory of possible vowels. In pre-tonic position, Germanic-component words tend to be limited to either [ə] (/gəzén/ 'seen') or [a] (/bakúmən/ 'get, receive', /antlójfn/ 'run away'; cf. Ger. *bekommen* 'get, receive', *entlaufen* 'run away'). Through input from the Hebrew and Aramaic, and Slavic components (as well as through more recent internationalisms), virtually any vowel/diphthong may occur in pre-tonic position (although here too there may be a tendency – especially in Yiddish dialects – toward a reduced inventory); e.g. /m[i]snágəd/ 'Orthodox Jewish opponent of Hasidism', /h[e]fkéjrəs/ 'neglect, wantonness, arbitrariness', /m[a]pólə/ 'defeat' /k[o]ntákt/ 'contact', /k[u]ndéjsəm/ 'urchins', /h[oj]dóə/ 'announcement'.

There is a strong general tendency in Yiddish for any post-tonic vowel or diphthong to reduce to schwa (with regional coloration). A schwa that – synchronically – is linked paradigmatically to a full vowel/diphthong is considered phonologically derived, as in: /kúnd[ə]s/ – /kund[éj]səm/ 'urchin-s', /tálm[ə]d/ – /talm[í]dəm/ 'pupil-s'. Non-linkable schwa is considered underlying in, e.g. /xánəkə/ 'Hanukkah' (cf. HA /ħănukkɔː/, /blótə/ 'mud' (cf. Pol. błoto). In varieties of Northeastern Yiddish there is some retention of vowel quality in post-tonic position: PYid. */óːlɔm/ 'world, public' > NEYid. [éjlɔm] (StYid. /ójləm/).

As part of the general weakening tendency, the sequence post-tonic vowel + tautosyllabic sonorant tend to be realized as syllabic sonorants. The deletion is not uniform, however; the tendency is strongest with nasals, less so for /l/, and generally does not occur in Standard Yiddish with /r/; thus: /nígn/ ([nigŋ]) 'melody' (cf. pl. /nigúnəm/; /mənúvl̩/ 'ugly/contemptible person' (pl. /mənuvóləm/), but /ʃíkər/ 'drunk' (pl. /ʃikúrəm/). Furthermore, when oblique marker -n is added to personal names ending in [ə], deletion does not occur: mójʃə-n → [mójʃən] 'Moyshe (obl.)'. Compare the oblique forms of /tátə/ meaning either 'father' or the proper name 'Dad': /tátə-n/ → [tatn̩] 'father (obl.)', versus [tatən] 'Dad (obl.)'. Deletion is also blocked where an unacceptable nasal cluster would otherwise result: deletion in /ʃrajb-ən/ → [ʃrajbm] 'to write', but no deletion in /kum-ən/ → [kumən] 'to come'. The historical apocope in the Germanic component which yields Yiddish /(ix) ʃrajb/, /kum/, /gas/, etc. (cf. StGer. (ich) schreibe, (ich) komme, Gasse) '(I) write, (I) come, street' occurred in the relevant source dialects of German pre-Jewish contact, and is not part of the internal phonological history of Yiddish.

A full vowel may be preserved in post-tonic position after an intervening morpheme boundary: after a strong boundary, as in: /frájnt#ʃaft/, 'friendship', /ʃéjn#kajt/ 'beauty', as well as after a weak boundary: /jid/ 'Jew' + /iʃ/ (adjective-forming suffix) → /jídiʃ/ 'Jewish'. There is a tendency in some dialects toward vowel reduction after weak boundary, thus: [jídiʃ] ~ [jídəʃ], [ʃéjd-im] ~ [ʃéjd-əm] 'ghost-s'. Again, non-alternating schwa in suffixes is synchronically underlying in Yiddish (e.g., in the adjective inflection /-ə/, in the feminine suffix /-kə/ (< Slav. /ka/), -ə (< HA /-ɔː/), or in the abstract noun suffix /-əs/ (< HA /-uːθ/)).

Consonants

The Standard Yiddish consonant system is given in Table 12.2. There is very little variation in the phonemic consonantal system across the Yiddish

Table 12.2   Standard Yiddish consonants

	Bilabial	Labiodental	Alveolar	Palatal	Velar	Glottal
Oral stops	p b		t d		k g	
Nasal stops	m		n	nʲ		
Fricatives		f	s	ʃ	x	h
		v	z	ʒ	—*	
Affricates			ts	tʃ ʤ		
Liquids			l	ļ r**		

Notes: *In some regions /r/ = [ɣ]; **Front /r/ = trill.

dialects. Many regional features (such as the confusion/collapse of hushing/ hissing distinctions (in Northeastern Yiddish) called *sabesdiker losn* 'Sabbath speech' < /*ʃabəs/ 'Sabbath', /*lɔːʃn/ 'tongue, language', or regional /h/-dropping: /ant/ < /hant/ 'hand' and non-organic /h/-insertion: /harbət/ < /arbət/ 'work') have largely disappeared under the pressure of standardization since the late nineteenth century.

Synchronically, Yiddish has a richer consonantism than Standard German, in terms of its (phonemic and allophonic) inventory and permissible consonant clusters. In the obstruents, there is fuller exploitation of the voicing distinction, including word-finally /zog/ '(I) say' – /zok/ 'sock'). In the affricates, Yiddish lacks /pf/ (StYid. /ferd/, /kop/, StGer. *Pferd*, *Kopf* 'horse', 'head'), but has /ts/, /tʃ/, /ʤ/.

The question of palatalized consonants (acquired largely through contact with Slavic) is problematic. In Standard Yiddish, the dentals (/t, d, s, z, n, l/) all have 'soft' (= palatalized) variants. However, only the distinctions /l – ļ/ and /n – nʲ/ have been universally phonemicized in Eastern Yiddish (and hence, Standard Yiddish): /mol/ 'time' – /moļ/ 'moth', /manʲə/ 'f. anthroponym' – /manjə/ 'mania'. Some Eastern Yiddish dialects have phonemicized /tʲ/, /dʲ/, and /sʲ/ as well. Allophonic palatalization of dentals and velars before a front vowel occurs regionally in varieties of Northeastern Yiddish and Southeastern Yiddish: /tir/ → [tʃir] 'door'. Standard Yiddish does not show – in Slavic loans – the distinction between 'hard' and 'soft' palato-alveolar fricatives and affricates; thus, Slavic /ʃ – ş/, /ʒ – j/, /tʃ – tç/, and /ʤ – dj/ are realized in Standard Yiddish only with /ʃ/, /ʒ/, /tʃ/, and /ʤ/, respectively. Standard Yiddish does not have final devoicing of obstruents. Like Standard German, Standard Yiddish, does not have geminate consonants.

Voiceless oral stops /p, t, k/ are unaspirated in Standard Yiddish. The phonemes /t, d, n/ are realized regionally as either dental or alveolar in their basic form.

Yiddish has a much fuller set of contrasts in the fricatives than does German. To a great extent this is due to the incorporation of lexical items of Hebrew/Aramaic and Slavic origin, which contributed more fricatives in more environments than are found in the German component. For example, Yiddish has initial /x/ in words of Hebrew/Aramaic, and Slavic origin, but not in German-component words (a possible exception: /xojzək/ 'fun; mockery' < Low German source); cf. /xojv/ 'debt' < HA vs /hojf/ 'courtyard' < German-component. Thus, when both Yiddish and German have borrowed a Slavic word with initial /x/, this /x/ was integrated into fundamentally different patterns; compare the incorporation of Slavic loan #/xr-/ in Yiddish /xrejn/ 'horseradish', German dialectal /kren/ (cf. Polish *chrzan*).

A discussion of Old High German */s/ in word-initial position is particularly instructive concerning the role of fricatives in Yiddish. Diachronically, in the relevant source dialects of German, word-initial /s-/ developed in two ways: /s/ > [z] /# ____ V (*sagan* > [zaːgən] 'say'); /s/ > [ʃ] / # ____ C (*slaːfan* > [ʃlaːfən] 'to sleep'). Thus, in Standard German, both /z/ and /ʃ/ occur word-initially (Modern German initial /ʃ/ before a vowel < */sk/; *scheinen* 'shine, appear' < /*skiːnan/); /s/ does not (natively). In contrast, Yiddish shows a full four-way opposition word-initially:

Word-initial Sybillant Oppositions

	Before a vowel	Before a consonant
s	/sojnə/ 'enemy'	/slup/ 'pole'
z	/zojnə/ 'prostitute'	/zlatə/ 'fem. anthroponym'
ʃ	/ʃabəs/ 'Sabbath'	/ʃlofn/ 'sleep'
ʒ	/ʒabəs/ 'frogs'	/ʒlob/ 'yokel, hick, boor'

Yiddish inherited a three-way (word-initial) contrast (/s/, /z/, and /ʃ/) from its Hebrew/Aramaic substrate. The German component only conributed words with initial /z/ or /ʃ/. Positional [ʒ] is found in Hebrew and Aramaic words ([xeʒbm̩] < /ħeʃboːn/ 'account'); however, the full phonemic status of /ʒ/ owes to Slavic-component input (/ʒabəs/ 'frogs').

The fullness of the set of fricative contrasts in Yiddish has also led to a richness in permissible consonant clusters beyond those found in the source languages, as illustrated, for example, by contrasting initial /sl-, zl-, ʃl-, ʒl-, str-, xr-/, etc. This richness is not limited to the fricatives, however; other non-Germanic initial clusters include, e.g. /dl-, tl-/, etc.

Eastern Yiddish dialects (as well as colonial German dialects) generally have an /l/ that is darker than in Standard German; Eastern Yiddish [l] is probably due to Slavic influence. Hard [ɫ] contrasts with soft [lʲ] in many Eastern Yiddish areas (with the exception of Northeastern Yiddish); thus:

/haltn/ 'to hold' – /palʲtn/ 'overcoat'. The distinction is marginally phonemic, but often allophonic ([lʲ] before stressed front vowels). There is a general association, however, of /lʲ/ and /nʲ/ with Slavicness', and Weinreich (1958) notes the creation of 'phonological pseudo-Slavicisms' with distinct semantic functions: /laxn/ 'to laugh' (< German component) vs /lʲaxn/ 'to guffaw', /knakər/ 'big shot' vs /knʲakər/ 'big shot' (more conceited than /knakər/). Thus, while /lʲ/ and /nʲ/ are recognized as phonemes in Standard Yiddish, they have a marginal status which merits special discussion.

Standard Yiddish /r/ may be realized as either front (apical) or back (uvular); these are the major variants found in Yiddish dialects.

Standard Yiddish has three nasal consonant phonemes: /n/, /m/, and (marginally) /nʲ/. /n/ → [ŋ] before a velar consonant; unlike English or Standard German, Standish Yiddish does not delete the [g] in /-ng-/ clusters: Eng. *long* [ŋ], StGer. *lang* [ŋ], StYid. /lang/ [ŋg]. The assimilation of /n/ to place of articulation of the adjacent consonant is general: /lip-n/ [m] 'lips', /lax-n/ [ŋ] 'to laugh'. Palatal /nʲ/ does not assimilate: /bankét/ [ŋk] 'banquet' vs /banʲkəs/ [nʲk] 'cupping glasses'.

Voicing Assimilation

In Northeastern Yiddish there is general anticipatory obstruent voicing assimilation (including across word boundaries). Thus: /(ix) ʃik bixər/ → [... g # b ...] '(I) send books', /(ix) lejg tfilən/ → [... k # t ...] '(I) put on phylacteries'. Central Yiddish generally lacks this assimilation, except in limited fashion in close juncture and rapid speech. Standard Yiddish has a limited form of anticipatory voicing assimilation. It is obligatory for devoicing: /ʃrajb/ + /st/ – > [ʃrajpst] 'you write', /ʃrajb/ # /tiʃ/ 'desk (= writing table)' → [ʃrajptiʃ]. It is mostly optional for voicing: /arojs + gejn/ – > [arojsgejn] ~ [arojzgejn] 'to go out'.

Syllable Types: Historical Development

Yiddish shows the results of two similar – yet historically and structurally distinct – processes of standardization of syllable quantity. Both processes occurred – independently – in pre-Yiddish times, and are reflected in the Hebrew/Aramaic, and German components of Yiddish, respectively. Both had the effect of making all stressed syllables *long*. However, what constituted *long* in the source languages differed. In the Hebrew and Aramaic component (as part of substratal pre-Yiddish Jewish vernacular), [+long] was defined as a single branching rime. Thus, original Hebrew and Aramaic long vowels in Pre-Yiddish were kept long in open syllables (HA /prɔː $ ṭíːm/ 'details' > Pre-Yid. */prɔ́ː $ tim/; StYid. /prótəm/ 'details'), shortened in (singly) closed syllables (HA /prɔːṭ/ > Pre-Yid. */prat/; StYid. /prat/ 'detail'). Original short vowels remained short in closed syllables, e.g. HA /mas $ qíːm/ > Pre-Yid. */más $ kim/; StYid. /máskəm + zajn/ ('be') 'agree', and lengthened in open syllables

(HA /tá $ ħaθ/ > Pre-Yid. */tɔ́ː $ xas/; StYid. /tóxəs/ 'buttocks, rump').

In the German process, short vowels were likewise lengthened in stressed open syllables (before underlying voiced consonants) /ta $ ga/ > /taː $ ge/ 'days'. However, there are two important deviations from the standardization of quantity found in the Jewish-vernacular substrate. First, long vowels were not shortened in (singly) closed syllables (Ger. /broːt/ 'bread' did not shorten). Second, in German there later occurred a paradigm-based analogical vowel lengthening; thus, [taːk] 'day' based on paradigm forms, e.g., [taːge], [taːgen], [taːges]. This analogical lengthening is not found in the Hebrew/ Aramaic component; cf. StYid. /tog/ 'day' (< *long vowel), but /prat/ vs /protəm/ 'detail-s', with no analogical lengthening. As a result of these independent processes, Yiddish has a number of morphophonemic vowel alternations which are typically limited to the Hebrew/Aramaic component: (StYid.) /oj – o/, /ej – e/, /a – o/, as well as full vowel or diphthong–with schwa (see Stress shift, below, pp. 397–8). Consonant degemination (found in all components of Yiddish) blurred many of the original environments for lengthening and shortening; thus, synchronically, Yiddish has all types of stressed syllable: short, long and overlong.

Prosodic Phonology

Stress

In its dominant German component, Yiddish shows the Germanic fixed stress on initial root syllables: /léb-n/, 'to live', /léb-ə-dik/ 'lively', /léb-ə-dik-ə/ 'lively' (inflected), /ba-léb-n/ 'to animate'. Two exceptions to initial root-syllable stress are: (a) 'Semitic-type' compounding (see below); and (b) stress on verb complements in verbs and nouns derived therefrom: /ojs/ (a perfectivizer) + /fregn/ 'to ask' – > /ójsfregn/ 'to interrogate', /er fregt ójs/ 'he interrogates'; noun: /(der) ójsfreg/ '(the) quiz'. The case for claiming initial root-syllable stress is further weakened by data from the Hebrew/Aramaic, and Slavic components, as well as recent internationalisms. Gernerally, however – with one important exception – whether stress is 'initial', penultimate, or otherwise classified, it is almost always fixed throughout paradigms.

The exception concerns a large number of words of Hebrew/Aramaic origin which exhibit movable stress in Yiddish. These are almost exclusively nouns paired either by number (singular – plural), or gender (masculine – feminine); for example, StYid. /gánəf/ 'thief' – /ganóvəm/ 'thieves', /xílək/ 'difference' – /xilúkəm/ 'differences', /tálməd/ '(male) pupil' – /talmídəm/ '(male) pupils', as well as /tálməd/ 'pupil' – /talmídə/ '(female) pupil'. A common claim is that Hebrew/Aramaic origin words in Yiddish reflect a shift from original ultimate stress (in Hebrew and/or Judeo-Aramaic) to penulti-mate stress, possibly as a partial adaptation to the Germanic pattern of (essentially) initial stress. More recently, a metrical analysis of the problem has suggested that there was a shift from the earlier Semitic stress pattern w͡s ('weak–strong') to a 'Germanic-like' pattern s͡w ('strong–weak'). The movable stress in related items like /tálməd/ – /talmídəm/ arose due to differences in embedded metrical structure (in pre-Yiddish times; these differences were the result of a pre-Yiddish linear retraction of stress based on vowel length). Additionally, in a number of derived adjectives and nouns consisting of a Hebrew/Aramaic origin noun plus a Germanic derivational affix the stress falls on the (original Hebrew) second syllable; thus: /gánəf/ 'thief' – /ganóvəm/ 'thieves', /ganéjviʃ/ 'thievish'; /tálməd/ 'Talmud' – /talmúdiʃ/ 'Talmudic', /kórəv/ 'relative' – /krójvəm/ 'relatives', /krójviʃ/ 'related, kindred', /krójviʃaft/ 'kinship'; but derivations also occur which are based on singular nouns: /xávər/ 'friend' – /xavéjrəm/ 'friends', /xávəriʃ/ 'friendly', /xávərʃaft/ 'comradeship'.

Synchronically, this inherited (< Pre-Yiddish, not Hebrew) movable stress shows a mild productivity in Yiddish. Under highly stipulated conditions, some non-Hebrew/Aramaic origin nouns are attracted into the paradigm with movable stress. Typically, these nouns are bisyllabic, monomorphemic, end in a consonant, and have stress on the first syllable. They thus resemble the Hebrew/Aramaic origin nouns of type /gánəf/ 'thief', /tálməd/ 'pupil', etc. Thus: /dóktər/ 'doctor' – /doktójrəm/ 'doctors' (< source?), /kúndəs/ 'urchin' – /kundéjsəm/ 'urchins' (< Slavic). The movable-stress paradigm is not an option if stress is not originally on the first syllable; thus, /kontákt/ 'contact (noun)' has plural /kontákt-n/, not /*kontákt-əm/.

Disrupting the general s͡w pattern are certain suffixes which require main word stress (usually internationalisms): /-al/, /-el/, /-ant/, etc.; e.g. aspiránt 'research student'.

A rhythmically determined secondary stress occurs two syllables before a main stress; thus, the unstressed /mə/ in /məʃúməd/ 'apostate' receives rhythmic secondary stress in the plural /məʃumódəm/. In this sense, rhythmic stress is related to foot formation rules, and the basic Yiddish foot s͡w.

Generally, Yiddish is a stress-timed language. Very little work has been done on Yiddish intonation; noteworthy is Weinreich (1956) on the 'rise-fall' intonation contour used in specific functions. In this rise-fall intonation, pitch goes from low to high, followed by a sharp fall (L–H–L). The initial L– must begin on the last primary stress of a construction. The realization of the subsequent H–L appears to be based on considerations of foot structure. The functions of the rise-fall intonation include: dramatic (semantic) transition between phrases, signalling of an incredulous question, and echo questions. The rise-fall intonation possibly may be traced back to pre-Ashkenazic Talmudic chant. It is not found in an identical form in languages co-territorial with Yiddish. The rise-fall contour in the above-mentioned functions has receded during the nineteenth and twentieth centuries, during the period of 'westernization'.

Word Boundaries

In words which begin with a vowel, Yiddish has a glottal stop which is much weaker than its Standard German counterpart. It readily disappears in context: StYid. /an epl/ – > [anepl] 'an apple'; cf. StGer. *ein Apfel* [ʔain ʔapfəl]. The weak Yiddish [ʔ] may be part of a general tendency in Yiddish to weaken word-boundary distinctions, linked with other boundary-associated phenomena (e.g. no initial aspiration of /p, t, k/; widespread loss of final obstruent devoicing) (King 1990). Nevertheless, morpheme and word boundaries are evident in a number of phonological rules in Yiddish, e.g. post-tonic reduction and compound-stress rules.

Compounding

Yiddish has compounds with the 'Germanic-type' stress pattern s͡w : /tógbùx/ 'diary' (< /tog/ [modifier] 'day' + /bux/ [head] 'book'), as well as with Hebrew/Aramaic-type' w͡s : /sèjfər-tójrə/ 'Torah scroll (lit. scroll of Torah)'. The latter type show Hebrew/Aramaic order of elements head–modifier. When two Hebrew/Aramaic origin words are compounded in Yiddish in modifier–head order, the stress pattern s͡w obtains: StYid. /jəʃívə-bòxər/ 'Yeshiva lad' (vs HA /bɔːhùːr-jəʃiːβɔ́ː/) is fully integrated into the dominant Germanic compounding pattern. The Hebrew/Aramaic-type compounds like /sèjfər-tójrə/ show partial, phonologically based, morphological integration into the Germanic pattern: gender and number are determined by the final element (as opposed to the head) in both source languages, Hebrew and German (Jacobs 1991).

Relation to orthography

Yiddish is written in a modified form of the Aramaic alphabet used in the writing of all Jewish languages (including Hebrew) since approximately the middle of the first millennium BCE. It is written from right to left. Yiddish orthography is often called 'phonetic' – except for words of Hebrew and Aramaic origin, which are written in their traditional (Hebrew or Aramaic) spelling. The development of modern Yiddish orthography has entailed a number of innovations in the use of an alphabet used for writing Semitic languages (based on consonantal roots) for writing a Germanic language where vowels are part of the root. Thus, vowels (and diphthongs) are represented as an integral part of the line of the written word (rather than with diacritics, in Semitic fashion). The modern Yiddish independent vowel symbols are innovations based on the Hebrew symbols for glides [j] and [w], and two consonants which were lost (as consonants) in the pronunciation of Ashkenazic Hebrew: ע (ayin; historically, *pharyngeal fricative /ʕ/) and א (alef; historically, *glottal stop /ʔ/). By orthographic convention (reflecting earlier Semitic orthography), Yiddish words which begin with a vowel are written with initial silent alef, or by a vowel letter based on alef: א /a/, and אָ /o/ – except for initial /e/, written with ע. (ע is also used to represent the

Table 12.3   The Yiddish alphabet

Letter	IPA	Romanization	Letter	IPA	Romanization
א	—	—	יי	[aj]	ay
אַ	[a]	a	כּ	[k]	k
אָ	[o]	o	כ (ך)	[x]	kh
בּ	[b]	b	ל	[l]	l
ב	[v]	v	מ (ם)	[m]	m
ג	[g]	g	נ (ן)	[n]	n
ד	[d]	d	ס	[s]	s
ה	[h]	h	ע	[e], [ə]	e
ו	[u]	u	פּ	[p]	p
וו	[v]	v	פ (ף)	[f]	f
וי	[oj]	oy	צ (ץ)	[ts]	ts
ז	[z]	z	ק	[k]	k
זש	[ʒ]	zh	ר	[r]	r
ח	[x]	kh	שׁ	[ʃ]	sh
ט	[t]	t	שׂ	[s]	s
י	[i], [j]	i, y	תּ	[t]	t
יי	[ej]	ey	ת	[s]	s

Note: Word-final forms given in parentheses.

unstressed vowel, [ə]. The Yiddish alphabet is given in Table 12.3.

The current century has seen the emergence of two main standardized orthographic systems: that of the YIVO (and the CYSHO (Central Jewish School Organization) of Poland), presented in 1936, and the Soviet orthography, developed after the Russian Revolution of 1917. The two systems are similar; the main difference is that Soviet orthography eliminated etymological spelling for words of Hebrew and Aramaic origin as part of a de-hebraization movement. Thus, Yid. /ʃojmər/ 'guard' is spelled traditionally in the YIVO orthography: שומר, and phonetically in the Soviet orthography: שוימער. (Less successful was the Soviet attempt to do away with the traditional convention of using the word-final variants of five consonants: פ – ף (/f/); צ – ץ (/ts/); כ – ך (/x/); מ – ם (/m/); נ – ן (/n/). These have been largely reintroduced in recent decades.) In the case of /xojzək/ 'fun, mocking', false etymology has led to 'Hebrew' spelling: חוזק, based on the common model in, e.g. /ʃojmər/: שומר. Conversely, Hebrew/Aramaic origin words no longer identified as such are spelled phonetically: מעקן /mekn/ 'to erase' (cf. Hebrew root מחק √mḥq). The rest of this discussion will be based on the YIVO orthography.

Six letters of the Hebrew alphabet are only used with Hebrew and Aramaic origin words: ב ח כ שׁ ת ת. In each case, there has been phonetic merger with other sounds: וו ב ק ס ט. (The latter are used generally, as the basic representations in Yiddish.) Thus, Yiddish /sojnə/ 'enemy' is written in the YIVO system: שׂונא, while in the Soviet system it is written: סוינע.

Yiddish consonant phonemes lacking an adequate corresponding single Hebrew letter are created through innovative combinations. Thus, the Yiddish affricate /c/ is represented by a single letter: צ, which was an affricate in Ashkenazic Hebrew (though fricative /ṣ/ in earlier Hebrew); Yid. /tʃ/ by טש (/t/ + /ʃ/), /ʒ/ by זש (/z + ʃ/), /ʤ/ by דזש (/d/ + /ʒ/).

In the YIVO system, the syllabicness of י when adjacent to another vowel is indicated by a dot underneath; thus: רויִק /ru $ ik/ 'peaceful' vs רויך /rojx/ 'smoke'. Sequences of וו (/v/) and ו (/u/) are disambiguated by a dot mid-level to the left of the vowel ו; thus ווּ /vu/ 'where', פרוּוון /pruvn/ 'to attempt'.

The marginal phonemes palatalized /lʲ/ and /nʲ/ are not systematically indicated in Standard Yiddish orthography (though they are sometimes represented by ני, לי); thus: שפּילקע /ʃpilʲkə/ 'pin', באַנקע /banʲkə/ 'cupping glass'.

The so-called 'phoneticness' of Standard Yiddish orthography is more a mixed (phonemic and morphophonemic) system. Morphophonemic voicing assimilations are not indicated: in /zog/ + /t/ 'say-s', /g/ – > [k] /____t, but is written זאָגט; similarly, /red/ + /t/ 'speak-s' is written רעדט. Consonant degemination (in non-compounds) is indicated: /hejs/ + /st/ – > הייסט '[you] are called' (= /hejs/ + /t/ – > הייסט 's/he is called'); thus also: /loz/ + /st/ – > לאָזט '[you] let', /zic/ + /st/ – > זיצט '[you] sit'.

In what follows, Yiddish forms will be referred to by means of the romanizations of Table 12.3.

12.3   Morphology

The Nominal Group

The Noun
Like German, Yiddish has a three-gender and two-number system. Gender is partially predictable from either the semantics or the ending of the noun. Thus words denoting males and females tend to be masculine (*rebe* 'rabbi'), feminine (*rebetsn* 'rabbi's wife'), respectively, and *-er* is associated with masculine (*fentster* 'window'), *-ik* with feminine (*gramatik* 'grammar'), and the diminutive suffixes *-l* and *-ele* with neuter (*hezl* < *hoz* 'hare'). In some cases the semantics and the ending may yield the same prediction, as with the feminizing suffix *-in* (*lererin* 'female teacher'), but they may be in conflict too, as with *meydl* 'girl' (diminutive from *moyd* 'maid'), which can be feminine or neuter. Gender differences between German and Yiddish cognates may result from variation in the ancestor Germanic dialects; Slavic

or Baltic influence (Yid. *klimat* (m.) 'climate' vs Ger. *Klima* (n.) but Pol. *klimat* (m.)); a different weighing of the semantics (Ger. *Mitglied* 'member' retains the neuter gender of *Glied* 'limb', but Yiddish *mitglid* has become masculine, even though it retained the neuter *glid*) or of the ending (Yid. *fentster* 'window' or *tsimer* 'room', both ending in *-er* and masculine, but Ger. *Fenster* and *Zimmer*, both neuter); or a syncretism between adjectival paradigms of different genders. The latter factor has been judged to be at work in the Northeastern dialects, where the loss of neuter gave rise to a complex two-gender system, with a feminine gender subdivided into three subgenders according to declensional differences in the adjectives and determiners.

Most Yiddish nouns can be singular or plural, much as in German, but with some small differences (e.g. Yiddish, different from German but like Polish, can pluralize *shney* 'snow' to refer to a large quantity of snow). There are two types of plural formation, Germanic vs Semitic. Germanic patterns involve the endings *-er* (*lider* 'songs') or *-(e)n* (*yorn* 'years'), vowel change (umlaut) (*tekhter* 'daughters' from *tokhter*), the combination of vowel change and *-er* (*beymer* 'trees' from *boym*), and in a few cases singular and plural are identical (*fraynt* 'friend(s)'). German and Yiddish do not always obey the same pluralization rule, primarily because Yiddish virtually lacks the *-e* plural (Ger. *Sohn-Söhne* 'sun(s)' vs Yid. *zun-zin*). There is also a Semitic-origin suffixation of *-im*, with or without other changes (*guf-gufim* 'body-bodies', *khaver* 'friend' – *khaveyrim* 'friends', *benyokhed* 'only son' – *bneyyekhidim* 'only sons'). Germanic patterns apply to many non-Germanic words, both Semitic (*sho* 'hour' – *shoen* 'hours') and Slavic (*sod-seder* – with umlaut – 'orchards'), and to a small extent Semitic *-im* is found on non-Semitic words (Yid. *nar-naronim* 'fool' vs Ger. *Narr-en*), sometimes with a pejorative ring (pejorative *profesoyrim* 'professors' next to neutral *profesorn* < *profesor*). Another Semitic plural ending is *-(e)s*. When written as תׁ, it only occurs on Semitic words (*khasene-s* 'wedding-s'), in which case there may be a vowel change as well (*dor* 'generation' – *doyres* 'generations'). But it can also be spelled as ס(ע) and then it attaches to Germanic words (*entfer-s* 'answers') as well as non-Semitic loans (*bobe-s* 'grandmother' < Slavic). The ס(ע) plural was often assumed to come from Romance, but is more plausibly seen as an extension of the תׁ plural to non-Semitic words. Though the plural is not phonologically predictable, regularities exist (nouns that end in *-er* and denote nationalities have a zero plural; feminine Semitic loans ending on ה get ות) and most productive are the suffixes *-(e)n* and *-(e)s*. A side effect of the synchronic productivity of the *-(e)s* rule is that English loans currently intruding in American Yiddish can keep their plurals (*sneks* 'snacks', *muvis* 'movies').

Yiddish has four cases: nominative, genitive, dative and accusative. They function more or less as in German, the biggest difference being that nearly all prepositions take the dative (except for *vi/mayse/betoyres* 'as' requiring the nominative). For the noun, case is of marginal relevance. Only nouns referring to people that are intimate or familiar to the speaker, like one's father, aunt or rabbi, have any case endings, and then only in the singular. The ending is -(e)n for the dative and the accusative and -(e)s (exceptionally -ns) for the genitive, irrespective of gender. Singular proper names too, when familiar, attract these inflexions.

Diminutives are formed by adding the suffixes -l or -ele to either the stem as such (tish/tishele from tish 'table') or a variation of it (umlaut as in gesl/gesele from gas 'street', epenthetic -kh- as in maylkhl/maylkhele from moyl 'mouth'). The plural suffix is -ekh, added to the diminutivizer (tishlekh/tishelekh), occasionally also used for non-diminutives ending on -l (shlislekh from shlisl 'key'). In the case of nouns that pluralize with -im and in a few nouns with -er plurals, the plural diminutive contains both the ordinary pluralizer and the diminutive one, separated by the diminutivizer (khokhem 'smart person' – khakhomim 'smart persons', khokheml – khakhomimlekh). From Slavic, Yiddish has borrowed the diminutivizers -inke, -shi, and -nju, mostly used on proper names, kinship and body terms (fusinke from fus 'foot', mamenju from mame 'mama'). This borrowing of Slavic suffixes is a more general phenomenon. Thus at least some speakers employ the Slavic augmentative-pejorative suffixes -atsh, -ak, -un, -uk, and -ets (yungatsh 'rascal') or feminizers -ke, -she, and -nitse (shnayderke 'female tailor'). Compounds are generally made in Germanic attribute-head fashion (folkslid 'folk-song'), but Yiddish also exhibits compounds of Semitic type, with head-attribute order (skhar-limed 'tuition fee' lit. 'fee-tuition').

Pronouns

The paradigm of the personal pronoun (Table 12.4) is similar to that of German, except that, whereas German has a dative-accusative syncretism only for the first- and second-person plural, Yiddish has it for the third-

Table 12.4   Personal pronouns

	Nominative	Accusative	Dative
1 sg.	ikh	mikh	mir
2 sg. fam.	du	dikh	dir
2 sg. pol.	ir	aykh	aykh
3 sg. m.	er	im	im
f.	zi	zi	ir
n.	es	es	im*
1 pl.	mir	undz	undz
2 pl.	ir	aykh	aykh
3 pl.	zey	zey	zey

Note: *Whether this form actually occurs is doubtful.

Table 12.5   Other pronouns

	Nominative	Accusative	Genitive	Dative
Demonstrative				
Distal, sg. m.	yener	yenem	yenems	yenem
f.	yene	yene	yeners	yener
n.	yen(t)s	yen(t)s	——	yenem
pl.	yene	yene	——	yene
Interrogative, human ('who')	ver	vemen	vemens	vemen
Indefinite, human ('someone')	emetser	emetsn	emetsns	emetsn
'everyone', m.	yederer	yedern	yederns	yedern
f.	yedere	yedere	yederers	yederer
'no one'	keyner	keynem	keynems	keynem

person masculine singular and third-person plural too, and in the Northeastern dialects this syncretism, with the dative form spreading to accusative use, is found for all the pronouns. As in some German dialects the nominative of the first-person plural is the same as the dative of the first-person singular.

The forms *ikh* 'I', *du* 'you', and *es* 'it' may cliticize to preceding or following verbs, sometimes reflected in the orthography, as in *hostu im gezen* 'have you seen him' and *s'ken zayn* 'maybe' (lit. 'it can be'). Intensification of the type 'I myself' is done by adding the invariable *aleyn* 'alone', yielding *ikh aleyn*.

Other frequent inflecting pronouns are listed in Table 12.5. Nominative, dative and accusative endings are the same as those for articles and adjectives (see below, pp. 405–6), while the genitive *-s* is shared with the genitive of the nouns. As with the personal pronouns, Yiddish has more dative-accusative syncretism than German; for the masculine forms the syncretism is complete. In contrast to this general morphological simplicity of Yiddish *vis-à-vis* German, however, the complexity of the 'double *-er*-form' *yederer*, unparalleled in German, is remarkable.

The proximal demonstrative has the same paradigm as the definite article (see below, pp. 405–6) – except for an additional genitive in *-s* – but apart from the neuter forms, it does not seem to be used often, and when it is used it is generally (perhaps always) understood as 'that' rather than 'this'. As in German, the words for 'what' (*vos*), 'something' (*epes*) and 'nothing' (*gornit*) are invariable. There is no separate relative pronoun; one uses forms of the interrogative pronoun *ver*, the originally adjectival *velkher* 'which', or the invariable *vos* with or without a resumptive personal pronoun or possessive determiner. The reflexive pronoun only has the form *zikh*. Pronominal adverbs exist with *der* (*derunter* 'under it').

Table 12.6   Determiners and adjectives

		Masculine 'the good pupil'	Feminine 'the good door'	Neuter 'the good book'
Singular				
Nom.	Yid.	der guter shiler	di gute tir	dos gute bukh
	Ger.	der gute Schüler	die gute Tür	das gute Buch
Acc.	Yid.	dem gutn shiler	di gute tir	dos gute bukh
	Ger.	den guten Schüler	die gute Tür	das gute Buch
Dat.	Yid.	dem gutn shiler	der guter tir	dem gutn bukh
	Ger.	dem guten Schüler	der guten Tür	dem guten Buch
Plural				
Nom./Acc.	Yid.	di gute shilers/tirn/bikher		
	Ger.	die guten Schüler/Türen/Bücher		
Dat.	Yid.	di gute shilers/tirn/bikher		
	Ger.	den guten Schülern/Türen/Bücher		

Determiners and Adjectives

The types of endings found with determiners and adjectives are the same as those found with pronouns. The biggest difference is that none of the former has any separate genitive form; for that function the dative has to be used (*dem altn yidns bukh* lit. 'the (dat.) old (dat.) Jew (gen.) book (= 'the book of the old Jew')). Table 12.6 illustrates the definite article and the adjective, and it contrasts them with German.

The definite article is unstressed. When stressed it acquires a proximal demonstrative meaning 'this', which may be made explicit by adding the Slavic particles *ot* or *ot o* in front of the article or the adjective *dozik-* also meaning 'this' or clitic *-o* following it. Allomorphs for the adjectival dative-accusative *-n* are *-en*, for adjectives ending on a stressed vowel or diphthong, or *-em*, for adjectives ending on *-n* (cf. also the *-em* and *-en* in the pronominal *yenem*, *vemen*, and *keynem* in Table 12.5). In post-prepositional position, *dem* usually cliticizes to the preposition (*nokhn* < *nokh dem* 'after the', *inem* < *in dem* 'in the'), a reduction process which can lead to a zero article in the case of a preposition ending in *-n* (*in park* 'in the park') and which in the Northeastern dialects can affect the feminine *der* (*oyfn* < *oyf der*).

In the case of the definite article, Yiddish is again distinguished from German by the greater degree of syncretism (which is complete in the plural and in the dative and accusative masculine singular). As to the differences in adjectival inflection, from the German perspective the Yiddish adjectival paradigm is a mixture of so-called 'strong' endings (nom. m. sg. and dat. f. sg. *-er* and pl. *-e*), 'weak' endings (nom./acc. n. sg. *-e*) and endings which fit either system. If it were not for the nominative/accusative neuter singular *-e* and the greater syncretism, one could say that Yiddish has generalized the strong inflection. Interestingly, a strong neuter ending (in *-s*) is possible too, but only when the adjective is predicative and preceded by the invariable indefinite article *a* (or *an* before a vowel), as in *dos bukh iz a guts* 'the book is a good (one)'. The neuter offers yet a third possibility: when the adjective following the indefinite article is used attributively, it either does not have any ending (nom./acc.) (*a gut bukh*) or the ending is optional (dat.) (*a gut(n) bukh*).

Both the inflection-diminishing effect of the indefinite article and the inflection extension of the predicative use are more general phenomena. Thus the determiner *ander* is sensitive to case and gender when preceded by the definite article: *der anderer shatkhn* 'the other matchmaker'. When preceded by the indefinite article, it is insensitive to case and gender e.g. *an ander shatkhn*, unless it is used predicatively: *er iz an anderer* 'he is another one'. The possessive determiners *mayn* 'my', *dayn* 'your', *zayn* 'his', *ir* 'her', *zayn* 'its', *undzer* 'our', *ayer* 'your', and *zeyer* 'their' are normally also insensitive to case and gender (*mayn/undzer shatkhn*), but not when used predicatively (*er iz mayner/undzerer*).

In the case of the possessives, there are two further uses that trigger inflection: (a) the attributive possessive is separated from the following noun by an indefinite article, as in *mayne a shvester*, yielding the special meaning 'a sister of mine'; and (b) the attributive possessive follows the noun, as in *der bankrot zeyerer* 'their bankruptcy'.

The synthetic comparative and superlative add *-er* and *-st*, respectively, to the stem or its umlaut version (*orem* – *oremer* – *oremst* 'poor'), but one also finds analytic forms with *mer* 'more' and Slavic *same* 'very'. Adjectives also have diminutive-like forms in *-lekh: kaltlekh* 'a little cold' from *kalt* 'cold'; and *-ink*, the latter conveying affection: *sheynink* 'lovingly pretty' from *sheyn* 'pretty'. Many adjectives can function as adverbs (*gut* 'well') or may turn into adverbs by the suffixes – *-erheyt* (*shtilerheyt* 'quietly'). Adverbs may also be formed from nouns, with the suffix *-vayz*, e.g. *masnvayz* 'massively', and there exist diminutive adverbs in *-lekh: shpetlekh* 'a bit late'.

The Verbal Group
Yiddish lacks the preterite and the subjunctive. Thus Yiddish verbs only have one synthetic paradigm, namely, the present indicative (*redn* 'speak': *red, redst, redt, redn, redt, redn*). There is little morphophonemic variation (as when the stem ends in *-s* and the second-person singular does not then add *-st* but only *-t*) and Yiddish has lost the distinction between strong and weak verbs as well as the distinction between singular modal verbs and their plurals and infinitives (Ger. *ich kann* – *wir können* < *können* 'can'; but Yid. *ikh ken* – *mir kenen* < *kenen*). Nearly all verbs are regular, exceptions being *zayn* 'be' and *hobn* 'have' and the *-t*-less third-person singular of the verbs *darfn* 'have to', *kenen* 'can, know', *megn* 'may', *muzn* 'must', *nit torn* 'not be permitted to', *zoln* 'should', as well as *veln* 'want' – *veln* is also used as the future auxiliary, but then it does have *-t* and it retains its vowel: *vil* – *vilst* – *vil* – *viln*

'want' vs *vel – vest – vet – veln* future auxiliary. Stems and second-person plurals also service the imperative.

As to non-finite forms, Yiddish has infinitives and both present and past participles. The infinitive is nearly always identical to the first- and third-person plural, with the exception of *gebn* 'give', *veln* 'want', *ton* 'do', *visn* 'know', whose present forms have different vowels (in all persons) (*ikh gib, du vilst, er tut, mir veysn*), and *geyn* 'go', *shteyn* 'stand', *zen* 'see', *zayn* 'be' (*mir geyen/shteyen/zeen/zaynen*). In the 'topicalization' construction (see section 12.4, Syntax), the infinitive has the shape of the finite verb stem followed by a syllabic *-n*. This is normally an ordinary infinitive, but we also find infinitives like *bin-en* and *izn*, both 'be'. The present participle is formed by adding *-ndik* to the stem, e.g. *shlofndik* 'sleeping'; though irregular infinitives have irregular present participles, e.g. *visndik* 'knowing'. The past participle is formed by prefixing the stem with *ge-* and suffixing it with *-t* (*geshikt* 'sent' < *shikn*), though many Germanic strong verbs follow the *ge-*stem-(*e*)*n* pattern, often with a vowel change (*gekumen* 'come' < *kumen*; *gekrogn* 'received' < *krign*). *ge-* is absent when the stem starts with an unstressed prefix (*gefunen* 'found' < *gefinen*) or ends with a stressed *-ir* suffix (*pasirt* 'happened' < *pasirn*).

The past tense is formed by *hobn* or *zayn* and the past participle, with *zayn* reserved for some intransitive *-(e)n* participles (*er hot geshribn* 'he wrote', *mir zaynen geblibn* 'we remained') and one also finds pluperfect with the participle of the main verb preceded by both a finite form of *hobn* or *zayn* and *gehat*, e.g. *er hot gehat geshribn* 'he had written'. The passive is formed by the auxiliary *vern* 'become' and the past participle; the future by the auxiliary *veln* and the infinitive; and the conditional takes the auxiliary *voltn* followed by either the past participle or (less often) the infinitive.

As in German, Yiddish verbs may contain prefixes, which if stressed and if the verb is finite, occur as separate words (particles) following the finite verb, e.g. *ikh heyb on* 'I start', *ikh vil onheybn* 'I want to start'. Under the influence of contiguous Slavic languages, which abound in verbal prefixes and assign them a central role in their verbal aspect systems, many of the Germanic prefixes of Yiddish greatly extended and changed their uses: thus *on-*, though the cognate of German *an-*, is the analogue of Slavic *na-*, in that it can express that the object of the verb is made in larger quantities, e.g. *onbakn* 'bake an accumulation of'.

12.4 Syntax

(Eastern) Yiddish syntax differs in a number of interesting respects from the syntax of other Germanic languages. Due to limitations of space, we shall discuss primarily those aspects where there is a significant difference, especially between Yiddish and its closest relative, German.

The Nominal Group

The [NP NP] Construction

One noteworthy feature of the nominal group is that adjectival modifiers, which may occur prenominally (*a sheyn meydl* 'a pretty girl', *di grine oygn* 'the green eyes', *mayn mishpokhe* 'my family') may also occur postnominally in an NP–NP structure: *a meydl a sheyne, di oygn di grine, di mishpokhe mayne*. (Interestingly, Semitic has such a construction.)

Not surprisingly, any noun phrase may in fact occur in second position, whether it includes an adjective or not, so long as it can be understood predicatively: *eyner a yid* 'one (who is) a Jew/guy', *a yid a melamed* 'a Jew/guy (who is) a teacher', *a melamed a kabstn* 'a teacher (who is) a pauper'. Note that the noun phrases may be iterated: *eyner a yid a melamed* 'one (who is a) Jew/guy (who is) a teacher'.

Anaphora

In Yiddish, noun phrases representing salient entities may sometimes be deleted/suppressed, although the exact discourse conditions are not entirely clear. Note that the suppression of subjects ('Subject pro-drop') behaves differently from the suppression of objects ('Object pro-drop').

Subject Pro-drop

In colloquial Standard Yiddish, salient main clause initial subjects can be deleted: Q: *vu iz der mentsh?* A: Ø *iz in shtub* 'where is the person? (he) is in the house'. Far less common, but equally grammatical, is the deletion of salient non-initial subjects and of salient subordinate clause subjects: *Efsher volst Ø mir gekent layen a finf rubl* 'maybe (you) could loan me about five roubles' and *shpring nit, vorem Ø vest araynfaln un Ø vest zikh tsebrekhn ruk un hent* 'don't jump, because (you) will fall in and (you) will break your neck', respectively. Note that the trace of the deleted initial subject suffices to fill Initial field (see below, p. 412).

Object Pro-drop

In contrast, all varieties of Standard Yiddish, formal as well as colloquial, manifest Object pro-drop. The inferred object may have specific reference: *hot er aroysgenumen fun keshene naynhundert nayn un nayntsik rubl un hot avekgevorfn Ø oyf der erd* 'so he took out 999 rubles from his pocket and threw (them) away on the ground'. Object pro-drop occurs freely in subordinate clauses: *zogt der politsmeyster, az, ven der rov farshteyt daytsh, vet er oykh farshteyn Ø* 'so the police sergeant says that, if the rabbi understands German, he'll also understand (it)'. Finally, both Subject pro-drop and Object pro-drop may occur in a single clause: *'ikh hob im oysgegebn, vos zol ikh ton?'* *Vert er in kas: 'Ø Host oysgegebn Ø? In eyn tog a gantsn rubl?'* '"I've spent it, what should I do?" So he gets angry: "(You) spent [it]? In a single day a whole ruble?"'

The Verbal Group

Tense
Yiddish, like Slavic, lacks sequence of tenses. That is, just as the reference time of the main clause is the time of the utterance, the reference time of a subordinate clause is the time of the clause in which it is embedded, with no sequence of tense modifications: *an oyrekh iz amol gezesn ban a balebos un hot gevart, biz me vet derlangen esn* 'a guest once sat in a gentleman's house and waited until they served (lit. will serve) the food'.

Periphrastic Verbs
Yiddish has a productive means for forming periphrastic verbs: a semantically weak auxiliary verb plus a nominal complement. In one type, the nominal is a nominalized verb, the standard nominalization being the zero affix on the verb stem; such periphrastic verbs are markedly perfective in meaning: *a kuk gebn* 'look', *a loz ton* 'let', *a freg ton* 'ask'. In the other major type, the nominal is a Semitic borrowing (often a passive form of the Hebrew verb) and the auxiliary verb is typically, though not necessarily, *zayn* 'be': *mekane zayn* 'envy', *khasene makhn* 'marry off', *nifter vern* 'die'.

Interestingly, in many dialects, if the periphrastic verb is transitive, it is conjugated in the present perfect with *hobn* 'have' even if its auxiliary verb is *zayn* 'be', which otherwise would be conjugated with *zayn*: *me hot im mekaber geven* 'one (has) buried him'. The syntax of periphrastic verbs is basically that of the verb + separable prefix.

Zayn-*deletion in Vos-*clauses
Finite forms of *zayn* 'be' may be gapped in all types of *vos*-clauses: *der doyerkayt, vos efsher Ø zey bashert* 'the posterity that (is) perhaps destined to them'; *vos Ø geven iz geven* 'what was (lit. been) was'.

Grammatical Relations: The Passive and Related Constructions
Yiddish lacks the 'impersonal passive' of German, often using instead an active form with *men* 'one' as subject: *ven men darf hobn moyekh, helft nit keyn koyekh* 'when brains are needed, brawn won't help', or else an active form of the verb with a reflexive pronoun and with the Patient as subject: *es brot zikh a katshke* 'a duck is being roasted'.

Unmarked Word Order
Yiddish is generally taken to be SVO, like English and the Scandinavian languages, with the added constraint that the finite verb is in second position in the clause (V2), as in all other Germanic languages except English. More unusual is the fact that, in Yiddish, verb-second applies categorically in subordinate as well as in main clauses. We shall look more closely at these generalizations by considering separately the different clause-types of Yiddish–declarative, imperative, and interrogative.

Declaratives

Declarative clauses include some main clauses and basically all subordinate clauses and are the most straightforward examples of both SVO word order and verb-second. On the surface, however, Yiddish appears to have two types of declaratives, those with clear SVO word order and verb-second and those that appear to be VSO without verb-second. We shall consider each of them and try to show that all may be subsumed under SVO with verb-second.

That Yiddish is SVO is shown in: *ikh hob gezen mitvokh, az ikh vel nit kenen kumen donershtik* 'I saw on Wednesday that I wouldn't be able to come on Thursday'; that it obeys verb-second in both main and subordinate clauses can be seen in: *mitvokh hob ikh gezen, az donershtik vel ikh nit kenen kumen* 'on Wednesday I saw that on Thursday I wouldn't be able to come', cf. **Mitvokh ikh hob . . . , *. . . az donershtik ikh vel . . .*

In addition to such canonical declaratives, Yiddish has 'Consecutive' declaratives, with an apparent VSO word order: *az a moyz falt arayn in a top milkh, varft men arayn in top a kats, un di kats frest op di moyz, ratevet men di milkh* 'when a mouse falls into a pot of milk, you throw a cat into the pot and the cat eats up the mouse, so one saves the milk'; *a telegram darf men shraybn kurts un sharf. Ot gib a kuk, ikh vel shraybn, vest du zen* 'a telegram you have to write short and to the point. Look here, I'll write it, so you'll see'. Such clauses necessarily follow some other clause and convey the understanding that the proposition they represent somehow follows from or is caused by the proposition represented by the preceding clause. They may not occur in subordinate clauses, nor may they be preceded by a conjunction: **ikh vel shraybn, ikh meyn (az) vest du zen* (lit.) 'I will write, I think (that) will you see'; **Ikh vel shraybn un vest du zen* (lit.) 'I will write and will you see'.

One way to account for the syntactic facts that such clauses may not be discourse-initial and may neither be embedded nor follow a conjunction is to say that these clauses are in fact SVO and verb-second, Initial field being filled, at some level, by the preceding clause. This would also account for the fact that Consecutive declaratives may undergo VP-deletion but not Gapping. Consider: *zi geyt arayn un er (geyt) aroys* 'she goes in and he goes out' (as two independent events); *zi geyt arayn, *(geyt) er aroys* 'she goes in, so he goes out'. In the first, we have a conjunction of two canonical clauses with the same verb and with the understanding of two independent events, and Gapping is possible. In the second, however, the second clause is a Consecutive clause, with the understanding that the event in this clause follows from, or is caused by, the event in the first clause, and with this understanding, Gapping is not possible. Likewise, Gapping is impossible where there is an initial subordinate clause: *az zi geyt arayn, *(geyt) er aroys* 'when she goes in, he *(goes) out'. If we say that the clause preceding a Consecutive declarative is in initial position, then the facts in the case of Consecutive declaratives are the same as the facts of this last example.

Similarly, consider: *zi geyt arayn un er vil (arayngeyn) oykh* (as two independent states) 'she goes in and he wants to (go in) also', where we have two conjoined clauses with the same verb phrase and where VP-deletion is possible. Likewise, where we have a Consecutive declarative following a clause with the same verb phrase, VP-deletion is also possible: *zi geyt arayn, vil er (arayngeyn) oykh* (as cause–effect) 'she goes in, so he wants to (go in) also'. Now consider: *az zi geyt arayn, vil er (arayngeyn) oykh* 'when she goes in, he wants to (go in) also', where we see that VP-deletion is also possible in a main clause when there is an identical verb phrase in an initial subordinate clause.

OV Relics

While basically SVO, Yiddish shows significant relics of an earlier SOV order: the syntax of the passive, of periphrastic verbs, and of separable prefixes, and clitic floating/climbing.

In the passive, the past participle of the main verb categorically precedes the past participle of the auxiliary verb: *di shtub iz opgebrent gevorn/*gevorn opgebrent* 'the house was burned down'.

Likewise, periphrastic verbs tend to have OV order, categorically when the verb-complement semantics is not transparent: *ven ikh hob khasene gehat/ *?gehat khasene, hob ikh gehat a groyse khasene* 'when I got married, I had a big wedding', *er vet maskim zayn/*zayn maskim* 'he will agree'.

Similarly, separable prefixes precede their verb, unless of course the verb has been moved to second position by verb-second: *er hot zikh ongeton/ *geton on* 'he got dressed'; *ir darft mikh oyfvekn/*vekn oyf* 'you must wake me up'.

Finally, Floating and Climbing are possible relics of an earlier OV order. In Floating, constituents in the verb phrase may cliticize on to the finite verb; in Climbing, constituents in an embedded infinitival clause may cliticize on to the (matrix) finite verb. In both cases, the displaced constituents may of course wind up preceding the verb which governs them. They may be pronouns: *mayn shviger hot **zikh** okorsht oyfgehongen* 'my mother-in-law just hanged **herself**' (Floating); prepositional phrases containing pronouns: *ir megt zikh **oyf mir** farlozn* 'you can depend **on me**' (Climbing); full noun phrases: *ober dos hot **dem rebn zaynem** shtark fardrosn* 'but this annoyed **his rabbi** a lot' (Floating); prepositional phrases containing full noun phrases: *eynmol iz **tsum rebn** gekumen a yidene* 'once an old bag came **to the rabbi**' (Floating); adverbials: *zey zenen **dortn** geleygn ban im in shtub* 'they were lying **there** in his house' (Floating); and miscellaneous particles: *me ken **dokh nokh**, khas vesholem, trefn imetsn in oyg!* '**After all**, one could, **God forbid**, hit someone in the eye' (Climbing). Note that such Climbing may occur not only out of bare infinitival phrases, as above, but also out of infinitival *tsu*-clauses: *ikh hob **aykh** fargesn tsu zogn* 'I forgot to tell **you**', and infinitival *wh*-clauses: *vos iz **zikh** do faran far vos tsu shemen?* 'what is there here to be ashamed of?' (lit. '... for which to shame **oneself**?').

Initial Field: Further Comments

Given an analysis whereby Consecutive declaratives have the preceding clause in Initial field, we can make the generalization that all declarative clauses in Yiddish are SVO and verb-second, at some level at least, and that Initial field is obligatorily filled. The default filler is the subject, whether it originates here or not, but just about any constituent may be moved into Initial Field by topicalization, to be discussed below.

If neither the subject nor a topicalized constituent occupies Initial field, then expletive *es* 'it' fills it. This expletive is merely a place-holder and not a dummy subject: *es iz mir kalt un nas* 'I'm cold and wet', *mir iz (*es) kalt un nas*; *es regnt shoyn a gantsn tog, iz (*es) mir kalt un nas* 'It's been raining all day so far, so I'm cold and wet'. Here we have a subjectless predicate, where the experiencer occurs in the dative case. In the first example, a canonical declarative where nothing has been topicalized, an expletive fills Initial field. In the second, the dative noun phrase has been topicalized and no expletive is possible. Likewise, in the third, a Consecutive declarative, the preceding clause fills Initial field (at some level) and no expletive is possible. We find the same expletive in canonical declaratives where the subject has been postposed and nothing has been topicalized: *es iz faran a goldshmid Roznblat in Moskve, ober ba undz in Varshe iz (*es) faran a goldshmid Rozntsvayg* 'there's a goldsmith Rosenblatt in Moscow, but at home in Warsaw there's a goldsmith Rosenzweig'.

Imperatives

Imperatives are, not surprisingly, verb-initial clauses: *gib mir epes tsum esn* 'give me something to eat', *lozt aykh got helfn* 'let God help you'. The imperative verb occurs in first position, Initial field being empty or non-existent, with no subject expressed, and with the same sort of floating/climbing found in declarative clauses. Thus it seems that, whatever position the finite verb moves to (or occurs in, regardless of how it got there) in declarative clauses, it moves to (or occurs in) the same position in imperatives, the only difference being the lack of an Initial field. However, the subject *may* be expressed, especially when it is contrastive: *gey du arayn, un ikh vel vartn* 'go in and I'll wait' (= 'You go in and I'll wait'), *der zogt: 'Nemt ir, Reb Yankl,' un yener zogt: 'Nemt ir, Reb Yitskhok'* 'one says, "You take [it], Mr Jake", and the other says, "You take (it), Mr Isaac"'.

It should be noted that, in spite of what has just been said, we do find apparent verb-second imperatives, that is, imperatives with a filled Initial field. This position may be filled by the subject: *du nem un loyf, un ikh vel mir geyn pamelekh* 'you start running and I'll walk slowly'; by a topicalized constituent: *dernokh gey dervayz, az du bist nit keyn ber!* 'then go and prove that you're not a bear!'; or by a particle: *to kush mikh nit in kop* 'then don't kiss me on the head'. Note that, as in the case of the expressed post-verbal subjects above, the initial material in such imperatives is often, though not necessarily, contrastive. In any event, one must acknowledge that there does appear to be a possible Initial field in imperatives. However, as we shall see in the case of interrogatives, this position may be outside the clause entirely, in which case all imperatives would be verb-initial.

In addition, Yiddish has a double imperative, where one imperative immediately follows the other and is its complement. The first imperative is typically a verb of coming or going: *gey red tsun im* 'go talk to him'; *kumt est* 'come eat'.

Finally, Yiddish has a letive construction etymologically related to *lozn* 'let', but with the frozen form *lomir* 'let us', followed by the infinitive. Like other imperatives, it is canonically verb-initial: *lomir shmusn* 'let's chat', triggers climbing: *lomir zikh eyn eyntsikn mol iberton di kleyder* 'let's just once exchange clothing', and can be preceded by particles: *ot lomir prubirn a freg ton dem ershtn yidn vos mir veln trefn* 'let's just try to ask the first guy we meet'.

Interrogatives

Interrogatives can occur, in somewhat different forms, in main clauses, i.e. as direct questions; and in subordinate clauses, i.e. as indirect questions. We shall discuss only main-clause interrogatives in this section and deal with subordinate clause interrogatives when we deal with subordination below (pp. 415–7).

Yiddish main-clause interrogatives (i.e. direct questions) are generally, as would be expected, verb-initial clauses (on the assumption that the initial question word is in the complementizer position rather than in the clause proper): *bist du meshuge?* 'are you crazy?'; *vu-zhe iz di tsveyte polke?* 'where on earth is the second drumstick?' As is the case with imperatives, interrogatives may be preceded by a topicalized element or a particle. However, if an interrogative complementizer is present, the topicalized element or particle precedes it, indicating that the clause is in fact verb-initial: *to far vos geyst du on hoyzn?* 'so why are you walking around without pants?, **far vos to geyst du on hoyzn?* On the whole, *wh*-Movement is possible out of subordinate clauses, sometimes with a verb-initial word order resulting in the subordinate clause: *vos meynt ir hot men derlangt tsum tish?* 'what do you think they served?' (lit. '... have they ...').

One noteworthy feature is that Yiddish has an optional overt complementizer for main clause yes/no interrogatives, *tsi* 'if, whether; or': *tsi zogst du mir ersht itst?* 'are you telling me now for the first time?' A minor point, which may be lexical rather than syntactic, is the occurrence of *vos* 'what' for *tsu vos* 'why; for what purpose'; *vos darf ikh a vayb?* 'what do I need a wife (for)?', *vos zol ikh dir plutsim gebn tsen kopikes?* 'what should I give you ten kopeks (for) all of a sudden?'

In addition, note that Yiddish has a *vos–far* split, analogous to German: *vos far a yontev iz dos?/vos iz dos far a yontev?* 'what kind of holiday is this?'

Finally, like many languages of Eastern Europe, Yiddish has multiple *wh*-fronting, about which very little is known: *hot zi nit gekent farshteyn ver mit vemen es shlogt zikh* 'so she couldn't understand who was fighting with whom'.

Marked Word Orders

Topicalization

Topicalization is very frequent in Yiddish, with just about any constituent being topicalizable, island effects aside. (By *island effects*, I mean the well-known effects of the constraints against moving constituents out of certain complex configurations, e.g. sentential subjects, relative clauses, however those constraints and effects are to be described.) One particularly noteworthy construction is Finite Verb Topicalization, where the stem of the finite verb is copied into Initial field with an infinitive ending affixed: *izn iz er a soykher un handlen handlt er mit tvue* 'as for what he is (lit. 'is' + inf.), he's a merchant, and, as for what he deals in (lit. 'deal' + inf.), he deals in grain'.

Subject Postposing

As noted above, subjects occur in Initial field (canonically) or in Middle field if Initial field is occupied by some other constituent or if the clause is a Consecutive declarative or verb-initial. In addition, subjects may be post-posed to the end of the verb phrase, Final field. If the clause is verb-second and if nothing is topicalized, dummy *es* occupies Initial field: *es iz geshtorbn a raykher goy* 'a rich gentile died', *es hobn breges oykh di yamen* '(even) the seas have their shorelines/limits'. The dummy noun phrase does not occur if the clause is (real or apparent) verb-initial: *der reboyney-shel-oylem hot derhert azelkhe diburim fun Moyshen, iz (*es) im ayngefaln dos harts* 'the Lord heard such words from Moses, his heart sank'; or if something is topicalized: *er zol oysrufn, az ba im iz (*es) farfaln gevorn a tsig* 'he should announce that a goat of his got lost'.

Prepositional phrases may and clauses must be extraposed beyond the postposed subject: *amol iz gekumen a yid fun a yor zibetsik tsum rov* 'once a guy of about 70 came to the rabbi', *tsum shenstn balebos fun shtot iz gekumen a shadkhn, redn a shidekh dem balebos' tokhter* 'to the finest gentleman in town came a matchmaker to arrange a marriage for the gentleman's daughter'.

Note that this construction is limited neither to 'presentational' verbs nor to indefinite subjects nor to intransitives, its felicitous occurrence constrained only by the discourse condition that the subject does not represent an entity already salient in the discourse model.

Existential Sentences

Canonical existential sentences consist of expletive *es* 'it' in Initial field, some form of the verb *zayn* 'be', the particle *do* (lit.) 'here' or *faran* (lit.) 'available' in Middle field, and the subject postposed to Final field: *es zenen faran oyf der velt gazlonim* 'there are robbers in the world', *es iz do nokh a kleyner khesorn* 'there's one more little flaw'. Of course, if the clause is a Consecutive declarative or if something is topicalized to Initial field, the expletive does not occur: *keyn gresere aveyre iz (*es) gor nito* (< *nit do* lit.'not here') 'there is no bigger sin'; *in di vagones tsveyte klas zenen (*es) dortn do shpiglen* 'in second-class trains there are mirrors there'. Notice, in this last example, that the occurrence of *dortn* 'there' shows that *do* truly lacks its literal sense 'here' in this construction. Finally, if the sentence is in the past tense, *do/faran* do not occur: *in a shtetl iz (*faran) geven a gvir* 'in a village there was a rich man'.

Dos-*sentences*
Yiddish has a construction wherein Initial field is filled by the expletive *dos* 'this', the subject occurring in Middle Field, and the understanding being that of the English *it*-cleft: *dos hot a folk tsvishn falndike vent dos lid gezungen mit naganes in di hent* 'it's a people between crumbling walls that sang this song with revolvers in their hand'.

Subordination

Verb Complements
Other than with modals or aspectuals, Yiddish has very few infinitival complements and no Raising: *dakht zikh, az du host khatoim nit veyniker fun andere!* 'you seem to have no fewer sins than the others' (lit. (It) seems (that) you ...'). The usual complementizer for finite verb complements is *az* 'that', which may be deleted; however, factives typically take *vos* (lit.) 'what': *iz der zun shoyn gevorn gor in kas, vos er darf altsding tsvey mol iberzogn* 'so the son got angry that he had to repeat everything twice'.

wh-*clauses*
There are the usual types of subordinate *wh*-clauses: indirect questions, free relatives and headed relatives. There is no preposition stranding, regardless of the type of clause or the complementizer used, all prepositions being fronted with their object noun phrases.

Indirect Questions/Free Relatives

Indirect questions/free relatives are syntactically identical; both are SVO clauses: *zol ikh nit visn fun beyz, vi ikh veys, fun vos di gvirim hobn aza hanoe!* 'I'll be damned if I know what rich men have such pleasure from!'; *git a kuk, vos di ganovim hobn gemakht* 'take a look at what the thieves have done'.

Like other subordinate clauses, indirect questions/free relatives are also verb-second, the finite verb being in second position even when some constituent other than the subject has been topicalized into initial position: *ir veyst efsher, avu do voynt Roznblat der goldshmid?* (lit.) 'you know perhaps where here lives Rosenblatt the goldsmith?'; *der yid zet, vi nokh dem oyrekh shlept zikh nokh a yungerman* 'the guy sees how behind the guest another young man has tagged along'.

Interestingly, when the subject has been extracted and when nothing has been topicalized, the dummy place-holder *es* 'it' must fill Initial field: *fregt der strazhnik dem yidn, ver es/*Ø iz mit im geven in tsimer* 'so the police officer asks the Jew who was with him in the room'; *ver es/*Ø vet trefn dem ber zol im hargenen* 'whoever finds the bear should kill it'.

Finally, Yiddish has infinitival indirect questions: *me hot nit gevust, vos tsu makhn* 'they didn't know what to do'. However, in contrast to English, Yiddish has infinitival free relatives as well: *zi hot nit vos tsu esn* 'she doesn't have anything (lit. what) to eat'.

Headed Relatives

Headed relative clauses are of two types, the expected gap-containing variety and those containing resumptive pronouns. The former are largely unexceptional within Germanic, except that they of course obey verb-second, as do all declarative clauses in Yiddish. They may have inflected relative pronouns: *arum 800 etiopishe yidn, velkhe zaynen geblibn shtekn in Sudan* 'about 800 Ethiopian Jews who (pl.) have remained in the Sudan'; *dem zelbikn hunderter, velkhn er git im* 'the same hundred dollar bill which (acc. m. sg.) he gives him'. Or they may have a more or less invariant complementizer: *yidn, vos shpiln in kortn* 'Jews (m. pl.) that play cards'; *di mayse, vos ikh vel aykh dertseyln* 'the story (f. sg.) that I'll tell you'. Note that, if a subject is relativized with nothing topicalized, we find a gap rather than a dummy noun phrase in Initial field, in contrast to the situation in free relatives/indirect questions.

Resumptive pronoun relative clauses are fully grammatical in Standard Yiddish (though those with a relativized subject predominate in the colloquial language). They occur only with the invariant complementizer *vos*, and the resumptive pronoun may occur in any position: *a yidene, vos zi/Ø hot geheysn Yente* 'an old hag that (she/Ø) was named Yenta'; *a melamed, vos es iz im/*?Ø zeyer shlekht gegangen* 'a teacher that (he/*?Ø) was very bad off'; *a shmole kladke, vos me hot kam gekent geyn oyf ir* 'a narrow footbridge that you could barely walk on (lit.)'. In fact, resumptive pronouns are strongly preferred to gaps when the relativized item is the dative Experiencer, as in the second example, and they are at least as frequent as gaps when the relativized item is the object of a preposition, as in the last example. In environments where a gap is as grammatical as a resumptive pronoun, the resumptive pronoun tends to occur either in non-restrictive relatives or, if in restrictives, where the head noun is indefinite, i.e. when the discourse entity evoked by the whole noun phrase is evoked by the noun phrase alone, the relative clause serving merely to predicate additional properties of that entity.

Negation

Yiddish has, like Bavarian German and Slavic, Negative Concord, whereby all non-referring arguments in a negative clause are negated: *keyner darf zikh keynmol nit ayln* 'no one should ever hurry' (lit. 'no one shouldn't ever not hurry'). Thus, an ambiguity that obtains in English, for example, with respect to specific vs non-specific indefinites does not obtain in Yiddish negative clauses: *er vil nit khasene hobn mit a/keyn norveger* 'he doesn't want to marry a certain/any Norwegian'. Note that negative concord distinguishes true arguments from complements of periphrastic verbs: *er hot nit khasene gehat* 'he didn't get married'; *er hot nit keyn khasene gehat* 'he didn't have a wedding'; *er hot khasene gehat, ober er hot nit gehat keyn (emese) khasene* 'he got married but he didn't have a (real) wedding'.

12.5 Lexis

The lexicon of modern Yiddish is predominantly Germanic, secondarily Semitic, and then Slavic, with percentage estimates going from 70–20–10 per cent to 85–12–3 per cent. Some Yiddishists insist on the importance of a Romance component, as in *leyenen* 'read' (Lat. *legere*) or *bentshn* 'bless' (Lat. *benedicere*), as a reflection of the fact that some Jews that settled in Germany must have spoken a form of Romance, but this component is minimal. For any piece of discourse, the actual proportion of Germanic, Semitic and Slavic depends in part on the topic of the discourse, with some matters of religion and Jewish culture being associated with a more heavily Semiticized Yiddish. The other factor is the provenance and background of the speaker. Thus Slavicisms tend to occur more in the speech of Slavic–Yiddish bilinguals. For many words with a Hebrew or Slavic origin, there is no obvious reason why it supplanted the native Germanic word (thus 'sea' is *yam* < HA and 'lake' is *ozere* < Slav. and neither Ger. *See* nor *Meer* have a Yiddish cognate). Despite the overall Germanic nature of the vocabulary, many of the common words are non-Germanic, e.g. the family names *tate* 'father', *zeyde* 'grandfather', and *bobe* 'grandmother', all from Slavic; and function words such as *tsi* 'whether' or *khotsh* 'although' from Slavic, and *tomer* 'if', *efsher* 'possibly', *afile* 'even', and *beys* 'while' from Semitic. Though the Germanic component of Yiddish is largely comprehensible by speakers of German, identifying a word as Germanic does not always mean that it has a German cognate or meaning. Sometimes Yiddish continues older Germanic words or meanings, e.g. *haint* 'today' < OHG *hînaht*, vs Ger. *heute*; *feter* retains the old 'uncle' meaning, different from Ger. *Vetter* 'cousin'; or makes new ones, e.g. *Ratnfarband* 'Soviet Union' vs Ger. *Sowjet union*, Yid. *yortsayt* developed the meaning 'anniversary of death', vs Ger. *Jahreszeit* 'season'. Words may furthermore 'look' Germanic but be Yiddishized borrowings ('loanblends'): *hargenen* 'kill' < Hebrew; or loan translations (calques): *oysgehaltn* 'consistent', cf. Russian *vyderžannyj* lit. 'out-held'. When one concept can be expressed by two words of different stocks, there is often a nuance of the Semitic stock word pertaining more exclusively to Jews; thus Germanic stock *aroysred* means 'pronunciation', but for the pronunciation of Hebrew Semitic stock *havore* is used.

Further Reading

Birnbaum, S. A. (1979) *Yiddish. A Survey and a Grammar*, Toronto: University of Toronto Press.

Diesing, M. (1990) 'Verb movement and the subject position in Yiddish', *Natural Language and Linguistic Theory* 8: 41–79.

Jacobs, N. G. (1990) *Economy in Yiddish Vocalism: A Study in the Interplay of Hebrew and Non-Hebrew Components*, Wiesbaden: Harrassowitz.

—— (1991) 'A reanalysis of the Hebrew *status constructus* in Yiddish', *Hebrew Union College Annual* LXII: 305–27.

Katz, D. (1987) *Grammar of the Yiddish Language*, London: Duckworth.

King, R. (1990) 'A konspiratsye un a frage-tseykhn', *Oksforder yidish* 1: 247–51.

Miner, K. (1990) 'Yiddish V/1 declarative clauses in discourse', *IPrA Papers in Pragmatics* 4.1/2: 122–49.

Prince, E. F. (1988a) 'The discourse functions of Yiddish Expletive *es* + Subject Postposing', *Papers in Pragmatics* 2: 176–94.

—— (1988b) 'Yiddish *Wh*-clauses, Subject-Postposing, and Topicalization', in J. Powers and K. de Jong (eds) *ESCOL '88*, Columbus, Ohio: Ohio State University, pp.403–15.

—— (1989) 'On pragmatic change: the borrowing of discourse functions', in A. Kasher (ed.), *Cognitive Aspects of Language Use*, Amsterdam: Elsevier, pp. 1–14.

—— (1990) 'Syntax and discourse: a look at resumptive pronouns', in K. Hall, J. P. Koenig, M. Meacham, S. Reinman and L. A. Sutton (eds), *Proceedings of the Sixteenth Annual Meeting of the Berkeley Linguistics Society*, Berkeley: Berkeley Linguistics Society, pp. 482–97.

Weinreich, M. (1980) *History of the Yiddish Language*, trans. S. Noble with the assistance of J. A. Fishman, Chicago: The University of Chicago Press (Yiddish original *Geshikhte fun der yidisher shprakh*, New York: Yivo Institute for Jewish Research, 1973).

Weinreich, U. (1956) 'Notes on the rise-fall intonation contour', in M. Halle, H. G. Lunt, H. MacLean and C. H. Van Schooneveld (eds), *For Roman Jakobson*, The Hague: Mouton, pp. 633–43.

—— (1958) 'Yiddish and Colonial German: the differential impact of Slavic', *American Contribution to the Fourth International Congress of Slavists*, The Hague, pp. 3–421.

—— (1971) *College Yiddish. An Introduction to the Yiddish Language and to Jewish Life and Culture*, New York: YIVO Institute for Jewish Research.
Weissberg, J. (1988) *Jiddisch. Eine Einführung*, Bern: Lang.
Wexler, P. (1987) *Explorations in Judeo-Slavic Linguistics*, Leyden: Brill.

13 Pennsylvania German

Silke Van Ness

13.1 Introduction

Pennsylvania German is the language spoken today by the modern descendants of German colonists who arrived in Pennsylvania before the Revolutionary War of 1776. Estimates put the number of native speakers between two- and three-hundred thousand distributed over at least twenty American states, parts of Central and South America, and southern Ontario, Canada.

Although the first Germans began to arrive in Pennsylvania in 1683, mass immigration did not take place until the 1720s. From the first settlement at Germantown, east of Philadelphia, the colonists spread into southeastern Pennsylvania, that is, the counties of Lancaster, Lehigh, Bucks, Berks and others. From the middle of the eighteenth century on, a southward expansion into parts of Maryland, North Carolina, Tennessee, Virginia and West Virginia took place, along with continuing migration into western Pennsylvania, the Mohawk Valley of New York, and southern Ontario, Canada. Finally, the nineteenth century carried German colonists westward into Ohio, Indiana, and beyond into many regions of the Americas. At the turn of this century, some 750,000 persons used Pennsylvania German in their daily life: 600,000 of them lived in the state of Pennsylvania.

The early German immigrants belonged to the religious sects of the Anabaptists, i.e., Mennonites, Amish, Dunkards, Schwenkfelders and Moravians. The years between 1727 and the American Revolution brought non-sectarian Germans, the Lutherans and Reformed, to Pennsylvania. These 'non-sectarians' surpassed the sectarians numerically and, until recently, constituted the largest segment of the Pennsylvania German speaking population. However, the non-sectarians will have completed the shift to English monolingualism by the early twenty-first century, and it is the ultra-conservative Anabaptist religious sects, the Old Order Amish and the Old Order Mennonites, who will maintain the Pennsylvania German language. With an above-average birth rate, the sectarian groups now greatly outnumber the non-sectarians (e.g.

420

the Old Order Amish population increased from 3,700 individuals in 1890 to 85,783 in 1979). The stable bilingualism in these communities is linked to the rigid enforcement of separate domains for language use – Pennsylvania German for in-group social interactions, most importantly in all religious functions; English with the outside world. Sermons are conducted in Pennsylvania German, with an archaic variety of Standard German, sometimes referred to as 'Amish High German', reserved for the reading of Bible passages and the singing of hymns. Although it has been claimed that ultra-conservative sectarians are trilingual, this is an overstatement; the 'Amish High German' is clearly restricted to orally recited passages from the Bible or prayerbook and is never used as a means of communication.

In spite of a large body of literary works ranging from comedy to prose, Pennsylvania German, as a written medium, never enjoyed wide currency. The problems created by the lack of uniform spelling conventions in combination with the fact that the language never functioned as the medium of instruction in the schools, restricted its use to a primarily oral tradition. A quasi writing system has been established for teaching grammars, where a Standard German orthography was merged with a Pennsylvania German sound system. Even though there are few native speakers who actually can read any form of Pennsylvania German, whether written in an English- or Standard German based orthography, some regional newspaper columns do attempt to keep a written form of the dialect alive. For the bilingual Anabaptist groups, Pennsylvania German is exclusively a spoken idiom. Some rudimentary instruction in Standard German is provided to aid in the studies of the Scriptures, but for many younger persons the English page of their bilingual Bible is what is really read. While some parts of the Bible have been available in the dialect, the translation of the entire New Testament into Pennsylvania German was completed by the Wycliffe Institute in 1993.

Pennsylvania German derives essentially from Middle High German and Early New High German dialects of the Palatinate, though there were also significant numbers of settlers from Switzerland, Württemberg, Alsace, Westphalia and Hesse. Due to a temporary halt in immigration in 1775, the processes of dialect mixture and accommodation allowed a relatively homogeneous dialect to crystallize, one that is distinct from other German dialects.

A synchronic analysis of Pennsylvania German must take into account the diverging developments of two primary groups of speakers: the orthodox Anabaptist sects (Old Order Amish, Old Order Mennonites, also referred to as 'plain' speakers because of their conservative dress and lifestyle), who keep themselves socially segregated from their surrounding American society, and the worldly non-sectarians, who are socially well integrated. This dichotomous situation reflects the present status of the language. On the one hand, the linguistically conservative language of the historically more numerous group, the non-sectarians, is facing extinction. There are no native

Pennsylvania German speakers under the age of fifty, yet, their language variety has traditionally formed the basis for the description of Pennsylvania German. On the other hand, the language of the sectarians, now the dynamic and numerically superior variety, with native speakers of all ages, is in the process of undergoing several linguistic changes. For these groups, the Pennsylvania German language provides the crucial barrier to assimilation and thus forms the nucleus of their unique communities, with religious conservatism as a watershed for language maintenance. An accurate description of the language must take this (socio-)linguistic reality into account. It is the language of the sectarian speakers that will define the linguistic parameters of Pennsylvania German in the future.

The subsequent sections describe a Generalized Pennsylvania German, in part following the descriptive tradition established by earlier scholars and based on the language of the non-sectarians. However, recent observations on dialect variations attributable to the rapidly changing Pennsylvania German of the sectarians will be added, in order to provide a balanced linguistic overview of Pennsylvania German.

13.2   Phonology

Vowels

Historically, Pennsylvania German (PG) has been considered to have an opposition between long and short vowels; however, this contrast appears to be more accurately described as one of quality rather than quantity. Therefore, the distinction will be symbolized phonemically as a tense–lax contrast. The phonology follows primarily the phonemic description that has become traditional in Pennsylvania German studies, but incorporates minor aspects of generative phonology in cases where the traditional approach fails to account successfully for details of Pennsylvania German phonology.

With the exception of /ə/, the reduced lax central vowel, all vowels can receive primary or secondary stress. A chart of vowels is displayed in Table 13.1.

Table 13.1   Basic vowel system of Pennsylvania German

i					u
ɪ				ʊ	
e				o	
ɛ		(ə)	ɔ		
(æ)	a	(ɑ)			

Diphthongs: ai, au, oi

Note: /æ/ is a borrowed phoneme from English; /ɑ/ frequently is indistinguishable from /a/ and even /ɔ/; schwa is detailed in the text.

The Middle High German high and mid vowels are regularly lowered to /a/ in the environment of a following /r/, as in, e.g. /marıɣə/ 'morning' < MHG *morgen*, /barıg/ 'mountain' < MHG *berc*. Pennsylvania German has no rounded front vowels; thus PG /i/ < MHG /y/ in an open syllable, e.g. /dir/ 'door' and PG /ı/ < MHG /y/ in a closed syllable, e.g. /ʃtıg/ 'piece'. The same process affected the Middle High German rounded mid front vowel /ø/ in open and closed syllables where Pennsylvania German has /e/ and /ɛ/ respectively (e.g. /el/ 'oil' and /kɛnd/ 'could').

The low front vowel /æ/ is theoretically a phoneme adopted from English and occurs only in English loans: e.g. /kæʃ/ 'cash', /hæwət/ 'dress/habit'; however, [æ] may also function as an allophone of /ɛ/ or /a/ before /r/, giving, e.g. /barig/ ~ /bærıg/ ~ /bɛrıg/ 'mountain'. Another phonetic variant of /a/ is the low back, rounded vowel [ɒ] in the environment before nasals, velars and /l/; e.g. /ʃaŋg/ ~ /ʃɒŋg/ 'closet', /man/ ~ /mɒn/ 'man', /ʃtal/ ~ /ʃtɒl/ 'stall/stable'. For many speakers [a] (/kats/ 'cat') and [ɒ] (/kɒdər/ 'tom cat') are not distinguishable from each other. At times overlap with [ɔ] (/kɔbxə/ 'cup') may even occur. Heavy nasalization of vowels before nasals, which are then lost, a common feature of continental Palatine and Swabian dialects, is becoming a relic feature associated with older speakers of Pennsylvania German, e.g. /tso/ ~ /tsõ/ 'tooth', /hihɔgə/ ~ /hĩhɔgə/ 'sit down'.

The phonemic status of schwa /ə/ is left unanswered. Schwa has derived from three different sources: (1) as an allophone of any Middle High German vowel in an unstressed position, e.g. PG /ʃanʃtə/ 'chimney' /besəm/ 'broom'; (2) in English loans, as in, e.g. PG /tʃægət/ 'vest' (from English 'jacket') /əbaut/ 'about'; (3) as an epenthetic vowel inserted between liquids and following labials or velars, giving, e.g. PG /darəm/ 'intestine' /marəɣə/ 'morning' /ʃɛləm/ 'rogue'. In modern Pennsylvania German it may occur as an unstressed positional variant of /e/ and at times /ə/ is introduced in particular environments mentioned above.

Pennsylvania German is surprisingly uniform across geographical regions, in spite of the fact that it developed out of a blend of different German dialects. This, however, does not imply homogeneous speech communities; in fact, much variation exists. At one level, there is variation in terms of region and sectarian vs non-sectarian features within Pennsylvania; at another level, there is regional variation outside of Pennsylvania. In the latter case, viable regional variants are of only one social variety, namely sectarian. The following examples illustrate the regional variations present in the vowel system. For example: /dir/ – /dɛr/ 'door', /fogəl/ – /fɔgəl/ 'bird', /karıx/ – /kɛrıx/ 'church'; some Canadian Mennonite groups say /wonə/ 'to live' versus the more common /wunə/ for other regions; a nearly extinct non-sectarian West Virginia community features the diphthong /ai/ in such words as, e.g. /flaiʃ/ 'meat', /hais/ 'hot' versus /fleʃ/ and /hes/ for most other non-sectarian and sectarian areas.

Table 13.2   Consonant phonemes of Pennsylvania German

	Bilabial	Labio-dental	Dental-alveolar	Palato-alveolar	Palatal	Velar	Glottal
Stops	p b		t d			k g	
Fricatives		f	s	ʃ		x	h
Affricates			ts	tʃ			
Nasals	m		n			ŋ	
Laterals			l r				
Semivowels	w				j		

Consonants

While Table 13.2 represents all of the consonant phonemes of Pennsylvania German, only those sounds that deviate from Standard German will be discussed.

The stop consonants have traditionally been treated as two sets, a series of voiceless lenis, represented as /b̥, d̥, g̊/, and another series of voiceless stops /p, t, k/, restricted in their occurrence to initial position preceding stressed vowels. Furthermore, /t/ in this environment is considered essentially a borrowed phoneme from English, since a Standard German /t/ corresponds to /d/ in Pennsylvania German (e.g. PG /dir/, StGer. *Tür* 'door'). There are exceptions of course, and the lenis/fortis opposition is obscured in those contexts where lenis sounds undergo voice assimilation in consonant clusters or occur finally in stressed contexts (cf. /ʃtori/ 'story' versus the traditional phonetic representation [ʃdori]).

In Standard German the voiceless fricative /ʃ/ may precede /t/ and /p/ only in morpheme-initial position, while Pennsylvania German extends the environment to include medial- and word-final positions, as in, e.g. /barʃt/ 'brush', /senʃt/ 'do you see', /fɛnʃtər/ 'window'.

Intervocalic lenition of /b/ and /g/ to [w] and [ɣ] respectively is a regular feature of Pennsylvania German, e.g. /wagə/ [wɑɣə] 'wagon', /habə/ [hawə] 'to have'. For younger sectarian speakers, underlying medial /g/ has two variants – [ɣ] before front vowels and [w] before back vowels, as in /weɣə/ 'roads', /awə/ 'eyes'. Phonemic overlap occurs where the [w] medial allophone of /g/ coincides with the variant of /b/, giving, e.g. /glagə/ [glawə] 'to complain' versus /glabə/ [glawə] 'to believe', thus causing homophony.

The phoneme /w/ is a voiced bilabial sound which for some speakers exhibits friction, [β], and for others, especially before rounded back vowels, is an approximant with the glide quality of the English labiovelar [w]. The voiceless fricatives /f/, /s/, and /ʃ/ occur in all environments and lack contrastive voiced counterparts.

Theoretically there are two principal affricates, i.e., /ts/ /tswe/ 'two' and

/tʃ/, the latter one of rare occurrence, e.g. /rɛtʃə/ 'to gossip', with the voiced /ʤ/ occurring in loans from English, e.g. /ʤɛnəreʃən/ 'generation'. In fact, phonetically only the voiceless variant exists, since English /ʤ/ is normally realized as [tʃ].

Influence from English, where it does occur, is limited to changes in phonetic quality. The liquids /l/ and /r/ show most strikingly English contact-induced variants. Velarized allophones of /l/ and retroflexed /r/ exist in variation with the traditional alveolar segments. As in Standard German, the /r/ phoneme of PG has an elaborate set of allophones, which may vary among speakers, from region to region, and from community to community. Generally, a pre-vocalic /r/ is pronounced as an alveolar trill, while in pre-consonantal position, /r/ may be weakly articulated or lost, e.g. /warʃt/ or /waʃt/ 'sausage'. Since Pennsylvania German has historically developed an epenthetic vowel between /r/ and a following labial or velar, this pre-consonantal /r/ is limited to occurrence before coronal sounds. In unstressed final position, the /r/ completely disappears and is realized as a central lax vowel [ɐ] PG /kɪnɐ/ 'children', represented traditionally in Pennsylvania German as schwa /ə/ plus /r/, i.e. /kɪnər/. Furthermore, when /r/ occurs after a short /a/ and before a dental it is realized as zero, e.g. /dat/ 'there' from MHG 'dort', /haʃ/ 'buck' from MHG *Hirsch* (see above for lowering of high and mid vowels to /a/).

13.3 Morphology
Pennsylvania German is a language without a standardized orthography. Written forms have been approximated by recourse to both English, and, more commonly, Standard German spelling systems. Neither approach is very satisfactory. To facilitate interpretation of the data, examples in the following sections will be cited in a broad phonetic transcription representing surface manifestations. The reader is encouraged to check the Phonology section for details.

Nominal Morphology
While Pennsylvania German basically maintains a two-case system (common and dative) for nouns among non-sectarian speakers and sectarians over the age of 60, convergence with English has resulted in the shift to a single, common case system of nominal inflection in sectarian Pennsylvania German. Three genders (masculine, feminine, neuter), and two numbers (singular and plural) have been retained by both groups. Nominal morphology is discussed in conjunction with the definite and indefinite article. Table 13.3 illustrates the traditional paradigm of noun declension.

Masculine, feminine and neuter genders are overtly realized in the three determiners, *dər*, *di* and *əs*. As in Standard German, animate objects are mostly assigned a natural gender, but gender is semantically unpredictable for

Table 13.3   Determiners and nouns

	Singular			Plural
	m.	f.	n.	All genders
Common				
def.	dər man 'the man'	di frɑ 'the woman'	əs kɪnd 'the child'	di kɪnər 'the children'
indef.	ən man 'a man'	ən frɑ 'a woman'	ən kɪnd 'a child'	
Dative				
def.	əm man	dər frɑ	əm kɪnd	də kɪnər
indef.	mə man	rə frɑ	mə kɪnd	

inanimate nouns. Barring a few exceptions, for example *dər budər* 'the butter' (StGer. *die Butter*), *di dan* 'the thorn' (StGer. *der Dorn*), gender conforms in most instances to the grammatical gender of Standard German. When nouns are borrowed from English, they need to be assigned gender in order to fit the morphological structure of Pennsylvania German. When this occurs, gender assignments may be based on: (a) natural gender, e.g. *dər dadi* 'the father', *dər træmp* 'the tramp', *di mæm* 'the mother'; (b) the gender of the displaced German noun, e.g. *dər hændəl*, PG *dər ftil* 'the handle'; *di gwɪld*, PG *di bɛd dɛg* 'the quilt'; *əs pɪgdər*, PG *əs bɪld* 'the picture'; (c) a suffix associated with a specific gender, e.g. StGer. *-ung* (Eng. *-ing*) and *-ie* (Eng. *-y*) for feminine: *di sɪlɪŋ* 'the ceiling', *di midɪŋ* 'the meeting' *di pærdi* 'the party', *di ftori* 'the story'; and StGer. *-er* suffix for masculine nouns, e.g. *dər kaundər* 'the counter', *dər parlər* 'the parlour'. It should be noted, however, that the assignment of gender to loanwords is by no means a predictable, consistent process, but rather, a general trend which still allows for many variations, e.g. what is *di bugi* 'the buggy' in one county will be *dər bugi* in another county.

Plural formation in Pennsylvania German is less profuse than in Standard German with only four main patterns discernible:

1   Zero allomorph: *karəb/karəb* 'basket/baskets' and with occasional stem vowel umlaut *abəl/ɛbəl* 'apple/apples';
2   Suffix *-er*: *hɛm/hɛmər* 'shirt/shirts' and with stem vowel umlaut when applicable *haus/haisər* 'house/houses';
3   Suffix *-ə*: *kix/kixə* 'kitchen/kitchens';
4   Suffix *-s* for some English loans: *ftor/ftors* 'store/stores'.

Although borrowings from English do have the choice of retaining their *-s* allomorph, as, for example in *sɪŋk/sɪŋks* 'sink/sinks', this option is not always the preferred one. Plurals are frequently forced into one of the above patterns, so that a general trend has emerged:

1   Plural morphology for masculine nouns with agentive suffix *-er* have identical singular and plural forms *dər ʃtorkipər – di ʃtorkipər* 'the storekeeper/storekeepers';

2   A variety of borrowed nouns alternate between an *-e* or zero plural morph: *di bɛl* 'the bell', *di bɛlə – di bɛl* 'the bells'; *di gaund* 'the (woman's) dress', *di gaund* 'the dresses' or *dər frag* 'the woman's dress' *di fragə* 'the dresses'; *di ɛgʃpɛns* 'the expense', *di ɛgʃpɛnsə* 'the expenses'.

At times, plurality is marked by vowel mutation *dər ʃɔp – di ʃɛp* 'the shop – the shops'.

A large number of diminutive forms, attributable to the varied linguistic background of the German colonists have been retained in Pennsylvania German speech communities. They are indicative of early settlement patterns along dialect/family lines. Regional Pennsylvania examples are: singular *-xə*, plural *-xər* and the compound suffixes *-əlxə*, *-lɪxə*, plural *-əlxər*, *-lɪxər* are prevalent in more northern and eastern parts, with singular *-li*, plural *-lm* in more southern and western sections of the state. Lancaster county shows greatest uniformity with singular *-(ə)li*, plural *(ə)lm* diminutives indicative of Alemannic remnants, e.g. *bɔbli – bɔblm* 'baby – babies'; *saili/wʊtsli – sailm/ wʊts(ə)lm* 'young pig – young pigs'.

The definite and indefinite article are unaccented forms which frequently cliticize and appear as contractions, e.g. *ʊnəm dax* 'under the roof', *dəmarɪyə* 'in the morning'. The accented counterparts of the definite articles are the demonstratives *dɛr*, *di*, *dɛs* 'this' and *sɛlər* 'that'. Constructions using a demonstrative are often supported by the adverb *do* 'here' as an emphatic, e.g. *dɛs do medəl* 'this (here) girl', or, as in the case of *sɛlər* by *dat* 'there', e.g. *sɛl haus dat ɪs alt* 'that house (there) is old'. *sɛlər* declines as shown in Table 13.4.

The case distinctions are carried by the preceding determiners (and/or adjectives). The form of the nominative serves for both the subject and the direct object, e.g. *ar lend mir dər wayə* 'he lent me the wagon'. For the linguistically conservative non-sectarians, the dative remains the case for the indirect object, e.g. *ix gɛb əm bu dər wayə* 'I give the wagon to the boy'. Furthermore, the functional load of the dative includes the formation of the possessive, as in *əm man sai bixər* 'the man's books'. In the Pennsylvania

Table 13.4 Demonstrative pronoun *sɛlər*

	Masculine	Feminine	Neuter	Plural All genders
Common	sɛlər	sɛli	sɛl	sɛli
Dative	sɛləm, sɛm	sɛlrə	sɛləm, sɛm	sɛlə

German construction, the possessor, in the dative case with a possessive adjective, precedes the (possessed) noun. In fact, this construction has undergone simplification in the speech of the sectarians, where a common case noun is now replacing the dative, e.g. *dər man sai bixər* 'the man's books'. A few relic forms of the old genitive remain in certain compounds and fixed idioms: *kmdskmd* 'grandchild', *owɛts* 'in the evening'.

In summary, the dative case is becoming a relic associated with non-sectarians or older sectarian speakers. The nominal morphology for the younger speakers continues to syncretize in its convergence toward English so that the common case will function not only as the subjective and objective case, but also as the indirect object, giving, e.g. *ıx gɛb dər bu dər wayə* 'I give the wagon to the boy'.

Adjectives

Adjectives are inflected in one of three ways, depending upon the preceding determiner, the gender and the case of the noun: (a) weak endings are used with adjectives that are preceded by a definite (*dər, di, əs* 'the') or demonstrative (*dɛr, di, dɛs* 'this', *sɛlər* 'that') article; (b) strong declensions are used with adjectives that are not preceded by a determiner; (c) mixed endings occur with adjectives that are preceded by an indefinitive article (*ən* 'a') or a possessive adjective (*mai* 'my', *dai* 'your', etc.).

Table 13.5 reflects a traditional inflectional paradigm; however, the preference for unstressed syllables is encouraging a trend to reduce inflections of all adjectives in all genders to a zero or -*ə* morph. The dative case forms are no longer viable in the speech of sectarian speakers. In addition, Pennsylvania German has a morphophonemic n-deletion rule which truncates a word-final underlying -*n* in the base form and restores the -*n* before the addition of inflections. We get the following citations: (a) uninflected PG *brau* 'brown' *də hʊnd is brau* 'the dog is brown'; (b) inflected *ən braunər hʊnd* (common case) 'a brown dog' or *əm braunə hʊnd* (dat.). For denominals derived from a source with an underlying -*n*, the same pattern prevails, giving, e.g. *ʃtenıx* 'stony' from *ʃte* 'stone' StGer. *Stein*. The adjectives *negʃt* 'next' and *lɛtʃt* 'last' frequently occur without inflectional endings, e.g. *negʃt mʊndag* 'next Monday', *lɛtʃt wɔx* 'last week'. Adjectival inflections for loans remain congruent with native Pennsylvania German patterns, for example: common case m. *ən ʃmartər man* 'a smart man' and f. *di madıxə ʃtros* 'the muddy street'; dat. pl. *uf plenə ʃtil* 'on plain chairs'.

The comparative of adjectives is regularly formed with an -*ər* suffix, e.g. *dif* 'deep', *difər* 'deeper' and the superlative with an -*ʃt* suffix, e.g. *difʃt* 'deepest'. As in Standard German, some adjectives have suppletive forms, e.g. *fil* 'much', *me* (*menər*) 'more', *menʃt* 'most'. The comparative particles are *wi* 'as', *as* 'than', or *as wi*. A cumulative comparative may be formed by using either *as* or *as wi*, e.g. *si hat menər kʊkis as* (*as wi*) *irə ʃwɛʃtər* 'she has more cookies than her sister'. To indicate a progressive change where

Table 13.5 Adjective inflections

	Singular Masculine	Feminine	Neuter	*Plural* All genders
Weak inflections				
Common	ald 'old'	ald 'old'	ald 'old'	aldə 'old'
Dative	aldə	aldə	aldə	aldə
Strong inflections				
Common	aldər	aldi	ald	aldə
Dative	aldəm	aldər	aldəm	aldə
Mixed inflections				
Common	aldər	aldi	ald(əs)	aldə
Dative	aldə	aldə	aldə	aldə

Standard German uses *immer* 'always', Pennsylvania German employs an *als* + comparative construction, e.g. *əs wat als kɛldər* 'it is getting colder'.

Personal Pronouns
The personal pronoun system is set out in Table 13.6. In the pronominal paradigm, only the non-sectarian Pennsylvania German has fully retained a distinct three-case system, i.e. nominative, accusative, and dative, while the Pennsylvania German language of the sectarians has reduced the pronominal cases to two, i.e. subject and object. There is only one pronoun of address, the informal singular *du* 'you' and the plural *dir* 'you (pl.)', although the latter form manifests regional variants.

Many pronouns are traditionally used as pro- or enclitics, thus unstressed and reduced forms are preferred: *mər, dər, nər, əm, ən, rə, nə* (see Verb morphology, p. 432). The second person singular pronoun is usually omitted in interrogatives, e.g. *wi bɪʃt?* 'how are you?', *was hɔʃt dat?* 'what do you have there?' In the first- and second-person plural, a variety of pronominal forms attest to linguistic remnants traceable to the original German dialect regions of the colonists, e.g. [miə] 'we' indicative of Palatine dialects, [diə] and [iə] 'your (pl.)' are of Alemannic origin.

By analogy to the English pronoun 'it', Pennsylvania German occasionally uses *əs, 's* 'it' when referring to inanimate objects, e.g. *wu ɪs dər brif?* 'where is the letter?' *si hat 's (əs) m irə bux* 'she has it in her book' in contrast with *si hat in m irə bux*. In the latter example, the pronoun *in* 'his' still reflects the masculine gender of *brif* 'letter'. The reflexive form is *sɪx* '-self', corresponding to Standard German *sich*.

Indefinite pronouns and adjectives are: *al* 'all' *alə* 'every, each', *aləs* 'everything', *del* 'some', *ɛbər* 'someone, somebody', *ɛbəs* 'something', *bɪsəl* 'a little bit', *enɪx* 'any', *wɛnɪx* 'a little, a bit', *nɪks* 'nothing', *fil* 'much, many'.

Table 13.6   Personal pronouns

| | Singular | | | Plural | | |
	1	2	3	1	2	3
Nom.	ɪx	du	ar, si, əs	mir/mər	dir/ir/dər/ər nər/nir	si
	'I'	'you'	'he, she, it'	'we'	'you'	'they'
Acc.	mɪx	dix	in, si, əs	ʊns	aix	si
Dat.	mir	dir	im, irə, im	ʊns	aix	inə

None of these words is declined; *del*, *ɛbər*, *ɛbəs*, and *nɪks* are used with third-person singular verbs only. There is a third-person singular indefinite pronoun *mər* 'one, people, they, you' equivalent to Standard German *man* 'one', e.g. *mər kʊmt gəwenlɪx ʊm sɛks ur* 'one usually arrives at six o'clock'. Besides the nominative form *mər*, there is also *em* used in accusative and dative functions, e.g. *sɛl ɪs nɛt gut far em* 'that is not good for one/people, etc.'.

The two interrogative pronouns *wɛr* 'who', *was* 'what' are similar to Standard German patterns. While *wɛr* has a common (*wɛr*) and a dative (*wɛm*) form, *was* remains invariant in both cases, e.g. *wɛr titʃt m airər ʃul?* 'who teaches in your (pl.) school', *was ɛst ar mariyəts?* 'what does he eat in the morning?', *wɛm hat ar sai bʊgi gɛwə* 'to whom did he give his buggy?' Possession is expressed with *wɛm* (common case *wɛr* for most sectarians) plus the invariant possessive adjective *sai*, as in *wɛm/wɛr sai brif ɪs sɛl?* 'whose letter is that'. The phrase *far was* renders the English meaning 'why', e.g. *far was heʃt nɛt?* 'why don't you listen?' The interrogative pronominal *wɛlər* 'which' follows the declensional paradigm of the demonstrative *sɛlər* 'that'.

The Verb System
Verbs fall into two broad categories: weak and strong. The strong class, which features an alternation of the stem vowel, still reflects the old Germanic ablaut series. Table 13.7 provides a basic paradigm for Pennsylvania German verb conjugations in the present tense. The pattern is the same for both weak and strong verbs. The prefix *ge-* is added to the stem of the majority of verbs to form the past participle, e.g. *gəbʊnə* 'bound'. The reduced vowel of the participle prefix has been lost historically in certain environments, i.e. before the voiceless fricatives /f/ *gfunə* 'found', /s/ *gsenə* 'seen', /ʃ/ *gʃrɪwə* 'written', and before the voiceless glide /h/ *ghesə* [kʰesə] 'known'. Voice assimilation, i.e. /g/ > [k], tends to accompany the reduced prefix, while a verb stem-initial /h/ generates a heavily aspirated [kʰ] as in [kʰadə] 'have had'. Assimilation processes have created further phonological changes in the past participle prefix; *ge* + morpheme initial /s/ or /ʃ/ assimilates in point of articulation, e.g.

Table 13.7   Verb morphology

	Weak	Strong
Infinitive	maxə 'to make'	nɛmə 'to take'
Present		
1 sg.	ɪx max	
2 sg.	du maxʃt	
3 sg. m.	ar maxt	
f.	si maxt	
n.	əs maxt	
1 pl.	mir maxə	
2 pl.	dir maxt (-ə, ət)	
3 pl.	si maxə	
Past participle	gəmaxt	gənʊmə
Imperative		
2 sg.	max	nɛm
2 pl.	maxt	nɛmt

gsenə > [tsenə] 'seen', *gʃpild* > [tʃpild] 'played'. Participles of strong verbs end in /-e/ (phonetically schwa [ə]), e.g. *gnʊmə* 'taken', those of the weak verbs in /-t/, e.g. *gəkɛnt* 'known'.

Both weak and strong verbs are inflected for person and number. Pennsylvania German verbs have only two principal parts – the infinitive and the past participle. The majority of verbs take *hawə* 'to have' as their auxiliary, with only a few verbs – albeit common ones – combining with *sai* 'to be'. Traditionally, the auxiliary *hawə* is used with all transitive verbs and with most intransitive ones, while *sai* is reserved for intransitive verbs expressing motion or change of condition. In some speech communities, the contrast between *hawə* and *sai* is being levelled and regularized so that *hawə* + past participle is becoming the preferred indicator of past action. Remnants of a former imperfect tense appear in some dialect poetry, but otherwise is limited to the subjunctive of a few isolated auxiliaries (*wɛr* 'would'). Besides the present and what is commonly referred to as the perfect tense, the spoken language has a pluperfect (past perfect), future, and future perfect tense formed periphrastically with *hawə*, *sai*, or *warə* 'to become' as auxiliary. To indicate the occurrence of two events in the past, Pennsylvania German employs the pluperfect to signal the one further removed in time. The pluperfect is expressed with the present perfect tense + the past participle of *hawə* or *sai* e.g. *ar hat gʃrɪwə ghat (ghadə)*, StGer. *er hatte geschrieben* 'he had written'; *ɪx bm gaŋə gəwɛst* 'I had gone'. A variant which replaces the auxiliary *sai* with its preterite *war* has been observed as the new auxiliary in past perfect constructions among sectarian speakers, e.g. *ar war gaŋə gəwɛst* 'he had gone'.

Although Pennsylvania German theoretically can indicate future tense periphrastically with *warə* 'to become' + infinitive of the main verb, this formal construction is rarely used and then only to express probability, e.g. *ar wat ʃʊn kʊmə* 'he (probably) will come'. Most commonly reference to the future is expressed either (a) with adverbials such as *glai*, *ʃʊn* 'soon' *marɪyə* 'tomorrow' and the present tense of the verb: *si hairə glai* 'they are soon getting married', *marɪyə genə mər nɑx əm dɔgdər* 'tomorrow we will go to the doctor'; (b) with the use of the present progressive + adverb: *ar ɪs wasəm am bluyə dənowəd* 'he is ploughing sod tonight'; or (c) with a construction using the auxiliaries *tsɛlə* 'to count on (doing something)' or *fɪgərə* 'to figure on (doing something)' e.g. *tsɛlət dir hairə?* 'are you (pl.) going to get married?' Evidence for *tsɛlə* as an expression of future time rather than simply intention is found in the fact that *tsɛlə* can occur in structures without a human subject, e.g. *sɛl tsɛlt nɛt kaundə* 'that won't count'. Future time constructions with the progressive as in (b) are more numerous in the speech of sectarians, while constructions with the auxiliary *tsɛlə* as in (c) do exist only in the sectarian communities. In fact, the latter form is so common among the Old Order Amish that *tsɛlə* is in the process of being grammaticalized.

The morphophonemic rule in Pennsylvania German which deletes underlying *-n* in word-final position (see adjectives), also operates in the verbal paradigm, that is, the Pennsylvania German infinitive, first- and third-person plural of verbs end in *-ə* not *-en*, as is the norm for Standard German.

Depending on regional usage, the pronominal and inflectional patterns for the second-person plural may show alternate forms, e.g., *dir/dər fragt* 'you (pl.) ask' in Berks, Center, Lancaster, Dauphin counties etc., or *ər/ir frayə* in East Lehigh, Northampton, and East Montgomery counties, or *nər/nir frayə* in Northwest Lehigh county, Pennsylvania (see Table 13.7). For sectarians, a second-person plural with *-ət* is the more common ending. When the word order is inverted, as in the fronting of verbs for yes/no questions, the pronoun following the verb cliticizes, or, as in the case of unaccented *du*, may be omitted, e.g. *ɪx hab* 'I have' but *hawəx?* 'do I have?', *du hɔft* 'you have' but *hɔft (ə)?* 'do you have?', *mər hɛn* 'we have' but *hɛmɐ* 'do we have', *dir hɛn* 'you (pl.) have' but *hɛnɐ?* 'do you (pl.) have?' Moreover, verbs with stems ending in a voiced velar stop undergo lenition when personal inflections render an intervocalic environment, e.g. *ɪx grig > mar griyə* 'I get' vs 'we get' (see Phonology).

Pennsylvania German has six modals: some of them manifest regional variants which are indicated parenthetically:

1   *mɪsə* 'must, to have to';
2   *kɛnə* 'to be able to';
3   *sɔlə (sɛlə)* 'should, to be supposed to';
4   *darəfə (daufə, dɛrfə)*;
5   *megə* 'may, to care to';
6   *wɔlə (wɛlə)* 'to want to'.

The verb *brauxə* (*braixə*) 'to need' can function as a modal, that is, either independently (with the meaning of 'to need') or in combination with a dependent infinitive preceded by *nɛt* 'not' (with the meaning of 'not to be required to'), e.g. *ar brauxt dər wayə* 'he needs the wagon' but *ar brauxt dər wayə nət kafə* 'he does not need to buy the wagon'.

Negation particles are *ke* (*kɛn*) and *nɛt* 'no, none', with *ke* negating preceding nouns and *nɛt* negating all other parts of speech. The common and dative case forms of *ke* are: *ke* (*kɛn*) for singular and plural of all genders in the common case; *kɛm* for masculine and neuter dative; *kɛnrə*, feminine dative singular; and *kɛn* plural dative, e.g. *mər gɛwə kɛm kɪnd kɛn kʊki*, which translates literally 'we give no child no cookie'. The particles *ke* and *kɛn* are used interchangeably, although *ke* is the older form. Emphasis is expressed with an additional negator *ni* 'never' or an emphatic *du* 'to do' (StGer. *tun*), e.g. *ɪx du nɛt ʃtrɪgə* 'I do not knit', *ɪx max ni ken panhɑs* 'I never make scrapple (US dish)'.

Loan Morphology
The inflectional morphology for borrowed verbs follows the native pattern, i.e. infinitives are created by adding the suffix -*ə* to the English loan, e.g. *titʃə* 'to teach': 1 sg. *ɪx titʃ*, 2 sg. *du titʃt*, 3 sg. *ar titʃt*, 1 pl. *mir titʃə*, 2 pl. *dir titʃt*, 3 pl. *si titʃə*. Past participles are based on the infinitive with a prefixed *gə*-morph, e.g. *gətiʃt* 'taught'. Other examples are: *gəfilt* 'felt', *gəʃtɔpt* 'stopped', *gəkokst* 'coaxed'. Only one occurrence of a loan participle being adapted to the pattern of a Pennsylvania German strong verb has been noted, i.e. *ausgəwɔrə* 'worn out' and *gəwɔrə* 'worn'.

When an English verb is borrowed with a verb particle, Pennsylvania German will convert the particle into a verb prefix, e.g. *ʊfgsoberəd* 'sobered up', *ausfɪgɛrə* 'to figure out'. In the case of a compound consisting of a preposition + verb, the preposition will be either translated or phonetically adapted, e.g. *ɪwərtʃardʒd* 'overcharged'. Verbal compounds are also created with the inseparable German prefix *fər*-, e.g. *fərbɔtʃt* 'all botched up', *fərmɪksə* 'completedly mixed up'.

Other loan derivations involve the combination of English reflexive verbs with German reflexive pronouns, e.g. *ɪx əntʃoi mɪx* 'I enjoy myself'. The durative affixes (-*ai*, *ge*-) readily compound to borrowed lexemes, e.g. *ʃmokərai* 'business of smoking', *bɔdərai* 'continual bother', *ən gəpʊʃ* 'a constant pushing'.

13.4   Syntax
The syntax, more than any other area of Pennsylvania German, closely resembles the structure of Modern Standard German (see chapter 11).

The discussion of syntax is limited to the following features:

1 Word order in main and subordinate clauses; word order with modals;
2 Progressive and iterative aspect;
3 Common subordinators and complementation in infinitival and relative clauses;
4 Passive voice;
5 Subjunctive mood.

Word Order
More recent analyses of Pennsylvania German syntax suggest SOV rather than SVO as the underlying word order for Pennsylvania German, in spite of the fact that the addition of elements to the right of the finite verb tends to be more numerous than in Standard German, e.g. *ɪx hab gǝwɪst as dǝr hut si nɛt fɪdǝ det an sɛlǝm ɛnd* StGer. *ich hab gewußt, daß ihr der Hut an dem Ende nicht passen würde* 'I knew that the hat would not fit her at that end'.

Despite this greater flexibility, word order has remained relatively consistent and outside the realm of English influence. As in Standard German, the position of the verb plays a pivotal role in the arrangement of clausal constituents. The major patterns are: the finite verb in first or second position in main clauses – e.g. *kafʃt du sɛlǝr gaul?* 'are you buying that horse?' *ar med ǝs gras* 'he mows the grass' and in final position in subordinate clauses, e.g. *tʃan hat nɛt gǝwɪst as si ǝs bux hat* 'John did not know that she has the book'. In some constructions, Pennsylvania German word order differs from Standard German. For example, if a dependent clause contains a double infinitive, Standard German precedes the multiple predicate with the finite form of *hawǝ* 'to have', e.g. StGer. *wenn ich so schön hätte singen können*, whereas Pennsylvania German places the finite verb medially between the double infinitive, e.g. *wan ɪx so ʃe sɪŋǝ hɛt kɛnǝ* 'if I could have sung that well'.

Word order in modal constructions generally follows the Standard German pattern. In main clauses, a modal functioning in an auxiliary capacity takes the position and function of the finite verb, while the infinitive of the main verb is placed sentence-final, e.g. *ar kan sɛl nɛt kafǝ* 'he cannot buy that'. In subordinate clauses, the modal appears in final and the infinitive, in the penultimate position, e.g. *ar wes, as ar sɛl nɛt kafǝ kan* 'he knows that he cannot buy that'. More prevalent, however, are constructions with a modal as the main verb, particularly when the notion of destination is implied, e.g. *ar mʊs nɑx ǝm dɔgdǝr* 'he has (to go) to the doctor'. Constructions with inversion of the modal and main verb infinitive, e.g. *ar hat mɪsǝ ʃafǝ* 'he had to work' rather than the traditional sentence-final placement of the modal *ar hat ʃafǝ mɪsǝ* have been observed in speech communities of younger Midwestern sectarian speakers.

Aspect
Pennsylvania German has constructions which mark aspectual information in conjunction with tense and/or adverbs. One construction – use of the auxiliary

sai + *am* + infinitive – corresponds to the English progressive in that it signals continuation or duration of an activity, e.g. *ar ɪs/war am brif ʃraiwə* 'he is/was writing a letter'. Although Standard German has no corresponding progressive construction, a form with *am* has been attested in some dialects of German. The past progressive combines the preterite of *sai* 'to be', i.e. *war* 'was' + *am* + infinitive of main verb + past participle – *gəwɛst* 'have been', e.g. *si wat am kɔxə gəwɛst* 'she had been cooking'. The aspectual marker *am* denoting a dative ending, is being replaced in the conservative religious groups with either [a] or [ə] + alveolar nasal /n/, e.g. *ɪx war mai bux an/ən lesə* 'I was reading my book'. More striking is the fact that for this group placement of constituent modifiers between *am* [an/ən] and the infinitive can occur, e.g. articles, possessive adjectives, as in *ar ɪs am/n sai bʊgi fiksə* 'he is fixing his buggy'. This form is in contrast with the more customary word order (i.e. in the speech of the non-sectarians) which does not permit modifiers to come between the object noun and *am*. Iterative aspect may be expressed in two ways: (a) with a present-tense form of the auxiliary *du* + infinitive *si dut ʃtrɪgə* 'she knits (habitually, for a living)'; and (b) the adverb *als* + past participle: *ar hat si als gəkɛnt* 'he used to know her', *ar hat əs gras als gəmet* 'he (repeatedly) mowed the grass'. Traditionally, *du* occurred with constructions in the present tense, while *als* was used with past time. This division no longer exits in the sectarian community, where recent studies have indicated the use of adverbial *als* as iterative aspect marker in past and present tense constructions: e.g. *marjəts dun mir als ʃafə* 'mornings we (usually) work'. While Standard German rarely employs the *tun* 'do' formation, evidence from spoken and written German indicates that it is in productive use.

Subordination

Pennsylvania German has the following subordinators and complementizers: *as* 'that', *as wan*, *as wi wan* 'as if', *bɪs* 'until, by the time (that)', *ɛp* 'before, whether', *nɔxdəm* 'after', *so as* 'so that, in order that', *wan* 'when, if', *wail* 'because, while', *wi* 'when (past occurrences), how, as', *tsɪdər* 'since'. Moreover, interrogatives like *wu* 'where', *wɛr* 'who' can function as subordinators as well. A common introducer of concessive clauses is the conjunction *ɛp* 'if, whether', e.g. *ɪx wes nɛt ɛp ar kʊmə kan* 'I don't know whether he is able to come'. Barring some exceptions, word order in dependent clauses generally agrees with Standard German; that is, the finite verb is placed in sentence-final position, e.g. *wan du tswe kʊkis haʃt* 'if you have two cookies' (see Word order).

Complementizers in Infinitival Clauses

Complementation in Pennsylvania German infinitival clauses differs in some instances from those in Standard German. Theoretically, four different strategies are at the disposal of Pennsylvania German speakers:

1   A *fər ... tsu* construction which most closely resembles StGer. *um ... zu*;
2   The use of only *tsu*;
3   The use of only *fər* as a complementizer;
4   A zero option with the infinitive alone.

Today the two options *fər ... tsu* or simply *tsu* are relic forms associated with older speakers, while *fər* or zero represent the viable construction. A clause of purpose, e.g. *... fər grʊmbɛrə (tsu) ɛsə ...* '(in order) to eat potatoes' will in modern Pennsylvania German omit *tsu* and maintain *fər* at the head of the clause. Inasmuch as English is influencing changes in Pennsylvania German, it has been suggested that in those cases where it is grammatical for English to use an infinitive or -ing form, Pennsylvania German opts for a zero construction, e.g. *si hat gʃtart lanə* 'she started/began to study/studying'. It appears that this trend towards simplification in complementation is a result of convergence with English.

Relativization

Mention has already been made of *as* 'that' as the introducer of subordinate clauses; it is in fact the invariant relativizing particle for relative clauses. Unlike Standard German, there are no true relative pronouns in Pennsylvania German. Historically, two complementizers *as* 'that' and *wu* 'which, who' were used to relativize elements in embedded clauses, e.g. *di med as/wu mər gsenə hɛn* 'the girls whom we saw'. Except for remnants of *wu* in dialect poetry and by older speakers, the usage of *as* 'that' is now the standard. The above notwithstanding, one genuine relative pronoun in possessive clauses has been substantiated by Pennsylvania German grammarians, e.g. *dəs ɪs dər man dəm sai hʊnd graŋg ɪs* 'that is the man whose dog is sick'. This construction requires a dative noun phrase + possessive pronoun. However, the single viable complementizer used today by sectarian speakers is *as*, e.g. *dəs ɪs dər man, as sai hʊnd graŋg ɪs*, which in (non-standard) English is 'that is the man that his dog is sick'.

Passive Voice

Another periphrasis to be considered is the passive, a grammatical contrast which Pennsylvania German and Standard German traditionally have shared. The marking occurs with the passive auxiliary *sai* 'to be' + past participle for perfective functions (statal passive), e.g. *dər pai ɪs gəbakə* 'the pie is baked' versus the auxiliary *warə* 'to become' + past participle to signal not yet completed activity (agentive passive), e.g. *dər pai wat gəbakə* 'the pie is being baked'. Events in the past are expressed with the present or preterite of *sai* + past participle + *warə* – here representing the participial form of the auxiliary *warə*, StGer. *(ge)worden* – as in, e.g. *dər pai ɪs/wat gəbakə warə* 'the pie was/had been baked'. An optional agent introduced by *fʊn* 'by' +

dative noun phrase may be added, e.g. *dər pai wat fʊn dər mæm gəbakə* 'the pie is being baked by (the) mother'. Influence from English has been suggested to account for an observed trend in some communities to (a) replace the auxiliary *warə* with *sai* in passive constructions; (b) replace the preposition *fun* 'by' with *bai* 'by'; (c) substitute the dative with a common case noun phrase; (d) postpose the prepositional phrase, e.g. *dər pai ɪs gəbakə bai di mæm* 'the pie is being baked by (the) mother'; (e) permit non-logical objects to passivize, e.g. *ɪx bɪn gsagt warə* 'I have been told'.

Subjunctive Mood
Changes in the subjunctive attest to the trend toward analysis, where the formerly synthetic form is being replaced with more isolating morphemes. Historically, the auxiliary *det* (subjunctive form of *du* 'to do') StGer. *täte* 'would/should' + infinitive of the main verb expresses the present subjunctive, e.g. *ɪx det sɛl fərfte* 'I would/should understand that'. There are a limited number of verbs which have retained distinct subjunctive forms, e.g. *kʊmə* (inf.) – *kemt* (subj.) 'come'; *me yə* (inf.) – *mext* (subj.) 'to care for'. However, these purely synthetic variants are exceptional for most speakers today and known only to older and linguistically conservative persons. In fact, a sentence like *ɪx wɔt si kemdə hem* 'I wish she would come home' is now formed as *ɪx wɔt si det hem kʊmə*. Only in the auxiliaries *hawə* 'to have' and *sai* 'to be' has Pennsylvania German preserved the historically synthetic forms, i.e. *hɛt* (subj.) StGer. *hätte* 'would/should have' and *wɛr* (subj.) StGer. *wäre* 'would/should have' respectively. These forms in combination with the past participle are essential in formation of the past subjunctive, e.g. *ɪx hɛt sɛl gədu* 'I would have done that'. Subjunctive forms of modal verbs have been maintained, e.g. *brauxə* 'to need' – *braixt* (subj.); *kɛnə* 'to be able' – *kɛnt* (subj.); *sɔlə* 'to be expected to' – *sɛt* (subj.).

Conditional clauses, usually introduced by *wan*, StGer. *wenn* 'if', are similar to Standard German, e.g. *wan ɪx raix wɛr det ɪx ir hɛlfə* StGer. *wenn ich reich wäre, würde (täte) ich ihr helfen* 'if I were rich, I would help her'.

13.5 Lexis
The lexical inventory is composed almost completely of words current in southwest German dialects during the latter part of the seventeenth and early part of the eighteenth century with some borrowings from Standard German and from English.

While borrowings from English are difficult to date, fossilized pronunciation of some of these lexemes testifies to their early incorporation into Pennsylvania German, e.g. *bailər* for 'boiler', *ɪnfɪŋ* for 'Indian', *bærjə* for 'bargain', *fmært* for 'smart', *pærdi* for 'party', *kær* for 'car'. Reflexes of Middle English [ă] before /r/ which become [æ] in the seventeenth century are preserved in the latter examples. The dialect word *pɪktɐ* 'picture' can be traced not only to early American speech, but also to the dialects of northern England. As a result, the qualitatively different pronunciation of these loans has aided in their acceptance now as part of the native lexicon.

English influence is conspicuously manifested in the numerous calques, e.g. *grʊndsau* for 'groundhog', *rɪgəlweg* 'railroad', *katsəfɪʃ* 'catfish', *(al) rɛxt* '(all) right, correct'. One of the more intriguing collocations occurred with the verb *glaixə* 'to like, to be fond of' as in *ɪx glaix ɛbəl boi* 'I like apple pie'. The semantic shift of *glaixə* from StGer. *gleichen* with the meaning of 'to be similar, to be like', a meaning not at all conveyed in the Pennsylvania German verb, may have been caused by interference from the English expressions *to like*, and *to be like*. Eventually, the meaning of *glaixə* came to denote 'to like' only and never 'to resemble'.

Further Reading

Buffington, A. F. and Barba, P. A. (1954) *A Pennsylvania German Grammar*, Allentown: Schlechter's.

Huffines, M. L. (1986) 'The function of aspect in Pennsylvania German and the impact of English', *Yearbook of German–American Studies* 21: 137–54.

Kelz, H. (1971) *Phonologische Analyse des Pennsylvaniadeutschen*, Hamburg: Buske.

Learned, M. D. (1988/9) 'The Pennsylvania German dialect', repr. in *American Journal of Philology* 9 (1988): 64–83, 178–97, 326–39, 425–45; 10 (1889): 288–315.

Louden, M. L. (1988) 'Bilingualism and syntactic change in Pennsylvania German', unpublished doctoral thesis, Cornell University.

Moelleken, W. W. (1983) 'Language maintenance and language shift in Pennsylvania German: a comparative investigation', *Monatshefte* 75: 172–85.

Penzl, H. (1938) 'Lehnwörter mit Mittelenglisch ă vor r im Pennsylvanisch–Deutschen Dialekt', *Journal of English and German Philology* 37: 396–402.

Reed, C. E. (1979) 'The syntax of Pennsylvania German', *Orbis* 28: 245–56.

Reed, C. E. and Seifert, L. W. (1954) *A Linguistic Atlas of Pennsylvania German*, Marburg/Lahn: Elwert.

Schach, P. (1951) 'Semantic borrowing in Pennsylvania German', *American Speech*, 26, 257–67.

Seifert, L. W. (1947) 'The diminutives of Pennsylvania German', *Monatshefte* 39: 285–93.

Van Ness, S. (1990) *Changes in an Obsolescing Language: Pennsylvania German in West Virginia*, Tübingen: Narr.

14 Dutch

Georges De Schutter

14.1 Introduction

Dutch is an official language in the Netherlands, Belgium, Surinam and the former Dutch Antilles (including Aruba). It is spoken as a first language by some 20 million people in Europe. The language has been and is known under a variety of names. In the Middle Ages it was called *Diets*(*ch*) or *Duits*(*ch*) (from which its English name derives), in the Renaissance period this was further specified as *Nederduits*(*ch*) (lit.) 'Nether Dutch', to distinguish it from its eastern neighbours (High and Low) German, which, in the course of time, monopolized the name *Duits*. The official modern name *Nederlands* ('Nether-landic') is fairly recent, and did not succeed in ousting popular designations like *Hollands* and *Vlaams* 'Flemish'; the latter names are largely restricted to the language as spoken in the Kingdom of the Netherlands and Belgium, respectively. Although the geographical distribution of Dutch is rather limited, there is a wide variety of regional dialects, the mutual intelligibility of which is often low. The diversity may be traced back to at least two sets of factors, one intra-, one extralinguistic in nature.

First of all, the language developed in a geographical area in which no fewer than three or even four major dialects of continental West Germanic come together: Frisian, Saxon and Low Franconian, of which the last split into a western and an eastern branch at a very early stage. Although Frisian, Saxon and East Low Franconian have been partly ousted, partly strongly influenced by the central dialects of Holland and Brabant, both of which have predominant Western Low Franconian characteristics, the old distinctions did to a certain degree live on in later evolutionary stages of dialects.

Apart from the associations based on the old tribal bonds, there is another, even hazier factor, connected with West Germanic history. In his *De Germania* Tacitus divided the Germanic tribes into Ingvaeones, Istvaeones and Erminones, of which the former occupied the coastal regions. It is not clear if this distribution maps in any definable way on to the division based on tribal bonds given above; but the term 'Ingvaeonism' has gained some popularity in Dutch historical linguistics, with reference to the quite considerable number of characteristics (morphophonemic, lexical and even

Figure 14.1   Dutch and Frisian dialects in the Netherlands, Belgium and the North of France

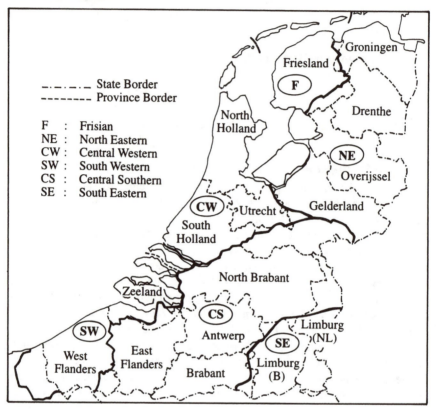

syntactic) common to a great many coastal dialects, irrespective of cataloguing as 'Franconian', 'Frisian' or 'Saxon'.

Even more important appears to be the extralinguistic diachronic factor: the Germanic-speaking Low countries grew together into one state at a fairly late date (late sixteenth century), and almost immediately broke up again into two political entities, due to the 'Reconquista' of the Southern Netherlands by the Spanish monarchy. In fact there was, until the end of the eighteenth century, a third state, that of Liège, to which most of the (Dutch-speaking) southeastern province of Belgian Limburg belonged. After the sixteenth century the southern dialects developed independently of a unifying standard language. For centuries, even up to the 1930s, most if not all administration was conducted in French, and most education was in French and Latin (the latter at the university). Regional dialects continued to be used in everyday life, but natural developments, as well as contact with the dominant language, French, continually drove them further apart, both *vis-à-vis* one another and with respect to the northern dialects. To all this may be added another external one. For the Roman Catholic clergy the northern dialects, especially those of the central provinces, were associated with Calvinism. Although most of the priests were favourable towards the local vernaculars (and not towards propagation of French), they tried to stop whatever linguistic influence might have come from the northern neighbour. The evolution in the northern dialects was less turbulent, and to some degree it was mitigated by a common written language. But even there the status of Dutch as a unifying language was not always undisputed, especially in a number of peripheral provinces. In Groningen, Low German was a formidable rival for some time, and the southern province of (eastern) Limburg was not attached to the Netherlands until 1848.

The original situation of pluriformity and the external historical facts converge on a picture of extreme dialectal diversification. Traditionally the modern dialects are divided into 5 large groups (Figure 14.1):

1 The central-western dialects (henceforth CW dialects), including all those in the provinces of North and South Holland and Utrecht, large parts of Gelderland, and the Zeeland Isles;
2 The northeastern (NE) dialects in Groningen, Drenthe, Overijsel and the eastern part of Gelderland;
3 The central-southern (CS) dialects in the Netherlands province of North Brabant and adjacent parts of Limburg, and in the Belgian provinces of Antwerp, Brabant and East Flanders; the language of the last province, together with the eastern part of the Netherlands territory of Zeeland Flanders, south of the River Scheldt, appears to be a blend between Brabantic characteristics and a substratum which must have been quite close to the southwestern dialects;
4 The southwestern (SW) dialects in the Belgian province of West Flanders, the western part of Zeeland Flanders; to the same stock belong the now obsolete dialects spoken until quite recently (in fact even up to this day by a dwindling number of elderly people) in the extreme northwestern part of France (French Flanders, between Dunkirk and Bailleul);
5 The southeastern (SE) dialects in the greater part of the Netherlands province of Limburg, and its Belgian namesake.

Of these groups the northeastern dialects are often called 'Saxon', the southeastern ones 'Eastern Low Franconian', the three other groups are supposed to derive more or less directly from 'Western Low Franconian'. Of course modern Frisian dialects, occupying the larger part of the province of Friesland, are not included in this overview, as they are usually considered to belong to another system.

Although there is little dispute among dialectologists concerning the general classification just presented, it is noteworthy that most linguistic differences cut across at least one of the groups, thus making it virtually impossible to give an overview of the characteristics of any single group. As a typical case we may refer to the effect of *i*-umlaut. This phonological process, common to West Germanic, has a rather limited effect on the western (CW and SW) dialects. In these varieties it does not affect long vowels, and is not generally used as a morphological device. In eastern (NE and SE) dialects it has a range that may be compared to that in Standard German. The central southern dialects, then, do not display a common picture: the western ones pattern together with the first two groups, and the same parallellism exists between eastern central-southern and northeastern/southeastern dialects. Between the extremes all gradations appear as one proceeds from one end of the area to the other. The picture may even be more complex, as is the case with the morphological opposition between *s*- and *n*-plural markers (see section 14.3). *S*-plurals are particularly frequent in southwestern dialects (in fact, they are considered as ingvaeonicisms by many historical linguists), and are almost absent in the southeastern region; in all other groups there is a wide range of choices, depending on the individual words rather than specific characteristics of noun classes. Another quite conspicuous feature is the distribution of palatalized forms of the diminutive suffix *tje* (as opposed to the older form with velar consonant *ke*). Only palatalized forms occur in central-western dialects; they also have a very regular distribution in southwestern dialects. In all other groups both forms occur in at least a number of dialects, but the distribution is blurred by a great number of interfering factors. Palatalized forms are growing less frequent as one moves from the west towards the east and south, and even vanish completely in a relatively small number of southern and eastern dialects.

It is clear from the examples given that the geographic area occupied by Dutch forms a continuum rather than a neat conglomerate of smaller entities, each with a fixed set of proper characteristics.

From the above examples it appears that most differences between regional dialects have an east–west distribution, which is in line with the general picture of an originally coastal (or 'Ingvaeonic') west, and a continental east. The interaction between these two entities is in fact often considered the main source of peculiarities of the Dutch language. But there is also a north–south opposition. Beginning in the Middle Ages, French had a strong influence both on Dutch dialects and on whatever standard there was in the Low Countries. This influence manifested itself not only in the lexicon, but also in a number of syntactic and morphological (derivational) aspects. Much of French influence passed through the mediation of the southern (especially SW and CS) dialects. After the separation of the Low Countries in the sixteenth century the north–south continuum broke down, and direct (though not necessarily indirect) influence from French halted at the border between the two countries, whereas it grew stronger in the southern provinces. In this way the border between Belgium and the

Netherlands turned from a purely political into a (partially) linguistic one. Up to this day the linguistic border has been maintained, and in some respects even reinforced, as dialects north of it are subject to different influences from those to the south. At least three (sets of) factors play a part in this: (a) the standard language, which serves as a reference point, differs in a number of respects; (b) more importantly, the cultural centres, from which linguistic trends and innovations spread, are different in the two countries: the Randstad (the urban area in South Holland and adjoining North Holland and Utrecht) is a highly dominant centre in the Netherlands, the Antwerp–Brussels region serves as a rather weak counterpart in Belgium; and (c) the Netherlands are directed almost exclusively towards the Anglo-Saxon world, whereas French still occupies a preferential position in the cultural and economic life of Belgium as a whole, including Flanders. This situation makes the relations between dialects, several non-standard varieties and the standard language even less conspicuous than might have been expected on the evidence of purely evolutionary processes.

The main difference between dialects in the Netherlands and in Belgium however lies in the social domain rather than in linguistic characteristics. In Belgium, dialects still serve as a common vernacular for people belonging to all social classes, whereas dialects in the Netherlands are restricted to use by a limited number of social groups, and in an ever decreasing set of situations and environments. One side-effect may be the intense use of regional dialects for literary works in the Netherlands. Dialects (or at least some of them) appear to be considered a valuable though rather impractical part of the cultural heritage. In Belgium there is no counterpart to this phenomenon. Dialects are taken as common, but at the same time rather stigmatized vernaculars, inappropriate in most formal domains such as public life.

For historical reasons the standard language, especially formal written Dutch, contains characteristics of the three Western Low Franconian dialect groups. In the sixteenth century the standard began to develop spontaneously on the basis of Brabantic (CS) dialects, which had themselves incorporated quite a lot of Flemish (SW) characteristics. The first *conscious* endeavour towards standardization may have been the Calvinist translation of the Bible (the famous 'Statenbijbel'), in which peculiarities of all dialect regions were incorporated. This fairly fixed form of written language was then widely adopted for all cultural purposes by the central provinces of the Republic of the Netherlands. It formed the basis of a common written standard, which in the course of time incorporated more and more characteristics from the Randstad dialects. The spoken language developed parallel to written styles, but with a more prominent contribution from central-western dialects. In this century it also succeeded in supplanting the old fashioned literary language in all domains, including written styles. Summarizing, we may say that Modern Standard Dutch is a direct heir of the dialects of the provinces of North and South Holland and Utrecht, with some rare admixtures of southern elements, especially in the rather formal written language. In this respect it is typical that the formal second-person pronoun *u* (su./obj.) developed from a southern form, whereas informal *jij* (su.)/*je* (su./obj./poss.)/*jou(w)* (obj./poss.) directly derived from older central-western forms.

The typically northern standard was also adopted in Belgium, though colloquial speech often includes lexical, morphological and syntactic characteristics from regional dialects, and often through these, from French. These deviations from the northern standard are partly general, partly regional. Consequently it is simply impossible to supply a general characterization of the differences between Belgian and Netherlands Dutch.

Dutch is an official language also in the former colonies of Surinam and the Dutch Antilles. In both countries (and in Aruba, which is separated form the Dutch Antilles) it is used side-by-side with a number of indigenous or imported languages: Sranan, Sarnami and a number of other ethnic languages in Surinam, Papiamento (a mainly Portuguese-based creole) and to a lesser degree English in the Antilles. There is a marked difference in the linguistic situation between those countries, however. In Surinam, Sranan and Sarnami are, to a very high degree, 'ethnic' languages of the two major groups of the population (Creoles and Hindustani), consequently neither language enjoys the status of a full-fledged 'national' language, even though Sranan is very widely used in everyday interethnic communication. That is why Dutch up to this day is, by and large, accepted as a national language for most cultural and administrative functions. This status as a national language is even being reinforced by the recent development of a specific Surinam Standard Dutch. Although the language follows the European standard in most respects, non-European characteristics are to be found as well. Among these we find (a) the lexicon, which not only contains words connected with local circumstances, but also displays a fairly large section of vocabulary which has become archaic in European Dutch; and (b) the pronunciation, e.g. retroflex [l], palatalization and nasalization of vowels in certain environments, and a loss of the [± voice] opposition between fricatives. In this way Dutch itself is gradually developing into a Surinam 'national' variety. None of this occurs in the Antilles, where Papiamento and English are ousting Dutch from all but some of the most formal domains.

14.2 Phonology

General Characteristics of Monomorphemic Words
Like all Germanic languages Dutch has a number of different morphological word types, including compound and derived ones. In this section we will concentrate on the phonemic structure of simplex (monomorphemic) words. These are of a widely varied stock. A first group consists of the Germanic heritage of monomorphemes, which during the course of time were all

reduced to mono- or disyllabic words with only one 'full' vowel (disyllabic words having [ə] in the second syllable). Then we have the originally derived or compound words, which lost their composite semantic structure. Most of these still reflect the original compound pattern by the fact that they retain two 'full' vowels, usually with stress on the first syllable (e.g. *antwoord* 'answer', *oorlog* 'war', *hertog* 'duke', *vennoot* 'business partner', but with final stress: *ellende* 'misery' and *forel* 'trout', a loan from German). Some of these polysyllabic words, like *gereed* 'ready', *begin* 'begin', *tevreden* 'content', have a phonological make-up that derives from, or is at least reminiscent of, prefix-derived words (the third one actually goes back to a prepositional phrase). Last, but not least, there are many words of 'foreign' origin, mostly borrowed from Romance, including Latin and the various stages in the development of French. The words of this category that were – and have remained – polysyllabic have a stress pattern which may be called 'final'. The overwhelming majority of those ending in heavy syllables (syllables consisting of tense vowel + consonant or lax vowel + consonant cluster) have stress on the last syllable, and the same applies to quite a number of words with light final syllables. Monomorphemic words may also have stress on the penultimate or antepenultimate syllable. The discrepancy with the Proto-Germanic stress pattern is of course the result of the overall tendency to reduce all non-stressed vowels to [ə] in a first stage, after which the syllable itself mostly disappeared. This tendency, which developed at a very early date, appears to have been stronger in Dutch than in German, though not nearly as strong as in English. It has remained in the language as a productive (though minor) rule throughout history, yielding such words as *cement* 'cement', *beton* 'concrete (noun)' (with [ə] in the first syllable) on the one hand, *pruik* 'wig', *krant* 'newspaper' and *kleur* 'colour' on the other (all from French disyllabic originals: *ciment*, *béton*, *perruque*, *courant* and *couleur*). Moreover most tri- and polysyllabic monomorphemes display reduction of full vowels to [ə] in non-peripheral syllables directly preceding or following the syllable which bears the main stress (e.g. the second syllables in *algebra, microfoon*). The latter tendency, however, is restricted to non-formal styles, and even then it does not affect all words to the same degree.

The Dutch Vowel System

The Modern Dutch vowel system is the result of a great number of changes, which left virtually each dialect group with a different set of 'full' vowels, with widely diverging distributions among sets of lexical items. In this section we will only go into the Standard system, which derives from the dialects of the leading 'Randstad' region. As far as systemic aspects of Standard Dutch phonology are concerned there is little or no variation in the whole language area, including Belgium.

The main phonetic oppositions, leading to 'distinctive features', are:

1 Tense–lax, rather than long–short, though there is in one sense a full correlation between both oppositions. Tense vowels are lengthened before homomorphic /r/; in other positions they may become long only in special cases (emphasis, very careful speech, etc.).

2 Front–back. Though distributional characteristics seem to prove that the open vowels /a/ (tense) and /ɑ/ (lax) do not partake in this opposition on the systematic (phonological) level, the opposition shows up at the phonetic level, the former being front, the latter back.

3 Rounded–unrounded. This opposition, with [+round] front vowels mainly the result of palatalization of back vowels in earlier stages of the development of Germanic, is not found with back vowels.

4 Monophthong–diphthong. On the systemic level Dutch has three diphthongs: /ɛⁱ/, /œʸ/ and /ɔᵘ/. Though the latter is subject to rather strong distributional restrictions, it is beyond doubt that it behaves as a single phoneme within the word, just like the other two. This is not true of, for example, the combination of /a/ + /j/, or /e/ + /w/ (as in waai(en) 'blow (verb)' and leeuw(en) 'lion(s)'), where the combination of vowel + glide is clearly treated as consisting of two single elements. The difference between the latter combinations and real diphthongs appears most clearly in the distributional characteristics.

5 Closed–open. Contrary to all preceding oppositions, this is a threefold one even at the phonological level: [+open] vs [–open, –closed] vs [+closed].

This leaves us with the phonological system shown in Table 14.1 (rounded vowels follow their non-rounded counterparts). As may be seen, the system of lax monophthongs is asymmetrical, both 'rounded' pairs /u/ – /ɔ/ and /y/ – /ʏ/ having merged in the Holland dialects. An opposition between a closed and a more open variant of /ɔ/ is often reported to exist on the systemic level, but with most (if not all) speakers these sounds are in complementary distribution. They vary according to phonological environments rather than phonological distribution. Oppositions like that between (semi-open) bot 'dull' and (semi-closed) bot '(hali)but' were mentioned in phonological

Table 14.1 The vowel system in Dutch

	Tense monophthongs		Lax monophthongs		Diphthongs	
	Front	Back	Front	Back	Front	Back
+closed	i/y	u	ɪ/–	—		
–closed, –open	e/ø	o	ɛ/ʏ	ɔ	ɛⁱ/œʸ	ɔᵘ
+open	a			ɑ		

treatments until some decades ago, but cannot be found in Standard Dutch as it is spoken today.

On the phonetic level, tense and lax vowels differ in quite a number of respects, especially in degree of 'openness'. Thus [ɪ] is more open than [i], [ɛ] more than [e], [ʏ] more than [ø].

Apart from the 'regular' vowels listed in Table 14.1, there exist what may be called loan phonemes, which occur exclusively in loanwords: though words as *frêle* 'frail', *ordinair* 'vulgar', *repère* 'reference' are well integrated into Dutch, they retain the tensed (and long) vowel [ɛː] of their French original. In the same way, though on a much more limited scale, the tensed counterparts of [ɔ] and [ʏ] occur. This would yield a four-level system *vis-à-vis* the open–closed opposition. Yet Dutch phonologists generally adhere to the system proposed in Table 14.1, these vowels being the only ones which may occur in any position available to their subclass. Loan phonemes on the other hand are subject to severe restrictions. For example, they are excluded from word-final position, though all native Dutch tense vowels may occur there.

As for the distribution of vowels, only one very general rule can be identified. Lax vowels do not occur in open syllables. This is of course especially clear in final syllables ending in a vowel (where tense vowels do occur, compare, e.g. *villa* 'villa', *hobo* 'oboe', *lelie* 'lily', *kneu* 'linnet' with /a/–/o/–/i/–/ø/ respectively). Other distributional restrictions concern mainly the positions before /r/, /j/ and /w/, where diphthongs, and to a large degree lax vowels do not occur. On the other hand dental obstruents /s/, /z/, /d/ and /t/ are very favourable to vowels excluded in other environments. For example, apart from the word *pauk* 'kettledrum', the diphthong /ɔ^u/ only occurs before dental obstruents.

The Consonant System (Including Glides)

On the whole, the consonant system which is generally reconstructed for Proto-Germanic, has survived very well in all Dutch dialects, at least at the systemic phonological level. Table 14.2 depicts the relationship between Indo-European, Proto-Germanic and Modern Dutch. Of course there were some changes. First, Proto-Germanic voiced and voiceless dental fricatives merged, yielding (in the end) uniformly stop /d/. The labials retained the original opposition to some degree. In word-initial position /v/ developed into /b/, /f/ in most words into /v/ (though in quite a number of words /f/ was retained), but in all other positions both Germanic fricatives were retained. It is generally held that the velars underwent the same processes as the labials, but even if that is so, the original situation was more or less restored afterwards: voiced /ɣ/ vs voiceless /x/, at least in post-vocalic position (/g/ became a fricative at a very early date in Dutch). In word-initial position /x/ developed into /h/, which in most dialects, including the Standard language, survived in pre-vocalic position, but was lost in all other positions.

Table 14.2   Dutch consonants and their forebears

Obstruents			Nasals, Liquids, Glides		
Dutch	Proto-Germanic	Indo-European	Dutch	Proto-Germanic	Indo-European
p	p	b	m	m	m
t	t	d	n	n	n
k	k	g	ŋ	n+g/k	n+gh/g
b	v	bh	l	l	l
d	θ/ð	t/dh	r	r/z	r/s
f	f	p	w	w/xw/ɣw	w/kʷ/gʷh
s	s	s	j	j	j
x	x	k	h	x/xw	k/kʷ
v	f/v	p/bh			
z	s	s			
ɣ	ɣ/g	k/gh			

Second, the opposition between voiced and voiceless fricatives word-initially is being lost. In the course of time most occurrences of /s/ and /f/ turned into /z/ and /v/ respectively, if followed by a voiced sound. Laryngeal /h/, which had developed from /x/ in this position, has been exempt from this process. In the modern language, especially in the northern variety, there is a very pronounced tendency to devoice initial fricatives /v/, /z/ and /ɣ/. It should be noted too that voiced obstruents (including stops) are on the whole less strongly voiced in Dutch than, for example, their English counterparts. As was mentioned before, Surinam Dutch, along with a considerable number of northern dialects in the mainland, has dropped the voiced–voiceless opposition completely with fricatives in any position.

Third, Dutch shares with German a devoicing rule through which final obstruents are devoiced. This accounts for the surface differences between *huis/huizen* 'house/houses', *raaf/raven* 'raven/ravens', *weg/wegen* 'road/roads', *goed/goede* (adj.) 'good', *eb/ebbe* 'ebb'. As the written examples show, the surface opposition is represented in the spelling of ‹f/v›, ‹s/z›, but not in the other oppositions: ‹g›, ‹d› and ‹b›, and not ‹ch›, ‹t› and ‹p› are written in endposition.

Fourth, /d/ is subject to a weakening tendency in the position between tense vowel and [ə]. This resulted in two minor rules. The first one applies if [ə] belongs to an affix, and converts /d/ into /w/ after the diphthong /ɔu/ or into /j/ (not written if preceded by a front vowel or diphthong, otherwise written ‹i›) in all other positions, including those after back vowels. The other rule deletes the whole onset and nucleus of the syllable [də(C)] in monomorphemic strings. Examples are *oude* 'old', *beneden* 'downstairs', *rijden* 'to ride', *goede* 'good', *rode* 'red' > *ouwe, beneeeën, rijen, goeie, rooie*; and *veder* 'feather', *teder* 'tender', *nader* 'near', *mede* 'with' > *veer, teer, naar, mee*. The first rule is restricted to informal usage; the second shows a wide range of lexical variation. With some words it is generally applied without any lexical consequences in all styles except very formal ones (e.g. *veder, moede* 'tired', *weder*$_{1-2}$ 'weather$_1$/again$_2$', *neder* 'down' > generally *veer, moe, weer, neer*), but it can also lead to word pairs with different meanings, which then appear in all possible styles (*moeder* 'mother' – *moer* 'doe', *nader* 'near' – *naar* 'towards', *teder* 'tender' – *teer* 'weak', *ijdel* 'vain' – *ijl* 'thin (air)'). As minor rules both phenomena are not only restricted stylistically. Quite a lot of words escape from them completely (e.g. *zaad+en* (pl. noun) 'seeds', *vader* 'father'), whereas others have undergone reanalysis (e.g. *vloei+en* flow', *zaai+en* (verb) 'sow (inf.)', cf. *vloed* 'flood', *zaad* 'seed' as singular nouns).

Finally, the velar nasal /ŋ/ originated as a product of assimilation before velar obstruents. As such it may have had the status of a combinatory variant. Phoneme status was (at least partially) achieved when /g/ after /ŋ/ was dropped word-finally, before another consonant and before [ə]. These are still the only positions where /ŋ/ occurs.

Syllable Structure
In Standard Dutch, syllables have exclusively vocalic nuclei, with either full vowels or [ə]. The vowel may be preceded and/or followed by one or more consonantal phonemes. A special restriction, mentioned before, is that lax vowels must be followed by at least one consonantal phoneme in word-final position. Even glides, which have a distribution arguably comparable with that of consonants, will not suffice in this case. Consonantal clusters between vowels in monomorphemes belong at least partly to the syllable controlled by the following vowel. This rule, combined with the necessity of closing the preceding syllable with at least one consonant if the vowel is lax, has led many phonologists to posit ambisyllabic consonants (thus belonging both to the preceding and the following syllable) in, for example, *pak-ken* 'packages', *tel-len* 'to count', *pas-sen* 'to fit'. As this is not corroborated by phonetic facts (Dutch has no gemination with consonants), nor by intuitions about natural syllabification in (even very careful) speech, it seems to be a purely theoretical construct, without factual basis, possibly also brought about by spelling conventions: double consonants are systematically used for marking laxness of the preceding vowel (see Orthography).

Pre-vocalic consonant clusters may contain as many as three elements (e.g. *spring* 'jump'), post-vocalic ones even four (e.g. *herfst* 'autumn'). It must be said however that such final clusters break up in parts of maximally two elements when the word is combined with a suffix beginning with a vowel. Part of the original cluster then forms the onset of the following syllable (e.g. *herf-stig* 'autumn-like', *burch-ten* (*burcht*) 'castle(s)', *oog-sten* (*oogst*) '(to) harvest'). This leaves us with an analysis of such final word clusters as consisting of a genuine syllable-final cluster of maximally two elements, possibly followed by an 'offset' of maximally two more consonants. The

Table 14.3   Onset combinations [obstruent + non-obstruent]

	m	n	l	r	w	j
p		×	+	+		
b			+	+		
t				+	+	×
d				+	+	
k		+	+	+	+	
f		×	+	+		
v			+	+		
s	+	+	+		×	+
z					+	
x			×	×		
ɣ		×	+	+		

'offset' forms the onset of a following syllable if the word becomes part of a derivation with a suffix beginning with [ə].

Consonant clusters, though very frequent in Dutch monomorphemic words, belong to a rather restricted set. Initial (onset) clusters always begin with an obstruent. The second phoneme may be a voiceless obstruent if the first one is /s/. Thus /st/, /sp/ and /sx/ are very commonly found, while /sk/ and /sf/ are restricted to loans, but are nonetheless considered 'normal' by native speakers. All obstruents may also be followed by non-obstruents, except for the velar nasal. Restrictions within this class of combinations may be derived from Table 14.3, in which the possible combinations are marked with + if they appear in the core lexicon, with × if peripheral.

On the whole, voiceless obstruents appear to have more possibilities than their voiced counterparts. An exception to this rule is of course the pair /x/ – /ɣ/, of which the former does not occur in initial position, except in a few loans. /s/ – /z/ represents another special case, as they are, by and large, in complementary distribution.

Clusters with three consonants all begin with /s/. They contain /spl/, /spr/, /str/, /sxr/ and peripheral /skl/.

Syllable-final clusters are somewhat more varied. Biconsonantal clusters may consist of:

1   Two voiceless obstruents: there are three subclasses, namely /s/ + stop (/sp/, /st/, /sk/); obstruent + /t/ (/pt/, /kt/, /ft/, /st/, /xt/); stop + /s/ (/ps/, /ts/, /ks/);
2   Nasal or liquid + obstruent: on the whole the nasals require the obstruent to have the same articulatory position: /n + dental/, /m + labial/, /ŋ + velar/ (e.g. *hand* 'hand', *kamp* 'camp', *plank* 'board'), but there are a few words with /m+d/ and /ŋ+s/ (e.g. *hemd* 'shirt', *langs* 'along');
3   Liquid + nasal: /lm/, /rm/, /rn/, but not */ln/ (e.g. *halm* 'stalk', *arm* 'arm',

kern 'kernel, core'). In informal talk the clusters /lm/, /rm/, /rn/ are broken by epenthetic [ə].

Phonological Rules

As mentioned before, Modern Standard Dutch does not manifest any large-scale variation as far as the phonological system is concerned. Still, it is relatively easy, even for people who do not know the language, to tell apart speakers from Belgium and those of the Netherlands; within either group there is no uniformity either. The limits of acceptability of phonetic variation in the standard language are a matter of debate. The variation itself is a function of the application of a number of phonetic rules. Five such rules are mentioned below.

1   Fricatives are at least partly devoiced in word-initial position. Though this rule is productive among all speakers of Dutch, it is expanding in the speech of Northerners, especially speakers from the Randstad. For many of these speakers the voiced–voiceless opposition is completely lost. This is also the case in Surinam Dutch. It should be noted that at least for those speakers there is no base left at all for the phonological distinction between /x/ and /ɣ/, as those elements are practically in complementary distribution on the phonological level.

2   If consonants with different specifications for voice meet, assimilation takes place, necessarily so between the elements of compound or derived words, preferably between final and initial clusters of subsequent words. The direction of this process (progressive or regressive) and the result (the voiced consonant assimilating to the voiceless one, or vice versa) differ according to the clusters. Though the general tendencies are the same in the whole linguistic area, there are a number of divergences between speakers of different geographical background, even if they use the Standard language.

3   As stated before, vowels immediately following or preceding stressed syllables are subject to a reduction rule, producing [ə] at the surface. On the whole, peripheral, especially final syllables are excluded from this rule, which, furthermore, is firmly restricted stylistically. The more informal the use of language is, the sooner and the more consistently it will be applied.

4   Tense vowels are subject to different tendencies. The most marked characteristic seems to be the diphthongization of /e/, /o/, /ø/ (the [–closed, –open] vowels) in the leading Randstad. Though strong diphthongization is socially stigmatized, a more moderate diphthongization has been widely accepted as a characteristic of the spoken Standard language. Most speakers from the east and south (including those in Belgium) prefer monophthongs however. It must be added that many Belgians (especially from the provinces of Antwerp and Brabant)

lengthen all tense vowels, including /i/, /y/, /u/, to a much greater degree than is accepted in the northern spoken Standard.

5   Standard Dutch has a rule of final-/n/ deletion after [ə], both in monomorphemes (except verb stems) and in derived word forms, e.g. in *regen* 'rain' (sg. noun), *merk+en*$_{1-2}$ 'brands$_1$ / notice$_2$ (verb)' (pl. noun or verb). The rule, which is productive in most regional dialects as well, is commonly applied in all styles of Standard Dutch, formal as well as informal. Many speakers from regions where it does not occur in the autochthonous dialects (the northeast of the Netherlands, and western Belgium), tend to disregard it if they switch over to Standard language. A special feature of the /n/-deletion rule is that it does not apply to verbal stems. Thus *(ik) teken* '(I) draw' is always pronounced with /n/, *(het) teken* 'the sign' will lose its final consonant in most styles of spoken Dutch. The restriction is generally traced back to the fact that verb stems were originally supplemented by an ending (in Middle Dutch [ə]) if used in the present tense or the imperative. Though the ending has been lost for several centuries now, it appears to have left at least some residue in linguistic consciousness.

Apart from these and a number of other rules, regional and/or social variation is reflected in suprasegmental phonology, e.g. pitch, intonation, and general stress patterns.

Orthography

Dutch orthography is based on the rules devised and published by the Dutch linguists De Vries and Te Winkel (1864), and was adopted officially both in Belgium and in the Netherlands in the second half of the nineteenth century. Though a number of fairly substantial changes have been officially adopted since then (the last ones in 1947), the set of basic principles has remained the same. The main criterion, that of 'received pronunciation', is mitigated by the principle of etymology, which leads to now phonetically unmotivated oppositions as, for example, between ‹ij› and ‹ei›, and between ‹ou› and ‹au› as graphemes for the diphthongs /ɛⁱ/ and /ɔᵘ/ respectively, for example, *(ik) lijd* '(I) suffer' – *(ik) leid* '(I) lead', and *rouw* 'mourning' – *rauw* 'raw'. It is further supplemented by the principles of analogy and uniformity, both of which take care of the homogeneous spelling of stems in various (morpho-) phonemic environments, e.g. *(ik) vind* '(I) find', despite final devoicing, because of *vinden* 'to find', and *(hij) vindt* '(he) finds' (= verb stem ending in /d/ + ending /t/, together pronounced as simple [t]), because of *(hij) vangt* 'he catches' (= stem *vang* + *t*). It should be noted that the principle of uniformity is not applied consistently, as it does not cover the oppositions between /s/ ~ /z/ and /f/ ~ /v/, e.g. *lees* ~ *lezen* '(I) read ~ to read', *raaf* ~ *raven* 'raven ~ ravens'.

Dutch spelling conventions include a rather extensive use of double letters (graphemes), both for vowels and for consonants. The doubling of consonants is consistently used between vowels (but never word-finally) to mark laxness of the preceding vowel, e.g. in *stellen* 'to put', *ballast* 'dead weight', *vullen* 'to fill', *mollig* 'plump', as opposed to (*ik*) *stel* '(I) put', *bal* 'ball', (*ik*) *vul* '(I) fill', *mol* 'mole'. The double consonant is not pronounced as a geminate. Doubling of vowels is used to mark tenseness in closed syllables, as in, for example, *vaas* 'vase' as opposed to the plural *vazen, steek* 'stick' vs *steken, rood* 'red' vs *rode*. The convention does not apply to /i/, which is written ‹ie› both in closed and in open syllables (except in most loans, where it is written ‹i›) or to /u/, which is written ‹oe›. As in French orthography, ‹u› (and double ‹uu›) are used for the sound /y/.

One of the main problems of Dutch orthography remains the spelling of loans of Romance (Latin or French) origin. Most of these are spelt in partial accordance with the rules of the Dutch system, but quite a number of graphemes are reminiscent of their origin. On the whole this does not bring about too many difficulties, except for /k/, which is spelt ‹k› in autochthonous words of Germanic origin, and in a great number of loans as well, e.g. *klasse* 'class', *praktijk* 'practice', *kwaliteit* 'quality', and generally all words which have undergone phonetic changes making them less conspicuous, e.g. *krant* 'newspaper', *kroon* 'crown', *kleur* 'colour'. On the other hand, a large number of more recent, and therefore potentially less integrated loanwords retain ‹c› or ‹qu› (e.g. *categorie* 'category', *compaan* 'companion', *syncope, quarantaine*). The experiment (started in 1953) by which the spelling of some sounds (including /k/) in loanwords was proclaimed 'free' has not been successful, and a popular claim nowadays is that a compulsory single spelling convention should be restored. In which way this has to be achieved is not clear at this moment.

14.3   Morphology

Dutch Word Structure

All word classes in Dutch contain both simplex (monomorphemic) and complex (polymorphemic) words. The latter include not only derivations and compounds, but also derivational compounds.

Compounds are very frequent in both spoken and written Dutch (see section 14.5, Polymorphemic words). They generally have the same categorial status as the last element (the first element then appears to function as a semantic adjunct to the second), though compound nouns in particular may be at variance with this general principle. Examples of compound nouns are (a) *vuilnisman* 'refuse collector', *arbeidersdochter* 'workman's daughter', *werkman* 'workman', *allemansvriend* 'everybody's friend', *binnenpretje* 'private joke', all of which belong to the regular type with a noun as their second element, the first element of the compound belonging either to the same or to another word category; and (b) *deugniet* 'good-for-nothing', *weetal* 'know-it-all', *vrijaf* 'day off', in which neither element is a noun in its own right. The elements of nominal compounds may be linked together with either of the elements *s* or *ə(n)* (written ‹s› and ‹en› or ‹e› respectively, both are originally genitive markers). Whether a 'linking sound', and if any, which one is used, is a matter of the lexicon.

Ik-/jijzelf 'I myself – you yourself', *elkander* 'each other', *iedereen* 'everybody' are pronominal. Many of these compounds have been reinterpreted as monomorphemic words in the course of history, e.g. *welk* 'which', *iemand* 'somebody'.

Examples of compound adjectives are *mierzoet* 'extremely sweet', *ingoed* 'extremely good', *aartslelijk* 'very ugly', and *geelgroen* 'yellowish green'. The second element is always an adjective, the first one may belong to different word classes. Most adverbs and particles, such as *nagenoeg* 'practically', *vrijwel* 'all but', *voorlangs* 'across in front', and *huiswaarts* 'home' are semantically opaque, i.e. their meaning can only partly be derived from that of the components.

As in most European languages, numerals are formed on the basis of the very limited set of nine names of units, nine names of tens, *elf* 'eleven', *twaalf* 'twelve', *honderd* 'hundred', *duizend* 'thousand', and a set of 'learned' words with *-joen* and *-jard* as a second element (e.g. *miljoen* '(a) million', *triljard* '(a) trilliard'). No remnants of a vigentesimal system survive. From 'thirteen' to 'ninety nine' numbers are formed by having units precede tens (the system that also persists in English numbers from 13 to 19). From 21 upwards units and tens (always in that order) are connected by *en* 'and': *vijftien* 'fifteen', but *vijfentwintig* 'five-and-twenty'. Hundreds and thousands are followed by tens and units (if necessary combined in the way described above), e.g. *honderd (en) vijfentachtig* '185'. Multiples of a hundred, a thousand, etc., are formed by a compound of the specifying number + *honderd*, etc. (e.g. *vijfentwintighonderd/duizend/miljoen* lit. 'five-and-twenty hundred/thousand/ million').

A special subcategory of compounds in Dutch is formed by pre- and postposition, e.g. *doorheen* 'throughout', *vanuit* 'starting from', *vanaf* 'from ... onwards'. Some of these combinations may be split by the noun phrase with which they combine, thus forming 'circumpositions', e.g. *om (het huis) heen* 'all around (the house)' (for further discussion see section 14.4, Adpositional phrases).

Compound nouns and verbs have the accent mostly on the first constituent. In most adjectives and numerals stress is not fixed at all: it varies according to the syntactic pattern in which the compound is incorporated. All other compounds typically have the accent on the last component.

Derivatives are both frequent and formally extremely diverse. They may contain prefixes (e.g. *be-legeren* 'beleager'), suffixes (e.g. *beleger-aar* 'besieger') and circumfixes; e.g. *ge-boef-te* 'riff-raff'. As neither **geboef* nor *boefte* exist as words in their own right, it is clear that *ge . . . te* as a whole is added to *boef* 'rascal'.

Prefixes do not, in general, take the main word stress, though the negative *on-* does so in nouns, and optionally in adjectives. Suffixes fall into three categories. Most suffixes of Germanic origin leave the stress pattern of the stem word intact, e.g. *'antwoord* 'answer' – *'antwoord-je* 'answer (dim.)'. Some suffixes draw the main stress towards the last syllable of the stem or the last element of a compound or derived word, e.g. *'algebra* – *alge'bra-isch* 'algebra – algebraic', *'afstand* – *af'stand-elijk* 'distance – distant', *'wonder-baar* – *wonder'baar-lijk* 'wonderful – miraculous'. There is a third class of predominantly (though not exclusively) loan suffixes; derivations with these require main stress on the suffix itself, e.g. *'landvoogd* – *landvoogd-'es* 'governor – governess', *'koning* – *koning-'in* 'king – queen'.

The gender of derived nouns is regular. Thus all diminutives are neuter, irrespective of the stem word, words with the suffix *-ing* are feminine (or non-neuter in those dialects which have given up the masculine–feminine dichotomy), and words with the prefix *ge-*, as well as those with the circumfix *ge-. . . -te* are neuter.

It is possible to derive ordinals by suffixing cardinal numbers with alternatively *-de* or *-ste*; the latter suffix is used in *eerste* '1st', *achtste* '8th', and from *twintigste* '20tn' upwards.

Derivational compounds consist of two or even more words, which are linked together by a suffix, and thus acquire word status. Instances are *eenogig* 'one-eyed' (= *(een+oog)+ig*), *meersyllabig* 'polysyllabic' (= *(meer+syllab(e))+ig*), *tweederangs* 'second rate' (= *(tweede+rang)+s*), *doordeweeks* 'commonplace' (= *door+de+week)+s*). To this class may also be added such words as *bijdehand* 'smart' (= *'bij+de+hand'*), *vanmorgen* 'this morning' (= *'van+morgen'*), which formally consist of a prepositional phrase, but have taken, like comparable concatenations with suffixes, fixed word stress on the last component.

Verbal Inflection

Dutch is no different from the other Germanic languages in having only a two-term tense distinction on the basis of inflectional contrasts: present and preterite. Apart from a few lexicalized remnants (e.g. *(het) zij (zo)* – *(het) moge (geschieden)* – *(als het) ware* 'it may be so/may it happen/as if it were (so)'), all traces of the subjunctive have disappeared. The imperative does not distinguish between singular and plural and is generally expressed by the verb stem without an explicit subject. If the addressee of the order or advice has to be foregrounded, the second-person (singular or plural) pronoun may be combined with the indicative verbal form. The clause then has 'inverted' word order (the order common in interrogative clauses), e.g. *maak jij/maken jullie (dat maar af)* 'you (and no other person(s)) better finish that'.

The present tense displays three different forms: (a) the verb stem, used with the first-person singular, and with *jij/je* 'you (sg.)' in clauses with 'inverted word order', i.e. with the finite verb preceding the subject pronoun; (b) verb stem + *t* (2 sg. except with *jij/je* in the inversion construction, and 3 sg.; the use of this form with the 2 pl. is obsolete); (c) verb stem + ə(*n*) (with plural subject, irrespective of 'person').

Most exceptions to this regular pattern are to be found with the third-person singular: (het) *is* '(it) is', *heeft* 'has', *mag* 'may', *kan* 'can', *wil* 'will', *zal* 'shall'. If *ben* is considered the regular singular stem related to *zijn* 'be', there is only one straightforward exception in second-person singular (*je/u mag* 'you may'), though all other preterite-presents whose 'plural' stems are commonly used to derive otherwise regular forms for the second-person singular, also have the same forms as with the third-person singular e.g. *je/u zult* (regular) or *zal* (deviant) 'you shall'. The first-person singular may be said to have no exceptions at all, given the same presupposition for *ben/zijn*. Plural forms are always identical with the infinitive. A few verbs whose stems end in a vowel or diphthong have *n*, which is of course not subject to the general rule of /n/-deletion (occurring after [ə]): *zijn* 'be', *doen* 'do', *gaan* 'go', *slaan* 'beat', *staan* 'stand', *zien* 'see', but *skiën* 'ski', *oliën* 'oil', *schreien* 'weep' and many other verbs have the regular ending.

Preterite formation may be traced back directly to the distinctions in Proto-Germanic between weak and strong verbs, with a few irregularities in both paradigms. Vowel alternations in strong verbs belong to a very large number of formal classes, though only a few groups contain more than ten different verbs ([i/o], [œ^Y/o], [ɛ^i/e], [ɪ/ɔ], [e/ɑ–a], [ɛ/ɔ], e.g. *bied/bood* 'offer(ed)', *buig/boog* 'bow(ed)', *rijd/reed* 'ride/rode', *bind/bond* 'bind/bound', *nemen/ nam – namen* 'take/took', *scheld/schold* 'abuse'. These larger classes in particular have over time attracted quite a number of originally 'weak' verbs, and thus the number of strong verbs remains considerable in the modern language. Vowel alternation in the preterite is now the 'normal' inflectional procedure for about 200 verbs, most of which belong to what may be called the 'core' (basic) lexicon.

Within the preterital paradigm of strong verbs there is only one formal opposition, that between the singular form, which is for all persons restricted to the stem, and the plural, which uniformly attaches ə(*n*) (written ‹en›) to it. Archaic language has one more form, stem + *t*, occasionally used with the second-person plural of strong verbs (*jullie waart/kwaamt* 'you (pl.) were/ came'). There is only one class of verbs left, which displays the Proto-Germanic opposition between singular and plural preterital stems, namely that of verbs with [e] or [ɪ] in the present (most deriving form Proto-Germanic classes IV and V), having [ɑ] in the preterite singular, and [a] in the plural, e.g. *stelen/stal – stalen* 'steal', *bidden/bad – baden* 'pray'. In most other classes the now uniform preterital stem goes back to the Proto-Germanic plural. As mentioned before, most preterite-presents still have two different forms, one used for the first- and third-person singular (*ik/hij zal/kan/mag*

'I/he shall/can/may'), the other one for the plural and for one form of the second-person singular (here the form for the third-person singular may be used as well): *we/jullie/ze + kunnen/zullen/mogen* ('we/you (pl.)/they + can/ shall/may'; *je kunt/zult* or *je kan/zal* 'you (sg.) can/shall', but only *je mag* 'you (sg.) may').

Weak verbs have only one preterite form in spoken Standard Dutch. It is derived from the present stem by suffixing *tə(n)* or *də(n)* to it (the variant with [t] is restricted to verb stems ending in voiceless obstruents). This, of course, covers a 'deep' opposition between (written) *te/de* (sg.) and *ten/den* (pl.), but a number of phonological rules, deleting [n] after [ə] in most environments, on the one hand, and inserting [n] between two [ə]-s, on the other, obscures the opposition to the ear. Of course speakers who do pronounce [n] after [ə] (see section 14.2, Phonological rules) preserve the opposition between both forms even in the spoken language.

Proto-Germanic 'irregular' weak verbs (e.g. **branx-ta*) dropped the vowel of the suffix, and from a synchronic point of view have merged with descendants of strong verbs, as far as the preterite is concerned: as is the case with strong verbs, there is a clear distinction, also phonetically, between singular and plural forms in e.g. *bracht/brachten* 'brought', *dacht/dachten* 'thought', *kocht/kochten* 'bought', *wist/wisten* 'knew'.

There are two infinitives, the bare and the *te*-infinitive. The former consists of the stem followed by the ending *ə(n)* or *n*, as in the plural present forms. The *te*-infinitive consists of *te* + bare infinitive. Though the two elements are still written apart, *te*, which originally was a preposition expressing Goal, followed by the then existing gerund (formally infinitive + *ə*), synchronically may be considered a marker, as, unlike in English, it may under no condition be separated from the rest of the verb form, cf. (*he kept on trying*) *to ultimately find out* (*that...*) = (*hij bleef maar proberen om*) *ten slotte te ontdekken* (*dat...*). The distribution between bare and *te*-infinitives depends on the syntactic environment. In Modern Dutch the *te*-infinitive appears to be constantly gaining ground on its bare counterpart. Apart from a few isolated fixed expressions, the *te*-infinitive has become the only possibility with prepositions, and the number of auxiliaries which require it is still growing: in the last century *durven* ('dare') and *weten* ('know (where something/ somebody lives, stands, etc.)') were added to the list of *te*-auxiliaries.

The present participle consists of stem + *ənd(ə)* or *nd(ə)*, the latter with verbs taking *n* in the infinitive and the plural present.

For the formation of the past participle, Dutch has a rule which prefixes all stems not preceded by a prefix (like *ver-*, *be-*, *ont-*, etc.) with *ge-*. Unlike its German cognate, the rule also applies to stems with final stress (e.g. *ge-inte'greer-d* = German *inte'griert* 'integrated'). Further the past participle displays the heritage of Proto-Germanic. From a synchronic point of view however we have four types, depending on both whether or not stem alternation is being applied, and the form of the suffix:

1   'Regular' weak verbs with the (infinitive) stem followed by /t/ or /d/, the
     first suffix being restricted to stems ending in a voiceless obstruent (cf.
     the parallel opposition with the weak preterite), e.g. *ge-maak-t* 'made',
     ge-waag-d 'ventured';
2   Strong verbs with the ending *ə(n)* attached to a special stem with vowel
     alteration, usually identical with the preterite stem, yet not for some
     descendants of Proto-Germanic *jan*-verbs, and verbs of the classes V and
     VI, e.g. *ge-bo(o)d-en* 'offered', *ge-bo(o)g-en* 'bowed', *ge-bond-en*
     'bound' (all of which have the same vowel as the preterite), but
     ge-sto(o)l-en 'stolen' (pret. *stal/stalen*), *ge-be(e)d-en* 'prayed, bidden'
     (pret. *bad/baden*);
3   'Strong' verbs with *ə(n)* suffixed to the present stem, most of them
     deriving from Proto-Germanic class V, VI or VII verbs, e.g. *lezen/*
     ge-lezen 'to read', *varen/ge-varen* 'to sail', *lopen/ge-lopen* 'to run';
4   'Irregular' verbs with special stem, identical with that of the preterite, e.g.
     ge-bracht 'brought', *ge-kocht* 'bought'.

As may be apparent from the details of the account, there is not much place
for what we might call 'irregularity' in verbal paradigms, unless stem
alternation in strong verbs is considered as such. Real exceptions to the
regular patterns are of course such verbs as *zijn* 'to be' and the preterite-
presents (e.g. *mogen* 'may' with singular present stem *mag*, dental preterite
mocht and past participle *gemoogd* or *gemogen*).

Nominal Inflection

All Dutch count nouns have plural forms which in one way or another differ
from the singular form. To this general statement two remarks have to be
added. First of all, some nouns referring to units, though having a plural form,
are not inflected if preceded by a numeral, in which case the noun phrase is
treated like a quantifier (e.g. *drie pond boter* '(the quantity of) three pounds
of butter', *vijf man* 'five people (forming a team)'). Second, with some nouns
singular and plural forms, though written differently, are pronounced in the
same way by the large majority of speakers (e.g. *kudde/kudden* 'herd(s)'). The
reason for this is the same as for the two forms of the weak preterite suffix
mentioned above. It should be noted that such phonetically null plural forms
are generally avoided, often by supplanting them with the *s*-plural (e.g.
kuddes).

Apart from the stacked suffix *-eren*, formed on the basis of Proto-West
Germanic *-V+r*, which is still the plural suffix of some fifteen neuter nouns
(e.g. *kind-eren* 'children', *ei-eren* 'eggs') there are two 'productive' for-
matives, the suffixes *ə(n)* and *s*. Though genuine rules cannot be given, there
is a very strong tendency for monosyllabic words to take *ə(n)*, and for
polysyllabic ones (both of Germanic and non-Germanic origin) to prefer *s*.
Moreover, quite a number of words may be suffixed with either, in which case

the *s*-plural tends to be less formal. While there is a semantic difference between *vaders* 'fathers' and *vaderen* '(spiritual) forebears', there is only a stylistic difference between *maten/maats* 'fellows', *benden/bendes* 'gangs', *leliën/lelies* 'lilies', *appelen/appels* 'apples'.

The origin of the plural ending *-s* is somewhat enigmatic. It is considered an ingvaeonicism by some, but as it is hardly to be found in early Middle Dutch, a direct derivation from the Proto-Germanic inflectional system (as is very probable for the homophonic ending in English) is at least problematic. The suffix *-s* might have spread as a 'clear' inflectional element (used originally for the genitive singular of vocalic stems), possibly also under the influence of French, which enriched Dutch vocabulary with hundreds of words, among those many polysyllabic nouns (the main 'harbour' of *s*-forms).

Stem variation between singular and plural forms is extremely rare in Standard Dutch. The only example of residual umlaut is *stad/steden* 'town(s)'. Some words have other types of vowel variation ([ɑ/a], [ɛ/e], [ɪ/e], [ɔ/o], [ɛⁱ/e]) when suffixed by *ə(n)*, but never with the alternative plural ending *-s* (e.g. *weg/wegen* 'roads, ways', *lid/leden* 'members, *pad/paden* 'paths', *professor/professoren* 'professors' (but as an alternative *professors*), *waarheid/waarheden* 'truth(s)').

Middle Dutch showed some systematic remnants of Proto-Germanic case inflection, but apart from a few set expressions (e.g. *ten getale van (drie)* 'three in number' *ten tijde van* 'at the time of', both nouns with dative *-ə*) almost nothing of this survives in the modern Standard language. The genitive *-s* survives with proper names and a few kinship names (e.g. *Karels auto* 'Charles' car', *(groot)moeders huis* '(grand)mother's house'), but in spoken Dutch even these have been supplanted either by a new formation with the possessive word following the whole noun phrase, or by a prepositional construction with *van* 'of' (e.g. *de vader/moeder van Karel* 'Charles' father/ mother', *Karel z'n/Mieke d'r auto* 'Charles'/Mary's car'). It should be noted that even the 'informal' construction with the possessive word attached to the noun phrase is hardly ever used with non-human noun phrases, and embedded genitival attributions, unlike in English, are avoided, cf. *de moeder van Karel d'r auto/de auto van Karel z'n moeder/de auto van de moeder van Karel/ ??Karel z'n moeder d'r auto* 'Charles' mother's car'. Attribution of noun phrases to other noun phrases is achieved by means of the prepositional group with *van*.

Most Dutch nouns have a diminutive formed with a *jə*-suffix, with the allomorphs *je*, *(e)tje*, *pje*, *kje*. The choice between the allomorphs depends on the syllable structure of the input noun. For the few nouns that have different singular and plural stems, there is no fixed rule for diminutive forms. Some even allow for more than one, e.g. *blad* 'leaf' (with plural *bladen* and *bladeren*) allows for *bladje(s)*, *blaadje(s)* and *bladertjes* (the latter only in the plural). Diminutive formation is not restricted to count input nouns, but always yields a count word. Thus the diminutive of *water* (*watertje*) always denotes a certain quantity, e.g. a glass, or a certain brand, etc. of water.

Pronominal Forms

In this section all substantival pronominal words will be dealt with; adjectival words (which function as determiners or specifiers to nouns) will be discussed in the section 'Determiners and quantifying words'. There is one notable exception to this: possessives are used attributively, and share some character- istics with determiners, but they are discussed here together with the personal pronouns they are directly related to. The reason for this is clear. Possessives function as the genitives of personal pronouns (in fact they either originated from genitive pronouns or from other pronominal forms, which had supplanted the regular genitives), and share many of their properties with this category.

Most pronominal categories distinguish between two forms according to the character of the concept they stand in for. There is a 'neutral' form, used for singular non-human referents, and one used for human referents, either plural or singular. Thus Dutch has the indefinite pronouns (*n*)*iemand* 'nobody/somebody', (*n*)*iets* 'nothing/something', *iedereen* 'everybody', *alles* 'everything', etc.; and the interrogative pronouns *wie* 'who(m)' *wat* 'what'. The deictic pronouns *die*, *dat* 'those, that', *deze*, *dit* 'these, this' have another distribution: *dat* and *dit* are used with reference to a neuter singular noun (whether human or non-human), *die* and *deze* in all other cases. The same applies to the relative pronouns, which are homophonous with both the interrogative and deictic pronouns (*die*/*dat* as well as *wie*/*wat*). The syntactic rules governing the choice between *die* and *wie*, and *dat* and *wat* are rather complex, and subject to considerable regional and stylistic variation. *Welk*, *hetwelk* 'which' as alternative relative pronouns, obsolete in the modern Standard, are restricted to highly formal written language now.

The regular forms listed above alternate with 'adverbial' forms, if combined with a pre- or postposition. The pronoun is then generally replaced by the corresponding locative adverbial (respectively (*n*)*ergens* 'nowhere/ somewhere', *overal* 'everywhere' *waar* 'where', *daar* 'there', *hier* 'here') with a postposition, e.g. (*hij dacht*) (*n*)*ergens aan* or *aan* (*n*)*iets'* '(he thought) of something/nothing'. If reference is to non-humans the replace- ment is obligatory with deictic and relative pronouns, and optional with interrogative and indefinite ones. If humans are referred to, standard usage prefers the combination of preposition + pronoun, and application of the replacement rule is a marker of a more colloquial style. It should be noted also that in Standard Dutch the two parts of the newly formed combination are usually discontinuous: the adverbial element is placed early in the sentence, together with other pronominal words, whereas the postposition is kept together with the clause-final verb group, e.g. (*ze heeft*) *daar* (*toen nog een hele tijd met haar ouders*) *over* (*gepraat*) '(she has then been talking) about that (for a long time with her parents)'. For the general principles governing Dutch constituent ordering, see section 14.4.

The pronouns referring to humans have genitive forms with -(n)s, some also with the combination of pronoun + z'n/d'r (iemands or iemand z'n/d'r 'somebody's', iedereens 'everybody's', wiens or wie z'n/d'r 'whose', diens or die z'n/d'r 'this one's' or 'these ones').

Personal pronouns are the only Dutch words that still have an opposition between subject and object forms. As corresponding possessives function as genitives, a threefold functional opposition may be set up, as in English. There is no difference between 'accusative' and 'dative' uses of the object forms, though a number of nineteenth-century school grammars propagated an opposition along that line between third-person plural hen and hun 'them'. The artificial distinction was not found in any regional dialect of Dutch (the opposition between accusative and dative had already been given up in pronouns in the earliest Middle Dutch), and has vanished from grammatical prescription in recent decades.

One peculiarity of Dutch among the Germanic languages is the (almost) general opposition between 'full' and 'reduced' forms in the three surface 'cases'. The reduced forms are used as clitics, and with subject pronouns both pro- and enclitics occur, with the exception of the exclusively enclitic third-person singular masculine ie, however. In Standard Dutch full pronouns appear only in stressed positions, though there is some variation as to the combination with a preposition. Belgian speakers of Dutch mostly prefer full forms in this position, even if unstressed ('Holland' met 'm vs 'Belgian' met hem 'with him'). The third-person singular shows a threeway distinction according to grammatical gender. As to the non-neuter forms hij/ie 'he', etc., and zij/ze 'she', etc. Northern Dutch has a distribution along lines which may be compared with the English usage. Apart from a few 'special cases' the feminine is restricted to reference to female humans. Masculine covers all other cases where the noun in question is grammatically non-neuter (either human or not). Southern varieties, especially those spoken in Belgium, preserve the historical distinction between masculine, feminine and neuter words, and use the pronouns accordingly.

Standard forms of personal pronouns, including possessive ones, are given in Table 14.4. In most cases the apostrophe ‹'› stands for [ə], though sometimes the consonantal form is used alone, without any vocalic element. In the reduced forms ‹e› also stands for [ə]. It should be noted that many speakers confuse the reduced object forms third-person singular feminine and third-person plural d'r ('her' (sg.)) and ze ('them' (pl.)). This can be accounted for by the fact that, for both pronouns, both the full subject forms and the reduced possessives are identical.

The second person displays a distinction between the common forms mentioned in Table 14.4, and formal u (su./obj.)/uw (poss.) (no reduced forms available), which is pragmatically determined by deference towards the

Table 14.4   Personal pronouns

	Subject		Object		Possessive	
	Full	Reduced	Full	Reduced	Full	Reduced
1 sg.	ik	'k	mij	me	mijn	m'n
2 sg.	jij	je	jou	je	jouw	je
3 sg. m.	hij	ie	hem	'm	zijn	z'n
f.	zij	ze	haar	ze/d'r	haar	d'r
n.	(dat)	het/'t	(dat)	het/'t	zijn	z'n
1 pl.	wij	we	ons	——	ons	——
2 pl.	jullie	je	jullie	je	jullie	je
3 pl.	zij	ze	hen/hun	ze/d'r	hun	d'r

addressee. The actual use of formal pronouns has decreased considerably in recent decades.

Apart from the two forms (full – reduced) mentioned before, there is a third set, the members of which are used if the pronoun is given contrastive function. In this case a compound form with *zelf* 'self' is used with the full subject and object forms (e.g. *ikzelf, onszelf*); *eigen* 'own' (written apart) is added to the full or reduced possessives (*m'n/mijn eigen*).

Mention should also be made of the adverbial pronoun *er* + postposition, which generally takes up the place of an adpositional phrase with a personal pronoun of the third person, if this has a non-human referent, in some styles also if a human referent is meant (see the adverbial indefinites, interrogatives, deictics and relatives discussed above).

Dutch did not originally have at its disposal any reflexive pronouns, not even in the third person. Since Middle Dutch this 'lack' has been remedied to some extent in two ways. First, for all persons the use of the contrastive possessives (*m'n/je/z'n/d'r/ons eigen*) expanded to the reflexive object function, though in informal speech only: *ze heeft d'r eigen in de spiegel bekeken* 'she looked at herself in the mirror'. Second, in the third person *zich* 'him-/her-/itself, themselves' was borrowed from literary German, and this word has become common even in everyday spoken language now. If some contrast is implied (only with transitive verbs used reflexively), the compound forms with *zelf* added to the reduced object form may be used (e.g. *ik schoor mezelf – hij schoor zichzelf* 'I/he shaved myself/himself (not anybody else)'.

Adjectival Inflection

The great profusion of adjectival endings in Proto-Germanic has been dramatically reduced to a mere twosome in the course of the history of Dutch: the stem on the one hand, the [ə]-extended form on the other. The latter is used attributively except with: (a) nouns denoting male human beings in some indefinite constructions, like *een goed man* 'a good man' – *een goed leraar* 'a good teacher' (the latter denotes somebody who is good as a teacher, different from *een goede leraar*, which would refer to a teacher who has a good character); and (b) indefinite noun phrases with singular neuter nouns. ə-less forms may sometimes be used in definite noun phrases with neutral nouns too, but this is only common in southern varieties of Dutch. In most standard variants the uninflected form is restricted to special types of definite neuter noun phrases, and is often also associated with a special meaning. Thus *ons oud huis* 'the house we used to live in before' is opposed to *ons oude huis* 'our house, which is old'.

Though most adjectives exhibit both forms, quite a number lack a special form with ə, among them those that end in [ə(n)], and most of the ones ending in monophthongal vowels, e.g. *open* 'open', *indigo, oranje* 'orange', but *gedwee+ë* 'meek'.

Comparative adjectives are formed with morphemes deriving directly from Proto-Germanic: *ər* in the comparative, *stə* in the superlative. Analytic constructions with *meer* 'more' and *meest* 'most', though not unknown in the language, are extremely rare, even with polysyllabic adjectives such as *interessant(er/st)* '(more/most) interesting' or *verbazingwekkend(er/st)* '(more/most) amazing'. Apart from *goed* 'good' with the inflectional comparative forms *beter/best* 'better/best', all derived adjectival forms are regular.

Stem variation occurs only (optionally) with one single adjective: *grof* 'coarse', yielding the ə-form *grove* and the comparative *grover*.

Two more facts deserve mentioning. First, Dutch adds *s* to the adjective if it is construed with an indefinite pronoun or quantifier such as (*n*)*iets* 'something/nothing', *veel* 'much', *weinig* 'little', e.g. *iets/veel fraais* 'something beautiful/many beautiful things'. Second, adjectives are used adverbially without any suffixation, but some may none the less take the (originally nominal) diminutive suffix, augmented with *s* ((*ə*)*tjəs*, etc.). Such words usually imply some sort of attitudinal involvement on the part of the speaker, e.g. *ze is stilletjes binnengekomen* 'she entered silently, which was wise/stupid/to be appreciated, . . .', vs neutral *ze is stil binnengekomen* 'she entered silently'.

Determiners and Quantifying Words

Most determiners (definite article, indefinite, interrogative, deictic words) have two forms, one combining with singular neuter nouns, the other being used in all other cases, e.g. *het/de* 'the', *welk/welke* 'which', *zulk/zulke* 'such', *elk/elke* 'each', *dat/die* 'that, those', *dit/deze* 'this, these'. A notable exception to this rule is the indefinite article, which nowadays has only the invariant singular form *een*, sometimes also written *'n*, pronounced [ən]. Possessive words, which were dealt with in the section on pronouns, have generally only one form left too, except for *ons/onze* 'our', which is an exception in another respect too, as it has no reduced form (see Table 14.4).

Quantifiers such as *veel*, 'much, many', *weinig* 'little, few', *enig* 'some', have two forms: with or without ə added to the stem. *Vele/weinige* is always used if preceded by a definite determiner, and sometimes, though not consistently, in other plural noun combinations (e.g. *het vele water* 'the great amount of water', *weinig(e) mensen* 'few people'). All other quantifying words have a regular distribution of the two forms. The one without ə is restricted to indefinite noun phrases with a singular neuter noun (for an exceptional use of *al* 'all' and *heel* 'whole' we refer the reader to section 14.4: The nominal group). Some quantifiers also have comparative and superlative forms, though for *veel* and *weinig* these happen to be irregular (*veel* – *meer(der)* – *meest* 'much/many – more – most' and *weinig* – *minder* – *minst* 'little/few – less/fewer – least/fewest').

Numerals do not have inflectional forms, with the exception of *een* 'one'. *Ene* is used after definite articles and other definite determiners (demonstratives, possessives and genitives). A very specific use is that with proper names, e.g. *ene Jan van Aken* 'a certain person, named Jan van Aken'.

Other Inflectional Phenomena

It is certainly remarkable that Dutch, with its very restricted set of inflectional categories, should have a few rather uncommon formal oppositions. First, some degree adverbs are formally adjusted to the attributive adjective they qualify: if the adjective takes ə the same ending may be added to the adverb, e.g. *een hele/erge kleine boom* 'a very small tree' vs *een heel/erg klein huis* 'a very small house'. Second, cardinal numbers take the ending ə(n) in substantival use, if they are the complement of a preposition, e.g (*ze waren*) *met (z'n) elven* '(they were) eleven', (*het was al*) *na zevenen* '(it was) after seven'. Numerals which have ə(n) as a plural marker (*honderd(en)* 'hundred(s)', *duizend(en)* 'thousand(s)', *miljoen(en)* 'million(s)', etc.) do not take the ending after prepositions, thus avoiding semantic ambiguity. So there is an opposition between (*ze kwamen*) *met (z'n) honderd* 'a hundred of them (came)' and (*ze kwamen*) *met honderden* 'hundreds of them (came)'. A third inflectional phenomenon is one that is not found in standard varieties of Dutch, but which is widespread in regional dialects from very different parts of the language area, namely, the inflection of complementizers (conjunctions and relative and interrogative pronouns) according to the number of the clause subject. In many Holland dialects e.g. (*ik hoop*) *datte ze kome* '(I hope) that they (will) come' is opposed with *dat hij komt* 'that he comes'. The phenomenon, known also from Bavarian dialects of German, has been well studied by a large number of linguists.

14.4 Syntax

Typological Features

Dutch is not easy to classify along the lines of current syntactic typology, though on the whole SOV or head-final patterns prevail. They are dominant in the verb phrase, noun phrase and adjective phrase and also occur in the prepositional phrase. A short survey will do here, as all relevant types of constituents will be dealt with in the following paragraphs.

First of all, there are two important features of Dutch surface word order which are characteristic of SVO rather than SOV: the existence of prepositions and sentence-initial complementizers, and the position of relative clauses after the antecedent. The prepositions are inherited from Proto-Germanic, and perhaps even further back, from Indo-European. In recent stages of the language a fairly large set of postpositions and circumpositions have developed, which are frequent in certain semantic functions, especially to denote temporal posteriority and spatial direction, but the bulk of adpositional phrases in Dutch do not fit the expected SOV picture. With respect to relative clauses, one may mention that formal, especially written Dutch shows a word-order pattern which is more in accordance with dominant SOV structure. Reduced clauses consisting of a participle preceded by any arbitrary combination of verbal complements or specifications (with the single exception of complement clauses), are possible before the noun they qualify: (*de*) *gisteren nog niet helemaal tot in de kleinste details door ons besproken* (*moeilijkheden*), (lit.) '(the) yesterday not yet completely into the smallest detail by us discussed (difficulties)' (= 'the difficulties we did not discuss . . .')

The overall picture of word ordering is as follows:

1   In noun phrases all determiners, quantifiers and adjectival specifiers (including participles) precede the head noun, e.g. *die drie mooie grote auto's* 'those three beautiful big cars'; prepositional phrases and clauses follow, as do adverbs: *die man daar/gisteren* 'that man (over) there/ yesterday'.

2   Adjectival phrases may contain noun phrases and adverbs, which precede their head: *het gebabbel meer dan beu* 'more than fed up with the chatter'. All constituents with prepositions or subordinating conjunctions may follow, though many prepositional phrases may precede as well (and even have to if the adjective is used attributively), especially in formal registers, e.g.: *de op dat ogenblik al erg grote oppositie* 'the opposition (which was) already quite large at that moment'. Among the constituents which have to follow is the standard of comparison (*ze is groter dan ik* 'she is taller than me'). In attributive usage this leads to a discontinuous expression, the adjective itself being positionally bound to the noun, cf. *een grotere man dan ik* 'a taller man than me', *een even grote man als ik* 'a man as tall as me'.

3   Clauses have the main verb at the end. But, there are two facts which blur the picture. First of all there is the rule which moves the finite verb to the first (interrogative or imperative) or second (declarative) position in main clauses. If there is no auxiliary in the clause this means that the main verb has to occupy that position, and that the canonical sentence-final verb place may become 'empty', e.g. *ik zoek (een nieuwe tafel voor mijn woonkamer)* 'I'm looking (for a new table for my living room)'. This is not necessary though, as complex verbs 'leave behind' their phrasal particles in sentence-final position, e.g.: *(ik) zette (de baby) neer* '(I) put down (the baby)'. Second, Dutch allows extraposition of a prepositional phrase or clause to the right of the canonical place of the verb (whether occupied or not). The rule is obligatory with complement clauses and optional with all other clauses and most prepositional constituents, but may be applied only once; e.g. *(je zult nog wat langer moeten wachten) op je bevordering/om bevorderd te worden* '(you will have to wait a little longer) for your promotion/to be promoted'.

We may conclude from all this that Dutch, from the point of view of surface typology, is a moderately verb-final (SOV) language. This mitigated status is further reflected in the fact that auxiliaries, if they form a continuous group with the main verb, may either follow (as is common in strict SOV languages) or precede the main verb: *(dat ze het) gezegd had/had gezegd* '(that she) had said (it)'. The latter ordering appears to be gaining ground in the modern language, especially in writing. With two auxiliaries there are sometimes different possibilities as well, e.g. *dat ze het gezegd zou hebben* or *zou hebben gezegd* (in Belgium also: *zou gezegd hebben*) 'that she would have told'. Most combinations, however, are only allowed with the auxiliaries preceding the main verb *(dat ze het) zal moeten zeggen*, not **zeggen zal moeten* '(that she) will be obliged to tell'.

Sentence Patterns
Three main patterns may be distinguished, although the differences only involve the initial elements: (a) subordinated clauses have the subordinating word or constituent in the first place (the finite verb stays at the end of the clause); (b) yes/no questions and imperatives start with the finite verb; all other elements remain in underlying order, i.e. the order they would also occupy in subordinate clauses; and (c) all other main clauses open with the finite verb preceded by an arbitrary constituent (or in *wh*-questions the *wh*-word/phrase). So subordinated clauses are the only type where the finite verb appears in the sentence-final verbal group. Instances are: (a) *(ik zei) dat ze mijn vriendje gisteren misschien ook uitgenodigd had* '(I said) that maybe she had invited my friend too'; (b) *had ze mijn vriendje gisteren misschien ook uitgenodigd?* 'had she perhaps also invited my friend yesterday?'; (c) *misschien had ze mijn vriendje gisteren ook uitgenodigd* 'maybe she had also

invited my friend yesterday'. It is noteworthy that Standard Dutch is the only Germanic language that does not allow complement clauses without an explicit subordinator: *ik zei dat ik het zou doen*/*ik zei ik zou het doen* (cf. Ger. *ich sagte dass ich es machen würde*/*ich sagte ich würde es machen*.) This characteristic of Dutch is sometimes attributed to the influence of French. Anyway, northern dialects, which did not undergo French influence as intensively as the southern ones, go along with other Germanic languages in this respect.

The clause is constructed roughly along the following lines in all sentence types. The opening block is followed by a block containing all personal pronouns and a number of other clitics, if any occur in the clause. The sentence closes with the verbal group (or whatever is left of it in main clauses, which have sentence-initial finite verbs), sometimes followed by a prepositional phrase or clause. The remaining constituents are ordered between the pronominal and the verbal block.

The rule of cliticization of the pronominal elements within the pronominal block, to either the complementizer or the finite verb, is not absolute however. Both the nominal and the pronominal subjects of clauses will in most cases precede all (other) pronouns in (relatively) sentence-initial position, e.g. *misschien heeft iemand het je verteld* (lit.) 'maybe has somebody it you told' (= 'maybe somebody told you'). This is all the more remarkable, as the subject is not bound to the first position after complementizer or finite verb in clauses where there are no pronouns, cf. (*blijkbaar hebben daar bij latere gelegenheden dan toch nog*) *andere mensen* (*aan gedacht*) '(apparently) other people (have thought of that on later occasions)'. This means that Dutch, contrary to German, does not regularly permit S–O inversion if O is a pronoun. Only non-agentive subjects, e.g. with verbs like *schijnen* 'seem', *verschijnen* 'appear', *voorbijgaan* 'pass', may break the regular S–O pattern, especially, if they are indefinite, e.g. (*er zijn*) *hem een paar mensen* (*voorbijgereden*) (lit.) '(there are) him a few people (passed)' (= 'a few people have passed him').

To sum up, the topology of declarative main clauses may thus be represented as: [X – finite verb/(subject) – pronouns/Y/verbal group/Z]. In this formula the positions X and Z may be occupied by topicalized or focused constituents (one in each). As mentioned before, Z may not contain argument noun phrases and a few types of complement prepositional phrases. Y is a concatenation of all remaining constituents: noun phrases, adjective phrases, prepositional phrases, clauses, adverbs and sentence particles. The relative order is rather free from a syntactic point of view, and is determined by the general sentence perspective, topical constituents mostly preceding focal ones. There are a few strict syntactic rules interfering with this simple pragmatic tendency however. Within Y three important rules apply, and partly compete with each other:

1   Argument noun phrases are invariably ordered: subject – indirect object – direct object. The prepositional phrase with *aan*, which often functions as an alternative for the noun phrase-indirect object, however, is free to either precede or follow the noun phrases, both subject and object, it is used with.

2   Non-noun-phrase complements (adjective phrases and prepositional phrases) follow all noun-phrase arguments.

3   Adverbials are usually ordered according to the degree in which the quality they denote is inherent in the verb: complements (e.g. directionals) generally follow phrasal adverbials (denoting e.g. manner, degree) which are in turn preceded by sentence adverbials (e.g. time, place). Cf.: (*ze heeft*) *vandaag₁ thuis₂ hard₃ aan haar proefschrift₄* (*gewerkt*) 'today₁ (she has been working) very hard₃ on her thesis₄ at home₂'.

Contrary to (1) and (2), rule (3) allows for deviations under strong pragmatic conditions.

If we look at constituent ordering diachronically, the impression prevails that syntactic rules such as those just mentioned are gaining ground on pragmatic ones, based on sentence perspective, etc.

The Nominal Group

Determiners (articles and demonstratives), possessives and genitival nouns, and 'absolute' quantifiers (*elk* 'each', *ieder* 'every', *geen* 'no', *sommige* 'some (specific)') all precede the noun, and they are mutually exclusive. As to the class of absolute quantifiers, it contains two words which show somewhat irregular behaviour, namely *al* 'all' and *heel* 'whole'. The former may be used in the same way as *elk*, etc., but may also be combined with determiners, possessives and genitives, e.g. *al de/die/mijn/Jan z'n* (*kleren*) 'all the/those/my/John's (clothes)'. In this usage *al* is not inflected (vs. *alle kleren* 'all clothes'). *Heel* may behave in a similar fashion; e.g. *heel de/die/ mijn/Jans* (*voorraad*) 'the/that/my/John's whole (stock)', and then this quantifier is not inflected either. It does take ə however in the alternating construction, comparable to that found in English, German, etc., where it follows one of the other words: *de/die/mijn/Jans hele* (*voorraad*) 'the/that/ my/John's whole (provision)'.

The basic distinction between definite and indefinite articles (either lexical or not) in Dutch runs parallel with that in most West European languages: it is predominantly a matter of (in)definiteness of reference. A few points deserve some attention.

1   Definite articles are not used with most types of proper names. They are however with the names of rivers, lakes, mountain ranges and mountains, and with some names of regions, territories and states, e.g. *de Schelde*

'the Scheldt', *de Alpen* 'the Alps', *de Eiger* 'Mount Eiger', *het Baikalmeer* 'Lake Baikal', *de Sahara* 'the Sahara', *(de) Libanon* 'Lebanon', *de Verenigde Staten* 'the United States'.

2   Indefinite articles are not generally used with plural and non-count singular nouns, except in a very specific meaning, to be described in (4) below. Such articles are generally also avoided if the noun is used to denote a function rather than the object or person occupying this function, a usage especially clear with noun phrases in predicative use, e.g.: *(hij is) arts* '(he is) a doctor', *(ze zegt dat als) arts* '(she says that as) a doctor'; cf also the section on Subject–verb agreement.

3   Noun phrases with definite articles may also be used with a categorial function, e.g. *de walvis is bijna uitgestorven* 'the whale is all but extinct'. Both definite and indefinite articles may apply in generic use: *een/de walvis heeft geen poten* 'a/the whale does not have legs', *walvissen hebben geen poten* 'whales do not have legs', but, as in English, the definite article is restricted to singular nouns.

4   Apart from the usage as a determiner, the indefinite article has developed a somewhat peculiar function: if combined with plural or non-count nouns, it expresses something like 'a great quantity (number) of *x*, in fact a greater quantity (number) than could be expected'; e.g. *(er waren daar toch) een mensen* 'an astonishing number of people (were present)'.

Numerals and 'relative' quantifiers such as *veel* 'much, many', *weinig* 'little, few', *enig* 'some (non-specific)', and all types of adjectives (in this order) line up between the determiner (if any) and the noun. Although there is some degree of freedom, adjectives are generally ordered in such a way that the more specific description precedes the more general one, e.g. *de mooie grote gele bloemen* 'the beautiful large yellow flowers'. Nouns may be followed by prepositional phrases and relative and complement clauses, as well as by adverbs (e.g. *die man daar* 'that man over there') and semi-pronominal words like *zelf* 'self', *allebei* 'both', *tezamen* 'together', *gezamenlijk* 'all together'. Instead of being incorporated into the noun phrase the latter may also occur as free adjuncts ('quantifier floating') e.g. both: *de twee delen tezamen kosten 40 gulden* and *die twee delen kosten tezamen 40 gulden* 'those two volumes together cost 40 guilders'.

From a structural point of view, noun phrases present the following pattern: [X – Y – Noun – Z – clause], in which X may be occupied by a member (very rarely more than one) of the determiner cluster, Y by one or more members of the numeral–adjective group, and Z by one or more prepositional phrases, adverbs and/or members of the *zelf* category.

The kernel (noun) position within the noun phrase may be occupied by (a) an inflected adjective, or (b) a bare infinitive. The restriction to inflected adjectives has to be taken literally: adjectives which lack the inflected form in attributive use (like *open* 'open', *verworpen* 'rejected', cf. *de verworpen voorstellen* 'the rejected proposals') do have such a form in just this construction, e.g. *de verworpene(n)* 'the outcast(s)'. Another consequence of the restriction is that substantivized adjectives referring to humans have both indefinite and definite uses (e.g. *de/een goede* 'the/a good (person)'), whereas those referring to (mainly abstract) objects are confined to definite descriptions. This is because neuter *een* strictly precludes the inflected form in all circumstances. So next to *het slechte* 'the bad things(s)/the wickedness' we do not find **een slecht(e)*; instead *iets slechts* 'something bad' is used (see section 14.3, Adjectival inflection). In regard to infinitives, many have, in the course of time, been reinterpreted as real nouns, also taking plural markers, cf. *het/de vermoeden(s)* 'the conjecture(s)', but as a result of a productive process the nominalized infinitive does not take nominal inflection: *het diepe nadenken ~ *de diepe nadenkens (over die zaak)* '(the) deep thinking ~ *deep thinkings (about that matter)'.

The Adpositional Phrases

Proto-Germanic does not seem to have had postpositions, but it did have a considerable number of prepositions. This situation lasted through the period of Middle Dutch. Along with the ongoing erosion of the inflection, and certainly also as a consequence of Renaissance 'learned' language use, Dutch developed a large number of new prepositions, mostly on the basis of verb stems, present and past participles, word combinations, etc. Simultaneously, a new category of 'postpositions' made its appearance. It is possible that these originated from constructions in which the prepositional phrase was further specified by addition of an adverb: the combination of prepositional phrase + adverb may then have been reinterpreted as a 'circumposition'. Circumpositions do persist in the modern language; e.g.: *(ze liep) om het huis heen* '(she walked) all around the house'. Circumpositions may eventually have lost their first elements, leaving the functional load completely to the nascent postposition. Whatever their origin, postpositions are now common, at least in Northern Dutch, and are gaining ground in Southern varieties. They are especially common in directional complements and adjuncts to verbs; e.g. *(ze klom) de boom in* 'she climbed into the tree', *(hij is) het huis uit (gelopen)* '(he walked) out of the house'. It should be mentioned that, contrary to prepositional phrases, postpositional ones functioning in clauses cannot be extraposed: e.g. *(hij is) de greppel over/over de greppel naar ons toe gesprongen* or *(hij is) naar ons toe gesprongen over de greppel* vs **(hij is) naar ons toe gesprongen de greppel over* 'he jumped towards us, across the ditch'. Another drawback for postpositional phrases is that they cannot be used as complements to nouns. Both restrictions seem to point in the same direction: only in those positions where the prepositional phrase precedes its head – which is not possible if the head is a noun – do postpositions appear to come into use.

As was mentioned before, prepositional phrases with pronominal complements are often avoided in Dutch: such combinations are replaced by the construction of corresponding adverb + postposition (see section 14.3, Pronominal forms). The resulting word group is frequently discontinuous, the first element being incorporated in the relatively sentence-initial 'pronominal block', whereas the postposition immediately precedes the final verb group. In Belgian Dutch it may even be incorporated into this group; e.g. Standard: *ze had er/daar heel wat over kunnen zeggen*, Belgian (also) *ze had er/daar heel wat kunnen over zeggen* 'she could have said quite a few things about it/that'.

Apart from the discontinuous construction just mentioned, stranded prepositions do not belong to the standard language, though such sentences as *zijn vader (had hij al heel lang niet meer) aan gedacht* 'his father (he had not been) thinking of (for a very long time)' do occur in a wide range of non-standard and regional varieties.

The Verbal Phrase

Dutch has developed a great number of auxiliaries and auxiliary-like verbs, covering such grammatical categories as voice, tense, mood and modality, causativity, and aspect. These auxiliaries can be combined to yield such combinations as *(dat ze het) had moeten kunnen laten gaan regenen* '(that she) should have been able to make (it) start raining'. One very special syntactic feature is the fact that most auxiliaries, if combined with a perfect-tense auxiliary, do not take the past participle, as would be expected for the syntactic complement of such verbs, but appear in the 'neutral form', i.e. the bare infinitive, cf. *(dat hij het) heeft kunnen doen/*heeft gekund doen/*heeft doen gekund* '(that he) has been able to do (it)'. This phenomenon, which is known from other Germanic languages also, is generally referred to as the 'IPP' (*infinitivus pro participio*) construction or the 'DIC' (double infinitive construction).

The passive voice is expressed by the auxiliary *worden* in the imperfect tenses and by *zijn* in perfect ones. These auxiliaries are restricted to direct passives, taking the natural direct object as the subject of the derived construction. A number of trivalent verbs, mostly compounds, may be construed with *krijgen* 'get' + past participle to form something comparable to English 'indirect passives', cf. *ze kregen het uiteindelijk toch nog toegestuurd* 'in the end they were sent it anyway'.

Most verbs form a perfect tense with *hebben* 'have', though *zijn* 'be' is used with (a) 'middle' verbs (nowadays often referred to as 'ergative' or 'unac-cusative' verbs): intransitive verbs with a non-agentive and non-causative subject like *verschijnen* 'appear', *sterven* 'die'; (b) intransitive 'directional' verbs like *vertrekken* 'leave', and verbs of motion like *lopen* 'walk', the latter only if they are combined with a directional complement; cf.: *ze is naar huis gelopen* 'she has walked home' vs *ze heeft nog wat gelopen* 'she has been walking for some time'; (c) a very small number of other verbs, e.g. *zijn* 'be', *(iets) verliezen* 'lose something', *vergeten* 'forget'. Especially in category (c) the usage in regional dialects, and even in non-standard Dutch is rather unstable.

Despite its name, the Dutch 'present perfect' is a preterital tense, and the difference between it and the inflectional preterite is very hard to state. The most conspicuous difference appears to be that between 'recording' (perfect) and 'narrating' (preterite), though quite a number of very special subfunctions must be added to this main opposition.

Future time does not usually require a special marker, though one of the auxiliaries *zullen* 'shall' (originally modal) or in some cases *gaan* (originally aspectual) may occur, especially in the absence of an overt adverb indicating future time. Of the two auxiliaries *zullen* mostly conveys some notion of uncertainty along with futurity; cf.: *hij komt volgende week terug* 'he will come back next week', vs *hij zal volgende week terugkomen* 'he is supposed to (or, intends to) come back next week'.

Although one can distinguish between at least three categories of modality – epistemic, deontic and factitive – on the whole each type makes use of the same set of auxiliaries: *zullen* 'shall', *moeten* 'must', *kunnen* 'can', *mogen* 'may', *willen* 'will', *hoeven* 'need', *(be)horen* 'be supposed to'. Those words may combine in complex verbal groups, in which case the epistemic auxiliary precedes the deontic one, and the last place is taken by the factitive one; cf.: *(ze) zal (het ook nog) moeten kunnen doen* '(it) is probable that (she also) has to get the opportunity to do (it)'. Modal particles (or adverbs) provide an alternative mode for epistemic modality.

Dutch also has a considerable number of aspectual auxiliaries, expressing durativity (*blijven* 'stay' + bare inf.), mutativity (*gaan* 'go' + bare inf.) inchoativity (*beginnen* 'begin' + *te*-inf.), stativity (*zijn* 'be' + *aan het* + bare inf., and other verbs like *staan* 'stand', *liggen* 'lie', *zitten* 'sit', *hangen* 'hang', *lopen* 'walk' + *te*-inf.). Examples are: *ze bleef praten* 'she talked on and on', *ze ging zitten* 'she sat down', *het begint te regenen* 'it starts raining', *ze zijn aan het praten/zitten te praten* 'they are talking'.

Causality and permission are expressed by the same auxiliary *laten* 'let' + inf.: *ik liet d'r komen* thus means both 'I allowed her to come' and 'I made her come'. Dutch used to have a specific causal auxiliary *doen* 'do', which has passed out of common use in the last century. It is still found however in set expressions, and sometimes even beyond these, especially if the subject is a non-human causer: *die opmerking deed me opschrikken* 'that remark made me jump'.

Negation

In Middle Dutch negation was expressed by the Proto-Germanic nasal particle *en/ne* cliticized to the finite verb, whatever the position of the latter in the clause. As in other Germanic languages a phonetically more distinct particle arose: *niet* (originally meaning 'nothing', i.e. 'in no respect') was first added to the negative expression, in the end making *en/ne* superfluous. Most dialects of Dutch, including the Standard variety, lost *en/ne* in the course of the last two centuries. *Niet* is canonically placed towards the end of the clause, in front of the verb group (if any). It is, however, moved to the front of the focal constituent, e.g. *ik heb die man niet gezien* 'I did not see that man' vs *ik heb niet 'die man gezien* 'I did not see 'that man (i.e. I saw another one)'. If the negative marker is moved in front of an indefinite noun phrase, it obligatorily merges with the article, yielding *geen* 'no', which is sometimes called a negative article, cf.: *ik heb geen films gezien* 'I did not see any movies'. In the same way it obligatorily merges with *iemand > niemand* 'somebody' – 'nobody', *iets > niets* 'something' – 'nothing', *ooit > nooit* 'ever' – 'never', *ergens > nergens* 'somewhere' – 'nowhere'.

Subject–Verb Agreement

On the whole, agreement (number and person) occurs between subject and finite verb. Some copula sentences with nominal predicates form an exception here: the verb usually agrees with non-third-person and/or plural predicate nouns if the subject is third-person singular; e.g. *dat ben ik/zijn wij* 'that's me/us', *het zijn leraren* 'they are teachers', *dat groepje zijn leraren* 'that group consists of teachers'. In this construction type the subject pronoun always takes the neuter (singular) form *het/dat* 'it/that', even if it refers to a plural entity or a human being. If the subject is first or second person or consists of a plural noun phrase, the verb agrees with the subject; e.g. *ik ben/ jij bent zijn vriend* 'I am/you are his friend', *die jongens daar zijn ons beste team* 'those boys over there are our best team'.

There is another copula construction with a bare noun, necessarily in the singular, as a predicate. It is used if the predicate designates the person's function. In this case the third-person pronoun is not neutralized, and agreement of the verb is with the subject; e.g. *hij is leraar* 'he is a teacher', *ze/die zijn leraar* 'they/those (people) are teachers'. So, the two Dutch clauses *hij is leraar* and *het is een leraar* (both to be translated as 'he is a teacher') are not equivalent: the function of *leraar* in the former may be called 'specifying/qualifying', that of *een leraar* in the latter 'identifying'.

The Expression of Pragmatic Functions

Although Dutch has the rule of verb-second, common to all Germanic languages, at least in main clauses, there is no equivalent for the English (or French) rule of 'subject-first'. This means that Dutch clauses may be construed along pragmatic lines such as 'topic-initial', 'focus-final', 'given-before-new', etc. Special topicalization (or thematization) constructions such as *wat Wibo betreft, die heb ik in tijden niet meer gezien* 'as for Wibo, I did not see him for years' do occur in Dutch. In most of these the constituent which is focused/topicalized, whatever its syntactic function, is taken up by a resumptive pronoun in the first constituent of the clause proper (in the example: *die* 'that one'). But special topicalized constructions such as this one are strongly marked, and thus extremely rare in everyday speech.

The same appears to be the case with cleft and pseudo-cleft sentences, which in some languages, as e.g. French, are customary tools for focusing, but which Dutch restricts to situations in which a previous statement has to be refuted or at least amended (e.g. *het is Wim die met d'r mee had moeten gaan* 'it is Bill who should have gone with her'). But even for this pragmatic function Dutch seems to prefer a simpler construction, consisting of a left-dislocated constituent that is taken up again by a resumptive pronoun in the sentence proper, preferably in the first, pre-verb position, cf. *Pieter, die moet komen* 'Peter, that one must come'. If the function of the left-dislocated constituent requires a preposition, this may be expressed twice, but it need only be expressed with the resuming pronoun: *(op) je vader, op die wachten we niet meer* 'your father we do not wait for any longer'. Informal language makes an extensive use of this left-dislocated construction.

14.5   Lexis

General Characteristics

Most formal characteristics of the Dutch lexicon have already been given in preceding sections. Words of Germanic stock constitute the overwhelming majority of the non-complex part of the basic vocabulary. These words generally contain only one 'full' vowel, though many have another syllable with [ə]. Examples of the latter category are *koren* 'corn', *korrel* 'grain', *geluk* 'luck'. It should be noted that of these only *koren* was monosyllabic in Proto-Germanic; in *korrel* and *geluk* the syllable with [ə] goes back to an affix. The basic vocabulary has been extended primarily by means of affixation and compounding, but to a considerable degree also with loans from neighbouring languages, in the first place French and its northern dialects (especially Picardian), and from classical and medieval Latin. Classical Greek contributed quite a lot of stems, especially in the fields of science and technology, often through the mediation of Latin. As was said before, this liberal attitude towards loans resulted in a rather complex pattern in the domains of phonology and (especially) accentuation of the modern language.

Quite a number of lexical divergences exist between the national varieties of Dutch. Belgian Dutch is most typically characterized by the existence of hundreds of dialectisms, gallicisms, and calques from French. Moreover lots of words which are considered archaic in the Netherlands are in everyday use in the language of most Belgians. The latter also applies to the variety of the language used in Surinam, where of course, a great number of 'local' circumstances have produced new words, unfamiliar to European varieties of Dutch – mostly borrowed from Sranan or Sarnami – and new meanings. Examples of archaisms common to Belgian and Surinam Dutch are *ijskast* (*koelkast* 'refrigerator'), *kleinzerig* (*lichtgeraakt* 'touchy'), *groen* (*onrijp* 'unripe'), *handlanger* (*hulpje* 'helper'), *stootkar* (*handkar* 'push car').

Monomorphemic Words

Not surprisingly, Dutch forms a group together with English, Frisian and German, deviating from the Scandinavian languages in vocabulary as well as in most other characteristics. Furthermore, it should be noted that its geographical situation between English and German is paralleled by a similar mid-position in the contents of the lexicon. Many Dutch words appear to belong to an Ingvaeonic ('North Sea') stock of words, most of which are also found in English, but not in High German. Among them *ladder* 'ladder', *klaver* 'clover', *wiel* 'wheel', *zwaaien* 'sway', *dus* 'thus', *jou* 'you (obj.)'. In the further evolution Dutch has been subject to a stronger influence from continental German than from insular English. Thus even for West Germanic words (including early loans from Latin), the distance from English, which seems to have been more considerable than that from High German from the very beginning of written evidence, anyway, has grown even larger in the course of time.

Reliable counts concerning the origin of Dutch words, in which such variables as frequency, register use, part of speech status, semantic category, etc., are taken into account, are not available. The following exercise, however, based on interim word counts by the Instituut voor Nederlandse Lexicologie (Leiden), is instructive. From the 500 most frequent words, and a random selection of 500 less frequent ones, taken from the lists for written language (totalling 600,000 tokens), and a comparable sample from those of spoken language (120,000 tokens), the monomorphemic words were selected. They were divided into five frequency classes (the most frequent words make up class 1, the least frequent ones class 5). From the point of view of etymology a division into three classes is made: words of direct Germanic origin (i.e. not through the mediation of any other language), loans, and new creations. The last category is an amalgam of types, ranging from completely new, sometimes onomatopoeic words, to words formed on the basis of existing stems, by means of non-productive procedures. Abbreviations, letter words, etc., are included here too. Examples are *fiets* 'bicycle', *sluw* 'sly' and *beha* 'bra'. The results of this division appear in Table 14.5, which contains only percentages. The number of words was between 100 and 200 in each frequency class both in written and spoken language:

Table 14.5   The origin of monomorphic words in Modern Dutch

| | Written Language | | | Spoken Language | | |
	Germanic	Loans	New	Germanic	Loans	New
Class 1	89.6	0.9	9.6	87.8	1.0	11.2
Class 2	62.9	18.1	19.0	62.0	17.0	21.0
Class 3	63.3	21.5	15.2	52.1	25.2	22.7
Class 4	40.9	46.6	12.5	48.5	34.7	16.8
Class 5	32.1	57.5	10.4	38.6	43.0	18.4

Words of Proto-Germanic origin constitute more than half of the mono-morphemic words among the 500 most frequent words (frequency classes 1, 2, 3), both in written and in spoken Dutch. There is a marked decline in the 4th class in the written language, but only in the 5th class (least frequent words) in spoken Dutch. In the two least frequent classes gaps are predominantly filled by loans, rather than by neologisms. Of course here only monomorphemic words are considered: new creation by means of compounding and affixation by far exceeds borrowing as a source of innovations, as illustrated below. Neologicisms are far more widespread in (more informal) spoken than in written language.

If we take a look at the parts of speech of the loans, it appears that the overwhelming majority are nouns, followed by adjectives. Not unexpectedly the other categories (verbs, adverbs, particles, conjunctions, pre- and postpositions, pronouns, determiners, numerals, etc.), have proven to be more immune to foreign influence, though each of them does include at least some loans.

Polymorphemic Words

As was repeatedly pointed out before, Dutch forms new words on the basis of existing ones, both by compounding and by affixation, both processes also allowing simultaneous and recurrent application. In the corpus described above the following percentages for composite words (i.e. words which are recognized as polymorphemic by native speakers) were found:

among the 500 most frequent words (classes 1–3): 26.9 per cent of the items in written, and 27.0 per cent in spoken language;
in the other frequency categories (classes 4–5): 55.1 per cent in written, 59.5 per cent in spoken language.

These percentages indicate that, on the whole, the existing lexicon is the main basis for naming new concepts and relations, derivation and compounding pushing aside borrowing in most domains. The latter restriction has to be made, because some fields, especially relating to the development of new technology, are more susceptible to massive borrowing from English, or – often through English – from international vocabulary. Complex words occur in all major classes of parts of speech, but appear to be most frequent with adverbs, adjectives and verbs.

Further Reading

Brachin, P. (1977) *La Langue Néerlandaise, Essai de Présentation*, Brussels: Didier.
De Schutter, G. and Van Hauwermeiren, P. (1983) *De structuur van het Nederlands. Taalbeschouwelijke grammatica*, Malle: De Sikkel.
De Vries, M. and te Winkel, L. A. (1864ff.) *Woordenboek der Nederlandsche Taal (WNT)*, The Hague/Leyden: Nijhoff, 1864 (1st issue; to be finished 1993).

Geerts, G., Haeseryn, W., de Rooij, J., van den Toorn, M. (1984) *Algemene Nederlandse Spraakkunst (ANS)*, Groningen/Leuven: Wolters-Noordhoff.

Koster, J. (1975) 'Dutch as an SOV language', *Linguistic Analysis* 1: 111–36.

Taeldeman, J. (1990) 'Ist die belgisch-niederländische Staatsgrenze auch eine Dialektgrenze?', in L. Kremer and H. Niebaum (eds), *Grenzdialekte, Germanistische Linguistik*, 101–3, Marburg/Lahn: Forschungsinstitut für deutsche Sprache, pp. 275–314.

Van den Toorn, M. C. (1979) *Nederlandse grammatica*, 6th edn, Groningen: Wolters-Noordhoff.

Van der Meer, M.J. (1927) *Historische Grammatik der niederländischen Sprache*, Heidelberg: Winter.

Van Loey, A. (1959) *Schönfelds Historische Grammatica van het Nederlands*, 6th edn, Zutphen: W. J. Thieme.

15 Afrikaans

Bruce Donaldson

15.1 Introduction

Although the concept of a new language policy for a post-apartheid South Africa is currently being debated, only Afrikaans and English are at present regarded as official languages in the Republic of South Africa. Government is thus officially bilingual, but due to the vast majority of bureaucrats (including the police, armed forces, railways, etc.) being Afrikaners and the fact that the traditional power base of the ruling party (in power since 1948) has been Afrikaans, Afrikaans dominates in that sphere, whereas in the sphere of commerce English dominates. In rural areas, with the exception of most of Natal, Afrikaans is more commonly spoken, whereas in the cities one hears more English.

It is not traditional to talk of the existence of dialects of Afrikaans, and yet certain regional variants do exist, as is to be expected over such distances in a language that has been evolving since the middle of the seventeenth century. Generally speaking three broad regional varieties are recognized (Figure 15.1): (a) the Western Cape, represented in its most extreme form by the highly distinctive speech of many so-called Cape coloureds (i.e. people of mixed race in the South African context) in that region; (b) the Eastern Cape together with the Orange Free State and the Transvaal, settlement of the latter two regions having taken place from the Eastern Cape Province; (c) Orange River Afrikaans, a term applied to a highly distinctive variant of the language that developed among the Griqua population (a subdivision of the coloureds whose ancestors were local Khoi (i.e. Hottentots) and white precursors of the later voortrekkers). The Griquas live(d) along the Orange River in the northern Cape and southern Free State. A group of these people trekked into South West Africa (now Namibia) in the 1860s and established Afrikaans there as an indigenous non-white language. Their present descendants in Namibia are the Rehoboth Basters. As far as the standard language is concerned, the variant of the former Boer Republics rules supreme, without any negative connotatons being applied to other variants, except where those variants, as is commonly the case, go hand in hand with ethnic differences. The quite deviant variety of Afrikaans spoken by many coloureds, for

Figure 15.1 Map of South Africa

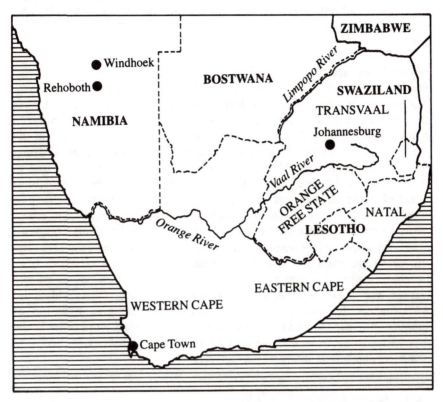

example, and sometimes referred to as 'advanced Afrikaans' in linguistic circles (implying that it is the product of pidginization), is one such 'dialect' that is looked down upon, even by many coloureds.

The standard language, which is based solely on the Afrikaans of whites and which is watched over by the *Taalkommissie* of the *Suid-Afrikaanse Akademie vir Wetenskap en Kuns*, has been nurtured since the last quarter of the nineteenth century, finally replacing Dutch as an official language in 1925.

One of the main problems of current standardization concerns the influence of English. Much has changed and is in the course of changing in Afrikaans because of the intimate contact with English and the high degree of bilingualism among native speakers of Afrikaans. Other than in the realm of international loanwords with cognate forms in English, the influence of English on the phonology of the language strangely enough seems to be minimal. The same is true of the morphology, syntax and even the lexis, the last due to a (too?) highly developed sense of purism. It is above all the idiom, and to a lesser degree the semantics, of Afrikaans that are being affected. In its idiom it is rapidly becoming a language of translation to which the many expressions like *jou sokkies optrek* 'to pull up your socks', *iemand se been trek* 'to pull someone's leg' and *uit die bloute* (*uit*) 'out of the blue' bear witness.

General Characteristics of Afrikaans
Phonologically Afrikaans is characterized by a preference for voiceless over voiced stops and fricatives (the exceptions being /b/ and /d/, but even these are devoiced in final position, and [g] only occurs as an allophone of /x/ in a few limited positions); by a great number of diphthongs (the result of the breaking of historically long vowels *inter alia*); as well as by a strong tendency to unrounding. Morphologically it is characterized by the lack of gender distinction; the lack of conjugation in the verbal system; the almost total lack of the original past tense, as well as a strong tendency to relate past events in the present tense; double negation; and the frequent occurrence of diminutives. The demise of the preterite has even led to Afrikaans losing two of the original characteristics of a Germanic language, i.e. the dental preterite and vowel gradation in strong verbs. Syntactically it differs very little from Dutch, retaining as it does verb-second word order in main and coordinate clauses and SOV word order in subordinate clauses. Characteristic of Afrikaans in this respect *vis-à-vis* Dutch is the common omission of subordinating *dat* leading to the retention of verb-second word order in the dependent clause, as well as the optional retention of interrogative inversion of subject and verb in indirect interrogatives.

15.2 Phonology

Short Vowels
/i/ occurs in loanwords too where it is represented by the grapheme ‹i› e.g. *artikel, titel*.

When followed by /r/, the vowels /i/, /u/, /y/, and /ɛ/ are pronounced long.

/ï/ is one of the sounds that typifies both Afrikaans and South African English *vis-à-vis* their mother forms. South African linguists traditionally transcribe stressed ‹i› as /ə/. The sound is best described either as a high schwa or a more central /i/, which is why /ï/ is used in Table 15.1. But in atonic position ‹i› is transcribed by schwa.

Table 15.1 Short vowels

i	y	u	dief	suutjies	boek
	ï			kind	
ɛ	œ	ɔ	bed	kus	bok
	a			kat	

/œ/ is commonly unrounded, thereby seeming to fall together with /ï/, e.g. *lug* 'air', *lig* 'light'.

Long Vowels

Table 15.2   Long vowels

iː	yː	uː	*mier*	*muur*	*boer*
ɛː	œː	ɔː	*skêr*	*rûe*	*sôe*
	aː			*kaart*	

/iː/, /yː/, /uː/, and /ɛː/ only occur before /r/ (although /ɛː/ can also be the result of compensatory lengthening), otherwise ‹ie›, ‹uu›, ‹oe›, and ‹e› are pronounced short. /œː/ and /ɔː/ occur in very few words. Consequently, of the long vowels only /ɛː/, and in particular /aː/, have a wide distribution, all other historically long vowels having undergone breaking (see Diphthongs). /ɛː/, or its allophone [æː], which occurs before /r/ + /d, s, t/, is only found before /r/ (+ consonant), e.g. *dertig* ['dæːrtəx] 'thirty', *perd* [pæːrt] 'horse', *wêreld* ['væːrəlt] 'world'. Otherwise /ɛː/, as well as all instances of /ɔː/, are the result of the few examples of compensatory lengthening that occurred when an intervocalic /x/ (or /x/ after /r/) was syncopated, e.g. *lêer* [lɛːər] 'file' (< Du. *legger*), *môre* [mɔːrə] 'morning' (< Du. *morgen*), *trôe* [trɔːə] 'troughs' (< Du. *troggen*).

In words like *dans* 'dance' [dãːs], *mens* 'person' [mɛ̃ːs], and *ons* 'we/us' [ɔ̃ːs], the long vowel is the result of compensatory lengthening, the loss of the nasal also causing nasalization of the vowel.

Diphthongs

Table 15.3   Diphthongs

əi				*wei/wy*		
	œi	œu	oə	*huis*	*koud*	*brood*
		øə			*seun*	
eə			ai	*weet*		*baie*

The long vowels of Afrikaans, compared with the vowels in cognate forms in Dutch, are characterized by (a) breaking; (b) raising; and (c) unrounding:

a   The vowels in *brood*, *seun*, and *weet* are traditionally transcribed without the schwa off-glide, implying that they are monophthongs, but such a view only has an historical validity;

b   ‹oo› and ‹ee› are also very commonly raised to /uə/ and /iə/.

c   The diphthongs /øə/ and /œi/ and the long vowel /yː/, as well as the short vowel /œ/, written ‹eu›, ‹ui›, ‹uu› and ‹u›, are all very commonly unrounded to /eə/, /əi/, /iː/ and /ï/. In so doing they become almost indistinguishable from the vowels represented by the graphemes ‹ee›, ‹ei›/‹y›, ‹ie› and ‹i›, e.g. *leun/leen, huis/hys, muur/mier, lug/lig*. The diphthong /œi/ is already somewhat unrounded when compared with its cognate in Dutch, /œy/.

/ai/ is limited to very few words, all ultimately of foreign origin, except where it occurs as the result of umlauting in the diminutive, in which case it is strictly speaking an allophone of /a/.

Diphthongization in Diminutive Formations

Addition of the palatal diminutive ending *-tjie*, or simply *-jie* if a noun already ends in ‹t› or ‹d› (both pronounced [t] in final position), causes umlauting of certain preceding vowels. The resulting diphthongs can in fact be regarded as allophones of the original vowels concerned which apply only when a word ends in [ci], e.g.

mat – matjie	'mat'	pron. [maici]
maat – maatjie	'mate'	pron. [maːici]
hand – handjie	'hand'	pron. [fiaiɲci]
aand – aandjie	'evening'	pron. [aːiɲci]
bed – bedjie	'bed'	pron. [bɛici]
kind – kindjie	'child'	pron. [kïiɲci]
pot – potjie	'pot'	pron. [pɔici]
poot – pootjie	'paw'	pron. [poici]
hond – hondjie	'dog'	pron. [fiɔiɲci]
oond – oondjie	'oven'	pron. [oiɲci]
voet – voetjie	'foot'	pron. [fuici]
put – putjie	'well'	pron. [pœici]
punt – puntjie	'point'	pron. [pœiɲci]

Double Vowels

Table 15.4 Double vowels

iu		ui	*sneeu*		*koeie*
		oːi			*nooi*
	aːi			*draai*	

Vowels in Atonic Syllables

There is a prevalence of schwa in atonic syllables, which is written in a number of ways depending on the etymology of the word, e.g. *Afrikaans* [afrəˈkãːs], *belangrik* [bəˈlaŋrək] 'important', *boere* [burə] 'farmers', *dikwels* ['dïkvəls] 'often', *gelukkig* [xə'lœkəx] 'happy', *onmiddellik* [ɔ'mïdələk] 'immediately', *kussing* ['kœsəŋ] 'cushion', *vereniging* [fə'reənəxəŋ] 'society'. The first vowel in the expressions *vanaand* 'this evening', *vandag* 'today', *vanmôre* 'this morning', etc., is a schwa too, i.e. [fə'naːnt], [fən'dax], [fə'mɔːrə]. In words of foreign origin schwa may also be represented by graphemes other than ‹e› and ‹i›, e.g. *krokodil* [krɔkə'dïl] 'crocodile', *kursus* ['kœrsəs] 'course'. The clusters /lm/ and /rm/ are broken up by a svarabhakti vowel (e.g. *psalm* and *storm*), but not /lk/ and /rk/ as is commonly the case in Dutch.

Consonants

Table 15.5   Consonants

p	t	k		pot	tafel	kat	
b	d			bom	dak		
f	s	x		Frans/vis	ses	goed	
v			ɦ	water			huis
m	n	ŋ		man	nooi	sing	
			l				lag
			r				rooi

The stops of Afrikaans are not aspirated at all. ‹b› and ‹d› are devoiced in final position, e.g. *bed* [bɛt], *hand* [ɦant]. It is traditional to transcribe diminutive forms ending in ‹djie›/‹tjie› as /ci/, but this [c] is essentially an allophone of /k/, e.g. *bakkie* [baci] 'bowl', *vroutjie* [frœuci] 'woman'. For historical reasons initial /f/ is represented by either ‹f› or ‹v›, more usually the latter. Although minimal pairs may exist where ‹f› and ‹v› seem to stand in contrast to each other, they have become homophones in Afrikaans, as they are in western Dutch, e.g. *Fin* 'Finn', *vin* 'fin'. The Dutch voiced fricatives /ɣ/ and /z/ are wanting in Afrikaans, as is the voiced pronunciation of the grapheme ‹v›; /v/ is represented by ‹w› in Afrikaans orthography. In certain intervocalic positions /d/ and /x/ are syncopated. /g/ does not occur in Dutch, other than as a result of sandhi, but has developed in Afrikaans as an allophone of /x/ after /r/ when followed by schwa, e.g. *burger* [bœrgər] 'citizen'. ‹h› is voiced in Afrikaans and as such is unique among Germanic languages. Initially it is often assimilated to preceding consonants, e.g. *gedoen het* [xə'dunət] 'did/ have done'. ‹ng› only occurs medially and word-finally, e.g. *vinger* 'finger', *sing* 'sing'. The cluster /nd/ is assimilated to [n] when it occurs intervocalically, but only in everyday words, i.e. it is in *hande* 'hands', *kinders* 'children', and *wonder* 'wonder', but is not in *bande* 'tyres', *handel* 'trade', and *monde* 'mouths'.

Syncope and Apocope of Consonants

Compared with their cognate forms in Dutch, many words in Afrikaans have lost sounds due to syncope or apocope.

Where /d/ and /x/ occur in Dutch after a long vowel or diphthong and are followed by schwa, they have been syncopated in Afrikaans, e.g. *leier* (< Du. *leider*) 'leader', *saal* (< Du. *zadel*) 'saddle', *nael* (< Du. *nagel*) 'nail', *spieël* (< Du. *spiegel*) 'mirror'. Less frequent is the syncope of intervocalic /v/ (written ‹w› in Afrikaans and ‹v› in Dutch), e.g. *naeltjie* (< Du. *naveltje*) 'navel', *oor* (< Du. *over*) 'over', *bo* (< Du. *boven*) 'above'. Exceptions to this are to be found in the many more learned sounding words that have been (re-)introduced from Dutch, e.g. *dodelik* 'fatal', *bespiegeling* 'conjecture', *owerheid* 'government', *te bowe kom* 'to get over'. This syncopation process is still productive in inflected forms, i.e. when a plural or adjectival -*e* ending is applied, e.g. *tyd > tye* 'time[s]'; *saag > sae* 'saw[s]'; *breed > breë* 'wide', *moeg > moeë* 'tired'. Also when forming the comparative in -*er* of such adjectives, e.g. *moeër, breër*. In *eg > êe* 'harrow[s]', *rug > rûe* 'back[s]', *trog > trôe* 'trough[s]' and *wig > wîe* wedge[s]' syncope causes compensatory lengthening.

Post-fricative /t/, written ‹d› or ‹t›, was apocopated in Afrikaans but returns when a plural or adjectival /ə/ ending is applied, e.g. *hemp > hemde* (< Du. *hemd*) 'shirt[s]', *kas > kaste* (< Du. *kast*) 'cupboard[s]', *nag > nagte* (< Du. *nacht*) 'night[s]'; *eg > egte* (< Du. *echt*) 'real', *lig > ligte* (< Du. *licht*) 'light'. This is also the case when forming the comparative in /ər/ of such adjectives, e.g. *egter, ligter*. Colloquially a /t/ is often inserted in the plural where historically there was none, e.g. *bus > busse/buste* (Du. *bussen*) 'bus[es]', *jas > jasse/jaste* (< Du. *jassen*) 'coat[s]'. On the other hand, in a few instances historical *t* does not return in the plural, e.g. *kos > kosse* (< Du. *kost*) 'food[s]', *wors > worse* (< Du. *worst*) 'sausage[s]'.

Orthography

Certain sounds that contrasted historically have fallen together in Afrikaans. This is the case in Dutch too, but is reflected less in the spelling of Dutch than of Afrikaans:

1 Whereas Dutch has the following voiced–voiceless couplets, which are faithfully reproduced in its spelling, Afrikaans has partially adapted its spelling to reflect the fact that this opposition is largely lacking, but certain remnants of the original opposition are still reflected in the spelling, the result of deliberate concessions to the Dutch spelling tradition so as to keep the two languages as close as possible on paper: Du. ‹g›/‹ch› > Afr. ‹g› (but always pronounced voiceless), Du. ‹v›/‹f› > Afr. ‹v›/‹f› (both pronounced voiceless), Du. ‹z›/‹s› > Afr. ‹s›, e.g. Du. *gaan* 'to go'/*lachen* 'to laugh' > Afr. *gaan/lag*, Du. *vader* 'father'/*fris* 'fresh' > Afr. *vader/fris*, Du. *zee* 'sea'/*suiker* 'sugar' > Afr. *see/suiker*.

2 The historically distinct diphthongs ‹ei› and ‹y› (the latter written ‹ij› in Dutch) have fallen together in standard Dutch and Afrikaans, but the distinction between the two is retained in the orthography of both languages. In some words the distinction helps distinguish between homonyms, e.g. *wei* 'pasture'/*wy* 'to devote', *hei* 'heather'/*hy* 'he', but on the whole it is retained purely for etymological reasons.

The spelling of the diminutive ending ‹-tjie›, pronounced [ci], has also been influenced by standard Dutch where the corresponding ending *-tje* reflects the way it is pronounced, i.e. [tjə].

The rules for the doubling of long vowels in closed syllables are as in Dutch, e.g. *aap/ape* 'monkey/monkeys', *boom/bome* 'tree/trees', as are those for the doubling of consonants after short vowels, e.g. *kat/katte* 'cat/cats', *pot/ potte* 'pot/pots'.

The rule of congruency demands that where words that contain a ‹b› or ‹d› in derived forms, are also spelt ‹b› and ‹d› when these consonants occur in word-final position and consequently undergo Auslautverhärtung, e.g. *ribbes* 'ribs' pronounced [rïbəs] < *rib* 'rib' pronounced [rïp]; *bande* 'tyres' pronounced [bandə] < *band* 'tyre' pronounced [bant]. Very few words end in *b* in fact.

The compound grapheme ‹gh› occurs initially in a few words of foreign origin to indicate that they retain the /g/ of the donor language, e.g. *gholf* [gɔlf] 'golf', *ghries* [gris] 'grease'; compare *golf* 'wave' [xɔlf].

The circumflex (*kappie*) is found most commonly on the letter ‹e› before /r/, e.g. *bêre* 'to put away', *militêr* 'military', but it is omitted when the /r/ is followed by a dental consonant, e.g. *perd* 'horse', *pers* 'purple'. In just a few isolated words it is applied to an ‹e›, ‹i›, ‹o› or ‹u› to indicate that compensatory lengthening has been applied after the syncopation of an intervocalic /x/ (or /x/ after /r/), e.g. *êe* 'harrows', *wîe* 'wedges', *sôe* 'sows', *môre* 'morning', *brûe* 'bridges'.

15.3 Morphology

Nouns and Adjectives

There is no longer any trace of case inflection to be found in nouns and adjectives outside of the numerous standard expressions where the origins of the remaining inflection have long since been forgotten, e.g. *van ganser harte* 'with all one's heart', *tenslotte* 'at last'. The only living examples of case in Afrikaans are to be found in the personal pronouns.

Given that when an adjective is inflected it takes an *-e*, the sound and spelling changes that occur in such cases are identical to those that apply when nouns take an *-e* in the plural (Du. *-en*), e.g. *boot/bote* 'boat[s]', *groot/ grotes* 'big/big ones'; *gebod/gebooie* 'commandment[s]', *dood/dooie* 'dead';

saag/sae 'saw[s]', *laag/lae* 'low'; *nag/nagte* 'night[s]', *sag/sagte* 'soft'. This parallel is the result of the identical phonological environment created in both categories when they are inflected.

Nouns

Plural Formation

Afrikaans makes no distinction in grammatical gender. It does distinguish number, the primary indicator of plurality being the suffix /ə/, with a substantial minority of nouns (more than in Dutch) taking the suffix /s/ and in addition there are several minor plural declensions that take other endings, e.g. *skoen – skoene* 'shoes', *boom – bome* 'trees', *pot – potte* 'pots'; *arm – arms* 'arms', *sokkie – sokkies* 'socks', *leeu – leeus* 'lions'; *aanwysing – aanwysings/-inge* 'instructions', *horing – horings* 'horns'; *bed – beddens* 'beds', *brug – brûe* 'bridges', *kalf – kalwers* 'calves'; *pad – paaie* 'roads', *skip – skepe* 'ships', *weg – weë* 'ways'.

Diminutization

The potential to diminutize any noun was inherited by Afrikaans from Dutch, and if Dutch makes extensive use of this morphological device to achieve certain semantic effects, this is all the more the case in Afrikaans where the diminutive is not noticeably less common in the written language than the spoken, which cannot be said of Dutch. This would seem to be in keeping with that general trait of Afrikaans *vis-à-vis* standard Dutch that it is based on an earlier spoken variant of that language. The diminutizing morpheme is *-tjie* (pronounced [ci] for historical reasons), with the allomorphs *-etjie, -ie, -jie, -kie,* and *-pie,* depending on the final sound in the noun, e.g. *vroutjie* (< *vrou*) 'woman', *deurtjie* (< *deur*) 'door', *stoeltjie* (< *stoel*) 'chair', *belletjie* (< *bel*) 'bell', *bakkie* (< *bak*) 'container', *paadjie* (< *pad*) 'road', *regerinkie* (< *regering*) 'government', *boompie* (< *boom*) 'tree'.

Many common words only occur in the diminutive form, e.g. *ertjie* 'pea', *mandjie* 'basket', *meisie* 'girl', *mossie* 'sparrow'. Such diminutives can be further diminutized, due to the attrition of the root from which they are derived, e.g. *ertjietjie, meisietjie,* etc.

Adjectives

Predicative adjectives are never inflected, but attributive adjectives often are. In all other Germanic languages that have preserved adjectival inflection, the criteria for inflecting an attributive adjective or not are determined by grammar. In Afrikaans inflection is determined primarily by the phonology of the adjective concerned, but also partially by its semantics (i.e. whether it is being used literally or figuratively, or even affectively). Inflection of the adjective in Afrikaans compared with the same concept in Dutch cannot be regarded as an example of simplification.

There are two main categories of adjectives that inflect, the inflectional ending being /ə/:

1 Adjectives of more than one syllable, which thus includes all derived adjectives, e.g. *belangrik – belangrike* 'important', *dankbaar – dankbare* 'grateful', *gemeen – gemene* 'common', *offisieel – offisiële* 'official', *perfek – perfekte* 'perfect', *relatief – relatiewe* 'relative', *vinnig – vinnige* 'quick'. As several of the examples above and below illustrate, inflection can cause certain changes to the phonology and spelling.

2 Monosyllabic adjectives ending in [t] (i.e. the allophone of /d/ in final position), /f/, /x/, and /s/, for example:

(a) Adjectives ending in [t], which is written ‹d›: if the adjective ends in a consonant + ‹d›, there is no spelling change, e.g. *blind – blinde* 'blind', *hard – harde* 'hard'. If the adjective contains a short vowel, the ‹d› remains and is doubled in writing to indicate preservation of the short vowel in the preceding closed syllable, e.g. *glad – gladde* 'smooth', but if it contains a long vowel or diphthong, it is syncopated (as is also the case in the formation of the plural of nouns), the inflectional ending taking a diaeresis if the root vowel is /eː/, e.g. *breed – breë* 'wide', *dood – dooie* 'dead', *goed – goeie* 'good', *koude – koue* 'cold'.

(b) Adjectives ending in /f/: if the adjective contains a short vowel, the final /f/ is voiced when /ə/ is added, i.e. ‹f› > ‹w›, and is doubled in writing to indicate preservation of the short vowel in the preceding syllable, e.g. *dof – dowwe* 'dull', *laf – lawwe* 'cowardly, silly', and if it contains a long vowel or diphthong, or a consonant precedes the /f/, the same voicing takes place but only one ‹w› is written, e.g. *doof – dowe* 'deaf', *eksklusief – eksklusiewe* 'exclusive', *gaaf – gawe* 'fine, good', *styf – stywe* 'stiff', *half – halwe* 'half'.

(c) Adjectives ending in /x/: if the adjective contains a long vowel or diphthong, the final /x/ is syncopated when /ə/ is added and a diaeresis is applied to the ‹e› where necessary to preserve the distinction between syllables, e.g. *droog – droë* 'dry', *hoog – hoë* 'high', *laag – lae* 'low', *leeg – leë* 'empty', *moeg – moeë* 'tired', *ruig – ruie* 'rugged, bushy'.

Adjectives which contain a short vowel, depending on their etymology, either add /tə/ or double the final ‹g› in writing to indicate preservation of the short vowel in the preceding syllable, e.g. *eg – egte* 'real', *lig – ligte* 'light', *reg – regte* 'right', *sleg – slegte* 'bad'; *stug – stugge* 'morose', *vlug – vlugge* 'quick'.

(d) Adjectives ending in /s/: adjectives which historically ended in /st/, but now end in /s/ due to apocope of final /t/, take /tə/, e.g. *bewus – bewuste* 'conscious', *juis – juiste* 'correct, exact', *vas – vaste* 'firm', whereas those that had no /t/ historically do not inflect, e.g. *fris* 'cool', *grys* 'grey', *los* 'loose', *pers* 'purple', *vars* 'fresh'. Only by comparing with Dutch can one know which words had a /t/ originally and which did not.

Adjectives which end in a consonant + /s/, take /ə/, e.g. *flukse – flukse* 'smart', *slaafs – slaafse* 'servile', *snaaks – snaakse* 'funny'.

The predicative adjectives *jonk* 'young', *lank* 'long, tall', and *oud* 'old' become *jong*, *lang*, and *ou* when used attributively, these reflexes being the result of a phonetic assimilation which occurred when the inflectional ending, which has since been apocopated, was added to the uninflected form.

Monosyllabic adjectives ending in any sound other than [t] (i.e. the allophone of /d/ in final position), /f/, /x/, and /s/ do not inflect, i.e. those ending in:

1   The voiceless stops /k/, /p/, and /t/, e.g. *sterk* 'strong', *ryp* 'ripe', *groot* 'big'.
2   The nasals /m/, /n/, and /ŋ/, e.g. *dom* 'stupid', *groen* 'green', *bang* 'frightened'.
3   The lateral and trill /l/ and /r/, e.g. *koel* 'cool', *swaar* 'heavy'.
4   Adjectives ending in a vowel or diphthong, e.g. *mooi* 'pretty', *blou* 'blue'.

For example: *die Groot Trek* 'the Great Trek', *'n groen deur* 'a green door', *dié/'n smal gangetjie* 'that/a narrow corridor', *hierdie/'n mooi meisie* 'this/a pretty girl'. When such adjectives are used affectively or figuratively, they may be subjected to inflection, but this aspect of inflection is somewhat hazy, e.g. *jou stomme kind* 'you silly child', *diepe tevredenheid* 'deep satisfaction', *die dorre Karoo* 'the arid Karoo'. They may also be inflected in standard expressions where they were inflected in Dutch, e.g. *in volle vertroue* 'in full confidence', *op vrye voet stel* 'to set free'.

Nominalized Adjectives

All adjectives take /ə/ when used nominally after determiners and possessives, e.g. *'n grote/die grote/hierdie grote/jou grote* 'a big one/the big one/this big one/your big one'. The plural of such forms is *die grotes* 'the big ones', etc. If the synonymous alternative construction with *een/ene/enetjie* (i.e. one) is used, the rules of inflection given above apply as the adjective is once again used attributively and not nominally, e.g. *'n/die/hierdie/jou groot een* (or colloquially also *ene* or *enetjie*) 'a/the/this/your big one'; in non-standard speech one hears these *een* constructions in the plural too, e.g. *(die) groot enes = (die) grotes* '(the) big ones'.

Adjectives Derived from Past Participles

Historically Weak Past Participles

The fact that many adjectives ending in /x/ and /s/ take a /tə/ ending when inflected, rather than simply an /ə/, is due to an historical sound change that occurred on a wide plane in Afrikaans. With nouns and adjectives final /t/ was apocopated after voiceless consonants, but in weak past participles final /t/, sometimes written ‹d›, was apocopated in all instances. However, in cases where an /ə/ is added to the participle, and the ‹t› or ‹d› are thus no longer in final position, they return in the form of the endings ‹te› or ‹de›. This is an issue which can only be fully understood in the light of certain historical factors.

Weak verbs in Dutch form their past participle by the addition of a ‹ge› prefix and a ‹t› or ‹d› suffix to the stem of the verb: ‹t› is added to stems ending in a voiceless consonant and ‹d› to those ending in a voiced consonant or a vowel, e.g. Du. *hopen – gehoopt* 'to hope', Du. *werken – gewerkt* 'to work', Du. *horen – gehoord* 'to hear', Du. *bouwen – gebouwd* 'to build'. As verbs, such forms appear in Afrikaans as *gehoop, gewerk, gehoor* and *gebou*, but when used as attributive adjectives, and thus inflected, they become *gehoopte, gewerkte, gehoorde* and *geboude*. To this point there is no problem.

One small difficulty in knowing whether to add ‹t› or ‹d› to a weak past participle in Dutch is presented by verbs with a ‹v› or ‹z› in the infinitive; verbs like *leven* 'to live' and *reizen* 'to travel', according to the rules of Dutch spelling, add the prefix ‹ge› and the suffix ‹d› to the stems *leef* and *reis*: these stems may end in voiceless consonants, but the ‹f› and ‹s› are derived from ‹v› and ‹z›, i.e. voiced consonants, and this fact determines the correct dental ending. But as such verbs in the infinitive form in Afrikaans are *leef* and *reis*, with no obvious sign of this ‹f› and ‹s› being derived from their voiced counterparts, it is difficult in such cases to know whether the correct inflected adjectival form of the verbal past participles *geleef* and *gereis* in Afrikaans is *geleefte/gereiste* or *geleefde/gereisde*; only the latter are strictly speaking correct, although with more obscure verbs speakers of Afrikaans are often in doubt themselves. In such cases their ear can no longer tell them what sounds correct, [-ftə]/[-stə] or [-fdə]/[-sdə], because in practice the voiced forms are seldom heard, they are only written; historically the /f/ and the /s/ were voiced before /də/ too, which is what the distinction was originally based on, but this is certainly no longer the case in Afrikaans. In Afrikaans this difficulty of choice not only affects verbs ending in ‹f› and ‹s›, but also those ending in ‹g›, as a ‹g› can be derived from a Dutch ‹ch› (unvoiced) or a Dutch ‹g› (historically voiced), e.g. *aangehegte/-de* (attached, officially only ‹te›).

Historically Strong Past Participles

Afrikaans abounds with the past participles of historically strong or irregular verbs, but none of them, with the exception of *gehad* 'had', is used verbally any more. Where they exist they are used and regarded as adjectives, *gebroke* 'broken' < *breek* 'to break', *handgeskrewe* 'handwritten' < *skryf* 'to write', *gesoute* 'salted' < *sout* 'to salt', *verbode* 'forbidden' < *verbied* 'to forbid'. As illustrated, adjectives derived from strong past participles end in ‹e› (< Du. ‹en›).

Many formerly strong verbs have lost their adjectival strong past participle and are now treated as if they have always been weak. This then raises the problem dealt with under historically weak past participles above – do they take a ‹te› or a ‹de›, given that in Dutch, where the strong participle is still used, they end in neither, e.g. *aanbeveel* 'to recommend' – *aanbeveelde* (< Du. *aanbevelen* – *aanbevolen*); *afspreek* 'to arrange' – *afgespreekte* (< *afspreken* – *afgesproken*). The forms given are considered correct because they are inflected as if they had been weak in Dutch too. But the originally strong forms of these two verbs – and also of many others – have not yet completely died out, i.e. *aanbevole* and *afgesproke*. The strong form of many other verbs, where it has survived at all, is infrequently used, e.g. *bak* – *gebakte* (< Du. *bakken* – *gebakken*) 'to bake', *vleg* – *gevlegte* (< Du. *vlechten* – *gevlochten*) 'to plait'.

Generally speaking it can be said that the better one's education, the greater one's familiarity with the strong forms; the lower down the social ladder the more one is likely to find analogically formed weak adjectival past participles, e.g. *bevrore/bevriesde* 'frozen', *gebonde/gebinde* 'bound', *voorgeskrewe/voorgeskryfde* 'prescribed', *verboë/verbuigde* 'inflected'. The tide of time is against the strong forms. But if all such weak forms, which after all did not exist in Dutch, still require that a choice be made between ‹te› and ‹de›, there is still room for error. Research has shown that Afrikaans speakers are very uncertain on this point, particularly with less familiar adjectives, whether originally weak or not.

In many instances the new analogically formed weak past participle exists side by side with the original strong form, but with a distinction in meaning (unlike those in the previous paragraph), the strong form usually denoting the more figurative meaning, e.g. *breek* 'to break' – *'n gebreekte koppie* 'a broken cup', *'n gebroke hart/gesondheid* 'a broken heart/shattered health'; *buig* 'to bend' – *'n gebuigde klerehanger* 'a bent clothes-hanger', *met geboë hoof* 'with a bowed head'.

Adjectival Inflection in /s/

Although traditional grammar states that when used after an indefinite pronoun an adjective takes /s/, an historically genitive ending still consistently used in such cases in Dutch and German, this ending is these days commonly omitted in Afrikaans, particularly in speech, but omission of the ending is considered non-standard by many, e.g. *ek het vandag iets interessants gehoor* 'I heard something interesting today', *kan shrywers aan niks beters dink as seks om oor te skryf nie?* 'can't authors think of anything better than sex to write about?' /s/ inflection is most commonly found after *iets* 'something' and *niks* 'nothing' and is now seldom heard after the pronouns *baie* 'a lot', *genoeg* 'enough', *iemand* 'someone' and *niemand* 'no one', e.g. *die kans dat sy iemand spesiaals sal ontmoet is bitter skraal* 'the chance that she'll meet someone special is remote'. /s/ inflection applies to comparatives too, e.g. *iets kleiners* 'something smaller', but even after *iets* and *niks* it is now commonly omitted from comparatives, e.g. *iets interessanter* 'something more interesting'.

Comparative and Superlative of the Adjective/Adverb
The comparative and superlative are formed as in Dutch, i.e. by the addition of /ər/ and /stə/ respectively. The difference between the two languages, if any, is to be found in a more frequent use of the periphrastic variants in *meer* and *mees*, a practice which seems to be gaining ground in Dutch too, but not to the same extent as in Afrikaans where the increased frequency may be due to the influence of English, e.g. *liefdevoller/liefdevolste*, *meer/mees liefdevolle* 'loving'.

Determiners
The definite article, *die*, is invariable in both the singular and the plural, e.g. *die man* 'the man', *die vrou* 'the woman', *die huis* 'the house', *die mans/ vrouens/huise* 'the men/women/houses'.

As the historically emphatic form of the demonstrative has survived as the definite article (compare Du. *die* and *de*), the demonstrative is simply expressed by stressing the definite article, written *dié*, e.g. *dié man* 'that man'. The distinction between the proximal and the distal demonstrative, common to other Germanic languages, is not necessarily made in Afrikaans, e.g. *dié week* 'this/that week'. But the compound forms *hierdie* 'this' and *daardie* 'that', although less common in the formal written language than *dié*, are commonly heard. The Dutch distal demonstrative *dat* has not survived in Afrikaans.

The indefinite article, *'n*, is pronounced [ə], even before nouns beginning with a vowel, although in some areas the nasal is also pronounced.

Pronouns

Personal Pronouns
The personal pronouns preserve the only living remnants of case in Afrikaans, but even here the distinction between subject and oblique case pronouns is only to be found in the singular, as the paradigm (Table 15.6) illustrates. Afrikaans has preserved only full (i.e. emphatic) pronouns.

It is a curious feature of Afrikaans that although grammatical gender no longer exists, *hy/hom* and *dit* (the Afrikaans reflexes of Dutch *hij/hem*, and *het*) alternate in free variation as anaphoric third-person singular pronouns with reference to inanimate objects, e.g. *het jy die nuwe plakkaat gesien. Ja, hy is/dis pragtig* 'have you seen the new poster. Yes, it's beautiful'. Note that

Table 15.6   Personal pronouns

	Subject		Object		Possessives		Independent possessives	
sg.	ek	I	my	me	my	my	myne	mine
	jy	you	jou	you	jou	your	joune	yours
	u	you	u	you	u	your	u s'n(e)	yours
	hy	he/it	hom	him/it	sy	his	syne	his
	sy	she	haar	her	haar	her	hare	hers
	dit	it	dit	it	sy	its	syne	its
pl.	ons	we	ons	us	ons	our	ons s'n(e)	ours
	julle	you	julle	you	julle, jul	your	julle s'n(e)	yours
	hulle	they	hulle	them	hulle, hul	their	hulle s'n(e)	theirs

dit is 'it is' is commonly said and written *dis*.

Jul and *hul* occur as variants of *julle* and *hulle*. Although they can theoretically function as subject and object pronouns, they most commonly occur as possessives or reflexives.

Somewhat analogous to Old Icelandic compounds in *þau*, e.g. *þau Guðrún* 'they and Guthrun', Afrikaans commonly adds *-hulle* as a suffix to personal names to indicate a collective in which the person named is seen as central, e.g. *pa-hulle/ma-hulle* 'mum and dad', *Koos-hulle* 'Koos and his wife, Koos and family, Koos' mob'.

The indefinite pronoun 'one' is rendered by ('n) *mens*, the object and possessive forms of which are *jou*. However, if in the same sentence 'one' is used a second time as a subject pronoun, *jy* is then used, not ('n) *mens*, e.g. *in die Kruger Wildtuin moet ('n) mens nooit uit jou kar klim nie en jy moet voor sonsondergang een van die kampe bereik* 'in the Kruger Game Park one should never get out of one's car and one has to get to one of the camps before sunset'. In the same way the reflexive pronoun belonging with ('n) *mens* is *jou*, e.g. ('n) *mens wil jou graag voorstel dat . . .* 'one rather likes to imagine that . . .'.

That reciprocal pronoun is *mekaar* 'each other', whose functions are the same as *elkaar* (colloquial *mekaar*) in Dutch.

Second-person Forms of Address

Although formally speaking the distinction between *jy* (pl. *julle*) and *u* (pl. *u*) is identical to that which exists in most European languages between the familiar and polite forms of address, in its use of these forms Afrikaans differs quite substantially from those other languages, even other Germanic languages. *U* is perhaps best regarded as a rather late (i.e. twentieth-century), somewhat learned borrowing from Dutch and is consequently seldom, if ever, heard in the speech of the common man. In his speech *jy* alternates with third-person forms of address, i.e. *ma* 'mother', *pa* 'father', *oom* 'uncle' (used towards any older male), *tannie* 'auntie' (used towards any older female), *dokter*, *professor*, *dame* 'madam', etc. In this respect Afrikaans is very conservative, but on the other hand this phenomenon goes hand in hand with a tendency to use *jy* towards strangers where the equivalent familiar form could not be used in the other languages that make a distinction between familiar and polite forms of address. This commonly occurs in combination with titulars like *meneer* 'Mr' and *mevrou* 'Mrs' which establish that the speaker is not being unnecessarily familiar, e.g. *goeie môre mevrou, kan ek vir jou help?* 'good morning, madam, can I help you?' = *goeie môre mevrou, kan ek vir mevrou help?* (very formal).

If Afrikaans speakers find themselves in a situation where they feel that one of these third-person forms of address is appropriate, they are usually very consistent in their use of that form, using it in lieu of subject, object, possessive and reflexive pronouns, e.g. *ek kan ma (= jou) ongelukkig nie nou help nie* 'unfortunately I can't help you now' (object), *ma moenie ma daaroor bekommer nie* 'you mustn't worry about that' (subject + reflexive), *sal ma (= jy) my ma se (= jou) kar leen?* 'will you lend me your car?' (subject + possessive).

Reflexive Pronouns

The reflexive pronouns are identical to the above object pronouns; the peculiarly third-person reflexive form *zich* of Dutch (< Ger. *sich*) is unknown in Afrikaans, where *hom*, *haar* and *hulle* are used. Where the third-person form of address is used, the same noun also functions as the reflexive pronoun.

The compound reflexive in *-self*, which prescriptive grammars maintain should only be used where one wishes to stress that the action is reflecting back on the subject, which is certainly the case in Dutch, is in practice more widely distributed than that in Afrikaans, probably due to the similarity with non-emphatic English reflexives in '-self', e.g. *gedra jouself* 'behave yourself'.

Relative Pronouns

The relative pronoun for all antecedents, whether they be singular or plural, personal or non-personal, is *wat*, e.g. *die man wat hier langsaan bly is 'n Amerikaner* 'the man who lives next door is an American', *die mense wat op hierdie plaas bly is Rhodesiërs* 'the people who live on this farm are Rhodesians', *die doringboom (doringbome) wat agter die motorhuis groei het te groot geword* 'the thorn tree(s) which is (are) growing behind the garage has (have) got too big'.

Because of the indeclinability of *wat*, the uniformity of verbal endings and the SOV word order of relative clauses, one is sometimes dependent on context to know whether a relative *wat* is the subject or the object of its clause, e.g. *die Engelse soldate wat dié Boere verslaan het, het na die oorlog medaljes gekry* 'the English soldiers who defeated those Boers/whom those Boers defeated, got medals after the war'. Because it is possible to put a *vir* before all personal direct objects (cf. Use of *vir* with personal objects, under section 15.4, Syntax), the ambiguity can be avoided here as follows: *die Engelse soldate wat vir dié Boere verslaan het* ... 'the English soldiers who defeated those Boers ...'.

When the relative is used in combination with a preposition, a distinction is made between personal and non-personal antecedents. In the former case standard Afrikaans does not allow prepositional stranding and requires preposition + *wie*, e.g. *die mense met wie jy nou net gepraat het is Portugese* 'the people to whom you were just talking are Portuguese/the people (who[m]) you were just talking to are Portuguese'.

With non-personal antecedents *waar* + preposition is required, e.g. *die program waarna jy nou net gekyk het was baie swak* 'the programme (which/ that) you were just watching was very weak', *dis dinge waarvan ons nooit praat nie* 'they are things (which/that) we don't talk about'. But *waar* + preposition is also possible with personal antecedents, e.g. *die mense waarmee jy nou net gepraat het is Portugese* 'the people you were just talking to (= to whom) are Portuguese'. Such compound relative pronouns are sometimes subjected to prepositional stranding, in which case the preposition is inserted later in the relative clause, prior to the verb(s) in that clause, e.g. *die mense waar jy nou net mee gepraat het is Portugese*. Prepositional stranding of this kind is not as common in Afrikaans as in Dutch, but on the other hand there is a growing preference in the spoken language for stranding in structures of the sort discussed in the next paragraph.

The above *waar* + preposition constructions are regularly replaced in the spoken language by *wat* + preposition (with stranding of the preposition before the verb(s) of the relative clause), e.g. *die program wat jy nou net na gekyk het was baie swak, dis dinge wat ons nooit van praat nie, die mense wat jy nou net mee gepraat het is Portugese.* (Compare the interrogative forms *waarna kyk jy/wat kyk jy na?* 'what are you looking at?') Stranding of the preposition in *waar* + preposition type constructions (i.e. both relative and interrogative), so common in Dutch, is no longer usual in Afrikaans, but it does occur, e.g. *die mense waar jy nou net mee staan en praat het is Portugese.* One's automatic reaction, if one splits in this fashion, at least in speech, is to replace *waar* with *wat.*

(Preposition +) 'whose', both relative and interrogative, with reference to personal antecedents is (preposition +) *wie se*, e.g. *dié mense wie se kinders ek baie gehelp het is nou albei dood* 'those people, whose children I have helped a lot, are now both dead', *hierdie mense is vriende met wie se kinders ek vroeër gespeel het* 'these people are friends whose children I once used to play with (= with whose)'. *Wie se* may also refer to animates other than people, e.g. *die koei wie se kalfie* ... 'the cow whose calf ...'.

'Whose' with reference to non-personal antecedents (i.e. = of which) is *waarvan* (or *wat se* in colloquial Afrikaans), e.g. *die huisie waarvan die grasdak/wat se grasdak herstel moet word, behoort aan die boer se plaaswerkers* 'the house whose thatch roof (= of which the thatch roof) has to be repaired belongs to the farmer's labourers'.

Interrogative Pronouns
Interrogative pronouns are as in Dutch, with the following exceptions. The Dutch word *welk(e)* 'which' has been largely replaced by *watter* but is still heard in standard expressions, e.g. *in welke mate* (= *in watter mate*) 'to what extent'. This interrogative also occurs in the expression *watter soort* (Du. *wat voor een*) 'what kind of a', and when used independently is optionally combined with *een*, i.e. *watter (een)* 'which one'. *Wat se* commonly replaces *watter* and *watter soort* in prenominal position in colloquial Afrikaans.

Possessive 'whose' is rendered by *wie se* (< Du. *wie z'n* (m.), *wie d'r* (f. and pl.)), the independent form being *wie s'n(e)*.

Prepositional stranding also occurs with interrogative pronouns (see Relative pronouns, p. 493).

Verbs

Tenses of the Verb
In common with certain other colonial dialects of Germanic (e.g. Yiddish, Pennsylvania German), the preterite has ceded to the perfect. A verb is therefore typically conjugated in the present and past tenses as in Table 15.7. In addition, there is no longer any distinction between strong and irregular verbs, all verbs being treated as weak in the perfect tense, and the traditional distinction between verbs that take 'to be' and 'to have' as an auxiliary in the perfect has disappeared in favour of *het* (finite form of *hê* 'to have').

Vestiges of the Preterite
Only the preterite of the following auxiliary verbs has been retained: *kan* 'to be able' – *kon*, *moet* 'to have to' – *moes*, *sal* 'will' – *sou*, *wil* 'to want to' – *wou*, and *wees* 'to be' – *was*. The preterite of *hê* 'to have' has not survived in standard Afrikaans, with the result that a formal pluperfect has also ceased to exist, general context or adverbs of time making it clear that an action is pluperfect. The following verbs, in addition to the possibility of forming their past tense regularly like all other verbs, have also retained their strong preterite forms, which exist in free variation with the regular forms: *dink* 'to think' – *dag/dog* and *het gedink* (also *het gedag/gedog*), *weet* 'to know' – *wis* and *het geweet*. *Wis* is now becoming rare, whereas there is a semantic distinction between *dag/dog/het gedag/het gedog* (all synonymous) on the one hand and *het gedink* on the other: although the latter can alternate with the former without any differentiation in meaning, it is not possible to use the former when 'thinking of someone or something, e.g. *ek het die hele dag aan*

Table 15.7   Tenses of the verb

Infinitive	*werk*	'to work'
Present tense		
1 sg.	ek werk	'I work, I am working, I do work, etc.'
2 sg.	jy/u werk	
3 sg. m.	hy werk	
f.	sy werk	
n.	dit werk	
1 pl.	ons werk	
2 pl.	julle werk	
3 pl.	hulle werk	
Progressive	ek is aan die werk	'I'm working'
	ek sit en werk	
Negative	ek werk nie	'I don't/am not working'
Imperative	werk	'work'
Negative imperative	moenie werk nie	'don't work'
Future tense	ek werk	'I'm working'
	ek sal werk	'I will work'
	ek gaan werk	'I'm going to work'
Past tense		
1 sg.	ek het gewerk	'I worked, I was working, I did work'
		'I have worked, I have been working'
		'I had worked, I had been working'
2 sg.	jy/u het gewerk	
3 sg. m.	hy het gewerk	
f.	sy het gewerk	
n.	dit het gewerk	
1 pl.	ons het gewerk	
2 pl.	julle het gewerk	
3 pl.	hulle het gewerk	
Progressive	ek was aan die werk (gewees)	'I was working'
	ek het (ge)sit en werk	'I have/had been working'
Negative	ek het nie gewerk nie	'I wasn't working/didn't work/haven't worked'

jou gedink 'I thought of you all day', nor is it possible to use those forms when referring to the mental activity of thinking, e.g. *Descartes het te veel in sy lewe gedink* 'Descartes thought too much in his life'. They can only alternate as an irrealis in contexts such as the following: *ek het gedag/gedog/gedink hy was jou broer* 'I thought (= believed) he was your brother'.

The Historic Present

The past tense is very frequently avoided when relating past events if it is obvious from the context (e.g. certain adverbs of time) that the action occurred in the past. Although this practice occurs in other Germanic languages too, it is particularly common in Afrikaans, just as much in the spoken, as the written language. Particularly when a clause in introduced by the conjunction *toe* ('when', on one occasion in the past) or contains the adverb *toe* ('then' in the past), the present tense is most usually used in that clause, whereas the verb in the main clause can be either in the present or the past, e.g. *toe hy tuis kom, sien hy dat sy vrou die hele dag niks gedoen het nie* (present + present + past [= pluperfect]) 'when he got home he saw that his wife had done nothing all day'.

The Pluperfect

With the loss of the preterite of *hê*, the pluperfect of all verbs was also lost, but this does not seem to have given rise to any undue ambiguity – Afrikaans usually relies simply on context to indicate whether a given event in the past occurred prior to another event in the past, but it can rely on the sequence of tenses to indicate a pluperfect.

Although one can say that there is no difference in form between the perfect and the pluperfect, there is one exception to this. The following structure occurs occasionally in both speech and writing when one wants to emphasize that a particular action had occurred prior to another: *hy het dit toe al gedoen gehad* 'he had already done it then'; i.e. the perfect of *hê* (in effect the equivalent of the English preterite 'had') is employed as the auxiliary of the verb. This practice is not unknown in other Germanic dialects. (See The Passive, below, for further comments on the pluperfect).

Idiosyncrasies of hê 'to have'

Hê is the only verb that has preserved an irregular past participle, i.e. *gehad*. It, like *wees*, also has a finite form that differs from the infinitive, i.e. *het*. Its preterite form *had* is now considered either dialectal or archaic. In compound tenses where the infinitive of 'to have' acts as an auxiliary in all other Germanic languages, Afrikaans employs the finite form *het*, e.g. *hy sal dit gedoen het* 'he will have done it', *hy moes dit gedoen het* 'he must have done it'.

Idiosyncrasies of wees 'to be'

In addition to *wees* being only one of two verbs whose finite form differs from the infinitive, i.e. *is*, it is also the only verb that still takes *wees* as its auxiliary in the past, e.g. *ek is gewees*. But this form is not often used. Although prescriptive grammar advocates that *was* is the past tense of *wees*, what one most commonly hears is *ek was gewees*, a structure which corresponds with the historical pluperfect, but which is semantically simply a past and therefore also a pluperfect, as indeed is the case with *was*, e.g. *ek was siek (gewees)* 'I was/have been/had been sick', *hulle het nie geweet dat ek siek was nie* 'they didn't know that I was/have been/had been sick'. As the previous example illustrates, when subordinate word order prevails, *was gewees* cedes to *was* or ocasionally *gewees het*.

The Passive

The auxiliary of the present passive is *word* 'to become', whereas that of the past passive is *wees*, e.g. *dit word/is deur my gedoen* 'it is being/was done by me'. Due to English influence *was* commonly alternates with *is* in the past, a form which corresponds with the historical pluperfect passive, but it is unlikely that a pluperfect passive really exists in Afrikaans as it is no longer extant in the active; nevertheless the existence of a pluperfect passive with *was* is commonly postulated in prescriptive grammars.

Subjunctive Mood

As is to be expected in a language with such a simplified verbal system as Afrikaans, all formal trace of the subjunctive has disappeared, mood being expressed periphrastically by means of *sou* 'would', should the need arise, e.g. *as jy nie so veel sou eet nie* ... 'if you didn't eat as much ...', *indien dit môre (sou) reën* ... 'should it rain tomorrow.../if it were to rain tomorrow ...'.

Reflexive Verbs

There are somewhat fewer reflexive verbs in Afrikaans than in Dutch. Quite a number are seldom, if ever, used reflexively any more; or the reflexive is at best now optional. It is highly likely that in most cases this development is due to English influence given that all cases where reflexivity is no longer required correspond with English verbs that are not reflexive, e.g. *haas* 'to hurry', *oorgee* 'to surrender', *skeer* 'to shave', *verskuil* 'to hide'.

Reflexive pronouns are identical to object pronouns. Afrikaans reference works now normally give the infinitive of reflexive verbs in the second, rather than the third person, e.g. *jou tuisvoel* 'to feel at home', rather than *hom tuisvoel*.

Reduplication

Adjectives, adverbs, nouns, numerals, and verbs can be reduplicated. Many such reduplications have become lexicalized, but the construction is still productive. Although they can be formed from all the above parts of speech, the reduplicated forms themselves function only as adverbs and verbs, most usually as the former, e.g. *hulle het vroeg-vroeg aangekom* 'they arrived very early', *sy swaar growwe hande het so liggies-liggies oor haar vel beweeg* 'his heavy, coarse hands moved lightly over her skin', *ryp sal plek-plek voorkom* 'there will be frost here and there', *sy kom toe lag-lag in* 'she came in laughing'. Although verbs can be reduplicated to produce adverbs, only reduplicated verbs, and not other reduplicated parts of speech, can function as verbs, e.g. *hy het sy ogies so geknip-knip* 'he kept blinking his eyes'. Reduplicated nouns can also give rise to new nouns, but this only occurs in the names of certain children's games, e.g. *huis(ie)-huis(ie)* 'mummies and daddies', *dokter-dokter* 'hospitals'.

15.4 Syntax

Order of Verbs
As in Dutch and German, in main and coordinate clauses verb-second word order applies to the finite verb, with all subsequent verbs (i.e. past participles or infinitives) standing at the end of the clause. The few exceptions to this are as in Dutch (e.g. they may precede prepositional adjuncts). In subordinate clauses, where SOV order applies, there is a fixed order for the transitive verb and all additional verbs, unlike in Dutch, which permits a certain variation, e.g. *dat ... sal doen* (Du. *dat ... zal doen/doen zal*), *dat ... gedoen het* (Du. *dat ... gedaan heeft/heeft gedaan*), *dat ... (sou) kon gedoen het* (Du. *dat ... zou hebben kunnen doen*), *dat ... sal laat doen* (Du. *dat .. zal laten doen*), *dat ... sal laat doen het* (Du. *dat ... zal hebben laten doen*), *om dit te gedoen het* (Du. ... *om het gedaan te hebben/te hebben gedaan*).

The subordinating conjunction *dat* is as commonly omitted in Afrikaans as in English, in which case the order of the dependent clauses reverts from SOV to verb-second, e.g. *Ek glo dat sy dit gedoen het* > *Ek glo sy het dit gedoen* 'I believe (that) she did it'.

Prenominal Modifiers
Sentential prenominal modifiers (i.e. with participles) of the kind so commonly used in German, and less commonly in spoken Dutch, do not occur at all in Afrikaans, i.e. Dutch *alle door de staat gesubsidieerde instellingen* 'all institutions that are subsidized by the state'. Afrikaans, like English, puts such information into a relative clause. But non-sentential prenominal modifiers which cannot be rephrased by means of a relative clause are possibly more common than in Dutch, presumably due to the influence of English, e.g. *'n drie jaar waglys* 'a three-year waiting list', *'n vier slaapkamer huis* 'a four-bedroomed house', *'n drie miljoen rand hospitaal* 'a three million rand hospital'.

Prepositional Groups Formed with *in ... in* and *uit ... uit*
In and *uit*, when designating motion rather than place, can be placed after the noun, as in Dutch, but more common, especially in the spoken language, is circumpositioning, e.g. *hy storm (in) die huis in/(uit) die huis uit* 'he storms into the house/out of the house'. In the case of *in*, this construction renders 'into' (motion), as opposed to 'in' (place). Either one postpositioned *in* or two

circumpositioned *in*'s are possible only with certain verbs indicating motion, particularly those with a separable prefix *in*, e.g. *hy het (in) die huis in gestorm/ingestorm*.

Although the prime purpose of circumpositioned *in* and *uit* is to express the idea of motion also inherent in a postpositioned *in* or *uit*, the construction now has a much wider distribution in Afrikaans, being applied in many contexts where there is not even a hint of motion and where a prepositioned *in* or *uit* would suffice, although this practice is much more common in the spoken than the written language, e.g. *die rob is deur tou gewurg en dit was binne in die vleis in* 'the seal had been strangled by rope and it was deep in its flesh', *jy moet sorg dat jy uit die tronk uit bly/uitbly* 'you'll have to make sure you stay out of prison'.

Possession

Use of the Linker *se*
The possessive particle *se*, historically an unemphatic form of *sy(n)* 'his' (< Du. *zijn/z'n*), functions in a similar fashion to apostrophe *s* in English, e.g. *die kind se toontjie* 'the child's toe', *die kinders se toontjies* 'the children's toes', *Suid-Afrika se hoofstad* 'South Africa's capital'. A succession of *se* constructions is possible, e.g. *ons bure se vriende se seun* 'our neighbours' friends' son', *dié kind se potlood se punt is stomp* 'the end of that child's pencil is blunt'. *Se*-structures are used with both animates and inanimates, e.g. *dié hond se stert* 'that dog's tail', *dié gebou se dak* 'the roof of that building', *die brief het die vorige dag se datum gehad* 'the letter had the previous day's date on it'. It is also used in adverbial expressions of time, e.g. *'n week se werk* 'a week's work', *hoeveel/twee uur se ry* 'how many/two hours' drive', as well as with measures, e.g. *vyf rand se biltong* 'five rands' worth of biltong (i.e. dried meat)', *miljoene rand se skade* 'millions of rands worth of damage', *tien kilo se aartappels* 'ten kilos (worth) of potatoes'.

As in colloquial English, the possessive can even follow a relative clause that is qualifying the noun to which it refers, e.g. *dit was die vrou wat so pas hier was se kind* 'it was the lady who was just here's child'. But the distribution of such constructions is wider in Afrikaans and is not limited to the spoken language, e.g. *vyf van die twaalf mense wat nog in die hospitaal behandel word, se toestand is kritiek* 'the condition of five of the twelve people that are still being treated in hospital is critical'.

The genitive of indefinite, reciprocal, interrogative, relative and demonstrative pronouns is also rendered by *se*, e.g. *elkeen se vakansie* 'everyone's holidays', *ons het mekaar se kinders baie lief* 'we love each other's children', *wie se handsak is dié?* 'whose handbag is this?', *die mense wie se plase deur die regering opgekoop is, moet nou 'n ander een probeer koop* 'the people whose farms have been bought up by the government now have to try and buy another', *dit is baie ou koppies. Kyk, hierdie (een) se/dié se oortjie het afgebreek* 'these are very old cups. Look, this one's/that one's handle has broken off'.

Use of the possessive form of the demonstrative can avoid the possible ambiguity of third-person possessive pronouns, e.g. *Koos en Jan en dié se pa* 'Koos and Jan and his (i.e. Jan's) father'.

Use of *s'n/s'ne*

Running parallel with the use of *se*, as well as that of *s'n(e)* in combination with the plural of independent possessive pronouns, is the use of these particles with nouns. In all the cases mentioned above in the discussion on *se*, *s'n/s'ne* renders possession where the noun or pronoun concerned is used independently, i.e. *Piet se vrou* 'Piet's wife', but *Piet s'n(e)* 'Piet's' (wife understood), e.g. *dis Amanda se ma se sambreel* 'it's Amanda's mother's umbrella', but *dis Amanda se ma s'n(e)*, 'it's Amanda's mother's', *ek weet nie wie s'n(e) dit is nie* 'I don't know whose it is', *vanjaar se oes is twee keer so groot soos verlede jaar s'n(e)* 'this year's harvest is twice as big as last year's'.

Use of *vir* with Personal Objects

The preposition *vir*, in addition to meaning 'for', also renders 'to' with reference to indirect personal objects, e.g. *ek het (vir) my tannie beloof dat ...* 'I promised my aunt that ...', *hy het dit vir my gesê/gegee* 'he told me/gave me it'.

But *vir* is also very commonly used before personal direct objects, although this practice tends to be limited to the spoken language, e.g. *ek sien vir jou later = ek sien jou later* 'I'll see you later', *hy het vir my geslaan* 'he hit me', *ons ken vir mekaar* 'we know each other'. This feature of Afrikaans is commonly cited as a possible instance of Portuguese influence.

Vir is also used with the relative pronoun *wie*, which turns a direct object *wat* into *wie* because relative *wie* is used after prepositions with reference to people, not *wat*, e.g. *dit is die vrou vir wie ek gister in die stad gesien het* (= *wat ek gister*) 'that's the woman I saw in town yesterday'.

Negation

Afrikaans has the following negators: *geen/g'n* 'no, not a/any', *geeneen* 'not one', *geensins* 'by no means, not in any way', *nêrens* 'nowhere', *nie* 'not', *niemand* 'no one, nobody', *niks* 'nothing', *nooit* 'never'. In certain limited contexts they function alone, but in the majority of cases they are complemented by a *nie*, termed the scope marker, which demarcates the extent of the negation, a function only clearly observable in compound sentences, e.g. *ek gaan dit nie koop nie hoewel ek genoeg geld het* 'I'm not going to buy it although I have enough money' – compare **ek gaan dit nie koop hoewel ek genoeg geld het nie*. If a sentence consists of only a subject and a finite verb, only a negator is required, e.g. *ek weet nie* 'I don't know', *hy bid nooit* 'he never prays'. If it consists of only a subject, a verb and a pronominal object, once again only a negator is required, e.g. *weet jy dit nie?* 'don't you know that?', *ek ken hom nie* 'I don't know him'. The negators *geen*, *geeneen*, *niemand*, and *niks*, being pronouns, can act as the subject of a sentence, in which case a scope marking *nie* is required, e.g. *geen mens weet nie* 'no one knows'.

If a nominal object, an adjective, an adverb or a separable prefix follows the verb, a scope marker is required, e.g. *ek ken nie daardie man nie* 'I don't know that man', *jy let nie op nie* 'you're not paying attention' (< *oplet*). If there is more than one verbal form in a negated clause, i.e. if the finite verb is followed by an infinitive or a past participle, a scope marker is also required, e.g. *hy sal nie kom nie* 'he won't come', *hy het nie gekom nie* 'he didn't come/hasn't come'. In effect this rule means that a sentence like *hy kom nie* requires only a negator in the present tense, but a negator plus a scope marker in the future and past tenses.

In a compound sentence consisting of a main clause and a subordinate clause, where the first clause is negated, a scope marker is most usually placed at the end of the second clause, not at the end of the first, e.g. *ek het nie geweet dat hy sou kom nie* 'I didn't know that he would be coming'. Although that is the norm, the following variants are possible: *ek het nie geweet nie dat hy sou kom*, *ek het nie geweet nie dat hy sou kom nie*. If only the second clause is negated, the following occurs: *ek het geweet dat hy nie sou kom nie* 'I knew he wouldn't be coming'. If both clauses are negated, the first clause contains a negator while the second contains a negator and a scope marker, e.g. *ek het nie geweet dat hy nie sou kom nie*. Where a negated relative clause is imbedded in a main clause, sense demands that the scope marker stand at the end of that relative clause, not at the end of the sentence, e.g. *mense wat nie rook nie lewe langer* 'people who don't smoke live longer'.

If a negated main clause is followed by a coordinate clause a scope marker is placed after the first clause, e.g. *hy kan nie kom nie want hy is siek* 'he won't be coming because he's sick'. If the clause following the negated main clause is an infinitive clause, a scope marker is placed at the end of the infinitive clause, e.g. *dis nie so moeilik om Afrikaans te leer nie* 'it isn't so difficult to learn Afrikaans'.

Where negators other than *nie* stand at the end of the sentence, addition of a scope marker is optional, e.g. *ek weet niks (nie)* 'I know nothing', *hy skryf nooit (nie)* 'he never writes', *ek ken niemand (nie)* 'I know nobody'. If *nooit*, *niks*, *niemand* or *nêrens* are uttered in isolation, i.e. not in the context of a sentence but as a reaction to something just stated, *nie* is optional, e.g. *gaan jy dit toelaat/ Nooit (nie)!* 'are you going to allow it? Never!'

The negators *nooit* and *nie* always follow pronominal objects, whether direct or indirect (i.e. those without a preposition), e.g. *hy het my nie gesien nie* 'he didn't see me'. A certain freedom exists as to the position of the negator in clauses containing nominal direct objects whether they be indefinite or definite, e.g. *ek het nog nooit 'n kar gehad nie* or *ek het 'n kar nog nooit gehad nie* 'I've never had a car', *ek het nog nie die sleutel gevind nie* or *ek het die sleutel nog nie gevind nie* 'I haven't found the key yet'.

15.5 Lexis

Afrikaans vocabulary is overwhemingly of Dutch origin, so much so that on paper at least the two are mutually intelligible, and even aurally after a minimum of exposure to the shifts in pronunciation of the vowels in particular. There are many common instances of Dutch words having either assumed or retained a different meaning from the cognate forms in Dutch, e.g. *aardig* 'peculiar' (Du. 'nice'), *leraar* 'preacher' (Du. 'teacher'), *stadig* 'slow' (Du. 'ceaselessly'). A number of terms previously only heard in the Dutch of seafaring folk have become everyday words in Afrikaans, e.g. *kombers* 'blanket' (Du. *kombaars* 'seaman's blanket'), *kombuis* 'kitchen' (Du. 'galley'), *spens* 'pantry'.

As many of the East India Company employees that stayed at the Cape had served in the Indies, as well as the fact that slaves were brought to the Cape from the Indies, a number of Malay words denoting everyday concepts have become an indispensable part of the language, e.g. *nooi* 'girl' (< *nonya*), *kapok* 'the/to snow', *piering* 'saucer', *piesang* 'banana'; *baie* 'much/many, very' (< *banjak*) has almost completely replaced Dutch *veel/heel*. It is possible that Malay had some role to play in the frequency of reduplicated forms in Afrikaans.

As Portuguese, like Malay, was a lingua franca of the Indies in the seventeenth century, some Portuguese loanwords also made their way into Afrikaans, e.g. *bredie* 'stew', *sambreel* 'umbrella', *tronk* 'prison'.

The influence of the indigenous languages (i.e. the Khoisan and Bantu languages) on the lexicon of Afrikaans has been minimal, being limited to a handful of cultural loanwords and a few exclamations.

Despite the fact that a very high proportion of Afrikaners have French surnames, the product of a substantial intake of Huguenot refugees in the 1680s, there is no trace of French influence to be found in Afrikaans, not even on the lexis, with the exception of course of the many French words which were present in Dutch.

Because of a perceived threat to the separate identity of Afrikaners *vis-à-vis* their English-speaking compatriots, there is a longstanding fear of those international loanwords with cognate forms in English such that they are now regarded as dispensable anglicisms with preference being given to indigenous synonyms. This phenomenon has lead to an overall impression of the vocabulary of Afrikaans being more Germanic than that of Dutch. Many ingenious neologisms, but above all loan translations from English, further contribute to the overall puristic impression of the vocabulary, e.g.

lugreëling 'air conditioning', *rekenariseer* 'to computerize', *toebroodjie* 'sandwich'; *droogskoonmaak* 'dry cleaning', *muurpapier* 'wall paper', *paneelklopper* 'panel beater'.

Further Reading

Donaldson, B. C. (1993) *A Grammar of Afrikaans*, Berlin: Mouton de Gruyter.
Ponelis, F. A. (1979) *Afrikaanse sintaksis*, Pretoria: Van Schaik.
—— (1993) *The Development of Afrikaans*, Frankfurt: Lang.
Raidt, E. H. (1983) *Einführung in Geschichte und Struktur des Afrikaans*, Darmstadt: Wissenschaftliche Buchgesellschaft.

16 Frisian

Jarich Hoekstra and Peter Meijes Tiersma

16.1 Introduction

Modern-day Frisian is commonly divided into three main dialectal areas: North, East, and West Frisian (see Figure 16.1). North Frisian is spoken by perhaps 10,000 people on the North Frisian islands and along the shores of the North Sea in Schleswig-Holstein, just below the Danish border. Remarkably, this small speech community is split into two major dialect groups: island and mainland North Frisian. Island North Frisian can be further subdivided into separate dialects for the islands of Söl (German *Sylt*), Feer (*Föhr*), Oomram (*Amrum*) and Helgoland. Mainland varieties also differ substantially from one another. No general variety of North Frisian has developed and the dialects are not always mutually intelligible.

The great linguistic variety in North Friesland is enhanced by the fact that this region is at the historic meeting point of the languages and territorial ambitions of Germany and Denmark. A number of people in North Friesland speak Danish, and that language (particularly the Jutish dialect) has influenced the Frisian spoken there. In addition, Low German, and more recently Standard German, have long served as lingua francas. Consequently, there are quadrilingual villages in which North Frisian, Jutish, Low and High German are all spoken, depending on the speaker and situation.

East Frisian is now spoken only in a small area of Germany known as Saterland, located between the city of Oldenburg and the Dutch frontier. Not to be confused with a type of Low German called *Ostfriesisch*, the real East Frisian was once extensively spoken throughout the countryside of what is known as *Ostfriesland*. Its use receded until the last speakers of the East Frisian island dialect of Wangeroog died at the beginning of this century, leaving Saterland as the remaining bastion of East Frisian. In the villages of Schäddel (German *Scharrel*), Strukelje (*Strücklingen*), and Roomelse (*Ramsloh*), there are presently some 1,000 speakers of East Frisian.

West Frisian is the language of the Dutch province of Friesland, although the provincial borders do not exactly mirror the Frisian-speaking region. Frisian has traditionally not been spoken in It Bilt (Dutch *Het Bildt*), an area reclaimed from the sea in the sixteenth century and settled by Dutch farmers.

Figure 16.1 The Frisian-speaking regions

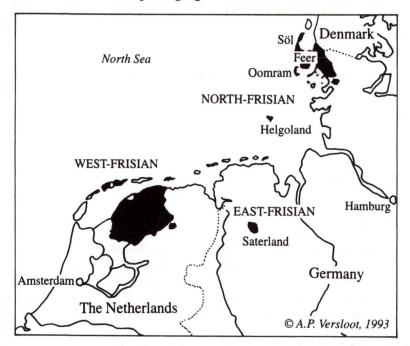

Furthermore, in the Stellingwerven, a strip of land between the river Tsjonger (*Kuinder*) and the province of Drenthe, and around Kollum in the northeast corner of the province, Saxon dialects are spoken, albeit with some Frisian influence. And residents of the larger West Frisian towns have for centuries spoken 'mixed' dialects that might be described as Frisian very heavily influenced by Dutch, or vice versa. These dialects, called *Stedfrysk* or 'Town Frisian', are found in Ljouwert (Dutch *Leeuwarden*), Snits (*Sneek*), Dokkum, Frjentsjer (*Franeker*), Boalsert (*Bolsward*), Harns (*Harlingen*) and Starum (*Staveren*). Both Town Frisian and, to a somewhat lesser extent, true West Frisian are under continual pressure from Dutch, the predominant language in the schools, churches, media and government. None the less, much progress has recently been made in promoting Frisian in the schools and elsewhere.

West Frisian has less dialectal diversity than North Frisian, which along with the greater number of speakers (some 400,000) does much to explain why it has developed a literary standard. Dialectical variation is mostly confined to the lexical and phonological level. Figure 16.2 shows the different dialects. The standard language is mainly based on *Klaaifrysk* (Clay Frisian). None the less, standard Frisian is rather tolerant as to the use of variants from the other main dialect, *Wâldfrysk* (Forest Frisian). The standard language does, however, avoid Dutch influence and is therefore more conservative than spoken Frisian.

Figure 16.2   The West-Frisian dialects

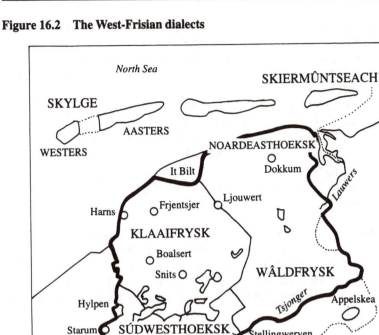

The dialects that differ most from the standard language are at the fringes of the Frisian-speaking area, in the city of Hylpen and on the islands Skiermûntseach and Skylge (where two Frisian dialects are spoken: *Aasters* and *Westers*). The most striking feature of these dialects is that they lack Modern West Frisian breaking (see section 16.2); where the central dialects underwent breaking, the peripheral dialects often exhibit shortening. Compare the alternation *peal* /pɪəl/ 'pole' – *peallen* /pjɛlən/ 'poles' in central dialects with Hylpen *pael – paelen*, Skiermûntseach *pail – pellen*, Aasters/Westers *peal – pellen*.

The dialect of the Súdwesthoeke (Southwest Corner) stands midway between the main dialects and the four dialects discussed above. It shows no breaking of *oa* and *oe* (cf. *doar* /doər/ 'door' – *dörren* /dœrən/, *foet* /fuət/ 'foot' – *futten* /føtən/), but it has imported breaking of *ie* and *ea* from the main dialects.

The Schiermûntseach dialect is the only West Frisian dialect that has retained the old three gender system: *dy baim* 'that tree' (m.); *jo tjark* 'that church' (f.); *dat búek* 'that book' (n.). Compare standard West Frisian: *dy beam*; *dy tsjerke*; *dat boek*.

The main dialects, *Klaaifrysk* (KF) and *Wâldfrysk* (WF), exhibit minimal differences:

1   The pronouns *my*, *dy*, *wy*, *sy* and the preposition *by* are pronounced with [ɛi] in *Klaaifrysk* and with [i] in *Wâldfrysk*.

2   The diphthong *ei* is pronounced [ai] or [ɔi] in *Klaaifrysk*, [ɛi] or sometimes [eː] in *Wâldfrysk*: *trein* 'train' [train], [trɔin] (KF), [trɛin], [treːn] (WF).

3   The diphthong *ea* before velar consonants is pronounced [ɪə] in *Klaaifrysk*, [ɛː] in *Wâldfrysk*: *each* 'eye' [ɪəx] (KF), [ɛːx] (WF).

4   *Klaaifrysk* [u] before *n* corresponds with *Wâldfrysk* [o(ː)]: *ûn-* 'un-' (prefix) (KF), *on-* (WF); *tûne* 'cask' (KF), *tonne* (WF); *hûn* 'dog' [hun] (KF), [hoːn] (WF).

5   *Klaaifrysk* [o] before *m* corresponds to *Wâldfrysk* [u]: *tomme* 'thumb' (WF), *tûme* (KF).

A subdialect of *Klaaifrysk*, the dialect of the *Noardeasthoeke* (Northeast Corner), basically follows *Wâldfrysk* with respect to properties (2–5).

Because it is, unfortunately, impossible to do justice to the diverse varieties of Frisian in one short article, standard West Frisian will form the basis for this description. East and North Frisian will receive special attention in an appendix.

16.2   Phonology

Vowels

Frisian has an extensive vowel inventory, containing nine short vowels, nine long vowels and a number of diphthongs. The vowels are shown on Table 16.1. In addition to the full vowels, Frisian has a schwa, which is phonetically quite similar to /ø/, but occurs only in unstressed syllables. There are furthermore a number of what are called falling diphthongs: full vowels followed by schwa, like /iə/. Other diphthongs consist of two full vowels, such as /ɛi/.

Several phonological processes affect the Frisian vowels. A vowel plus /n/ combination becomes a nasalized vowel when it precedes one of the continuant consonants /s, z, f, v, j, r, l, w/. For example, *ûns* 'ounce' is pronounced [ũːs]. This example shows that a nasalized vowel before /s/ or /z/ is also lengthened.

Shortening is a morphophonemic process that affects mainly long vowels in monosyllabic stems. Most commonly, this occurs when a plural or diminutive suffix is appended to a noun, as when the long vowel in *faam* /faːm/ 'girl, maid' alternates with the corresponding short vowel in *fammen* /famən/ 'girls' and *famke* /famkə/ 'young girl'. Less frequently, shortening occurs before other suffixes. Compare *heech* /heːx/ 'high' with *hichte* /hɪxtə/ 'height' and *baarch* /baːrx/ 'pig' with *bargje* /barɣjə/ 'make a mess'.

Another process, called 'breaking', refers to the alternation in which falling

Table 16.1   The Frisian vowels and diphthongs

Vowel	Spelling
[i]	*i* in orthographically open and *y* in closed syllables (*Piter/Pyt*)
[iː]	*i* in orthographically open and *ii* in closed syllables (*wider/wiid*)
[ɪ]	*i**
[eː]	*e* in orthographically open and *ee* in closed syllables
[ɛ]	*e**
[ɛː]	*ê*
[a]	*a**
[aː]	*a* in orthographically open and *aa* in closed syllables
[ɔ]	*o* (or *a* before dentals)*
[ɔː]	*â, ô*
[o]	*o**
[oː]	*o* in orthographically open and *oo* in closed syllables
[u]	*û, oe*
[uː]	*û, oe*
[y]	*u* in orthographically open and *ú* in closed syllables
[yː]	*u* in orthographically open and *ú* in closed syllables
[ø]	*u**
[øː]	*eu*
[ə]	mostly *e* (in unstressed syllables)

Diphthongs	Spelling
[iə]	*ie*
[ɪə]	*ea*
[uə]	*oe*
[oə]	*oa*
[yə]	*ue*
[øə]	*eo, eau*
[ɛi]	*y, ij*
[øy]	*ui*
[ui]	*oei*
[oəi]	*oai*
[aːi]	*aai*
[ai]	*ei, ai*
[au]	*ou, au*

Note: *Generally only occurs in orthographically closed syllables.

diphthongs in monosyllabic stems alternate with rising (broken) diphthongs when a suffix is added to the stem. Unfortunately, breaking is usually not reflected in the orthography. There are four main sets of alternating pairs of diphthongs (with the falling and rising diphthongs presented in that order): /iə/ – /jɪ/ (*stien* /stiən/ 'stone', *stiennen* /stjɪnən/ 'stones'); /ɪə/–/jɛ/ (*beam* /bɪəm/ 'tree', *beammen* /bjɛmən/ 'trees'); /uə/ – /wo/ (*foet* /fuət/ 'foot', *fuotten* /fwotən/ 'feet'); and /oə/ – /wa/ (*doar* /doər/ 'door', *doarke* /dwarkə/

'small door'). As with shortening, breaking is probably most common in noun diminutives and plurals, although it also occurs in derivation and compounding. For instance, broken diphthongs are found in words like *beammich* /bjɛməx/ 'wooded', *jierdei* /jɪdi/ 'birthday', *siedzje* /sjɪdzjə/ 'sow', and *Iester* /jɪstər/ 'resident of (the village of) Ie'.

Shortening and breaking occur in roughly the same morphological environments. A generalization that holds for many cases is that if the plural of a noun undergoes either shortening or breaking, the diminutive does also. None the less, it is impossible to state that certain stems invariably undergo the process. For example, *tiid* 'time' is not shortened in the plural, but *is* as the first member of the compound *tydskrift* 'periodical'. *Hân* 'hand', by contrast, undergoes the process in the plural (*hannen*), but not as first member of the compound *hânskrift* 'manuscript'.

Consonants

A list of the Frisian consonants is presented in Table 16.2. For the most part, the phonetic symbols for the consonants overlap with the orthography. Observe, however, that [x] is spelled as ‹ch›, while [ɣ] is generally written ‹g›. [ŋ] is ‹ng›, and [v] is ‹w› when in initial position.

Various types of assimilation and sandhi occur in Frisian. For example, /n/ assimilates to the place of articulation of the following stop, as when *yn* /in/ 'in' and *bine* /binə/ 'bind' are combined to form *ynbine* [imbinə] 'bind into'. When a voiceless stop at the end of one word encounters a voiced stop at the beginning of the next, both are generally voiced. For example, *ik bin* 'I am' is phonetically [ɪg bɪn]. But when what follows is a function word such as *dit* 'this', *dat* 'that', *dizze* 'this', *dyn* 'your', the adjoining consonants tend to become voiceless: *op dyn* is pronounced [op tin]. Similarly, a voiceless fricative in final position followed by a vowel or voiced consonant becomes voiced: *hûs is* 'house is' is pronounced [huːz ɪs].

Also common to spoken Frisian is syllabification. A syllable consisting of schwa plus a liquid or nasal usually becomes syllabified. For example, *bûter* 'butter' is phonetically [butr̩]. The process is quite common with the plural

Table 16.2 The Frisian consonants

	Bilabial	Labiodental	Dental	Palatal	Velar	Labiovelar	Glottal
Stops	p b		t d		k g		
Fricatives		f v	s z		x ɣ		
Trill			r				
Lateral			l				
Glides				j		w	h
Nasals	m		n		ŋ		

suffix *-en*, which not only becomes a syllabified *n*, but also generally assimilates to the place of articulation of the preceding consonant: *skippen* 'ships' becomes [skɪpm̩] and *ljurken* 'larks' becomes [ljørkŋ̩]

As in German and Dutch, word-final obstruents are always unvoiced, although the process appears to be of recent origin in Frisian. Compare *reed* /reːt/ 'road, lane' with its plural *reden* /reːdən/ and *slab* /slap/ 'bib' with *slabben* /slabən/. Before a suffix, the situation is more complex. Devoicing always takes place before a diminutive suffix: *reedsje* /reːtsjə/; *slabke* /slapkə/. It is less regular with other suffixes. Compare *soarchlik* /swarxlək/ 'sorrowful' with *deeglik* /deːɣlək/ 'proper'.

There are various types of consonant cluster simplification in Frisian. For example, degemination applies to identical obstruents that become contiguous. Also, the stem-final cluster /st/ is often reduced to /s/ before the diminutive suffix or the verbal suffixes *-ke* or *-je*: the diminutive of *kwast* 'paint brush' is *kwastke* /kwaskə/, while *hoastje* 'cough' is pronounced /wasjə/. *Hoastje* shows that before a glide, *h* is deleted in most dialects, as reflected also in *hierren* /jɪrən/ 'hairs'. Additionally, a stem-final /t/ is generally deleted before the suffix *-st*: *bytst* '(you) bite' is phonetically /bist/.

One might also refer to the deletion of /r/ before the dental consonants /t, d, n, l, s, z/ as a type of consonant cluster simplification. In most cases, the *r* is present orthographically, so to a large extent this is a rule of pronouncing written Frisian. The word *bern* 'child, children' is phonetically [bɛːn] or [bɛn] and *gers* 'grass' is [gɛːs]. The *r* also disappears when it comes to stand before a dental consonant through inflection, as can be seen by comparing *far* [far] '(I) sail' with *farst* '(you) sail' and *fier* [fiər] 'far' with its superlative form *fierst* [fjɪst] (this form, incidentally, also undergoes breaking).

Affrication of stem-final /t/ and /d/ to /ts/ and /dz/, respectively, occurs before the *-je* suffix. Hence, past tense forms *skodde* 'shook' and *rotte* 'rotted' have the infinitives *skodzje* and *rotsje*.

In standard West Frisian, a final *d* has been dropped historically from a few words like *sie* 'seed', *trie* 'wire', and *dea* 'death', although it often remains in inflected forms such as *siedzje* 'sow', *triedden* 'wires', and *deade* 'dead'. Likewise, the *d* has disappeared from verbs like *soe* 'should', *woe* 'would' and *die* 'did', but remains when the clitic *er* 'he' follows one of these verbs: *woed er* 'would he'. Many speakers have reanalysed this phenomenon into a rule that the clitic *er* has the variant *der* when directly preceded by a vowel or sonorant: *woe der* 'would he'; *foel der* 'fell he'. Insertion of /d/ occurs mandatorily between a stem ending in /r/ and the suffix *-er*, but is optional with stems ending in /l/ and /n/: *djoer* 'expensive, dear' – *djurder* 'more expensive'; *hiere* 'rent' – *hierder* 'renter'; *rinne* 'walk' – *rinder* or *rinner* 'walker'.

The consonants written as ‹g› or ‹ch› also deserve brief mention. What is written as ‹g› is generally the voiced velar stop [g] at the beginning of a word, as in *gean* 'go', but usually represents a voiced velar fricative [ɣ] elsewhere, as in *bargje* 'make a mess'. This fricative undergoes devoicing and assimilation as do other voiced fricatives, producing words like *baarch* [baːrx] 'pig'. In addition, if /x/ comes to stand before an /s/, it usually dissimilates to [k]: *heechst* 'highest' [heːkst].

Syllable Structure

Frisian syllable structure is in many respects similar to German and Dutch, differing most dramatically in the large variety of complex consonant clusters allowed in initial position. Most of these clusters are the same as those permitted in German or Dutch, but allow the addition of a /j/ or /w/ as final element of the cluster. Not surprisingly, clusters that end in /j/ or /w/ are often the result of breaking.

For example, /j/ and /w/ can follow most initial consonants: *poarte* /pwatə/ 'gate', *peallen* /pjɛlən/ 'poles', *doarren* /dwarən/ 'doors', *djoer* /djuər/ 'expensive', *wjirm* /vjɪrm/ 'worm' and *woarst* /vwast/ 'sausage'. Where German and Dutch allow two initial consonants (generally an obstruent plus liquid), Frisian permits clusters of three (an obstruent, liquid and glide): *priuwe* /prjowə/ 'taste', *triuwe* /trjowə/ 'push', *knoarre* /knwarə/ 'a lot', *bruorren* /brworən/ 'brothers' and *snoarkje* /snwarkjə/ 'snore'. Clusters of four consonants are also possible: *strjitte* /strjɪtə/ 'street', *skriuwe* /skrjowə/ 'write' and *skroarje* /skrwarjə/ '(to) tailor'.

Prosodic Phenomena

Generally, native monomorphemic words of more than one syllable are stressed on the first element: *'suster* 'sister', *'hynder* 'horse', *'biezem* 'broom'. Exogenous (especially French) words often receive stress on the final syllable, unless that syllable contains a schwa or syllabic consonant: *pa'pier* 'paper', *restau'rant* 'restaurant', *ge'raazje* 'garage'.

As a very rough principle, compounds with an adjective as first element are stressed on the second part, as with *jong'faam* 'young woman'. Those with nouns as first element are generally stressed on the first part: *'heitelân* 'fatherland'. Most suffixes are unstressed: *'skriuwster* '(woman) writer'; *'boadskip* 'message'; *'smoargens* 'dirt'. Exceptions to this rule are *-esse* and *-inne* (both creating a female agent) and *-erij*: *freon'dinne* 'girlfriend'; *prin'sesse* 'princess'; *bakke'rij* 'bakery'. Prefixes operate much like those in Dutch and German. Some are never stressed (such as *be-*, *fer-* and *te-*), others (like *oar-* in *oarsaak* 'cause' and *ant-* in *antwurd* 'answer') always are. In addition, Frisian parallels German and Dutch in having separable and inseparable prefixes, with similar stress patterns.

16.3   Morphology

The Nominal Group

The indefinite article *in* [ən] 'a, an' occurs only with singular count nouns. *De* [də] and *it* [ət] are the definite articles, *it* preceding singular neuter nouns and *de* singular common nouns and all plurals. The classification into neuter and common nouns is largely arbitrary from a synchronic standpoint, at least with respect to natural gender. Neuter nouns in German are usually neuter in Frisian, and masculine and feminine nouns in German are usually common in Frisian.

It is often reduced to *'t* both in speech and writing: *fan't jier* 'this year'; *'t wie hjerst* 'it was autumn'. Furthermore, *de* is often rendered *'e* in prepositional phrases like *op 'e mar* 'on the lake'. This occurs primarily following *op* 'on', *yn* 'in', *nêst* 'next to', *om* 'around', *út* 'out of', *tsjin* 'against', *fan* 'from', *ûnder* 'under', *efter* 'behind' and *tusken* 'between'. Some temporal expressions with the preposition *fan* or *by* may use the neuter article even if the following noun is common. Compare *de maitiid* 'spring' and *de simmer* 'summer' with *fan 't maitiid* 'this spring' and *fan 't simmer* 'this summer' or *by 't simmer* 'in the summer'.

The determiner *gjin* 'no, none' is never inflected. On the other hand, *sok* 'such', which occurs before mass neuter nouns (*sok gers* 'such grass'), becomes *sa'n* before singular count nouns (*sa'n hynder* 'such a horse'), and *sokke* before plural nouns (*sokke tosken* 'such teeth') and mass common nouns (*sokke sûpengroattenbrij* 'such buttermilk porridge'). This determiner can also be used substantively: *soks* 'something like that'; *sa'nen ien* 'one like that'; *sokken* 'those kind of things/people'.

The demonstrative pronouns are *dat* 'that' and *dit* 'this' for singular neuter nouns: *dat famke* 'that girl'; *dit hea* 'this hay'. *Dy* 'that, those' and *dizze* 'this, these' precede common nouns (*dy frou* 'that woman'; *dizze wjerljocht* 'this lightening') and all plural nouns (*dy froulju* 'those women'; *dizze famkes* 'these girls').

Predicative adjectives are uninflected: *de loft is skier* 'the sky is grey'. Attributive adjectives are inflected with *-e* before common singular nouns and all plurals: *de skiere loft* 'the grey sky'; *in griene beam* 'a green tree'; *goede buorlju* 'good neighbours'. Before a neuter singular noun, the *-e* ending is added only when the adjective follows *it*, *dit*, or *dat*. Compare *droech waar* 'dry weather' and *sok droech waar* 'such dry weather' with *dit droege waar* 'this dry weather'.

The adjective may optionally be uninflected in the following types of phrases: (a) before *man* and words referring to occupations (*in ryk boer* 'a rich farmer'); and (b) when the adjective, particularly *âld*, *nij*, *jong*, *lyts* and *grut*, and the following noun enter into a fixed collocation, becoming virtually a compound: *de jongfaam* 'the young woman'; *dy âld skuorre* 'that old shed'.

When an adjective is preceded by *in*, *gjin*, or *sa'n* and followed by *ien* 'one' or no nominal element at all, it takes the suffix *-en*, as in the phrase *in minnen* (*ien*) 'a bad one'. After certain words, most commonly *wat* 'something', *neat* 'nothing' and *wat foar* 'what kind of', adjectives take the ending *-s*: *neat nijs* 'nothing new'.

The comparative is formed by affixing *-er* to the stem. This form is inflected like the positive: *in grienere beam* 'a greener tree'; *droeger waar* 'dryer weather'; *dit droegere waar* 'this dryer weather'.

Superlatives are created by the suffix *-ste* when used attributively, regardless of gender: *de grienste beam* 'the greenest tree'; *it wietste sân* 'the wettest sand'. In predicate position the suffix may be either *-ste* or *-st*: compare *dy beam is it grienst* with its equivalent *dy beam is it grienste* 'that tree is greenest' and *dat sân is it wietst* with *dat sân is it wietste* 'that sand is wettest'.

There are no real case markings in contemporary West Frisian, with the possible exception of the genitive *-s*. Possession is most commonly indicated by phrasal constructions, discussed in the section on syntax. Consequently, the main morphological phenomenon in nouns is plural and diminutive formation. These suffixes are determined primarily by phonological criteria, not gender. The plural marker for native words ending in *em, en, el, er, ert* is generally *-s*: *wurkers* 'workers'; *woartels* 'carrots'. The same *-s* plural is also used with all diminutives: *kealtsjes* 'small calves'. Most other native words take *-en*: *seinen* 'scythes'; *tsjerken* 'churches'. Many borrowings take the *-s* plural despite their phonetic structure, as in *auto's*. And, of course, several nouns have irregular plural formation, which may include invariable plurals (*bern* 'child/children'; *skiep* 'sheep'), double plural marking (*reed/ redens* 'skate/skates') and synchronically less transparent phenomena (*ko/kij* 'cow/cows'; *skoech/skuon* 'shoe/shoes').

Diminutives are quite commonly used to indicate that something is small or to express affection. When a stem ends in a vowel, a labial consonant /m, p, b, f/, or /s/ or /r/, the regular suffix is *-ke*: *kaike* 'small key'; *wyfke* 'small woman'. With words ending in the dentals /l, n, t, d/, the suffix is *-tsje*, as in *kealtsje* 'small calf' and *pûdsje* 'small bag'. Finally, when a stem ends in the velars /k/ or /x/, the ending is *-je*: *barchje* 'small pig'. After the velar nasal /ŋ/, the suffix is *-kje*: *ring* 'ring', *rinkje* 'small ring'.

As noted above, many nouns undergo shortening or breaking of the stem vowel in both the plural and the diminutive. Furthermore, there is a very small number of nouns that resist diminutive formation, particularly words for periods of time (*dei* 'day'; *wike* 'week'; *moanne* 'month'), and certain monetary units (*gûne* 'guilder'; *sint* 'cent').

The Frisian pronouns are listed on Table 16.3. The second-person singular is divided into familiar and polite forms. It is common to use terms of address in place of the second-person pronoun, especially (but not exclusively) among family members. These might be referred to as *pronoun substitutes*. While it is not improper to address an older family member with the polite form *jo*,

Table 16.3   Frisian pronouns

Person/number	Subject	Object	Possessive
1 sg.	ik 'I'	my 'me'	myn 'my'
2 sg. fam.	do 'you'	dy 'you'	dyn 'your'
2 sg. pol.	jo 'you'	jo 'you'	jo/jins 'your'
3 sg. m.	hy 'he'	him 'him'	syn 'his'
f.	hja/sy 'she'	har 'her'	har 'her'
n.	it 'it'	it 'it'	syn 'its'
indefinite	men 'one'	jin 'him/her'	jins 'one's'
1 pl.	wy 'we'	ús 'us'	ús 'our'
2 pl.	jimme 'you'	jimme 'you'	jimme 'you'
3 pl.	hja/sy 'they'	har(ren) 'them'	har(ren) 'their'

it is more usual to use a term of address (like *heit* 'father', *muoike* 'aunt' or *dokter* 'doctor') and the third-person verb: *wol mem in bakje kofje?* 'does mother (do you) want a cup of coffee?'; *hoe giet it mei pake?* 'how is grandfather?' (or 'how are you, grandfather?'). This usage avoids the distance created by the formal *jo* pronoun. Furthermore, a person's name may also be used as a pronoun substitute: *Durk moat ris by ús útfanhûs* 'Durk (you) should come stay with us some time'. The third-person pronoun *hy* or *hja/sy* may be used in speaking to children: *hy moat stil wêze* 'you must be quiet'.

The pronoun *do* is optionally deleted: *bist let* 'you are late'. *Jo* takes a plural verb. The pronoun for 'she' or 'they' is in spoken Frisian almost always *sy* or *se*. In literary and formal contexts *hja* is preferred, largely because *sy* is felt to reflect Dutch influence. The means of distinguishing these two uses of *hja* (or *sy*) is, of course, the number of the associated verb. The indefinite pronoun *men* [mən], used with a singular verb, generally includes the speaker. Sometimes *jo* or *do* is used in an indefinite sense also, as is the third person plural.

There are reduced or cliticized versions of many of the pronouns. For example, *ik* and *it* may be reduced in casual speech to [k] and [t] when phonotactic constraints allow, producing sentences such as *'k wie thús* 'I was at home' and *'k hie 't sjoen* 'I had seen it'. *Jimme* is often pronounced *jim*. *Hy* has the clitic form *er*, which occurs directly following a finite verb or subordinating conjunction: *docht er alles?* 'is he doing everything?' *Do* has the clitic form *-de* or *-te* in the same environment, or may be dropped entirely: *giesto/gieste/giest fuort?* 'are you going away?'; *ik wit datsto/datste/datst hjir bist* 'I know that you are here'.

The possessive pronouns, when modifying a noun, are not inflected: *ús nije wein* 'our new wagon'. Predicatively, however, they receive the suffix *-es*: *dat aai is dines* 'that egg is yours'; *dy aaien binne uzes* 'those eggs are ours'.

There are no separate reflexive pronouns in Frisian. Rather, the object forms of the personal pronouns perform this function: *omke skeart him* 'Uncle is shaving (himself)'. In order to add emphasis, or to make it clear that the pronoun is being used reflexively, *-sels* can be added: *it bern sjocht harsels yn 'e spegel* 'the child sees herself in the mirror'. Reciprocal pronouns are *inoar* or *elkoar* 'each other': *hja seagen inoar yn 'e eagen* 'they looked each other in the eyes'. These pronouns are often appended to a preposition: *meiinoar* 'with one another'; *opelkoar* 'on top of each other'.

The relative pronouns are *dy't* (common) and *dat* (neuter): *de kij dy't oer it fjild rinne* 'the cattle which are walking over the field'. *Dêr't* is used to designate places: *it doarp dêr't er wennet* 'the village where he lives'.

Question words include *wat* 'what'; *wat foar* 'what kind of'; *wa* 'who'; *waans* or *wa's* 'whose'; *hoe* 'how'; *hoefolle* 'how much'; *wannear* 'when'; and *wêr* 'where'. *Hoe'n, hok, hokke,* and *hokker* all mean 'what kind of' or 'which'. *Hok* occurs before mass neuter nouns (*hok sân?* 'what kind of sand?'); *hokke* before plurals and mass common nouns (*hokke sjippe?* 'what kind of soap?'); *hoe'n* is used with singular count nouns (*hoe'n hûn?* 'what kind of dog?'); and *hokker* before all types of nouns (*hokker sân?*; *hokker sjippe?*; *hokker hûn?*).

The Verbal Group

Although Germanic verbs are often divided into weak and strong, a more sensible division in modern West Frisian is between Class I (ending in *-e*) and Class II (ending in *-je*). Class membership determines which endings a verb takes. The present-tense forms for the two classes are illustrated on Table 16.4. Recall that *jo* takes plural endings.

Strong verbs mainly end in *-e* and are therefore conjugated according to Class I. Verbs with stem changes ending in *-je*, of course, take the endings of Class II verbs. A number of verbs have irregular present-tense formation, often showing vowel changes in the second- and third-person singular forms: *ik gean* 'I go'; *do giest* 'you go'; *hy giet* 'he goes'; *wy geane* 'we go'. Other verbs reflect historical alternation between *k* and *ts(j)*: *ik meitsje* 'I make'; *do makkest* 'you make'; *hja makket* 'she makes'; *wy meitsje* 'we make'.

It is possible to analyse all verbs as having the same personal endings in

Table 16.4   Present-tense verb endings

Person/Number	Class I	Class II
Infinitive	meane 'to mow'	harkje 'to listen'
1 sg.	ik mean 'I mow'	ik harkje 'I listen'
2 sg.	do meanst 'you mow'	do harkest 'you listen'
3 sg.	hja meant 'she mows'	hja harket 'she listens'
pl.	wy meane 'we mow'	wy harkje 'we listen'

the simple past: no marker in the first- and third-person singular; -st in the second-person singular; and -en for all plurals and the jo form.

The simple past-tense stem for regular Class I verbs is formed by adding -de to the stem, or -te if the stem ends in a voiceless obstruent. Thus, the past tense of meane is meande, while that of rûke 'smell' is rûkte. The personal endings are added to these forms. When a suffix with a schwa is added to a stem ending in schwa, only one schwa remains: meande plus -en produces meanden. Class II verbs regularly produce the preterite by the addition of -e to the stem. Thus, the past tense of harkje 'listen' is harke. Strong verbs form the past tense by changes in the stem vowel and, less commonly, also by consonant changes. Compare fergeat 'forgot' and hong 'hung' with the infinitive ferjitte and hingje. The same personal endings are used: do fergeatst 'you forgot'.

The formation of the past tense is illustrated on Table 16.5. The table also shows that the present participle is formed by adding -nd to the infinitive. The past participle is irregular for many historically strong verbs. For Class II verbs, it is identical to the past-tense stem. And for regular Class I verbs it is formed by the addition of -d or -t, the -t being suffixed to stems that take -te as the past-tense marker.

The present perfect consists of the inflected verb hawwe 'have' and the past participle, while the past perfect uses the preterite of hawwe as the auxiliary: ik ha songen 'I have sung', hja hiene songen 'they had sung'. The future consists of the inflected verb sille 'shall' and the infinitive (do silst sjonge 'you will sing'), and the future perfect consists of sille and the past participle of the verb, followed by hawwe in infinitive form (wy sille songen hawwe 'we will have sung'). Finally, the conditional is formed with the auxiliary soe (the past tense of sille) and the infinitive; the perfect conditional is also formed with soe, followed by the past participle and hawwe: jo soene harkje 'you would listen', do soest harke hawwe 'you would have listened'. Conditionals may also be created with past tense morphology. As in other Germanic

Table 16.5 Non-present verb forms

Person/Number	Class I	Class II	Strong verb
Infinitive	meane 'mow'	harkje 'listen'	sjonge 'sing'
Past 1 sg.	meande	harke	song
2 sg.	meandest	harkest	songst
3 sg.	meande	harke	song
pl.	meanden	harken	songen
Present participle	meanend	harkjend	sjongend
Past participle	meand	harke	songen
Imperative	mean	harkje	sjong

languages, certain verbs, particularly those referring to changes in state and motion, take *wêze* 'be' in place of *hawwe*.

Present-tense passives are created with the conjugated form of the verb *wurde* 'become' and the past participle: *do wurdst sjoen* 'you are seen'. The preterite passive is similar but uses the past tense of *wurde*: *ik waard sjoen* 'I was seen'. The present and past perfect passives are formed by the present and preterite inflected forms of *wêze*, then the past participle, and followed optionally in some dialects by *wurden* (the past participle of *wurde*): *ik bin sjoen* (*wurden*) 'I have been seen', *ik wie sjoen* (*wurden*) 'I had been seen'. The future passive consists of the auxiliary *sille*, the past participle, and *wurde* in infinitive form (*ik sil sjoen wurde* 'I will be seen'), while the conditional passive is the same but uses *soe* (*ik soe sjoen wurde* 'I would be seen'). Finally, the future perfect passive consists of *sille*, the past participle, optionally includes *wurden*, and then the infinitive form *wêze*: *ik sil sjoen* (*wurden*) *wêze* 'I will have been seen'. The perfect conditional passive is the same, but uses *soe* in place of *sille*: *ik soe sjoen* (*wurden*) *wêze* 'I would have been seen'.

Adverbs
As in Dutch and German, many adjectives can function as adverbs with no particular morphological marker. *Goed* can be either the adjective 'good' or the adverb 'well'. Some distinct adverbs consist of a noun or adjective with suffixes such as *-ling* (*hoasfuotling* 'on stockinged feet') or the diminutive + *s* (*súntsjes* 'softly'). Certain adverbs that derive from adjectives and serve an intensifying function take an *-e* suffix when preceding the adjective they modify: *it wie ferskriklike kâld* 'it was terribly cold' (cf. *ferskriklik* 'terrible'). Finally, nouns referring to time become adverbs with the addition of *-s*, as in *middeis* 'in the afternoons'; *sneons* 'on Saturdays'. When referring to a specific time instead of a period of time generally, the article is added: *de sneins* 'that Sunday'; *de moarns* 'that morning'.

Word Formation
Frisian follows the general patterns of Germanic word formation. As in other Germanic languages, the most frequent type of compound combines two nouns: *bûsdoek* 'handkerchief' (lit. 'pocket cloth'), *appelsop* 'apple juice', *sinneljocht* 'sunlight'. Also very common is the verb-noun type: *sliepkeamer* 'bedroom' (lit. 'sleeping room'), *waskmasine* 'washing machine', *printflater* 'printer's error'. Like German and Dutch, Frisian makes extensive use of 'link morphemes': *koken-s-doar* 'kitchen door', *bern-e-boek* 'children's book', *riz-en-brij* 'rice pudding', *rol-tsje-redens* 'roller-skates', *hing-el-brêge* 'suspension-bridge', *boart-ers-guod* 'playthings'.

Rather specific to Frisian is the relatively large number of noun-verb and adjective-noun compounds. The noun-verb type consists of lexicalized noun-incorporation verbs: *koffjedrinke* (lit.) 'coffee-drink', *lokwinskje* (lit.) 'luck-wish', *sykhelje* (lit.) 'breath-take'. Whereas noun-incorporation is limited to adjacent nouns and verbs (see section 16.4), these lexicalized verbs may appear in any verb position, for example, in the verb-second position: *hja noassnute lûd* (lit.) 'she nose-blew loudly'.

Adjective-noun compounds originate from syntactic phrases which have been reanalysed as one word, generally with loss of the adjective's inflection. Some examples are *jongkat* 'kitten' (lit. 'young-cat'), *kweageast* 'evil spirit', *swierwaar* 'thunderstorm' (lit. 'heavy weather'), *Goedfreed* 'Good Friday'.

Prefixes include verbal prefixes like *be-* (*beprate* 'talk over'), *fer-* (*ferslite* 'wear out'), *te-* (*teskuorre* 'tear to pieces') and *ûnt-* (*ûntkrije* 'take away'), which all have a transitivizing and/or perfectivizing effect. Most other prefixes combine with adjectives and serve a negative or intensifying function: *ûn-* (*ûnwier* 'untrue'); *poer-* (*poermin* 'very bad'); *witte-* (*witteheech* 'very high'); *troch-* (*trochwiet* 'very wet'); *yn-* (*ynwyt* 'very pale') and the negative polarity item *oer-* ((*net*) *oersnoad* '(not) very clever').

Among the suffixes deriving nouns from nouns are the diminutive, the collective suffixes *-t* and *-guod* (*fûgelt*, *fûgelguod* 'birds'), feminine suffixes *-inne*, *-esse* and *-ske* (*boerinne* 'farmer's wife', *profetesse* 'prophetess', *foarsitterske* 'chairwoman') and the quantifying suffix *-mannich* (*in rigelmannich* 'some lines').

The suffix *-er* derives agentive nouns and, more marginally, object, instrument and action nouns from verbs: *bodder* 'toiler', *omparter* 'hand-out', *hierdroeger* 'hair dryer', *snjitter* 'brief rain shower'. Descriptive nouns are derived from adjectives by suffixes like *-ert* (*leffert* 'coward'), *-eling* (*healwizeling* 'fool') and, interestingly, by *-sma* (*ferfelendsma* 'bore'), which originates from the ending *-sma* in Frisian surnames like *Tiersma*. The ending *-stra* in surnames like *Hoekstra* has also become marginally productive in the formation of descriptive nouns, as in *typstra* 'freak'.

The most important suffixes deriving nouns from verbs and adjectives are perhaps the nominalizing suffixes. The suffixes *-en*, *-ing* and *-erij* (as well as the prefix *ge-*) are added to verbs to form action nouns. Whereas *-en* is normally used for transparent nominalizations (*praten* 'talking'), *ing*-derivations are more open to semantic drift (*blieding* 'bleeding', *útstalling* 'exhibition'). The affixes *-erij* and *ge-* form collective (often somewhat pejorative) nominalizations: *skriuwerij* 'writing', *geëamel* 'chatter, drivel'.

This pattern is repeated with de-adjectival nominalizations. The suffix *-ens* forms transparent abstract nouns (*goedens* 'goodness', *blauwens* 'blueness'), while derivations with *-heid* often show meaning specification: *iensumheid* 'loneliness, lonely place', *aardichheid* 'something nice'. The suffix *-ichheid* produces collective (often slightly pejorative) abstract nouns: *grutskichheid* 'haughtiness'.

Verbs can be derived from verbs by the iterative/diminutive suffix *-k*: *drave – drafkje* 'trot', *aaie – aikje* 'caress', *gnize – gnyskje* 'sneer'. The derivation of verbs from other (non-verbal) categories proceeds by means of conversion, which involves simply the addition of verbal morphology: *healwiizje* 'act foolish' (*healwiis* 'foolish'), *fjouwerje* 'gallop' (*fjouwer* 'four'), *útfanhúzje* 'stay, lodge' (*út fan hûs* 'out of (the) house'). The stem of a converted verb may be augmented by a semantically empty *k-/t*-element: *fûstkje* 'shake hands', *briefkje* 'write letters', *sintsje* 'sunbathe'. Note that verbs derived by suffixation or conversion invariably belong to what is probably the unmarked conjugation class in Frisian, Class II.

16.4   Syntax

Noun Phrase

The minimal noun phrase in Frisian consists of a pronoun or a proper name (*do* 'you', *Jan* 'John'). Otherwise noun phrases at least contain a determiner and a nominal head: *de hûn* 'the dog'; *in boek* 'a book'. The determiner may be a zero article in the case of plural and mass nouns: Ø *wolkens* 'clouds', Ø *rein* 'rain'.

Attributive adjectives precede the nominal head: *de kreaze faam* 'the pretty girl'. Modifiers and complements, which take the shape of clauses or prepositional phrases, follow the nominal head. Compare *it hûs by de feart* 'the house near the canal', *de man dy't fermoarde wie* 'the man who was killed', *in boek oer de oarloch* 'a book about the war', *syn besykjen om ús te helpen* 'his attempt to help us'.

Numerals and quantifiers are prenominal and normally precede the adjective if there is one: *fjouwer reade auto's* 'four red cars', *guon moaie gebouwen* 'some beautiful buildings'. Numerals precede indefinite determiners like *sa'n, sok(ke)* 'such a, such', while they follow definite determiners like *dy* 'that, those, these': *tsien sokke stuollen* 'ten such chairs', *dy tsien stuollen* 'those ten chairs'. Most indefinite quantifiers occur before an indefinite determiner: *in soad sok ark* 'a lot of such tools', *ferskate sokke minsken* 'various such people', *gâns in stêd* 'quite a city'. Some may also follow a definite determiner: *de ferskate minsken* 'the various people'. Definite quantifiers like *alle* 'all' and *elk* 'each' are probably determiners themselves and cannot co-occur with other determiners.

A few quantifiers may appear on either side of the nominal head: *genôch jild/jild genôch*, 'enough money', *by 't soad ideeën/ideeën by 't soad* 'plenty of ideas', *tefolle skroeven* 'too many screws', *tsien skroeven tefolle* 'ten screws too many'.

Possession can be expressed by a prepositional phrase, containing the preposition *fan* 'of' and the possessor noun phrase, following the possessed noun: *it tsjil fan 'e fyts* 'the wheel of the bicycle', *de broer fan Piter* 'the brother of Piter'. If the possessor is a pronoun, the predicative form of the possessive pronoun is used in the *fan*-phrase, just as in English: *in omke fan mines* 'an uncle of mine'. If the possessor is animate, a possessive pronoun, which can be preceded by a possessor noun phrase, may appear in the determiner position: *syn broer* 'his brother', *Piter syn broer* 'Piter's brother', *de boer syn hinnen* 'the farmer's chickens'. This construction of the form 'possessor + possessive pronoun + possessum' is the normal one with a noun phrase possessor. The use of the genitive *-s* has become almost obsolete in Frisian, although it can still be employed with proper names: *Piter's broer*.

Finally, at the leftmost periphery of the nominal phrase (before any noun phrase possessors) we find the universal quantifier *al* and the partitive quantifier *fan* (historically related to the preposition *fan* 'of'). In contrast to the determiner *alle*, the quantifier *al* must co-occur with a determiner: *al sokke dingen* 'all such things', *al dy bern* 'all those children', *al jimme kij* 'all your (pl.) cows'. Partitive *fan* is used in sentences like *der rûnen fan buorman syn hinnen yn ús tún* 'some of the neighbour's chickens walked in our garden' (lit. 'there walked of neighbour's chickens in our garden'), *dit binne mei fan 'e moaiste fersen dy 't er skreaun hat* 'these are among the most beautiful poems he has written' (lit. 'these are along of the most beautiful poems that he has written').

The nominal head may remain empty, if preceded by a determiner (but not an article on its own), an adjective or a quantifier: *ik keapje dy/reade/trije/in pear* 'I will buy those/red (ones)/three/a few'. The dummy noun *ien* 'one' may be inserted after adjectives and indefinite determiners ending in *-en*: *ik ha in readen/sa'nen (ien) kocht* 'I have bought a red/such a (one)'. In all these cases the content of the head should, of course, be recoverable from the context.

A noun phrase consisting of an indefinite article, a comparative adjective and a nominal head may be rather drastically reduced in negative (or perhaps existential) contexts. Thus, in the phrase *in kreazere frou* 'a prettier woman' in the sentence *in kreazere frou wie der net* 'there was no prettier woman' (lit. 'a prettier woman was there not'), one can successively drop the adjective ending (*in kreazer frou wie der net*), the article (*kreazer frou wie der net*) and – if contextually recoverable – the nominal head (*kreazer wie der net*). Compare also *is der (in) aakliker(e) (dea) te betinken?* 'is there (a) more horrible (death) to imagine?'

Adjective Phrase

An adjective phrase minimally consists of a bare adjective: *(ik bin) siik* '(I am) ill'. The adjective can be preceded by degree adverbs (*sa/hoe/te/like/tige/ôfgryslike siik* 'so/how/too/as/very/terribly ill') and descriptive adverbs (*ûnferwinlik siik* 'incurably ill'). The degree adverb *genôch* 'enough; too' is suffixed to the adjective as *-ernôch*: *grutternôch* 'big enough, too big'; *follernôch* 'full enough, too full'.

Adjectives in the comparative form and those preceded by the degree adverbs *sa* and *te* may have a measure phrase in front of them: *tsien meter heger* 'ten meters higher', *fjouwer kear sa lang* 'four times as long', *in stap te fier* 'a step too far'.

Complements and modifiers in the shape of prepositional phrases or clauses normally follow the adjective: *sljucht op iis* 'crazy about ice cream', *ree om ús te helpen* 'willing to help us'. As most other Germanic languages, Frisian possesses a small, closed class of transitive adjectives. These adjectives take a direct object to their left: *it libben sêd* 'weary of life', *de problemen treast* 'able to cope with the problems', *har freonen trou* 'faithful to her friends'.

Adpositional Phrase

Frisian has both prepositions and postpositions. Prepositions take a full noun phrase complement or (sometimes) a clausal complement: *njonken it postkantoar* 'next to the post office'; *sûnder dat er in wurd sei* 'without saying a word'. Postpositions, on the other hand, only take pronouns as their complement, more specifically adverbial *r*-pronouns like *der/dêr* 'there', *hjir* 'here' and *wêr* 'where': *deryn* 'in it', *hjirnjonken* 'next to this'. Traditionally, combinations of *r*-pronouns and postpositions are called 'pronominal adverbs'.

In addition to simple adpositions, the language has a relatively large number of circumpositions: *ta it rút út* 'out of the window', *foar de tsjerke oer* 'across from the church', *oer de sleat hinne* 'over the ditch'. Circumpositions also show up as postpositions: *deroerhinne* 'over it'.

In some exceptional cases, prepositions or circumpositions and their postpositional congeners do not have the same form: *nei Ljouwert ta* 'to Ljouwert' – *derhinne* 'to it' (not: *der neita*), *út Ljouwert wei* 'from Ljouwert' – *derwei* 'from it' (*derútwei*), *fan 'e dûkplanke ôf* 'off of the divingboard' – *derôf* 'off it' (*derfanôf*). Furthermore, some prepositions lack a postpositional counterpart: *fanwegen de pine* 'because of the pain' – *derfanwegen* 'because of it'.

Adpositions can be preceded by a measure phrase (*in telmannich nei it skot* 'some seconds after the shot', *hjir in eintsje ôf* 'a short distance from here') or a specifying adverb (*lyk yn 't gesicht* 'right in the face', *der roerdelings lâns* 'narrowly past it').

Verb Phrase

The basic word order in the Frisian verb phrase is O(bject) V(erb), normally found in embedded clauses: (*dat er*) *it stek ferve* '(that he) painted the fence', (*om*) *in nije auto te keapjen* '(to) buy a new car'. In main clauses OV-order is obscured by the effects of verb-second, discussed below.

Frisian has a good deal of 'noun incorporation'. A direct object may be incorporated into the verb in certain contexts: (*dat er*) *sneons altyd autowasket* (lit.) '(that he) always car-washes on Saturdays'; (*dat se*) *oan it boekjelêzen is* '(that she) is book-reading', (*dat wy*) *ophoden te toarnbeisykjen* '(that we) stopped blackberry-picking'.

The order of elements in the 'middle field' – the part of the sentence between the complementizer and the verb(s) – is relatively 'free'. For example, in the sentence *(dat er) juster mei in stôk de hûn sloech*, which is literally '(that he) yesterday with a stick the dog hit', the object and the two adjuncts may appear in any order: *(dat er) juster de hûn mei in stôk sloech, (dat er) mei in stôk juster de hûn sloech, (dat er) mei in stôk de hûn juster sloech, (dat er) de hûn mei in stôk juster sloech, (dat er) de hûn juster mei in stôk sloech*. There is, however, no freedom in a strict sense, as the actual order is governed by factors having to do with the information (given/new) structure of the sentence.

Within the verbal complex there is a rigid right-to-left order: A governed verb invariably appears to the left of its governor: *(dat er) swimme kin* '(that he) can swim', *(dat ik) har rinnen seach* '(that I) saw her walking', *(datst) wachtsje moatten hiest* '(that you) should have waited'. An exception is infinitives preceded by the infinitival marker *te*: *te*-infinitives, or at least verbal *te*-infinitives (see below), occupy the rightmost position in a verbal group: *(dat se) it boek besocht hat te lêzen* '(that she) has tried to read the book', *(dat jimme) sliepe skine te wollen* '(that you) seem to want to sleep'.

Finite sentential complements as well as non-finite sentential complements introduced by the conjunction *om* occur in postverbal position: *(dat er) hope, dat it moai waar wurde soe* '(that he) hoped, that the weather would be fine', *(dat se) fan doel wie, om de blikke te meanen* '(lit.) (that she) of intention was, for the lawn to mow'.

Finally, prepositional phrases may appear on either side of the verb: *(dat de bern) op it hiem boarten/boarten op it hiem* '(that the children) played in the yard'. Prepositional complements of verbs denoting a position or motion, however, are strictly preverbal: *(dat ik) yn 'e hûs bin/*bin yn 'e hûs* '(that I) am in the house', *(dat jimme) nei Snits ta geane/*geane nei Snits ta* '(that you) go to Snits'. The same holds for prepositional phrases forming part of an idiom: *(datst) noch wolris fan 'e bok dreame silst/*dreame silst fan 'e bok* 'that you will have bad experiences sometime' (lit. 'that you will dream of the buck sometime').

The Sentence

Verb-second

Like all Germanic languages except English, Frisian displays the so-called 'verb-second' phenomenon: in declarative main clauses the finite verb occupies the second position in the clause. The first position can be filled by all sorts of constituents. Compare: *Germen hat juster it ankel ferkloft* 'Germen sprained his ankle yesterday', *juster hat Germen it ankel ferkloft, it ankel hat Germen juster ferkloft, ferkloft hat Germen juster it ankel*. In yes/no questions and in imperatives, the finite verb opens the clause: *wolst my it jiskepantsje efkes oerjaan?* 'would you pass me the ashtray?', *kom my net oan!* (lit.) 'come me not on!' (i.e. 'don't touch me!').

In embedded clauses the verb normally remains in its clause-final position:

hy fertelde, dat Germen koarts hie 'he said that Germen has a fever', *it is net noflik, om koarts te hawwen* 'it's no fun to have a fever'. Conditional clauses, however, may have either verb-initial or, if the complementizer is expressed, verb-final order. Compare *jout er my hûndert gûne, dan doch ik it* 'if he gives me one hundred guilders, I'll do it' with *at er my hûndert gûne jout, dan doch ik it.*

Verb-second may also show up in an embedded clause which is the complement of verbs of belief and assertion. Next to *hy sei, dat er skille hie* 'he said that he had called', it is possible to say *hy sei, hy hie skille* and *hy sei, dat hy hie skille.* The same three possibilities can be found in result clauses: *wy wiene sa benaud, dat de knibbels ús oan staten* 'we were so afraid, that our knees shook', *wy wiene sa benaud, de knibbels staten ús oan, wy wiene sa benaud, dat de knibbels staten ús oan.*

Furthermore, verb-second optionally occurs in embedded clauses introduced by the adverbial conjunctions *omt* 'because', *mits* 'provided that', *hoewol* 'although': Compare *hja kin net sjonge, omt se heas is* 'she can not sing, because she is hoarse', where the verb is in final position, with *hja kin net sjonge, omt se is heas.*

Finally, verb-second is found in the so-called '*en* + imperative' construction. In this construction an embedded clause is introduced by the conjunction *en* (which has lost its original coordinating function), followed by a verb in the imperative form (but without the imperative function). The *en* + imperative construction comes in two types. In the first type the *en*-clause is an adjunct: *hy woe syn wurk derhinne smite en wurd skriuwer* 'he wanted to give up his job and become a writer', *jimme moatte efkes nei de bakker ta gean en nim in bôle mei* 'you should go to the baker's and get a loaf of bread'. Compare this to a normal coordinated sentence, *jimme moatte efkes nei de bakker ta gean en in bôle meinimme*, in which the verb is in clause-final position.

In the second type of *en* + imperative construction, the *en*-clause is a complement of the main clause verb: *ik bin fan doel en skriuw in boek* 'I plan to write a book' (lit. 'I am of intention and write a book'), *hy ferpoft it en doch altyd de smoarge putsjes* 'he refuses to always do the dirty jobs' (lit. 'he refuses it and do always the dirty jobs').

Historically the formal imperative in the *en* + imperative construction derives from an infinitive. Until this century the *en* + infinitive and the *en* + imperative construction occurred side by side. Presently, the infinitive has been completely replaced by the imperative.

Complementizers

Frisian possesses a relatively complex complementizer system. There are two finite complementizers, i.e. *dat* 'that' and *oft* 'whether': *hy hope, dat se komme soe* 'he hoped, that she would come', *hy wist net, oft se komme soe* 'he didn't know, whether she would come'.

Both these complementizers sometimes appear in the cliticized form *'t*. The cliticized form is optional if the complementizer is selected by the main-clause verb. Thus, for example, in *wh*-complements the complementizer may appear as *oft* or cliticized to the *wh*-word as *'t*: *ik wist net, wa oft/wa't komme soe* 'I didn't know who (whether) would come'.

If the complementizer is not selected, cliticization is obligatory. This is the case in relative clauses (*de jonge dy't* (**dy oft*) *nêst ús wennet* 'the boy who (whether) lives nextdoor'). Note, however, that cliticization does not apply if there is no simple relative pronoun available to host the clitical complementizer: *de jonge dy syn fyts oft* (**'t*) *stellen wie* 'The boy whose bike (whether) had been stolen'.

With adjunct clauses we must distinguish between those introduced by a preposition and those that are not. In the former case the preposition can be said to select the complementizer. Accordingly, the complementizer may appear in full or cliticized form, attached to the preposition: *neidat/nei't er toskboarstele hie, gie er op bêd* 'after (that) he had brushed his teeth, he went to bed'. In the latter case, complementizer cliticization applies obligatorily: *doe't* (**doe dat*) *se de kat fretten jûn hie, begûn se te krantlêzen* 'when (that) she had fed the cat, she began reading the newspaper'.

Infinitival clauses containing a *te*-infinitive are headed by the complementizer *om*. The complementizer is optional (although normally present in common usage) when the embedded clause is a complement: *it is in griis, (om) dy skuon wei te smiten* 'it is a pity to throw away those shoes', *ik ried dy oan, (om) op te hâlden fan smoken* 'I advise you to stop smoking'. *Om* is obligatory when the clause is an adjunct: *hy joech it bern in bal om mei te boartsjen* 'he gave the child a ball to play with', *hja wie te wurch om de keamer op te rêden* 'she was too tired to tidy up the room'.

Infinitives

Infinitives come in three types in Frisian: (a) *e*-infinitives (*rinne* 'walk'); (b) *en*-infinitives (*rinnen*); and (c) *te*-infinitives (*te rinnen*). The distribution of these infinitives is a rather complicated matter.

Modal verbs like *kinne* 'can', *wolle* 'want', *moatte* 'must', *meie* 'may', *sille* 'shall', and the causative verb *litte* 'let' select an *e*-infinitive: *Antsje wol sliepe* 'Antsje wants to sleep'; *hy liet ús in beam tekenje* 'he made us draw a tree'.

An *en*-infinitive is selected by perception verbs like *sjen* 'see', *hearre* 'hear', *fiele* 'feel' and *fernimme* 'notice': *ik seach har it hier kjimmen* 'I saw her comb her hair'; *hja fernaam har bloed sieden* 'she felt her blood boil'.

The verbs *gean* 'go' and *bliuwe* 'stay' may function as aspectual (inchoative and durative, respectively) verbs in Frisian, when combined with the *en*-infinitive of the posture verbs *stean* 'stand', *sitte* 'sit', *lizze* 'lie' and *hingje* 'hang'. Consider *Jitske gie op 'e stoel sitten* 'Jitske sat down on the chair' and *Fedde bliuwt de hiele dei op bêd lizzen* 'Fedde stays in bed the whole day'.

Both *e*-infinitives and *en*-infinitives may show up in nominal infinitives:

sjonge/sjongen is syn wille en tier 'singing is his love and passion'. Nominal *e*-infinitives may be accompanied by objects and modifiers: *under 'e brûs aria's sjonge is syn wille en tier* 'singing aria's in the shower is his love and passion'. With *en*-infinitives this is only possible if the nominalization is headed by a determiner: *it ûnder 'e brûs aria's sjongen is syn wille en tier* 'the singing of aria's in the shower is his love and passion'. Nominal *e*-infinitives are never introduced by a determiner.

We may distinguish four types of *te*-infinitives: (a) verbal *te*-infinitives; (b) adjectival *te*-infinitives; (c) prepositional *te*-infinitives; and (d) sentential *te*-infinitives.

Verbal *te*-infinitives appear in extraposed clauses introduced by the complementizer *om*: ...*om de fisk ta te meitsjen* 'to clean the fish'. Furthermore, as noted in the section on the verb phrase, they are obligatorily raised from an intrasentential clausal complement to a postverbal position: ... *dat er de fisk ûnthiet te bakken* 'that he promised to fry the fish'.

Adjectival and prepositional *te*-infinitives are always located to the left of the verb (barring the effects of verb-second). Adjectival *te*-infinitives may be preceded by an adverb: ... *dat it boek (slim) te lêzen is* 'that the book is (hardly) readable'. Furthermore, they may occur attributively and, in that case, may be optionally inflected: *dy net te ferjitten(e) dei* 'that unforgettable day'. Prepositional *te*-infinitives appear in the complement of the verbs *wêze* 'be' and *gean* 'go'. They may exhibit noun incorporation, which is impossible with verbal and adjectival *te*-infinitives. Compare ... *dat er te fiskjen is* 'that he is out fishing' and ... *dat se te skiepmelken giet* (lit. 'that she goes to sheep-milk').

Sentential *te*-infinitives differ from adjectival and prepositional *te*-infinitives by the fact that they are always in postverbal position. This puts them on par with verbal *te*-infinitives. They are distinguished from the latter, however, by the fact that they may show noun incorporation. Consider the following examples: *Boate begjint te tafelklearmeitsjen* 'Boate is beginning to set the table' (lit. 'to table-ready-make'); *wy sille jimme helpe te itensieden* 'we will help you cook dinner' (lit. 'to dinner-cook'); *Hiltsje stiet te hierkjimmen* 'Hiltsje is combing her hair' (lit. 'stands to hair-comb').

Pro-drop

In Frisian, the second-person singular pronoun *do* may remain unexpressed when not used emphatically. In other words, Frisian displays partial pro-drop. *Do*-drop occurs after a preposed finite verb (*komst (do) jûn?* 'are you coming tonight?') or after an inflected complementizer (*oftst (do) jûn komst* 'whether you are coming tonight'). Note that the complementizer is inflected, whether the second-person singular pronoun is present or not.

When the second-person singular pronoun *do* is relativized, the relative clause contains an unexpressed *do*: *do, dy'tst de âldste bist* 'you, who are the eldest' (cf. Ger. *du, der du der älteste bist*). Although *do* is not phonetically realized, it is recoverable from the inflection marker *-st* on the complementizer (*'t*).

Split Phrases

Adpositional phrases may be split: the adpositional object may appear in clause-initial position, stranding the adposition. Like Dutch (and some dialects of German), Frisian shows postposition stranding with *r*-pronouns: *dêr harke net ien nei* (lit. 'there listened no one at'); *wêr hat er om frege?* 'what did he ask for?' The *r*-pronoun may also show up in a clause-internal position, separated from the postposition: *net ien woe dêr jild foar jaan* (lit. 'no one would there money for give'). Unlike Dutch, Frisian allows stranding with 'normal' noun phrases as well: *dy sifers haw ik my slim oer fernuvere* (lit.) 'those figures have I myself much about puzzled', *wa hast juster mei praat?* 'who did you talk with yesterday?', *hy fûn fioelmesyk neat oan* (lit.) 'he found violin music nothing on' ('he didn't like violin music').

In contrast to Dutch, but like German, Frisian allows split noun phrases, i.e. nouns separated from their determiner or quantifier: *strikken haw ik wol hûndert* (lit. 'neck-ties have I as many as hundred'), *aaien lizze der noch guon yn 'e kuolkast* (lit. 'eggs lie there still some in the refrigerator'), *drege boeken hoech ik gjin* (lit. 'difficult books need I none').

Interrogatives, Relatives

Apart from 'simple' interrogatives and relatives (*wa komt jûn?* 'who is coming tonight?', ... *de man, dy't jûn komt* '... the man, who is coming tonight'), Frisian allows questioning and relativization of elements in embedded clauses: *wa tinkst dat jûn komt?* 'who do you think will come tonight?'; ... *de man, dy'tst tinkst dat jûn komt* ... 'the man who you think will come tonight'. It is even possible to question or relativize elements in embedded questions: *wa fregest dy ôf hoe let oft jûn komt?* (lit.) 'who do you wonder at what time will come tonight?'; ... *it famke, dat ik net wit, wêr't wennet* (lit.) '... the girl who I don't know where lives'.

In addition to *wa tinkst dat jûn komt?*, Frisian has two other strategies for questioning an element in an embedded clause. First, a copy of the *wh*-word may appear in the first position of the embedded clause: *wa tinkst wa't jûn komt?* And second, the neuter *wh*-word *wat* 'what' may head the main clause, functioning as a scope marker for the *wh*-word in the embedded clause: *wat tinkst wa't jûn komt?*

Negation

To negate a phrase or a sentence Frisian makes use of the negative adverb *net*: *hy hat it net dien* 'he did not do it'. *Net* may also appear in its cliticized form *n't*: *ik wit n't* 'I don't know'; *moai waar, n't wier?* 'Nice weather, isn't it?' When *net* is followed by an indefinite article (*in* or *Ø*), it may fuse with this article into the negative article *gjin*: *wy ha gjin* (< *net in*) *auto* 'we don't own a car', *gjin* (< *net Ø*) *moal* 'no flour'.

Frisian exhibits occasional double negation. Negative elements like *nea* 'never', *nearne* 'nowhere', *nimmen* 'no one' may be followed by an optional *net*: *hja binne nea net op 'e tiid* 'they are never on time'; *der wie nimmen net op 'e strjitte* 'there was no one in the street'. Some speakers use a clause-final *net* in addition to another negative element: *hja binne nea op 'e tiid net* 'they are never on time'.

16.5 Lexis

Historically Frisian is closely related to English. Some features of its lexicon still bespeak these old bonds. Consider palatalization of *k* to *ts(j)* (*tsiis* 'cheese', *tsjêf* 'chaff') and *g* to *j* (*dei* 'day', *rein* 'rain', *jern* 'yarn'), loss of *n* before voiceless fricatives (*ús* 'us', *goes* 'goose') and strong fronting of back vowels (*swiet* 'sweet', *bliede* 'bleed'). Furthermore, there are lexical parallels like *kaai* 'key', *jit* 'yet' (but only in the sense of Dutch/German *nog/ noch*)' and *boai* 'boy'.

None the less, present-day Frisian shows much more resemblance, both lexically and structurally, to its direct neighbours than it does to English. For example, like Dutch and German, Frisian possesses a large inventory of modal particles. Frisian modal particles include *no* (*dat wie no net sa moai fan him* 'that was ‹now› not very nice of him'), *dan* (*it is dan wûnder* 'it is ‹then› strange'), *oars* (*hja hearde oars net sa fleurich* 'she did not ‹otherwise› sound very happy'), *ek* (*do bist ek in raren* 'you are ‹also› a funny sort of person'), *mar* (*hy wie mar bluisterich* 'he was ‹but› boisterous') and *ris* (*kom hjir ris* 'come here ‹once›'). These particles may co-occur in numerous combinations; *dat wie no dan oars ek mar ris tige bêst oanbean* 'that was ‹now then otherwise also but once› a very nice offer' is an extreme example.

Somewhat surprising is the considerable number of French loanwords in Frisian, some not or no longer used in Dutch: *avensearje* 'hurry' (< French *avancer*); *jin oppenearje* 'express one's feelings; present oneself, occur' (< *opiner*); *argewaasje* 'annoyance' (< *arguer*); *maleur* 'bad luck; breakdown' (< *malheur*) and *krupsje* 'disease' (< *corruption*). Presumably, this is 'gesunkenes Kulturgut' from the time when French was used in higher circles in the Netherlands.

Frisian is heavily influenced by Dutch, especially in the spoken language. Even in standard Frisian, Dutch influence is clearly visible, from accepted Dutch-isms like *gesellich* 'cosy' (Dutch *gezellig*) and *toaniel* 'stage' (*toneel*) to a large number of loan translations: *belesting* 'tax' (*belasting*); *fleanfjild* 'airport' (*vliegveld*); *pjutteboartersplak* 'playgroup' (*peuterspeelplaats*).

There have long been efforts to prevent the language from Dutchifying too much. This has sometimes been done by borrowing from languages other than Dutch; some grammatical terminology, for example, consists of loan translations from German and Scandinavian: *tiidwurd* 'verb' (Ger. *Zeitwort*); *doetiid* 'past' (Dan. *datid*). In addition, a word like *yndie* 'indeed' is modelled on the English example. But Frisian also coins new words using its own linguistic resources: *brûs* 'shower' (from *brûs* 'nozzle of a watering can'); *reau* 'vehicle' (from the more concrete *reau* 'carriage') and *reinerij* 'field sprinkler' (*reine* 'rain + -*erij*).

Appendix: East and North Frisian

Within the scope of this article it is simply impossible to do justice to the various quite distinct North Frisian dialects and the East Frisian dialect of Saterland. Therefore, this section can only highlight some of their more noteworthy attributes.

Phonology

The vowel and consonant inventory of Saterlandic East Frisian is quite similar to that of West Frisian. Some special developments in the Saterlandic consonants are reflected in words like *gjucht* 'right' (WFris. *rjucht*), *fjund* 'friend' (WFris. *freon*, older *frjuen*), *kolich* 'calf' (WFris. *keal*) and *bäiden* 'child' (WFris. *bern*).

Many North Frisian dialects have various palatalized consonants, including in word-final position: Mooring *schölj* 'school', *üülj* 'old'; Fering *aatj* 'father'; *lidj* 'people'; Sölring *litj* 'small', *winj* 'wind'.

The dialect of the island Söl retained the voiced alveolar fricative ([ð]) up to this century. In word-final position [ð] has changed to [r] (cf. *biir* 'both'); intervocalically [ð] has become [l] or [r], although it is still written ‹ð›: *faaðer* 'father', *brööðer* 'brother'.

An interesting historical development is that Old Frisian long *i* was shortened in North Frisian, producing words like *is* 'ice'. Short *i* was generally lowered to *e* or *a*: mooring *frasch*; Fering *fresk* 'Frisian'. Furthermore, some North Frisian dialects, like Mooring on the mainland, have no final devoicing.

The dialect of Helgoland has a considerable number of compounds with primary stress on the second part, a phenomenon it shares with West Frisian: *baad'kant* 'bed board' (WFris. *bêds'planke*); *helli'doagen* 'holy days' (WFris. *hjel'dagen*); *keeken'deer* 'kitchen door' (WFris. *kokens'doar*).

Morphology

The most common plural suffix on the North Frisian mainland is -*e*: Mooring *hüne* 'dogs'. The island plural marker is generally -*en* or -*er*: Fering *düüwen* 'doves', *diker* 'dikes'; Sölring *gleesen* 'glasses', *wainer* 'wagons'; Helgolandic *booamen* 'trees', *baader* 'beds'. East Frisian generally uses -*e*: Saterlandic *bouke* 'books'.

Mainland dialects like Mooring have three genders, as reflected by the strong forms of the definite article: *di moon* 'the man' (m.); *jü wüset* 'the woman' (f.); *dåt bjarn* 'the child' (n.); *da hüne* 'the dogs' (pl.). Incidentally, Mooring and Fering have a double article paradigm. In addition to the strong forms mentioned above, Mooring has the corresponding weak forms: *e, e, et, e*. The choice between the strong and weak paradigm is determined by the referentiality of the definite noun phrase. The dialects of the islands Söl, Feer, Oomram and Helgoland and that of Saterland have two genders.

What stands out in the North Frisian pronoun system is the presence of dual forms: Mooring *wat* 'the two of us'; *jat* 'the two of you'. Use of the name or third-person pronoun to address older persons is attested in North Frisian, as it is in West Frisian.

As for verbal inflection, all Frisian dialects distinguish two infinitives, the former ending in *-e/-i* or *-Ø* and the latter in *-(e)n*. Furthermore, most of them distinguish two classes of weak verbs, deriving from the verbs ending in *-a* and *-ia* in Old Frisian.

Syntax

North Frisian has an interesting construction with the coordinate conjunction 'and' introducing an embedded infinitival clause: Mooring *dåt as ai gödj än heew douen ma ham* (lit.) 'it is not easy and have doings with him'; Sölring *hat es beeter en maaki di düür tö* (lit.) 'it is better and close the door'. This construction is reminiscent of the *en* + imperative in West Frisian. It is, however, at least partly due to the influence of similar constructions in Jutish, where *at* 'to' and *og* 'and' have fused together into *å*.

In Saterlandic the verb *dwoo* 'do' can be used as an auxiliary expressing durative aspect, a phenomenon also well known from Low German: *Joo dieden Eed greeue* (lit.) 'they did peat dig'.

Lexis

North Frisian vocabulary has been influenced a good deal by Danish (Jutish). Consider the word for 'not' (Mooring *ai*, Fering *ei*, Sölring *ek*) and Mooring *jül* 'Christmas', Fering *skaas* 'spoon' and Sölring *köör* 'drive'. Both East and North Frisian contain many lexical borrowings from Low German; Low German was used by Frisians to communicate with speakers of other Frisian dialects and Low German. Low German loanwords include Helgolandic *kark* 'church', Mooring *frööge* 'be happy', Fering *boowen* 'above', Sölring *leewent* 'life'. More recently, the growing influence of High German has left its marks on the East and North Frisian lexicon (and on the overall structure of these languages).

Further Reading

General

Århammar, N. (1975) 'Friesiche Dialektologie', *Zeitschrift für Mundartforschung*, Beiheft, New Series 5: 264–317.

Markey, T. L. (1981) *Frisian*, Trends in Linguistics, State of the Art Reports 13, The Hague: Mouton.

Ramat, P. (1967) *Il Frisone, Introduzione allo studio della Filologia Frisone*, Firenze: Sansoni; Revised and translated into German as *Das Friesische, Eine sprachliche und kulturgeschichtliche Einführung*, Innsbrucker Beiträge zur Sprachwissenschaft 14, Innsbruck, 1976.

Sjölin, B. (1969) *Einführung in das Friesische*, Stuttgart: Metzger.

West Frisian

Anglade, J. (1966) *Petit manuel de Frison Moderne de l'Ouest*, Groningen: Wolters.

Feitsma, A. (1989) 'The history of the Frisian linguistic norm', in I. Fodor and C. Hagège (eds), *Language Reform, History and Future*, vol. IV, Hamburg: Buske, pp. 247–72.

Gorter, D., Jelsma, Gj., van der Plank, P. and de Vos, K. (1984) *Taal yn Fryslân*. Fryske Akademy, Leeuwarden; English summary: *Language in Friesland*, Leeuwarden: Fryske Akademy, 1988.

Kodama, H. (1992) *Furijiagobunpoo-oranda no moohitotsu no gengo-*, Tokyo: Daigakusyorin.

Sipma, P. (1913) *Phonology and Grammar of Modern West Frisian*, Oxford: Clarendon; Photo-reprint: Leeuwarden: Fryske Akademy, 1966.

Tiersma, P. M. (1979) *Aspects of the Phonology of Frisian, Based on the Language of Grou*, Meidielingen 4, Frisian Program of the Vrije Universiteit in Amsterdam.

—— (1985) *Frisian Reference Grammar*, Dordrecht: Foris.

Zhluktenko, Yu. A. and Dvuchzilov, A. V. (1984) *Frizski Yazyk*, Kiev: Naukova Dumka.

East and North Frisian

Århammar, N. (1967) *Die Syltringer Sprache. Die Syltringer Literatur*, Itzehoe: Voßkate.

—— (1976) *Die Amringer Sprache. Die Amringer Literatur*, Itzehoe: Voßkate.

Bauer, E. (1925) *Die Moringer Mundart*, Heidelberg: Winter.

Borchert, M. and Århammar, R. and N. (1987) *Wi lear Halunder*, Helgoland: Verein zum Wiederaufbau des früheren Helgoländer Nordseemuseums e.V.

Hofmann, D. (1956) 'Probleme der nordfriesischen Dialektforschung', *Zeitschrift für Mundartforschung* 24: 78–112.

Kramer, P. (1982) *Kute Seelter Sproakleere: Kurze Grammatik des Saterfriesischen*, Rhauderfehn: Ostendorp Verlag.

Löfstedt, E. (1968/1971) *Beiträge zu einer nordfriesischen Grammatik*, Pts I, II, Acta Universitatis Upsaliensis, Studia Germanistica Upsaliensia 6, Uppsala: Almquist and Wiksells.

Schmidt-Petersen, J. and Cragie, J. (1928) *The North Frisian Dialect of Föhr and Amrum*, Edinburgh: Hutchen.

Walker, A. (1989) 'Frisian', in C. Russ (ed.) *The Dialects of Modern German*, London: Routledge, pp. 1–30.

17 English

Ekkehard König

17.1 Introduction

Although second to Chinese in terms of the number of native speakers, English is probably the most important language of the world in terms of geographic dispersion and in terms of the role it plays in international communication. From its original home base English has spread to Ireland, Scotland, North America, Australia, New Zealand, South Africa and is now the sole official language in more than thirty countries, including Ghana, Liberia, Nigeria, Uganda, Zimbabwe, Jamaica and the Bahamas. In other countries like India, Singapore, the Philippines, Western Samoa, Tanzania and Cameroon, English shares official status with one or two other languages, so that it has an official status in over 60 of the world's territories. Over 300 million speak English as a mother tongue and at least another 400 million use English as a first foreign (i.e. second or international) language. English is the main language of newspapers and of advertising. It is the official international language of airports and air-traffic control. It is the lingua franca of international business and academic conferences, of diplomacy, of sport and it is one of the six official languages used by the United Nations.

Given this diffusion of English around the globe and its role as an official language in so many countries, it should not come as a surprise that there is considerable variation, both in the standard varieties and especially in the non-standard varieties of that language. In many countries English has been undergoing a process of 'nativization'. Whether or not the results should be recognized as a new indigenous norm, independent of one common outside norm, be it national (British) or supranational ('Common English'), is a matter of some debate. The view that there are several interacting centres, each providing a national variety with its own norms, is forcefully expressed by the new plural *Englishes*, now frequently found in the sociolinguistic literature, and by the characterization of English as a 'pluricentric language'.

From a more traditional point of view, standard varieties of English can roughly be divided into two branches: British English, which also includes standard varieties spoken in Ireland, Australia, New Zealand and South Africa, and (North) American English, which includes the varieties spoken by

532

educated speakers in the United States and in Canada. Another typology cuts across this division and draws a first distinction between northern and southern English, both of which can be found in Britain and North America. Differences between standard varieties are primarily matters of pronunciation, lexis and perhaps also discourse. In Britain, there are various regional standards of pronunciation, but there is also a non-regional superstandard, namely Received Pronunciation (RP). Originally a regional accent of the Southeast and of London, used primarily by the court and the upper classes, RP later became the accent taught in public schools and was used by the BBC as well as other national institutions in the UK. Today it is best described as an 'educated accent' with its own spread of variation, which gives no information as to the regional origin of its speakers. In the United States, there are regional pronunciation standards rather than a national one. The move from a vernacular to a standard is essentially a change within a regionally defined set of parameters. In contrast to speech, standards of writing are fairly uniform and permit surprisingly little variation in morphology, syntax and orthography. Differences are more often than not a matter of frequency.

Non-standard varieties of English, which can further be subdivided into regional (accents, dialects) and social ones (social dialects), manifest a much more striking latitude and degree of variation. Such non-standard varieties can, as a first step, be divided into British and American varieties. In Britain, regional and social variation are connected in such a way that regional variation tends to decrease the higher one moves up the social scale. The major regional division in England is the one between Northern and Southern, and within this broad framework the North can be further distinguished from the Midlands and further east–west divisions can be made within the Midlands as well as within the South. It is a significant fact of the dialect situation in Britain that the rural dialects defined by such divisions as Yorkshire, West Country, Home Counties, Lancashire, etc. are becoming less significant than the broad regional types defined by major conurbations, such as London, Edinburgh, Leeds, Bristol, Tyneside, etc. Other important (national) varieties within the British group are identified by such labels as Scots, Irish English, Australian English, etc.

Despite some differences, Canadian and US English are similar enough, so that it is possible to view them as regional variants of a single type. Within the United States, three major dialect areas are now distinguished by most dialectologists: the North, the Midlands and the South, although recent research suggests that the Midlands constitute no more than a very broad transition zone between only two distinct dialects. This division has replaced an older one into Eastern, Southern and General American. Among the non-standard varieties of English spoken in the United States, several ethnically based varieties can clearly be identified, notably Black English, arguably a semi-creole in the final stages of decreolization, and Chicano English.

Table 17.1   Consonant phonemes

	Labial	Labiodental	Dental	Alveolar	Palatal/ palato- alveolar	Velar	Glottal
Stops/affricates	p, b			t, d	tʃ, dʒ	k, g	
Fricatives		f, v	θ, ð	s, z	ʃ, ʒ		h
Nasals	m			n		ŋ	
Liquids/ approximants	w			l, r	j		

17.2   Phonology

The description of the segmental inventories given in Table 17.1 and Table 17.2 is primarily based on Southern British English, in general, and RP in particular. Striking deviations from that system and the phonetic realizations associated with it will briefly be mentioned.

Like all Germanic languages, English has two more or less parallel series of voiceless and voiced obstruents (stops, fricatives, affricates). The contrast between the phonetic realizations of members of each pair is not always one of presence vs absence of vocal-cord vibration, however. Aspiration or the length of the preceding vowel may also play an important role for the identification of the relevant phonemes. In American English voiceless stops tend to become voiced in intervocalic position, so that pairs like *writer* and *rider* or *latter* and *ladder* may not be distinct phonetically. In nearly all British, but also some American, accents voiceless stops in final position are reinforced by a glottal stop, which has the effect of shortening the preceding vowel.

The contrast between /θ/ and /ð/ does not carry the same functional load as that between the other related pairs. In word-initial position, there is a certain complementarity: all words with initial /ð/ are members of minor word classes (*this, that, than, then, though, them, the*, etc.). In intervocalic position only /ð/ is found (*lather, weather, bother*) and there are only a few minimal pairs, all of them with the relevant contrast in final position: *teeth* vs *teethe*; *wreath* vs *wreathe*. The phonemes grouped together as liquids and approximants do not form a completely homogeneous set from a phonetic point of view, but share the properties of being devoiced after voiceless consonants (*twin, play, pray, tune*) and of occurring after /s/ + stop (*squeal, spray, splash, stew*).

This system is found in nearly all varieties of English. The only additions made to it in some cases are /x/ and /w̥/. Some northern English dialects, Scots as well as some North American dialects differentiate pairs of words like *wail* and *whale* or *witch* and *which* and the velar fricative /x/ can be found in Scots, South African and Yiddish English. The phoneme /r/ has a large number of phonetic realizations across dialects and exhibits a great deal of allophonic variation within a specific variety. In most British accents it is realized as a post-alveolar frictionless continuant or as an alveolar flap. In North American varieties /r/ is realized either as a retroflex sound or as an essentially velar sound with secondary articulation in the pharynx. Voiceless stops are aspirated in the initial position of a syllable, unless /s/ precedes. The lateral liquid /l/ has a velarized [ɫ] and a non-velarized allophone [l] in Southern British English and Southern American English, but not in most other varieties of American English, in Australian English or in Scots. Finally, a very important distinction concerns the distribution of /r/. As a result of the loss of /r/ in post-vocalic position, which began in the South of England in the seventeenth century, rhotic and non-rhotic dialects can be distinguished. Rhotic dialects (most North American varieties, Scots, Irish) have /r/ in all positions, whereas non-rhotic ones (England, Australia, New Zealand, South Africa, southern coastal US) exclude /r/ from word-final position and the position before a consonant.

Vowels

Like other Germanic languages, English has three types of vowels: short vowels, long vowels and diphthongs. In contrast to most of its sister languages, however, there are no rounded front vowels. Furthermore, it is not possible to set up pairs of vowels that are solely or primarily distinguished by length, with the possible exception of /ə/ and /ɜː/. Phonetically similar vowels such as /ɪ/ and /iː/ differ strikingly in the quality of their phonetic realization in addition to length. For a variety of phonological reasons, long vowels and diphthongs can be grouped together as a class:

1   Distribution: both long vowels and diphthongs occur in stressed open syllables, short vowels do not.
2   Equivalence across dialects: short vowels in one dialect typically correspond to other short vowels, albeit of a different phonetic quality, in other dialects; long vowels correspond to other long vowels or diphthongs.
3   Allophonic variation: long vowels and diphthongs are equivalent in length and subject to some variation in quantity. Both are shortened before 'voiceless' obstruents (*plays – place, league – leak*). Thus the vowel system of Southern British English, including RP, can be represented as in Table 17.2.

The diphthongs in Table 17.2 have been arranged according to the phonetic quality of their second element: a front vowel in the first row, a back vowel in the second and a central schwa in the third row ('centering diphthongs'). This phonological system differentiates words such as the following:

Table 17.2   Vowel phonemes

Short		Long Monophthongs		Diphthongs		
ɪ ʊ		iː uː		eɪ aɪ ɔɪ		
e ə		3ː ɔː		əʊ ɑʊ		
æ ɒ		ɑː		ɪə ɛə ʊə		

pit	put	reed	rude	fate	fight	boy
pet putt			pert	port	oat	out
pat	pot		part	here	there	poor

The exact phonetic realization of the different vowel phonemes and partly also the system itself differs, of course, enormously across dialects. To give just one example of such variation, in standard varieties of American English, the low back vowel in words like *pot*, *hot* is unrounded and thus better represented as /ɑ/, whereas the long mid back vowel /ɔː/ in RP in words like *port*, *short* may either correspond to a more closed vowel /oː/ (*force*, *four*) or to a lower vowel /ɒː/ (*thought*, *law*) in American English. In nearly all varieties of English, long vowels, diphthongs and sometimes also combinations of short vowel + nasal are shorter before voiceless obstruents than before the relevant voiced counterparts. Minimal pairs like the following are thus primarily distinguished through the length of their vowels: *joys – Joyce*; *ride – write*; *rude – root*; *and – ant*.

Syllable Structure

The onset (initial part) of a syllable in English can consist of one, two or three consonants, the final part (coda) can consist of up to four consonants. There are no restrictions for the most simple cases, except that /h/ is only possible in the onset and /ŋ/ is excluded from this position. For combinations of two consonants, the following restrictions can be formulated: (a) the cluster /sC/ is permitted both in onsets and codas: *skill*, *desk*; (b) /Cs/ is only permitted in codas: *mix*; and (c) stop + liquid clusters are confined to onsets, liquid + stop clusters to codas, having thus mirror-image properties: *cloud* vs *cold*. Another instance of such complementarity of clusters across two syllables can be found in rhotic dialects: if /Cr/ occurs in the onset of the first syllable only /Cl/ can occur in the second and vice versa (cf. *blubber*, *bramble*; *bristle*, *blister*). Nasal + stop clusters are restricted to codas: *kind*, *link*. Overall, only about 10 per cent of all possible combinations of consonants are permitted. If the onset takes the form CCC the first consonant must be an /s/, the second must be a voiceless stop and the third must be one of /r, l, j, w/ (cf. *sprinkle, scrape, splash, stew*). In codas many more clusters are permitted than in onsets, but a major proportion of the more complex clusters are morphologically complex too (cf. *glimpsed, desks, bridles*, etc.). It is a particularly interesting fact of English that certain constraints apply to both onsets and codas: (a) clusters of obstruents always agree in voicing. The word *exit*, for example, has two possible pronunciations /egzɪt/ and /eksɪt/, which illustrate this; (b) no two members of the sibilant class /s, z, ʃ, ʒ, tʃ, dʒ/ may be combined and neither can two stops of the same place of articulation. These restrictions have interesting repercussions for the shapes of certain grammatical suffixes: the fact that the plural morpheme has the allomorph -*s* after voiceless stops, -*z* after voiced stops and -*ɪz* after sibilants is a reflection of this regularity. There are only a few restrictions within the nuclear part of the syllable ('peak'), but that nuclear part together with the coda plays an important role for the assignment of stress.

Word Stress
English is sometimes characterized as a free-stress language, since stress is not simply determined by the numerical value of a syllable within a word, as in Finnish (stress on first syllable), French (stress on last syllable), Polish (stress on penultimate syllable), etc. Compared to these simple word-prosodic systems, the variety found in English is baffling: there are polysyllabic words with the stress on the first syllable (*'mother, 'controversy*), the second syllable (*be'hold, can'teen*), the third syllable (*tele'vision*) and the last one (*inter'nee*). Moreover, there are a small number of minimal pairs like *'abstract – ab'stract, 'accent – ac'cent* or *'transport – trans'port*, which just differ in the location of the stress as well as the word-class membership and a larger class of pairs such as *'contract – con'tract*, where such a difference in stress assignment and word-class membership goes together with some variation in vowel quality. Such differential stress marking is fairly regular in English, but it shows that stress assignment cannot simply be a matter of counting syllables.

In so far as this characterization suggests that stress assignment to words in English is unpredictable, it is highly misleading. There are major regularities describable by rules that are applicable to a vast section of the English vocabulary. These rules differ for the vocabulary derived from Germanic and that derived from Romance, but they happen to coincide for the vast majority of cases.

The rule for the native part of the vocabulary is the one familiar from other Germanic languages: the word stress is assigned to the first syllable of any lexical root including compounds: *mother, heaven, nightingale, cut-throat*. Stress placement in that part of the vocabulary contributed by Romance is sensitive to two properties of syllables: (a) their distance from the end of the word; (b) their weight. Stress is generally not more than three syllables away from the end of the word and only heavy syllables, i.e. syllables with the structure -VV(C) or -VCC can be stressed. Thus the following Main Stress Rule can be formulated for English: (a) stress falls on the rightmost heavy syllable in the word (cf. 'blossom, 'human vs di 'vine, dis 'turb); (b) the search for a heavy syllable is restricted to the last three syllables (cf. 'history, cri 'terion, 'narrative, me 'tropolis). This rule coincides with the one that is relevant for native words, since these are generally mono- or disyllabic. It is not applicable to derived words with affixes inherently marked for stress (e.g. -ee in employee) or stress attraction (e.g. -ity, -ic, -ian, -ial) and to cases of differential stress marking (e.g. 'transfer – trans 'fer). The regularity for differential stress marking is that nouns or adjectives tend to be stressed on the first syllable and verbs on the second.

Orthography

Modern English orthography is generally regarded as highly irregular, or even chaotic. This impression is particularly created by the fact that 400 of the most frequently used words (e.g. could, eye, rough, great, people, of, etc.) are extremely irregular in their spelling. But even a general assessment of the relationship between phonology and the orthography for the language as a whole has to admit that the distance between them is greater than in other Germanic languages, even if over 70 per cent of the vocabulary is spelled according to general patterns.

Old English was first written down by Roman missionaries, whose Latin alphabet was not quite adequate for the representation of the Old English phonemic inventory. This orthographic system was modified by French scribes after the Norman Conquest. The result of the introduction of printing was a certain standardization in spelling. William Caxton chose the system that reflected the speech of the London area and apart from minor modifications this system is still the one used today. Phonological changes that occurred in the fifteenth and in subsequent centuries are not reflected in the spelling system: (a) the Great Vowel Shift, as a result of which the long vowels of Middle English (/eː, ɛː, aː, ɔː, oː/) were raised, with the two highest vowels (/iː/, /uː/) being diphthongized (/aɪ/, /aʊ/); (b) the loss of /k/ and /g/ before nasals: knee, know, gnash, gnat; (c) the loss of post-vocalic /r/ in British English and the development of non-rhotic dialects; and (d) the split in the further development of Middle English /u/, which developed into /ʌ/ in Southern British English (hut, cut), but remained /ʊ/ after labials: pull, push, wool.

If English is not very transparent and consistent as far as the differentiation and representation of phonemes is concerned, it certainly scores higher from a morphological point of view. Morphemes are generally represented by one form (e.g. -s, -ed), even if there is allomorphic variation. Moreover, the connection between words related by derivational processes is clearer in the orthography than in speech, for example: divine, divinity; serene, serenity; indicate, indicative of; profane, profanity.

17.3. Morphology

In the course of its historical development, English has lost most of its inflectional contrasts. In the noun phrase, nearly all case distinctions have disappeared. Articles and adjectives are invariant in Modern English. The verb morphology was also greatly simplified during the Middle English period: the distinction between mood categories (indicative, subjunctive, imperative) largely disappeared and the system of person–number distinctions was largely reduced, too. Originally an inflecting language like its Germanic neighbours, English has developed into a largely isolating or analytic language.

Nouns and Pronouns

The only case distinction preserved in English nouns is the one between the genitive (*John's book*, *the President's men*) and the morphologically unmarked 'common case'. Since the ending -*s* can also be attached to a whole phrase ('the group genitive') it is frequently analysed not as a case ending, but as a phrasal affix: *someone else's girlfriend, the King of Denmark's court.* Only pronouns have preserved a three-term distinction between a nominative ('subjective'), accusative ('objective') and a genitive ('possessive') form: *I, me, my; he, him, his; she, her, her; we, us, our*, etc. The second-person pronoun *you*, which also lacks a plural counterpart (except in some American dialects, which use *you all, y'all* in this function), is an exception to this regularity. A parallel distinction in the 'paradigm' of the relative and interrogative pronoun *who* is rarely preserved in spoken varieties of English. *Whom* tends to be replaced by *who*. In contrast to Old English, grammatical gender does not play a role as an inflectional category in Modern English. What is relevant for the choice of anaphoric pronouns are natural or metaphorical sex distinctions: *the uncle . . . he, the aunt . . . she, the family . . . it/they, the ship/engine . . . she.* The only inflectional category that has been preserved for nouns throughout the history of English is number (singular vs plural). Whereas the singular form is morphologically unmarked, the plural is indicated by the suffix ‹-*s*›, with -*s*, -*z*, and -*ɪz* as allomorphs depending on the phonological environment. In addition to this major pattern, there are a few irregular plurals, signalled by the suffix -*en* (*oxen, children*), by internal vowel change (*foot–feet, goose–geese*), by zero (*sheep, series*) as well as by a few foreign affixes. *One* is used as a pro-form for count nouns (*I like old books better than new ones*) and there are two different sentential pro-forms in English: *it* and *so*. The regular neuter pronoun *it* is used after factive verbs (*I regret/resent/know it*) and a few other subclasses of verbs (*I tried/proved/ suggested it*), whereas the originally deictic expression *so* is used after verbs of saying, of wishing and of thinking: *I think/guess/assume/suppose so, if you so wish/desire . . ., she said so.*

Adjectives

Adjectives are invariant in both predicative and attributive position: *the girl is intelligent, an intelligent girl....* Comparative and superlative forms of gradable adjectives can either be formed with the suffixes *-er, -est* or, analytically, with the inherently comparative and superlative adverbs *more* and *most.* Which of these two strategies is used depends primarily on the syllable structure of the adjective. Monosyllabic adjectives take the inflectional form: *big, bigger, biggest*; adjectives with three syllables take the analytic form: *intelligent, more intelligent, most intelligent.* Disyllabic adjectives accept both strategies. Disyllabic adjectives with synthetic comparatives are frequently found with adjectives ending in an unstressed vowel, in /l/ or in /ə(r)/: *funny, narrow, feeble, clever.* Another relevant factor for the choice of these two strategies is frequency of usage. Rare adjectives tend to take the analytic form even if they are monosyllabic.

Verbal Inflection

Verbs inflect for tense and marginally also for person and number. As in other Germanic languages only two tenses are differentiated by means of inflection: the present (non-past) and the past. Weak verbs such as *walk, raise, mend* form their past tense by adding a dental suffix (*walked, raised, mended*), whereas strong verbs (*eat, dig, drink, rise, throw*) exhibit vowel gradation (*ablaut*) in their past tense forms and past participles (*ate, dug, drank, rose, threw*). As in other Germanic languages, the class of strong verbs in English is a closed class and contains very common and frequent verbs.

Apart from the copula *be*, which exhibits more contrasts in its inflectional paradigm than any other verb in English (*I am, you are, she is*; *I was, you were*, etc.), verbs only inflect for person and number in the present tense and the only contrast is that between the third-person singular and the rest. In addition to these different finite forms, all verbs (except the modal auxiliaries) can occur in three different non-finite forms: the infinitive (base form), the present participle (*-ing* form), which is formed by adding the suffix *-ing* to the base form, and the past participle, which is formed by adding a dental suffix (weak verbs), by adding the suffix *-en* or by changing the vowel (strong verbs). There are no specific imperative forms in Modern English, the base form of a verb is used in imperative sentences (*sit down!*). There is also no consistent inflectional distinction between an indicative and a subjunctive mood. Where other Germanic languages use a specific subjunctive form, English uses the past tense: *if he knew the answer...*, *I wish I had not said this*; the base form: *long live the Queen!*, *I demand that he go immediately*; or a modal verb: *may the Lord bless you, I insist that he should go.* The only remainder of a former subjunctive mood is the form *were* as used with the first or third-person singular: *if I were you....* But in such contexts many speakers already use *was.*

Apart from the copula *be*, each verb thus occurs in maximally four (weak

Figure 17.1 Verb inflection

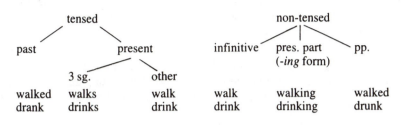

verbs) or five different inflectional forms (strong verbs) and the inflectional paradigms of verbs in English are therefore best represented by diagrams such as Figure 17.1.

Tense and Aspect

If the tense system of English is analysed from a purely structural point of view, there is only a two-term opposition: only the contrast between past and non-past (present) is marked in the morphology of the verb: *John plays tennis, John played tennis*. In addition to these two tenses, already distinguished in Old English, a 'future tense' is developing as a result of combining the present tense of the volitional auxiliary *will* with the infinitive of main verbs: *John will play tennis next week*. But there are also other ways of referring to future time. The other so-called 'relative tenses' (present perfect, past perfect, future perfect) are combinations of the three 'absolute' tenses with the perfect marker *have* and the past participle of a main verb: *John has played tennis before, John had played tennis, John will have played tennis*. The standard terminology nicely reflects the compositional character of these 'relative tenses' in English. From a semantic point of view, however, these 'relative tenses' are not perfectly compositional and it is therefore not uncommon to analyse the English tense system as comprising six rather than only two terms, or at least as being on the way towards developing such a system:

John plays tennis (present)
John played tennis (past)
John will play tennis next week (future)
John has played tennis before (present perfect)
John had played tennis (past perfect)
John will have played tennis by that time (future perfect)

In addition to *will*, *shall* (only first person, Br. Eng.), and *to be going to*, the simple present and the present progressive can also be used to refer to future time. None of these devices expresses pure future time reference: *will* is typically used in contingent statements (e.g. conditionals or predictions implying a conditional antecedent) and for the distant future, *to be going to* expresses intention of the speaker (statements) or hearer (interrogatives) and the simple present can be used in sentences relating to general schedules or regularities. The present progressive expresses that an arrangement has been made at the time of utterance.

Will you play tennis next week? (Will you have the time?)
Are you going to play tennis next week? (What are your plans?)
Are you playing tennis next week? (Have you booked a court?)

Moreover, the combination of *will* + progressive can be used to express 'future-as-a-matter-of-course': *will you be passing through Manchester, do you think?*

The present perfect is in sharp paradigmatic contrast with the past tense and only combines with time adverbials that include or may include the moment of utterance: *I have not seen him so far, I have not had breakfast this morning.* The past tense, by contrast, combines with time adverbials that identify a time before the moment of utterance: *two days ago I saw George.* Whether the perfect marker *have* + *-ed* is a tense marker or an aspectual marker is a matter of some debate. What is clear, however, is that the present perfect is used if a time span is under consideration that starts in the past and goes up to the moment of utterance ('extended now'). The 'gesamtbedeutung' of the present perfect can therefore be described as 'current relevance'. This general meaning manifests itself differently in the context of different classes of verbs (aktionsarten):

I have known the Jones for a long time (state up to the present)
I have been to the States (perfect of experience, existential perfect)
The taxi has arrived (resultative perfect)
Anthony Perkins has died from Aids at the age of sixty (13 September 1992)

If the verb expresses an event, its combination with the present perfect expresses an event plus a resultant state at the moment of utterance. There is a slight contrast between British English and American English in so far as the past rather than the present perfect is used in American English in the contexts of adverbials that require the present perfect in British English: *did you ever see such a thing?, I was never there before, did you sell your car yet?* In other words, the new category in the tense system of English is more restricted in its use in American English than in British English.

If the perfect cannot easily be identified as either a tense or an aspectual category, the opposition between the progressive (expanded form) and the non-progressive (simple form) is clearly an aspectual one (e.g. *John is eating fish – John eats fish*). The simple form of the verb is morphologically unmarked, whereas the progressive aspect is expressed by the copula *be* and the suffix *-ing* added on to the main verb following the copula. This progressive marker can combine with all tenses, and with all verbs, except for a few stative ones and modal auxiliaries: *contain*, *own*, *belong to*, *consist of*, *know*, etc. It also combines with the copula *be* and adjectives or noun phrases: *he is being impertinent, I am being a policeman*. In combination with verbs the progressive denotes a process or situation that forms an open interval around a moment of reference and is part of a more comprehensive situation or event (subinterval property). In the following examples these moments of reference are the moment of utterance (a); a moment specified by a time adverbial (b); a moment specified by an event (c); and a moment specified by a series of such events (d):

(a) John is working in the library.
(b) John was sleeping at eight.
(c) When I left the party, John was playing the piano.
(d) Whenever I visit him he is mowing the lawn.

As a result of the location of the point of reference, the situation is seen from within i.e. a process is seen as ongoing, whereas a situation described in the simple form is seen from outside. Due to the subinterval property, the progressive does not combine with time adverbials expressing an upper bound (**Mary was dancing until the music stopped*), it expresses possible incompleteness in combination with event verbs (*when I came to the river the child was drowning*) and an unbounded situation in combination with adverbials of duration. On the basis of this general meaning more specific uses can be identified in certain contexts: 'temporal frame' in contexts like (c), backgrounding as opposed to temporal sequence ((c) and (e)), omission i.e. deliberate non-acting (f), a function in the mathematical sense or a continuous process (g), etc.

(e) I look at Mary. She was smiling.
(f) Nobody was answering the phone.
(g) The temperature is rising.
      This is costing you too much.
      More people are dying of cancer this year than in previous years.

In addition to these central aspects of meaning, the English progressive also has some minor extended uses: (a) the futurate use mentioned above, an emotive use in combinations with frequency adverbials (*he is always getting into trouble with the police, I am constantly forgetting people's names*), which invariably expresses an element of hyperbole or exaggeration, and an interpretative use, where the progressive is used for a second more elaborate interpretation of a situation described by a preceding simple form and expresses something like 'situation A amounts to B': *those on the roll who do not vote will in effect be voting no; if you fail to plan you are planning to fail; I'm not insisting, I'm merely suggesting.* Combinations of the progressive with the present perfect are not easy to describe in completely compositional terms. In contrast to the simple present perfect, such combinations may describe repetition (vs single occurrence), concomitant effects (vs results), indefinite quantity (vs definite quantity), incompleteness (vs completion) and relate a specification of duration to the activity rather than to the resultant state.

> The baby has been falling out of its bed. vs The baby has fallen out of bed.
> I have been mowing the lawn. vs I have mowed the lawn.
> It has been snowing a lot. vs It has snowed two inches.
> Perhaps we have been spoiling her a little. vs We have spoilt her a little.
> They have been leaving for half an hour. vs They have left for half an hour.

Starting from modest beginnings in Old English and Middle English, the progressive has continuously extended its territory and now also combines with the passive (*the road is being repaired*), occasionally even with the perfect + passive (*how long has this bridge been being built?*), and with the copula + adjectives or noun phrases (*aren't you being a little defensive?, I am being a policeman*). In the combinations with adjectives and noun phrases the progressive expresses temporary wilful behaviour and/or role playing. This use of the progressive seems to be closely related to the interpretative use: only agentive subjects are possible (*John is being rude/noisy, *the river is being noisy*) and only adjectives that denote properties that are subject to manipulation are selected: *Mary is being polite/frank/sincere/obscure, *Mary is being old/tall/fair-haired*. Furthermore, such sentences can be used to tell somebody what s/he is doing, what his or her behaviour amounts to: *you are being very rude/good/obnoxious*. In other words, sentences like these specify a non-obvious, more far-reaching interpretation for some event than some description already given. The simple (non-progressive) form is used in habitual and generic sentences (*this bucket leaks, do you drive?*), but also for instantaneous events and in explicitly performative formulae (*I promise you ...*).

17.4. Syntax

The Nominal Group

The Noun Phrase
The typical make-up of a complex noun phrase in terms of constituents and the linear sequence of these constituents can be illustrated by the following example:

The last two hectic days in Stratford, which we spent together . . .

Noun phrase complements and relative clauses follow the head noun, attributive adjectives generally precede it. Articles typically occur at the left periphery. There are two semantically and distributionally overlapping genitive constructions. Genitives marked by the suffix -*'s* precede the head noun: *John's book*; those introduced by the preposition *of* follow their head noun: *the leader of the band*. In examples like *a friend of my father's* or *a friend of my parents'* the two constructions are combined to form the 'double genitive'. In contrast to other Germanic languages, English does not allow complex pre-nominal modifiers. Adjectives or participles together with complements can only follow their head noun: *a typically negative remark* but *a country rich in natural resources*. Only if the adjective is incorporated into an adjectival or participial compound can such combinations occur in pre-nominal position: *an avenue lined with trees* vs *a tree-lined avenue*. This constraint can plausibly be connected with two other regularities: (a) the constraint that adjectival modifiers have to be adjacent to the head nouns, found in all Germanic languages; and (b) the rule that complements strictly follow their adjectival heads in English: *she is proud of her achievements*.

Relative Clauses
Relative clauses in Standard English can be introduced by the pronouns *who* (*whose, whom*) and *which* (also used as interrogative pronouns), by the invariant marker *that*, by zero and marginally also by *as*. The choice between these markers depends on factors such as properties of the antecedent (noun or sentence, personal or non-personal noun), the grammatical function of the relativized constituent (subject or object), the type of relative clause (restrictive or non-restrictive), the environment of the relative pronoun (presence of a preposition), etc. *As* is marginal and only occurs after *such*: *such women as he knew were teachers*. *Who* (*whom*) is used after personal antecedents, *which* is used after non-personal antecedents: *the students who* vs *the chair which*. Relative markers can generally be omitted in restrictive relative clauses unless the position relativized into is the subject position: *the people I have talked to* vs *people who know me*. The omission of relative pronouns functioning as subjects is only possible after existential *there*: *there is a man wants to see you*. *That* can generally be used in restrictive relative clauses unless the clause is introduced by a preposition: *the room that the child is hiding in* vs *the room in which the child is hiding*. Headless relatives are introduced by *who/which/what + ever* or by *what*: *whatever I gave them was spent quickly*. Accessible to relativization are not only all subjects and all types of objects, but also the second argument of a comparative construction (the so-called 'standard of comparison'):

> *Trying to decide whom Luellen reminded her of, she traced a flimsy memory back to her mother's distant admiration for a film actress, ... Madelein Cross, than whom no one could have looked less murderous.*
>
> (A. Cross, *Death in the Faculty*)

Another specific feature of English relatives (and interrogatives) is a phenomenon known as 'unbounded dependencies': the grammatical function borne by a clause-initial *who, which* or *what* can be that of a subject or object in that clause, i.e. with respect to the closest verb, but it can also be some grammatical function inside a smaller constituent properly contained inside the clause: *this is exactly what the British government is now trying to find ways to do.* In the preceding example *what* bears no grammatical function with respect to the verb *try* or the verb *find* for that matter, but functions as object of the verb *do.*

Reflexive and Reciprocal Pronouns

Reflexive (e.g. *herself, ourselves*) and reciprocal pronouns (*each other, one another*) are non-referential expressions (anaphors) that depend for their reference on antecedents given somewhere else within a certain domain, typically within the same clause: *John admires himself, John and Mary admire each other*. Reflexives express co-reference, reciprocals indicate that the relation expressed by the verb holds in both directions for the arguments given (i.e. *John admires Mary and Mary admires John*). In Old English there were no true reflexives. The opposition between co-reference (*John$_i$ admires himself$_i$*) and disjoint reference in the same clause (*John$_i$ admires him$_j$*) could only be suggested rather than clearly expressed, since personal pronouns did double duty for both functions. To indicate more clearly that co-reference was intended in such contexts, the emphatic focus particle *self* (*sylf, seolf*) – i.e. the Old English counterpart of German *selbst* or Dutch *zelfs* – gradually came to be used after the pronoun in later Old English and Middle English (*he hyne sylfne ahang* 'he hanged himself'). These combinations of pronoun + emphatic particle lost their compositionality in late Middle English and were ultimately fused into one word. As a result of this grammaticalization process, Modern English developed 'complex' or 'strong' reflexives (like Spanish *si mismo*) in contrast to the weak reflexives of German (*sich*) and Scandinavian (*sig*). A certain number of properties of the English reflexive pronouns are clearly connected with or even follow from this historical development. First, there are distinct forms for all persons, for the singular and plural and for three genders in the third-person singular (*myself, yourself, himself, herself, itself, ourselves, yourselves, themselves*) and reflexives agree with their antecedents in person, number and gender (*she injured herself, we injured ourselves*, etc.) Moreover, there is a special indefinite form (*oneself*). In contrast to Scandinavian, however, there are no possessive reflexives in English. Second, there are hardly any inherently reflexive verbs, such as *to pride oneself upon,* *to absent oneself from*, *to avail oneself of* and verbs of grooming, typically reflexive in other languages, may combine with, but do not require a reflexive pronoun: *to wash/dress/shave (oneself)*. Third, there is no clear contrast in English between reflexive pronouns and so-called emphatic reflexives, i.e. combinations of pronouns and nouns with the emphatic focus particle corresponding to German *selbst*. The Old English particle *self* did not survive into Modern English and exactly the same expressions that are used as reflexive pronouns are also used as such emphatic focus particles: *the President himself won't come, the President won't come himself*. In the core cases, reflexive pronouns in English have their antecedents within the same clause and these antecedents are subjects: *John allowed himself a rest*. The antecedent typically c-commands the reflexive: **himself hates John*; and split antecedents are excluded: *John$_i$ spoke to Mary$_j$ about *themselves$_{ij}$*. Furthermore, personal pronouns and reflexive pronouns are typically in complementary distribution: *John$_i$ admires *him$_i$/himself$_i$* vs *John$_i$ thinks that Mary admires him$_i$/*himself$_i$*. Whether antecedent and reflexive are also clause mates in the so-called 'Raising' or 'Exceptional Case-marking Construction' (*John believes himself to be clever*) is not a perfectly safe, but a plausible assumption. In addition to these simple regularities, however, reflexives in English also manifest some more complex and surprising properties: not only subjects, but also objects can be antecedents for reflexives: *John talked to Mary about herself*. First-person and second-person reflexives are possible without any antecedent in the same or a preceding clause: *this would be difficult for my wife and myself*. Moreover, reflexives and plain pronouns are not always in complementary distribution. In certain contexts either pronoun may be used to express co-reference: *John hid the book behind him/himself, John pulled the blanket towards him/himself, Mary told John that there was a picture of him/himself in the newspaper*. The difference in meaning between members of such minimal pairs concerns the point of view: the reflexive obliges us to take the protagonist's perspective whereas the use of the pronoun allows the normal 'objective' point of view. Finally, we find plain pronouns in clauses where we would expect reflexives, since the antecedent is in the same clause: *John found a snake near him, we have a whole day before us, John left his family behind him*. In most of these contexts, the meaning of the sentence requires co-reference, i.e. the pronoun given is the only possible choice and does not contrast with anything else. And we also find reflexives with antecedents beyond the immediate clause: *Zapp sat down at the desk and opened the drawers. In the top right hand one was an envelope addressed to himself*.

Indefinite Pronouns

The traditional class of indefinite pronouns is a very heterogeneous group of expressions and includes subclasses with widely differing syntactic behaviour: expressions like *some, any, every, each, either, all* behave partly like articles (*each book, every copy, some people*) and are therefore often grouped together with the latter as 'determiners'. *Half, both* and *all*, by contrast, may precede the definite article (*half/all the money*). Expressions like *many, few, much, several* and partly also *every* manifest a more adjective-like behaviour: *the many/few people who were there, your every move*; and expressions like *someone, anybody, everyone, nothing, somewhere* or *sometime* function like noun phrases: *something is happening.* On the basis of semantic criteria all of these expressions are often grouped together as quantifiers. Among the striking features of English in this domain is the internal make-up of noun-phrase-like expressions: such indefinites have been formed and lexicalized in the history of English by combining 'determiners' like *some, any, every, no* with generic nouns like *body, thing, time, place*, or pronouns: *somewhere, somehow; someone, everyone.* Remarkable from a comparative perspective are also certain lexical differentiations: the selection of *much* vs *many* or (a) *little* vs (a) *few* is sensitive to inherent properties of the noun following (mass vs count: *There is not much wine left* vs *There are not many bottles left*). The distinction between *each* and *every*, too, has no parallel in other Germanic languages. *Each*, as opposed to *every*, is used as a universal quantifier if a restricted domain of quantification is specified in the context: *Every student is asked to fill in this form* vs *Seven students were there. Each one had brought an instrument.* More attention than any other lexical differentiation in this domain, however, has been devoted to the one between *some* and *any*. Ambiguous sentences like *I would not give this to anybody* and certain contrasts in meaning and distribution (*anybody can come to the party* vs *I didn't see anybody*) suggest that a free-choice *any* has to be distinguished from an existential *any*. The latter use is only found in negative-polarity ('downward entailing') contexts, i.e. overt negation, implicit negation, interrogatives, conditionals, emotive predicates, etc. (*if you see anybody, please let me know; I regret that I said anything*), and is partly in complementary distribution with *some* (*I saw somebody, I said something*). Existential *any* and *some* also overlap in their distribution, however, and may express a distinction of scope (*he didn't talk to some students – he didn't talk to any students*), a distinction of illocutionary force (*would you like anything to eat? – would you like something to eat?*), of expectation with respect to an answer (*don't you have any children? – don't you have some children?*), etc. to mention only some common oppositions. What the exact relationship between *some* and *any* is is a matter of considerable controversy.

Verbs and Verb Phrases

Main Verbs and Auxiliary Verbs

Within the huge class of English verbs, a small subclass of auxiliary verbs can be singled out and opposed to the main verbs on the basis of the following criteria: first, auxiliary verbs cannot function as main predicate of a sentence, but have to combine with a main verb to form a sentence (*I will follow you* vs *I followed him*). Sentences like *he could the Bible in the holy tongue* or *I must to the king* were still possible at the time of Shakespeare, but are ungrammatical in Modern English. Second, a number of constructions require auxiliary verbs: (a) the negation marker *not* invariably follows the first auxiliary in a tensed sentence, unless it precedes another scope-bearing element: *many arrows did not hit the target* vs *not many arrows hit the target*. If the corresponding affirmative sentence does not contain an auxiliary, the dummy verb *do* has to be inserted into its negative counterpart: *I cannot hear you* vs *I do not know*; (b) in a variety of constructions the tensed verb precedes the subject and it is only auxiliary verbs that are affected by this process of inversion: *can you hear me? little does she know ...* ; (c) auxiliary verbs carry the sentence stress and are thus required if the affirmative polarity of a sentence (as opposed to its negation) is focused: *he **must** help us*, I *do know*; (d) auxiliary verbs are also required in case of post-verbal ellipsis, as in question tags, etc.: *he found out, didn't he?, you are going, are you?* Within the class of auxiliary verbs, two subgroups can be distinguished: the primary auxiliary verbs: *be, have, do*; and the secondary or modal auxiliary verbs: *will, shall, must, can, may*. Modal auxiliaries do not have finite forms and can therefore not be combined (except in Scottish English), they do not take the inflectional suffix *-s* in the third-person singular of the present tense nor do they combine with the infinitive marker *to*: *I tried to see her* vs *I could see her*. The phonological forms *do* and *have* have several uses. The verb of possession *have*, for example, can function as a main verb in British English, but not in (all varieties of) American English. This means that all of the following constructions are allowed in Br.Eng., but are usually excluded in Am.Eng.: *I haven't any books, have you any books? I have a few books.*

It is a characteristic property of English sentences that the verb phrase, i.e. the verb and its complements, is generally preceded by an auxiliary complex (also called 'Infl.'), i.e. by one or more auxiliary verbs, which carry the tense, person and number marker. Only in the most simple structures is there no such auxiliary and the main verb inflects for tense, person and number (*John snores* vs *John could have been killed*). The maximal number of such auxiliary verbs is four and the order between them, expressed in terms of their function, is as follows: modal – perfect – progressive – passive. The last three of these functions are expressed by discontinuous expressions: (*have + ed*) (*be + ing*) (*be + ed*), i.e. the perfect marker *have* is followed by the past participle of the next verb (*to have organized*), the progressive marker *be* is followed by the *-ing*-form of the following verb (*to have been organizing*) and the passive auxiliary *be* co-occurs with a following past participle. It is this auxiliary complex that occurs in sentence-final position when the verb phrase is preposed: *he said he would never kill deer again, but kill deer he did*; or omitted: *he wasn't killed, but he could have been.* Within the verb phrase all

complements follow the verb and noun-phrases invariably precede prepositional phrases: *she provided food for the refugees, she provided the refugees
with food.* In so-called 'split infinitives', which are frowned upon by
prescriptive grammarians but quite common in modern usage, adverbs are
inserted between the infinitive marker *to* and the main verb: *to even think of
that would be a crime, he decided to hastily withdraw.*

Grammatical Relations

Grammatical relations between a verb and its arguments are exclusively
marked by the position of the relevant arguments. Except for a few marked
patterns of word order, the subject precedes and the object follows the verb
in declarative sentences. But even in these marked patterns, the normal order
between subject and main verb is normally preserved: *John I don't like, never
have I seen such a sight.* Only pronouns have different inflectional forms for
subjects and objects: *he saw him, she wrote to her.* The finite verb agrees with
its subject in person and number, but this is only visible in the third-person
of the present tense: *Mary writes poems, I write essays.* There are no
subjectless sentences of the German type *mich friert* in English, nor is it
possible to leave the subject position unspecified if the relevant information
is contextually given, as in Italian or Spanish. If no other subject can be used
a dummy subject (*it, there*) has to be inserted: *it is raining, there are good
linguists and bad linguists.* The subject position is normally filled by a noun
phrase, but prepositional phrases (*under the bed is a good place to hide,
between nine and ten would suit me*) and adverbs are also marginally possible
(*tomorrow will be cloudy in most places*). Objects are not differentiated
paradigmatically, but only syntagmatically. In other words, only if there is
more than one object are they differentiated through word order (*I will spare
you the details*) or through prepositions (*Mary gave all her money to her
children*). All single (direct) objects in simple transitive clauses are treated
alike, i.e. they are not – and cannot – be differentiated as dative objects,
accusative objects, etc. On the other hand, direct objects are of course kept
apart from prepositional objects: *I trust George* vs *I trust in God.* Objects are
always adjacent to the verb that governs them. Only focus particles like *only,
even* can be inserted between main verb and object: *I saw only John.* Manner
adverbs are rarely found in that position.

On the basis of its valency (number and kinds of arguments) different basic
sentence patterns can be distinguished in a language. Not only straightforward
intransitive verbs (*John snores/dined/sneezed*), and transitive verbs with
missing arguments (*he drinks/knows/drives*), but also symmetric predicates
with plural or conjoined subjects can be constructed without objects in
English: *they separated, John and Mary met/agreed/kissed/married.* The
difference in meaning between such constructions with conjoined subjects
and the alternative transitive construction (*John met/kissed/married Mary,
John agrees with Mary*) concerns such aspects as empathy, initiative, control,

etc. Verbs with prepositional objects are sometimes indistinguishable, but have to be distinguished, from phrasal verbs (particle verbs) with direct objects: *he talked about the situation* vs *he brought along some friends.* Phrasal verbs are monosyllabic or disyllabic verbs of Germanic origin (with the stress on the first syllable) that combine with adverbial particles like *about, across, down, in, off, on, out, up, through, away, along, by,* i.e. with expressions that can also be used as prepositions. The usual valency distinctions also apply here: there are intransitive phrasal verbs (*to speak up, to work away*), transitive ones (*to eat up, to bring along*) and phrasal verbs that combine with prepositional objects (*to put up with something, to come up with something*). There are, however, a number of syntactic properties that differentiate between transitive phrasal verbs and verbs taking prepositional objects: the adverbial particles of phrasal verbs can follow an object and must follow it, if it is a pronoun: *he threw it up* vs *he talked about it.* In contrast to such particles, prepositions may precede an interrogative or relative pronoun: *about what did he talk? what did he talk about?* vs *what did he throw up?* Manner adverbials may be inserted between verbs and prepositions, but not between verbs and particles: *he talked loudly about the situation.* What these tests show is that the adverbial particle forms a constituent with the verb.

Ditransitive verbs show up in two different syntactic patterns: (a) in the double-object construction (*Mary gave John a book, I threw him some nuts*); and (b) in constructions with noun phrase + prepositional phrase (*Mary gave a book to John, Fred blamed John for the accident, Fred blamed the accident on John*). These two objects are terminologically distinguished either as 'primary' and 'secondary object': Mary gave John$_{pr}$ the book$_{sec}$; or as 'direct' vs 'indirect' object: Mary gave the book$_{dir.obj}$ to John$_{indir.obj}$. Terminology varies considerably for such constructions depending on which object is grouped together with those of simple transitive verbs and depending on how the relationship between the two structures *Mary gave John a book* and *Mary gave a book to John* is seen. The complements following verbs like *elect, consider, make, call,* etc., are traditionally distinguished as direct object and predicative complement, but are sometimes also analysed as a specific type of non-finite clause, a 'small clause': *they elected [him President]$_S$, we consider [Bill a genius]$_S$.*

The system of 'voice' comprises three options in English: the active, the passive and the 'middle' voice (mediopassive). The passive and the middle voice involve a reduction of the basic valency of a verb. The passive in English is formed with the auxiliary *be* and the past participle of the verb: *this house was built by a famous architect.* In addition to *be, get* can also be used as a passive auxiliary in informal spoken English. The choice of *get,* as opposed to *be,* indicates either a certain emotional involvement of the speaker: *I got stung,* or partial responsibility of the Patient, i.e. of the person denoted by the object in the relevant active sentence: *he got (himself) run over by a car, the students got arrested to prove their point.* Not all transitive verbs (e.g. *fit, suit, lack, survive*) can occur in the passive voice. The relevant constraint is a semantic-pragmatic one: the subject of the passive construction must be a true Patient, i.e. be genuinely affected by the action of the verb. Ditransitive verbs have two passives: *John was offered a big cigar, a big cigar was offered to John.* In both cases it is the object adjacent to the verb in the active counterpart that shows up as subject of the passive version. In contrast to other Germanic languages, verbs with prepositional objects also permit passivization (*I have been lied to, hard drinks are best abstained from*) and even verbs with directional complements and sentences with intransitive verbs and local adjuncts are compatible with this construction, provided the constraint mentioned above is met: *this bed has been slept in, this lake has been gone across many times in winter.* Simple intransitive verbs (*dance, snore, sneeze*) do not occur in passive constructions. In contrast to passivized intransitive sentences with locative adjuncts (*this bed has been slept in, this cup has been drunk out of*) the passive version of a sentence with *snore* or *dance* would not have a subject and, as was mentioned before, there are no subjectless sentences in English. Expressions like *to make fun/use/a mess of, to take stock/advantage/care of,* etc. are analysable either as complex verbs or as combinations of verbs plus objects and these two possible analyses are reflected in two possible passives: *John was taken advantage of – advantage was taken of John.* In the so-called 'middle' voice, transitive verbs are constructed like intransitive ones and what is normally selected as object appears in subject position: *Shakespeare does not translate, this bed folds up easily, this tent puts up in five minutes, this paint applies evenly.* In contrast to other Germanic languages, English does not use a reflexive marker in such constructions, whose meaning can roughly be described as expressing inherent properties of objects in a basically transitive construction.

There are no productive morphological processes in English as a result of which the basic valency of a verb is increased. A phenomenon that could, however, be mentioned in this context is the existence of a large number of verbs that have both an intransitive and a transitive use such that the type of subject selected in the intransitive use corresponds exactly to the type of object selected in the transitive use: *the baby sat up – John sat the baby up, the ball bounced – Mary bounced the ball, you work too hard – don't let the boss work you too hard, tomatoes grow in this valley – the farmers grow tomatoes in this valley.* The second of such pairs of sentences expresses the causation of the event denoted by the first. Because of the correspondence in the selectional restrictions of the two uses of such verbs they are often called 'ergative' verbs or verbs with 'double orientation'. Another interesting phenomenon that can briefly be mentioned in this context is the existence of complex verbal constructions like the following: *to take a look, to give a smile, to do a dance, to get a feel.* These constructions are composed of a semantically very unspecific verb (*have, take, do, get, give*) and a de-verbal noun exactly identical to the underlying verb. Such constructions with *have*, which are more common in British and Australian than in American English, express intentional actions (*Fred had a swim*) that are limited in time, but not momentary (*after lunch we had a chat in the library*), repeatable, but not goal-directed (*he had a bite of my sandwich, let's have a stroll*). In contrast to *have*, *take* is used if there is an external goal and the action has a specific beginning and end: *let's take a walk to the railway station, the lovers took a last long look at each other*.

Both subjects and objects are rather vague and unspecific in English, as far as their interpretation in terms of syntagmatic semantic relations (thematic roles) are concerned. In other words, a wide variety of such thematic roles can be coded as subject or objects. There is no close tie-up between the thematic role 'Agent' and the grammatical function of subject and, more generally, no consistent mapping of thematic roles onto grammatical functions. In the following examples the thematic role of the argument coded as subject is given in brackets:

This advert will sell us a lot of dog food. (Instrument)
The road was rustling with dead leaves. (Location)
The dead bird was dripping blood. (Source)
The trial cannot proceed. (Theme)
Tomorrow will be cloudy in most places. (Time)
The car burst a tyre. (Possessor)

In addition to this remarkable option, there is of course also the possibility of encoding the arguments in a way more common in European languages:

He will sell a lot of dog food with this advert.
Dead leaves were rustling on the road.
Blood was dripping from the dead bird.
We cannot proceed with this trial.
A tyre of the car burst.

From a functional point of view we could see these options as compensatory mechanisms for the lack of flexibility exhibited by English word order. It is the choice in the selection of a subject that allows English a certain flexibility in the selection of a sentence topic, i.e. for the entity which the rest of the sentence is about.

The Sentence
English is a strict SVO language. SVO is the linear sequence of the major building blocks in a declarative sentence, regardless of whether it is a main clause or a subordinate clause: *John wrote a letter, I know that John wrote a letter*. It is also the order found in imperatives with a subject: *you mind your*

own business! Deviations from this basic pattern of constituent order are marked and therefore called 'inversion'. In most cases it is the auxiliary verb that changes its position with respect to the subject ('Subject-Auxiliary Inversion'), but inversion of subject and main verb is also possible. Whether or not such inversion is a reflex of an earlier verb-second rule is not clear. Such marked patterns of constituent order are triggered by very specific conditions and roughly three broad functions can be distinguished.

First of all, Subject-Auxiliary Inversion is used in English to distinguish non-declarative sentence types from declarative ones. As in all Germanic languages, word order is used in English to distinguish interrogative sentences from declaratives. Polar interrogatives and related exclamative sentences invariably manifest inversion: *will he find us?, do you speak Spanish?, isn't this great!* Constituent interrogatives (*wh*-questions) exhibit inversion only if a constituent other than the subject is questioned: *who has eaten all the sandwiches?* vs *where does he live?* Conditional protases may also manifest inversion, but this possibility is highly restricted in English and confined to the auxiliary forms *should, had* and *were: had I known this, I would not have gone, should he arrive late, we could always change our plans, were it to reveal its secrets, that house would collapse in shame.* It is interesting to note in this connection that two of these modal verbs could not be used in questions. Finally, there are some archaic phrases with that word order: *be it ever so humble there is no place like home, suffice it to say that. . . .*

A second function of inversion is essentially semantic, since it indicates wide scope of negation and other downward-entailing operators: *never have I seen such a sight, no sooner had he opened the door than he saw . . ., rarely does he also drink whiskey.* The crucial trigger for this kind of inversion is often seen in the presence of a 'negative' adverbial (*no, not, never, seldom, rarely, little, only*) or degree adverbial (*so often had John been disappointed that . . .*) in initial position. That the presence of such an adverbial is not a sufficient condition, however, is shown by the fact that certain adverbials with negation markers do not trigger inversion: *in no time he had solved the problem, not for the first time the government is lying*; and that there are minimal pairs of sentences only one of which manifests Subject-Auxiliary Inversion: *with no job, John would be happy – with no job would John be happy, not even a year ago they made a profit – not even a year ago did they make a profit.* In such minimal pairs, which also differ in intonational phrasing, the difference in word order is associated with a difference in the scope of negation and thus in the interpretation. Only if the negation has wide scope over the whole sentence ('there is no job John would be happy with', 'They didn't even make a profit a year ago') do we find inversion.

Discourse-pragmatic factors are responsible for a third type of inversion, which also involves main verbs. The preposing of locative and directional adverbials as well as of the non-finite part of certain progressive constructions permits the shifting of subjects which introduce new discourse referents into final position: *round the bend came a long train, down the cobbled lane walked a strange-looking man, staring me right in the eye was a green-eyed monster.*

Adverbials typically occur at the left or right periphery of a clause: *yesterday I lost my wallet, I lost it yesterday.* In addition to adverbs, prepositional phrases and clauses, noun phrases may also function as adverbials in English: *the following day he left, I did it my way.* Certain types of adverbs (adjuncts rather than disjuncts) can also be found between auxiliary verbs and main verbs: *he has probably not done it.* As far as the order within phrases is concerned, English comes close to being a head-initial language. Lexical heads generally precede their phrasal co-constituents: *eat the apple, aware of the difficulties, in the morning, because I like you.* The relatively fixed word order of English does not provide much flexibility for the presentation of information in terms of theme < rheme, given < new or for highlighting and backgrounding certain constituents simply by shifting them into certain positions. The major marked patterns of word order have already been mentioned: Subject-Auxiliary Inversion, Subject–Main-Verb Inversion, Topicalization: *the last part I haven't read yet*; VP-Shift: *but fight they did.* There are, however, specific constructions which provide the possibility of highlighting and backgrounding certain constituents or of presenting the same information in different ways. The most important of these are various types of cleft constructions (*what he lost was the keys, it was the keys that he lost, that's what I mean, is that what he said?*) and various types of presentational or existential constructions (*there is a man following us, there was no one present, there blew a strong wind*). Cleft sentences separate a highlighted part ('exhaustive listing focus') from a backgrounded one. Existential and presentational sentences, on the other hand, provide the possibility to shift a non-topical subject away from the beginning of the sentence. Such constructions are introduced by the originally locative adverb *there* and a finite form of the copula *be* or an intransitive verb (e.g. *arrive, come, appear, go, emerge, rule, wave, blow*) with locational and existential import, i.e. a verb that can establish something on the scene. The noun phrases following these predicates are typically indefinite, but can also be a list of proper names or definite descriptions: *there is a house on a hill; who will help me? well, there's always George and Bill.* Given that English is a strict SVO language it does not come as a surprise that this existential *there* should have some subject properties: *there* precedes the finite verb; inverts with auxiliary verbs in the relevant constructions: *is there any milk left*; is not omissible in tags and in cases of verb phrase-deletion: *there are some potatoes left, aren't there; are there any potatoes left? – yes, there are*; and occurs in Raising constructions after verbs like *expect*, just like any other subject: *I expect there to be no problems; England expects every man to do his duty.* As far as verb agreement is concerned, it is still typically the noun phrase following the finite verb that determines its form (*there were no students present*), but even this criterion does not always clearly characterize the noun phrase following the finite verb as subject. There are sentences like *there is a bottle of wine and a glass on the table* and in some varieties of spoken English it is clearly *there* that determines the form of the finite verb: *there's lots of people waiting outside for you.*

Non-declarative Sentence Types

As in all other Germanic languages, word order is the most important device for distinguishing interrogative from declarative sentences in English. All polar interrogatives (yes/no questions) exhibit inversion and so do constituent interrogatives unless the subject is questioned: *what do you think?* vs *who cares?* There are separate morphologically simplex interrogative pronouns for animate (human) and inanimate subjects and objects (*who, whose, who*(*m*) vs *which*) as well as for temporal (*when*), local (*where*), causal (*why*) and manner adverbials (*how*). These pronouns introduce interrogative sentences used as normal questions or requests. If the noun phrase of a prepositional phrase or of a genitive construction is questioned, either the whole prepositional phrase or complex noun phrase is moved to the front or only the questioned noun phrase itself. In the latter case the preposition is left behind (Preposition Stranding): *about what did you talk? – what did you talk about?, the daughter of which professor did she marry? – which professor did he marry the daughter of?* A questioned constituent does not necessarily belong to the highest clause in some complex sentence, but can also fulfil some function in an embedded clause: *which mountain did they say they tried to climb to the top of?* Such unbounded dependencies can also be found in relative clauses. It is a specific feature of English that reduced interrogative clauses can be added as so-called 'question tags' to declarative and imperative sentences: *you know this, don't you?, sit down, won't you?, keep on the pavement, will you?* Such question tags consist of an auxiliary verb and a pronominal copy of the (understood) subject given in the main clause. Reversed-polarity tags, i.e. tags which reverse the polarity of the preceding clause (*she is very happy, isn't she? – she isn't very happy, is she?*) are found in all varieties of English. Constant-polarity tags, by contrast, only occur in British English and all related varieties: *you know him, do you? it's cold outside, is it?* Such utterances are used to express inferences, based on the hearer's current verbal or non-verbal behaviour.

Exclamative sentences, if they can be distinguished at all from interrogatives as a separate sentence type, are closely related to the latter. Negative polar interrogatives with gradable expressions can be used as exclamations (*isn't this marvellous!*) and constituent interrogatives with declarative word order are also used in this function (*what a wonderful memory you have!*). Imperatives typically lack an overt subject, which may, however, show up in the interrogative tags: *go to the door!, fill up my glass, would you?* Imperatives addressed to hearer(s) and the speaker himself are introduced by *let's*: *let's sit over there, shall we?*; and negative imperatives are introduced by *don't*: *don't trust that guy!, don't you look at my girlfriend!* Affirmative imperatives introduced by *do* are emphatic and presuppose a preceding failure of the addressee to perform the relevant action: *do come over tomorrow, do tell your wife and make my excuses.* In contrast to other Germanic languages, there are passive imperatives in English. The auxiliary verb in such sentences is always *get* rather than *be*: *get lost!, don't get run over by a car!* Another peculiarity of English is the possibility of having a constituent before the verb, either a subject or a manner adverbial: *you take the left side!, Quickly change into lower gear, Never say 'never'!, thoroughly mix the sand, cement and gravel together.*

Subordination

In contrast to many other Germanic languages, there are no differences in the word order exhibited by main and subordinate clauses. The distinction between coordination and subordination must therefore be based on other criteria, such as (a) whether one clause occupies a structural position within the other: *I regret this fact/that I said anything*; (b) whether one clause depends on another for the identification of its subject, tense, mood: *not seeing anyone, Fred left the building*; (c) whether a clause can be shifted or preposed: *Max found it appalling, whereas Fred liked it* vs *whereas Fred liked it Max found it appalling*; (d) whether an anaphoric pronoun in one clause can precede its antecedent in the other: *although he$_i$ was sick John$_i$ went to work* vs *he went to work although John was sick*; etc. Subordinate clauses are traditionally subclassified according to their function (sentential complements, adverbial clauses, relative/adjectival clauses) and according to finiteness (finite clauses vs infinitive constructions and participial constructions). Finite subject and object clauses in English are introduced by the subordinating conjunctions (complementizers) *that, whether, what, how* or *if*, depending on the clause type that is embedded: *she remembered what a struggle it had been, she asked me whether tomorrow would be convenient.* Non-finite subordinate clauses are typically subjectless, but English also has non-finite subject and object clauses with overt subjects: *for people to love their children is common, I arranged for my son to go to Stanford.* Subordinate clauses of this type are introduced by the complementizer *for* and are the result of reanalysing prepositional complements introduced by the preposition *for* as subjects of a following clause: *[It is good for a man] [not to drink wine]* > *[It is good] [for a man not to drink wine].* That *for* in such constructions is no longer a preposition expressing a benefactive relationship is shown by the fact that this preposition and the complementizer *for* can occur side by side: *it is good for me for my children to go to Stanford.* Such *for*-clauses differ in meaning from the corresponding *that*-clauses: *it offends him that men act weak* vs *it offends him for men to act weak, but fortunately they don't*; and in a variety of contexts these two types of subordinate clauses are in complementary distribution: *for/*that you to be here is imperative* vs *that/*for the earth is flat is untrue*. A *for*-clause generally denotes the thing (i.e. something virtual) that a *that*-clause names an instance of. *For*-clauses are generally more common in American English than in British English. Examples like the following are unacceptable for many British speakers: *I'd like for you to see my parents, he said for us to come immediately, we expect for it to rain any second*.

Subjectless non-finite object clauses (infinitive constructions) are typically introduced by the infinitive marker *to*: *he tried to reach the glass*. Only a few verbs can be followed by the bare infinitive: *Ed helped repair the car, Ed let Liz repair it*. Among the verbs that combine with infinitival complements, two subclasses can be distinguished: (a) those that only combine with such a complement: *she managed to convince him*; and (b) those that combine with both a nominal and an infinitival complement: *Mary persuaded John to buy the picture*. In the former subclass a further subdivision can be made: some verbs are genuinely transitive and select a personal subject as well as an infinitival complement (e.g. *like, love, prefer, try, manage, hate*), whereas others (e.g. *seem, happen, begin, appear, fail*) are basically sentential predicates, even though they also show up in the transitive construction: *I happen to like George* vs *it so happens that I like George*. In the group of verbs that combine both with an object and with an infinitival complement in surface structure a distinction is generally drawn between verbs taking three arguments, one of which can be an infinitive complement, like *persuade, convince, assist, invite, ask* and basically transitive or bivalent verbs that allow Raising (Exceptional Case Marking) of the underlying subject of the object clause (*intend, suppose, expect, guarantee, believe, assume*). Various syntactic tests like the equivalence of embedded active and passive sentences (*Ed intended Liz to photograph the child* vs *Ed intended the child to be photographed by Liz*) and the possibility of replacing the apparent object by *there* (*Ed had intended there to be a reporter at the meeting*) differentiate between these two types of infinitive constructions. Raising (of underlying subjects to objects) is more frequent and often more acceptable in gerundial or participial clauses than in main clauses: *while assuming John to be innocent, ?They assume John to be innocent*. Furthermore, this phenomenon is more often found in relative and interrogative clauses than in main clauses: *John is the man they assume to be innocent, L. claims that Proto-Germanic, a language he concludes to have been OV, can be divided into three branches*; *?L. concludes Proto-Germanic to have been OV*). The unacceptability of Raising in main clauses is often a consequence of the non-permissibility of having one or even two objects after the relevant non-finite verb: *?we thought the boy to be honest* vs *a boy we thought to be honest*; *this entity was always mentioned in connection with some dreary object which Nan was trying to persuade him to be unavoidably necessary*. Passivization in Raising constructions can be applied either to the object clause alone (*the authorities believe* *the bomb to have been planted by the IRA*) or to the whole sentence (*the IRA is believed to have planted the bomb*). Another specific feature of English is an infinitive construction with basically monovalent adjectives in which the superficial subject is understood as underlying object of a following verb: *Fred is hard to miss, Mary is interesting to work with*.

Within the family of Germanic languages, gerunds (nominal gerund phrases) are a specifically English phenomenon. Gerunds may or may not have subjects (*Congress legalized the President's sending troops to the Middle East* vs *I enjoyed reading that book*) and also seem to be semantically parallel to subordinate clauses. They are, however, unlike clauses in several respects and in fact manifest in their distribution and in their internal syntax both noun-phrase-like and verb-phrase-like properties. Like noun phrases they can occur as subjects (*sighting UFOs makes John nervous*), direct objects (*you risk getting caught*) and prepositional objects (*they didn't approve of my leaving without a word*). Unlike clauses, but like ordinary noun phrases, they can undergo Subject-Auxiliary Inversion: *would my leaving now be taken as an admission of guilt?* Like verb phrases, on the other hand, gerunds take bare verb-phrase objects (*his doing that*), they combine with the full range of auxiliary verbs (*his having been doing that*) and they can contain the negation marker *not* (*I am proud of not having done that*). A large proportion of verbs that combine with nominal gerund phrases (e.g. *regret, resent, welcome, enjoy*) are factive, i.e. the proposition expressed by the gerund is presupposed to be true. Verbs like *risk, consider, contemplate, avoid*, however, also combine with gerunds and there is thus no perfect match between the type of verb in the main clause and the selection of a gerund as complement.

Adverbial clauses are introduced by conjunctions such as *if* (conditional), *because, since* (causal), *when, while* (temporal), *although, even though* (concessive) or *so as, in order to/that* (purposive). Some of the relevant expressions (*before, after, since, until, for*) can be used both as prepositions and conjunctions: *I will stay until lunch/John arrives*. Adverbial clauses may generally precede or follow the main clause in English and more often than not this topological contrast is accompanied by a clear difference in the discourse role played by the relevant clause. One of the more remarkable facts of English in the domain under discussion is the existence of three different types of purpose clauses. Only the first type (now often called 'rational clause') can be finite and be introduced by a conjunction like *in order to, so as to*, or *so that*: *we said nothing in order not to be recognized as foreigners, we made lots so everyone would get enough, we are getting up early tomorrow so as to catch the first train*. The other two types of purpose clauses, for which this term is now often reserved, must have a gap in their structure, which can either be in the subject position (*she hired a nurse to look after her mother*) or a non-subject position (*he bought a skillet to fry eggs in*). In contrast to rationale clauses, such purpose clauses cannot be preposed and are subject to severe restrictions on the selection of the verb in the main clause.

A specific feature of English within the context of Germanic languages is also the extensive use made of non-finite adverbial constructions, specifically of adverbial participles (free adjuncts, same-subject converbs) and absolute constructions (different-subject converbs) such as the following: *taking my car out of the garage, I noticed that a window was broken, persuaded by our optimism, he gladly contributed time and money, no further discussion arising, the meeting was brought to a close.* Whereas absolute constructions have an overt subject, this position is left unspecified in free adjuncts. The understood subject in this type of converbs is typically the same as the subject of the main clause: *using a sharp axe, he fought his way into the building*; but unrelated or 'dangling' participles – often frowned upon by prescriptive grammarians – are also possible: *even allowing for fast driving, twenty minutes was optimistic, there must – knowing my grandfather – have been enough angry oaths about the man who had done this.* The subject of absolute constructions typically stands in a part–whole relationship or some other close relation to the subject of the main clause: *'that's better!' he said, his spirits rising a little.* The link between either type of converbs and the main clause is more often than not an asyndetic one. Free adjuncts can also be introduced, however, by conjunctions such as *while, when, before, after, since, although*: *while waiting for his nurse, the doctor was pacing the room*; and absolute constructions may be introduced by *with, without* or *what with*: *you never know what will happen, with Gary driving.* As far as their interpretation is concerned, free adjuncts and absolutes are vague and unspecific in their meaning and depend for their interpretation as conditional, causal, temporal or concessive clauses on a variety of syntactic factors (sequence of main clause and converb); semantic factors (internal make-up of main clause, presence of a modal verb, frequency adverbial, etc.); and pragmatic factors (background assumptions). In examples like the following a free adjunct varies in its interpretation with different main clauses: *crossing the street, John was hit by a car* (temporal, simultaneity); *crossing the street, John entered a bank* (temporal sequence); *crossing the street, John entered a different country* (instrumental). The relevance of the polarity of the adjunct is illustrated by the following minimal pair: *Mary enjoyed the idea of going home over the weekend, knowing that her uncle would be there*; *Mary enjoyed the idea of going home over the weekend, not knowing that her uncle would be there.* In a context where Mary likes her uncle the first example would receive a causal, the second a concessive interpretation. Free adjuncts have a wider range of interpretations than absolutes and within the latter class unaugmented constructions allow a wider range of interpretations than those introduced by *with* or *without*.

Negation

Negation in English is expressed by the 'adverb' *not*, the 'determiner' *no*, or by one of a series of a complex expressions containing one of these two markers as a component (*nobody, nothing, none, neither, never, nowhere, no way,* etc.). Sentences with one of these expressions manifest a specific syntactic behaviour which distinguishes them from sentences with affirmative polarity: (a) they provide the right environment for a class of contextually restricted items ('negative-polarity items') like *ever, at all, any, so much as, let alone*: *I couldn't get any sleep*; (b) they are followed by positive question tags: *this doesn't make much sense, does it?*; (c) they allow a continuation with *not even* or *neither/nor*: *I never get sufficient sleep, not even over the weekend/ and neither does George*; (d) they manifest Subject-Auxiliary Inversion if the negative expression occurs in initial position: *not until he wanted to pay did he realize.* . . . Since these syntactic tests show the same results for sentences containing expressions like *hardly, rarely, seldom, barely, only, little, few,* the latter can also be considered as negative words: *I seldom get any sleep, not even over the weekend, rarely does crime pay so well.* Within this large class of negation expressions, *not* has a special status, however, in so far as it is only sentences with *not* that always have a straightforward affirmative counterpart. Whereas *not* could still follow main verbs in Early Modern English (*I know thee not*), this expression can only occur after the first auxiliary in Modern English (*he might not have been working*), unless it precedes another scope-bearing element (*many arrows didn't hit the target* vs *not many arrows hit the target*). The focusing negation marker *not . . . but* is not positionally restricted in this way: *not John but Bill gave the order.* If the affirmative counterpart of a negative sentence does not already contain an auxiliary verb, the dummy verb *do* has to be introduced: *he snores* vs *he doesn't snore.* The grammatical-ization of *do*-Support began in the seventeenth century. The negation marker *not* can be cliticized on to the preceding auxiliary: *he doesn't give a damn, he hasn't lifted a finger lately.* Together with the preceding auxiliary, enclitic *not* can undergo Subject-Auxiliary Inversion: *didn't Mary get the job?* vs *did Mary not get the job? Not* and *no* alternate in sentences with indefinite complements. In contrast to *not, no* may follow the main verb: *I didn't hear any noise* vs *I heard no noise.* Such minimal pairs differ in their meaning in subtle ways. One of the differences is that *no* tends to express the contrary, whereas *not* tends to express the contradictory proposition relative to the underlying affirmative sentence: *he is no friend of mine* vs *he is not a friend of mine.* Furthermore, the information expressed by the sentence with *no* tends to be given rather than newly introduced: *don't make any noise; she's asleep* vs *you've been warned; make no noise.*

The syntactic tests given above only apply, of course, if the relevant negation has scope over a whole clause or sentence. As already mentioned before, a negative adverbial in initial position does not trigger inversion if the negation has scope only within a phrase: *not infrequently it rains very hard*

here, with only ten dollars in his pockets he went to this expensive restaurant.
The negative prefixes *un-*, *in-* and *non-* never have clausal scope in this sense:
he is unhappy, isn't he? If a sentence contains another scope-bearing
expression in addition to negation, the relative scope of these two items can
simply be indicated by their linear sequence: the leftmost expression takes
wide scope over the expression following: *she often doesn't accept our
decisions* vs *she doesn't often accept our decisions.* Since the latest possible
position for *not* in a sentence is the one after the first auxiliary, relative scope
cannot always be indicated in this way, however. Scope-bearing expressions
in final position may or may not have scope over a preceding negation. In such
cases intonational phrasing (tonality) is one of the devices employed in
English for marking the intended scope: [*I wasn't listening all the time*] vs [[*I
wasn't listening*] *all the time*]. In the second example the time adverbial has
wide scope over the preceding *not.* The scope of *not* is also not clearly
identifiable on the basis of linear sequence whenever this expression follows
a modal auxiliary: *he may not know, you must not do this, you need not worry.*
In combination with *can*, *not* can have either wide scope over the whole
sentence (*John cannot help us*) or narrow scope only over the main predicate
(*he can (also) not do it*). In most cases, however, only one of the two general
options is available: wide scope (*you need not do it*) or narrow scope (*you
must not smoke here, he may not be at home*).

Negation is often accompanied by emotion and emphasis and thus often
expressed either by emphatic lexical means: *I didn't sleep a wink, he didn't
lift a finger, I haven't eaten a single bite*, or in a cumulative fashion. It is
therefore not surprising that in older stages of English and in non-standard
dialects multiple negation should be found: *you ain't seen nothing yet, I didn't
tell John to buy none of these.* The present standard forms which do not allow
more than one negation per clause were imposed in the eighteenth century. In
Black English, we find a proliferation of negation. In contrast to white
dialects, negative concord, i.e. the replacement of all non-assertive forms with
any or *ever* by negative expressions is obligatory: *you better not never steal
nothing from me.*

17.5   Lexis

As a result of having been fed by two major sources (Germanic and Romance)
the vocabulary of English is particularly rich. Major dictionaries like
Webster's Third International Dictionary and the *Oxford English Dictionary*,
together with their various supplements, list about half a million different
words. The fact that the English vocabulary derives from two major stocks is
most clearly visible in the coexistence of a wide variety of near-synonyms,
one deriving from Germanic and the other from Romance: *go on – continue,
dig up – excavate, let on – admit, let up – diminish, make up – invent, own
up – confess, admit, go through – succeed, suffer*, etc. Borrowings before the

Norman conquest mainly came from Latin and from other Germanic tongues, notably Scandinavian, and again this is illustrated by pairs of related words: *garden – yard, skirt – shirt, scar – shear*, etc. During the Renaissance, English borrowed extensively from Latin and more recent borrowings came from a wide range of donor languages including French, Spanish, Italian, Latin, Greek, German, Yiddish, Japanese, Russian, Chinese and Arabic, to mention only the most important ones. From earliest times on, English has proved to be particularly open and flexible in attracting and integrating loanwords.

One of the most striking properties of the vocabulary of Modern English is that – as a result of morphological attrition – a large proportion of the phonological forms can be assigned to more than one word class. In other words, no clear morphological distinction is drawn between nouns, verbs and adjectives in a wide variety of cases. A phonological form like *right* can be assigned to four different classes (N, V, Adj, Adv), the form *light* has to be assigned to the class of nouns, to the class of verbs as well as to that of adjectives and forms like *book, border, burn, risk, stand* are used both as nouns and verbs. Furthermore, as has already been mentioned, expressions like *before, after, until, since, for* are used both as prepositions and conjunctions and are often cited in support of the claim that adverbial conjunctions are basically prepositions subcategorized for sentential complements. The relatedness between these morphologically identical and semantically similar, but syntactically distinct forms is generally explicated by a rule of word formation ('conversion') that changes the word class of the input expression, but is not associated with any concomitant morphological process (noun > verb: *to butter, to bottle, to mail*; verb > noun: *a call, a guess, a touch*; adjective > verb: *to dirty, to empty, to clean*; adjective > noun: *a regular, a daily, blacks*). The direction of derivation is based on semantic criteria: *to bottle* 'to put into/store in a bottle'. In some cases conversion is accompanied by a shift of stress: *re 'fill* vs *'refill, to take off* vs *'take off*). In addition to conversion there are, of course, other derivational processes that also result in a change of word class, but clearly differentiate between related members of different classes through affixation. Clear examples are provided by such related expressions as the following: *indicate – indicative of – indication; describe – descriptive of – description; reminisce – reminiscent of – reminiscence; suspect – suspicious of – suspicion; deserve – deserving of – deserts*, etc. By and large the same types of word formation are found in English as in the other Germanic languages: compounding: *candlelight, cut-throat, overkill, fallout*; prefixation: *familiar* vs *unfamiliar, charge* vs *discharge*; suffixation: *sincere* vs *sincerity, manage* vs *manageable*; blending: *smog, Chunnel, stagflation*; and clipping: *telephone > phone, influenza > flu, advertisement > ad*.

As far as properties of specific lexical subsystems are concerned, a few examples have already been given, in particular the existence of a large class of verbs (like *burn, change, break, grow*) which can be used both intransitively and transitively and whose selectional restrictions for subjects in the intransitive use are identical to those for objects in the transitive use: *the leaves are burning – John is burning the leaves* (inchoative–causative alternation). Deictic expressions exhibit a two-term opposition between a proximal and a distal term: *this – that*; *here – there*; *now – then*. Further differentiations in the distal terms (*that* vs *yon, yonder*) are archaic, but still used in regional dialects. The subsystem of deictic expressions involving such directional contrasts as *hither – hence, thither – thence, whither – whence* has almost completely disappeared from current usage. This system of originally local deixis is structured in terms of proximity vs distance (signalled by *h-* vs *th-*) and source vs goal (signalled by *-ence* vs *-ither*). If these expressions are used at all today they are used in a temporal (*hitherto, henceforth*) or epistemic sense (*hence, whence*). The contrast between *come* and *go* is not only used for movement towards and away from a centre of orientation, but also for movement towards or away from normal or positively evaluated states (*go crazy* vs *come to one's senses*). Remarkable lexical differentiation is found in English as far as copulas expressing change of state are concerned (*become annoyed, get angry, grow old, go stale, come alive*), whereas comparatively few distinctions are made in certain verbal subsystems depending on the type of object the verb combines with. Whereas German differentiates, for example, between a large number of verbs of dressing and undressing, depending on the position of the garment, English only has two, or perhaps four, very unspecific ones (*put on – take off*; *don – doff*). Also in contrast to other Germanic languages, there are no modal particles in English. To translate modal particles in German, Dutch or Swedish, prosodic devices, tags, emphatic *do* or adverbs like *ever* are used in English. Similarly, English has relatively few focus particles (focusing adjuncts) like *also, too, even, only, merely*. Certain distinctions like the one between *nur* and *erst* in German are not drawn at all and some particles like *even* do duty in all contexts where six or seven different expressions are used in German. Constructions like *as early as, of all times, not least because*, etc. are used to fill the relevant gaps.

Further Reading

Bailey, R. W. and Görlach, M. (1982) *English as a World Language*, Ann Arbor: University of Michigan Press.

Baker, C. L. (1989) *English Syntax*, Cambridge, Mass.: The MIT Press.

Bolinger, D. (1971) *The Phrasal Verb in English*, Cambridge, Mass.: Harvard University Press.

Chomsky, N. and Halle, M. (1968) *The Sound Pattern of English*, New York: Harper & Row.

Crystal, D. (1988) *The English Language*, Harmondsworth: Penguin Books.

Declerck, R. (1991) *Tense in English. Its Structure and Use in Discourse*, London and New York: Routledge.

Dixon, R. M. W. (1991) *A New Approach to English Grammar on Semantic Principles*, Oxford: Clarendon Press.

Giegerich, H. J. (1992) *English Phonology*, Cambridge: Cambridge University Press.

Hawkins, J. (1986) *A Comparative Typology of English and German*, London: Croom Helm.

Huddleston, R. D. (1984) *Introduction to the Grammar of English*, Cambridge: Cambridge University Press.

Kortmann, B. (1991) *Free Adjuncts and Absolutes in English*, London and New York: Routledge.

Lass, R. (1987) *The Shape of English*, London: J. M. Dent & Sons.

Levin, B. (1993) *English Verb Classes and Alternations*, Chicago: University of Chicago Press.

McCawley, J. D. (1988) *The Syntactic Phenomena of English*, 2 vols, Chicago: University of Chicago Press.

Palmer, F. (1988) *The English Verb*, 2nd edn, London: Longmans.

Plank, F. (1984) 'Verbs and objects in semantic agreement. Minor differences that might suggest a major one', *Journal of Semantics* 3: 305–60.

Pullum, G. K. (1991) 'English nominal gerund phrases as noun phrases with verb-phrase heads', *Linguistics* 29: 763–99.

Quirk, R., Greenbaum, S., Leech, G. and Svartvik, J. (eds) (1985) *A Comprehensive Grammar of English*, London: Longman.

Strang, B. M. H. (1970) *A History of English*, London: Methuen.

Trudgill, P. (1984) *Language in the British Isles*, Cambridge: Cambridge University Press.

Zribi-Hertz, A. (1989) 'Anaphor binding and narrative point of view: English reflexive pronouns in sentence and discourse', *Language* 65: 695–727.

18 Germanic Creoles

Suzanne Romaine

18.1 Introduction

In this chapter I will provide an overview of the structure of creole languages whose vocabulary is derived from a Germanic language. In practice, this will include discussion of English-, German- and Dutch-based creoles (see below for a list of the languages included). Although there is no agreement on how to define pidgins and creoles or where they came from, all linguists recognize that there is such a group of languages. Their distinctiveness lies not in areal or genetic relationships, but in shared circumstances of sociohistorical development and use. At present there is no way of deciding whether a language constitutes a pidgin or creole unless reference is made to three criteria: linguistic, social and historical. The term 'creole' is generally applied to pidgins which have become nativized, although not all linguists agree that creoles need have a prior pidgin stage. Pidgins, by contrast, are nobody's first language. They come into existence in contact situations, where they are used by speakers with different language backgrounds to fulfil certain restrictive communicative purposes, typically, trade. They are simplified languages characterized by a minimal lexicon, little or no morphology and limited syntax.

The standard view sees pidginization and creolization as mirror-image processes and assumes a prior pidgin history for creoles. This implies a two-stage development. The first involves rapid and drastic restructuring to produce a language variety which is reduced and simplified. The second step consists of the elaboration of this variety as its functions expand and it becomes nativized. From a sociological point of view, what linguists call a creole serves as the native or primary language of most of its speakers. Pidgin speakers, who have another language, can get by with a minimum of grammatical apparatus, but the linguistic resources of a creole must be adequate to fulfil the communicative needs of human language users.

The term '-based' means that the bulk of the lexicon is drawn from that language, while the grammatical structure typically shows influence from other (usually non-Indo-European) languages. These other languages are referred to as the 'substrate'. Thus, when scholars speak of English-based creoles, they are referring to all those creoles which have taken most of their vocabulary from English. Terms such as 'English-lexicon or lexifier creole' are also used and the lexifier language is sometimes called the superstrate. While it has often been the case that scholars have treated English-based creoles as dialects of English and French creoles as Romance languages, etc., most creolists now recognize that creoles are languages in their own right with an independent structure. They are not parasitic systems or corrupted versions of the languages to which they are most closely related at the lexical level, i.e. the superstrate language. The term 'Germanic creole' is not generally used as a cover label for all these languages with a Germanic lexicon, probably because most of the languages which could be so classified are English-based anyway, but I will adopt it here for convenience. In doing so, I make no claim that these languages are genetically related to the Germanic languages. The genetic classification of languages is based on lexical rather than grammatical affinities and it is in this sense that the creoles under discussion here can be thought as part of the Germanic family, despite their formation under rather different sociohistorical circumstances from those of other languages whose membership in the Germanic family is not disputed.

Theories of Origin

Monogenesis vs Polygenesis

Traditional approaches to historical change have relied on the family-tree model, which is based on the assumption that over time languages gradually diverge from a common ancestor. This model has been widely applied to explain the historical origins of pidgin and creole languages and has been referred to as the 'monogenetic hypothesis', i.e. that pidgins and creoles are to be derived from a single common ancestor. Many espoused the view that all the European-based pidgins and creoles were originally descended from a fifteenth century Portuguese pidgin first used along the African coast and later carried to India and the Far East. This proto-pidgin may have been a relic of Sabir, the medieval lingua franca believed to have been the language of the Crusaders and a common Mediterranean trading language. While a common Portuguese origin would account well for certain lexical similarities found across the Atlantic and Pacific pidgins and creoles (see especially 18.5), one has to invoke the notion of 'relexification' to account for the many differences which exist between the Romance and Germanic creoles. Relexification is a change in lexical base. Of course, the monogenetic theory would have nothing to say about the origins of non-European-based pidgins and creoles.

Most linguists reject the monogenetic view because pidgins and creoles are typically formed through a convergence of linguistic structures from more than one genetic stock. It was the Romance linguist, Schuchardt (1842–1927), often called the father of creole studies, who used data from pidgin and creole languages to argue against prevailing nineteenth-century views on the regularity of sound change.

Conversely, polygenetic theories stress the idea that pidgins and creoles arose independently but developed in parallel ways because they used common linguistic material and were formed in similar sociohistorical terms. Stated in this way, there is a universalist element to the polygenetic view (see further below).

Substratum or Superstratum

Proponents of substratum explanations for the origins of pidgins and creoles claim that models for many of the structures common to these languages can be found in the substratum, particularly the languages of West Africa are believed to have had a great influence on the Atlantic creoles. Similar arguments about the importance of the Oceanic substrate have been made more recently for the Pacific pidgins and creoles.

Universal Principles of Language Structure

Typologically, it could be argued that creoles show more similarities to one another regardless of their base language than they do to their lexifier or base language. Some linguists find the concept of a 'creole syntax' uncontroversial, even though there might be disagreements about exactly which features are included (see further in 18.3 and 18.4). Others, however, are sceptical about the extent to which creoles can be regarded as a distinct structural type. This has led many scholars to explain the origin of pidgins and creoles in universalist terms. At one level, one can appeal to universal pressures of a functional type which exist in any communicative situation where speakers do not share each other's language. There will be pressure towards simplification, greater reliance on context, slower rate of speaking, etc. The language used to foreigners or 'foreigner talk' is a good example of these strategies and may result in an incipient pidgin. Some of these same features can be found in the speech addressed to young children, or 'baby talk'. In situations where the communicative partners are not social equals, the access of the subordinate group to the language of the dominant group may be only partial. Therefore, imperfect learning may lead to the emergence of a reduced version of the upper group's language.

A more far-reaching type of universalist explanation based on an alleged innate 'bioprogram' which contains an innate blueprint for the features the creole must have (see further in 18.3). The bioprogram hypothesis links the emergence of creoles with first-language acquisition as well as with the evolution of language in the human species more generally. It claims that the features which children learn early and effortlessly are among those prominent in creole languages. The existence of a bioprogram is argued for by appeal to the alleged lack of adequate input which children receive in a pidgin-speaking community. Under such circumstances children fall back on the bioprogram to produce rules for which they had no models in the input from the older generation. This theory has provoked a great deal of controversy, particularly since its claims cannot be tested directly. No children are currently acquiring a creole language under the relevant circumstances required to validate the operation of the bioprogram. Many linguists prefer not to invoke only one source, but appeal instead to a convergence of forces to account for the development of creole features. Some examples are given in sections dealing with particular characteristics. Thus, while some characteristics of particular creoles obviously have their origin in particular substratum languages, others require a universalist explanation.

Life Cycles

The decision to delimit the discussion to creoles rather than pidgins is inevitably arbitrary since the boundary between these two types of varieties cannot be defined in purely linguistic terms. Thus, some languages such as Tok Pisin 'talk pidgin', an English-based variety spoken in Papua New Guinea, and West African Pidgin English, spoken widely in West Africa, may exist in both pidgin and creole forms, which display different degrees of structural expansion and stability depending on whether they are used by first- or second-language speakers. Creolization can take place at any point during the pidgin's life cycle, ranging from a jargon to an expanded pidgin. The term 'jargon' refers to a speech variety with a minimal linguistic system and great individual variation used for communicating in limited situations between speakers of different languages, for example, trade, while a pidgin has a certain degree of stability. Three possible routes to creolization are depicted in Figure 18.1.

Figure 18.1   Three types of Creolization

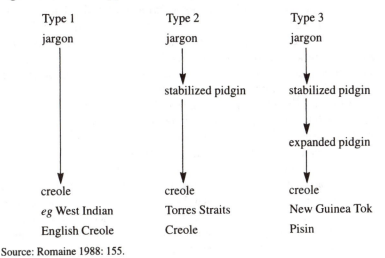

Source: Romaine 1988: 155.

Figure 18.2   The Guyanese Creole continuum

Guyanese creole < – > English
basilect   mesolect   acrolect

Guyanese Creole (basilect) mi gii am
                                 mi bin gii am
                                 mi bin gii ii
                                 mi bin gi ii
                                 mi di gii ii
                                 mi di gi hii
                                 a di gii ii
mesolect   a di gi ii
                                 a did gi ii
                                 a did giv ii
                                 a did giv hii
                                 a giv ii
                                 a giv im
                                 a giv him
                                 a geev ii
                                 a geev im
                                 a geev him
English (acrolect)   I gave him

Source: O'Donnell and Todd 1980: 52.

Once creolization has occurred, the evolutive changes that take place thereafter may make it impossible to identify a prior creole or pidgin stage, as in the case of Black English in the United States, which many linguists believe to be a variety in the late stages of decreolization. The term 'decreolization' is used to refer to changes which bring a creole closer to its superstrate language, and there is some dissatisfaction with it because some changes may not be motivated by influence from the lexifier language. In other words, not all changes are unidirectional. The terms 'basilect', 'mesolect' and 'acrolect' are used to describe the range of varieties often found after creolization, as shown in Figure 18.2 illustrating the Guyanese creole continuum. They are arranged along a post-creole continuum which has acrolectal (or those varieties closest to the superstrate) at one end and basilectal (or those varieties furthest from it) at the other. Mesolectal varieties are intermediate. The ordering of the varieties in the model presented here makes no claim about their diachronic development since it seems likely that in many cases mesolectal and acrolectal varieties were present even in the earliest phases of creole formation and do not always develop after creolization in adaptation to the superstrate. Thus, acrolectal varieties cannot be regarded as necessarily 'later' than basilectal ones. Creolization and decreolization can be coexistent, as they are for instance, in Papua New Guinea. Tok Pisin is in the process of being nativized by the younger generation at the same time as increased accessibility to English schooling is creating a range of varieties which are neither Tok Pisin nor English.

Because creolization can occur at any stage in the development continuum from jargon to expanded pidgin, different kinds and degrees of structural repair may be necessary to make the pidgin fully adequate to meet the demands placed on it for use as a primary language. Sources for new structures vary too. Bickerton (1981), whose primary interest is the first type of creolization where a pidgin is abruptly transformed into a creole within one generation, believes that bioprogram universals provide the most important input into the newly emerging creole.

Some important consequences follow from this view of the pidgin life cycle. If creolization occurs at the jargon stage, then the amount of expansion will be more considerable than that required to make an expanded pidgin structurally adequate. This means that formal attempts to characterize pidgins as distinct from creoles will fail because they ignore the fact that those languages are developing systems which may overlap in terms of the structural complexity reached at any point in their life cycle depending on their functions. When linguists talk of pidgins or creoles, they are often comparing entities which are not at comparable stages of development and this is one reason why attempts to identify structural similarities fail.

It also follows that creolization is not a unique trigger for complexity. A pidgin may expand without nativization, and there will be few structural differences between an expanded pidgin and a creole which develops from it. Moreover, it is by no means clear that all of the kinds of changes which typically go on in the expansion of a pidgin and under creolization involve an increase in complexity. For instance, it is not readily apparent how the signalling of tenses by means of particles instead of temporal adverbs (which is a general feature of many creole languages, see 18.4) introduces greater complexity into a system. It is just a restructuring. Such change does not increase the referential adequacy or power of the language or add a new category. Many routes can be followed in the expansion of an impoverished pidgin so that competing solutions may coexist for some time.

The fact that pidgins and creoles share some structural features with each other and with other language varieties which are reduced in function indicates that the same solutions tend to recur to some degree wherever acquisition and change occurs, regardless of contact, but especially in cases of contact. Thus, while the term *pidginization* can be used to refer to all kinds of simplification, not all of them will necessarily result in a variety that we want to call a true pidgin. The common emergent features can be regarded as natural developmental solutions to processing problems posed by non-optimal structural configurations. These are discussed in more detail in 18.3 and 18.4.

Checklist of Germanic Creoles

As a starting point, I will provide a list of the languages which come under the scope of this chapter and give some background information about their

Figure 18.3   Germanic Pidgins and Creoles

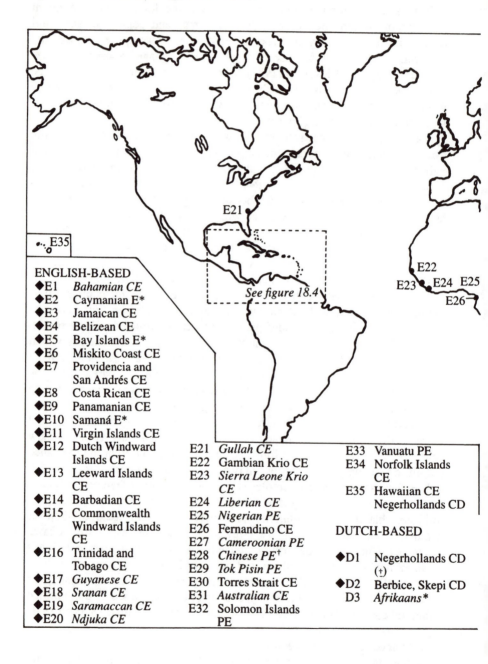

E21

E22
E23 ● E24 E25
E26

E35

ENGLISH-BASED
◆E1 *Bahamian CE*
◆E2 Caymanian E*
◆E3 Jamaican CE
◆E4 Belizean CE
◆E5 Bay Islands E*
◆E6 Miskito Coast CE
◆E7 Providencia and
San Andrés CE
◆E8 Costa Rican CE
◆E9 Panamanian CE
◆E10 Samaná E*
◆E11 Virgin Islands CE
◆E12 Dutch Windward
Islands CE
◆E13 Leeward Islands
CE
◆E14 Barbadian CE
◆E15 Commonwealth
Windward Islands
CE
◆E16 Trinidad and
Tobago CE
◆E17 *Guyanese CE*
◆E18 *Sranan CE*
◆E19 *Saramaccan CE*
◆E20 *Ndjuka CE*

E21 *Gullah CE*
E22 Gambian Krio CE
E23 *Sierra Leone Krio
CE*
E24 *Liberian CE*
E25 *Nigerian PE*
E26 Fernandino CE
E27 *Cameroonian PE*
E28 *Chinese PE*[†]
E29 *Tok Pisin PE*
E30 Torres Strait CE
E31 *Australian CE*
E32 Solomon Islands
PE

E33 Vanuatu PE
E34 Norfolk Islands
CE
E35 Hawaiian CE
Negerhollands CD

DUTCH-BASED

◆D1 Negerhollands CD
(†)
◆D2 Berbice, Skepi CD
D3 *Afrikaans**

See figure 18.4

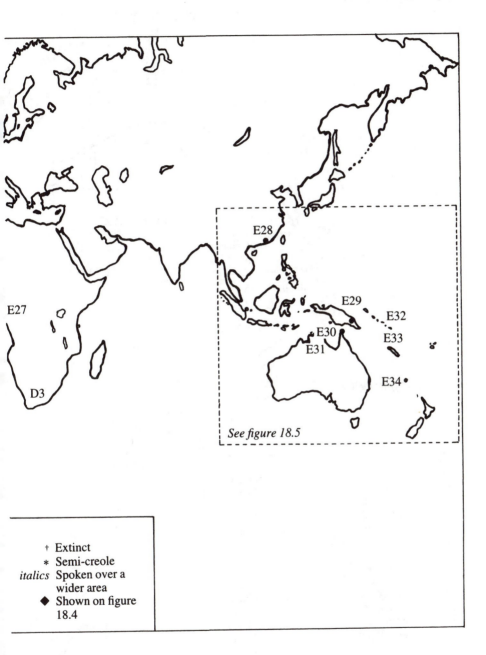

E27

D3

E28

E29

E32

E30

E33

E31

E34

See figure 18.5

† Extinct
* Semi-creole
italics Spoken over a
    wider area
◆ Shown on figure
    18.4

Source: Holm 1988: vol. 1, xvi–xvii.

Figure 18.4   Caribbean Creoles

ENGLISH-BASED

E1	*Bahamian CE*	E14	Barbadian CE	
E2	Caymanian E*	E15	Commonwealth Windward Islands CE	
E3	Jamaican CE			
E4	Belizean CE			
E5	Bay Islands E*	E16	Trinidad and Tobago CE	
E6	Miskito Coast CE			
E7	Providencia and San Andrés CE	E17	*Guyanese CE*	
		E18	*Sranan CE*	
E8	Costa Rican CE	E19	*Saramaccan CE*	
E9	Panamanian CE	E20	*Ndjuka CE*	
E10	Samaná E*			
E11	Virgin Islands CE			
E12	Dutch Windward Islands CE	DUTCH-BASED		† Extinct
		D1	Negerhollands CD (†)	* Semi-creole
E13	Leeward Islands CE	D2	Berbice, Skepi CD	*italics* Spoken over a wider area

ATLANTIC
OCEAN

VIRGIN ISLANDS   Anguila
E10   E11 D1   St Martin
HAITI DOMINICAN   E12   Antigua
       REP.   E13   Montserrat
                   Saba
PUERTO   St. Kitts   Guadeloupe
RICO   Nevis   Dominica
LEEWARD ISLANDS   Martinique

SEA   WINDWARD ISLANDS   St. Lucia
                St. Vincent   Barbados
                         E15   E14
                         Grenada
Aruba   Bonaire   Tobago
       Curaçao   Trinidad
                            E16

VENEZUELA   E17   D2   E18
             GUYANA   FRENCH
                    E19   E20 GUIANA
                 SURINAME

0   500   1000 *km*

0   500 *miles*

Source: Holm 1988: vol. 1, xviii–xix.

users and uses as well as their present day status. Figure 18.3 shows where these languages are spoken. The relevant sections of Holm (1989: vol. 2) can be consulted for short sample texts. The following have been excluded from discussion: Gastarbeiterdeutsch and Russenorsk. Not all linguists agree that the variety of German spoken by foreign workers is a 'true' pidgin, although it displays some of the structural characteristics typical of pidgins, for example, simplification, morphological reduction, etc. Similar arguments have been put forward in favour of recognition of a pidgin or pidginized Swedish as spoken by immigrants in Stockholm. Russenorsk (Russo-Norwegian), a trade pidgin used in northern Norway by Russian merchants and Norwegian fishermen for 140 years up until World War I, probably did not develop beyond the stable pidgin stage. (Also excluded are dubious cases such as Middle English, which some have suggested is a creole because it underwent sufficient borrowing from French and Latin so as to undermine its historical continuity and identity as a Germanic language.) I will stick to a narrower definition of creole and creolization here (see further below), while at the same time recognizing that the development of pidgins and creoles can offer many insights into traditional views of change and linguistic reconstruction.

It is customary practice to label pidgins and creoles with a formula which includes their location and their principal lexifier language, e.g. Chinese Pidgin English, Berbice Creole Dutch, Rabaul Creole German, etc. Since some pidgins and creoles may change their lexical affiliation through relexification, such as Berbice Dutch did when Dutch was superseded by English as the superstrate language, these labels are not entirely satisfactory. Other creoles such as Tok Pisin and Sranan, an English-based variety spoken in Surinam, have been affected by this kind of change too. However, no one has suggested replacing the name Berbice Creole Dutch with Berbice Creole English. These labels are unsatisfactory for other reasons too. One is that they imply a separation between lexicon and syntax and give more weight to the lexicon in deciding relationships among languages. Another difficulty is that the first term in such labels may be ambiguous as to whether it specifies a language, a group of speakers or a geographical location. Thus, in the name 'Hawaiian Creole English' the adjective 'Hawaiian' is ambiguous because it could refer to the geographical location of Hawai'i, to people of Hawaiian descent, or to the Hawaiian language.

Linguists' names for pidgins and creoles are not always widely used by the speakers of the language themselves. Thus, Tok Pisin has sometimes been referred to by linguists as 'Neomelanesian' or 'New Guinea Pidgin English', while its speakers call it 'Tok Pisin'. Similarly, speakers of Torres Strait Creole English call their language 'Broken' (i.e., broken English), while speakers of Australian Creole English call their language 'Kriol' and Hawai'i Creole English speakers call their variety 'Pidgin', etc. Sranan is sometimes also called 'Sranan Tongo' ('Suriname tongue') or 'Taki-Taki' ('talktalk').

Although they are often widely used by the majority of the population, throughout their history most of the Germanic creoles have not had any official status in the countries where they are spoken. In the Pacific, for instance, only Tok Pisin and Bislama have received some official recognition. Tok Pisin is a *de facto* official language in Papua New Guinea spoken by more than half of the population; however, English is the official medium of education. There is also another pidgin language, Hiri Motu, 'trade Motu', based on the indigenous language, Motu, which shares the same *de facto* official status as Tok Pisin. In practice, all this means is that Hiri Motu and Tok Pisin may be used in the House of Assembly, the country's main legislative body. In fact, most business is conducted in Tok Pisin, which is the most widely shared language among the members. While Bislama is recognized by the constitution of Vanuatu as the national language of the country, paradoxically it is forbidden in the schools. English and French, the languages of the former colonial powers, are still the official languages of education. Although Australian Kriol does not have any official status, it has been used in bilingual education programmes. While many linguists in both the Caribbean and Pacific have argued for an increase in status and standardization of the pidgins and creoles spoken in these regions so that they can be used in education, the governments concerned have generally ignored these issues and preferred instead simply to continue the colonial legacy of using the metropolitan European language already in place. French-based Haitian Creole is the only one which appears to have been given serious attention by government planners.

English-based Creoles

Pidgin and creole languages based on English are more numerous than those based on any other language (Germanic or otherwise), attesting to the greater spread of English than any other metropolitan language. Two major groups, the Atlantic and the Pacific, are recognized according to historical, geographic and linguistic factors. The Atlantic creoles shown in further detail in Figure 18.4 were established primarily during the seventeenth and eighteenth centuries in the Caribbean and West Africa, while the Pacific group originated primarily in the nineteenth. The Atlantic creoles were largely products of the slave trade in West Africa, which dispersed large numbers of West Africans to the Caribbean. They share a common substrate and display many common features. Holm (1989) includes 33 Atlantic creoles. However, different sources will give slightly different figures due to the lack of unanimity in defining which languages count as pidgins or creoles.

In the Pacific, different languages formed the substratum and sociocultural conditions which gave rise to the 11 or so pidgin and creole languages shown in Figure 18.5 were somewhat different than in the Atlantic. Although the plantation setting was crucial for pidginogenesis in both areas, in the Pacific labourers were recruited and indentured rather than slaves. Apart from Hawai'i, a history of gradual creolization has distinguished the Pacific from

Figure 18.5 Pacific varieties of Pidgin and Creole English

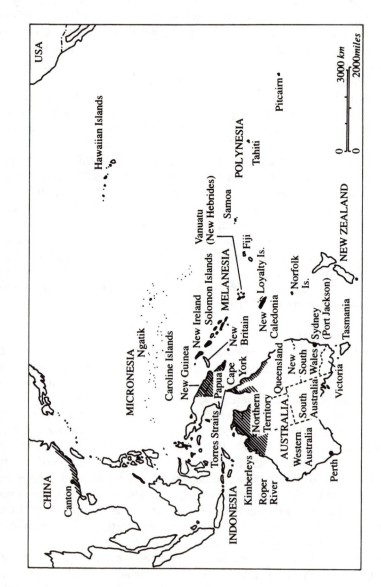

Source: Holm 1989: vol. 2, 513.

the Atlantic (particularly Caribbean) creoles, whose transition has been more abrupt. While this traditional grouping is geographically convenient, it may obscure a far more complex picture of interrelationships. It also does not take into account that there was probably some interaction between Atlantic and Pacific, and that judgements about the degree to which creolization was abrupt depend on historical evidence which is usually lacking.

Linguistic evidence to support the view that sailors played an important role in spreading linguistic features across vast areas can be found in the fact that there is some lexical sharing among distant pidgins such as Hawai'i Pidgin English, Chinook Jargon, a contact language used for trade in the Pacific Northwest, and Eskimo Jargon. The term *kanaka* (< Hawaiian 'human being, person, man') occurs in both English- and French-based pidgins and creoles throughout the Pacific, although its meaning and, in particular, connotations vary somewhat from language to language. In Tok Pisin, for instance, it was originally a term used by Europeans to refer to the indigenous population, often pejoratively, and it has these negative overtones in Tok Pisin today. To refer to someone as a *kanaka*, especially a *bus kanaka* 'bush kanaka' is insulting because it implies that they are backward and unsophisticated. In the French overseas territory of New Caledonia, however, the term is used as a symbol of Melanesian unity and pride in the face of the continuing French colonial administration. In 1984 Melanesian activists declared an independent state to which they gave the name 'Kanaky', but independence has yet to be recognized by France. Interestingly, in Hawai'i English Creole, the term is not much used, despite its presence in the Hawaiian language. The word *kanaka* is also found in non-European-based varieties such as Chinook Jargon, where it and other items spread after the development of the fur trade along the northwest coast of North America in the late eighteenth century. Similarly, Eskimo Jargon has *kaukau* 'food', itself a loanword in Hawaiian, introduced from Chinese Pidgin English *chowchow*. The term *kaukau* is still used in Hawai'i Creole English to mean 'food' or 'eat', although most of the younger generation use the term *grind* in the sense of 'eat'. During the nineteenth century contacts across the North Pacific became routine. The Hawaiian Islands became a frequent port of call and a wintering place for ships. Recent work places a great deal of emphasis on sailors in the spread and stabilization of pidgin English in the Pacific.

Among the grammatical features widely shared by both the Atlantic and Pacific group are the following:

1   Use of zero copula, as in: *de pikni sik* (Jamaican Creole English) 'the child is sick' and *pikinini sik* (Tok Pisin) 'the child is sick';
2   Use of *get/got* for 'have', as in: *dem get wan uman we get gyal pikni* (Guyanese Creole English) 'there is a woman who has a daughter' and *get wan wahine shi get wan data* (Hawai'i Creole English) 'there is a woman who has a daughter'.

3   Pre-verbal negation, as in: *hongri man no de set dan won ples* (Kru Pidgin English) 'a hungry man doesn't sit down in one place' and *melabat no kaan go garram yumob* (Australian Kriol) 'we can't go with you'.

These features are, however, believed to be shared by all pidgins and creoles, whatever their lexical base. Their common existence thus suggests either a much broader genetic relationship or universal principles of development.

Nevertheless, there are other creoles which do not share these features. Compare, for instance, *ori wa fiki* (Berbice Creole Dutch) 'he was ill', where the particle *wa* performs some of the functions of a copula, and *hemia se wanem ia?* (Bislama) 'what is that?', where *se* (probably from French *c'est* 'that is') acts like a copula in some contexts.

Atlantic Creoles

The Atlantic creoles can be grouped into five subdivisions on the basis of settlement patterns: those of West Africa; Suriname; the Eastern Caribbean; the Western Caribbean; and North America. English-based pidgins and creoles are spoken in West Africa from Gambia in the northwest to Cameroon in the southeast. They are found mainly along the coast, particularly in urban areas, where the population is heterogeneous, but they have spread into the rural hinterland too. Most of these languages are spoken in countries where the official language is English, e.g. the Gambia, Sierra Leone, Liberia, Ghana, Nigeria and Cameroon, but some varieties are used where the official language is English or French. The West African varieties, like many of those spoken in the Pacific, exist in both pidgin and creole form, i.e. are used as both first and second languages. The degree of their structural complexity thus depends on their extent of use. These fall into three major groups: Krio, Liberian and West African Pidgin English as spoken in Ghana, Nigeria and Cameroon. Krio and West African Pidgin share a number of similarities and thus a certain degree of mutual intelligibility thanks to their interconnected histories.

The English-based creoles of Suriname are spoken in what was formerly the Dutch part of the Guyanas in northern South America before its independence in 1975. There are three groups: Sranan, the language spoken along the coast by people of African and mixed descent; Saramaccan and Ndjuka, spoken by descendants of slaves who escaped into the interior from coastal plantations in the seventeenth and eighteenth centuries. The Suriname creoles have been of great interest to linguists because the records of the Moravian mission provide a historical perspective on the development of these languages. These creoles were also separated from English influence over 300 years ago when after scarcely a generation the colony founded by the English was taken over by the Dutch.

By contrast, the Caribbean creoles either remained in contact with English from the seventeenth century or were settled from such areas later. It is this constant contact with English that led to the development of post-creole continua. English settlement of the Caribbean took place primarily from east to west and one can distinguish an Eastern group including the lesser Antilles, Trinidad and Guyana and a Western group including Miskito Coast, Belize and Jamaica. Varieties of Caribbean creoles have also been transplanted to the United Kingdom by West Indian immigrants.

There are historical as well as linguistic reasons to separate all these creoles from those which originated on the North American mainland. Among the latter are Bahamas Creole English; Gullah spoken in parts of coastal South Carolina and Georgia; United States Black English; Afro-Seminole spoken in Texas; Samana Creole English spoken in the Dominican Republic; and American Indian Pidgin/Creole English.

Pacific Group

The precise historical relationships among the Pacific pidgins and creoles are still being disputed and intensely debated. English was first brought to the Pacific by explorers and traders. Many linguists have used the term 'Pacific Jargon English' to refer to the early formative stages of the modern English-based Melanesian pidgins. Multilingual whaling vessels in the Pacific from the late 1700s are known to have carried and spread a contact form of English used between Europeans and Pacific Islanders. Subsequent waves of trading focused on sandalwood (dominant in the 1830s) and the *bêche-de-mer* or sea slug (primarily 1840s and 1850s). Both of these gave their names to the contact language used in trade. Some observers of the time used the phrase 'South Seas English' as a cover term for the kind of English that was spoken throughout Melanesia and elsewhere by the late 1880s, suggesting that it was considered a single language wherever it was spoken. Some writers have also used the term 'Beach La Mar' in this way to cover the entire Melanesian Pidgin-speaking area during the nineteenth century (see e.g. Churchill 1911, who includes material from New Guinea, Queensland, Torres Strait, Samoa and Fiji). Melanesian pidgin later evolved into a number of distinctly named varieties, including Tok Pisin, spoken in Papua New Guinea, Bislama, spoken in Vanuatu, and Pijin, spoken in the Solomon Islands. The term 'Beach La Mar', which has given rise to modern Bislama, comes from the Portuguese *bicho do mar* 'small sea creature', which was the term used to refer to the sea slug. It was incorporated into French as *biche de mar* and later into English in a variety of forms. Beach La Mar of the 1840s gradually evolved in structure and social function to become the language called *Bislama* today in Vanuatu. The word *bislama* is also used in Tok Pisin, where it refers to the sea slug, but it is also used as a term of abuse. To call someone a sea slug is to imply that they are lazy and good for nothing. In Bislama the term is also used as a general term to refer to a variety of Melanesian pidgin. Thus, one commonly hears Tok Pisin referred to as 'Bislama bilong PNG', i.e., the pidgin spoken in Papua New Guinea.

Figure 18.6   The historical relations of Pacific varieties of Pidgin English and Creole English

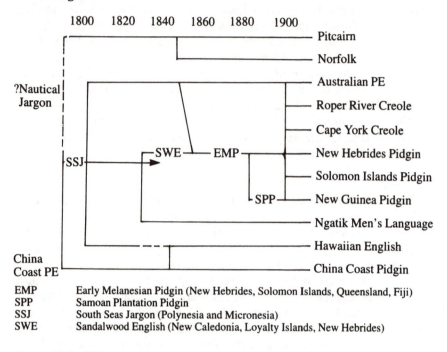

EMP	Early Melanesian Pidgin (New Hebrides, Solomon Islands, Queensland, Fiji)
SPP	Samoan Plantation Pidgin
SSJ	South Seas Jargon (Polynesia and Micronesia)
SWE	Sandalwood English (New Caledonia, Loyalty Islands, New Hebrides)

Source: Clarke 1979.

While some scholars have claimed a relationship between the English-based pidgins and creoles with those elsewhere, evidence for a world-wide English nautical pidgin English is not clear. Although a number of characteristics have been identified which are shared by the Pacific varieties with those in the Atlantic, the Atlantic features were drawn from contemporary rather than historical records, and not enough research has been done in the Atlantic area to support a historical connection.

During the nineteenth century Melanesians from a variety of Pacific Islands began to work on sandalwood ships as crew members alongside both Europeans and Polynesians. The Labor Trade, or 'blackbirding' as it was called, uprooted and transported thousands of Melanesians as indentured plantation workers to Queensland, Samoa and elsewhere. These conditions were conducive to pidginization since for over a quarter of a century there was continual contact of a commercial kind, both on shore, first at *bêche-de-mer* stations and later in plantations, and on ship between Melanesians and Europeans, Melanesians and Polynesians, and among Melanesians who did not share a common language. The present-day varieties of Melanesian Pidgin are the result of a gradually stabilizing and expanding contact language.

Clark (1979) proposed the diagram shown in Figure 18.6 to illustrate the historical relationships among the pidgin and creole languages of the Pacific. Clark's reconstruction was based on the distribution of 30 grammatical and lexical items in 11 pidgin and creole languages.

Of the languages indicated in this diagram only Chinese Pidgin English can be omitted from discussion since there is no evidence to indicate creolization. It was once thought to have been the common ancestor of other Pacific varieties. There is some dispute over the status of the variety of English spoken on Pitcairn and Norfolk Islands. The conditions under which this variety developed were exceptional. Before 1790 Pitcairn Island was uninhabited, but the arrival of 28 people (9 of them mutineers from HMS *Bounty*, and the others Polynesians) marked the beginning of a community which existed in isolation for 33 years. Most people were resettled on Norfolk Island after 1856. Although there have been a few studies of Pitcairn-Norfolk speech, no consensus on its classification has emerged. Pitcairnese is clearly identifiable as having an English-based lexicon and shares many features with English-based and other creoles, though it also shows some 'exceptional' features. For example, the presence of consonant clusters, which are not found in Tahitian, is hard to explain. From one description it appears that Pitcairn-Norfolk displays at least nine of the characteristics mentioned by Bickerton and others as typical of creoles more generally. However, it does not show any distinctly Pacific characteristics. This is not surprising since it has no historical link with Pacific Jargon English and developed in isolation from other varieties of Pacific Pidgin English.

The only clear-cut groupings by genetic affiliation in this diagram are those between varieties of Melanesian Pidgin and between the Australian varieties. Clark's evidence suggested a connection between these two groups which subsequent work has confirmed. Clark found that Melanesian Pidgin and Australian Pidgin shared a number of features not found in the other Pacific varieties. In particular, he discovered at least four important features which were established in Australia significantly earlier than in Melanesian Pidgin, for example, the use of *by and by* as a future marker.

Dutch-based Creoles

Although Dutch existed in various parts of the New World, such as New York and New Jersey, there is direct evidence to support the existence of only three varieties of fully creolized Dutch: Negerhollands 'Black Dutch' spoken in the Virgin Islands, Berbice Creole Dutch and Skepi Creole Dutch, spoken in the former Dutch colonies of Berbice and Essequibo, now part of Guyana. These languages resulted from the presence of seventeenth- and eighteenth-century Dutch traders and settlers, but are nearly extinct now. According to one source, the last native speaker of Negerhollands died in September 1987. Berbice Dutch is apparently spoken only by those over 60.

In addition, some have argued for at least partial creolization of Afrikaans, and the existence of pidginized varieties of Afrikaans called *Taal* 'talk, language' or *Tsotsi Taal* among speakers of Bantu languages in black ghetto townships such as Soweto has been reported. Pidginized varieties of Dutch presumably preceded the emergence of creole Dutch in the Caribbean and pidginized varieties may also have existed in West Africa and Asia.

It is remarkable there are so few linguistic remnants of the Dutch empire. Apart from the Dutch colonies in the Caribbean which are soon likely to become independent, most Dutch possessions were lost to Britain by the nineteenth century. By contrast, the Portuguese empire, despite its earlier collapse, left a greater legacy of surviving creole languages. The Dutch, like the Germans and French, were not always the first or only Europeans to arrive in the places they colonized, and in most cases they did not stay as long. Also like the Germans in Africa, the Dutch were apparently reluctant to spread their language among the colonized. At least one authority says that the Dutch regarded their language as a sort of caste-language and did not want it learned by others whom they regarded as their inferiors. There are other cases where languages have been deliberately withheld from potential learners to maintain social distance.

The Dutch language secured a place for itself only where the Dutch were the first European settlers, i.e. in New York, Guyana and the Cape, and predominated numerically over other settlers, e.g. in the Virgin Islands. The success of Berbice and Skepi Dutch may be attributed to the fact that when the Dutch West India Company established settlements along the Essequibo and Berbice Rivers on the Guyana coast of South America, neither the Spanish nor Portuguese had settled there. In 1667, however, the Dutch colony of New Amsterdam became the English colony of New York in exchange for Suriname in the Guyanas. The establishment of a settlement in South Africa in 1652 was the high point of Dutch colonial power. The persistence of Afrikaans owes much to the settlers of Dutch descent who resisted British efforts to marginalize them and their language. Elsewhere, in Suriname, the Dutch Windward Islands and in the Virgin Islands (which were never Dutch, but Danish, and since 1917 belong to the United States), Dutch creoles were replaced by English creoles or local varieties of English. In the Dutch Leeward Islands Dutch lost out to Spanish/Portuguese-based Papiamentu.

German-based Creoles

The only example of a German-based creole is Rabaul Creole German, called *Unserdeutsch* 'our German', which arose at the turn of the century as a lingua franca of the Catholic mixed-race community in Vunapope near Rabaul in what is now East New Britain Province of Papua New Guinea. This was formerly part of the German colony Kaiserwilhelmsland from 1884 to 1914. This language was apparently used by children at a mission boarding school and creolized in one generation. Because Germany lost most of its colonies after World War I, German never had a chance to spread as widely as other colonial languages such as French and English. While there was a significant input from German into Tok Pisin during the period of German colonial rule, as can still be seen today in words such as *rausim* 'to get rid of' (< *heraus*), others are falling into disuse, e.g. *beten* is being replaced by *prea* 'prayer'. Other items such as *blaistik* (< *Bleistift*) 'pencil', *winkel* 'carpenter's square', *slos* (< *geschlossen*, past participle of *schliessen*) 'lock' have long since disappeared. Remnants of a rudimentary pidgin German may still be heard in parts of the country where men were sent to mission schools and taught in German by German-speaking missionaries. Although the Germans did not want Tok Pisin to be the lingua franca of their colony, knowledge of it was so widespread that there was little they could do to combat it. In East Africa, however, where Germany also had colonies, the language was withheld and a specially fabricated variety was proposed for spread among the populace.

18.2   Phonology

On the whole, the phonology of creoles has been less well investigated than their syntax, and within the domain of phonology, there is scant information on suprasegmental phenomena such as tone, stress and intonation. As in morphosyntax, the relative contribution of universals vs substratum influence to constraints on size and membership of phonological inventories and phonotactic constraints as well as on suprasegmental features, needs further investigation in particular cases before more general conclusions can be stated. It is not always possible to trace the origin of a particular creole feature to a unique source.

Size of Phonological Inventory

Many scholars have commented on the small size or reduction of pidgin and creole phonological inventories when compared to both their lexifier and substratum languages. Although it has been sometimes argued that creoles represent the lowest common denominator of the source languages, this is not always true. Pidgins and creoles may also have segments which are not found in the superstrate. The Tok Pisin consonantal system used by Usarufa speakers actually has a much greater range of diversity than the Usarufa system both in terms of distribution and phonetic variety. Many speakers of Tok Pisin, for example, particularly those from the Highlands, have pre-nasalized stops, e.g. *ngut* 'gut'. In the orthography pre-nasalization is indicated only when it is used by both Europeans and Melanesians, e.g. *sindaun* 'sit down', *pundaun* 'to fall down', *krungut* 'crooked'. That is, just in cases where it is a stabilized and regular feature of Tok Pisin and not a variation due to the speaker's first language. In Saramaccan, a creole English spoken by some 20,000 'Bush Negroes' or Maroons, whose ancestors escaped into the interior part of Suriname from plantations nearer the coast during the late seventeenth and early eighteenth centuries, the double stops /k͡p/ and /g͡b/ have been retained from the African substratum languages. The same is true for some varieties of West African Pidgin English.

Although a pan-creole phonological inventory has been proposed, it can be difficult to determine the size of a phonological inventory in a particular creole. Pidgins and creoles do not have a single phonology and phonology remains the least stable system in otherwise stabilized pidgins. Phonological variability may be due to substratum and/or superstrate influences as well as universal developmental tendencies, and is affected by external factors such as education, sex, age, acquisitional history, etc. This means that variant pronunciations may be found for the same items even within a small group of speakers. Expansion of a pidgin usually involves a steady increase in phonological distinctions, the use of what were formerly free variants for stylistic purposes, and the emergence of phonological rules which separate underlying from surface forms. During decreolization, when the superstrate exerts pressure on the creole, the creole phonological system may merge partially with that of the superstrate language. Thus, the phonology of individual speakers of Tok Pisin varies from heavily anglicized to what some have called a 'core phonology'. The core phonology is shared by all speakers of the language, while the anglicized phonology makes the most of the consonant and vowel distinctions in English. In principle, the fluent bilingual speaker of Tok Pisin and English has the whole phonological inventory of English to draw on when speaking Tok Pisin.

Sounds that are typically absent or infrequent in creole phonologies are often those that are absent or vary in phonological status in the substrate languages. Both Jamaican Creole and Tok Pisin, for instance, do not regularly contrast /p/ and /f/. In Tok Pisin as well as Sranan /r/ and /l/ are not distinct. This has been attributed to the fact that in the substratum languages for Jamaican Creole and Sranan and many of the languages of Papua New Guinea there is no systematic contrast between /p/ and /f/, and /r/ and /l/.

In Tok Pisin, for example, ‹p› is used in words deriving from English /p/ such as *pik* 'pig', *planti* 'many, plenty', etc. Tok Pisin ‹p› derived from English ‹f› is pronounced in one of three ways: as English [pf], as English [f], or as [p]. This means that some Tok Pisin speakers use [p] for every use of English ‹p› and ‹f›, e.g. /pik/ 'pig', /prut/ 'fruit'. Other speakers use [pf] only for words derived from ‹p› and they use [f] or [p] for words deriving from English ‹f›, e.g. *pik, frut*. Most speakers use [f] for words written with ‹f›, e.g. /fut/ 'foot'.

Nevertheless, at the same time as creole phonology reflects pressures from the substratum, there are also universal tendencies of first- and second-language acquisition which will tend to eliminate marked segments and to reduce the overall number of phonological contrasts. We can note, for instance, the general avoidance of fricatives and affricates in pidgin phonological inventories. From a markedness perspective, fricatives are more marked than stops. Their presence in a language presupposes the existence of stops. This is a good example of how substratum influence and universal pressures converge on a common solution. However, other sounds commonly not found may be due to superstratum influence. For example, the fact that /h/ is generally absent in Jamaican Creole and Tok Pisin is probably due to the variable omission of /h/ in non-standard varieties of English to which creole speakers were exposed.

The original process of pidginization involved the application of natural phonological processes, which obscured the etymological connections between English and Tok Pisin items. A case in point is Tok Pisin *abus*, which is derived from English *animals* via /l/ vocalization, loss of unstressed syllable and replacement of /n/ with homorganic stop. In this case the origin of the item is opaque to both the English and Tok Pisin speaker. This is evidenced by the fact that *animal* has been 're-borrowed' into Tok Pisin and used alongside *abus*. Learners do not have access to underlying phonological representations and the phonological relatedness of lexical items in the lexifier language is no longer realized in the derived jargon. Phonological information is further lost through the conflation of sounds from the English inventory by the learners, resulting in the disappearance of many contrasts and the increased likelihood of homophones, e.g. *sol* 'salt', 'shoulder', *hat* 'hot'/'hard', etc.

Now, however, by virtue of increasing exposure to English, where such contrasts are significant, speakers are beginning to remodel Tok Pisin forms on their English cognates. This is the phonological dimension of decreolization. New phonological distinctions are being introduced, particularly in the Tok Pisin spoken by the younger generation of speakers in urban areas. This can be seen in Table 18.1. Tok Pisin /p/ corresponds to English ‹p› in 73 per cent of the cases and to English ‹f› in the remaining 27 per cent. However, Tok Pisin /f/ does not always correspond to English ‹f›, although it does so most of the time (85 per cent). This means that there are cases where *pig* becomes /fig/. Pronunciations such as these (along with others such as /foroman/ (< *poroman* 'friend': Eng. *foreman*), /fisin/ (< *pisin* 'bird': Eng. *pigeon*), and /fot/ (< *pot* 'pot')) occur mainly in rural areas rather than in urban centers. In urban areas Tok Pisin /f/ almost always corresponds to

Table 18.1 Correspondences between English and Tok Pisin for p/f in rural and urban areas (per cent)

Area	Tok Pisin [p] = Eng. ‹p› e.g. *pik* 'pig'	= Eng. ‹f› *prut* 'fruit'	Tok P. [f] = Eng. ‹f› *frut* 'fruit'	= Eng. ‹p› *fik* 'pig'
Rural	74	26	75	25
Urban	72	28	95	5
Total	73	27	85	15

Source: Romaine 1992, ch. 6.

English ‹f›, e.g. /frut/ 'fruit'. Forms such as /fig/ are new hypercorrections motivated by imperfect acquisition of English.

Phonotactics

There is a notable tendency towards CV structure in creoles. The preference for open syllables may, however, derive from universal developmental tendencies as well as from substratum influence. For example, in Table 18.2, we can see that Negerhollands syllable structure is much closer to its African substratum languages, Akwamu, Fanti, Ga and Ewe than it is to its superstrate language, Dutch. Although there is adjustment towards CV structure in Negerhollands, etymological consonants and consonant clusters are also preserved to some extent, particularly in syllable-initial position. Many of the clusters permissible in syllable-initial position in the African languages are identical to those of the Germanic languages.

However, processes such as vowel epenthesis and paragoge, i.e. vowel addition word-finally, are widely found in Negerhollands and other creoles, which serve to maintain canonical CV shape, e.g. Tok Pisin /giraun/ vs /graun/ from English *ground*, Negerhollands /filis/ vs /fles/ from Dutch *vleis* 'meat' (cf. StDu. *vlees*), and West African Pidgin English /sikin/ from English *skin*. Compare Jamaica Creole /taki/ from English *talk* and /habi/ from English *have* as cases where paragoge applies. Secondary consonant clusters are generally the product of decreolization. Marked segments tend to be replaced by unmarked ones, for example, in English-based creoles the interdental fricatives of English are replaced by the corresponding stops /t/ and /d/. However, lack of this contrast is also found in Hiberno-English and other regional varieties of English which provided input to the creole, so we cannot conclude that its absence in many pidgins and creoles is due entirely to universal principles.

In other respects, however, creoles have been conservative in preserving phonological patterns found in the superstrate during the time of creole

Table 18.2   Percentage of words which conform to CV syllable structure

Language	% CV
Dutch	6
English	8
Danish	15
Akwamu	44
Fanti	50
Ga	72
Ewe	78
Negerhollands	77

Source: Sabino 1990: 98.

formation. For example, in Jamaican Creole the palatalization of /k/ and /g/ as in /kyar/ 'car' and /gwain/ 'going' was customary in some of the varieties of British English transported to Jamaican in the eighteenth century.

Suprasegmental Phonology

Many have commented that the suprasegmental phonology of the Atlantic English-based creoles has been influenced by the tonal systems of the African substrate languages. In Jamaican Creole, tone is lexical in a few minimal pairs. Thus, /at/ with a high level tone means 'hat' or 'hurt', while with a high falling tone it means 'heart'. Another contrastive set is /bit/, which with a high level tone means 'bit' and with a high falling tone means 'beat' or 'beet'. There are three tones: high falling, high level and low level. Stress is non-phonemic. Because rising tone occurs before final pause, speakers of Standard English often mistake statements for questions. Some take these phenomena as sufficient grounds for recognizing Jamaican Creole as a separate language rather than a dialect of English. Explicit parallels between the tonal systems of West African languages such as Efik, Ewe, Yoruba and Ibo have been drawn. It has also been claimed that West African Pidgin English is a tone language with two tones, high and low.

Orthography

Most pidgins and creoles are not written languages and therefore, not standardized. The few such as Tok Pisin which have been reduced to writing and undergone some degree of standardization have been used primarily by missionaries for proselytization. Many of those who tried to develop orthographies for creoles assumed they were dealing with a version of English or another European language. As a result of these perceived similarities, writing systems based on European languages often did the creoles a disservice in suggesting that they were inferior and amusing versions of European languages.

Often literacy in the creole was promoted as an explicit bridge to the acquisition of literacy in the related European language. This underlined the importance of using an orthography which emphasized the similarities between the creole and its lexifier and did not distort etymological connections.

18.3   Morphology

There is relatively little to be said about morphology in pidgins and creoles since lack of it is one of the defining characteristics of the pidginization process. The absence of highly developed inflectional morphology was generally equated with lack of grammar and thought to reflect the primitiveness of both the language and its speakers. Pidginization can entail loss of all bound morphology, many free grammatical morphemes and even a large part of the vocabulary. Some morphemes are, however, more robust than others. It has been suggested that grammatical morphemes fall into two classes: those which if lost will not be reconstituted (1), and those that if lost must be reconstituted (2), as listed below.

1 *Morphemes not reconstituted*
gender agreement
number agreement
bound verbal morphology
derivational morphology
pronoun case and gender forms
most prepositions

2 *Reconstituted morphemes*
tense, aspect, modality forms
question words
pluralizer
pronouns for all persons and numbers
forms to mark oblique cases
general locative preposition
an irrealis complementizer
a relativizing particle
reflexives and reciprocals

Thus, loss of gender, which in European languages only vaguely corresponds with the semantic concept of sex, will not involve a conceptual loss, but will result in a substantial simplification. Lexicalization of gender results in irregularity, as can be seen in the English sets like *sow/boar, cow/bull, mare/stallion* as compared to Tok Pisin *pik meri/pik man, bulmakau meri/ bulmakau man, hos man/hos meri* (where *meri* means 'woman' and *man* means 'man'). Compare also Jamaican Creole *man hag/uman hag* 'boar'/ 'sow'. In Rabaul Creole German there is an invariant definite article, *de*, instead of the three-way gender distinction found in Standard German. This article does not take any case marking and the infinitive forms of verbs are often used instead of the standard inflected forms, e.g. *wenn de baby weinen, de mama muss aufpicken* 'if/when the baby cries, the mother must pick (it) up'. Pidgins and creoles also have few prepositions. In Tok Pisin, for instance, two forms, *long* and *bilong*, indicate all grammatical relations, as in *mi go long taun* 'I went to town'; *em givim tupela pik long mi* 'he gave me two pigs', *haus bilong papa bilong mi i stap long hap* 'my father's house is over there', *em man bilong spak* 'a drunkard or man who likes to drink', *mi raitim dispela buk long ol i ken ridim* 'I wrote this book so that they could read it'. Others such as Bislama have up to five prepositions, but none appears to have a range anything like its superstrate languages.

If the items in list (2) are lost, then lexical forms will be recruited to perform these functions. There are many similarities in the source morphemes used by creoles to grammaticalize these functions. The semantics of the grammatical morphemes are highly constant as are their etymologies; and in almost all cases they are drawn from the superstrate language. Thus, for English-based creoles the indefinite article is usually derived from the numeral *one*, as in Hawai'i Creole English *I get one car* 'I have a car', the irrealis marker from a verb meaning 'go', as in Hawai'i Creole *I go tel um* 'I'll tell him', the completive marker from a verb meaning 'finish', as in Tok Pisin *ol go pinis long ples bilong ol* 'they returned to their village', and a complementizer from a reflex of *for*, as in Miskito Coast Creole English *ai fried fo guo tek di tingz* 'I'm afraid to go take the things', etc.

Question words are usually bimorphemic, e.g. Guyanese Creole *wisaid* (< which side) 'where', Cameroons Creole *wetin* (< what thing) 'what', and Tok Pisin *wanem* (< what name) 'what'. It has been claimed that no creole shows any difference in syntactic structure between questions and statements. If a creole has special question particles, they are sentence-final and optional. In Guyanese Creole an utterance such as *i bai di eg dem* 'he bought the eggs' is not formally distinguishable as an interrogative or declarative. The difference is marked by intonation.

This is an interesting and salient typological feature of creoles when taken in conjunction with the fact that most creoles tend to have SVO word order. Greenberg (1963: 81) proposes an implicational universal to the effect that if a language has sentence external question particles, these tend to occur initially in prepositional (e.g. SVO) languages, but sentence-externally in postpositional (e.g. SOV) languages. The creole prototype violates this expectation since most are SVO languages.

It has been suggested that if the notion of morphological simplification is to be understood in any meaningful way, with respect to creoles, it should be with respect to the selection of the unmarked options of universal grammar. Bickerton's more recent versions of the bioprogram hypothesis (see Bickerton 1984) are framed in terms of the unmarked parametric settings of Universal Grammar. Nevertheless, there are quite a few cases where creoles have marked settings or are typologically at odds with implicational universals. These are often, though not always, explained by substratum. A case in point which is attributable to substratum is the inclusive–exclusive distinction in Melanesian Pidgin first-person plural and dual pronouns, e.g. *yumi* 'we' (inclusive of speaker and hearer) vs *mipela* 'we' (exclusive of the hearer). Thus, an utterance such as *mipela go long taun* 'we (exc.) are going to town' would exclude the hearer from those going to town.

As far as other parameters are concerned, the evidence is not straightforward. If we look at Pacific Jargon English, we can find many utterances without overt subject pronouns, e.g. *now got plenty money, no good work* 'now I have lots of money so I do not need to work'. Null subjects also emerged in experimental studies, which try to simulate the conditions under which pidgins are formed by giving people a limited vocabulary of a few hundred words in a language they do not know and asking them to perform various communicative tasks. In one such experiment using Farsi Pidgin, speakers produced utterances such as, *naxeir fahmidan* 'no understand'. In the case of Farsi pidgin the first language of the students was mainly English and since English is not a pro-drop language, transfer was not operative. This does not explain why subjects are obligatorily present in Portuguese- and Spanish-based creoles when the respective base languages are pro-drop, unless there is a transfer of the marked setting. Thus, the parameter of pro-drop is not completely general among creole languages, but part of the problem may be that we are comparing entities which are different stages of development. Since creoles may become more complex over time, it may be that an earlier stage, present-day non-pro-drop creoles were formerly pro-drop.

Bickerton (1988) believes that all parametric variation is in the lexicon and that the concept of markedness is no longer helpful. Rather than claim that creoles have (largely) unmarked lexical and morphological properties, due to the stripping process of pidginization, they may inherit fewer such properties from the input languages. It is this paucity, rather than a particular (unmarked) type of property that gives creole languages their high degree of similarity.

It may be that in cases where the grammars of creole languages adopt unmarked settings initially, these fall out from more general cognitive principles. Other properties of pidgin/creole grammar such as the elimination of allomorphy and allotaxy can likewise be seen to follow from more general cognitive principles which are at work in the learner's processing of input, for example, pay attention to the order of words, phonic saliency, semantic transparency, preference for ease of segmentability, etc.

18.4 Syntax

It is in the area of syntax that the boldest claims have been made for the distinctiveness of creoles. In fact, some time ago, scholars noted in connection with Jamaican Creole that the most striking differences between basilectal and acrolectal varieties lay not so much in phonology and vocabulary as in grammar. Although the reason offered by many was that creole grammar had African origins, the conclusion was that basilectal Jamaican Creole could not be regarded simply as a dialect of English, but was instead a new and different language.

Complex Syntax

Pidgin grammars tend to be shallow with no syntactic devices for subordination or embedding. They generally use no formal marking to indicate that one part of an utterance is subordinate to another. Distinctive marking of structures such as relative clauses comes later in the stabilization or expansion phase of the pidgin life cycle, or arises in the process of creolization. While most creoles lack passives, most have relative clauses.

Bickerton (1981: 62–3, 291–2) suggests that deletion was the 'original' strategy of relativization for pidgin and creoles. There is some support for that hypothesis intuitively in that pidgins have little room for redundancy. They favour production strategies. Bickerton's explanation for the lack of relatives is structural, but he goes on to emphasize that such a grammar without overt relative markers does not necessarily satisfy functional considerations such as ease of processing. If the lack of surface relativizers poses processing problems, then over time there would be pressure to adopt explicit marking of relative clauses, particularly in subject position. Bickerton found that markers were present in subject position in Hawai'i English creole at least twice as often as in object position.

When relative clauses begin to be marked, quite often there is no special marker. In many creoles the third-person singular pronoun is used. Deictics often provide a source for relativizers. The use of *we* (< *where*) occurs in West African Pidgin English, Krio, Nigerian Pidgin English, Cameroon Pidgin English, Torres Strait Broken, Guyanese Creole, Tok Pisin and other English-based pidgins and creoles.

I have observed a diachronic trend towards more explicit marking of relative clauses in Tok Pisin. These examples illustrate the different strategies which now exist for subject marking. The relative clauses are enclosed in brackets: *em go nau lukim dispela rabit ia [Ø stap insait long wanpela hul]* (zero marking) 'he went now and saw this rabbit (that) was in a hole', *narapela ia [em draivim kar ia] mi no save nem bilong em.* (third-person singular pronoun) 'the other one [she (who) drives the car] I don't know her name', *em kilim man [husat stilim samting]* (interrogative pronoun) 'he killed the man who stole something', and *man ia [we i maritim wanem meri ia]* ... (locative/interrogative pronoun) 'the man where (who) married that woman ...'.

New strategies of relativization have begun to appear in subject position, e.g. *husat* 'who'. Comparative evidence from other English-based creoles suggests a similar trend, though the precise details need checking. Of the 33 Anglophone creoles surveyed by Hancock (1986) only 7 have been said to have zero relativization (Bahamian, Belizean, Black English, Guyanese, Hawaiian, Liberian English and Providencia). All the others have some overt relativizer, which in 13 of them is a *wh*-form. It may not be possible to reconstruct an original state of relativization by deletion in all the relevant cases. Even where this is not possible, however, there is some evidence to indicate an increase in explicitness through the addition of strategies which use case-variable pronouns rather than invariant complementizers.

Table 18.3 Tense and aspect markers in various creole and African languages

	Unmarked	Anterior	Progressive	Anterior	Habitual	Anterior	Completive	Anterior	Irrealis	Anterior
São Tomé CP	Ø	ta(va) –	s(a)ka –	tava ka –	ka –	tava ka –	–za		ka –	ka –
Cape Verde CP	Ø	– ba	ta –	ta – ba	ta –	ta – ba	–ja		ta –	ta – be
Papiamentu CS	Ø		ta –	tabata –	ta –	tabata –	– kaba	a – kaba	lo S–	lo S a –
Palenquero CS	Ø		ta –	taba –	ase –	aseba –	a –	a – ba	tan –	tanba –
Negerhollands CD	Ø	(h)a –	lo –	a lo –	lo ~ ka(n) –	a ka –	ka –	a ka –	lo ~ sa(l) –	a sa –
Lesser Antillean CF	Ø	te –	ka –	te ka –	ka –	te ka –	– fin?		ke –	te ke –
Haitian CF	Ø	t(e) –	ap –	t-ap –	Ø ~ ap –	t(e) –	fin – ?		(v)a –	t-a –
Sranan CE	Ø	(b)en –	(d)e –	ben e –	Ø ~ (d)e –		– kaba		(g)o ~ sa –	ben o –
Jamaican CE	Ø	ben –	(d)a ~ de –	(b)ena –	Ø ~ a –	(b)en –	don – ~ / –don	don – ~ / –don	go ~ wi –	wuda –
Gullah CE	Ø	bin –	(d)a – ~ / – in	bina –	da ~ doz –	doz –	don –	don –	gwāi –	wuda –
Yoruba	Ø	ti –	ń –	ti ń –	maa ń –	ti maa ń –	– tán	ti – tán	á ~ yió –	yio ti –
Bambara	Ø		bɛ –	tun bɛ –	bɛ –	tun bɛ –	ye – ka ban	tun ye – ka ban	bena –	tun bena –

Source: Holm 1989: 148.
Notes: –, position of verb; S, subject.

Tense-Mood-Aspect

The most discussed feature of creole morphosyntax is the system of verbal markers. As early as the nineteenth-century scholars commented on markers of tense, mood and aspect which were shared across creoles with different lexical bases. Many have claimed that although these markers are lexically related to the superstrate language, they behave syntactically and semantically like the pre-verbal tense, mood and aspect markers in the substrate languages. Table 18.3 shows some of the similarities across unrelated Atlantic creoles and two African languages, Yoruba and Bambara. Bickerton (1981), however, has largely ignored the similarities in tense-mood-aspect marking between creoles and their substrate languages and instead has claimed that the common features are due to the operation of the bioprogram.

The following similarities can be observed:

1   The simple form of the verb without any markers refers to whatever time is in focus. In this example a speaker of Nicaraguan Miskito Coast Creole English is explaining how each jungle spirit guides the animals under his protection to hide them from hunters:

Him a di uona. Him tek dem an put dem an dis wie ... die kom an him liiv dem all hiia an guo de.
'He is their owner. He takes them and puts them on the right path ... they come and he leaves them all in that place and goes off.'

All the verbs refer to a permanent state of affairs. In this next one, however, unmarked verb forms refer to the past:

Wi liiv from der an kom doun hiir fo stodi.
'We left there and came down here so I could study.'

2   Each creole language tends to have three markers; one to mark anterior tense (simple past for states and past before past for actions), one to mark irrealis mood (future and conditional) and one to mark non-punctual aspect (progressive and habitual). In the case of Hawai'i Creole English, for instance, the markers are *bin* (anterior), *go* (irrealis) and *ste* (punctual), as in these examples:

A bin go si Toni abaut go spansa da kidz, ae, da baesketbawl tim, da wan ai ste koch fo.
'I went to see Tony about sponsoring the kids, eh, the basketball team, the one I am coaching'
Bambai til tumoru he go teli telifon.
'Later, by tomorrow, he'll call.'

3   Where there is more than one particle accompanying a verb, the particles always have a fixed order before the verb:

Tense Mood Aspect. Although all combinations are not found in all creoles, examples of this pattern can be seen in conservative creoles such as Saramaccan and Sranan, as in this example from Sranan, *me ben sa e go* 'I would have been going' and this one from Jamaican Creole *mi en a go sing* 'I was going to be singing'.

The best examples of the full three-term system of tense-mood-aspect marking tend to be found in the Atlantic rather than the Pacific, although there has been significant development in Tok Pisin, for instance, in recent decades. As recently as the late 1960s and early 1970s there appears to have been a constraint in Tok Pisin against having two particles in pre-verbal position. This has since been clearly abandoned by some speakers, as is evident in these examples, where combinations of various particles occur, *ok, yu ken bai kisim* 'OK, you can take it' and *yumi mas bai helpim* 'we (inc.) will have to help'. The reasons for these differences between the Atlantic and Pacific creoles are not yet clear, but they may have to do with time-depth since the Pacific creoles are all relatively younger. The contribution of decreolization to the development of tense-mood-aspect systems is also unclear.

While most creoles have pre-verbal particles rather than inflections, Berbice Dutch is unique among basilectal creoles of the Caribbean in its use of a mixture of pre-verbal particles and suffixes in its tense-mood-aspect system.

Verb Serialization

Another common feature of creole syntax is serialization of verbs. Serial verb constructions are chains of two or more verbs which have the same subject, e.g. *im tek im fut kik me* (Jamaican Creole) (lit. 'he take his foot kick me') 'he kicked me'. In creoles they are used for marking functions such as direction, benefaction, dative and instrumental, which in other languages are marked either by inflectional case or prepositions, as in these examples: *a waka go a wosu* (Sranan) (lit. 'he walk go to house') 'he walked home', and *a teke nefi koti a meti* (Ndujka) (lit. 'he take knife and cut meat') 'he cut the meat with a knife'.

This is yet another instance where syntax makes up for losses in other areas (compare circumlocution discussed in 18.5). In many cases the verbs involved in serialization can be translated into English with a single verb, and the first verb in the series is often *come, go, take,* etc. The length of such constructions is apparently not constrained in some languages and thus in Nigerian Pidgin English three or more verbs may be concatenated together across a multiple clause structure as in this example: *dem come take night carry di wife, go give di man* (lit. 'they come take night carry the wife go give the man') 'they came at night, got the wife and gave her to her husband'.

It is widely believed that serialization in the Atlantic pidgins and creoles is to be attributed to substratum from the African languages, particularly the Kwa group. The parallels can be seen in examples such as:

Akoroma no kyeree akoko no wee. (Twi)
Di haak kets di tskikin iit it. (Jamaican Creole)
(lit.) 'the hawk catch the chicken eat it'
'the hawk caught the chicken and ate it'.

Similarly, in the Pacific, it has been suggested that there may be Austronesian substratum influence in the serial constructions found in Tok Pisin. Compare, for instance: *boro di-rau-mate-i* (Manam) (lit.) 'pig they hit die it' and *ol i kilim indai pik* (Tok Pisin) (lit. 'they hit die pig') 'they killed the pig'. However, serialization has a much more limited occurrence in the Pacific creoles and is arguably of a different character.

18.5 Lexis

As far as the content of the lexical items in pidgin and creole languages is concerned, at least two general points can be made. One is the common existence of a nautical element, which is not surprising given the fact that most pidgins and creoles tend to be located near a marine expanse. Another is presence of a common core of items shared across unrelated pidgins and creoles. Among these are words such as *pikinini* 'child, baby' (< Port. *pequeño* or *pequeniño* 'small'), as found in Jamaican Creole, Tok Pisin and many others, and *save* (< Sp./Port. *saber/sabir* 'know') as found again in Tok Pisin and most of the Atlantic creoles. The latter has since passed into more general English usage, e.g. *he has a lot of business savvy.*

Creoles generally take at least 80 per cent or more of their lexicon from the superstrate language. Consider, for instance, Negerhollands, which has at least 84 per cent of its vocabulary derived from Dutch, 7.5 per cent from English, 2 per cent from Iberian languages, 1.4 per cent from Danish, and 5 per cent from African languages. This estimate is based on 1,300 words recorded in the 1920s. The African element seems to be largely shared with other languages in that region, e.g. *bukra* 'white man' (< Twi, Efik, Ibo *mbakara*) (cf. also Jamaican Creole) and *funtji* 'cornmeal dish'.

By comparison, Tok Pisin is estimated to contain from 11 per cent to 20 per cent of its lexicon from indigenous languages such as Tolai, spoken in New Britain. There are also words from Malay such as *binatang* 'insect' and at least 5 per cent from German, though much of the latter is now archaic and has been replaced by English. It is not always possible to trace creole lexical items to a unique source, for example, Tok Pisin *gaden* may be equally from German *Garten* or English *garden*. Similarly, *bel* 'stomach' may be derived from English *belly* or Tolai *bala* 'stomach'. The residue of faulty analyses is particularly evident in the lexicons of pidgins and creoles. Tok Pisin, for example, has incorporated *bow and arrow* as one lexical item, *bunara* and *tortoise shell* as *trausel*. These fused forms persist partly through lack of access to correct target models.

Bickerton (1988: 281) suggests that it is the massive pruning of lexical properties from the target language which gives rise to the typological similarities of creoles. In older, more established languages complexity arises through the addition of a wide range of lexical and morphological properties through centuries of change. Languages such as Tok Pisin and Nigerian Pidgin English have begun to develop productive, although, limited word-formation processes. In general, borrowing has been preferred over exploiting internal morphological processes, where these exist. In my discussion of simplicity and impoverishment in the lexicon I will make reference in particular to the consequences which follow from the fact that a pidgin language has a small number of items, namely semantic generality, greater lexicalization, circumlocution and multifunctionality.

Semantic Generality

The number of items in the lexicon of a pidgin is highly restricted. Estimates of size vary from about 300–1,500 words, depending on the language. In the case of the younger generation of Tok Pisin speakers, for example, it ranges from about 800 in rural areas to about 2,500 in urban areas, where a greater number of English words have been incorporated. Compare the number of lexical items which a speaker of an ordinary language like English has, e.g. 25–30,000, by comparison with the number of lexical items in Tok Pisin, i.e. 1,500. However, these 1,500 words can be combined into phrases so as to say anything that can be said in English. The implication is that there is no reduction in the overall semantic domains covered by a pidgin, but merely in the number of items used to map them.

Thus, reduction of number of items does not in itself simplify a language, though it entails certain adjustments in lexical structure which may make a language more regular. Lexical items in pidgin languages cover a wider semantic domain than in the base language. Not only is the number of actual pidgin lexical items highly restricted, but also the conventions as to the lexical information found within each item. Tok Pisin has the term *pisin* (< English *pigeon*) for 'bird'. Historically, this represents a case of extension of reference from the English term *pigeon* which refers to a specific kind of bird in English to a term with more general reference.

Multifunctionality

Due to their small inventory of items pidgins associate different grammatical information with the same semantic and phonological items, although this violates the principle of one form/one meaning. This is generally referred to as multifunctionality, i.e. use of the same lexical item in more than one grammatical function. For example, in Tok Pisin *askim* can function as both noun and verb: *mi gat wanpela askim* 'I have a question', *mi laik askim em* 'I want to ask him/her/it'. The freedom from lexical specification increases the information content of each unit in the lexicon. The use of the same lexical item in a number of grammatical functions constitutes a gain in simplicity of the lexical entry. The existence of multifunctionality also calls into doubt the extent to which traditional grammatical categories such as noun, verb, etc., are applicable to creoles.

As a consequence of phonological reduction pidgins also have widespread homophony, where one form stands for a number of meanings. Homophony rarely leads to ambiguity since the items concerned are usually quite disparate, for example, Tok Pisin *sip* may be 'sheep', 'ship' or 'jeep', so that context usually supports only one interpretation.

Circumlocution: Morphological vs Semantic Complexity

It is obvious that there will be gaps in the pidgin lexicon, particularly in the early stages of its development. These may be filled by borrowing or circumlocution. Only at a later stage in its development does the pidgin develop productive internal resources for expanding its lexicon. Circumlocution is a strategy which involves letting the syntax make up for the lack of productive morphological processes which would be used to form words in the lexifier language.

Europeans have been eager in the past to cite mythical circumlocutions to demonstrate the inadequacy of pidgin, one of the most notable being that for 'piano' in Melanesian Pidgin, e.g. *big fellow bokkes, suppose missis he fight him, he cry too much* 'the big box, if the European woman hits it, it cries a lot'. Although it is possible that such a description was used in the first encounter with the piano, it is highly unlikely that it persisted. Nonce circumlocutions such as the following in Bislama for 'burp': *oli pulum win afta sakem bakegen* 'they breathe air in and then throw it out again', probably occur quite frequently. Once an innovation has caught on and is used, it will become conventionalized and shortened. Initially, these expressions served as descriptions. At this stage there was a preference for high analytical coding at the expense of economy. Later, however, in response to the demands of efficient communication, speakers economized. Once these forms had been used several times they were reduced and stabilized.

As the lexicon expands, the clumsy but motivated compounds and periphrastic expressions disappear, for example, Tok Pisin *kot bilong ren* 'raincoat' is now *kotren* or *renkot* and *bel bilong mi hat* (lit. 'stomach of me hot') is now *mi belhat* 'I am angry'. This is motivated by the desire to give common concepts a reduced expression.

Lexicalization

It is direct consequence of their small vocabulary that pidgins and creoles exhibit a high degree of motivation and transparency in compounding. There is an inverse correlation between the lexical expansion of a language and the iconicity of its grammar. The greater the lexicon, the greater the opacity, the smaller the lexicon, the greater the transparency and iconicity. The more exceptions a language has, the harder it is to learn. Haiman (1985) distinguishes between lexical and grammatical languages. In general a lexical language has a large stock of primary roots, while a grammatical one has a small stock and makes up the deficit in periphrastic constructions. Long-established languages are relatively more lexical and arbitrary, while pidgins, second language learner varieties and child language are more grammatical.

Many aspects of the lexicon and grammar of Tok Pisin reflect a semantic orientation which is basically non-European, while other aspects draw on universal principles which determine maximum regularity of encoding of grammatical categories and lexical distinctions. In some areas of the lexicon we see a conspiracy between these factors. As an example, we can take the following semantic field lexicalized by the Tok Pisin term *gras* (< English *grass*), which can be used to refer to 'head hair', 'body hair', 'fur', 'feathers', 'moustache', and make a partial comparison with Warapu, a non-Austronesian language spoken in northwest New Guinea etc.

Tok Pisin	English	Warapu
gras	'hair'	pei
gras bilong fes	'beard'	
mausgras	'moustache'	
gras antap long ai	'eyebrow'	
gras bilong pisin	'bird's feather'	ndru pei
gras bilong dog	'dog's fur'	naki pei
gras nogut	'weed'	

The fact that meanings such as 'grass', 'beard', 'feather' and 'weed' are all expressed by separate, unrelated lexemes in English is an indication of its greater degree of lexicalization. Note too that we would not even consider this to be a coherent semantic field in English. In Tok Pisin, however, there is a kind of iconic relation between these items, which is expressed by the fact that they are all encoded by means of constructions incorporating the word *gras*. In other words, the terms in Tok Pisin are motivated, whereas in English they are arbitrary. This represents a good illustration of what is called dia-grammatic iconicity, i.e. a systematic arrangement of signs, none of which necessarily resembles its referent, but whose relationships to each other mirror the relationships to their referents. Thus, one could say that *grass* has the same relationship to the ground or earth that feathers have to a bird, a beard to a face, etc. They are all coverings on different surfaces. In this particular semantic domain the optimal solution to the problem of encoding is reinforced by the existence of a similar system in the indigenous languages.

Many of the languages of Papua New Guinea (both Austronesian and non-Austronesian) have the same lexical item for 'feather' and 'hair'. Often 'fur' and 'leaf' are included within the scope of reference of this same term. Thus, the languages of the Huon Peninsula have the same lexical item for 'feather' and 'hair'. Often 'fur' and 'leaf' are included within the scope of reference of this same term. In Warapu, a single lexical item is used for 'head hair' and 'leaf'. The same item in Warapu also means 'body hair', 'fur' and 'feathers', as seen above. This is also true of Karam, a New Guinea Highlands language. This distribution of domains is not uncommon in Austronesian languages of New Guinea, but a more normal set for non-Austronesian languages is to have one word for all kinds of hair and a separate word for 'leaf'. We can now see how Tok Pisin serves to channel an alien concept system into a native conceptual system, while constituting at the same time a simplified means of expression which creates pressure for the grammatical complexities often found in other languages to be eliminated or sharply reduced.

Nevertheless, there is an inverse correlation between the lexical expansion of a language and the iconicity of its grammar. Now English terms like *feda* ('feather') are increasingly used, especially by the younger generation of urban speakers, who are rapidly expanding the vocabulary of Tok Pisin. In such cases borrowing from English is making the structure of Tok Pisin more irregular and complex.

Names for body parts such as *ai* 'eye' and *maus* 'mouth' function as metaphors in both Tok Pisin and Cameroon Pidgin. For example, Tok Pisin has *aipas* 'blind' (< 'close' + 'eye'). Compare also Cameroon Pidgin *lokai* and also Tok Pisin *mauspas* 'silent' and *yaupas* 'deaf' (< 'ear' + 'close'). Tok Pisin also has *ai bilong sua* 'head of a sore', *ai bilong botol* 'lid of a bottle', and *ai bilong kokonas* 'hole of a coconut'. Of course English has metaphorical extensions of body parts too such as 'eye of a storm', and 'ear of corn', but the fact that it has many more arbitrary terms like 'blind', 'deaf' and 'dumb' to encode meanings which are all formerly linked in Tok Pisin is an indication of the greater degree of lexicalization of English.

Another more general process of grammaticalization is probably at work here too. Body parts provide the most important source domain for spatial concepts in language. Thus, locative pre- and postpositions in many languages are cognate with or derived from body parts. Thus, mouth and eye frequently provide the source for the spatial dimension of 'front'. In Tok Pisin *sanap long ai bilong ol* means 'to stand up in front of everyone'. Similarly, the word for 'head' in many languages comes to encode the dimension of 'on' or 'front', while the word for 'back' comes to encode the location of 'behind'; and the word for 'buttocks' or 'anus', the location of 'under'. In Tok Pisin, for example, we have *as bilong diwai/flaua* 'the base of the tree/flower' and *asples* 'one's place of origin' as well as *as bilong kros* 'the reason/cause for anger'. In the latter case we have a metaphorical extension from the concrete domain of body parts to a more abstract concept which does not have an inherent spatial dimension of 'bottomness' or 'under'.

In pidgins and creoles these metaphorical uses are an important means of extending a restricted vocabulary with limited syntactic means. Borrowing from English, however, is threatening to disrupt the unity of a great many semantic fields which are linked by these metaphors. While the borrowing of *lid* represents an economy at one level over periphrastic *maus* or *ai bilong pot* 'mouth/eye of the pot', at another level it leads to complexity.

The price that has to be paid when a concept is fully lexicalized is that it has to be learned as a totally new item. Presumably this requires cognitive 'cost'. However, overt morphological motivation can lead to an increase in length of time/units required to enclode a concept, which must also involve some cost. Nevertheless, there comes a point beyond which motivation ceases to be morphological and is semantic. Thus, the alleged circumlocution for the concept of 'piano' is semantically motivated, but still relatively opaque to someone who has no idea of keyboard instruments, as is the one for 'saw' (*brata bilong tamiak, yu kisim i go subim i kam* 'brother of tomahawk which you push back and forth'). Nothing has been said about the interface between semantic and morphological complexity in motivating linguistic expression.

Further Reading

Bickerton, D. (1981) *Roots of Language*, Ann Arbor: Karoma.
—— (1984) 'The language bioprogram hypothesis', *The Behavioural and Brain Sciences* 7: 173–221.
—— (1988) 'Creole languages and the bioprogram', in F. Newmeyer (ed.) *Linguistics. The Cambridge Survey, Vol. II. Linguistic Theory: Extensions and Implications*, Cambridge: Cambridge University Press, pp. 268–84.
Churchill, W. (1911) *Beach-La-Mar, the Jargon Trade Speech of the Western Pacific*, Washington, DC: Carnegie Institution Publication No. 164.
Clark, R. (1979) 'In search of Beach-la-mar', *Te Reo* 22: 3–64.
Devonish, H. (1986) *Language and Liberation. Creole Language Politics in the Caribbean*, London: Karia Press.
Greenberg, J. (1963) 'Some universals of grammar with particular reference to the order of meaningful elements', in J. Greenberg (ed.), *Universals of Language*, Cambridge, Mass.: MIT Press, pp. 58–90.
Haiman, J. (1985) *Natural Syntax. Iconicity and Erosion*, Cambridge: Cambridge University Press.
Hall, R. A. (1966) *Pidgin and Creole Languages*, New York: Cornell University Press.
Hancock, I. (1986) 'A preliminary classification of the Anglophone Atlantic creoles: with syntactic data from 33 representative dialects', in G. Gilbert (ed.) *Pidgin and Creole Languages: Essays in Memory of John Reinecke*, Honolulu: University of Hawaii Press, pp. 264–333.
Holm, J. (1988–9) *Pidgins and Creoles*, 2 vols, Cambridge: Cambridge University Press.
Keesing, R. (1988) *Melanesian Pidgin and The Oceanic Substrate*, Stanford: Stanford University Press.
Mühlhäusler, P. (1986) *Pidgin and Creole Linguistics*, Oxford: Blackwell.
O'Donnell, W. R. and Todd, L. (1980) *Variety in Contemporary English*, London: George Allen and Unwin.
Reinecke, J. E., DeCamp, D., Hancock, I, and Wood, R. E. (1975) *A Bibliography of Pidgin and Creole Languages*, Honolulu: University of Hawaii Press.

Romaine, S. (1988) *Pidgin and Creole Languages*, London: Longman.
—— (1992) *Language, Education and Development: Urban and Rural Tok Pisin in Papua New Guinea*, Oxford: Oxford University Press.
Sabino, R. (1990) 'Towards a Phonology of Negerhollands: An Analysis of Phonological Variation', unpublished doctoral thesis, University of Pennsylvania.
Singler, J. V. (ed.) (1990) *Pidgin and Creole Tense-Mood-Aspect Systems*, Amsterdam: John Benjamins.
Wurm, S. A. and Mühlhäusler, P. (eds) (1985) *Handbook of Tok Pisin*, Pacific Linguistics C-70, Canberra: Australian National University.

Index

Italics indicate major references